GENDERED
READINGS FROM THE AMERICAN EXPERIENCE
VOICES

GENDERED

READINGS FROM THE AMERICAN EXPERIENCE

VOICES

KARIN BERGSTROM COSTELLO
Santa Monica College

HARCOURT BRACE COLLEGE PUBLISHERS

Fort Worth Philadelphia San Diego New York Orlando Austin
San Antonio Toronto Montreal London Sydney Tokyo

Vice President, Publisher ●	Ted Buchholz
Editor in Chief ●	Christopher P. Klein
Executive Editor for English ●	Michael Rosenberg
Developmental Editor ●	Camille Adkins
Project Editor ●	Elizabeth Cruce Alvarez
Senior Production Manager ●	Kathleen Ferguson
Senior Art Director ●	Don Fujimoto

Cover Image: Henri Matisse, *The Dance*. Hermitage, St. Petersburg, Russia. Copyright 1995 Succession H. Matisse, Paris/Artist Rights Society, New York.

ISBN: 0-15-501578-8

Library of Congress Catalog Card Number: 94-79795

PREFACE

Gendered Voices: Readings from the American Experience offers a unique approach to a challenging topic that is at once timely and timeless: gender. Our chromosomes determine our sex. But gender refers to the way we define femininity and masculinity, the psychological and social meanings we attach to our identity as women and men. Although gender begins with biology, it is finally the result of culture—"the acquired knowledge that people use to interpret their world and generate social behavior."[1]

As Americans we share a culture, but each of us also reflects both smaller communities of class, region, and ethnicity and, of course, our individual experiences. Our acquired concepts of masculinity and femininity influence the personal qualities we cherish or discourage in ourselves, our relationships, what and how we learn, our work and play, our goals, and how we participate in the political and social life of our communities. Gender matters.

Because gender affects every aspect of our lives, it should engage our critical interest. But its influence is so pervasive and ingrained that often we don't question our assumptions about it or the reactions that those assumptions lead us to. As a result, everyone is an "expert" on gender, although there are frequently as many opinions as there are people to voice them. Our heated arguments often conceal confusion and discomfort. Now, as traditional gender roles change, confusion and discomfort grow.

Gendered Voices invites readers to question their assumptions about gender, in light of new information, and perhaps to adjust their values. It introduces a variety of American perspectives on and experiences with gender in order to provide topics for critical analysis, discussion, and writing.

Organization

The book is divided into nine chapters. In the first, several biologists, a cultural anthropologist, and a psychologist debate the relative roles of biology (nature) and culture (nurture) in shaping gender. In the second chapter, historical documents trace the development of and discussion about gender roles in America. These two chapters provide theoretical and analytical tools for later use. Succeeding chapters explore how gender is defined and experienced in key stages and aspects of our lives: family, coming of age, education, love and marriage, friendship, work, and popular culture.

Although the chapters follow the progress of our life experiences, the book is *flexible:* individual chapters are self-contained and may be assigned out of sequence; and

---

[1] James P. Spradley and David W. McCurdy, *Conformity and Conflict,* 7th ed., (Glenview, IL: Scott, Foresman/Little Brown, 1990) 4.

individual selections within chapters may be grouped with readings from other chapters.

All chapters contain theoretical and analytical selections that frame the issues. Chapters focusing on the private sphere—family, coming of age, love and marriage, and friendship—bring these issues to life primarily through short fiction, poetry, personal narratives, and personal essays. Chapters focusing on the public sphere—the nature versus nurture debate, history, education, work, and popular culture—emphasize nonfiction and historical documents, but also include some fiction and poetry.

Each chapter begins with a short introductory essay, and each reading selection is introduced by a headnote. In addition, most selections are preceded by two segments that encourage writing: Journal Topics and As You Read. Journal Topics encourages students to write about their own experiences and ideas about a topic *before* they read what another writer has said. As You Read, on the other hand, contains questions designed to improve comprehension by directing students to write about some of the selection's major themes and organization. Writing Assignments, which follows most readings, often builds on the issues raised in Journal Topics and As You Read.

An Instructor's Manual suggests several reading assignment combinations that focus on themes other than gender (for example, race, class, communication, religion, and violence). It also contains a Table of Contents identifying selections by genre or rhetorical strategy.

Special Features

The following features make *Gendered Voices* accessible, relevant, and interesting to all students:

- Masculinity and femininity receive equal focus.
- All readings explore the American experience.
- A polyphonic chorus of *voices* is heard: from Native-, Latin-, African-, Asian-, and European-American backgrounds; from urban, suburban, and rural settings; from the North, East, South, and West; from the rich, poor, and middle class; from heterosexual and homosexual orientations; from scholarly and sophisticated to popular and sometimes nàive perspectives; from traditional and conservative to liberal and radical views; from reasoned to passionate, serious to humorous, impersonal to confessional tones.
- Variety in the format of reading selections includes fiction, poetry, scholarly and popular nonfiction, journalism, essays, letters, and speeches.
- Reading selections and writing assignments emphasize how issues of ethnicity, race, and class intersect with gender.
- Selections vary in perspective and difficulty to accommodate the differing backgrounds of students.
- While organized to address the specific needs of composition classes, the book (as well as the Instructor's Manual) is also useful for American studies,

psychology, women's studies, cult and anthropology, and introductory literature classes.

Writing Assignments

With the exception of the "History" chapter and most poems, writing assignments of varying difficulty follow each selection and are organized into three categories: (1) Analysis, (2) Argument, and (3) Personal Writing and Writing from Research. (In the "History" chapter, the shorter readings are clustered, and writing assignments follow each cluster.) Rather than proceeding from less to more difficult, writing assignments are organically arranged to follow the development of each reading selection. Diversity in format, perspective, and style of reading selections provide models for student writing.

Writing assignments also include Collaborative Projects. To avoid predetermining the nature of the collaboration, directions are not spelled out, although the Instructor's Manual provides specific suggestions. Several assignments for each selection ask students to work with more than one reading. These multiple readings are usually drawn from the same chapter.

Both the research done for this book and personal experience have lead the author to believe that ideas about masculinity and femininity should reflect fewer stereotypes and polarities, and more flexibility and inclusiveness. A more ideal America would not inhibit or devalue its members by rigidly assigning gender to personal qualities (tenderness or ambition), activities (nursing or mountain climbing), skills (cooking or map reading), or perspectives (rational or intuitive). Indeed, most of what makes us human is not strictly tied to gender anyway. Finally, no matter how culture and biology shape us, no human being is "all masculine" or "all feminine."

Acknowledgments

My interest in this project began in the crucible of family experiences and conversations. I owe special thanks to my husband, Ed, whose feminism has sometimes antedated mine and whose keen intelligence has helped me refine my thinking. He is my best friend. I have also learned much from our three admirable daughters— Catharine, Kristin, and Katherine. Their engagement with the issues raised in this book has yielded quite individual and satisfying results for them and has given me insights into and hopes for their generation.

Various chapters of this book have been refined over the last two years with the help of my English 1 students at Santa Monica College, a microcosm of multicultural America and the larger world. Their suggestions about writing assignments have been invaluable, and their enthusiasm for the material, inspiring. My colleagues, physical anthropologist Jan Austin and cultural anthropologist Johanna Barker, helped me develop the book's conceptual framework and find some of the readings. Their friendship sustained me.

I would like to thank the reviewers whose comments on drafts and sections of the manuscript helped make *Gendered Voices* lively, balanced, truly reflective of American diversity, and useful as both a reader and composition text: Stephen Caldwell Wright, Seminole Community College; Toni-Lee Capossela, Stonehill College; Margaret Ford, Houston Community College; Lisa Gerrard, UCLA; Rob Koelling, Northwest College; Eric Pankey, Washington University; and Irwin Weiser, Purdue University.

I also want to express my appreciation to the professional team at Harcourt Brace College Publishers for their work on this book. Michael Rosenberg, executive editor for English, provided initial encouragement, sustained support, and both vision and attention to detail. Camille Adkins, development editor, was unfailingly thoughtful, patient, practical, and good-humored. Beth Alvarez, project editor; Kathy Ferguson, senior production manager; Don Fujimoto, senior art director; and Cheri Throop, permissions researcher, skillfully shepherded the project through its metamorphosis from manuscript to book. Working with all of them made writing *Gendered Voices* a pleasure.

CONTENTS

3 THE FAMILY   *160*

4 Coming of Age *225*

5 EDUCATION   *290*

7 FRIENDS 454

GENDERED
READINGS FROM THE AMERICAN EXPERIENCE
VOICES

NATURE VERSUS NURTURE

Boys will be boys . . .
Take it like a man . . .
Isn't that just like a woman?

Have you ever uttered these words, or heard them?

Whether said fondly or in exasperation, these and other familiar expressions reveal how deeply embedded in us are our assumptions about the essential nature of each sex. Are such expressions just verbal habits, archaic legacies of a time when gender roles were more rigidly defined and gender stereotyping went unchallenged?

Or do they still reflect what we secretly believe, perhaps even fear to be true: that men and women occupy different emotional, intellectual, spiritual, and social worlds, destined to be complementary halves, at best, and wary adversaries, at worst?

The debate about whether and why men and women differ continues unabated. Opinions about whether the differences matter and what to do about them, if they exist, proliferate. Where you stand on these issues probably depends on a number of factors: your age, religious beliefs, politics, experiences, maybe even your academic orientation, among other considerations.

This chapter doesn't try to answer all the specific questions or resolve the larger issues. Instead, it lays out a number of approaches to thinking about them. It begins with two selections written in the late 1970s, not coincidentally, in the wake of the second American feminist movement. The first selection, by David Barash, a zoologist, posits evolutionary, biological origins of social differences between the sexes. Barash finds confirmation for his position in human cultures around the world and in analogies to the behavior of non-human animals. Stephen Jay Gould, also a zoologist, challenges both the conclusions and methodology of sociobiologists like Barash and worries about the social and political implications of their ideas.

More recently, journalist Christine Gorman surveys scientific research on gender differences in the brain. Then, poet Sharon Olds observes young boys at her son's birthday party and raises questions about the origins and consequences of traits traditionally associated with masculinity.

Next, psychologist Sandra Bem acknowledges biological differences between the sexes but laments our obsession with them and dismisses them as a smokescreen that conceals the real causes of differences in the way men and women live. She locates these causes in our cultural environment, not our evolutionary biology.

Continuing the emphasis on culture, anthropologist Ernestine Friedl examines the sexual division of power and prestige in hunter-gatherer peoples and draws conclusions for men and women in contemporary, highly technological societies like ours.

Sexism
Strategies of Reproduction, or When Is Beeswax Like a Ferrari?

David P. Barash

David P. Barash received his PhD in zoology from the University of Washington, where he is professor of psychology and zoology. He is the author of *Sociobiology and Behavior* (1977), *Stop Nuclear War* (1982), *The Caveman and the Bomb* (1985), and *The Whisperings Within* (1979), from which this selection is excerpted. These "whisperings" refer to evolutionary adaptations made by our ancestors which, he believes, survive as imprints on our genes to influence our social behavior.

Journal Topics: List the traits, behaviors and tendencies that you believe are essentially masculine or feminine. Where possible, explain their origin and function.

As You Read: (1) Make a list of the times that Barash's language attributes human feelings or consciousness to animals. How does his anthropomorphic treatment of animals help him develop his theme? (2) Describe the essay's style and tone. (3) Why does Barash believe that the difference between males and females is one of sociobiology's most important concerns? (4) Might historians, sociologists, psychologists, anthropologists, or even other biologists and zoologists offer different interpretations of the human behaviors for which Barash provides biological explanations? (5) List the occasions when Barash's analysis of human behavior reinforces stereotypes about men and women.

1   Generations of Tom Sawyers and Huck Finns set out on their boisterous adventures and come home covered with mud, while we chuckle indulgently. Little girls, though, are made of sugar and spice. "Boys will be boys," we're told, but "nice girls don't do that." "Vive la différence," echoes the French Parliament. *La différence* is one of sociobiology's most important concerns.

2   There has been no human society that has not distinguished the sexes, by their anatomies and by their behavior. But we tend to focus on the superficial differences— dress, hair, length, body shape—and most of us don't really know what makes a woman female and a man male.

3   We all know how a human male differs physically from a female. Likewise for male and female chimpanzees, elephants and lions. But how do we differentiate birds, for example, which generally lack a penis or vagina? And what about oysters? Not much visible there, but biologists, at least, are absolutely confident in distinguishing the sexes. What is the underlying biological meaning of male and female?

4   The answer is quite simple. In almost all living species there are two different kinds of sexual individuals. One kind, the female, produces a relatively small number of large sex cells, called eggs. The other kind, the male, produces a relatively large number of rather small sex cells, or sperm. In many cases, the difference between male and female sex cells is dramatic. Birds may lay eggs that weigh 25 percent or more of their total body weight, while their mates produce only a few drops of sperm. Mammals seem to be exceptions to this, since their eggs are quite small; a human egg is only about the size of a pinhead. But the sperm are even smaller; a single male ejaculation produces enough of them to fertilize every woman in North America. Zoologist Richard Dawkins points out that the exploitation of women by men probably began very long ago, when the smaller, more active sperm began to take advantage of the rich food reserves present in the larger, less active eggs.

5   The biological consequences of fertilization and pregnancy are immense, falling only on the woman. Eggs are fertilized by sperm, not vice versa. And women become pregnant, not men. It is the woman who must produce a placenta and nourish her unborn child; who must undergo the metabolic and hormonal stresses of pregnancy; who must carry around an embryo that grows in bulk and weight, making her more and more ungainly as her pregnancy advances; and who, when the child is born, must nurse it.

6   Because women become pregnant, they simply cannot produce as many children as can men. We may regret this fact, glory in it or simply accept it, but it remains, nevertheless, an indelible part of our biology. Although Priam's wife Hecuba, the queen of Troy, was said to have had more than twenty children, twelve or so is a more realistic maximum for one woman, and in most societies, six or seven children is considered quite a few. By contrast, there is little in their biology that limits the number of children that men can produce. For instance, Ismail, a seventeenth-century king of Morocco, is reported to have fathered 1,056 offspring.

7   In some ways, Western society is a great equalizer. By our promotion of monogamy, we have narrowed the reproductive gap between men and women. We are even less likely to tolerate a modern-day Ismail than a Hecuba, and, with the exception of successful sperm donors, most men today really have little opportunity to father more children than women have to mother them. However, we are still perfectly good mammals, and the biology of maleness and femaleness continues to apply to us, just as it does to a mouse or monkey. There is good reason to believe that we are, in fact, primed to be much less sexually egalitarian than we appear to be. We may not be entirely comfortable with *la différence,* but we had better try to understand it.

8   The biological difference between men and women is absolutely crucial to comprehending sociobiology's arguments for the behavioral differences between them. Natural selection dictates that individuals will behave in ways that maximize their fitness, so, clearly, different strategies will be appropriate for the two sexes, given their dramatically different biological characteristics.

9   Sperm are cheap. Eggs are expensive. Accordingly, females have a much greater stake in any one reproductive act. Biologist George C. Williams points out that in virtually all species, males are selected to be aggressive—sexual advertisers—while females are selected to be choosier—comparison shoppers. Again, these behaviors

follow directly from the biology of what it is to be male or female. For males, reproduction is easy, a small amount of time, a small amount of semen, and the potential evolutionary return is very great if offspring are produced. On the other hand, a female who makes a "bad" choice may be in real evolutionary trouble. If fertilization occurs, a baby is begun, and the ensuing process is not only inexorable but immensely demanding. In certain species of flies, copulating with a male from the wrong species results in the death of the female. The male, however, loses little. Among birds, a comparable error by the female in choosing a mate can lead to the production of sterile eggs—a potential wastage of one-fourth of her body weight. She may also be unable to breed again for a full year. The cost to the male? Again, little, if anything. Small wonder that females in virtually every species are more discriminating than males in the choice of sexual partners.

10   The evolutionary mechanism should be clear. Genes that allow females to accept the sorts of mates who make lesser contributions to their reproductive success will leave fewer copies of themselves than will genes that influence the females to be more selective. Accordingly, genes inducing selectivity will increase at the expense of those that are less discriminating. For males, a very different strategy applies. The maximum advantage goes to individuals with fewer inhibitions. A genetically influenced tendency to "play fast and loose"—"love 'em and leave 'em"—may well reflect more biological reality than most of us care to admit.

11   According to Zorba the Greek, God has a very big heart, but "there is one thing that He will not forgive—when a woman calls a man to her bed, and he will not come!" Presumably, had the situation been reversed and a man called a woman to his bed, and she demurred—that He *would* forgive. Sociobiology helps us understand why this should be so.

12   In a well-known custom of medieval Europe, when a serf got married, the lord of the manor had the right—the *droit du seigneur*—to spend the wedding night with the new bride. Intolerable to today's morality, perhaps, but it probably did wonders for the lord's fitness. And why was it the lord who slept with the bride and not the lady of the manor who slept with the groom? Such a practice would probably not have helped milady's fitness and, not surprisingly, there never was a *droit de la madame*.

RAPE

13   In her book *Against Our Will*, Susan Brownmiller claimed that only human beings engage in rape. The facts are otherwise. Rape is common among the birds and bees, and is epidemic among the mallard ducks.[1] In fact, large groups of drakes sometimes

---

[1] Some people may bridle at the notion of rape in animals, but the term seems entirely appropriate when we examine what happens. Among ducks, for example, pairs typically form early in the breeding season, and the two mates engage in elaborate and predictable exchanges of behavior. When this rite finally culminates in mounting, both male and female are clearly in agreement. But sometimes strange males surprise a mated female and attempt to force an immediate copulation, without engaging in any of the normal courtship ritual and despite her obvious and vigorous protest. If that's not rape, it is certainly very much like it.

descend on an unsuspecting female and rape her repeatedly, often causing death, as the victim's head may be held under water for a long period of time. What's going on here? When mallards pair up for breeding, there often remain a number of unmated males, since there are more males than females in most such species (probably owing to the risks involved in defending eggs against predators). These bachelors have been excluded from normal reproduction, and so they engage in what is apparently the next best strategy: raping someone else's female.

14   What about the victim's "husband"? Clearly, his fitness is threatened when his mate is raped, and we would expect him to do something about it. He does, and once again his behavior is remarkably consistent with sociobiological theory. He tries to intervene, beating the attackers away with his wings. However, if his mate is the victim of a gang rape, his chances of success are low and the likelihood of his being injured in the attempt are high, so he usually just stands by. Furthermore, if the rapists indicate by their behavior that the rape has been successful, the victim's mate does a most remarkable—and ungentlemanly—thing. He proceeds to rape the just-raped female himself! His mating is not quite as brutal as the initial violation of the female, but it clearly differs from the usual copulations of mated pairs, with their rather drawn-out courtship rituals. In this case the male simply forces himself upon his hapless and exhausted mate, without even the by-your-leave of "head pumping," *de rigueur* in mallard boudoir etiquette.

15   Again, what is going on here? Once more, the mallard drake is maximizing his fitness. If he can prevent the rape, well and good. If he cannot, either because he is outnumbered or because he is simply too late, the next best thing he can do is to introduce his sperm as quickly as possible, to compete with that of the rapists. Of course, behavior of this sort does not require any awareness by the drake that he is maximizing his fitness. Any genetically influenced tendency to respond in such a fashion will be favored by natural selection, and this behavior will ultimately become characteristic of the species.

16   Compare the behavior of a mallard drake whose female has just been raped with the response of a male mountain bluebird who has been led to suspect that his mate had been adulterous. The mallard does not seek to drive away his female, whereas the bluebird does, at least early in the season. This difference in reaction is not simply one of greater tolerance, understanding or nobler character among mallards. Rather, it simply reflects the cold, unyielding calculus of evolutionary fitness. On Mount Rainier in Washington State, where I conducted my study, there is an apparent surplus of unmated female bluebirds. Accordingly a suspect female can be replaced, and the male is well advised—that is, most fit—to do so. Female mallards, by contrast, are in short supply, so that even after a female has been raped she is still too valuable a mate to drive off, since it is unlikely that the male will get another. Besides, he may have successfully fertilized her. Selection among mallards therefore favors male behaviors that lead to retention of the mate, and maximum protection of the evolutionary investment.

17   Rape in humans is by no means as simple, influenced as it is by an extremely complex overlay of cultural attitudes. Nevertheless, mallard rape and bluebird adultery may have a degree of relevance to human behavior. Perhaps human rapists, in their

own criminally misguided way, are doing the best they can to maximize their fitness. If so, they are not that different from the sexually excluded bachelor mallards. Another point: Whether they like to admit it or not, many human males are stimulated by the idea of rape. This does not make them rapists, but it does give them something else in common with mallards. And another point: During the India-Pakistan war over Bangladesh, many thousands of Hindu women were raped by Pakistani soldiers. A major problem that these women faced was rejection by husband and family. A cultural pattern, of course, but one coinciding clearly with biology.

COMPETITION, AGGRESSION, AND RISK-TAKING

18 It may seem by now as if evolution—and human culture—have given males an overwhelming reproductive and personal advantage over females. Not so. Remember, whenever a given child is produced, it is still a product of just one male and one female. The child is their triumph, their ticket to evolutionary success. When King Ismail of Morocco fathered 1,056 children, it was at the expense of 1,055 other Moroccan males. While he was reproducing, they weren't. On balance, the two sexes are equally successful, always. However, *individuals* of the two sexes need not be and, in fact, rarely are. In most animal species, there is a rather large variation in the number of offspring that different males produce, that is, in their fitness. Some males (the King Ismails) father many children, while others (the eunuchs, either literally or figuratively) have few or none. Among females, however, there is much less difference between the most and the least fit. No woman could produce 1,056 children, but most women are successful in bearing a rather small number. Certainly, the difference between the "haves" and the "have-nots" is less significant than among males.

19   A useful theory of male-female differences bearing on this point has been developed by Harvard's Robert L. Trivers, who has proposed the notion of "parental investment," defined as any expenditure of time, energy or risk that a parent makes on behalf of its offspring. Every expenditure of this sort carries a cost along with it, and an element in this cost is a reduction in the ability of the investing parent to rear additional successful offspring. As with everything in life, investing in a child is a double-edged sword. Give a child food and you have less for yourself and your other children; defend it from a predator, and you run the risk of losing your own life, along with any chance of breeding again. It is clear that women (indeed, females of nearly all species) necessarily invest more in each child than do men, quickly reaching a point where they exhaust their potential and can invest no more. But men have the biological potential to do more, and evolution favors those who attempt to do so.

20   Trivers's theory of parental investment emphasizes that, because of the high cost of offspring to women, they are limited in how many they can produce. During the nine months that she is pregnant, a woman cannot reproduce again—she is already occupied. A man continues to produce perfectly good sperm during that period. Furthermore, after the child is born, a woman is biologically primed to nurse it, often for

several years. Her parental investment is "taken" and will not be available to her hus-band again for quite a while. In most animal species, therefore, the best reproductive arrangement for males is that they be mated to many females. As long as the females are also fulfilling their reproductive potential, this arrangement is satisfactory to their fitness as well.

21   Biology dictates that women provide more initial investment in their offspring than do men, and in the technical language of sociobiology, the sex investing more becomes a limiting resource for the sex investing less. For human beings, this means that men will compete with other men for access to women much more often than will women compete with other women for access to men. After all, the reproductive success of men is limited largely by the number of women they inseminate—more wives or lovers, more children. The reproductive success of women, however, is only rarely limited by the number of men with whom they copulate. For a man to be suc-cessful in making his sperm an evolutionary success, he must obtain, at a minimum, a woman's investment of an egg and placenta not already in use. This may not always be easy. What a woman needs to project her genes into the future is only a small con-tribution from the opposite sex, and it is unlikely that she will be unable to find a man willing to oblige.

22   The difference between male success and failure is likely to be enormous, result-ing in strong competition for selection among males, for whom the payoff is so great. Because the payoff for females is much less, competition is also much less. As might be expected, this difference has wide-ranging consequences for the behavior of males and females.

23   Certain animal species exaggerate male-female differences with particular clarity. Among elephant seals, sea-going mammals that breed off the California coast, the adult males are truly elephantine, weighing about three tons, while the females are less than one-quarter of that size. Typically, these seals breed in large harems, presided over by one or a few adult males. If the harem is a small one, fifty females or so, a single male, the harem master, usually does most of the breeding. In larger harems, because a single male is hard-pressed to service all his females and also to defend them from the advances of other males, several other males may also father some pups. A successful harem master may well father 150 pups in a single year, a phenomenal evolutionary achievement.

24   Of course, success by the harem master is balanced by failure among the other males; harems make for many bachelors who do not father any offspring. There is no payoff for being such an evolutionary failure, and males therefore engage each other in titanic battles with high stakes and high mortality. Adult females do not fight. As with the males, their fitness is maximized by breeding, but, unlike the males, they are virtually guaranteed the opportunity to do so. Their successes, of course, are more restrained. There is simply no such thing as an evolutionary jackpot for fe-males, who do well to produce a single pup every year. Since she may live twelve to fifteen years, a female can hope to produce no more than 12 offspring or so during her lifetime. (Compare that ability with 150 offspring in a single year for a successful harem master.)

25   People aren't elephant seals, of course, but we do share the same mammalian reproductive biology. And there may be reason to suppose that, through most of our evolutionary history, we ourselves were harem makers and that even today we carry indelible signs of this heritage in our bodies and perhaps, as well, in our behavior.

26   It is recognized increasingly that there are real differences between little boys and little girls, behavioral differences that begin early in life and that derive at least in part from our biology. For example, boys tend to be more active and more aggressive than girls. Girls accidentally exposed to testosterone, the male sex hormone, while still in their mother's uterus were found to be "masculinized" as children. They often developed into tomboys, favoring rough-and-tumble outdoor play, and were generally more active than other, "normal" girls, even though their parents seemingly did not treat them any differently. In fact, the parents of such children were so disturbed by their daughters' "boylike" behavior that the children were brought to a doctor—the basis of the discovery of the testosterone exposure.

27   The biology of male-female differences suggests a reason why little boys are more likely than girls to climb trees, get into fights, get covered with mud and wander far from home. Their behavior is more risky and more flamboyant. Natural selection and parental investment theory make intelligible much of what seems to be going on.

28   There are many possible predictions of differing male and female behavior that can be made and that would be worth testing. For example, male-male competition is likely to be greater when harems occur than when all of a group's members are monogamously mated. The reasoning is that harems are likely to leave some males sexually disenfranchised, but in situations where every male gets mated, there is little call for sexual competition. We also expect, and find, a greater male-female difference in behavior in harem-forming species, since reproductive success in males requires fighting success as well. It would be interesting to learn whether male-female differences in children's play are greater in polygynous than in monogamous societies. Such findings would not necessarily suggest a genetically influenced difference between males in the two types of societies, but if risky, aggressive behavior is more valued and more rewarded in one society than in another, we might expect that that society would be the polygynous one.

29   It has been observed that infant boys seem to be more "colicky" than girls. Perhaps they have more gastrointestinal distress, or simply a greater "need to cry," but whatever the cause, one result is that they receive greater parental attention, perhaps even more food and nursing. Such behavior can be risky, since it may backfire and anger the parent, but, as with the elephant seals, boys have probably been selected to take such risks.

OTHER THEORIES

30   What theories are available to account for the differences between men and women, both in sexual proclivities and in aggressiveness? The few that exist are woefully unconvincing. One theory proposed by Sigmund Freud has, for better or worse, been

highly influential. According to Freud, most of our adult behavior derives from sexual impulses redirected early in life, with male-female differences proving no exception. Just as the mythical Greek Oedipus is supposed to have murdered his father and married his mother, little boys are believed to develop an early sexual yearning for their mothers. This potential incest is inhibited only because the mother is "already taken" by the much larger and more formidable father. The healthy male must work out his Oedipal conflict by identifying with his father and by seeking out other women who will ultimately substitute for the forbidden mother. In the process, of course, he may compete with other young males and may further act out his frustrated inability to dominate his father.

31   And little girls? As infants, they too are sexually inclined toward their mothers but soon make the shocking discovery that they (the little girls) don't have a penis. They develop "penis envy," and may resent their mothers for having irreparably castrated them. They cannot achieve their original goal—possession of the mother—because they are the "wrong" sex, and unfortunately father is also unavailable, because mother is around. So girls are resigned to a passive acceptance of their unhappy lot, producing babies as a "penis substitute."

32   Another theory, common in social science, is that boys act as they do because such behavior is taught to them, and the same for girls. There is no question about it, we do do a great deal to inculcate gender identity among our children. Girls are more likely to be given dolls to play with, and boys tend to receive toy airplanes. Much of this early conditioning may be quite unconscious, even by the most sexually unstereotyped parent. For example, we tend to hold girl babies differently—often, more tenderly—than boys, and we are more inclined toward rough-and-tumble play with boy babies. These differences, which almost certainly contribute to differences among adults, are not limited to Western societies. Among the world's warlike non-industrialized societies, boys are treated quite unlike girls. Beginning in infancy, they are rewarded for intemperate, aggressive behavior, which doubtless makes for intemperate, aggressive men.

33   This point is significant and carries a real message if we are to ameliorate our own sexist society. Dick-and-Jane books must show Jane doing exciting, interesting things too, if real-life Janes are to grow up believing that they can do so. But as an all-encompassing explanation for male-female differences, early social experience is simply insufficient. If we are to believe that there are no real male-female differences in behavior, and that such differences as we see are simply a result of the differential experiences that society provides little boys and little girls, we must also explain why such differences are promulgated independently by every society on earth. Anthropologist Marvin Harris has written: "Not a shred of evidence, historical or contemporary, supports the existence of a single society in which women controlled the political and economic lives of men."[2] It strains belief that around the globe and

[2] However, I don't wish to misrepresent Harris, who then provides a rather standard social science approach: "The appropriate response . . . is an investigation of the cultural conditions that have nurtured and sustained male sexism. . . . Male supremacy is not a biological imperative or a genetically programmed characteristic of the human species."

throughout history women have been the victims of a coordinated and sustained plot by churlish males who have conspired to manipulate the social structure to exploit women by forcing them into unwanted roles.

34 Granted, human societies tend to "make" girls distinct from boys. In addition, different societies do so in different ways and to different degrees. But *they all do it,* and the most reasonable explanation is that, at least to some extent, such differences express something of the biological dissimilarities between males and females. Such a conclusion is unavoidable. Society may exaggerate sex differences between people but it does not create them. Lionel Tiger and Robin Fox have pointed out that we learn aggressiveness as we learn love—easily. The same may well be true of sex role differences.

35 Another common explanation of male-female differences holds that the two sexes differ in their hormone levels, with testosterone prevailing in men and estrogen in women. Certainly, male-female hormone variations are very real, and no farmer needs to be told the difference between a bull and an ox, a stallion and a gelding, or a rooster and a capon. But endocrine action is an immediate, proximal cause, not an ultimate, evolutionary one. To say that men are more aggressive because of testosterone is like saying that internal-combustion engines are noisier than electric motors because of gasoline. In a sense, the statement is true, but a deeper fact is that internal-combustion engines use gasoline and other combustible (that is, noisy) fuels because that is they way they are designed. We are inquiring here into the design features of human behavior—in the present case, why we respond to testosterone in the way we do, and why men secrete more of it than women. Why is sugar sweet? Ask evolution.

36 Actually, there are two other biological factors that might contribute to the differences between men and women. Greater male size and aggressiveness may also be due in part to a long evolutionary history of selection for male ability to defend the group and family against predators and enemies, as well as for the ability to hunt successfully. While these notions are fine up to a point, they don't explain such other phenomena as greater male sexual availability. Furthermore, they beg the question of why males were selected for defense and/or hunting in the first place. Perhaps this was because males are biologically the more expendable sex.

37 The fact remains: in all animals, human and otherwise, males are selected for a reproductive strategy different from that of females. In nearly all of these cases, males compete with other males for sexual access to females, as a consequence of their biologically defined maleness. Among some species, the contest is open and rather brutal. Elephant seals, elk and mountain sheep rams must defeat all rivals to win their harems. Females in these species are passive; they maximize their fitness by acquiescing to the results of the male contests, just as the males maximize their fitness by contesting. In other species, however, competition is often much more subtle. Males and females must still engage in fitness-maximizing strategies, but the male may either have to gain control of important environmental resources or make himself attractive to the female. This sort of self-advertisement introduces a whole new, exciting dimension to reproductive strategies—female choice.

FEMALE CHOICE

38   In resource-based mating systems, males are selected to compete with other males for control of the best resources, and females are selected to mate preferentially with the winners for use of those resources. As the saying goes, "Those that have, get." The orange-humped honeyguide is a brilliant-colored bird that lives in Nepal and loves to eat beeswax. Beehives are, therefore, highly valued and are defended energetically by males. To obtain beeswax, a female must copulate with the proprietor male, and, as an indication of the importance of the resource, only males defending hives do any copulating. While females find non-beehive-owning males totally resistible, one particularly "wealthy" male was observed to mate forty-six times with at least eighteen different females during one breeding season! Females probably gain twofold in this system. By copulating with proprietor males they gain access to a valued food; furthermore, by mating only with proprietors, they insure that they will be inseminated by the best males, those selected to compete for control of the hives. Those that win are likely to be the *best;* by winning, they have proven themselves.

39   A similar case has been described by Syracuse University biologist Larry Wolf for purple-throated Carib hummingbirds on the island of Dominica. In this instance, the valued resource is certain trees that have an abundance of flowers. Hummingbirds are particularly fond of these blooms, and the males defend territories containing as many flowering trees as possible, aggressively driving off other males that attempt to feed there. Interestingly, they drive off females as well, unless the females copulate with them. Males, then, give food in exchange for sex. Wolf reported his observations in a scientific paper he entitled "Prostitution Behavior in a Tropical Hummingbird," and his use of this term is probably correct, since what is human prostitution if not the exchange of sexual favors for resources? In human prostitution the male client may not be trying to impregnate his companion, and she is almost certainly not trying to become pregnant by him. However, it is still consistent with biology that males seek sex and are willing to pay for it, and that females have something that males desire for which they demand payment.

40   The relevant point for human sociobiology is that we almost certainly base much of our mating on resources, although perhaps less directly than do red-winged blackbirds, tropical hummingbirds or Himalayan honeyguides. Certainly we have modified, sometimes even redirected, the internal whisperings of fitness maximization that control so much of animal behavior. With our remarkable ability to be subtle and complex, we encrust our biological impulses with culture, learning and psychological satisfactions that are often several steps removed from our biology. When we are sexually excited, reproducing our genes may be the last thing on our minds, but natural selection is under no obligation to let us in on its designs. It is probably no accident that when it comes to reproduction, men are nearly always treated as "success objects," which is how beeswax may be very much like a Ferrari—and vice versa.

41   The connection between resources and human mating is particularly apparent in polygynous societies, where, not surprisingly, the standard pattern is for a man to acquire wives as he acquires resources. He may acquire his first wife at age twenty to

twenty-five, his second at thirty-five to forty, his third at forty-five to fifty, and so on. There appears to be a strong connection between polygyny and gerontocracy, with older men having more wives. It may not be coincidental that older men also have more resources. In addition, senior members of a society have often proved themselves in hunting, war or other activities valued by the group. The practice of trophy hunting and collecting is nearly universal; it may well have evolved as a technique for males to display their competence to attentive females. Among Muslims, who may have up to four wives, the number, appropriately, is controlled rather strictly by the man's wealth.

42   To consider such societies as exploiting women is to be both nearsighted and culture bound. A woman may be far better off, in terms of both personal amenities and reproductive success, as the third wife of a wealthy sheik than as the only wife of a pauper.

43   Among many Australian aboriginals,

> The women tended to aggregate themselves in collectives of co-wives around the men at the peak of their productive capacity, and this tendency reached its maximum when the women had their greatest child-rearing burdens. It will be immediately noted that in this explanation it was the women and not the men who took the active role to establish polygynous units, and that this type of family provided the optimum conditions for the rearing of the younger generation inside the collectives of co-wives of the polygynous families.

44   Note that men are at the "peak of their productive capacity" when they are in their mid-forties—that is, when they are most able to provide resources for their families, and not when they are at their sexual peak, which occurs in the teens. Sperm are produced in such amounts, even in middle age, that potency takes a back seat to other considerations.

45   Throughout the world, "May-December" marriages are common, almost always with the man December and woman May. It is fascinating that shortly after taking the Senate floor to denounce the "immorality" of former United States Supreme Court Justice William O. Douglas for taking a wife less than half his age, South Carolina's Senator Strom Thurmond did the same thing, marrying a woman young enough to be his granddaughter! Although tongues may occasionally wag at such behavior, it is not generally regarded as discrediting, perhaps because of grudging, if unconscious, recognition that the people involved are maximizing their fitness, or at least behaving in ways consistent with evolutionary strategies of resources and mate selection. But consider the scandal when an older woman associates with a much younger man! This relationship is somehow "against nature." Given the sociobiology of mate selection, the movie *Harold and Maude,* which told the story of a sexual liaison between a seventeen-year-old-boy and an eighty-year-old woman, had no alternative but to be tragicomic.

46   Hypergamy (literally, "marrying up") is widespread among humans. Predictably, it is especially a strategy of women. It is much more common for women to be influenced by the accomplishments of potential husbands than for men to be concerned

with similar traits in their wives. Which situation seems more incongruous, a male doctor, college professor or business executive whose wife has only a high-school education, or a female doctor, college professor or business executive whose husband hasn't gone to college? This tendency to hypergamy places successful females in our own society in a difficult position. They are much more limited in their choices of suitable mates than are equally successful males. Men can find mates from the entire spectrum of female population, while women tend to be uncomfortable with men who are "beneath" them. Although in fairy tales there is always the princess who runs off with the gypsy, it requires a man with an especially strong ego to accept a mate who is more successful than he is.

47   The tendency for female animals to select males that provide resources that contribute most to their fitness and the corresponding tendency of males to oblige them has had some bizarre results. Males of many different species of birds and insects present their females with food as part of courtship. In certain cases, the male even gives his female the ultimate gift: himself. The female dines on the male during or after, or, in some cases, before copulating with him. This behavior can be seen as the gruesome result of a female's selection of males who provide her with additional food, that is, males who will contribute to her fitness. A male concerned with his own fitness has no alternative but to accede.

48   Courtship in the natural world often involves gift giving and receiving, and because males and females are constituted differently, they almost never go "Dutch treat."

49   Among the small carnivorous insects known as empid flies, females are larger than males, and, not uncommonly, an unlucky male finds himself being a meal rather than a mate. This is fine with the females, so long as they are eventually fertilized by an occasional "lucky" male. In certain empid species, males avoid this fate by first securing a ritual offering, generally a smaller fly of another species, and presenting this juicy morsel to their chosen female. While she feeds happily, he may copulate unmolested. Males of other empid fly species first adorn their gifts with silk, perhaps in order to make them more conspicuous to the female. This decoration may also ensure that it takes longer for the female to open the package, thereby giving the male more time to copulate. Males of yet another species suck the prey dry themselves— and wrap it in an especially large amount of silk. Presumably, once the deception is discovered by their paramours it is too late. Other empids dispense with the prey altogether and simply take a twig or piece of leaf, making certain only to wrap it well. And in one species the males don't even bother with the contents; they go a-courtin' with an elaborate silken balloon containing . . . nothing whatever!

CONCLUSION

50   We have offered here a powerful mix of theory and animal data, all pointing toward several general behavior patterns: (1) Male aggressiveness, along with insistent and relatively undiscriminating sexuality, as opposed to female docility and sexual fussiness;

(2) male-male competition; (3) a widespread tendency toward polygyny (harem formation); (4) a major role for female choice, acting through preference for mates with "good genes," access to important resources, and/or appropriate—that is, fitness maximizing—behavior.

51   When it comes to the human species, the situation is obviously more fuzzy. We are very special animals, since we are also linguistic and cultural creatures with much behavior that seems arbitrary, symbolic and stylistic. At this point, it is only possible to point out the similarity between the predictions of natural selection, confirmed time and again in all other species, and the reality of human behavior. We may then decide simply to marvel at the coincidence. Or we may deny it as altogether irrelevant, misleading or perhaps even dangerous. Or finally we may consider it suggestive enough to warrant some very careful examination. This last choice points toward the establishment of the new field of human sociobiology, and it is on that choice that I am betting.

52   This is, in many ways, a troublesome chapter. I hope, of course, that it will not incur the wrath of feminists, but more than that, I worry that it will be misinterpreted and used as support for the continued oppression of women. My intent has been only to explore the evolutionary biology of male-female differences, not to espouse any particular social, political or ethical philosophy. Evolution simply *is*—or, better yet, evolution *does*. It says nothing whatever about what ought to be. It does have its share of imperatives, of course, but they're not moral imperatives. If females appear to be scheming and yet basically passive, males are nasty and aggressive, sometimes ridiculous and, given modern weaponry, very, very dangerous. There is probably a risk that the sociobiological understanding of male-female differences will be used to justify sexist attitudes, to defend the view that it is only "natural" for men to be aggressive and for women to be more passive, and all the rest. But, as we've said before, what is natural is not necessarily what is good. Furthermore, the inclinations predicted by sociobiology are just that: inclinations. They are not certainties.

53   It will be a gross abuse of science if evolution's insights are used to support the culturally mediated exaggeration of sex differences in behavior. Modern society continues to exploit women intolerably and to deprive them of their rights to an extent that demands redress. We owe it to ourselves both to evaluate the differences in the treatment of males and females and to understand the differences that do exist. A just society demands objective, unbiased facts. We need far more information in order to understand the real nature of men and women. The Jeffersonian principle is that all people are created equal, not that they are identical (which would be the case only if we were all born from one single egg). If society has an obligation to provide all of its members with the fullest realization of their potential, we had better explore that potential and give up being intellectual ostriches.

54   To my thinking, sexism occurs when society differentially values one sex above another, providing extra opportunities for one (usually the males) and denying equal opportunities for the other (usually the females). As such, it has nothing to do with sociobiology. On the other hand, sexism is also sometimes applied to the simple identification of male-female differences, and on this count, sociobiology is, I suppose,

sexist. No one would think it awful to state that a man has a penis and a woman, a vagina. Or that a man produces sperm and a woman, eggs. But when we begin exploring the behavioral implications of these facts somebody is sure to cry "Foul." If male-female differences are sexist, we should put the blame where it really belongs, on the greatest sexist of all: "Mother" Nature!

Notes

My technical papers reported on mallard rape (Barash, 1977b). Robert L. Trivers is a brilliant sociobiologist who has made several major contributions to the field with important theoretical papers during the 1970s. His work on parental investment and its influence on mate selection (1972) is already a modern classic. Burney LeBoeuf, a professor at the University of California at Santa Cruz, was originally trained as a psychologist. He subsequently saw the light and began biological studies of social behavior in a spectacular mammal, the elephant seal. His technical account (1974) is a valuable reference on competition in these oversized animals. Johns Hopkins University researcher John Money is one of our foremost experts on the hormonal aspects of male-female differences. His book, *Man and Woman, Boy and Girl* (1972), written with psychiatrist Anke Ehrhardt, especially emphasizes the role of hormones during child development. The Marvin Harris quotation is from his article (1977b) in the *New York Times*, titled "Why Men Dominate Women." I think he is wrong about why, although clearly right about whether. His ideas of "cultural materialism" are actually quite close to sociobiology in that they look at the adaptive value of seemingly non-adaptive traits.

For hummingbird prostitution, see the report by Syracuse University biologist Larry Wolf (1975), and for the important role of beeswax in determining the mating system of Himalayan honeyguides, see Cronin and Sherman (1977). Stephen Emlen and Lewis Oring (1977) presented a technical account of resource-based mating systems in general, emphasizing that social systems may well be predictable from the local pattern of environmental resources. For gerontocracy and polygyny among Australian aborigines, see Rose (1968). New Mexico entomologist Randy Thornhill (1976) discusses cannibalism of the male by the female as an especially dramatic aspect of parental investment.

The strange courtship of empid flies was described by Kessel (1955).

WRITING ASSIGNMENTS

Analysis

1. Write the text for a class lecture that explains how Barash's concept of biologically determined male and female reproductive strategies applies to *one* of the following: greater female "docility and sexual fussiness," rape by males, male-male competitiveness, male in the breadwinner role, courtship behavior, and the criteria for mate selection. Draw additional evidence from the selection in this chapter by Gorman and examples from your own experiences.

2. Write the text of a class lecture in which you provide alternative explanations for one of the behaviors given a sociobiological explanation by Barash. Where relevant, draw on material from the selections in this chapter by Sandra Bem, Stephen Jay Gould, and Ernestine Friedl and examples from your own experiences.

3. As a class, use topics two and three in No. 1 as the basis of a class debate on the "nature and/or nurture" basis of gender.

4. In his conclusion, Barash says, "We are very special animals, since we are also linguistic and cultural creatures. . . ." Compared to biology, what role do language and culture play in Barash's explanation of human behavior?

5. First, list Barash's references to literature and popular culture (e.g., Tom Sawyer and Huck Finn, *Harold and Maude*), and then evaluate their logical relevance and stylistic effectiveness.

6. List Barash's attributions of humanlike consciousness to animals, as in the following: "While females [bees] find non-beehive-owning males totally resistible, one particularly 'wealthy' male. . . ." Explain how such attributions reinforce Barash's thesis.

7. As an advertising executive, you have just convinced a major client to hire you to produce the campaign for a new product. Write two advertisements (one aimed at men, the other at women) for the client's new line of sports clothing or for an automobile. Include a description of the visuals and text, indicate the publications where the advertisements will run, and use evidence from Barash to explain the gender-linked basis of the advertisements' appeal.

Argument

1. Note the underlined metaphors in this selection:

> Certainly we have modified, sometimes even redirected the <u>internal whisperings</u> of fitness maximization that control so much of animal behavior. With our remarkable ability to be subtle and complex, we <u>encrust</u> our biological impulses with culture, learning and psychological satisfactions that are often several steps removed from our biology.

List these and other such metaphors in Barash's essay and argue whether they fairly characterize the roles of biology and culture in shaping human behavior.

2. Barash concludes his essay by saying, "If male-female differences are sexist, we should put the blame where it really belongs, on the greatest sexist of all: 'Mother' Nature!" Do you agree? Explain your position.

3. Use Barash's essay to support maintaining the traditional nuclear family as a way to control "natural" but unfortunate human inclinations.

4. Use Barash's essay to argue that the nuclear family and monogamy are doomed because they are "unnatural."

Personal Writing and Writing from Research

1. What are the implications of Barash's sociobiological interpretation of human behavior for the politics of rape, increased women's participation in historically male activities, prostitution, or violence?

2. Write a research paper on the cultural and historical origins of one of the following: prostitution in nineteenth-century England, the medieval European custom of *le droit du seigneur,* the Punjabi Bedi-Sikh practice of daughter-killing, Inuit (Eskimo) female infanticide, or the rape of "enemy" women by soldiers in war.

3. Imagine that you are an adult advising your adolescent child about dating behavior or an adult friend about choosing a spouse. What advice would you give if you agreed with Barash? Write your advice in the form of a letter. Would the sex of your child or friend affect what you say?

4. Does science's current understanding of how genes operate support Barash's view that genes control complex human behaviors like courtship, mating behavior, marriage patterns, competition, and aggression? Research this question and present your findings as the text of a 15-minute lecture to your class.

Biological Potentiality vs. Biological Determinism

Stephen Jay Gould

Stephen Jay Gould is the Alexander Agassiz Professor of Zoology at Harvard University. A prolific author, he has won the National Book Award, the National Book Critics Circle Award, and the Phi Beta Kappa Science Award (twice) and was in the first group of MacArthur Award winners. "Biological Potentiality vs. Biological Determinism" first appeared in *Ever Since Darwin* (1979).

Gould refers throughout his essay to Edmund O. Wilson's *Sociobiology: The New Synthesis* (1975). Wilson, a noted entomologist and a leading figure in sociobiology, is the Baird Professor of Science and professor of zoology at Harvard.

Journal Topics: Describe an incident when you or another person could have been aggressive or peaceful, dominant or submissive, spiteful or generous. In describing what happened, attempt to explain why the person acted as he or she did. Did these responses seem to demonstrate potentiality or determinism?

As You Read: (1) Why does Gould begin his essay with a reference to the Linnaean system of classification? (2) How does Gould's introductory reference to the

Socratic injunction, *nosce te ipsum*—"know thyself," foreshadow one of his major points about human behavior? (3) In your own words, explain the difference between "homologous" and "analogous" features, and provide examples. (4) Why is Gould's distinction between potentiality and determinism so important?

1   In 1758, Linnaeus faced the difficult decision of how to classify his own species in the definitive edition of his *Systema Naturae*. Would he simply rank *Homo sapiens* among the other animals or would he create for us a separate status? Linnaeus compromised. He placed us within his classification (close to monkeys and bats), but set us apart by his description. He defined our relatives by the mundane, distinguishing characters of size, shape, and number of fingers and toes. For *Homo sapiens,* he wrote only the Socratic injunction: *nosce te ipsum*—"know thyself."

2   For Linnaeus, *Homo sapiens* was both special and not special. Unfortunately, this eminently sensible resolution has been polarized and utterly distorted by most later commentators. Special and not special have come to mean nonbiological and biological, or nurture and nature. These later polarizations are nonsensical. Humans are animals and everything we do lies within our biological potential. Nothing arouses this ardent (although currently displaced) New Yorker to greater anger than the claims of some self-styled "ecoactivists" that large cities are the "unnatural" harbingers of our impending destruction. But—and here comes the biggest *but* I can muster—the statement that humans are animals does not imply that our specific patterns of behavior and social arrangements are in any way directly determined by our genes. *Potentiality* and *determination* are different concepts.

3   The intense discussion aroused by E. O. Wilson's *Sociobiology* (Harvard University Press, 1975) has led me to take up this subject. Wilson's book has been greeted by a chorus of praise and publicity. I, however, find myself among the smaller group of its detractors. Most of *Sociobiology* wins from me the same high praise almost universally accorded it. For a lucid account of evolutionary principles and an indefatigably thorough discussion of social behavior among all groups of animals, *Sociobiology* will be the primary document for years to come. But Wilson's last chapter, "From Sociobiology to Sociology," leaves me very unhappy indeed. After twenty-six chapters of careful documentation for the nonhuman animals, Wilson concludes with an extended speculation on the genetic basis of supposedly universal patterns in human behavior. Unfortunately, since this chapter is his statement on the subject closest to all our hearts, it has also attracted more than 80 percent of all the commentary in the popular press.

4   We who have criticized this last chapter have been accused of denying altogether the relevance of biology to human behavior, of reviving an ancient superstition by placing ourselves outside the rest of "the creation." Are we pure "nurturists"? Do we permit a political vision of human perfectibility to blind us to evident constraints imposed by our biological nature? The answer to both statements is no. The issue is not universal biology vs. human uniqueness, but biological potentiality vs. biological determinism.

5   Replying to a critic of his article in the *New York Times Magazine* (October 12, 1975), Wilson wrote:

> There is no doubt that the patterns of human social behavior, including altruistic behavior, are under genetic control, in the sense that they represent a restricted subset of possible patterns that are very different from the patterns of termites, chimpanzees and other animal species.

6   If this is all that Wilson means by genetic control, then we can scarcely disagree. Surely we do not do all the things that other animals do, and just as surely, the range of our potential behavior is circumscribed by our biology. We would lead very different social lives if we photosynthesized (no agriculture, gathering, or hunting—the major determinants of our social evolution) or had life cycles like those of the gall midges. (When feeding on an uncrowded mushroom, these insects reproduce in the larval or pupal stage. The young grow within the mother's body, devour her from inside, and emerge from her depleted external shell ready to feed, grow the next generation, and make the supreme sacrifice.)

7   But Wilson makes much stronger claims. Chapter 27 is not a statement about the range of potential human behaviors or even an argument for the restriction of that range from a much larger total domain among all animals. It is, primarily, an extended speculation on the existence of genes for specific and variable traits in human behavior—including spite, aggression, xenophobia, conformity, homosexuality, and the characteristic behavioral differences between men and women in Western society. Of course, Wilson does not deny the role of nongenetic learning in human behavior; he even states at one point that "genes have given away most of their sovereignty." But, he quickly adds, genes "maintain a certain amount of influence in at least the behavioral qualities that underlie variations between cultures." And the next paragraph calls for a "discipline of anthropological genetics."

8   Biological determinism is the primary theme in Wilson's discussion of human behavior; chapter 27 makes no sense in any other context. Wilson's primary aim, as I read him, is to suggest that Darwinian theory might reformulate the human sciences just as it previously transformed so many other biological disciplines. But Darwinian processes cannot operate without genes to select. Unless the "interesting" properties of human behavior are under specific genetic control, sociology need fear no invasion of its turf. By interesting, I refer to the subjects sociologists and anthropologists fight about most often—aggression, social stratification, and differences in behavior between men and women. If genes only specify that we are large enough to live in a world of gravitational forces, need to rest our bodies by sleeping, and do not photosynthesize, then the realm of genetic determinism will be relatively uninspiring.

9   What is the direct evidence for genetic control of specific human social behavior? At the moment, the answer is none whatever. (It would not be impossible, in theory, to gain such evidence by standard, controlled experiments in breeding, but we do not raise people in *Drosophila* bottles, establish pure lines, or control environments for invariant nurturing.) Sociobiologists must therefore advance indirect arguments

based on plausibility. Wilson uses three major strategies: universality, continuity, and adaptiveness.

10   1. Universality: If certain behaviors are invariably found in our closest primate relatives and among humans themselves, a circumstantial case for common, inherited genetic control may be advanced. Chapter 27 abounds with statements about supposed human universals. For example, "Human beings are absurdly easy to indoctrinate—they *seek* it." Or, "Men would rather believe than know." I can only say that my own experience does not correspond with Wilson's.

11   When Wilson must acknowledge diversity, he often dismisses the uncomfortable "exceptions" as temporary and unimportant aberrations. Since Wilson believes that repeated, often genocidal warfare has shaped our genetic destiny, the existence of nonaggressive peoples is embarrassing. But, he writes: "It is to be expected that some isolated cultures will escape the process for generations at a time, in effect reverting temporarily to what ethnographers classify as a pacific state."

12   In any case, even if we can compile a list of behavioral traits shared by humans and our closest primate relatives, this does not make a good case for common genetic control. Similar results need not imply similar causes; in fact, evolutionists are so keenly aware of this problem that they have developed a terminology to express it. Similar features due to common genetic ancestry are "homologous"; similarities due to common function, but with different evolutionary histories, are "analogous" (the wings of birds and insects, for example—the common ancestor of both groups lacked wings). I will argue below that a basic feature of human biology supports the idea that many behavioral similarities between humans and other primates are analogous, and that they have no direct genetic specification in humans.

13   2. Continuity: Wilson claims, with ample justice in my opinion, that the Darwinian explanation of altruism in W. D. Hamilton's 1964 theory of "kin selection" forms the basis for an evolutionary theory of animal societies. Altruistic acts are the cement of stable societies, yet they seem to defy a Darwinian explanation. On Darwinian principles, all individuals are selected to maximize their own genetic contribution to future generations. How, then, can they willingly sacrifice or endanger themselves by performing altruistic acts to benefit others?

14   The resolution is charmingly simple in concept, although complex in technical detail. By benefiting relatives, altruistic acts preserve an altruist's genes even if the altruist himself will not be the one to perpetuate them. For example, in most sexually reproducing organisms, an individual shares (on average) one-half the genes of his sibs and one-eighth the genes of his first cousins. Hence, if faced with a choice of saving oneself alone or sacrificing oneself to save more than two sibs or more than eight first cousins, the Darwinian calculus favors altruistic sacrifice; for in so doing, an altruist actually increases his own genetic representation in future generations.

15   Natural selection will favor the preservation of such self-serving altruist genes. But what of altruistic acts toward non-relatives? Here sociobiologists must invoke a related concept of "reciprocal altruism" to preserve a genetic explanation. The altruistic act entails some danger and no immediate benefit, but if it inspires a reciprocal act by the current beneficiary at some future time, it may pay off in the long run: a

genetic incarnation of the age-old adage: you scratch my back and I'll scratch yours (even if we're not related).

16   The argument from continuity then proceeds. Altruistic acts in other animal societies can be plausibly explained as examples of Darwinian kin selection. Humans perform altruistic acts and these are likely to have a similarly direct genetic basis. But again, similarity of result does not imply identity of cause (see below for an alternate explanation based on biological potentiality rather than biological determinism).

17   3. Adaptiveness: Adaptation is the hallmark of Darwinian processes. Natural selection operates continuously and relentlessly to fit organisms to their environments. Disadvantageous social structures, like poorly designed morphological structures, will not survive for long.

18   Human social practices are clearly adaptive. Marvin Harris has delighted in demonstrating the logic and sensibility of those social practices in other cultures that seem most bizarre to smug Westerners (*Cows, Pigs, Wars, and Witches,* Random House, 1974). Human social behavior is riddled with altruism; it is also clearly adaptive. Is this not a prima facie argument for direct genetic control? My answer is definitely "no," and I can best illustrate my claim by reporting an argument I recently had with an eminent anthropologist.

19   My colleague insisted that the classic story of Eskimos on ice floes provides adequate proof for the existence of specific altruist genes maintained by kin selection. Apparently, among some Eskimo peoples, social units are arranged as family groups. If food resources dwindle and the family must move to survive, aged grandparents willingly remain behind (to die) rather than endanger the survival of their entire family by slowing an arduous and dangerous migration. Family groups with no altruist genes have succumbed to natural selection as migrations hindered by the old and sick lead to the death of entire families. Grandparents with altruist genes increase their own fitness by their sacrifice, for they enhance the survival of close relatives sharing their genes.

20   The explanation by my colleague is plausible, to be sure, but scarcely conclusive since an eminently simple, nongenetic explanation also exists: there are no altruist genes at all, in fact, no important genetic differences among Eskimo families whatsoever. The sacrifice of grandparents is an adaptive, but nongenetic, cultural trait. Families with no tradition for sacrifice do not survive for many generations. In other families, sacrifice is celebrated in song and story; aged grandparents who stay behind become the greatest heroes of the clan. Children are socialized from their earliest memories to the glory and honor of such sacrifice.

21   I cannot prove my scenario, any more than my colleague can demonstrate his. But in the current context of no evidence, they are at least equally plausible. Likewise, reciprocal altruism undeniably exists in human societies, but this provides no evidence whatever for its genetic basis. As Benjamin Franklin said: "We must all hang together, or assuredly we shall all hang separately." Functioning societies may require reciprocal altruism. But these acts need not be coded into our consciousness by genes; they may be inculcated equally well by learning.

22   I return, then, to Linnaeus's compromise—we are both ordinary and special. The central feature of our biological uniqueness also provides the major reason for

doubting that our behaviors are directly coded by specific genes. That feature is, of course, our large brain. Size itself is a major determinant of the function and structure of any object. The large and the small cannot work in the same way. The study of changes that accompany increasing size is called "allometry." Best known are the structural changes that compensate for decreasing surface/volume ratios of large creatures—relatively thick legs and convoluted internal surfaces (lungs, and villi of the small intestine, for example). But markedly increased brain size in human evolution may have had the most profound allometric consequences of all—for it added enough neural connections to convert an inflexible and rather rigidly programmed device into a labile organ, endowed with sufficient logic and memory to substitute non-programmed learning for direct specification as the ground of social behavior. Flexibility may well be the most important determinant of human consciousness; the direct programming of behavior has probably become inadaptive.

23 Why imagine that specific genes for aggression, dominance, or spite have any importance when we know that the brain's enormous flexibility permits us to be aggressive or peaceful, dominant or submissive, spiteful or generous? Violence, sexism, and general nastiness *are* biological since they represent one subset of a possible range of behaviors. But peacefulness, equality, and kindness are just as biological—and we may see their influence increase if we can create social structures that permit them to flourish. Thus, my criticism of Wilson does not involve a nonbiological "environmentalism"; it merely pits the concept of biological potentiality—a brain capable of the full range of human behaviors and rigidly predisposed toward none—against the idea of biological determinism—specific genes for specific behavioral traits.

24 But why is this academic issue so delicate and explosive? There is no hard evidence for either position, and what difference does it make, for example, whether we conform because conformer genes have been selected or because our general genetic makeup permits conformity as one strategy among many?

25 The protracted and intense debate surrounding biological determinism has arisen as a function of its social and political message. Biological determinism has always been used to defend existing social arrangements as biologically inevitable—from "for ye have the poor always with you" to nineteenth-century imperialism to modern sexism. Why else would a set of ideas so devoid of factual support gain such a consistently good press from established media throughout the centuries? This usage is quite out of the control of individual scientists who propose deterministic theories for a host of reasons, often benevolent.

26 I make no attribution of motive in Wilson's or anyone else's case. Neither do I reject determinism because I dislike its political usage. Scientific truth, as we understand it, must be our primary criterion. We live with several unpleasant biological truths, death being the most undeniable and ineluctable. If genetic determinism is true, we will learn to live with it as well. But I reiterate my statement that no evidence exists to support it, that the crude versions of past centuries have been conclusively disproved, and that its continued popularity is a function of social prejudice among those who benefit most from the status quo.

27 But let us not saddle *Sociobiology* with the sins of past determinists. What have been its direct results in the first flush of its excellent publicity? At best, we see the

beginnings of a line of social research that promises only absurdity by its refusal to consider immediate nongenetic factors. The January 30, 1976, issue of *Science* (America's leading technical journal for scientists) contains an article on panhandling that I would have accepted as satire if it had appeared verbatim in the *National Lampoon*. The authors dispatched "panhandlers" to request dimes from various "targets." Results are discussed only in the context of kin selection, reciprocal altruism, and the food-sharing habits of chimps and baboons—nothing on current urban realities in America. As one major conclusion, they find that male panhandlers are "far more successful approaching a single female or a pair of females than a male and female together; they were particularly unsuccessful when approaching a single male or two males together." But not a word about urban fear or the politics of sex—just some statements about chimps and the genetics of altruism (although they finally admit that reciprocal altruism probably does not apply—after all, they argue, what future benefit can one expect from a panhandler).

28   In the first negative comment on *Sociobiology,* economist Paul Samuelson (*Newsweek,* July 7, 1975) urged sociobiologists to tread softly in the zones of race and sex. I see no evidence that his advice is being heeded. In his *New York Times Magazine* article of October 12, 1975, Wilson writes:

> In hunter-gatherer societies, men hunt and women stay at home. This strong bias persists in *most* [my emphasis] agricultural and industrial societies and, on that ground alone, appears to have a genetic origin. . . . My own guess is that the genetic bias is intense enough to cause a substantial division of labor even in the most free and most egalitarian of future societies. . . . Even with identical education and equal access to all professions, men are likely to continue to play a disproportionate role in political life, business and science.

29   We are both similar to and different from other animals. In different cultural contexts, emphasis upon one side or the other of this fundamental truth plays a useful social role. In Darwin's day, an assertion of our similarity broke through centuries of harmful superstition. Now we may need to emphasize our difference as flexible animals with a vast range of potential behavior. Our biological nature does not stand in the way of social reform. We are, as Simone de Beauvoir said, "l'être dont l'être est de n'être pas"—the being whose essence lies in having no essence.

WRITING ASSIGNMENTS

Analysis

1. Summarize Gould's logical objections to applying biological determinism to human social behavior.
2. Where does Gould fit in along the "nature versus nurture" spectrum? In a short essay, classify Gould, Barash, Bem, and Friedl according to their placement on this spectrum, and define the criteria for your placements.
3. *Collaborative Project:* How might a scholar's discipline, which defines the subjects of inquiry, the evidence to be examined, and the methods of examina-

tion, distort a scholar's perceptions and thus predispose the scholar toward certain conclusions? Barash and Gould are zoologists; Bem, a psychologist; and Friedl, a cultural anthropologist. What influence might their disciplines have on the ways these scholars view the nature versus nurture controversy? If such distortion occurs, what can be done about it?

4. Explain the relevance of the anecdote about aged Eskimos' self-sacrifice to the nature versus nurture debate.
5. Gould suggests that, "Flexibility may well be the most important determinant in human consciousness." In an essay, analyze the role that flexibility, a consequence of large brains, plays in shaping the hunter-gatherer societies described by Friedl, one of the human behaviors described by Barash, or your handling of an obstacle in your own life.

Argument

1. *Collaborative Project:* Apply the concepts of "kin selection" and "reciprocal altruism" to explain these situations and defend your positions in essays for debate:

   - A retiree campaigns for a congressional candidate pledged to lowering the deficit by reducing Social Security and Medicare benefits.
   - Parents oppose an affirmative action program at their college *alma mater* even though their children, who have applied to or already attend the school, would probably benefit from it.
   - Family members oppose taking a terminally ill relative off of life-support machines even though the medical expenses are bankrupting the family.

2. *Collaborative Project:* In essays or debate, develop explanations other than "kinship" or "reciprocal altruism" for the above situations.
3. After listening to the debate between the above groups, or reading their papers, other class members write argument essays supporting either side or offering a synthesis of the groups' positions.
4. Gould published his essay in the late 1970s. Do any of the recent scientific experiments described in Gorman's article provide the kind of empirical evidence, which Gould said was lacking, to prove or disprove genetic control of specific human social behaviors?
5. Citing evidence from current events, write an essay supporting or opposing Gould's claim that ". . . peacefulness, equality, and kindness are just as biological—and we may see their influence increase if we can create social structures that permit them to flourish."

Personal Writing and Writing from Research

1. Explore the potential consequences of widespread public acceptance of specific sex-linked genes for aggression, dominance, spite, passivity, manipulativeness, submissiveness, or generosity.
2. *Collaborative Project:* Gould says, "If genetic determinism is true, we will learn to live with it. . . ." Write a research paper on the historical resistance given to

a scientific theory that was later confirmed or refuted, or to a technological development that altered society dramatically. Describe the sources and explain the reasons for this resistance.

3. Gould says, ". . . biological determinism has always been used to defend existing social arrangements as biologically inevitable." Write a research paper describing either historical or contemporary examples of such rationalizing.

Sizing Up the Sexes
Scientists Are Discovering that Gender Differences Have as Much to Do with the Biology of the Brain as with the Way We Are Raised

Christine Gorman

The cover story in the January 20, 1992, issue of *Time* magazine, Christine Gorman's article surveys the scientific activity that is part of the debate over biology's role in gender differences.

Journal Topics: (1) Recall your feelings about and experiences with math and science in junior and senior high school. What factors influenced your attitudes toward these subjects? (2) What are your preconceptions about how the hormones estrogen and testosterone influence human behavior?

As You Read: (1) Summarize the gender-related findings from research on the hypothalamus. (2) Note the direct quotations from all of the scientists that Gorman interviewed; do the scientists' words confirm *significant, permanent* differences in male and female brains? (3) Is Gorman's presentation of their findings at all sensationalized? If so, how?

> What are little boys made of?
> What are little boys made of?
> Frogs and snails
> And puppy dogs' tails,
> That's what little boys are made of.
>
> What are little girls made of?
> What are little girls made of?
> Sugar and spice
> And all that's nice,
> That's what little girls are made of.
> —Anonymous

1 Many scientists rely on elaborately complex and costly equipment to probe the mysteries confronting humankind. Not Melissa Hines. The UCLA behavioral scientist is hoping to solve one of life's oldest riddles with a toybox full of police cars, Lincoln Logs and Barbie dolls. For the past two years, Hines and her colleagues have tried to determine the origins of gender differences by capturing on videotape the squeals of delight, furrows of concentration and myriad decisions that children from 2½ to 8 make while playing. Although both sexes play with all the toys available in Hines' laboratory, her work confirms what most parents (and more than a few aunts, uncles and nursery-school teachers) already know. As a group, the boys favor sports cars, fire trucks and Lincoln Logs, while the girls are drawn more often to dolls and kitchen toys.

2 But one batch of girls defies expectations and consistently prefers the boy toys. These youngsters have a rare genetic abnormality that caused them to produce elevated levels of testosterone, among other hormones, during their embryonic development. On average, they play with the same toys as the boys in the same ways and just as often. Could it be that the high levels of testosterone present in their bodies before birth have left a permanent imprint on their brains, affecting their later behavior? Or did their parents, knowing of their disorder, somehow subtly influence their choices? If the first explanation is true and biology determines the choice, Hines wonders, "Why would you evolve to want to play with a truck?"

3 Not so long ago, any career-minded researcher would have hesitated to ask such questions. During the feminist revolution of the 1970s, talk of inborn differences in the behavior of men and women was distinctly unfashionable, even taboo. Men dominated fields like architecture and engineering, it was argued, because of social, not hormonal, pressures. Women did the vast majority of society's child rearing because few other options were available to them. Once sexism was abolished, so the argument ran, the world would become a perfectly equitable, androgynous place, aside from a few anatomical details.

4 But biology has a funny way of confounding expectations. Rather than disappear, the evidence for innate sexual differences only began to mount. In medicine, researchers documented that heart disease strikes men at a younger age than it does women and that women have a more moderate physiological response to stress. Researchers found subtle neurological differences between the sexes both in the brain's structure and in its functioning. In addition, another generation of parents discovered that, despite their best efforts to give baseballs to their daughters and sewing kits to their sons, girls still flocked to dollhouses while boys clambered into tree forts. Perhaps nature is more important than nurture after all.

5 Even professional skeptics have been converted. "When I was younger, I believed that 100% of sex differences were due to the environment," says Jerre Levy, professor of psychology at the University of Chicago. Her own toddler toppled that utopian notion. "My daughter was 15 months old, and I had just dressed her in her teeny little nightie. Some guests arrived, and she came into the room, knowing full well that she looked adorable. She came in with this saucy little walk, cocking her head, blinking her eyes, especially at the men. You never saw such flirtation in your life." After 20

years spent studying the brain, Levy is convinced: "I'm sure there are biologically based differences in our behavior."

6   Now that it is O.K. to admit the possibility, the search for sexual differences has expanded into nearly every branch of the life sciences. Anthropologists have debunked Margaret Mead's work on the extreme variability of gender roles in New Guinea. Psychologists are untangling the complex interplay between hormones and aggression. But the most provocative, if as yet inconclusive, discoveries of all stem from the pioneering exploration of a tiny 3-lb. universe: the human brain. In fact, some researchers predict that the confirmation of innate differences in behavior could lead to an unprecedented understanding of the mind.

7   Some of the findings seem merely curious. For example, more men than women are lefthanded, reflecting the dominance of the brain's right hemisphere. By contrast, more women listen equally with both ears while men favor the right one.

8   Other revelations are bound to provoke more controversy. Psychology tests, for instance, consistently support the notion that men and women perceive the world in subtly different ways. Males excel at rotating three-dimensional objects in their head. Females prove better at reading emotions of people in photographs. A growing number of scientists believe the discrepancies reflect functional differences in the brains of men and women. If true, then some misunderstandings between the sexes may have more to do with crossed wiring than cross-purposes.

EMOTIONS

FEMALE INTUITION: THERE MAY BE SOMETHING TO IT

Do women really possess an ability to read other people's hidden motives and meanings? To some degree, they do. When shown pictures of actors portraying various feelings, women outscore men in identifying the correct emotion. They also surpass men in determining the emotional content of taped conversation in which the words have been garbled. This ability may result from society's emphasis on raising girls to be sensitive. But some researchers speculate that it has arisen to give women greater skill in interpreting the cues of toddlers before they are able to speak.

MALE INSENSITIVITY: IT'S A CULTURAL RELIC

If men seem less adept at deciphering emotions, it is a "trained incompetence," says Harvard psychologist Ronald Levant. Young boys are told to ignore pain and not to cry. Some anthropologists argue that this psychic wound is inflicted to separate boys from their mothers and prepare them for warfare. Many men, says Levant, can recognize their emotions only as a physical buzz or tightness in the throat—a situation that can be reversed, he insists, with training.

---

9   Most of the gender differences that have been uncovered so far are, statistically speaking, quite small. "Even the largest differences in cognitive function are not as large as the difference in male and female height," Hines notes. "You still see a lot of overlap." Otherwise, women could never read maps and men would always be left-handed. That kind of flexibility within the sexes reveals just how complex a puzzle gender actually is, requiring pieces from biology, sociology and culture.

10   Ironically, researchers are not entirely sure how or even why humans produce two sexes in the first place. (Why not just one—or even three—as in some species?) What is clear is that the two sexes originate with two distinct chromosomes. Women bear a double dose of the large X chromosome, while men usually possess a single X and a short, stumpy Y chromosome. In 1990 British scientists reported they had identified a single gene on the Y chromosome that determines maleness. Like some kind of bio-molecular Paul Revere, this master gene rouses a host of its compatriots to the complex task of turning a fetus into a boy. Without such a signal, all human embryos would develop into girls. "I have all the genes for being male except this one, and my husband has all the genes for being female," marvels evolutionary psychologist Leda Cosmides, of the University of California at Santa Barbara. "The only difference is which genes got turned on."

11   Yet even this snippet of DNA is not enough to ensure a masculine result. An elevated level of the hormone testosterone is also required during the pregnancy. Where does it come from? The fetus' own undescended testes. In those rare cases in which the tiny body does not respond to the hormone, a genetically male fetus develops sex organs that look like a clitoris and vagina rather than a penis. Such people look and act female. The majority marry and adopt children.

12   The influence of the sex hormones extends into the nervous system. Both males and females produce androgens, such as testosterone, and estrogens—although in different amounts. (Men and women who make no testosterone generally lack a libido.) Researchers suspect that an excess of testosterone before birth enables the right hemisphere to dominate the brain, resulting in lefthandedness. Since testosterone levels are higher in boys than in girls, that would explain why more boys are southpaws.

13   Subtle sex-linked preferences have been detected as early as 52 hours after birth. In studies of 72 newborns, University of Chicago psychologist Martha McClintock and her students found that a toe-fanning reflex was stronger in the left foot for 60% of the males, while all the females favored their right. However, apart from such reflexes in the hands, legs and feet, the team could find no other differences in the babies' responses.

14   One obvious place to look for gender differences is in the hypothalamus, a lusty little organ perched over the brain stem that, when sufficiently provoked, consumes a person with rage, thirst, hunger or desire. In animals, a region at the front of the organ controls sexual function and is somewhat larger in males than in females. But its size need not remain constant. Studies of tropical fish by Stanford University neurobiologist Russell Fernald reveal that certain cells in this tiny region of the brain swell markedly in an individual male whenever he comes to dominate a school.

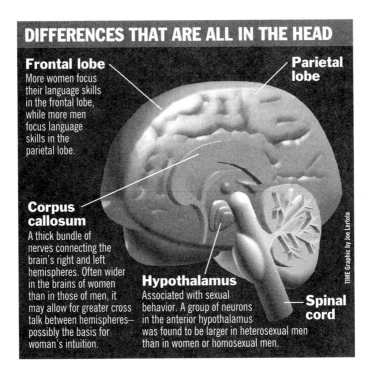

DIFFERENCES THAT ARE ALL IN THE HEAD

Frontal lobe
More women focus their language skills in the frontal lobe, while more men focus language skills in the parietal lobe.

Parietal lobe

Corpus callosum
A thick bundle of nerves connecting the brain's right and left hemispheres. Often wider in the brains of women than in those of men, it may allow for greater cross talk between hemispheres— possibly the basis for woman's intuition.

Hypothalamus
Associated with sexual behavior. A group of neurons in the anterior hypothalamus was found to be larger in heterosexual men than in women or homosexual men.

Spinal cord

TIME Graphic by Joe Lertola

Unfortunately for the piscine pasha, the cells will also shrink if he loses control of his harem to another male.

15   Many researchers suspect that, in humans too, sexual preferences are controlled by the hypothalamus. Based on a study of 41 autopsied brains, Simon LeVay of the Salk Institute for Biological Studies announced last summer that he had found a region in the hypothalamus that was on average twice as large in heterosexual men as in either women or homosexual men. LeVay's findings support the idea that varying hormone levels before birth may immutably stamp the developing brain in one erotic direction or another.

16   These prenatal fluctuations may also steer boys toward more rambunctious behavior than girls. June Reinisch, director of the Kinsey Institute for Research in Sex, Gender and Reproduction at Indiana University, in a pioneering study of eight pairs of brothers and 17 pairs of sisters ages 6 to 18 uncovered a complex interplay between hormones and aggression. As a group, the young males gave more belligerent answers than did the females on a multiple-choice test in which they had to imagine their response to stressful situations. But siblings who had been exposed in utero to synthetic antimiscarriage hormones that mimic testosterone were the most combative of all. The affected boys proved significantly more aggressive than their unaffected brothers, and the drug-exposed girls were much more contentious than their unexposed sisters. Reinish could not determine, however, whether this childhood aggression would translate into greater ambition or competitiveness in the adult world.

17   While most of the gender differences uncovered so far seem to fall under the purview of the hypothalamus, researchers have begun noting discrepancies in other parts of the brain as well. For the past nine years, neuroscientists have debated whether the corpus callosum, a thick bundle of nerves that allows the right half of the brain to communicate with the left, is larger in women than in men. If it is, and if size corresponds to function, then the greater crosstalk between the hemispheres might explain enigmatic phenomena like female intuition, which is supposed to accord women greater ability to read emotional clues.

18   These conjectures about the corpus callosum have been hard to prove because the structure's girth varies dramatically with both age and health. Studies of autopsied material are of little use because brain tissue undergoes such dramatic changes in the hours after death. Neuroanatomist Laura Allen and neuroendocrinologist Roger Gorski of UCLA decided to try to circumvent some of these problems by obtaining brain scans from live, apparently healthy people. In their investigation of 146 subjects, published in April, they confirmed that parts of the corpus callosum were up to 23% wider in women than in men. They also measured thicker connections between the two hemispheres in other parts of women's brains.

19   Encouraged by the discovery of such structural differences, many researchers have begun looking for dichotomies of function as well. At the Bowman Gray Medical School in Winston-Salem, N.C., Cecile Naylor has determined that men and women enlist widely varying parts of their brain when asked to spell words. By monitoring

---

LANGUAGE
IN CHOOSING HER WORDS, A WOMAN REALLY USES HER HEAD
For both sexes, the principal language centers of the brain are usually concentrated in the left hemisphere. But preliminary neurological studies show that women make use of both sides of their brain during even the simplest verbal tasks, like spelling. As a result, a woman's appreciation of everyday speech appears to be enhanced by input from various cerebral regions, including those that control vision and feelings. This greater access to the brain's imagery and depth may help explain why girls often begin speaking earlier than boys, enunciate more clearly as tots and develop a larger vocabulary.

IF JOHNNY CAN'T READ, IS IT BECAUSE HE IS A BOY?
Visit a typical remedial-reading class, and you'll find that the boys outnumber the girls 3 to 1. Stuttering affects four times as many boys as girls. Many researchers have used these and other lopsided ratios to support the argument that males, on average, are less verbally fluent than females. However, the discrepancy could also reflect less effort by teachers or parents to find reading-impaired girls. Whatever the case, boys often catch up with their female peers in high school. In the past few years, boys have even begun outscoring girls on the verbal portion of the Scholastic Aptitude Test.

---

increases in blood flow, the neuropsychologist found that women use both sides of their head when spelling while men use primarily their left side. Because the area activated on the right side is used in understanding emotions, the women apparently tap a wider range of experience for their task. Intriguingly, the effect occurred only with spelling and not during a memory test.

20   Researchers speculate that the greater communication between the two sides of the brain could impair a woman's performance of certain highly specialized visual-spatial tasks. For example, the ability to tell directions on a map without physically having to rotate it appears stronger in those individuals whose brains restrict the process to the right hemisphere. Any crosstalk between the two sides apparently distracts the brain from its job. Sure enough, several studies have shown that this mental-rotation skill is indeed more tightly focused in men's brains than in women's.

21   But how did it get to be that way? So far, none of the gender scientists have figured out whether nature or nurture is more important. "Nothing is ever equal, even in the beginning," observes Janice Juraska, a biopsychologist at the University of Illinois at Urbana-Champaign. She points out, for instance, that mother rats lick their male offspring more frequently than they do their daughters. However, Juraska has demonstrated that it is possible to reverse some inequities by manipulating environmental factors. Female rats have fewer nerve connections than males into the hippocampus, a brain region associated with spatial relations and memory. But when Juraska "enriched" the cages of the females with stimulating toys, the females developed more of these neuronal connections. "Hormones do affect things—it's crazy to deny that," says the researcher. "But there's no telling which way sex differences might go if we completely changed the environment." For humans, educational enrichment could perhaps enhance a woman's ability to work in three dimensions and a man's ability to interpret emotions. Says Juraska: "There's nothing about human brains that is so stuck that a different way of doing things couldn't change it enormously."

22   Nowhere is this complex interaction between nature and nurture more apparent than in the unique human abilities of speaking, reading, and writing. No one is born knowing French, for example; it must be learned, changing the brain forever. Even so, language skills are linked to specific cerebral centers. In a remarkable series of experiments, neurosurgeon George Ojemann of the University of Washington has produced scores of detailed maps of people's individual language centers.

23   First, Ojemann tested his patients' verbal intelligence using a written exam. Then, during neurosurgery—which was performed under a local anesthetic—he asked them to name aloud a series of objects found in a steady stream of black-and-white photos. Periodically, he touched different parts of the brain with an electrode that temporarily blocked the activity of that region. (This does not hurt because the brain has no sense of pain.) By noting when his patients made mistakes, the surgeon was able to determine which sites were essential to naming.

24   Several complex sexual differences emerged. Men with lower verbal IQs were more likely to have their language skills located toward the back of the brain. In a number of women, regardless of IQ, the naming ability was restricted to the frontal lobe. This disparity could help explain why strokes that affect the rear of the brain seem to be more devastating to men than to women.

25   Intriguingly, the sexual differences are far less significant in people with higher verbal IQs. Their language skills developed in a more intermediate part of the brain. And yet, no two patterns were ever identical. "That to me is the most important finding," Ojemann says. "Instead of these sites being laid down more or less the same in everyone, they're laid down in subtly different places." Language is scattered randomly across these cerebral centers, he hypothesizes, because the skills evolved so recently.

26   What no one knows for sure is just how hardwired the brain is. How far and at what stage can the brain's extraordinary flexibility be pushed? Several studies suggest that the junior high years are key. Girls show the same aptitudes for math as boys until about the seventh grade, when more and more girls develop math phobia. Coincidentally, that is the age at which boys start to shine and catch up to girls in reading.

27   By one account, the gap between men and women for at least some mental skills has actually started to shrink. By looking at 25 years' worth of data from academic tests, Janet Hyde, professor of psychology and women's studies at the University of Wisconsin at Madison, discovered that overall gender differences for verbal and mathematical skills dramatically decreased after 1974. One possible explanation, Hyde notes, is that "Americans have changed their socialization and educational patterns over the past few decades. They are treating males and females with greater similarity."

28   Even so, women still have not caught up with men on the mental-rotation test. Fascinated by the persistence of that gap, psychologists Irwin Silverman and Marion Eals of York University in Ontario wondered if there were any spatial tasks at which women outperformed men. Looking at it from the point of view of human evolution, Silverman and Eals reasoned that while men may have developed strong spatial skills

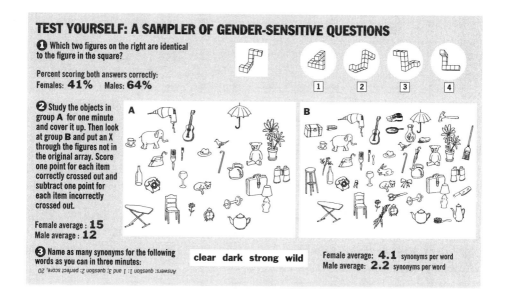

TEST YOURSELF: A SAMPLER OF GENDER-SENSITIVE QUESTIONS

❶ Which two figures on the right are identical to the figure in the square?

Percent scoring both answers correctly:
Females: **41%**   Males: **64%**

| 1 | 2 | 3 | 4 |

❷ Study the objects in group **A** for one minute and cover it up. Then look at group **B** and put an X through the figures not in the original array. Score one point for each item correctly crossed out and subtract one point for each item incorrectly crossed out.

Female average : **15**
Male average : **12**

A

B

❸ Name as many synonyms for the following words as you can in three minutes:

clear   dark   strong   wild

Female average: **4.1** synonyms per word
Male average: **2.2** synonyms per word

Answers: question 1: 1 and 3; question 2: perfect score, 20

PERCEPTION
HE CAN READ A MAP BLINDFOLDED, BUT CAN HE FIND HIS SOCKS?
It's a classic scene of marital discord on the road. Husband: "Do I turn right?" Wife, madly rotating the map: "I'm not sure where we are." Whether men read maps better is unclear, but they do excel at thinking in three dimensions. This may be due to ancient evolutionary pressures related to hunting, which requires orienting oneself while pursuing prey.

IF LOST IN A FOREST, WOMEN WILL NOTICE THE TREES
Such prehistoric pursuits may have conferred a comparable advantage on women. In experiments in mock offices, women proved 70% better than men at remembering the location of items found on a desktop—perhaps reflecting evolutionary pressure on generations of women who foraged for their food. Foragers must recall complex patterns formed of apparently unconnected items.

in response to evolutionary pressures to be successful hunters, women would have needed other types of visual skills to excel as gatherers and foragers of food.

29   The psychologists therefore designed a test focused on the ability to discern and later recall the location of objects in a complex, random pattern. In series of tests, student volunteers were given a minute to study a drawing that contained such unrelated objects as an elephant, a guitar and a cat. Then Silverman and Eals presented their subjects with a second drawing containing additional objects and told them to cross out those items that had been added and circle any that had moved. Sure enough, the women consistently surpassed the men in giving correct answers.

30   What made the psychologists really sit up and take notice, however, was the fact that the women scored much better on the mental-rotation test while they were menstruating. Specifically, they improved their scores by 50% to 100% whenever their estrogen levels were at their lowest. It is not clear why this should be. However, Silverman and Eals are trying to find out if women exhibit a similar hormonal effect for any other visual tasks.

31   Oddly enough, men may possess a similar hormonal response, according to new research reported in November by Doreen Kimura, a psychologist at the University of Western Ontario. In her study of 138 adults, Kimura found that males perform better on mental-rotation tests in the spring, when their testosterone levels are low, rather than in the fall, when they are higher. Men are also subject to a daily cycle, with testosterone levels lowest around 8 p.m. and peaking around 4 a.m. Thus, says June Reinisch of the Kinsey Institute: "When people say women can't be trusted because they cycle every month, my response is that men cycle every day, so they should only be allowed to negotiate peace treaties in the evening."

32   Far from strengthening stereotypes about who women and men truly are or how they should behave, research into innate sexual differences only underscores humanity's awesome adaptability. "Gender is really a complex business," says Reinisch. "There's no question that hormones have an effect. But what does that have to do with the fact that I like to wear pink ribbons and you like to wear baseball gloves? Probably something, but we don't know what."

33   Even the concept of what an innate difference represents is changing. The physical and chemical differences between the brains of the two sexes may be malleable and subject to change by experience: certainly an event or act of learning can directly affect the brain's biochemistry and physiology. And so, in the final analysis, it may be impossible to say where nature ends and nurture begins because the two are so intimately linked.

WRITING ASSIGNMENTS

Analysis

1. Make a list of all the differences in male and female brains, including hormonally triggered differences, described by Gorman. Write an essay evaluating their significance.

2. Analyze Gorman's direct statements, specific word choice, and phrasing to discover her point of view on the differences in male and female brains discussed in her article. Write a brief essay reporting and illustrating your findings.

3. Make a list of all the experimental evidence, comments by scientists, and authorial statements that suggest biological differences in men's and women's brains may be unverifiable, not permanent, small, malleable, reversible, or compensable by education. In an essay, explain the implications of this evidence for the article's overall assertion of significant biologically based differences in male and female brains.

4. Write a two-page summary of Gorman's article for a group of public education policy-makers who will use your summary to draft recommendations on curriculum and classroom organization. Begin your summary with one of these two statements from the article itself, selecting the one that more accurately reflects the evidence she presents: "Perhaps nature is more important than nurture after all," or ". . . it may be impossible to say where nature ends and nurture begins because the two are so intimately linked."

Argument

1. Use the evidence presented in Gorman's article to support or oppose *one* of the following proposals and explain your reasoning:

   • Monitoring female estrogen and male testosterone levels in test-takers and decision-makers.
   • Limiting space for women in academic disciplines requiring ability in mathematics and with spatial arrangements.

- Limiting space for men in academic disciplines requiring verbal ability or in fields requiring emotional sensitivity.
- Administering estrogen or testosterone prenatally to influence fetal development.

2. Argue causes other than biological or hormonal for the following:

- Despite parents' attempts to counter sexism, boys favor trucks and Lincoln Logs while girls favor dolls and kitchen toys.
- Men suffer heart disease at a younger age than women.
- Women show more moderate physiological response to stress than do men.
- Psychology professor Jerre Levy's 15-month-old daughter is "flirtatious."
- Adolescent girls fall behind boys in math.
- Adolescent boys catch up with girls in reading.

Personal Writing and Writing from Research

1. Describe your childhood experiences with games and toys and your elementary school academic experiences. How do these memories correlate to gender-typed behaviors described by Gorman? How do you explain your preferences and experiences?
2. *Collaborative Project:* Conduct follow-up research on one or more of the scientific projects described in Gorman's article, such as the effects on girls of uterine exposure to the male hormone, testosterone. Report your findings to the class.
3. As a group or individually, conduct primary research on young children's behavior. On several occasions, observe children playing in a park, schoolyard, day-care center, or home. Ideally, observe the same child or children several times and in the same setting(s). Note any gender-related behaviors. Note also any signs of environmental influence on child behavior. If possible, interview the care-givers to determine their attitudes on gender-related behavior in children. Correlate your findings with those described in Gorman's article.

Rite of Passage

Sharon Olds

Born in San Francisco in 1942, Sharon Olds earned her BA from Stanford University in 1964 and her PhD from Columbia University in 1972. The recipient of numerous awards, she has taught poetry at many schools and institutions and is currently associate professor of English at New York University.

Her work depicts personal family life as well as global political events. Critics describe her poetry as intense, urgent, candid, erotic, powerful, and touching. Says one critic, "Out of private revelations she makes poems of universal truth of sex, death, fear, love. Her poems are sometimes jarring, unexpected, bold, but always loving and deeply rewarding." Her books include *Satan Says* (1980), *The Gold Cell* (1987), *The Matter of This World* (1987), *The Sign of Saturn* (1991), and *The Father* (1992). "Rite of Passage" comes from *The Dead and the Living* (1984).

Journal Topics: (1) Describe what you would consider to be "typical" behavior by the children at a birthday party for a 7-year-old girl, and for a 7-year-old boy. (2) What kinds of activities would you, as an adult, plan for either event? Explain your choices.

As You Read: (1) List the behaviors of the boys at this party that the mother notes. Then list the words that reveal the mother's interpretation of those behaviors. To what extent do her comments reflect traditional ideas about masculinity? In your opinion, is she an accurate interpreter, or could the boys' actions be viewed in a different way? (2) Are the implications of this poem consistent with David Barash's or Stephen Jay Gould's views about masculinity?

> As the guests arrive at my son's party
> they gather in the living room—
> short men, men in first grade
> with smooth jaws and chins.
> 5 Hands in pockets, they stand around
> jostling, jockeying for place, small fights
> breaking out and calming. One says to another
> *How old are you? Six. I'm seven. So?*
> They eye each other, seeing themselves
> 10 tiny in the other's pupils. They clear their
> throats a lot, a room of small bankers,
> they fold their arms and frown. *I could beat you
> up,* a seven says to a six,
> the dark cake, round and heavy as a
> 15 turret, behind them on the table. My son,
> freckles like specks of nutmeg on his cheeks,
> chest narrow as the balsa keel of a
> model boat, long hands
> cool and thin as the day they guided him
> 20 out of me, speaks up as a host
> for the sake of the group.
> *We could easily kill a two-year-old,*
> he says in his clear voice. The other
> men agree, they clear their throats
> 25 like Generals, they relax and get down to
> playing war, celebrating my son's life.

Transforming the Debate on Sexual Inequality
From Biological Difference to Institutionalized Androcentrism

Sandra L. Bem

Sandra Bem, professor of psychology and women's studies at Cornell University, is noted for her research on sex roles, androgyny, and the development of psychosexual identity and maturity. This article is excerpted from an address delivered at Claremont McKenna College on February 24, 1992. It was later published in *The Lenses of Gender: Transforming the Debate on Sexual Equality* (1993).

Journal Topics: (1) Describe any physical characteristic of yours that has resulted in your facing unnecessary and unfair discrimination. (2) Briefly identify the important people and events that come to mind when you think about American history. (3) Contrast the role of men and women in a religious tradition with which you are familiar. (4) Describe any examples in either the law or the workplace where men and women are treated differently.

As You Read: (1) Why does Bem begin by reviewing the history of discussions about male and female biological differences? (2) According to Bem, how has technology affected the significance of male and female biological differences? (3) How have environmental features combined with biological differences to create different, unequal roles for men and women? (4) How does Bem explain the persistence of these differences and inequalities?

1   Because I am a feminist psychologist, I am frequently asked to lecture on the question: What biological sex differences are there, *really?* This question puts me in an awkward position because I not only don't have the answer to it, I don't even think it's the question we ought to be asking. This lecture will tell you why.

2   I begin my talk today with a single historical fact—which is that since the middle of the nineteenth century (and especially during times of intense feminist activity), America has been literally obsessed with the question of whether women and men are fundamentally the same as one another or fundamentally different from one another. In other words, the question of biological difference has been the focal point of almost all American discussions of sexual inequality.

3   This focus on biological difference came into being almost immediately after feminists like Elizabeth Cady Stanton and Susan B. Anthony first started pushing to get women the most basic rights of citizenship, including the right to vote, own property,

speak in public, and have access to higher education. Threatened by these extraordi-narily radical proposals for social change, anti-feminists tried to argue against them by raising the specter of biological difference. I'll mention just three examples of this anti-feminist argument, all by highly regarded scientists and scholars of the period. Paul Broca argued against higher education for women by claiming that their brains were too small; Edward Clarke argued against higher education by claiming it would divert women's limited complement of blood from their reproductive organs to their brains—hence their reproductive organs would atrophy and they would be unable to bear children; and finally, Herbert Spencer argued against giving women the right to vote on the grounds that they had too much maternal instinct to allow only the fittest in society to survive.

4   These nineteenth-century arguments against women's equality, I should note, were heavily tinged with racism as well as sexism. With educated white women be-ginning to have many fewer babies than uneducated women, and with America also experiencing a gigantic increase in the number of immigrants from Eastern and Southern Europe, the feminist proposals for social change were seen as threatening to not just male dominance but white dominance. When G. Stanley Hall argued that higher education for women would spell "race suicide," it was thus not the sui-cide of the human race that he was worried about but the suicide of the white, or Eu-ropean, race.

5   In response [to] all of this biological and anti-feminist theorizing on the part of some of the most respected scientists of the nineteenth century, by the early twenti-eth century, many *feminists* were beginning to focus on the question of biological difference as well. I'll give but one example. Beginning in 1903, two of the very first women PhDs in the new field of empirical psychology took it upon themselves to try and refute all this anti-woman theorizing by not only doing their own carefully con-trolled studies of male-female difference on a whole variety of intellectual and other abilities, they also began to publish a whole slew of review articles carefully compil-ing and evaluating the results of all the research on male-female difference then available. This work by Helen Thompson Woolley and Leta Stetter Hollingworth is not only recognized today as being among the best science of its time, it is also what started the century-old tradition of research in psychology on sex differences, which tries to figure out once and for all what alleged sex differences really exist. The very existence of this research tradition is itself an example, of course, of the American obsession with biological sex difference that I am talking about.

6   Although our obsession with the question of biological difference died down a bit after women finally got the vote in 1920, it exploded onto the scene again after the second major wave of American feminism in the late 1960s and early 1970s and has been with us ever since. This modern focus on whether males and females are fun-damentally the same or fundamentally different is now so integrated into American culture that you can see it in almost any magazine article on women and men that you happen to pick up at your local supermarket. To remind you of just a few of the most popular of today's sex diffrence themes: There's the idea from sociobiology that male dominance (including even the male predisposition to rape) is encoded in our

genes; there's the idea from prenatal hormone theory that in-utero testosterone is responsible for male aggression; there's the idea that some kind [of] male math gene explains why males do better at mathematics; there's the idea that some difference in brain structure having to do with the corpus callosum makes males right-brained and females left-brained; and finally, there's the idea from a popular stream of modern feminism that says females are naturally concerned about relationships and caring whereas males are naturally concerned about autonomy and justice—which is why, it is suggested, they have such a hard time relating to one another.

7   There are two reasons why I have begun my talk today by point[ing] out that America *organizes* almost all of its discussion about gender and sexual inequality around the issue of biological difference. First, I wanted to shift your angle of vision a little and have you focus—if only for a moment—on the *question* America is always asking instead of the *answer* to that question. Put somewhat differently, I wanted you to stop taking America's focus on sexual difference for granted as something completely natural and unremarkable and instead begin to say to yourself: Why *is* this the question America is always asking? And even more importantly: Is there some other question America could or should be asking instead? Second, I wanted to set the stage for my major argument today—which is that America needs to finally shift the focus of its discussion of sexual inequality from biological difference to institutionalized androcentrism. That is, America needs to reframe its discussion of sexual inequality so that it focuses not on male-female difference per se but on how our androcentric (or male-centered) institutions transform male-female difference into female disadvantage.

8   My overall argument is going to have two parts. First, I will argue that the focus on biological difference is based on a false assumption and hence is misguided both intellectually and scientifically. Next I will argue that we need to accept at least a certain level of biological difference as given or axiomatic and thereby shift the starting point of our discussion from difference per se to society's situating of women in a social structure so androcentric that it not only transforms what is really just male-female difference into female disadvantage, it also disguises what is really just a male standard or norm as gender neutrality.

THE FOCUS ON BIOLOGICAL DIFFERENCE IS MISGUIDED

9   The reason America has become so obsessed with the biology of sex differences is that for 150 years now, feminists have been saying that we need to change our culture in order to make women more equal; and for that same 150 years, the culture has been saying back that our biological differences may not even allow for the kind of equality that feminists like me are always advocating. Implicit in this response, however, is a false assumption, which is that biology is a kind of bedrock beyond which social change is not feasible. And not only is that assumption false in and of itself, it also leads to the misguided conclusion that the question of biological sex difference is urgent, both politically and scientifically. I disagree. As I see it, social change—or [what] I would rather call cultural invention—can so radically transform the situational

context in which biology operates that the human organism can actually be liberated from what had earlier seemed to be its intrinsic biological limitations. Consider but three examples.

10 1. As a biological species, human beings require food and water on a daily basis, which once meant that it was part of universal human nature to live as survivalists. But now human beings have invented agricultural techniques for producing food, and storage and refrigeration techniques for preserving food, which means that it is no longer part of universal human nature to live as survivalists.

11 2. As a biological species, human beings are susceptible to infection from many bacteria, which once meant that it was part of universal human nature to die routinely from infection. But now human beings have invented antibiotics to fight infection, which means that it is no longer part of universal human nature to die routinely from infection.

12 3. As a biological species, human beings do not have wings, which once meant that it was part of universal human nature to be unable to fly. But now human beings have invented airplanes, which means that it is no longer part of universal human nature to be unable to fly.

13 As dramatically liberating as these three examples of technological innovation clearly are, the general principle that they illustrate is so mundane and noncontroversial that even sociobiologists would unhesitatingly endorse it. Simply put, the impact of any biological feature depends in every instance on how that biological feature interacts with the environment in which it is situated.

14 Of course, the question that immediately arises is the following: If this whole idea of biology interacting with the social context is right, then why have women and men played such different and unequal roles in virtually every society on earth? The biology-in-context answer is that throughout human history, there have not only been certain indisputable and universal differences between men's and women's bodies, with only women being able to become pregnant and to breastfeed and with men, on average, being bigger and stronger. There have also been certain indisputable and universal features of the environment, with all cultures everywhere having no effective means of controlling fertility, no digestible substitutes for mother's milk, few technological instruments for extending the strength of the human body, and relatively little work that was mental rather than physical.

5 Now, in that sociohistorical context, the argument continues, the bodily differences between the sexes not only made it likely that most women would be either pregnant or breastfeeding during most of the years from menarche to menopause; they also made it likely that the culture would develop both a division of labor based on sex and an institutionalized system of male political dominance. In the current sociohistorical context, however, those very same bodily differences do not need to impact on people's lives in quite the same way.

6 But of course, this biology-in-context answer then raises another question that is almost always presented as the ultimate challenge to modern feminism: If cultural invention has now so transformed the situational context of human life that the

bodily differences between the sexes are no longer as functionally significant as they once were, then why is it that males and females continue to play such different—and unequal—roles in even a modern technological society like our own, which has not only effective control over fertility and digestible substitutes for mother's milk, but little or no labor for which the sex of the laborer is truly decisive? There is both a short answer to this question and a long answer, both of them historical.

17   The long answer is spelled out in my book, *The Lenses of Gender: Transforming the Debate on Sexual Inequality.* The short answer is that women and men are both politically and economically unequal even in America today because we live in an androcentric (or male-centered) social structure that continues to invisibly transform what is really just a biological difference between males and females into a massive female disadvantage. I'll shift in a moment to a discussion of what androcentrism is and how it works, but first I want to make one more point about biology per se. In particular, I want to answer the question that many of you are silently asking in your minds, which is: Do I really believe that all biology does in the context of sex and gender is to produce male and female bodies? Put somewhat differently, do I really believe there are no biological differences between the sexes beside the very obvious differences in their anatomy and physiology?

18   The truth is that I'm very much of an agnostic with respect to this question. For all I know, there may well be a kernel of truth in Alan Alda's argument that men are more physically aggressive than women because they are suffering from prenatal "testosterone poisoning"; there may also be a kernel of truth in Alice Rossi's argument that women are more maternal than men because of their female hormones; and there may even be a kernel of truth in Camilla Benbow's argument that males are better at higher mathematics than females because of their having some special biological ability to reason mathematically.

19   But there are three related issues about which I am not at all agnostic, and about which I would not be very likely to become agnostic, even if it should turn out that human males and females differed biologically with respect to any number of specific abilities or predispositions:

20   1. There would be so much overlap between the sexes in all of these cases that the differences would pale into insignifance next to the bigger and more obvious differences between male and female bodies. Even if they should someday be shown to have a biological component, these differences would thus add little or nothing to our understanding of why it is that women and men have universally played such different—and unequal—roles in virtually every society on earth.

21   2. These biological differences would be so poorly matched to the requirements of the jobs that women and men currently hold in American society that they would again add little or nothing to our understanding of why American women and men currently hold the different—and unequal—positions that they do. So yes, women might well turn out to be more biologically nurturant than men on the average, but that should make them psychiatrists, not

secretaries. And yes, men might also turn out to have a higher aptitude for mathematics than women on the average, but that would not explain why there are so many more women with a high aptitude for mathematics than there are women in careers requiring a high aptitude for mathematics. Stated more generally, no matter what subtle biological differences there may someday prove to be between women and men on the average, those differences will never justify the sexual inequality that has, for centuries, been a feature of human social life.

22   3. No matter how many subtle biological differences between the sexes there may someday prove to be, both the size and the significance of those biological differences will depend, in every single instance, on the situational context in which women and men live their lives. The feature of the situational context that I've focused on so far is the historically universal absence of modern technology. At least as important in the development of sexual difference and sexual inequality, however, is the male-centeredness that has resulted in every single culture from the institutionalization of male political power. And that feature of the environment, I'll talk about now.

ANDROCENTRISM

23   The concept of androcentrism was first articulated in the early twentieth century by Charlotte Perkins Gilman, who wrote in *The Man-Made World or Our Androcentric Culture* (1911/1971) that:

> all our human scheme of things rests on the same tacit assumption; man being held the human type; woman a sort of accompaniment and subordinate assistant, merely essential to the making of people. She has held always the place of a preposition in relation to man. She has always been considered above him or below him, before him, behind him, beside him, a wholly relative existence—"Sydney's sister," "Pembroke's mother"—but never by any chance Sydney or Pembroke herself. . . . It is no easy matter to deny or reverse a universal assumption. . . . What we see immediately around us, what we are born into and grow up with, . . . we assume to be the order of nature. . . . Nevertheless, . . . what we have all this time called "human nature" . . . was in great part only male nature. . . . Our androcentric culture is so shown to have been, and still to be, a masculine culture in excess, and therefore undesirable. (pp. 20–22)

24   Without actually using the term itself, Simone de Beauvoir brilliantly elaborated on the concept of androcentrism, and integrated it more completely into a theory of sexual inequality, in *The Second Sex* (1952), which was originally published in France in 1949. According to de Beauvoir, the historical relationship of men and women is not best represented as a relationship between dominant and subordinate, or between high and low status, or even between positive and negative. No, in all male-dominated cultures,

> man represents both the positive and the neutral, as is indicated by the common use of *man* to designate human beings in general; whereas woman represents only the

negative, defined by limiting criteria, without reciprocity. . . . It amounts to this: just as for the ancients there was an absolute vertical with reference to which the oblique was defined, so there is an absolute human type, the masculine. Woman has ovaries, a uterus; these peculiarities imprison her in her subjectivity, circumscribe her within the limits of her own nature. It is often said that she thinks with her glands. Man superbly ignores the fact that his anatomy also includes glands, such as the testicles, and that they secrete hormones. He thinks of his body as a direct and normal connection with the world, which he believes he apprehends objectively, whereas he regards the body of woman as a hindrance, a prison, weighed down by everything peculiar to it . . . Thus humanity is male and man defines woman not in herself but as relative to him; she is not regarded as an autonomous being. . . . She is defined and differentiated with reference to man and not he with reference to her; she is the incidental, the inessential as opposed to the essential. He is the Subject, he is the Absolute—she is the Other. (pp. xv–xvi)

25   These quotations make androcentrism pretty clear, but let me describe it a few different ways and then give you some concrete examples to illustrate it. As I see it, androcentrism is the privileging of males, male experience, and the male perspective. There are many different ways to describe this privileging. For example, you could say it's the treating of males as the main characters in the drama of human life around whom all action revolves and through whose eyes all reality is to be interpreted, and the treating of females as the peripheral or marginal characters in the drama of human life whose purpose for being is defined only in relation to the main—or male—character. This goes along with Gilman's idea that women are always defined in relation to men. On the other hand, you could say that androcentrism is the treating of the male as if he were some kind of universal, objective, or neutral representative of the human species, in contrast to the female who is some kind of a special case—something different, deviant, extra, or other. This goes along with de Beauvoir's idea that man is the human and woman is the other.

26   There are lots of examples of androcentrism that you already know about even if you haven't ever thought to label them as androcentric. In language, for example, there's the generic use of "he" to mean "he or she," which treats "he" as universal, human, genderless, and "she" as specifically female. In the Old Testament story of Adam and Eve, there's the fact that not only is Adam created first (in God's image), Eve is created (out of Adam) to be his helper. Only Adam, you'll recall, is explicitly given the power to name every creature on earth from his own perspective. And then, of course, there's Freud's theory of penis envy, which treats the male body as so obviously being the human norm—and the female body as so obviously being an inferior departure from that norm—that the mere sight of the other sex's genitals not only fills the three-year-old boy with "a horror of the mutilated creature he has just seen," it also leads the three-year-old girl to "make her judgment and her decision in a flash; she has seen it and knows that she is without it and wants to have it."

27   Let me shift now to some examples of androcentrism that are both more modern and more pertinent to everyday life. As long as we've been talking about the presumed inferiority or otherness of the female body, let's begin with the U.S. Supreme

Court's rulings related to pregnancy—in particular, the Court's rulings on whether employers can exclude pregnancy from the package of disability insurance benefits that they provide to their employees. The situation is this: An employer says their insurance benefits will cover you for every medical condition that keeps you away from work, *except* pregnancy and giving birth. Is this exclusion okay? Supreme Court says yes. Question: Why is it okay to exclude pregnancy if discrimination against women is now illegal? The Court has explained this in a number of different ways.

28   In *Geduldig v. Aiello* (1974), the Court reasoned that the exclusion of pregnancy from a disability insurance program does not "amount . . . to invidious discrimination" against women because it does not involve "discrimination based upon gender as such. . . . While it is true that only women can become pregnant," the Court conceded,

> it does not follow that every legislative classification concerning pregnancy is a sex-based classification. . . . The lack of identity between the excluded disability and gender . . . becomes clear upon the most cursory analysis. The program divides potential recipients into two groups—pregnant women and nonpregnant persons. While the first group is exclusively female, the second includes members of both sexes. The fiscal and actuarial benefits of the program thus accrue to members of both sexes. (Lindgren & Taub, 1988, p. 53)

29   According to the Court, the neutrality of the pregnancy exclusion can be seen in yet another way:

> There is no risk from which men are protected and women are not. Likewise, there is no risk from which women are protected and men are not. (Quoted in Lindgren & Taub, 1988, p. 53)

30   The Court expanded on this very same reasoning in yet another case in 1976. "Pregnancy-related disabilities constitute an *additional* risk, unique to women," the Court wrote, "and the failure to compensate them for this risk does not destroy the presumed parity of the benefits . . . [that accrue] to men and women alike." (Quoted in Lindgren & Taub, 1988, pp. 117–118)

31   There are some problems with the Court's reasoning here because, as I hope you see, it is androcentrically defining whatever is male as the standard and whatever is female as something "additional" or "extra." Justices Brennan, Douglas, and Marshall came within millimeters of exposing this androcentrism when they wrote in a dissenting opinion that

> by singling out for less favorable treatment a gender-linked disability peculiar to women . . . [while simultaneously giving] men . . . full compensation for all disabilities suffered, including those that affect only or primarily their sex, such as prostatectomies, circumcision, hemophilia, and gout, . . . the State . . . [is creating] a double standard for disability compensation.

32   Justice Stevens came even closer to exposing the Court's androcentrism when he argued in his dissent that

> [i]t is not accurate to describe the program as dividing "potential recipients into two groups—pregnant women and nonpregnant persons." . . . The classification is

between persons who face a risk of pregnancy and those who do not. . . . By defini-tion, such a rule discriminates on the basis of sex; for it is the capacity to become pregnant which primarily differentiates the female from the male. . . . Nor is it accu-rate to state that under the plan "[t]here is no risk from which men are protected and women are not" . . . If the word "risk" is used narrowly, men are protected against the risks associated with a prostate operation whereas women are not. If the word is used more broadly to describe the risk of uncompensated employment caused by physical disability, men receive total protection . . . against that risk whereas women receive only partial protection. (Quoted in Lindgren & Taub, 1988, pp. 118–119)

33   What is going on in these pregnancy cases should be clear. Just like Sigmund Freud himself, the Court is androcentrically defining the male body as the standard human body; hence it is seeing nothing unusual or inappropriate about giving that standard human body the full insurance coverage that it would need for each and every condition that might befall it. Consistent with this androcentric perspective, the Court is also defining equal protection as the granting to women of every con-ceivable benefit that this standard human body might require—which, of course, does not include disability coverage for pregnancy.

34   Had the Court had even the slightest sensitivity to the meaning of androcentrism, there are at least two truly gender-neutral standards that it would have surely consid-ered instead. In set-theory terms, these are: (a) the *intersection* of male and female bodies, which would have narrowly covered only those conditions that befall both men and women alike; and (b) the *union* of male and female bodies, which would have broadly covered all those conditions that befall both men and women separately. In fact, however, the Court was so blind to the meaning of androcentrism that it saw nothing the least bit amiss when, in the name of equal protection, it granted a whole package of special benefits to men and men alone.

35   Let me now move to a final example of an androcentric law that looked gender-neutral even to me until just a couple of years ago. This final example has to do with our culture's legal definition of self-defense, which holds that a defendant can be found innocent of homicide only if he or she perceived imminent danger of great bod-ily harm or death and responded to that danger with only as much force as was neces-sary to defend against it. Although that definition had always seemed to have nothing whatsoever to do with gender and hence to be perfectly gender-neutral, it no longer seemed quite so gender-neutral once feminist legal scholars finally pointed out how much better it fit with a scenario involving two men in an isolated episode of sudden violence than with a scenario involving a woman being battered, first in relatively minor ways and then with escalating intensity over the years, by a man who is not only bigger and stronger than she is, but from whom she can also not get police pro-tection because he is her husband. The "aha" experience here is the realization that if this woman and this situation had been anywhere near the center of the policy-makers' consciousness on the day when they were first drafting our culture's supposedly neu-tral definition of self-defense, they might not have placed so much emphasis on the de-fendant's being in imminent danger at the particular instant when the ultimate act of self-defense is finally done.

36   Of course, it isn't only in the context of insurance and self-defense that the male difference from women is "affirmatively compensated" by American society while the female difference from men is treated as an intrinsic barrier to sexual equality. To quote Catharine MacKinnon, who is perhaps the most distinguished feminist lawyer in America today:

> [V]irtually every quality that distinguishes men from women is . . . affirmatively compensated in this society. Men's physiology defines most sports, their needs define auto and health insurance coverage, their socially designed biographies define workplace expectations and successful career patterns, their perspectives and concerns define quality in scholarship, their experiences and obsessions define merit, their objectification of life defines art, their military service defines citizenship, their presence defines family, their inability to get along with each other—their wars and rulerships—defines history, their image defines god, and their genitals define sex. For each of their differences from women, what amounts to an affirmative action plan is [thus] in effect, otherwise known as the structure and values of American society. (MacKinnon, 1987, p. 36)

37   Of all the androcentric institutions on MacKinnon's list that are typically thought of as gender-neutral, there is perhaps no institution more directly responsible for denying women their rightful share of America's economic and political resources than the structure of the American work world. Although that work world may seem to many Americans to be as gender-neutral as it needs to be now that explicit discrimination against women has finally been made illegal, in fact, it is so thoroughly organized around a worker who is not only presumed to be male rather than female, but who is also presumed to have a wife at home to take care of all of the needs of his household—including the care of his children—that, as I've said several times already, it "naturally" and automatically ends up transforming what is intrinsically just a male/female difference into a massive female disadvantage.

38   Imagine how differently our social world would be organized if all of the workers in our workforce were women rather than men, and hence most of the workers in our workforce—including those at the highest levels of government and industry—were also either pregnant or responsible for childcare during at least a certain portion of their adult lives. Given such a workforce, "working" would so obviously need to coordinate with both birthing and parenting that institutions facilitating that coordination would be built into the very structure of the social world. There would thus be not only such things as paid pregnancy leave, paid days off for sick children, paid childcare, and a match—rather than a mismatch—between the hours of the work day and the hours of the school day, there would probably also be a completely different definition of a prototypical work life, with the norm being not a continuous forty hours or more per week from adulthood to old age, but a transition from less than forty hours per week when the children are young to forty hours or more per week when the children are older.

39   The lesson of this alternative reality should be clear. It is not women's biological and historical role as mothers that is limiting their access to America's economic and political resources. It is a social world so androcentric in its organization that it

provides but one institutionalized mechanism for coordinating work in the paid labor force with the responsibilities of being a parent, that one institutionalized mechanism being the having of a wife at home to take care of one's children.

40   Now, to people who don't yet appreciate either what androcentrism is or how it operates institutionally, the suggestion that we need to change our social institutions so that they are more accommodating to women or more inclusive of women's experience seems completely wrong-headed. As they would surely describe it, it seems like a move away from gender neutrality and hence in the absolutely wrong direction of where America ought to be going.

41   But in fact, America's institutions have been so thoroughly organized for so long from an androcentric perspective—that is, they have for so long been taking care of men's special needs automatically while women's special needs have been either treated as special cases or simply left unmet—that the only way for them to even begin to approximate gender neutrality is for our society to finally begin giving as complete a package of special benefits to women as it has always given to men and men alone.

42   I want to end my lecture today with an analogy that may help you see even more clearly that the gender problem in America today isn't about the difference between women and men; it's about the transformation of that difference into female disadvantage by an androcentric social structure that looks not only gender-neutral but even god-given, because we're just so used to it by now that we don't realize it's literally *man*-made until that fact is forced upon us.

43   This analogy plays on another one of my own non-privileged attributes, not my femaleness this time, but my shortness. (I happen to be only 4 feet, 9 inches tall.) Imagine, if you will, a whole community of short people like myself. Given the argument sometimes made in our society that short people are unable to be firefighters because they are neither tall enough nor strong enough to do the job, the question arises: Would all the houses in this community eventually burn down? Well yes, if we short people had to use the heavy ladders and hoses designed by and for tall people. But no, if we (being as smart as short people are) could instead construct lighter ladders and hoses usable by both tall and short people. The moral here should be obvious: It isn't short biology that's the problem; it's short biology being forced to function in a tall-centered social structure.

44   It should be clear that there are two related morals in both this final story and my whole lecture today:

45   The first moral is that as important as the biological difference between the sexes may appear on the surface, the impact of that biological difference depends in every single instance on the environment in which it is situated. This interaction of biology and the situational context can be liberating, as in the case of antibiotics, refrigeration, airplanes, and baby formula. This interaction can also be discriminating, as in the case of women being disadvantaged—and men being advantaged—by a male-centered social structure.

46   The second moral is that as familiar, comfortable, gender-neutral, and natural as our own culture's institutions may appear to be now that explicit discrimination

against women has finally been made illegal, in fact, our institutions are so thoroughly saturated with androcentrism that even those that do not discriminate against women explicitly—like the definition of self-defense—must be treated as inherently suspect.

WRITING ASSIGNMENTS

Analysis

1. Why does Bem consider "America's focus on sexual difference" to be cyclical, obsessive, and misguided?
2. In a letter to *Time* magazine using Bem's perspective, provide an alternative assessment of the male-female brain differences described in Gorman's article.
3. Compare Bem's emphasis on technology to Friedl's focus on economics to explain human social arrangements. Are these approaches mutually exclusive or complementary?
4. Compare and contrast Bem's and Barash's views on the *relative* roles of biology and culture in shaping human behavior.

Argument

1. *Collaborative Project:* Debate Bem's proposition: "Social change— or [what] I would rather call cultural invention—can so radically transform the situational context in which biology operates that the human organism can actually be liberated from what had earlier seemed to be its intrinsic biological limitations." Draw material for both supporting and opposing arguments from the other readings in this chapter.
2. Use the comments of Bem, Gilman, de Beauvoir, *or* MacKinnon to confirm or refute the role of androcentrism (male-centeredness) in one of these areas: American political life, sports, language, movies, or workplace conditions.

Personal Writing and Writing from Research

1. *Collaborative Project:* Write a research paper on the anti-feminist arguments of one of these nineteenth-century figures: Paul Broca, Edward Clarke, Herbert Spencer, or G. Standley Hall. (Edward Clarke's speech, "Sex in Education," is a selection in Chapter 5.)
2. Compare and contrast Clarke or Spencer with Barash on the role of biology, specifically women's reproductive role, in determining women's role in society.
3. *Collaborative Project:* Write a paper on Helen Thompson Woolley and Leta Stetter Hollingworth's research into male-female differences.
4. How has any one of the following made your life different from that of your parents or altered your future plans: a recently developed medical technology, computers, video, satellite communications, VCRs, portable and car telephones, or genetic engineering?

Society and Sex Roles

Ernestine Friedl

Ernestine Friedl is the James B. Duke Professor of Cultural Anthropology, Emeritus, and former Chair of the Department of Cultural Anthropology at Duke University. She has done fieldwork among the Chippewa Indians in Wisconsin, the Pomo Indians of California, and villagers in Greece. "Society and Sex Roles" appeared in *Human Nature* (April 1978).

Journal Topics: (1) In American society, are more highly compensated activities also more prestigious? Provide examples to support your answer. (2) Describe the customary handling of money in your family and among your friends. Who decides how money will be spent? Who actually handles financial transactions? (3) Is money handled the same way when "friends" as compared to "dates" go out?

As You Read: (1) Compare and contrast the features of hunter-gatherer and contemporary industrial societies. How does Friedl explain male dominance, and differences in degree of male dominance, in these societies? (2) How does the expression "bringing home the bacon" suggest a connection between highly complex, industrialized societies like ours and hunter-gatherers?

1 "Women must respond quickly to the demands of their husbands," says anthropologist Napoleon Chagnon, describing the horticultural Yanomamö Indians of Venezuela. When a man returns from a hunting trip, "the woman, no matter what she is doing, hurries home and quietly but rapidly prepares a meal for her husband. Should the wife be slow in doing this, the husband is within his rights to beat her. Most reprimands . . . take the form of blows with the hand or with a piece of firewood. . . . Some of them chop their wives with the sharp edge of a machete or axe, or shoot them with a barbed arrow in some nonvital area, such as the buttocks or leg."

2 Among the Semai agriculturalists of central Malaya, when one person refuses the request of another, the offended party suffers *punan,* a mixture of emotional pain and frustration. "Enduring *punan* is commonest when a girl has refused the victim her sexual favors," reports Robert Dentan. "The jilted man's 'heart becomes sad.' He loses his energy and his appetite. Much of the time he sleeps, dreaming of his lost love. In this state he is in fact very likely to injure himself 'accidentally.'" The Semai are afraid of violence: a man would never strike a woman.

3 The social relationship between men and women has emerged as one of the principal disputes occupying the attention of scholars and the public in recent years. Although the discord is sharpest in the United States, the controversy has spread throughout the world. Numerous national and international conferences, including one in Mexico sponsored by the United Nations, have drawn together delegates from

all walks of life to discuss such questions as the social and political rights of each sex and even the basic nature of males and females.

4   Whatever their position, partisans often invoke examples from other cultures to support their ideas about the proper role of each sex. Because women are clearly subservient to men in many societies, like the Yanomamö, some experts conclude that the natural pattern is for men to dominate. But among the Semai no one has the right to command others, and in West Africa women are often chiefs. The place of women in these societies supports the argument of those who believe that sex roles are not fixed, that if there is a natural order, it allows for many different arrangements.

5   The argument will never be settled as long as the opposing sides toss examples from the world's cultures at each other like intellectual stones. But the effect of biological differences on male and female behavior can be clarified by looking at known examples of the earliest forms of human society and examining the relationship between technology, social organization, environment, and sex roles. The problem is to determine the conditions in which different degrees of male dominance are found, to try to discover the social and cultural arrangements that give rise to equality or inequality between the sexes, and to attempt to apply this knowledge to our understanding of the changes taking place in modern industrial society.

6   As Western history and the anthropological record have told us, equality between the sexes is rare; in most known societies females are subordinate. Male dominance is so widespread that it is virtually a human universal; societies in which women are consistently dominant do not exist and have never existed.

7   Evidence of a society in which women control all strategic resources like food and water, and in which women's activities are the most prestigious, has never been found. The Iroquois of North America and the Lovedu of Africa came closest. Among the Iroquois, women raised food, controlled its distribution, and helped to choose male political leaders. Lovedu women ruled as queens, exchanged valuable cattle, led ceremonies, and controlled their own sex lives. But among both the Iroquois and Lovedu, men owned the land and held other positions of power and prestige. Women were equal to men; they did not have ultimate authority over them. Neither culture was a true matriarchy.

8   Patriarchies are prevalent, and they appear to be strongest in societies in which men control significant goods that are exchanged with people outside the family. Regardless of who produces food, the person who gives it to others creates the obligations and alliances that are at the center of all political relations. The greater the male monopoly on the distribution of scarce items, the stronger their control of women seems to be. This is most obvious in relatively simple hunter-gatherer societies.

9   Hunter-gatherers, or foragers, subsist on wild plants, small land animals, and small river or sea creatures gathered by hand; large land animals and sea mammals hunted with spears, bows and arrows, and blow guns; and fish caught with hooks and nets. The three hundred thousand hunter-gatherers alive in the world today include the Eskimos, the Australian aborigines, and the Pygmies of Central Africa.

10   Foraging has endured for two million years and was replaced by farming and animal husbandry only ten thousand years ago; it covers more than 99 percent of human

history. Our foraging ancestry is not far behind us and provides a clue to our understanding of the human condition.

11   Hunter-gatherers are people whose ways of life are technologically simple and socially and politically egalitarian. They live in small groups of 50 to 200 and have neither kings, nor priests, nor social classes. These conditions permit anthropologists to observe the essential bases for inequalities between the sexes without the distortions induced by the complexities of contemporary industrial society.

12   The source of male power among hunter-gatherers lies in their control of a scarce, hard to acquire, but necessary nutrient—animal protein. When men in a hunter-gatherer society return to camp with game, they divide the meat in some customary way. Among the !Kung San of Africa, certain parts of the animal are given to the owner of the arrow that killed the beast, to the first hunter to sight the game, to the one who threw the first spear, and to all men in the hunting party. After the meat has been divided, each hunter distributes his share to his blood relatives and his in-laws, who in turn share it with others. If an animal is large enough, every member of the band will receive some meat.

13   Vegetable foods, in contrast, are not distributed beyond the immediate household. Women give food to their children, to their husbands, to other members of the household, and rarely, to the occasional visitor. No one outside the family regularly eats any of the wild fruits and vegetables that are gathered by the women.

14   The meat distributed by the men is a public gift. Its source is widely known, and the donor expects a reciprocal gift when other men return from a successful hunt. He gains honor as a supplier of a scarce item and simultaneously obligates others to him.

15   These obligations constitute a form of power or control over others, both men and women. The opinions of hunters play an important part in decisions to move the village; good hunters attract the most desirable women; people in other groups join camps with good hunters; and hunters, because they already participate in an internal system of exchange, control exchange with other groups for flint, salt, and steel axes. The male monopoly on hunting unites men in a system of exchange and gives them power; gathering vegetable food does not give women equal power even among foragers who live in the tropics, where the food collected by women provides more than half the hunter-gatherer diet.

16   If dominance arises from a monopoly on big-game hunting, why has the male monopoly remained unchallenged? Some women are strong enough to participate in the hunt and their endurance is certainly equal to that of men. Dobe San women of the Kalahari Desert in Africa walk an average of 10 miles a day carrying from 15 to 33 pounds of food plus a baby.

17   Women do not hunt, I believe, because of four interrelated factors: variability in the supply of game; the different skills required for hunting and gathering; the incompatibility between carrying burdens and hunting; and the small size of seminomadic foraging populations.

18   Because the meat supply is unstable, foragers must make frequent expeditions to provide the band with gathered food. Environmental factors such as seasonal and annual variation in rainfall often affect the size of the wildlife population. Hunters

cannot always find game, and when they do encounter animals, they are not always successful in killing their prey. In northern latitudes, where meat is the primary food, periods of starvation are known in every generation. The irregularity of the game supply leads hunter-gatherers in areas where plant foods are available to depend on these predictable foods a good part of the time. Someone must gather the fruits, nuts, and roots and carry them back to camp to feed unsuccessful hunters, children, the elderly, and anyone who might not have gone foraging that day.

19   Foraging falls to the women because hunting and gathering cannot be combined on the same expedition. Although gatherers sometimes notice signs of game as they work, the skills required to track game are not the same as those required to find edible roots or plants. Hunters scan the horizon and the land for traces of large game; gatherers keep their eyes to the ground, studying the distribution of plants and the texture of the soil for hidden roots and animal holes. Even if a woman who was collecting plants came across the track of an antelope, she could not follow it; it is impossible to carry a load and hunt at the same time. Running with a heavy load is difficult, and should the animal be sighted, the hunter would be off balance and could neither shoot an arrow nor throw a spear accurately.

20   Pregnancy and child care would also present difficulties for a hunter. An unborn child affects a woman's body balance, as does a child in her arms, on her back, or slung at her side. Until they are two years old, many hunter-gatherer children are carried at all times, and until they are four, they are carried some of the time.

21   An observer might wonder why young women do not hunt until they become pregnant, or why mature women and men do not hunt and gather on alternate days, with some women staying in camp to act as wet nurses for the young. Apart from the effects hunting might have on a mother's milk production, there are two reasons. First, young girls begin to bear children as soon as they are physically mature and strong enough to hunt, and second, hunter-gatherer bands are so small that there are unlikely to be enough lactating women to serve as wet nurses. No hunter-gatherer group could afford to maintain a specialized female hunting force.

22   Because game is not always available, because hunting and gathering are specialized skills, because women carrying heavy loads cannot hunt, and because women in hunter-gatherer societies are usually either pregnant or caring for young children, for most of the last two million years of human history men have hunted and women have gathered.

23   If male dominance depends on controlling the supply of meat, then the degree of male dominance in a society should vary with the amount of meat available and the amount supplied by the men. Some regions, like the East African grasslands and the North American woodlands, abounded with species of large mammals; other zones, like tropical forests and semideserts, are thinly populated with prey. Many elements affect the supply of game, but theoretically, the less meat provided exclusively by the men, the more egalitarian the society.

24   All known hunter-gatherer societies fit into four basic types: those in which men and women work together in communal hunts and as teams gathering edible plants, as did the Washo Indians of North America; those in which men and women each collect

their own plant foods although the men supply some meat to the group, as do the Hadza of Tanzania; those in which male hunters and female gatherers work apart but return to camp each evening to share their acquisitions, as do the Tiwi of North Australia; and those in which the men provide all the food by hunting large game, as do the Eskimo. In each case the extent of male dominance increases directly with the proportion of meat supplied by individual men and small hunting parties.

25   Among the most egalitarian of hunter-gatherer societies are the Washo Indians, who inhabited the valleys of the Sierra Nevada in what is now southern California and Nevada. In the spring they moved north to Lake Tahoe for the large fish runs of sucker and native trout. Everyone—men, women, and children—participated in the fishing. Women spent the summer gathering edible berries and seeds while the men continued to fish. In the fall some men hunted deer, but the most important source of animal protein was the jackrabbit, which was captured in communal hunts. Men and women together drove the rabbits into nets tied end to end. To provide food for the winter, husbands and wives worked as teams in the late fall to collect pine nuts.

26   Since everyone participated in most food-gathering activities, there were no individual distributors of food and relatively little difference in male and female rights. Men and women were not segregated from each other in daily activities; both were free to take lovers after marriage; both had the right to separate whenever they chose; menstruating women were not isolated from the rest of the group; and one of the two major Washo rituals celebrated hunting while the other celebrated gathering. Men were accorded more prestige if they had killed a deer, and men directed decisions about the seasonal movement of the group. But if no male leader stepped forward, women were permitted to lead. The distinctive feature of groups such as the Washo is the relative equality of the sexes.

27   The sexes are also relatively equal among the Hadza of Tanzania, but this near-equality arises because men and women tend to work alone to feed themselves. They exchange little food. The Hadza lead a leisurely life in the seemingly barren environment of the East African Rift Gorge, which is, in fact, rich in edible berries, roots, and small game. As a result of this abundance, from the time they are ten years old, Hadza men and women gather much of their own food. Women take their young children with them into the bush, eating as they forage, and collect only enough food for a light family meal in the evening. The men eat berries and roots as they hunt for small game, and should they bring down a rabbit or a hyrax, they eat the meat on the spot. Meat is carried back to the camp and shared with the rest of the group only on those rare occasions when a poisoned arrow brings down a large animal—an impala, a zebra, an eland, or a giraffe.

28   Because Hadza men distribute little meat, their status is only slightly higher than that of the women. People flock to the camp of a good hunter and the camp might take on his name because of his popularity, but he is in no sense a leader of the group. A Hadza man and a woman have an equal right to divorce, and each can repudiate a marriage simply by living apart for a few weeks. Couples tend to live in the same camp as the wife's mother, but they sometimes make long visits to the camp of the

husband's mother. Although a man may take more than one wife, most Hadza males cannot afford to indulge in this luxury. In order to maintain a marriage, a man must supply both his wife and his mother-in-law with some meat and trade goods, such as beads and cloth, and the Hadza economy gives few men the wealth to provide for more than one wife and mother-in-law. Washo equality is based on cooperation; Hadza equality is based on independence.

29   In contrast to both these groups, among the Tiwi of Melville and Bathurst Islands off the northern coast of Australia, male hunters dominate female gatherers. The Tiwi are representative of the most common form of foraging society, in which the men supply large quantities of meat, although less than half the food consumed by the group. Each morning Tiwi women, most with babies on their backs, scatter in different directions in search of vegetables, grubs, worms, and small game such as bandicoots, lizards, and opossums. To track the game, they use hunting dogs. On most days women return to camp with some meat and with baskets full of *korka,* the nut of a native palm, which is soaked and mashed to make a porridge-like dish. The Tiwi men do not hunt small game and do not hunt every day, but when they do they often return with kangaroo, large lizards, fish, and game birds.

30   The porridge is cooked separately by each household and rarely shared outside the family, but the meat is prepared by a volunteer cook, who can be male or female. After the cook takes one of the parts of the animal traditionally reserved for him or her, the animal's "boss," the one who caught it, distributes the rest to all near kin and then to all others residing with the band. Although the small game supplied by the women is distributed in the same way as the big game supplied by the men, Tiwi men are dominant because the game they kill provides most of the meat.

31   The power of Tiwi men is clearest in their betrothal practices. Among the Tiwi, a woman must always be married. To ensure this, female infants are betrothed at birth and widows are remarried at the gravesides of their late husbands. Men form alliances by exchanging daughters, sisters, and mothers in marriage, and some collect as many as twenty-five wives. Tiwi men value the quantity and quality of the food many wives can collect and the many children they can produce.

32   The dominance of the men is offset somewhat by the influence of adult women in selecting their next husbands. Many women are active strategists in the political careers of their male relatives, but to the exasperation of some sons attempting to promote their own futures, widowed mothers sometimes insist on selecting their own partners. Women also influence the marriages of their daughters and granddaughters, especially when the selected husband dies before the bestowed child moves to his camp.

33   Among the Eskimo, representative of the rarest type of forager society, inequality between the sexes is matched by inequality in supplying the group with food. Inland Eskimo men hunt caribou throughout the year to provision the entire society, and maritime Eskimo men depend on whaling, fishing, and some hunting to feed their extended families. The women process the carcasses, cut and sew skins to make clothing, cook, and care for the young; but they collect no food of their own and depend on the men to supply all the raw materials for their work. Since men provide all

the meat, they also control the trade in hides, whale oil, seal oil, and other items that move between the maritime and inland Eskimos.

34 Eskimo women are treated almost exclusively as objects to be used, abused, and traded by men. After puberty all Eskimo girls are fair game for any interested male. A man shows his intentions by grabbing the belt of a woman, and if she protests, he cuts off her trousers and forces himself upon her. These encounters are considered unimportant by the rest of the group. Men offer their wives' sexual services to establish alliances with trading partners and members of hunting and whaling parties.

35 Despite the consistent pattern of some degree of male dominance among foragers, most of these societies are egalitarian compared with agricultural and industrial societies. No forager has any significant opportunity for political leadership. Foragers, as a rule, do not like to give or take orders, and assume leadership only with reluctance. Shamans (those who are thought to be possessed by spirits) may be either male or female. Public rituals conducted by women in order to celebrate the first menstruation of girls are common, and the symbolism in these rituals is similar to that in the ceremonies that follow a boy's first kill.

36 In any society, status goes to those who control the distribution of valued goods and services outside the family. Equality arises when both sexes work side by side in food production, as do the Washo, and the products are simply distributed among the workers. In such circumstances, no person or sex has greater access to valued items than do others. But when women make no contribution to the food supply, as in the case of the Eskimo, they are completely subordinate.

37 When we attempt to apply these generalizations to contemporary industrial society, we can predict that as long as women spend their discretionary income from jobs on domestic needs, they will gain little social recognition and power. To be an effective source of power, money must be exchanged in ways that require returns and create obligations. In other words, it must be invested.

38 Jobs that do not give women control over valued resources will do little to advance their general status. Only as managers, executives, and professionals are women in a position to trade goods and services, to do others favors, and therefore to obligate others to them. Only as controllers of valued resources can women achieve prestige, power, and equality.

39 Within the household, women who bring in income from jobs are able to function on a more nearly equal basis with their husbands. Women who contribute services to their husbands and children without pay, as do some middle-class Western housewives, are especially vulnerable to dominance. Like Eskimo women, as long as their services are limited to domestic distribution they have little power relative to their husbands and none with respect to the outside world.

40 As for the limits imposed on women by their procreative functions in hunter-gatherer societies, childbearing and child care are organized around work as much as work is organized around reproduction. Some foraging groups space their children three to four years apart and have an average of only four to six children, far fewer than many women in other cultures. Hunter-gatherers nurse their infants for extended periods, sometimes for as long as four years. This custom suppresses ovulation and limits

the size of their families. Sometimes, although rarely, they practice infanticide. By limiting reproduction, a woman who is gathering food has only one child to carry.

41   Different societies can and do adjust the frequency of birth and the care of children to accommodate whatever productive activities women customarily engage in. In horticultural societies, where women work long hours in gardens that may be far from home, infants get food to supplement their mothers' milk, older children take care of younger children, and pregnancies are widely spaced. Throughout the world, if a society requires a woman's labor, it finds ways to care for her children.

42   In the United States, as in some other industrial societies, the accelerated entry of women with preschool children into the labor force has resulted in the development of a variety of child-care arrangements. Individual women have called on friends, relatives, and neighbors. Public and private child-care centers are growing. We should realize that the declining birth rate, the increasing acceptance of childless or single-child families, and de-emphasis on motherhood are adaptations to a sexual division of labor reminiscent of the system of production found in hunter-gatherer societies.

43   In many countries where women no longer devote most of their productive years to childbearing, they are beginning to demand a change in the social relationship of the sexes. As women gain access to positions that control the exchange of resources, male dominance may become archaic, and industrial societies may one day become as egalitarian as the Washo.

WRITING ASSIGNMENTS

Analysis

1. Friedl says, "Male dominance is so widespread that it is virtually a human universal. . . ." In a short essay for a newsletter directed at workingwomen, explain this universal male dominance.
2. Compare and contrast Barash's, Bem's and Friedl's explanations of male dominance.
3. Compare and contrast the kinds of evidence that Barash and Friedl use to support their claims. Which is more persuasive? Why?
4. How does Friedl explain differences in male dominance in hunter-gatherer societies?
5. Why don't women in hunter-gatherer societies perform the tasks that earn men power and prestige?
6. Compare and contrast the conditions that limit women's economic role in hunter-gatherer and in contemporary agricultural and industrial societies. You may want to draw on the concepts and evidence in Barash's or Bem's essays.

Argument

1. Friedl says, "Throughout the world, if a society requires a woman's labor, it finds ways to care for her children." Beginning with a summary of how hunter-gatherer societies combine women's work and child care, write an essay

containing recommendations on how American society can use its resources to achieve this goal.

2. Do you find Barash's primarily biological or Friedl's primarily cultural explanation of male dominance more persuasive? Explain your answer in the form of a critique of the writer with whom you disagree.

3. Friedl says, "Women who contribute services to their husbands and children without pay, as do some middle-class Western housewives, are especially vulnerable to dominance." Do you agree? What other factors in American society affect women's power and status, making some women even more vulnerable than nonworking middle-class wives? Classify groups of women in terms of their vulnerability or power.

4. *Collaborative Project:* Friedl says, "To be an effective source of power, money must be exchanged in ways that require returns and create obligations. In other words, it must be invested." In a report, describe the ways that contemporary Americans "invest," such as hospitality, gift-giving, and traditional investing. Are these activities gender-linked?

Personal Writing and Writing from Research

1. *Collaborative Project:* Research how other industrialized societies have or have not provided for child care when women work outside the home. In an oral or written report, include your evaluation of these societies' provisions and your recommendations on whether the United States should adopt any of them.

2. Either as a collaborative or individual project, interview women who have combined child-rearing with work outside the home. Use Friedl's article as a model for your limited-scope report on American society and sex roles. Cover these topics:

   - when and why the women began working
   - who else, if anyone, contributes to the family's income
   - how the women's income is used and perceived by the family
   - how the women's income affects their status and role in the family, particularly their child-care responsibilities and decision-making power
   - the existence outside the immediate family of supports for the women's work and family responsibilities

3. Interview fathers whose wives work outside the home, adapting the topics from No. 2.

4. Interview mothers who do not work outside the home and are dependent on their husband's incomes. Compare your findings with the responses from working mothers in No. 2.

HISTORY AND VISION

The chronologically sequenced documents in this chapter illustrate an ongoing debate about the roles of women and men in American society. Proclaiming that the "personal is political," feminists—both female and male—in the late twentieth century linked elections and jobs to the politics of sex, etiquette, housework, and child care. But even in the early nineteenth century, it was clear, at least to some, that when it came to gender roles, personal, political, economic, religious, racial, and social issues were, like the filaments of a spider's web, all interconnected. Pulling any one strand of the web threatened to unravel them all. Understandably and predictably, resistance to change has been strong, and confusion and anxiety persist.

One of the first formal records of this debate neatly coincides with the Continental Congress's deliberations about declaring independence from England. On March 31, 1776, Abigail Adams wrote to her husband, John, asking him to "Remember the Ladies" when he and his male colleagues were drafting the Declaration of Independence. In 1797, John Adams succeeded George Washington to become the second president of the United States. The relevant portions of Abigail's letter and John's reply, private correspondence between a very public wife and husband on the subject of male and female relations, are the first documents in this chapter.

A generation later, in 1838, Sarah Moore Grimke, a Southerner active in the movement to abolish slavery, wrote what is perhaps the first American feminist critique of the woman's "sphere." Her letter, an analysis of biblical authority for female subordination, responds to "The Pastoral Letter of the General Association of Congregational Ministers of Massachusetts," which is also partially reproduced here.

The third selection comes from Alexis de Tocqueville's *Democracy in America*. A Frenchman, Tocqueville is credited with writing the most detailed, penetrating, and perceptive analysis of American society and the new republic to appear in their early years. Noting the difference between the status of women in Europe and in the United States, he praises both the relative equality of American women and men and their separate spheres.

In 1848, 18 years after Tocqueville's observations were published, American feminists first gathered to protest formally what they saw as the separate and unequal status of American women. Elizabeth Cady Stanton, who would emerge as a leader of the new women's movement, and a number of coeditors drafted the "Seneca Falls Convention Declaration of Sentiments," modeled on the Declaration of Independence. Frederick Douglass, the ex-slave whose autobiography and lifelong advocacy made him the most prominent African-American leader in the abolitionist movement, immediately connected race and gender issues in "The Rights of Women."

Three years later, in 1851, another ex-slave, the illiterate but eloquent Sojourner Truth, addressed an audience that included opponents of women's rights at the Akron Women's Rights Convention. In "Ain't I a Woman," she refuted the myth of women's sheltered, privileged lives and vividly testified to the particularly harsh conditions endured by African-American women.

The next three selections redefine woman's place. When Lucy Stone and Henry Brown Blackwell, both reformers, married in 1855, they repudiated the specific sexual inequalities enshrined in American marriage laws and customs. Included here are their protest and the words of the man who married them, Rev. Thomas Wentworth Higginson.

The Bible had long been invoked to justify the subjugation, or even the inferiority, of women, as demonstrated by the pastoral letter to which Sarah Grimke responded. Just before her 80th year, Elizabeth Cady Stanton collaborated with other women's rights advocates to write *The Woman's Bible.* Their comments on the creation of man and woman in Genesis are included here.

As Sojourner Truth's speech made clear, the experience of African-American women, although in some respects like that of other women, was much harder. The 1895 "Address to the First National Conference of Colored Women" by Josephine St. Pierre Ruffin reflects the aspirations of African-American women who were more socially privileged than Sojourner Truth, but equally oppressed by the racial prejudice that all African-American women and men continued to endure.

Defenders of tradition spoke as loudly as proponents of change, and they framed their arguments in the language of morality, history, and science. Theodore Roosevelt, our 26th president, shows in his speeches that it is impossible to understand the roles of either women or men in isolation. Changes in one inevitably affect the other. Roosevelt's 1899 speech in Chicago defines the American character and national destiny in traditionally virile images. Six years later, in his "Address before the National Congress of Mothers," he defined the respective domestic roles of women as homemakers, wives, and mothers, and of men as breadwinners.

By the middle of the twentieth century, psychological formulations had often supplanted traditional religious and moral perspectives in discussions about gender. But the conclusions drawn could sound the same. In *Modern Woman: The Lost Sex,* a popular advice book published in 1947, just after the end of World War II, Ferdinand Lundberg and Marynia F. Farnham, MD, urge women to resume their traditional and—they argue—natural feminine roles. In "Mother and Child," a passage from "The Slaughter of the Innocents," a section of their book, they emphasize the primary responsibility of mothers for the psychological health of their children.

Although many women remained in the post-war workforce, millions heeded the call to return to domestic life. Some, such as Betty Friedan, were highly educated. In 1957, Friedan sent a questionnaire to her Smith College classmates. Their answers led Friedan to write her 1963 book, *The Feminine Mystique,* which is widely credited with launching the second wave of American feminism. An excerpt from the book's first chapter is included here.

The women's movement aroused opposition and raised concerns among many. In a 1970 *Time* essay, Gloria Steinem attempts to reassure skeptics as she speculates about the major changes that American society would undergo if the feminist movement succeeded.

Speaking for an overlooked group, Mitsuye Yamada describes and rejects the invisibility and powerlessness of Asian Americans, particularly Asian-American women.

The next three selections present very different challenges, by women, to mainstream feminism. In the first of these, "Understanding the Difference," Phyllis Schlafly attacks the women's liberation movement and defends the value and power of traditional femininity. Then, poet Maya Angelou uses images from fairy tales and history to show how race and class have divided women and created skepticism among black women toward mainstream American feminism. Last, bell hooks calls upon her black sisters to embrace an expanded definition of feminism.

The last four selections present a chorus of men's voices exploring the meaning of contemporary masculinity and the proper relationship between men and women. Educator Cooper Thompson calls for a rejection of traditional masculinity, and Warren Farrell responds with a spirited defense. Robert Reich, secretary of labor in the Clinton administration, issued his "Wake-Up Call" in 1989 when he was a lecturer and economic theorist at Harvard. Already sensitized to gender issues, Reich was outraged when his wife was denied academic tenure for what he considered to be gender bias. He analyzes her experience, offers his own observations of lingering, deep-seated sexism, and urges feminist men like himself to become actively involved in changing both attitudes and behavior.

Finally, in "My Life in the Military Closet," José Zuniga, the Sixth Army's Soldier of the Year turned gay rights activist, explores what he calls the inherent contradictions in military psychology. He also traces his experiences, and those of others, that led him out of the closet, ending the military career he loved.

IN THE BEGINNING

Correspondence

Abigail and John Adams

Historians have called Abigail Adams the "first fully emancipated woman in American history." In addition to being a prolific writer, she was also her husband's full partner. As president (1797–1801), he discussed important problems with her and engaged her help in drafting semiofficial letters. One historian called her a "minister without portfolio." But more than 20 years earlier, his April 14, 1776, response to her March 31, 1776, letter sounds a different note. He was then a delegate to the Continental Congress, which was deliberating independence from England.

On March 31, 1776, Abigail Adams wrote to her husband while the Continental Congress was deliberating independence. After describing the arrival of spring in Massachusetts, she admonished him to "Remember the Ladies" when writing the new code of laws. In his reply of April 14, 1776, he treated her "extraordinary Code of Laws" as his dear wife's little joke.

ABIGAIL TO JOHN

1 . . . I long to hear that you have declared an independancy—and by the way in the new Code of Laws which I suppose it will be necessary for you to make I desire you would Remember the Ladies, and be more generous and favourable to them than your ancestors. Do not put such unlimited power into the hands of the Husbands. Remember all Men would be tyrants if they could. If perticuliar care and attention is not paid to the Laidies we are determined to foment a Rebelion, and will not hold ourselves bound by any Laws in which we have no voice, or Representation.

2 That your Sex are Naturally Tyrannical is a Truth so thoroughly established as to admit of no dispute, but such of you as wish to be happy willingly give up the harsh title of Master for the more tender and endearing one of Friend. Why then, not put it out of the power of the vicious and the Lawless to use us with cruelty and indignity with impunity. Men of Sense in all Ages abhor those customs which treat us only as the vassals of your Sex. Regard us then as Beings placed by providence under your protection and in immitation of the Supreem Being make use of that power only for our happiness.

JOHN TO ABIGAIL

3 . . . As to your extraordinary Code of Laws, I cannot but laugh. We have been told that our Struggle has loosened the bands of Government every where. That Children and Apprentices were disobedient—that schools and Colledges were grown turbulent—that Indians slighted their Guardians and Negroes grew insolent to their Masters. But your Letter was the first Intimation that another Tribe more numerous and powerfull than all the rest were grown discontented.—This is rather too coarse a Compliment but you are so saucy, I wont blot it out.

4 Depend upon it. We know better than to repeal our Masculine systems. Altho they are in full Force, you know they are little more than Theory. We dare not exert our Power in its full Latitude. We are obliged to go fair, and softly, and in Practice you know We are the subjects. We have only the Name of Masters, and rather than give up this, which would compleatly subject Us to the Despotism of the Peticoat, I hope General Washington, and all our brave Heroes would fight. I am sure every good Politician would plot, as long as he would against Despotism, Empire, Monarchy, Aristocracy, Oligarchy, or Ochlocracy.—A fine Story indeed. I begin to think the Ministry as deep as they are wicked. After stirring up Tories, Landjobbers, Trimmers, Bigots, Canadians, Indians, Negroes, Hanoverians, Hessians, Russians, Irish Roman Catholicks, Scotch Renegadoes, at last they have stimulated the [Ladies] to demand new Priviledges and threaten to rebell.

Response to "The Pastoral Letter of the General Association of Congregational Ministers of Massachusetts"

Sarah Moore Grimke

Although Sarah Grimke (1792–1873) had been raised as part of the slave-holding class on a South Carolina plantation, she and her sister Angelina became celebrated activists in the movement to abolish slavery. Their prominence in the antislavery crusades of the 1830s drew them into a second controversy over the propriety of women's participation in public affairs. Grimke herself draws attention to an underlying connection between the movements to end slavery and to liberate women by addressing her *Letters on the Equality of the Sexes* (1838), from which this selection comes, to Mary S. Parker, president of the Boston Female Anti-Slavery Society. Excerpts from the Pastoral Letter precede Grimke's letter of response.

EXCERPTS FROM THE PASTORAL LETTER

1 We invite your attention to the dangers which at present seem to threaten the female character with wide spread and permanent injury.

2   The appropriate duties and influence of women, are clearly stated in the New Testament. Those duties and that influence are unobtrusive and private, but the sources of mighty power. When the mild, dependant, softening influence of woman upon the sternness of man's opinions is fully exercised, society feels the effects of it in a thousand forms. The power of woman is in her dependence, flowing from the consciousness of that weakness which God has given her for her protection and which keeps her in those departments of life that form the character of individuals and of the nation. There are social influences which females use in promoting piety and the great objects of christian benevolence, which we cannot too highly commend. We appreciate the unostentatious prayers and efforts of woman, in advancing the cause of religion at home and abroad:—in Sabbath schools, in leading religious inquirers to their pastor for instruction, and in all such associated effort as becomes the modesty of her sex; and earnestly hope that she may abound more and more in these labours of piety and love. But when she assumes the place and tone of a man as a public reformer, our care and protection of her seem unnecessary, we put ourselves in self defence against her, she yields the power which God has given her for protection, and her character becomes unnatural. If the vine, whose strength and beauty is to lean upon the trellis work and half conceal its clusters, thinks to assume the independence and the overshadowing nature of the elm, it will not only cease to bear fruit, but fall in shame and dishonour into the dust.

3   We cannot, therefore, but regret the mistaken conduct of those who encourage females to bear an obtrusive and ostentatious part in measures of reform, and countenance any of that sex who so far forget themselves as to itinerate in the character of
public lecturers and teachers.

4   We especially deplore the intimate acquaintance and promiscuous conversation of
females with regard to things "which ought not to be named;" by which that modesty
and delicacy which is the charm of domestic life, and which constitute the true influence of women in society are consumed, and the way opened, as we apprehend, for de-
generacy and ruin. We say these things, not to discourage proper influences against
sin, but to secure such reformation as we believe is scriptural and will be permanent.

GRIMKE'S RESPONSE

Haverhill, 7th Mo. 1837

5 DEAR FRIEND,—When I last addressed thee, I had not seen the Pastoral Letter of the
General Association. It has since fallen into my hands, and I must digress from my intention of exhibiting the condition of women in different parts of the world, in order
to make some remarks on this extraordinary document. I am persuaded that when
the minds of men and women become emancipated from the thraldom of superstition
and "traditions of men," the sentiments contained in the Pastoral Letter will be recurred to with as much astonishment as the opinions of Cotton Mather and other distinguished men of his day, on the subject of witchcraft; nor will it be deemed less
wonderful, that a body of divines should gravely assemble and endeavor to prove that
woman has no right to "open her mouth for the dumb," than it now is that judges
should have sat on the trials of witches, and solemnly condemned nineteen persons
and one dog to death for witchcraft.

6   But to the letter. It says, "We invite your attention to the dangers which at present
seem to threaten the FEMALE CHARACTER with wide-spread and permanent injury." I rejoice that they have called the attention of my sex to this subject, because I
believe if woman investigates it, she will soon discover that danger is impending,
though from a totally different source from that which the Association apprehends,—danger from those who, having long held the reins of *usurped* authority, are
unwilling to permit us to fill that sphere which God created us to move in, and who
have entered into league to crush the immortal mind of woman. I rejoice, because I
am persuaded that the rights of woman, like the rights of slaves, need only be examined to be understood and asserted, even by some of those, who are now endeavoring
to smother the irrepressible desire for mental and spiritual freedom which glows in
the breast of many, who hardly dare to speak their sentiments.

7   "The appropriate duties and influence of women are clearly stated in the New Testament. Those duties are unobtrusive and private but the sources of *mighty power.*
When the mild, *dependent,* softening influence of woman upon the sternness of
man's opinions is fully exercised, society feels the effects of it in a thousand ways." No
one can desire more earnestly than I do, that women may move exactly in the sphere

which her Creator has assigned her; and I believe her having been displaced from that sphere has introduced confusion into the world. It is, therefore, of vast importance to herself and to all the rational creation, that she should ascertain what are her duties and her privileges as a responsible and immortal being. The New Testament has been referred to, and I am willing to abide by its decisions, but must enter my protest against the false translation of some passages by the MEN who did that work, and against the perverted interpretation by the MEN who undertook to write commentaries thereon. I am inclined to think, when we are admitted to the honor of studying Greek and Hebrew, we shall produce some various readings of the Bible a little different from those we now have.

8   The Lord Jesus defines the duties of his followers in his Sermon on the Mount. He lays down grand principles by which they should be governed, without any reference to sex or condition:—"Ye are the light of the world. A city that is set on a hill cannot be hid. Neither do men light a candle and put it under a bushel, but on a candlestick, and it giveth light unto all that are in the house. Let your light so shine before men, that they may see your good works, and glorify your Father which is in Heaven." I follow him through all his precepts, and find him giving the same directions to women as to men, never even referring to the distinction now so strenuously insisted upon between masculine and feminine virtues: this is one of the anti-christian "traditions of men" which are taught instead of the "commandments of God." Men and women were CREATED EQUAL; they are both moral and accountable beings, and whatever is *right* for man to do, is *right* for woman.

9   But the influence of woman, says the Association, is to be private and unobtrusive; her light is not to shine before man like that of her brethren; but she is passively to let the lords of the creation, as they call themselves, put the bushel over it, lest peradventure it might appear that the world has been benefitted by the rays of her candle. So that her quenched light, according to their judgment, will be of more use than if it were set on the candlestick. "Her influence is the source of mighty power." This has ever been the flattering language of man since he laid aside the whip as a means to keep woman in subjection. He spares her body; but the war he has waged against her mind, her heart, and her soul, has been no less destructive to her as a moral being. How monstrous, how anti-christian, is the doctrine that woman is to be dependent on man! Where, in all the sacred Scriptures, is this taught? Alas! she has too well learned the lesson which man has labored to teach her. She has surrendered her dearest rights, and been satisfied with the privileges which man has assumed to grant her; she has been amused with the show of power whilst man has absorbed all the reality into himself. He has adorned the creature whom God gave him as a companion, with baubles and gewgaws, turned her attention to personal attractions, offered incense to her vanity, and made her the instrument of his selfish gratification, a plaything to please his eye and amuse his hours of leisure. "Rule by obedience and by submission sway," or in other words, study to be a hypocrite, pretend to submit, but gain your point, has been the code of household morality which woman has been taught. The poet has sung, in sickly strains, the loveliness of woman's dependence upon man, and now we find it re-echoed by those who profess to teach the religion of the Bible. God says, "Cease ye from man whose breath is in his nostrils, for wherein is

he to be accounted of?" Man says, depend upon me. God says, "HE will teach us of his ways." Man says, believe it not, I am to be your teacher. This doctrine of dependence upon man is utterly at variance with the doctrine of the Bible. In that book I find nothing like the softness of woman, nor the sternness of man: both are equally commanded to bring forth the fruits of the Spirit, love, meekness, gentleness, &c.

10   But we are told, "the power of woman is in her dependence, flowing from a consciousness of that weakness which God has given her for her protection." If physical weakness is alluded to, I cheerfully concede the superiority; if brute force is what my brethren are claiming, I am willing to let them have all the honor they desire; but if they mean to intimate, that mental or moral weakness belongs to woman, more than to man, I utterly disclaim the charge. Our powers of mind have been crushed, as far as man could do it, our sense of morality has been impaired by his interpretation of our duties; but no where does God say that he made any distinction between us, as moral and intelligent beings.

11   "We appreciate," says the Association, "the *unostentatious* prayers and efforts of woman in advancing the cause of religion at home and abroad, in leading religious inquirers TO THE PASTOR for instruction." Several points here demand attention. If public prayers and public efforts are necessarily ostentatious, then "Anna the prophetess, (or preacher,) who departed not from the temple, but served God with fastings and prayers night and day," "and spake of Christ to all them that looked for redemption in Israel," was ostentatious in her efforts. Then, the apostle Paul encourages women to be ostentatious in their efforts to spread the gospel, when he gives them directions how they should appear, when engaged in praying, or preaching in the public assemblies. Then, the whole association of Congregational ministers are ostentatious, in the efforts they are making in preaching and praying to convert souls.

12   But woman may be permitted to lead religious inquirers to the PASTORS for instruction. Now this is assuming that all pastors are better qualified to give instruction than woman. This I utterly deny. I have suffered too keenly from the teaching of man, to lead any one to him for instruction. The Lord Jesus says,—"Come unto me and learn of me." He points his followers to no man; and when woman is made the favored instrument of rousing a sinner to his lost and helpless condition, she has no right to substitute any teacher for Christ; all she has to do is, to turn the contrite inquirer to the "Lamb of God which taketh away the sins of the world." More souls have probably been lost by going down to Egypt for help, and by trusting in man in the early stages of religious experience, than by any other error. Instead of the petition being offered to God,—"Lead me in thy truth, and TEACH me, for thou art the God of my salvation,"—instead of relying on the precious promises—"What man is he that feareth the Lord? him shall HE TEACH in the way that he shall choose"—"I will instruct thee and TEACH thee in the way which thou shalt go—I will guide thee with mine eye"—the young convert is directed to go to man, as if he were in the place of God, and his instructions essential to an advancement in the path of righteousness. That woman can have but a poor conception of the privilege of being taught of God, what he alone can teach, who would turn the "religious inquirer aside" from the fountain of living waters, where he might slake his thirst for spiritual instructions, to

those broken cisterns which can hold no water, and therefore cannot satisfy the panting spirit. The business of men and women, who are ORDAINED OF GOD to preach the unsearchable riches of Christ' to a lost and perishing world, is to lead souls to Christ, and not to Pastors for instruction.

13   The General Association say, that "when woman assumes the place and tone of man as a public reformer, our care and protection of her seem unnecessary; we put ourselves in self-defence against her, and her character becomes unnatural." Here again the unscriptural notion is held up, that there is a distinction between the duties of men and women as moral beings; that what is virtue in man, is vice in woman; and women who dare to obey the command of Jehovah, "Cry aloud, spare not, lift up thy voice like a trumpet, and show my people their transgression," are threatened with having the protection of the brethren withdrawn. If this is all they do, we shall not even know the time when our chastisement is inflicted; our trust is in the Lord Jehovah, and in him is everlasting strength. The motto of woman, when she is engaged in the great work of public reformation should be,—"The Lord is my light and my salvation; whom shall I fear? The Lord is the strength of my life; of whom shall I be afraid?" She must feel, if she feels rightly, that she is fulfilling one of the important duties laid upon her as an accountable being, and that her character, instead of being "unnatural," is in exact accordance with the will of Him to whom, and to no other, she is responsible for the talents and the gifts confided to her. As to the pretty simile, introduced into the "Pastoral letter," "If the vine whose strength and beauty is to lean upon the trellis work, and half conceal its clusters, thinks to assume the independence and the overshadowing nature of the elm," &c. I shall only remark that it might well suit the poet's fancy, who sings of sparkling eyes and coral lips, and knights in armor clad; but it seems to me utterly inconsistent with the dignity of a Christian body, to endeavor to draw such an anti-scriptural distinction between men and women. Ah! how many of my sex feel in the dominion, thus unrighteously exercised over them, under the gentle appellation of *protection*, that what they have leaned upon has proved a broken reed at best, and oft a spear.

Thine in the bonds of womanhood,
Sarah M. Grimke

How the Americans Understand the Equality of the Sexes

Alexis de Tocqueville

Alexis de Tocqueville, a Frenchman, spent nine months in 1831–1832 touring the United States and preparing a report on America's new penitentiary system for his government. But he was an observer of much more than our prisons. His impressions of the new republic and its society, published in two volumes under the title *Democracy in America* (1835, 1840), became a bestseller in both France and the United States. His mainly laudatory views are still discussed today and were widely influential in the decades before the Civil War. Attributing much of the success of American democracy to the character of American women, he praises Americans for proclaiming equality as their highest ideal while restricting women to the domestic sphere of hearth and home.

1   I have shown how democracy destroys or modifies the different inequalities that originate in society; but is this all, or does it not ultimately affect that great inequality of man and woman which has seemed, up to the present day, to be eternally based in human nature? I believe that the social changes that bring nearer to the same level the father and son, the master and servant, and, in general, superiors and inferiors will raise woman and make her more and more the equal of man. But here, more than ever, I feel the necessity of making myself clearly understood; for there is no subject on which the coarse and lawless fancies of our age have taken a freer range.

2   There are people in Europe who, confounding together the different characteristics of the sexes, would make man and woman into beings not only equal but alike. They would give to both the same functions, impose on both the same duties, and grant to both the same rights; they would mix them in all things—their occupations, their pleasures, their business. It may readily be conceived that by thus attempting to make one sex equal to the other, both are degraded, and from so preposterous a medley of the works of nature nothing could ever result but weak men and disorderly women.

3   It is not thus that the Americans understand that species of democratic equality which may be established between the sexes. They admit that as nature has appointed such wide differences between the physical and moral constitution of man and woman, her manifest design was to give a distinct employment to their various faculties; and they hold that improvement does not consist in making beings so dissimilar do pretty nearly the same things, but in causing each of them to fulfill their respective tasks in the best possible manner. The Americans have applied to the sexes the great principle of political economy which governs the manufacturers of our age, by carefully dividing the duties of man from those of woman in order that the great work of society may be the better carried on.

4   In no country has such constant care been taken as in America to trace two clearly distinct lines of action for the two sexes and to make them keep pace one with the other, but in two pathways that are always different. American women never manage the outward concerns of the family or conduct a business or take a part in political life; nor are they, on the other hand, ever compelled to perform the rough labor of the fields or to make any of those laborious efforts which demand the exertion of physical strength. No families are so poor as to form an exception to this rule. If, on the one hand, an American woman cannot escape from the quiet circle of domestic employments, she is never forced, on the other, to go beyond it. Hence it is that the women

of America, who often exhibit a masculine strength of understanding and a manly energy, generally preserve great delicacy of personal appearance and always retain the manners of women although they sometimes show that they have the hearts and minds of men.

5   Nor have the Americans ever supposed that one consequence of democratic principles is the subversion of marital power or the confusion of the natural authorities in families. They hold that every association must have a head in order to accomplish its object, and that the natural head of the conjugal association is man. They do not therefore deny him the right of directing his partner, and they maintain that in the smaller association of husband and wife as well as in the great social community the object of democracy is to regulate and legalize the powers that are necessary, and not to subvert all power.

6   This opinion is not peculiar to one sex and contested by the other; I never observed that the women of America consider conjugal authority as a fortunate usurpation of their rights, or that they thought themselves degraded by submitting to it. It appeared to me, on the contrary, that they attach a sort of pride to the voluntary surrender of their own will and make it their boast to bend themselves to the yoke, not to shake it off. Such, at least, is the feeling expressed by the most virtuous of their sex; the others are silent; and in the United States it is not the practice for a guilty wife to clamor for the rights of women while she is trampling on her own holiest duties.

7   It has often been remarked that in Europe a certain degree of contempt lurks even in the flattery which men lavish upon women; although a European frequently affects to be the slave of woman, it may be seen that he never sincerely thinks her his equal. In the United States men seldom compliment women, but they daily show how much they esteem them. They constantly display an entire confidence in the understanding of a wife and a profound respect for her freedom; they have decided that her mind is just as fitted as that of a man to discover the plain truth, and her heart as firm to embrace it; and they have never sought to place her virtue, any more than his, under the shelter of prejudice, ignorance, and fear.

8   It would seem in Europe, where man so easily submits to the despotic sway of women, that they are nevertheless deprived of some of the greatest attributes of the human species and considered as seductive but imperfect beings; and (what may well provoke astonishment) women ultimately look upon themselves in the same light and almost consider it as a privilege that they are entitled to show themselves futile, feeble, and timid. The women of America claim no such privileges.

9   Again, it may be said that in our morals we have reserved strange immunities to man, so that there is, as it were, one virtue for his use and another for the guidance of his partner, and that, according to the opinion of the public, the very same act may be punished alternately as a crime or only as a fault. The Americans do not know this iniquitous division of duties and rights; among them the seducer is as much dishonored as his victim.

10   It is true that the Americans rarely lavish upon women those eager attentions which are commonly paid them in Europe, but their conduct to women always

implies that they suppose them to be virtuous and refined; and such is the respect entertained for the moral freedom of the sex that in the presence of a woman the most guarded language is used lest her ear should be offended by an expression. In America a young unmarried woman may alone and without fear undertake a long journey.

11   The legislators of the United States, who have mitigated almost all the penalties of criminal law, still make rape a capital offense, and no crime is visited with more inexorable severity by public opinion. This may be accounted for; as the Americans can conceive nothing more precious than a woman's honor and nothing which ought so much to be respected as her independence, they hold that no punishment is too severe for the man who deprives her of them against her will. In France, where the same offense is visited with far milder penalties, it is frequently difficult to get a verdict from a jury against the prisoner. Is this a consequence of contempt of decency or contempt of women? I cannot but believe that it is a contempt of both.

12   Thus the Americans do not think that man and woman have either the duty or the right to perform the same offices, but they show an equal regard for both their respective parts; and though their lot is different, they consider both of them as beings of equal value. They do not give to the courage of woman the same form or the same direction as to that of man, but they never doubt her courage; and if they hold that man and his partner ought not always to exercise their intellect and understanding in the same manner, they at least believe the understanding of the one to be as sound as that of the other, and her intellect to be as clear. Thus, then, while they have allowed the social inferiority of woman to continue, they have done all they could to raise her morally and intellectually to the level of man; and in this respect they appear to me to have excellently understood the true principle of democratic improvement.

13   As for myself, I do not hesitate to avow that although the women of the United States are confined within the narrow circle of domestic life, and their situation is in some respects one of extreme dependence, I have nowhere seen woman occupying a loftier position; and if I were asked, now that I am drawing to the close of this work, in which I have spoken of so many important things done by the Americans, to what the singular prosperity and growing strength of that people ought mainly to be attributed, I should reply: To the superiority of their women.

WRITING ASSIGNMENTS

Analysis

1. Explain the division of power between men and women and the consequences of this division, according to Abigail Adams and Sarah Moore Grimke. Why does Abigail Adams use the term "Naturally Tyrannical" to describe men and Grimke express concern about the danger to women from the "*usurped au-*thority" of men?

2. Both the Congregational ministers and Grimke use figurative language. Analyze the effect of the following images on the theme and tone of both the Pastoral Letter and Grimke's response:

From the Pastoral Letter, "If the *vine,* whose strength and beauty is to lean upon the trellis work and half conceal its clusters, thinks to assume the independence and the overshadowing nature of the *elm,* it will not only *cease to bear fruit,* but fall in shame and dishonour into the dust" [emphasis added].

From Grimke's response, "Ah! how many of my sex feel in the dominion, thus unrighteously exercised over them, under the gentle appellation of *protection,* that what they have leaned upon has proven a *broken reed* at best, and oft a *spear*" [emphasis added].

3. Explain the division of power between men and women and its justification according to John Adams and the Congregational ministers.
4. Grimke says of woman, "She has surrendered her dearest RIGHTS, and been satisfied with the privileges which man has assumed to grant her." Define the difference between rights and privileges in this context. Given Grimke's distinction, does Abigail Adams seem concerned with "rights" or "privileges"?
5. What aspect of femininity is Grimke attacking when she says that man "has adorned the creature whom God gave him as a companion, with baubles and gewgaws, turned her attention to personal attractions, offered incense to her vanity, and made her the instrument of his selfish gratification, a plaything to please his eye and amuse his hours of leisure"? Is her observation valid today?
6. Use Tocqueville's observations to compare the status of European and American women of his time.
7. Explain what Tocqueville means by attributing the prosperity and growing strength of the American people to the "superiority of their women."

Argument

1. Argue that the Bible either does or does not provide authority for male domination. Support your evidence with scriptural citations.
2. Is Tocqueville's explanation of the naturally separate-but-equal spheres of men and women logically demonstrated? Explain your answer.
3. Agree or disagree with Tocqueville that it is possible to achieve moral and intellectual equality between the sexes while preserving social inequality.
4. Agree or disagree with Tocqueville's observation that American women are content with their status, using his evidence along with information from other relatively contemporaneous selections from this chapter.
5. Argue whether or not Tocqueville respects American women. Explain your position.
6. Drawing on the correspondence between Abigail and John Adams, the pastoral letter and Grimke's response, and Tocqueville, argue whether or not women were respected by law, custom, religion, and men in early nineteenth-century America.

Personal Writing and Writing from Research

1. Grimke dismisses the Congregationalist ministers' views on women as superstition and compares them to the discredited views of Cotton Mather and

other men of his day on witchcraft. Write a research paper on Mather and the witchcraft trials.

2. In an essay, compare the uses of scriptural evidence by both Grimke in her response and Martin Luther King Jr. in his "Letter from Birmingham Jail" to refute their clerical opponents, who also cited Scripture.
3. In a research paper, trace the historical use of the Bible to defend slavery and attempt to prove the inferiority of African Americans.
4. Tocqueville says that in America, "No families are so poor as to form an exception to the rule" that women are exempt from field work or labor demanding physical strength. Which women did Tocqueville overlook? Research their status and experiences.

PROTEST

Seneca Falls Convention Declaration of Sentiments

Elizabeth Cady Stanton

Elizabeth Cady Stanton (1815–1902) was the well-read daughter of a wealthy family in upstate New York. She married Henry B. Stanton, an abolitionist and lawyer, and had seven children, the last in 1859.

Together, Elizabeth Cady Stanton and Susan B. Anthony directed the women's movement during the second half of the nineteenth century. But before they joined forces in 1851, Cady Stanton had already worked to pass landmark legislation in New York that gave property rights to married women. Active in the movement to abolish slavery, she and her husband had traveled to England for an abolitionist convention that refused to allow women to speak. In 1848, she helped organize the Seneca Falls Convention, the first formal gathering of what soon became the women's movement for equal rights. Along with Elizabeth Cady Stanton, the drafters of the Declaration of Sentiments included Lucretia Mott, Martha C. Wright, and Mary Ann McClintock. They worked together in McClintock's parlor. Notice that their declaration closely echoes Thomas Jefferson's Declaration of Independence and draws much of its power from that parallelism. One-third of the signatories to the Declaration of Sentiments were men.

When, in the course of human events, it becomes necessary for one portion of the family of man to assume among the people of the earth a position different from that which they have hitherto occupied, but one to which the laws of nature and of nature's God entitle them, a decent respect to the opinions of mankind requires that they should declare the causes that impel them to such a course.

We hold these truths to be self-evident: that all men and women are created equal; that they are endowed by their Creator with certain inalienable rights; that among these are life, liberty, and the pursuit of happiness; that to secure these rights governments are instituted, deriving their just powers from the consent of the governed. Whenever any form of government becomes destructive of these ends, it is the right of those who suffer from it to refuse allegiance to it, and to insist upon the institution of a new government, laying its foundation on such principles, and organizing its powers in such form, as to them shall seem most likely to effect their safety and happiness. Prudence, indeed, will dictate that governments long established should not be changed for light and transient causes; and accordingly all experience hath shown that mankind are more disposed to suffer, while evils are sufferable, than to right themselves by abolishing the forms to which they were accustomed. But when a long train of abuses and usurpations, pursuing invariably the same object evinces a design to reduce them under absolute despotism, it is their duty to throw off such government, and to provide new guards for their future security. Such has been the patient sufferance of the women under this government, and such is now the necessity which constrains them to demand the equal station to which they are entitled.

The history of mankind is a history of repeated injuries and usurpations on the part of man toward woman, having in direct object the establishment of an absolute tyranny over her. To prove this, let facts be submitted to a candid world.

He has never permitted her to exercise her inalienable right to the elective franchise.

5   He has compelled her to submit to laws, in the formation of which she had no voice.

He has withheld from her rights which are given to the most ignorant and degraded men—both natives and foreigners.

Having deprived her of this first right of a citizen, the elective franchise, thereby leaving her without representation in the halls of legislation, he has oppressed her on all sides.

He has made her, if married, in the eye of the law, civilly dead.

He has taken from her all right in property, even to the wages she earns.

10   He has made her morally, an irresponsible being, as she can commit many crimes with impunity, provided they be done in the presence of her husband. In the covenant of marriage, she is compelled to promise obedience to her husband, he becoming, to all intents and purposes, her master—the law giving him power to deprive her of her liberty, and to administer chastisement.

He has so framed the laws of divorce, as to what shall be the proper causes, and in case of separation, to whom the guardianship of the children shall be given, as to be wholly regardless of the happiness of women—the law, in all cases, going upon a false supposition of the supremacy of man, and giving all power into his hands.

After depriving her of all rights as a married woman, if single, and the owner of property, he has taxed her to support a government which recognizes her only when her property can be made profitable to it.

He has monopolized nearly all the profitable employments, and from those she is permitted to follow, she receives but a scanty remuneration. He closes against her all the avenues to wealth and distinction which he considers most honorable to himself. As a teacher of theology, medicine, or law, she is not known.

He has denied her the facilities for obtaining a thorough education, all colleges being closed against her.

15 He allows her in Church, as well as State, but a subordinate position, claiming Apostolic authority for her exclusion from the ministry, and, with some exceptions, from any public participation in the affairs of the Church.

He has created a false public sentiment by giving to the world a different code of morals for men and women, by which moral delinquencies which exclude women from society, are not only tolerated, but deemed of little account in man.

He has usurped the prerogative of Jehovah himself, claiming it as his right to assign for her a sphere of action, when that belongs to her conscience and to her God.

He has endeavored, in every way that he could, to destroy her confidence in her own powers, to lessen her self-respect, and to make her willing to lead a dependent and abject life.

Now, in view of this entire disfranchisement of one-half the people of this country, their social and religious degradation—in view of the unjust laws above mentioned, and because women do feel themselves aggrieved, oppressed, and fraudulently deprived of their most sacred rights, we insist that they have immediate admission to all the rights and privileges which belong to them as citizens of the United States.

20 In entering upon the great work before us, we anticipate no small amount of misconception, misrepresentation, and ridicule; but we shall use every instrumentality within our power to effect our object. We shall employ agents, circulate tracts, petition the State and National legislatures, and endeavor to enlist the pulpit and the press in our behalf. We hope this Convention will be followed by a series of Conventions embracing every part of the country.

The following resolutions were discussed by Lucretia Mott, Thomas and Mary Ann McClintock, Amy Post, Catharine A. F. Stebbins, and others, and were adopted:

WHEREAS. The great precept of nature is conceded to be, that "man shall pursue his own true and substantial happiness." Blackstone in his Commentaries remarks, that this law of Nature being coeval with mankind, and dictated by God himself, is of course superior in obligation to any other. It is binding over all the globe, in all countries and at all times; no human laws are of any validity if contrary to this, and such of them as are valid, derive all their force, and all their validity, and all their authority, mediately and immediately, from this original; therefore,

Resolved, That such laws as conflict, in any way, with the true and substantial happiness of woman, are contrary to the great precept of nature and of no validity, for this is "superior in obligation to any other."

Resolved, That all laws which prevent woman from occupying such a station in society as her conscience shall dictate, or which place her in a position inferior to that of man, are contrary to the great precept of nature, and therefore of no force or authority.

25 *Resolved,* That woman is man's equal—was intended to be so by the Creator, and the highest good of the race demands that she should be recognized as such.

Resolved, That the women of this country ought to be enlightened in regard to the laws under which they live, that they may no longer publish their degradation by declaring themselves satisfied with their present position, nor their ignorance, by asserting that they have all the rights they want.

Resolved, That inasmuch as man, while claiming for himself intellectual superiority, does accord to woman moral superiority, it is pre-eminently his duty to encourage her to speak and teach, as she has an opportunity, in all religious assemblies.

Resolved, That the same amount of virtue, delicacy, and refinement of behavior that is required of woman in the social state, should also be required of man, and the same transgressions should be visited with equal severity on both man and woman.

Resolved, That the objection of indelicacy and impropriety, which is so often brought against woman when she addresses a public audience, comes with a very ill-grace from those who encourage, by their attendance, her appearance on the stage, in the concert, or in feats of the circus.

30 *Resolved,* That woman has too long rested satisfied in the circumscribed limits which corrupt customs and a perverted application of the Scriptures have marked out for her, and that it is time she should move in the enlarged sphere which her great Creator has assigned her.

Resolved, That it is the duty of the women of this country to secure to themselves their sacred right to the elective franchise.

Resolved, That the equality of human rights results necessarily from the fact of the identity of the race in capabilities and responsibilities.

Resolved, therefore, That, being invested by the Creator with the same capabilities, and the same consciousness of responsibility for their exercise, it is demonstrably the right and duty of woman, equally with man, to promote every righteous cause by every righteous means; and especially in regard to the great subjects of morals and religion, it is self-evidently her right to participate with her brother in teaching them, both in private and in public, by writing and by speaking, by any instrumentalities proper to be used, and in any assemblies proper to be held; and this being a self-evident truth growing out of the divinely implanted principles of human nature, any custom or authority adverse to it, whether modern or wearing the hoary sanction of antiquity, is to be regarded as a self-evident falsehood, and at war with mankind.

At the last session Lucretia Mott offered and spoke to the following resolution:

35 *Resolved,* That the speedy success of our cause depends upon the zealous and untiring efforts of both men and women, for the overthrow of the monopoly of the

pulpit, and for the securing to woman an equal participation with men in the various trades, professions, and commerce.

The only resolution that was not unanimously adopted was the ninth, urging the women of the country to secure to themselves the elective franchise. Those who took part in the debate feared a demand for the right to vote would defeat others they deemed more rational, and make the whole movement ridiculous.

But Mrs. Stanton and Frederick Douglass seeing that the power to choose rulers and make laws, was the right by which all others could be secured, persistently advocated the resolution, and at last carried it by a small majority.

Thus it will be seen that the Declaration and resolutions in the very first Convention, demanded all the most radical friends of the movement have since claimed— such as equal rights in the universities, in the trades and professions; the right to vote; to share in all political offices, honors, and emoluments; to complete equality in marriage, to personal freedom, property, wages, children; to make contracts; to sue, and be sued; and to testify in courts of justice. At this time the condition of married women under the Common Law, was nearly as degraded as that of the slave on the Southern plantation. The Convention continued through two entire days, and late into the evenings. The deepest interest was manifested to its close.

The Rights of Women

Frederick Douglass

Born a slave, Frederick Douglass (1817–1895) never knew his mother or father. He was raised by his grandmother on a plantation in Maryland, then sent to work as a house slave in Baltimore at age 8. In Baltimore, his mistress, a Northerner by birth, taught him to read, an act forbidden by law. But she later regretted doing so and staunchly imposed the conditions of slavery on Douglass. Returned to work on the plantation as a field hand and tortured by a "slave breaker," he eventually escaped, at age 21, to New York City and New Bedford, Massachusetts, where he took the last name of Douglass.

Invited to speak to an antislavery gathering in 1841, he was so eloquent that he was engaged as an agent for the Massachusetts Anti-Slavery Society and became a leading speaker. He wrote his autobiography in 1845 in part to answer critics who doubted his authenticity. But fearing that he might be recaptured and returned to slavery, he spent two years abroad on a lecture tour. With the money he earned, he purchased his freedom and launched his own abolitionist paper, the *North Star,* in Rochester, New York, in 1847.

One year later, he made common cause with the women's movement by publishing "The Rights of Women" in the July 28, 1848, edition of the *North Star.*

He continued to urge African Americans to fight racial discrimination after the Civil War, and he worked for passage of the Thirteenth, Fourteenth, and Fifteenth amendments, even as reaction began that set the stage for Jim Crow laws and segregation.

One of the most interesting events of the past week, was the holding of what is technically styled a Woman's Rights Convention at Seneca Falls. The speaking, addresses, and resolutions of this extraordinary meeting was almost wholly conducted by women; and although they evidently felt themselves in a novel position, it is but simple justice to say that their whole proceedings were characterized by marked ability and dignity. No one present, we think, however much he might be disposed to differ from the views advanced by the leading speakers on that occasion, will fail to give them credit for brilliant talents and excellent dispositions. In this meeting, as in other deliberative assemblies, there were frequent differences of opinion and animated discussion; but in no case was there the slightest absence of good feeling and decorum. Several interesting documents setting forth the rights as well as the grievances of women were read. Among these was a Declaration of Sentiments, to be regarded as the basis of a grand movement for attaining the civil, social, political, and religious rights of women. We should not do justice to our own convictions, or to the excellent persons connected with this infant movement, if we did not in this connection offer a few remarks on the general subject which the Convention met to consider and the objects they seek to attain. In doing so, we are not insensible that the bare mention of this truly important subject in any other than terms of contemptuous ridicule and scornful disfavor, is likely to excite against us the fury of bigotry and the folly of prejudice. A discussion of the rights of animals would be regarded with far more complacency by many of what are called the *wise* and the *good* of our land, than would a discussion of the rights of women. It is, in their estimation, to be guilty of evil thoughts, to think that woman is entitled to equal rights with man. Many who have at last made the discovery that the Negroes have some rights as well as other members of the human family, have yet to be convinced that women are entitled to any. Eight years ago a number of persons of this description actually abandoned the anti-slavery cause, lest by giving their influence in that direction they might possibly be giving countenance to the dangerous heresy that woman, in respect to rights, stands on an equal footing with man. In the judgment of such persons the American slave system, with all its concomitant horrors, is less to be deplored than this *wicked* idea. It is perhaps needless to say, that we cherish little sympathy for such sentiments or respect for such prejudices. Standing as we do upon the watch-tower of human freedom, we cannot be deterred from an expression of our approbation of any movement, however humble, to improve and elevate the character of any members of the human family. While it is impossible for us to go into this subject at length, and dispose of the various objections which are often urged against such a doctrine as that of female equality, we are free to say that in respect to political rights, we hold woman to be justly entitled to all we claim for man. We go farther, and express our conviction that all political rights which it is expedient for man to exercise, it is equally so for woman. All that distinguishes man as an intelligent and accountable being, is equally true of woman, and if that government only is just which governs by the free consent of the governed, there can be no reason in the world for denying to woman the exercise of the elective franchise, or a hand in making and administering the laws of the land. Our doctrine is that "right is of no sex." We therefore bid the women engaged in this movement our humble Godspeed.

Ain't I a Woman?

Sojourner Truth

She was born a slave in 1797 and given the name Isabella by her master. In 1827, when mandatory emancipation freed the slaves in the state of New York, she was reunited with 2 of her 13 children and moved to New York City, where she first did missionary and then domestic work.

In 1843, she rejected her slave name, took the name of Sojourner Truth, and began to travel and preach again. Although illiterate, she was a charismatic speaker and became famous as an abolitionist and preacher in the 1840s and 1850s. Nearly six-feet-tall, powerful, and gaunt, she was an imposing figure who defied the conventional notions about women's delicacy and helplessness, notions that were often invoked to justify refusing women the right to vote. There were even rumors that she was a man who dressed in women's clothes to speak about women's rights. She supposedly refuted that charge by baring a breast at one of her appearances. She delivered "Ain't I a Woman?" at the 1851 Akron Women's Rights Convention.

1 The tumult subsided at once, and every eye was fixed on this almost Amazon form, which stood nearly six feet high, head erect, and eyes piercing the upper air like one in a dream. At her first word there was a profound hush. She spoke in deep tones, which, though not loud, reached every ear in the house, and away through the throng at the doors and windows.

2 "Wall, chilern, whar dar is so much racket dar must be somethin' out o' kilter. I tink dat 'twixt de niggers of de Souf and de womin at de Norf, all talkin' 'bout rights, de white men will be in a fix pretty soon. But what's all dis here talkin' 'bout?

3 "Dat man ober dar say dat womin needs to be helped into carriages, and lifted ober ditches and to hab de best place everywhar. Nobody eber helps me into carriages, or ober mud-puddles, or gibs me any best place!" And raising herself to her full height, and her voice to a pitch like rolling thunder, she asked, "And a'n't I a woman? Look at me! Look at my arm! (and she bared her right arm to the shoulder,

showing her tremendous muscular power). I have ploughed, and planted, and gathered into barns, and no man could head me! And a'n't I a woman? I could work as much and eat as much as a man—when I could get it—and bear de lash as well! And a'n't I a woman? I have borne thirteen chilern, and seen 'em mos' all sold off to slavery, and when I cried out with my mother's grief, none but Jesus heard me! And a'n't I a woman?

4   "Den dey talks 'bout dis ting in de head; what dis dey call it?" ("Intellect," whispered some one near.) "Dat's it, honey. What's dat got to do wid womin's rights or nigger's rights? If my cup won't hold but a pint, and yourn holds a quart, wouldn't ye be mean not to let me have my little half-measure full?" And she pointed her significant finger, and sent a keen glance at the minister who had made the argument. The cheering was long and loud.

5   "Den dat little man in black dar, he say women can't have as much rights as men, 'cause Christ wan't a woman! Whar did your Christ come from?" Rolling thunder couldn't have stilled that crowd, as did those deep, wonderful tones, as she stood there with outstretched arms and eyes of fire. Raising her voice still louder, she repeated, "Whar did your Christ come from? From God and a woman! Man had nothin' to do wid Him." Oh, what a rebuke that was to that little man.

6   Turning again to another objector, she took up the defense of Mother Eve. I can not follow her through it all. It was pointed, and witty, and solemn; eliciting at almost every sentence deafening applause; and she ended by asserting: "If de fust woman God ever made was strong enough to turn de world upside down all alone, dese women togedder (and she glanced her eye over the platform) ought to be able to turn it back, and get it right side up again! And now dey is asking to do it, de men better let 'em." Long-continued cheering greeted this. "'Bleeged to ye for hearin' on me, and now ole Sojourner han't got nothin' more to say."

WRITING ASSIGNMENTS

Analysis

1. Compare the Seneca Falls Declaration to the Declaration of Independence and explain the benefits of such modeling.
2. Use Frederick Douglass's editorial and Sojourner Truth's speech to critique Tocqueville's position. Or use Tocqueville to critique Douglass and Truth.

Argument

1. Is it easier to base an argument against slavery or in favor of women's rights on religious authority or on political rights? Draw your examples from the selections in this chapter and explain your position.
2. Does the Seneca Falls Declaration too exclusively express the concerns of middle- and upper-middle-class white women, ignoring the concerns of poor women and women of color? Explain your answer.

Personal Writing and Writing from Research

1. *Collaborative Project:* Research the historical evidence on *one* of the following grievances named in the Seneca Falls Declaration: women's property rights, child-custody laws, a married woman's legal status, a married woman's legal liability for acts committed in her husband's presence, a husband's right to "chastise" his wife, divorce laws, women's access to education, women's role in organized religion, or a double standard in morals.
2. Trace the connections between the antislavery and the women's rights movements in nineteenth-century America.
3. Profile Sojourner Truth, Frederick Douglass, or one of the activists who attended the Seneca Falls Convention.

WOMAN'S PLACE REDEFINED

Protest
with a note by
Rev. Thomas Wentworth Higginson

Henry Brown Blackwell and Lucy Stone

Born in Massachusetts, Lucy Stone (1818–1893) was the eighth of nine children. When her family refused to help her attend college, she taught school and saved enough to enter Oberlin College, the first in the United States to admit women. She became a famous abolitionist and feminist speaker.

Henry Blackwell was a reformer and member of an exceptional family. He argued that a woman's retention of a career after marriage was essential to the survival of an equal union. His sister, Elizabeth Blackwell, was the first woman admitted to an American medical school; she spent much of her life fighting for the right of women to obtain a medical education and to practice medicine.

When Stone and Blackwell married in 1855, they devised a marriage contract to protest the laws that subjected the wife to her husband. To symbolize her separate identity, Stone kept her maiden name, a highly unusual step in that era. They helped to establish the National American Woman Suffrage Association in 1869 and founded the *Woman's Journal,* a major suffrage journal.

MARRIAGE OF LUCY STONE UNDER PROTEST.

It was my privilege to celebrate May day by officiating at a wedding in a farm-house among the hills of West Brookfield. The bridegroom was a man of tried worth, a leader in the Western Anti-Slavery Movement; and the bride was one whose fair name is known throughout the nation; one whose rare intellectual qualities are excelled by the private beauty of her heart and life.

I never perform the marriage ceremony without a renewed sense of the iniquity of our present system of laws in respect to marriage; a system by which "man and wife are one, and that one is the husband." It was with my hearty concurrence, therefore, that the following protest was read and signed, as a part of the nuptial ceremony; and I send it to you, that others may be induced to do likewise.

Rev. Thomas Wentworth Higginson

1 While acknowledging our mutual affection by publicly assuming the relationship of husband and wife, yet in justice to ourselves and a great principle, we deem it a duty to declare that this act on our part implies no sanction of, nor promise of voluntary obedience to such of the present laws of marriage, as refuse to recognize the wife as an independent, rational being, while they confer upon the husband an injurious and unnatural superiority, investing him with legal powers which no honorable man would exercise, and which no man should possess. We protest especially against the laws which give to the husband:

1. The custody of the wife's person.
2. The exclusive control and guardianship of their children.
3. The sole ownership of her personal, and use of her real estate, unless previously settled upon her, or placed in the hands of trustees, as in the case of minors, lunatics, and idiots.
4. The absolute right to the product of her industry.
5. Also against laws which give to the widower so much larger and more permanent an interest in the property of his deceased wife, than they give to the widow in that of the deceased husband.
6. Finally, against the whole system by which "the legal existence of the wife is suspended during marriage," so that in most States, she neither has a legal part in the choice of her residence, nor can she make a will, nor sue or be sued in her own name, nor inherit property.

2 We believe that personal independence and equal human rights can never be forfeited, except for crime; that marriage should be an equal and permanent partnership, and so recognized by law; that until it is so recognized, married partners should provide against the radical injustice of present laws, by every means in their power.

3 We believe that where domestic difficulties arise, no appeal should be made to legal tribunals under existing laws, but that all difficulties should be submitted to the equitable adjustment of arbitrators mutually chosen.

4   Thus reverencing law, we enter our protest against rules and customs which are unworthy of the name, since they violate justice, the essence of law.

(Signed), Henry B. Blackwell, Lucy Stone

Comments on Genesis

Elizabeth Cady Stanton and the Revising Committee

In the years following the Seneca Falls Convention Declaration of Sentiments, Elizabeth Cady Stanton expanded her writing and speaking efforts on behalf of women's rights and continued to raise her seven children. With Susan B. Anthony, she also edited *The Revolution,* a radical weekly paper addressing issues related to the woman question. In 1878, she was instrumental in getting the Woman Suffrage Amendment introduced into Congress for the first time. It was reintroduced at every succeeding Congress until it was passed in 1920.

As shown by Sarah Grimke's 1838 response to the Pastoral Letter, religion was often invoked to maintain women's subordinate position and to prove their inferiority. To redress this injustice, Stanton, then 79, and a revising committee of eight women convened in 1895 to write *The Woman's Bible,* a commentary on the Old and New Testaments. Stanton wrote, "The Old Testament makes woman a mere after-thought in creation; the author of evil; cursed in her maternity; a subject in marriage; and all female life, animal and human, unclean. The Church in all ages has taught these doctrines and acted on them, claiming divine authority therefor." Some of the women who agreed to participate in this project withdrew their names, fearing association with such a radical project. The comments on Genesis included here were written by Stanton, Ellen Battelle Dietrick, and Lillie Devereux Blake, all feminist activists. When Part I was published in 1895, it received wide coverage. Some members of the clergy called it "the work of women, and the devil." Several editions were published, and an expanded Revising Committee prepared Part II, which was published in 1898.

Genesis i:26, 27, 28.

26 And God said, Let us make man in our image, after our likeness: and let them have dominion over the fish of the sea, and over the fowl of the air, and over the cattle, and over all the earth, and over every creeping thing that creepeth upon the earth.

27 So God created man in his *own* image, in the image of God created he him; male and female created he them.

28 And God blessed them, and God said unto them, Be fruitful, and multiply, and replenish the earth, and subdue it; and have dominion over the fish of the sea, and over the fowl of the air, and over every living thing that moveth upon the earth.

1 Here is the sacred historian's first account of the advent of woman; a simultaneous creation of both sexes, in the image of God. It is evident from the language that there was consultation in the Godhead, and that the masculine and feminine elements were equally represented. Scott in his commentaries says, "this consultation of the Gods is the origin of the doctrine of the trinity." But instead of three male personages, as generally represented, a Heavenly Father, Mother, and Son would seem more rational.

2 The first step in the elevation of woman to her true position, as an equal factor in human progress, is the cultivation of the religious sentiment in regard to her dignity and equality, the recognition by the rising generation of an ideal Heavenly Mother, to whom their prayers should be addressed, as well as to a Father.

3 If language has any meaning, we have in these texts a plain declaration of the existence of the feminine element in the Godhead, equal in power and glory with the masculine. The Heavenly Mother and Father! "God created man in his *own image, male and female.*" Thus Scripture, as well as science and philosophy, declares the eternity and equality of sex—the philosophical fact, without which there could have been no perpetuation of creation, no growth or development in the animal, vegetable, or mineral kingdoms, no awakening nor progressing in the world of thought. The masculine and feminine elements, exactly equal and balancing each other, are as essential to the maintenance of the equilibrium of the universe as positive and negative electricity, and the centripetal and centrifugal forces, the laws of attraction which bind together all we know of this planet whereon we dwell and of the system in which we revolve.

4 In the great work of creation the crowning glory was realized, when man and woman were evolved on the sixth day, the masculine and feminine forces in the image of God, that must have existed eternally, in all forms of matter and mind. All the persons in the Godhead are represented in the Elohim the divine plurality taking counsel in regard to this last and highest form of life. Who were the members of this high council, and were they a duality or a trinity? Verse 27 declares the image of God male and female. How then is it possible to make woman an afterthought? We find in verses 5–16 the pronoun "he" used. Should it not in harmony with verse 26 be "they," a dual pronoun? We may attribute this to the same cause as the use of "his" in verse II instead of "it." The fruit tree yielding fruit after "his" kind instead of after "its" kind. The paucity of a language may give rise to many misunderstandings.

5 The above texts plainly show the simultaneous creation of man and woman, and their equal importance in the development of the race. All those theories based on the assumption that man was prior in the creation, have no foundation in Scripture.

6   As to woman's subjection, on which both the canon and the civil law delight to dwell, it is important to note that equal dominion is given to woman over every living thing, but not one word is said giving man dominion over woman.

7   Here is the first title deed to this green earth giving alike to the sons and daughters of God. No lesson of woman's subjection can be fairly drawn from the first chapter of the Old Testament.

E. C. S.

8   The most important thing for a woman to note, in reading Genesis, is that that portion which is now divided into "the first three chapters" (there was no such division until about five centuries ago), contains two entirely separate, and very contradictory, stories of creation, written by two different, but equally anonymous, authors. No Christian theologian of to-day, with any pretensions to scholarship, claims that Genesis was written by Moses. As was long ago pointed out, the Bible itself declares that all the books the Jews originally possessed were burned in the destruction of Jerusalem, about 588 B.C., at the time the people were taken to Babylonia as slaves to the Assyrians, (see II Esdras, ch. xiv, v. 21, Apocrypha). Not until about 247 B.C. (some theologians say 226 and others 169 B.C.) is there any record of a collection of literature in the re-built Jerusalem, and, then, the anonymous writer of II Maccabees briefly mentions that some Nehemiah "gathered together the acts of the kings and the prophets and those of David" when "founding a library" for use in Jerusalem. But the earliest mention anywhere in the Bible of a book that might have corresponded to Genesis is made by an apocryphal writer, who says that *Ezra* wrote "all that hath been done in the world since the beginning," after the Jews returned from Babylon, under his leadership, about 450 B.C. (see II Esdras, ch. xiv, v. 22, of the Apocrypha).

9   When it is remembered that the Jewish books were written on rolls of leather, without much attention to vowel points and with no division into verses or chapters, by uncritical copyists, who altered passages greatly, and did not always even pretend to understand what they were copying, then the reader of Genesis begins to put herself in position to understand how it can be contradictory. Great as were the liberties which the Jews took with Genesis, those of the English translators, however, greatly surpassed them.

10   The first chapter of Genesis, for instance, in Hebrew, tells us, in verses one and two, "As to origin, created the gods (Elohim) these skies (or air or clouds) and this earth . . . And a wind moved upon the face of the waters." Here we have the opening of a polytheistic fable of creation, but, so strongly convinced were the English translators that the ancient Hebrews must have been originally monotheistic that they rendered the above, as follows: "In the beginning God created the heaven and the earth. . . . And the spirit of God (!) moved upon the face of the waters."

11   It is now generally conceded that some one (nobody pretends to know who) at some time (nobody pretends to know exactly when), copied two creation myths on the same leather roll, one immediately following the other. About one hundred years ago, it was discovered by Dr. Astruc, of France, that from Genesis ch. i, v. 1 to Genesis

ch. ii, v. 4, is given one complete account of creation, by an author who always used the term "the gods" (Elohim), in speaking of the fashioning of the universe, mentioning it altogether thirty-four times, while, in Genesis ch. ii, v. 4, to the end of chapter iii, we have a totally different narrative by an author of unmistakably different style who uses the term "Iahveh of the gods" twenty times, but "Elohim" only three times. The first author, evidently, attributes creation to a council of gods, acting in concert, and seems never to have heard of Iahveh. The second attributes creation to Iahveh, a tribal god of ancient Israel, but represents Iahveh as one of two or more gods, conferring with them (in Genesis ch. xiii, v. 22) as to the danger of man's acquiring immortality.

12   Modern theologians have, for convenience sake, entitled these two fables, respectively, the Elohistic and the Iahoistic stories. They differ, not only in the point I have mentioned above, but in the order of the "creative acts;" in regard to the mutual attitude of man and woman, and in regard to human freedom from prohibitions imposed by deity. In order to exhibit their striking contradictions, I will place them in parallel columns:

ELOHISTIC.

Order of Creation:
First—Water.
Second—Land.
Third—Vegetation.
Fourth—Animals.
Fifth—Mankind; male and female.

In this story male and female man are created simultaneously, both alike, in the image of the gods, *after* all animals have been called into existence.

Here, joint dominion over the earth is given to woman and man, without limit or prohibition.

Everything, without exception, is pronounced "very good."

Man and woman are told that "every plant bearing seed upon the face of the earth and *every tree*. . . . "To you it shall be for meat." They are thus given perfect freedom.

IAHOISTIC.

Order of Creation:
First—Land.
Second—Water.
Third—Male Man, only.
Fourth—Vegetation.
Fifth—Animals.
Sixth—Woman.

In this story male man is sculptured out of clay, *before* any animals are created, and *before* female man has been constructed.

Here, woman is punished with subjection to man for breaking a prohibitory law.

There is a tree of evil, whose fruit, is said by Iahveh to cause sudden death, but which does not do so, as Adam lived 930 years after eating it.

Man is told there is *one tree* of which he must not eat, "for in the day thou eatest thereof, thou shalt surely die."

ELOHISTIC.	*IAHOISTIC.*
Man and woman are given special dominion over all the animals—"every creeping thing that creepeth upon the earth."	An animal, a "creeping thing," is given dominion over man and woman, and proves himself more truthful than Iahveh Elohim. (Compare Genesis chapter ii, verse 17, with chapter iii, verses 4 and 22.)

13 Now as it is manifest that both of these stories cannot be true; intelligent women, who feel bound to give the preference to either, may decide according to their own judgment of which is more worthy of an intelligent woman's acceptance. Paul's rule is a good one in this dilemma, "Prove all things: hold fast to that which is good." My own opinion is that the second story was manipulated by some Jew, in an endeavor to give "heavenly authority" for requiring a woman to obey the man she married. In a work which I am now completing, I give some facts concerning ancient Israelitish history, which will be of peculiar interest to those who wish to understand the origin of woman's subjection.

E. B. D.

14 Many orientalists and students of theology have maintained that the consultation of the Gods here described is proof that the Hebrews were in early days polytheists— Scott's supposition that this is the origin of the Trinity has no foundation in fact, as the beginning of that conception is to be found in the earliest of all known religious nature worship. The acknowledgment of the dual principal, masculine and feminine, is much more probably the explanation of the expressions here used.

15 In the detailed description of creation we find a gradually ascending series. Creeping things, "great sea monsters," (chap. I, v. 21, literal translation). "Every bird of wing," cattle and living things of the earth, the fish of the sea and the "birds of the heavens," then man, and last and crowning glory of the whole, woman.

16 It cannot be maintained that woman was inferior to man even if, as asserted in chapter ii, she was created after him without at once admitting that man is inferior to the creeping things, because [he was] created after them.

L. D. B.

Address to the First National Conference of Colored Women

Josephine St. Pierre Ruffin

Josephine St. Pierre Ruffin (1843–1924) grew up in Boston and attended public schools there after they were desegregated in 1855. Married at 16 to George Lewis Ruffin, a member of a prominent

Boston family, she returned to America from England after the outbreak of the Civil War. Her husband attended Harvard Law School
and became the first black municipal judge in Massachusetts. The
couple raised five children.

A reform activist from the Civil War years onward, Josephine Ruffin established the Woman's Era Club in 1894, served as its president for 10 years, and edited its newspaper, *The Woman's Era,* for
many years. To consolidate the efforts of many clubs, Ruffin organized the first national conference of black women in 1895, to
whom she delivered the address included here.

In 1900, as a delegate from the Woman's Era Club and the Massachusetts State Federation of Women's Clubs, Ruffin attended the
convention of the General Federation of Women's Clubs in Milwau-
kee. The General Federation's credentials committee refused to seat
her as a delegate of a black club, but offered to admit her as a representative of the Massachusetts State Federation of Women's Clubs, a
"white club." She refused. The segregationist policies of the General
Federation of Women's Clubs persisted long into the twentieth century. Ruffin remained a community leader until her death, founding
and serving a number of social-welfare organizations in Boston.

1 It is with especial joy and pride that I welcome you all to this, our first conference. It
is only recently that women have waked up to the importance of meeting in council, and
great as has been the advantage to women *generally,* and important as it is and
has been that they should confer, the necessity has not been nearly so great, matters
at stake not nearly so vital, as that *we,* bearing peculiar blunders, suffering under especial hardships, enduring peculiar privations, should meet for a "good talk" among
ourselves. Although rather hastily called, you as well as I can testify how long and
how earnestly a conference has been thought of and hoped for and even prepared for.
These women's clubs, which have sprung up all over the country, built and run upon
broad and strong lines, have all been a preparation, small conferences in themselves,
and their spontaneous birth and enthusiastic support have been little less than inspi-
rational on the part of our women and a general preparation for a large union such as
it is hoped this conference will lead to. Five years ago we had no colored women's
clubs outside of those formed for special work; to-day, with little over a month's notice, we are able to call representatives from more than twenty clubs. It is a good
showing, it stands for much, it shows that we are truly American women, with all the
adaptability, readiness to seize and possess our opportunities, willingness to do our
part for good as other American women.

2 The reasons why we should confer are so apparent that it would seem hardly necessary to enumerate them, and yet there is none of them but demand our serious
consideration. In the first place we need to feel the cheer and inspiration of meeting

each other, we need to gain the courage and fresh life that comes from the mingling of congenial souls, of those workings for the same ends. Next, we need to talk over not only those things which are of vital importance to us as women, but also the things that are of especial interest to us as *colored* women, the training of our children, openings for our boys and girls, how they can be prepared for occupations and occupations may be found or opened for them, what *we* especially can do in the moral education of the race with which we are identified, our mental elevation and physical development, the home training it is necessary to give our children in order to prepare them to meet the peculiar conditions in which they shall find themselves, how to make the most of our own, to some extent, limited opportunities, these are some of our own peculiar questions to be discussed. Besides these are the general questions of the day, which we cannot afford to be indifferent to: temperance, morality, the higher education, hygienic and domestic questions. If these things need the serious consideration of women more advantageously placed by reason of all the aid to right thinking and living with which they are surrounded, surely we, with everything to pull us back, to hinder us in developing, need to take every opportunity and means for the thoughtful consideration which shall lead to wise action.

3   I have left the strongest reason for our conferring together until the last. All over America there is to be found a large and growing class of earnest, intelligent, progressive colored women, women who, if not leading full useful lives, are only waiting for the opportunity to do so, many of them warped and cramped for lack of opportunity, not only to do more but to *be* more; and yet, if an estimate of the colored women of America is called for, the inevitable reply, glibly given, is, "For the most part ignorant and immoral, some exceptions, of course, but these don't count."

4   Now for the sake of the thousands of self-sacrificing young women teaching and preaching in lonely southern backwoods, for the noble army of mothers who have given birth to these girls, mothers whose intelligence is only limited by their opportunity to get at books, for the sake of the fine cultured women who have carried off the honors in school here and often abroad, for the sake of our own dignity, the dignity of our race and the future good name of our children, it is "mete, right and our bounden duty" to stand forth and declare ourselves and principles, to teach an ignorant and suspicious world that our aims and interests are identical with those of all good aspiring women. Too long have we been silent under unjust and unholy charges; we cannot expect to have them removed until we disprove them through *ourselves*. It is not enough to try to disprove unjust charges through individual effort, that never goes any further. Year after year southern women have protested against the admission of colored women into any national organization on the ground of the immorality of these women, and because all refutation has only been tried by individual work the charge has never been crushed, as it could and should have been at the first. Now with an army of organized women standing for purity and mental worth, we in ourselves deny the charge and open the eyes of the world to a state of affairs to which they have been blind, often willfully so, and the very fact

that the charges, audaciously and flippantly made, as they often are, are of so humiliating and delicate a nature, serves to protect the accuser by driving the helpless accused into mortified silence. It is to break this silence, not by noisy protestations of what we are not, but by a dignified showing of what we are and hope to become that we are impelled to take this step, to make of this gathering an object lesson to the world. For many and apparent reasons it is especially fitting that the *women* of the race take the lead in this movement, but for all this we recognize the necessity of the sympathy for our husbands, brothers and fathers.

5   Our woman's movement is woman's movement in that it is led and directed by women for the good of women and men, for the benefit of *all* humanity, which is more than any one branch or section of it. We want, we ask the active interest of our men, and, too, we are not drawing the color line; we are women, American women, as intensely interested in all that pertains to us as such as all other American women; we are not alienating or withdrawing, we are only coming to the front, willing to join any others in the same work and cordially inviting and welcoming any others to join us.

6   If there is any one thing I would especially enjoin upon this conference it is union and earnestness. The questions that are to come before us are of too much import to be weakened by any trivialities or personalities. If any differences arise let them be quickly settled, with the feeling that we are all workers to the same end, to elevate and dignify colored American womanhood. This conference will not be what I expect if it does not show the wisdom, indeed the absolute necessity of a national organization of our women. Every year new questions coming up will prove it to us. This hurried, almost informal convention does not begin to meet our needs, it is only a beginning, made here in dear old Boston, where the scales of justice and generosity hang evenly balanced, and where the people "dare be true" to their best instincts and stand ready to lend aid and sympathy to worthy strugglers. It is hoped and believed that from this will spring an organization that will in truth bring in a new era to the colored women of America.

WRITING ASSIGNMENTS

Analysis

1. Which interpretation of Genesis do you find more credible—the traditional one or the Revising Committee's? Why?
2. How did biblical scholarship, the study of ancient languages, history, and archeology influence the Revising Committee's interpretation of Genesis?
3. What can you infer about Ruffin's political principles and social values from her conference address?
4. Compare and contrast the content, attitude, and style of Ruffin's address and the Seneca Falls declaration; or compare Ruffin's address and Sojourner Truth's "Ain't I a Woman?"

Argument

1. In a marriage, is equality either desirable or possible?
2. Does the Bible present a negative view of woman's nature and woman's role relative to man's?
3. Stanton, the Revising Committee, and, earlier, Grimke accuse male interpreters, rather than the Bible itself, of justifying male dominance and superiority. Are they right?
4. Explain why you believe that Ruffin's address speaks or does not speak relevantly to African-American women today.
5. The documents in this chapter show that while black and white women shared many concerns, their experiences often differed dramatically. Does this pattern of shared and divergent interests persist today?

Personal Writing and Writing from Research

1. Stone and Blackwell's protest was a radical gesture for its time. During the 1960s and 1970s, many couples wrote their own wedding vows in order to redefine the traditional roles of husband and wife. Explain why you believe a couple should or should not write its own vows.
2. Write and explain your own wedding vows.
3. If you are married, explain how your assumptions before marriage about your role as husband or wife compare with the reality of the role as you live it.
4. Write a research paper on the Lucy Stone Society, whose membership includes women who retain their birth name after marriage.
5. *Collaborative Project:* Research the arguments used to support the laws and customs that Blackwell and Stone protest. Present your findings to the class.
6. *Collaborative Project:* Compare the laws of your state between the mid-1800s and now governing one of the following: child custody, property rights in marriage and divorce, or inheritance.
7. Survey the contemporary responses to the publication of *The Woman's Bible,* Part I.
8. Explore the role that biblical or religious teaching plays in your views on marriage and the respective roles of husbands and wives.
9. Compare Genesis to other creation myths, particularly Native American myths. Specifically, what role does gender play in each creation story?
10. Ruffin cites the following line to illustrate the unfavorable image of "colored" women: "For the most part ignorant and immoral, some exceptions, of course, but these don't count." Trace the image of African-American women in American culture. You may want to consult the writings of bell hooks, Vivian Gordon, Paula Giddings, Katie G. Cannon, and Gerda Lerner on this subject.
11. Trace the political and social history of African-American women's clubs.

TRADITION REAFFIRMED AND UPDATED

Excerpts from **In Praise of the Strenuous Life** (1899) *and* **Address Before the National Congress of Mothers** (1905)

Theodore Roosevelt

Born to a wealthy New York family, Theodore Roosevelt (1858–1919) was a physical weakling as a child, but he plunged into physical activity and became a vigorous outdoorsman. After graduating from Harvard, he briefly attended Columbia Law School before turning to politics and historical writing. At age 23, he was elected to the New York State Legislature.

When Alice, his first wife, died, he forbade her name to be mentioned in his presence. He wrote in his diary, "For joy or sorrow, my life has now been lived out." Despite this testimony to his love for and his dependence on her, his energies were not exhausted. He plunged deeper into Republican Party politics, suffered several defeats, and spent two years ranching in the Dakota Territory. Widowed less than two years, he became engaged to a childhood friend, Edith Carow. They were married for 33 years and had four children.

Back in New York, he served as police commissioner and then as assistant secretary of the Navy in the McKinley administration. He resigned in 1898 to lead a troop of volunteers, known as the Rough Riders, in the Spanish-American War. His heroics in Cuba won him the governorship of New York. There he alienated the Republican machine boss, who "got rid" of him by making him the vice-presidential nominee on McKinley's ticket in 1900. When McKinley was assassinated in 1901, Roosevelt became the 26th president of the United States.

He delivered "In Praise of the Strenuous Life" in 1899, shortly after he became governor of New York. Six weeks before, William Jennings Bryan had spoken in Chicago, denouncing imperialism. In responding to Bryan, Roosevelt articulates a distinctly masculine definition of citizenship and America's role in the world.

Six years later, in his Washington, DC, "Address Before the National Congress of Mothers," Roosevelt sets out the complementary duties of men and women, in particular the roles of the "husband-breadwinner" and the "wife-mother-homemaker."

IN PRAISE OF THE STRENUOUS LIFE

1 In speaking to you, men of the greatest city of the West, men of the state which gave to the country Lincoln and Grant, men who preeminently and distinctly embody all that is most American in the American character, I wish to preach not the doctrine of ignoble ease but the doctrine of the strenuous life; the life of toil and effort; of labor and strife; to preach that highest form of success which comes not to the man who desires mere easy peace but to the man who does not shrink from danger, from hardship, or from bitter toil, and who out of these wins the splendid ultimate triumph. . . .

2 As it is with the individual so it is with the nation. It is a base untruth to say that happy is the nation that has no history. Thrice happy is the nation that has a glorious history. Far better it is to dare mighty things, to win glorious triumphs, even though checkered by failure, than to take rank with those poor spirits who neither enjoy much nor suffer much because they live in the gray twilight that knows neither victory nor defeat. If in 1861 the men who loved the Union had believed that peace was the end of all things and war and strife a worst of all things, and had acted up to their belief, we would have saved hundreds of thousands of lives, we would have saved hundreds of millions of dollars. Moreover, besides saving all the blood and treasure we then lavished, we would have prevented the heartbreak of many women, the dissolution of many homes; and we would have spared the country those months of gloom and shame when it seemed as if our armies marched only to defeat. We would have avoided all this suffering simply by shrinking from strife. And if we had thus avoided it we would have shown that we were weaklings and that we were unfit to stand among the great nations of the earth. Thank God for the iron in the blood of our fathers, the men who upheld the wisdom of Lincoln and bore sword or rifle in the armies of Grant! Let us, the children of the men who proved themselves equal to the mighty days—let us, the children of the men who carried the great Civil War to a triumphant conclusion, praise the God of our fathers that the ignoble counsels of peace were rejected, that the suffering and loss, the blackness of sorrow and despair, were unflinchingly faced and the years of strife endured; for in the end the slave was freed, the Union restored, and the mighty American Republic placed once more as a helmeted queen among nations.

3 We of this generation do not have to face a task such as that our fathers faced, but we have our tasks, and woe to us if we fail to perform them! We cannot, if we would, play the part of China, and be content to rot by inches in ignoble ease within our borders, taking no interest in what goes on beyond them; sunk in a scrambling commercialism; heedless of the higher life; the life of aspiration, of toil and risk; busying ourselves only with the wants of our bodies for the day; until suddenly we should find, beyond a shadow of question, what China has already found, that in this world the nation that has trained itself to a career of unwarlike and isolated ease is bound in the end to go down before other nations which have not lost the manly and adventurous qualities. If we are to be a really great people, we must strive in good faith to play a great part in the world. We cannot avoid meeting great issues. All that we can determine for ourselves is whether we shall meet them well or ill. Last year we could

not help being brought face to face with the problem of war with Spain. All we could decide was whether we should shrink like cowards from the contest or enter into it as beseemed a brave and high-spirited people; and, once in, whether failure or success should crown our banners. So it is now. We cannot avoid the responsibilities that confront us in Hawaii, Cuba, Puerto Rico, and the Philippines. . . .

4   The timid man, the lazy man, the man who distrusts his country, the overcivilized man, who has lost the great fighting, masterful virtues, the ignorant man and the man of dull mind, whose soul is incapable of feeling the mighty lift that thrills "stern men with empires in their brains"—all these, of course, shrink from seeing the nation undertake its new duties; shrink from seeing us build a navy and army adequate to our needs; shrink from seeing us do our share of the world's work by bringing order out of chaos in the great, fair tropic islands from which the valor of our soldiers and sailors has driven the Spanish flag. These are the men who fear the strenuous life, who fear the only national life which is really worth leading. . . .

5   I preach to you, then, my countrymen, our country calls not for the life of ease, but for the life of strenuous endeavor. . . .

ADDRESS BEFORE THE NATIONAL CONGRESS OF MOTHERS

1   . . . Far more important than the question of the occupation of our citizens is the question of how their family life is conducted. No matter what that occupation may be, as long as there is a real home and as long as those who make up that home do their duty to one another, to their neighbors and to the State, it is of minor consequence whether the man's trade is plied in the country or the city, whether it calls for the work of the hands or for the work of the head.

2   But the nation is in a bad way if there is no real home, if the family is not of the right kind; if the man is not a good husband and father, if he is brutal or cowardly or selfish, if the woman has lost her sense of duty, if she is sunk in vapid self-indulgence or has let her nature be twisted so that she prefers a sterile pseudo-intellectuality to that great and beautiful development of character which comes only to those whose lives know the fulness of duty done, or effort made and self-sacrifice undergone.

3   In the last analysis the welfare of the State depends absolutely upon whether or not the average family, the average man and woman and their children, represent the kind of citizenship fit for the foundation of a great nation; and if we fail to appreciate this we fail to appreciate the root morality upon which all healthy civilization is based.

4   No piled-up wealth, no splendor of material growth, no brilliance of artistic development, will permanently avail any people unless its home life is healthy, unless the average man possesses honesty, courage, common sense, and decency, unless he works hard and is willing at need to fight hard; and unless the average woman is a good wife, a good mother, able and willing to perform the first and greatest duty of

womanhood, able and willing to bear, and to bring up as they should be brought up, healthy children, sound in body, mind, and character, and numerous enough so that the race shall increase and not decrease.

5   There are certain old truths which will be true as long as this world endures, and which no amount of progress can alter. One of these is the truth that the primary duty of the husband is to be the home-maker, the bread-winner for his wife and children, and that the primary duty of the woman is to be the helpmeet, the housewife, and mother. The woman should have ample educational advantages; but save in exceptional cases the man must be, and she need not be, and generally ought not to be, trained for a lifelong career as the family bread-winner; and, therefore, after a certain point the training of the two must normally be different because the duties of the two are normally different. This does not mean inequality of function, but it does mean that normally there must be dissimilarity of function. On the whole, I think the duty of the woman the more important, the more difficult, and the more honorable of the two; on the whole I respect the woman who does her duty even more than I respect the man who does his.

6   No ordinary work done by a man is either as hard or as responsible as the work of a woman who is bringing up a family of small children; for upon her time and strength demands are made not only every hour of the day, but often every hour of the night. She may have to get up night after night to take care of a sick child, and yet must by day continue to do all her household duties as well; and if the family means are scant she must usually enjoy even her rare holidays taking her whole brood of children with her. The birth-pangs make all men the debtors of all women. Above all our sympathy and regard are due to the struggling wives among those whom Abraham Lincoln called the plain people, and whom he so loved and trusted; for the lives of these women are often led on the lonely heights of quiet, self-sacrificing heroism.

7   Just as the happiest and most honorable and most useful task that can be set any man is to earn enough for the support of his wife and family, for the bringing up and starting in life of his children, so the most important, the most honorable and desirable task which can be set any woman is to be a good and wise mother in a home marked by self-respect and mutual forbearance, by willingness to perform duty, and by refusal to sink into self-indulgence or avoid that which entails effort and self-sacrifice. Of course there are exceptional men and exceptional women who can do and ought to do much more than this, who can lead and ought to lead great careers of outside usefulness in addition to—not as substitutes for—their home work; but I am not speaking of exceptions; I am speaking of the primary duties. I am speaking of the average citizens, the average men and women who make up the nation. . . .

8   . . . I do not in the least believe in the patient Griselda type of woman, in the woman who submits to gross and long-continued ill treatment, any more than I believe in a man who tamely submits to wrongful aggression. No wrong-doing is so abhorrent as wrong-doing by a man toward the wife and children who should arouse every tender feeling in his nature. Selfishness toward them, the lack of tenderness

toward them, lack of consideration for them, above all, brutality in any form toward them, should arouse the heartiest scorn and indignation in every upright soul.

9   . . . I regard marriage as a partnership, in which each partner is in honor bound to think of the rights of the other as well as of his or her own. But I think that the duties are even more important than the rights; and in the long run I think that the reward is ampler and greater for duty well done, than for the insistence upon individual rights, necessary though this, too, must often be. Your duty is hard, your responsibility great; but greatest of all is your reward. I do not pity you in the least. On the contrary, I feel respect and admiration for you. . . .

10   There are many good people who are denied the supreme blessing of children, and for these we have the respect and sympathy always due to those who, from no fault of their own, are denied any of the other great blessings of life. But the man or woman who deliberately foregoes these blessings, whether from viciousness, coldness, shallow-heartedness, self-indulgence, or mere failure to appreciate aright the difference between the all-important and the unimportant—why, such a creature merits contempt as hearty as any visited upon the soldier who runs away in battle, or upon the man who refuses to work for the support of those dependent upon him, and who, though able-bodied, is yet content to eat in idleness the bread which others provide.

11   The existence of women of this type forms one of the most unpleasant and unwholesome features of modern life. If any one is so dim of vision as to fail to see what a thoroughly unlovely creature such a woman is, I wish he would read Judge Robert Grant's novel, "Unleavened Bread," ponder seriously the character of Selma, and think of the fate that would surely overcome any nation which developed its average and typical woman along such lines. Unfortunately, it would be untrue to say that this type exists only in American novels. That it also exists in American life is made unpleasantly evident by the statistics as to the dwindling families in some localities. It is made evident in equally sinister fashion by the census statistics as to divorce, which are fairly appalling; for easy divorce is now, as it ever has been, a bane to any nation, a curse to society, a menace to the home, an incitement to married unhappiness, and to immorality, an evil thing for men, and a still more hideous evil for women. . . .

12   The woman's task is not easy—no task worth doing is easy—but in doing it, and when she has done it, there shall come to her the highest and holiest joy known to mankind; and having done it, she shall have the reward prophesied in Scripture; for her husband and her children, yes, and all people who realize that her work lies at the foundation of all national happiness and greatness, shall rise up and call her blessed.

Mother and Child

Ferdinand Lundberg
and Marynia F. Farnham, MD

"Mother and Child" is an excerpt from a popular advice book published in 1947, two years after World War II ended. Featured in
newsreels, Dr. Farnham urged "Rosie the Riveter" to leave the workforce and return to her home, for only in full-time domesticity
could she find true feminine fulfillment, avoid marital problems,
and, most important, raise healthy children. But according to Lundberg and Farnham, while the mother's role was critical to her children's mental health, few mothers successfully performed this
essential role.

1 The spawning ground of most neurosis in Western civilization is the home. The
basis for it is laid in childhood, although it emerges strongly later, usually from late
adolescence until middle age, provoked by circumstances and conditions encountered in life. And as we have pointed out, the principal agent in laying the ground-
work for it is the mother. Many women classified as housewives and mothers are just
as disturbed as were the feminists, and for the same general reasons. There are mothers, for example, who, although not neurotic, feel dissatisfied with the life they are
leading. The home offers them few energy outlets. The work they do in it does not
bring them prestige. Others, neurotic by reason of their own childhood upbringing
and the failure of life to provide them with satisfactory outlets, suffer from the same
general affliction as the feminists—penis-envy. It is more repressed than it was in the
feminists, but it is at work in the psychic depths.

2   The feminists, turning their backs on a feminine life, lived out, expressed, their
penis-envy, and obtained great satisfaction thereby. The neurotically disturbed
women who find themselves mothers and housewives, however, have *consciously* accepted the feminine way of life, are not aware that deep within them they suffer from
the same general affliction as the feminists. For they were reared in homes greatly re-
sembling those of the feminists, and they were subject to the same cultural influences. They could not escape.

3   Unlike the feminists, they have made sure of libidinal outlets in their lives. But
they have increasingly foregone ego outlets, and have been unable at the same time
to utilize their libidinal opportunities. Many of them, even though not neurotic, cannot help but feel passed by, inferior, put upon by society's denial of ego outlets for
them. When they are neurotic they feel the lack even more. To a certain extent a
woman can derive great ego satisfaction from playing a fully feminine role, but there
are dangers in it both to herself and to her children. Too many women today are
forced to derive their entire ego-support from their children, which they do at the

expense of the children, to the danger of society. A child can never be an adult play-thing and turn out well.

4   The mothers of neurotics and of persons with marked neurotic character traits, with very few exceptions break down into four broad categories, each susceptible of further breakdown until one reaches the great personal complexity of individuals. These categories, in each of which the mother carries out the pattern of her own up-bringing and of the culture around her, are as follows:

1. The rejecting mother, who in various degrees from extreme to subtle, apes society around her and rejects the child. She ordinarily has no more than one, or at most two.
2. The oversolicitous or overprotective mother, who underneath closely resembles the rejecting mother but whose entire activity represents a conscious denial of her unconscious rejection.
3. The dominating mother, who is also very often a strict disciplinarian. This type obtains release for her misdirected ego-drives at the expense of the child. Denied other opportunities for self-realization, she makes her children her pawns, usually requires of them stellar performance in all their undertakings.
4. The over-affectionate mother, who makes up for her essentially libidinal disappointments through her children. Her damage is greatest with her sons, whom she often converts into "sissies"—that is, into passive-feminine or passive-homosexual males.

5   There is, on the other hand, the fully maternal mother, who fortunately accounts for perhaps 50 per cent or more of the births because she has more children than the other types. She does not reject her children, attempt to overprotect them out of her guilty anxiety, dominate them or convert them into lap dogs. She merely loves her children.

6   It is the first three types who produce the delinquents, the difficult behavior-problem children, some substantial percentage of criminals and persons who, al-though moving in socially approved channels, are a trouble to themselves, to close associates and often to society. Along with the over-affectionate mother, they also produce a large percentage of the confirmed alcoholics. Since somewhere around 40 to 50 per cent of the mothers are in the first three categories, the wide damage they do is obvious and warrants fuller discussion.

WRITING ASSIGNMENTS

Analysis

1. How do Roosevelt's views on American citizenship and America's role in the world correlate with the traditional definition of masculinity?
2. Compare Roosevelt's vision of the "strenuous life" to other heroic or mythic images of the American man, such as the pioneer, the mountain man, the

cowboy, GI Joe, or the entrepreneur. What traits do these figures share? What traits are incompatible with these images?

3. Define Roosevelt's idea of masculine and feminine duty. What should men and women be prepared to sacrifice in order to fulfill their duty?

4. Compare Roosevelt's and Tocqueville's understanding of the proper relationship between men and women and their respective roles.

5. How does Roosevelt's contempt for ease and idleness compare to late-twentieth-century versions of the American dream?

6. Attempt to define what Lundberg and Farnham mean by "the fully maternal mother" who "merely loves her children."

7. What can you infer about Lundberg and Farnham's masculine ideal from this short selection on mothering?

8. Lundberg and Farnham's book was published in 1947, shortly after World War II. How might the book's content and its timing be related?

Argument

1. Explain why you agree or disagree with either Roosevelt's vision of America's proper role in the world or his concept of good citizenship.

2. Roosevelt says, "On the whole, I think the duty of the woman the more important, the more difficult, and more honorable of the two; on the whole I respect the woman who does her duty even more than I respect the man who does his." Explain why you do or do not agree with him.

3. Are Roosevelt's ideas about men's and women's economic and social roles and divorce old-fashioned? Which, if any, survive in American culture today? How are they expressed?

4. Do you agree with Lundberg and Farnham that the mother is primarily, even exclusively, responsible for her children's upbringing?

5. Does American society generally value mothers and mothering?

Personal Writing and Writing from Research

1. Assess how Roosevelt's personal life helped shape his concept of masculinity and the American character.

2. Trace the background of the National Congress of Mothers held in Washington DC, March 13, 1905, before which Roosevelt gave his speech.

3. What was the status of the women's movement during Roosevelt's presidency? What were its political and social goals? Did it speak with a unified or fragmented voice?

4. Read Robert Grant's novel, *Unleavened Bread,* which Roosevelt praises, and write an essay comparing it to a contemporary novel that presents a positive or negative female role model.

5. Compare the perspective on mothering, or on parenting, of a contemporary advice book to that offered by Lundberg and Farnham.

MODERN FEMINISM

The Problem That Has No Name

Betty Friedan

Betty Friedan graduated from Smith College in 1942 and then studied psychology at the University of California, Berkeley. She married Carl Friedan in 1947. In 1957, she sent a questionnaire to her Smith College classmates, and their answers led to her writing *The Feminine Mystique* (1963). An excerpt of its introductory chapter is included here.

Her book was not the first to explore women's discontent with the life of domesticity recommended to them by seemingly every expert and spokesperson for popular culture in the post-World War II years. But in synthesizing their discontents, Friedan placed the blame not on women, but on the role that middle-class women were required to play. *The Feminine Mystique* became an instant bestseller and remains a classic in the modern feminist movement.

Friedan has remained a leader of the liberal wing of the women's movement. In 1966, along with several other women, she founded NOW, the National Organization for Women. She is also the author of *It Changed my Life* (1976), *The Second Stage* (1981), and *Fountain of Age* (1993).

1   The problem lay buried, unspoken, for many years in the minds of American women. It was a strange stirring, a sense of dissatisfaction, a yearning that women suffered in the middle of the twentieth century in the United States. Each suburban wife struggled with it alone. As she made the beds, shopped for groceries, matched slipcover material, ate peanut butter sandwiches with her children, chauffeured Cub Scouts and Brownies, lay beside her husband at night—she was afraid to ask even of herself the silent question—"Is this all?"

2   For over fifteen years there was no word of this yearning in the millions of words written about women, for women, in all the columns, books and articles by experts telling women their role was to seek fulfillment as wives and mothers. Over and over women heard in voices of tradition and of Freudian sophistication that they could desire no greater destiny than to glory in their own femininity. Experts told them how to catch a man and keep him, how to breastfeed children and handle their toilet training, how to cope with sibling rivalry and adolescent rebellion; how to buy a dishwasher, bake bread, cook gourmet snails, and build a swimming pool with their own hands; how to dress, look, and act more feminine and make marriage more

exciting; how to keep their husbands from dying young and their sons from growing into delinquents. They were taught to pity the neurotic, unfeminine, unhappy women who wanted to be poets or physicists or presidents. They learned that truly feminine women do not want careers, higher education, political rights—the independence and the opportunities that the old-fashioned feminists fought for. Some women, in their forties and fifties, still remembered painfully giving up those dreams, but most of the younger women no longer even thought about them. A thousand expert voices applauded their femininity, their adjustment, their new maturity. All they had to do was devote their lives from earliest girlhood to finding a husband and bearing children.

3   By the end of the nineteen-fifties, the average marriage age of women in America dropped to 20, and was still dropping, into the teens. Fourteen million girls were engaged by 17. The proportion of women attending college in comparison with men dropping from 47 per cent in 1920 to 35 per cent in 1958. A century earlier, women had fought for higher education; now girls went to college to get a husband. By the mid-fifties, 60 per cent dropped out of college to marry, or because they were afraid too much education would be a marriage bar. Colleges built dormitories for "married students," but the students were almost always the husbands. A new degree was instituted for the wives—"Ph.T." (Putting Husband Through).

4   Then American girls began getting married in high school. And the women's magazines, deploring the unhappy statistics about these young marriages, urged that courses on marriage, and marriage counselors, be installed in the high schools. Girls started going steady at twelve and thirteen, in junior high. Manufacturers put out brassieres with false bosoms of foam rubber for little girls of ten. And an advertisement for a child's dress, sizes 3–6x, in the *New York Times* in the fall of 1960, said: "She Too Can Join the Man-Trap Set."

5   By the end of the fifties, the United States' birthrate was overtaking India's. The birth-control movement, renamed Planned Parenthood, was asked to find a method whereby women who had been advised that a third or fourth baby would be born dead or defective might have it anyhow. Statisticians were especially astounded at the fantastic increase in the number of babies among college women. Where once they had two children, now they had four, five, six. Women who had once wanted careers were now making careers out of having babies. So rejoiced *Life* magazine in a 1956 paean to the movement of American women back to the home.

6   In a New York hospital, a woman had a nervous breakdown when she found she could not breastfeed her baby. In other hospitals, women dying of cancer refused a drug which research had proved might save their lives; its side effects were said to be unfeminine. "If I have only one life, let me live it as a blonde," a larger-than-life-sized picture of a pretty, vacuous woman proclaimed from newspaper, magazine, and drugstore ads. And across America, three out of every ten women dyed their hair blonde. They ate a chalk called Metrecal, instead of food, to shrink to the size of the thin young models. Department-store buyers reported that American women, since 1939, had become three and four sizes smaller. "Women are out to fit the clothes, instead of vice-versa," one buyer said.

7   Interior decorators were designing kitchens with mosaic murals and original paintings, for kitchens were once again the center of women's lives. Home sewing became a million-dollar industry. Many women no longer left their homes, except to shop, chauffeur their children, or attend a social engagement with their husbands. Girls were growing up in America without ever having jobs outside the home. In the late fifties, a sociological phenomenon was suddenly remarked: a third of American women now worked, but most were no longer young and very few were pursuing careers. They were married women who held part-time jobs, selling or secretarial, to put their husbands through school, their sons through college, or to help pay the mortgage. Or they were widows supporting families. Fewer and fewer women were entering professional work. The shortages in the nursing, social work, and teaching professions caused crises in almost every American city. Concerned over the Soviet Union's lead in the space race, scientists noted that America's greatest source of unused brain-power was women. But girls would not study physics: it was "unfeminine." A girl refused a science fellowship at Johns Hopkins to take a job in a real-estate office. All she wanted, she said, was what every other American girl wanted—to get married, have four children and live in a nice house in a nice suburb.

8   The suburban housewife—she was the dream image of the young American women and the envy, it was said, of women all over the world. The American housewife—freed by science and labor-saving appliances from the drudgery, the dangers of childbirth and the illnesses of her grandmother. She was healthy, beautiful, educated, concerned only about her husband, her children, her home. She had found true feminine fulfillment. As a housewife and mother, she was respected as a full and equal partner to man in his world. She was free to choose automobiles, clothes, appliances, supermarkets; she had everything that women ever dreamed of.

9   In the fifteen years after World War II, this mystique of feminine fulfillment became the cherished and self-perpetuating core of contemporary American culture. Millions of women lived their lives in the image of those pretty pictures of the American suburban housewife, kissing their husbands goodbye in front of the picture window, depositing their stationwagonsful of children at school, and smiling as they ran the new electric waxer over the spotless kitchen floor. They baked their own bread, sewed their own and their children's clothes, kept their new washing machines and dryers running all day. They changed the sheets on the beds twice a week instead of once, took the rug-hooking class in adult education, and pitied their poor frustrated mothers, who had dreamed of having a career. Their only dream was to be perfect wives and mothers; their highest ambition to have five children and a beautiful house, their only fight to get and keep their husbands. They had no thought for the unfeminine problems of the world outside the home; they wanted the men to make the major decisions. They gloried in their role as women, and wrote proudly on the census blank: "Occupation: housewife."

10   For over fifteen years, the words written for women, and the words women used when they talked to each other, while their husbands sat on the other side of the

room and talked shop or politics or septic tanks, were about problems with their children, or how to keep their husbands happy, or improve their children's school, or cook chicken or make slipcovers. Nobody argued whether women were inferior or superior to men; they were simply different. Words like "emancipation" and "career" sounded strange and embarrassing; no one had used them for years. When a Frenchwoman named Simone de Beauvoir wrote a book called *The Second Sex,* an American critic commented that she obviously "didn't know what life was all about," and besides, she was talking about French women. The "woman problem" in America no longer existed.

11   If a woman had a problem in the 1950's and 1960's, she knew that something must be wrong with her marriage, or with herself. Other women were satisfied with their lives, she thought. What kind of a woman was she if she did not feel this mysterious fulfillment waxing the kitchen floor? She was so ashamed to admit her dissatisfaction that she never knew how many other women shared it. If she tried to tell her husband, he didn't understand what she was talking about. She did not really understand it herself. For over fifteen years women in America found it harder to talk about this problem than about sex. Even the psychoanalysts had no name for it. When a woman went to a psychiatrist for help, as many women did, she would say, "I'm so ashamed," or "I must be hopelessly neurotic." "I don't know what's wrong with women today," a suburban psychiatrist said uneasily. "I only know something is wrong because most of my patients happen to be women. And their problem isn't sexual." Most women with this problem did not go to see a psychoanalyst, however. "There's nothing wrong really," they kept telling themselves. "There isn't any problem."

12   But on an April morning in 1959, I heard a mother of four, having coffee with four other mothers in a suburban development fifteen miles from New York, say in a tone of quiet desperation, "the problem." And the others knew, without words, that she was not talking about a problem with her husband, or her children, or her home. Suddenly they realized they all shared the same problem, the problem that has no name. They began, hesitantly, to talk about it. Later, after they had picked up their children at nursery school and taken them home to nap, two of the women cried, in sheer relief, just to know they were not alone.

13   Gradually I came to realize that the problem that has no name was shared by countless women in America. As a magazine writer I often interviewed women about problems with their children, or their marriages, or their houses, or their communities. But after a while I began to recognize the telltale signs of this other problem. I saw the same signs in suburban ranch houses and split-levels on Long Island and in New Jersey and Westchester County; in colonial houses in a small Massachusetts town; on patios in Memphis; in suburban and city apartments; in living rooms in the Midwest. Sometimes I sensed the problem, not as a reporter, but as a suburban housewife, for during this time I was also bringing up my own three children in Rockland County, New York. I heard echoes of the problem in college dormitories and semi-private maternity wards, at PTA meetings and luncheons of the League of Women Voters, at suburban cocktail parties, in station wagons waiting for trains, and

in snatches of conversation overheard at Schrafft's. The groping words I heard from other women, on quiet afternoons when children were at school or on quiet evenings when husbands worked late, I think I understood first as a woman long before I understood their larger social and psychological implications.

14   Just what was this problem that has no name? What were the words women used when they tried to express it? Sometimes a woman would say "I feel empty somehow . . . incomplete." Or she would say, "I feel as if I don't exist." Sometimes she blotted out the feeling with a tranquilizer. Sometimes she thought the problem was with her husband, or her children, or that what she really needed was to redecorate her house, or move to a better neighborhood, or have an affair, or another baby. Sometimes, she went to a doctor with symptoms she could hardly describe: "A tired feeling . . . I get so angry with the children it scares me . . . I feel like crying without any reason." (A Cleveland doctor called it "the housewife's syndrome.") A number of women told me about great bleeding blisters that break out on their hands and arms. "I call it the housewife's blight," said a family doctor in Pennsylvania. "I see it so often lately in these young women with four, five and six children who bury themselves in their dishpans. But it isn't caused by detergent and it isn't cured by cortisone."

15   Sometimes a woman would tell me that the feeling gets so strong she runs out of the house and walks through the streets. Or she stays inside her house and cries. Or her children tell her a joke, and she doesn't laugh because she doesn't hear it. I talked to women who had spent years on the analyst's couch, working out their "adjustment to the feminine role," their blocks to "fulfillment as a wife and mother." But the desperate tone in these women's voices, and the look in their eyes, was the same as the tone and the look of other women, who were sure they had no problem, even though they did have a strange feeling of desperation.

16   A mother of four who left college at nineteen to get married told me:

> I've tried everything women are supposed to do—hobbies, gardening, pickling, canning, being very social with my neighbors, joining committees, running PTA teas. I can do it all, and I like it, but it doesn't leave you anything to think about—any feeling of who you are. I never had any career ambitions. All I wanted was to get married and have four children. I love the kids and Bob and my home. There's no problem you can even put a name to. But I'm desperate. I begin to feel I have no personality. I'm a server of food and putter-on of pants and a bedmaker, somebody who can be called on when you want something. But who am I?

17   A twenty-three-year-old mother in blue jeans said:

> I ask myself why I'm so dissatisfied. I've got my health, fine children, a lovely new home, enough money. My husband has a real future as an electronics engineer. He doesn't have any of these feelings. He says maybe I need a vacation, let's go to New York for a weekend. But that isn't it. I always had this idea we should do everything together. I can't sit down and read a book alone. If the children are napping and I have one hour to myself I just walk through the house waiting for them to wake up. I don't make a move until I know where the rest of the crowd is going. It's as if ever

since you were a little girl, there's always been somebody or something that will take care of your life: your parents, or college, or falling in love, or having a child, or moving to a new house. Then you wake up one morning and there's nothing to look forward to.

18   A young wife in a Long Island development said:

> I seem to sleep so much. I don't know why I should be so tired. This house isn't nearly so hard to clean as the cold-water flat we had when I was working. The children are at school all day. It's not the work. I just don't feel alive.

19   In 1960, the problem that has no name burst like a boil through the image of the happy American housewife. In the television commercials the pretty housewives still beamed over their foaming dishpans and *Time*'s cover story on "The Suburban Wife, an American Phenomenon" protested: "Having too good a time . . . to believe that they should be unhappy." But the actual unhappiness of the American housewife was suddenly being reported—from the *New York Times* and *Newsweek* to *Good Housekeeping* and CBS Television ("The Trapped Housewife"), although almost everybody who talked about it found some superficial reason to dismiss it. It was attributed to incompetent appliance repairmen (*New York Times*), or the distances children must be chauffeured in the suburbs (*Time*), or too much PTA (*Redbook*). Some said it was the old problem—education: more and more women had education, which naturally made them unhappy in their role as housewives. "The road from Freud to Frigidaire, from Sophocles to Spock, has turned out to be a bumpy one," reported the *New York Times* (June 28, 1960). "Many young women—certainly not all—whose education plunged them into a world of ideas feel stifled in their homes. They find their routine lives out of joint with their training. Like shut-ins, they feel left out. In the last year, the problem of the educated housewife has provided the meat of dozens of speeches made by troubled presidents of women's colleges who maintain, in the face of complaints, that sixteen years of academic training is realistic preparation for wifehood and motherhood."

20   There was much sympathy for the educated housewife. ("Like a two-headed schizophrenic . . . once she wrote a paper on the Graveyard poets; now she writes notes to the milkman. Once she determined the boiling point of sulphuric acid; now she determines her boiling point with the overdue repairman. . . . The housewife often is reduced to screams and tears. . . . No one, it seems, is appreciative, least of all herself, of the kind of person she becomes in the process of turning from poetess into shrew.")

21   Home economists suggested more realistic preparation for housewives, such as high-school workshops in home appliances. College educators suggested more discussion groups on home management and the family, to prepare women for the adjustment to domestic life. A spate of articles appeared in the mass magazines offering "Fifty-eight Ways to Make Your Marriage More Exciting." No month went by without a new book by a psychiatrist or sexologist offering technical advice on finding greater fulfillment through sex.

22   A male humorist joked in *Harper's Bazaar* (July, 1960) that the problem could be solved by taking away woman's right to vote. ("In the pre-19th Amendment era, the American woman was placid, sheltered and sure of her role in American society. She left all the political decisions to her husband and he, in turn, left all the family decisions to her. Today a woman has to make both the family *and* the political decisions, and it's too much for her.")

23   A number of educators suggested seriously that women no longer be admitted to the four-year colleges and universities: in the growing college crisis, the education which girls could not use as housewives was more urgently needed than ever by boys to do the work of the atomic age.

24   The problem was also dismissed with drastic solutions no one could take seriously. (A woman writer proposed in *Harper's* that women be drafted for compulsory service as nurses' aides and baby-sitters.) And it was smoothed over with the age-old panaceas: "love is their answer," "the only answer is inner help," "the secret of completeness—children," "a private means of intellectual fulfillment," "to cure this toothache of the spirit—the simple formula of handing one's self and one's will over to God."

25   The problem was dismissed by telling the housewife she doesn't realize how lucky she is—her own boss, no time clock, no junior executive gunning for her job. What if she isn't happy—does she think men are happy in this world? Does she really, secretly, still want to be a man? Doesn't she know yet how lucky she is to be a woman?

26   The problem was also, and finally, dismissed by shrugging that there are no solutions: this is what being a woman means, and what is wrong with American women that they can't accept their role gracefully? As *Newsweek* put it (March 7, 1960):

> She is dissatisfied with a lot that women of other lands can only dream of. Her discontent is deep, pervasive, and impervious to the superficial remedies which are offered at every hand. . . . An army of professional explorers have already charted the major sources of trouble. . . . From the beginning of time, the female cycle has defined and confined woman's role. As Freud was credited with saying: "Anatomy is destiny." Though no group of women has ever pushed these natural restrictions as far as the American wife, it seems that she still cannot accept them with good grace. . . . A young mother with a beautiful family, charm, talent and brains is apt to dismiss her role apologetically. "What do I do?" you hear her say. "Why nothing. I'm just a housewife." A good education, it seems, has given this paragon among women an understanding of the value of everything except her own worth . . .

27   And so she must accept the fact that "American women's unhappiness is merely the most recently won of women's rights," and adjust and say with the happy housewife found by *Newsweek:* "We ought to salute the wonderful freedom we all have and be proud of our lives today. I have had college and I've worked, but being a housewife is the most rewarding and satisfying role. . . . My mother was never included in my father's business affairs . . . she couldn't get out of the house and away from us children. But I am an equal to my husband; I can go along with him on business trips and to social business affairs."

28   The alternative offered was a choice that few women would contemplate. In the sympathetic words of the *New York Times:* "All admit to being deeply frustrated at times by the lack of privacy, the physical burden, the routine of family life, the confinement of it. However, none would give up her home and family if she had the choice to make again." *Redbook* commented: "Few women would want to thumb their noses at husbands, children and community and go off on their own. Those who do may be talented individuals, but they rarely are successful women."

29   The year American women's discontent boiled over, it was also reported (*Look*) that the more than 21,000,000 American women who are single, widowed, or divorced do not cease even after fifty their frenzied, desperate search for a man. And the search begins early—for seventy per cent of all American women now marry before they are twenty-four. A pretty twenty-five-year-old secretary took thirty-five different jobs in six months in the futile hope of finding a husband. Women were moving from one political club to another, taking evening courses in accounting or sailing, learning to play golf or ski, joining a number of churches in succession, going to bars alone, in their ceaseless search for a man.

30   Of the growing thousands of women currently getting private psychiatric help in the United States, the married ones were reported dissatisfied with their marriages, the unmarried ones suffering from anxiety and, finally, depression. Strangely, a number of psychiatrists stated that, in their experience, unmarried women patients were happier than married ones. So the door of all those pretty suburban houses opened a crack to permit a glimpse of uncounted thousands of American housewives who suffered alone from a problem that suddenly everyone was talking about; and beginning to take for granted, as one of those unreal problems in American life that can never be solved—like the hydrogen bomb. By 1962 the plight of the trapped American housewife had become a national parlor game. Whole issues of magazines, newspaper columns, books, learned and frivolous, educational conferences and television panels were devoted to the problem.

31   Even so, most men, and some women, still did not know that this problem was real. But those who had faced it honestly knew that all the superficial remedies, the sympathetic advice, the scolding words and the cheering word, were somehow drowning the problem in unreality. A bitter laugh was beginning to be heard from American women. They were admired, envied, pitied, theorized over until they were sick of it, offered drastic solutions or silly choices that no one could take seriously. They got all kinds of advice from the growing armies of marriage and child-guidance counselors, psychotherapists and armchair psychologists, on how to adjust to their role as housewives. No other road to fulfillment was offered to American women in the middle of the twentieth century. Most adjusted to their role and suffered or ignored the problem that has no name. It can be less painful for a woman, not to hear the strange, dissatisfied voice stirring within her.

32   It is no longer possible to ignore that voice, to dismiss the desperation of so many American women. This is not what being a woman means, no matter what the experts say. . . .

33   I think the experts in a great many fields have been holding pieces of that truth under their microscopes for a long time without realizing it. . . .

34   If I am right, the problem that has no name stirring in the minds of so many American women today is not a matter of loss of femininity or too much education, or the demands of domesticity. It is far more important than anyone recognizes. It is the key to these other new and old problems which have been torturing women and their husbands and children, and puzzling their doctors and educators for years. It may well be the key to our future as a nation and as a culture. We can no longer ignore that voice within women that says: "I want something more than my husband and my children and my home."

What It Would Be Like If Women Win

Gloria Steinem

Gloria Steinem, the founder of *Ms.* magazine, has created bridges between feminists and an uncomprehending, often apprehensive, public. She provoked controversy through an early article that described her humiliating experiences as an "undercover" Playboy bunny, at a time when the Playboy Club and magazine still symbolized sexual liberation and the fulfillment of fantasy for millions of Americans. Her books, *Outrageous Acts and Everyday Rebellions* (1983), *Marilyn: Norma Jean* (1986), and *Revolutions from Within* (1992), have given mainstream America an idiom with which to discuss and understand the modern women's movement. Her magazine, *Ms.*, gave the women's movement a voice in popular journalism. "What It Would Be Like If Women Win" is another example of her translating, in reassuring terms, the feminist vision for the American public. It appeared in *Time* magazine in 1970.

1   Any change is fearful, especially one affecting both politics and sex roles, so let me begin these utopian speculations with a fact. To break the ice.

2   Women don't want to exchange places with men. Male chauvinists, science-fiction writers and comedians may favor that idea for its shock value, but psychologists say it is a fantasy based on ruling-class ego and guilt. Men assume that women want to imitate them, which is just what white people assumed about blacks. An assumption so strong that it may convince the second-class group of the need to imitate, but for both women and blacks that stage has passed. Guilt produces the question: What if they could treat us as we have treated them?

3   That is not our goal. But we do want to change the economic system to one more based on merit. In Women's Lib Utopia, there will be free access to good jobs—and decent pay for the bad ones women have been performing all along, including

housework. Increased skilled labor might lead to a four-hour workday, and higher wages would encourage further mechanization of repetitive jobs now kept alive by cheap labor.

4   With women as half the country's elected representatives, and a woman President once in a while, the country's *machismo* problems would be greatly reduced. The old-fashioned idea that manhood depends on violence and victory is, after all, an important part of our troubles in the streets, and in Viet Nam. I'm not saying that women leaders would eliminate violence. We are not more moral than men; we are only un-corrupted by power so far. When we do acquire power, we might turn out to have an equal impulse toward aggression. Even now, Margaret Mead believes that women fight less often but more fiercely than men, because women are not taught the rules of the war game and fight only when cornered. But for the next 50 years or so, women in politics will be very valuable by tempering the idea of manhood into something less aggressive and better suited to this crowded, post-atomic planet. Consumer protection and children's rights, for instance, might get more legislative attention.

5   Men will have to give up ruling-class privileges, but in return they will no longer be the only ones to support the family, get drafted, bear the strain of power and responsibility. Freud to the contrary, anatomy is not destiny, at least not for more than nine months at a time. In Israel, women are drafted, and some have gone to war. In England, more men type and run switchboards. In India and Israel, a woman rules. In Sweden, both parents take care of the children. In this country, come Utopia, men and women won't reverse roles; they will be free to choose according to individual talents and preferences.

6   If role reform sounds sexually unsettling, think how it will change the sexual hypocrisy we have now. No more sex arranged on the barter system, with women pretending interest, and men never sure whether they are loved for themselves or for the security few women can get any other way. (Married or not, for sexual reasons or social ones, most women still find it second nature to Uncle-Tom.) No more men who are encouraged to spend a lifetime living with inferiors; with housekeepers, or dependent creatures who are still children. No more domineering wives, emasculating women, and "Jewish mothers," all of whom are simply human beings with all their normal ambition and drive confined to the home. No more unequal partnerships that eventually doom love and sex.

7   In order to produce that kind of confidence and individuality, child rearing will train according to talent. Little girls will no longer be surrounded by air-tight, self-fulfilling prophecies of natural passivity, lack of ambition and objectivity, inability to exercise power, and dexterity (so long as special aptitude for jobs requiring patience and dexterity is confined to poorly paid jobs; brain surgery is for males).

8   Schools and universities will help to break down traditional sex roles, even when parents will not. Half the teachers will be men, a rarity now at preschool and elementary levels; girls will not necessarily serve cookies or boys hoist up the flag. Athletic teams will be picked only by strength and skill. Sexually segregated courses like auto mechanics and home economics will be taken by boys and girls together. New courses

in sexual politics will explore female subjugation as the model for political oppression, and women's history will be an academic staple, along with black history, at least until the white-male-oriented textbooks are integrated and rewritten.

9   As for the American child's classic problem—too much mother, too little father—that would be cured by an equalization of parental responsibility. Free nurseries, school lunches, family cafeterias built into every housing complex, service companies that will do household cleaning chores in a regular, businesslike way, and more responsibility by the entire community for the children: all these will make it possible for both mother and father to work, and to have equal leisure time with the children at home. For parents of very young children, however, a special job category, created by Government and unions, would allow such parents a shorter work day.

10   The revolution would not take away the option of being a housewife. A woman who prefers to be her husband's housekeeper and/or hostess would receive a percentage of his pay determined by the domestic relations courts. If divorced, she might be eligible for a pension fund, and for a job-training allowance. Or a divorce could be treated the same way that the dissolution of a business partnership is now.

11   If these proposals seem farfetched, consider Sweden, where most of them are already in effect. Sweden is not yet a working Women's Lib model; most of the role-reform programs began less than a decade ago, and are just beginning to take hold. But that country is so far ahead of us in recognizing the problem that Swedish statements on sex and equality sound like bulletins from the moon.

12   Our marriage laws, for instance, are so reactionary that Women's Lib groups want couples to take a compulsory written exam on the law, as for a driver's license, before going through with the wedding. A man has alimony and wifely debts to worry about, but a woman may lose so many of her civil rights that in the U.S. now, in important legal ways, she becomes a child again. In some states, she cannot sign credit agreements, use her maiden name, incorporate a business, or establish a legal residence of her own. Being a wife, according to most social and legal definitions, is still a 19th century thing.

13   Assuming, however, that these blatantly sexist laws are abolished or reformed, that job discrimination is forbidden, that parents share financial responsibility for each other and the children, and that sexual relationships become partnerships of equal adults (some pretty big assumptions), then marriage will probably go right on. Men and women are, after all, physically complementary. When society stops encouraging men to be exploiters and women to be parasites, they may turn out to be more complementary in emotion as well. Women's Lib is not trying to destroy the American family. A look at the statistics on divorce—plus the way in which old people are farmed out with strangers and young people flee the home—shows the destruction that has already been done. Liberated women are just trying to point out the disaster, and build compassionate and practical alternatives from the ruins.

14   What will exist is a variety of alternative life-styles. Since the population explosion dictates that childbearing be kept to a minimum, parents-and-children will be only

one of many "families": couples, age groups, working groups, mixed communes, blood-related clans, class groups, creative groups. Single women will have the right to stay single without ridicule, without the attitudes now betrayed by "spinster" and "bachelor." Lesbians or homosexuals will no longer be denied legally binding marriages, complete with mutual support agreements and inheritance rights. Paradoxically, the number of homosexuals may get smaller. With fewer overpossessive mothers and fewer fathers who hold up an impossibly cruel or perfectionist idea of manhood, boys will be less likely to be denied or reject their identity as males.

15   Changes that now seem small may get bigger:

MEN'S LIB

16   Men now suffer from more disease due to stress, heart attacks, ulcers, a higher suicide rate, greater difficulty living alone, less adaptability to change and, in general, a shorter life span than women. There is some scientific evidence that what produces physical problems is not work itself, but the inability to choose which work, and how much. With women bearing half the financial responsibility, and with the idea of "masculine" jobs gone, men might well feel freer and live longer.

RELIGION

17   Protestant women are already becoming ordained ministers; radical nuns are carrying out liturgical functions that were once the exclusive property of priests; Jewish women are rewriting prayers—particularly those that Orthodox Jews recite every morning thanking God they are not female. In the future, the church will become an area of equal participation by women. This means, of course, that organized religion will have to give up one of its great historical weapons: sexual repression. In most structured faiths, from Hinduism through Roman Catholicism, the status of women went down as the position of priests ascended. Male clergy implied, if they did not teach, that women were unclean, unworthy and sources of ungodly temptation, in order to remove them as rivals for the emotional forces of men. Full participation of women in ecclesiastical life might involve certain changes in theology, such as, for instance, a radical redefinition of sin.

LITERARY PROBLEMS

18   Revised sex roles will outdate more children's books than civil rights ever did. Only a few children had the problem of a *Little Black Sambo,* but most have the male-female stereotypes of "Dick and Jane." A boomlet of children's books about mothers who work has already begun, and liberated parents and editors are beginning to pressure for change in the textbook industry. Fiction writing will change more gradually, but romantic novels with wilting heroines and swashbuckling heroes will be reduced to historical value. Or perhaps to the sado-masochist trade. (*Marjorie Morningstar,* a romantic novel that took the '50s by storm, has already begun to seem as unreal as its

'20s predecessor, *The Sheik.*) As for the literary plots that turn on forced marriages or horrific abortions, they will seem as dated as Prohibition stories. Free legal abortions and free birth control will force writers to give up pregnancy as the *deus ex machina.*

MANNERS AND FASHION

19 Dress will be more androgynous, with class symbols becoming more important than sexual ones. Pro- or anti-Establishment styles may already be more vital than who is wearing them. Hardhats are just as likely to rough up antiwar girls as antiwar men in the street, and police understand that women are just as likely to be pushers or bombers. Dances haven't required that one partner lead the other for years, anyway. Chivalry will transfer itself to those who need it, or deserve respect: old people, admired people, anyone with an armload of packages. Women with normal work identities will be less likely to attach their whole sense of self to youth and appearance; thus there will be fewer nervous breakdowns when the first wrinkles appear. Lighting cigarettes and other treasured niceties will become gestures of mutual affection. "I like to be helped on with my coat," says one Women's Lib worker, "but not if it costs me $2,000 a year in salary."

20 For those with nostalgia for a simpler past, here is a word of comfort. Anthropologist Geoffrey Gorer studied the few peaceful human tribes and discovered one common characteristic: sex roles were not polarized. Differences of dress and occupation were at a minimum. Society, in other words, was not using sexual blackmail as a way of getting women to do cheap labor, or men to be aggressive.

21 Thus Women's Lib may achieve a more peaceful society on the way toward its other goals. That is why the Swedish government considers reform to bring about greater equality in the sex roles one of its most important concerns. As Prime Minister Olof Palme explained in a widely ignored speech delivered in Washington this spring: "It is *human beings* we shall emancipate. In Sweden today, if a politician should declare that the woman ought to have a different role from man's, he would be regarded as something from the Stone Age." In other words, the most radical goal of the movement is egalitarianism.

22 If Women's Lib wins, perhaps we all do.

Invisibility Is an Unnatural Disaster
Reflections of an Asian American Woman

Mitsuye Yamada

Poet and fiction writer Mitsuye Yamada is a second-generation Japanese American who was born in 1923 and was interned in Idaho during World War II. In *Camp Notes and Other Poems* (1976) and *Desert Run: Poems and Stories,* she explores the internment experience, cultural identity, and racial interaction. This 1981 selection appeared in the collection *This Bridge Called My Back: Writings by Radical Women of Color,* edited by Cherrie Moraga and Gloria Anzaldua.

1 Last year for the Asian segment of the Ethnic American Literature course I was teaching, I selected a new anthology entitled *Aiiieeeee!* compiled by a group of outspoken Asian American writers. During the discussion of the long but thought-provoking introduction to this anthology, one of my students blurted out that she was offended by its militant tone and that as a white person she was tired of always being blamed for the oppression of all the minorities. I noticed several of her classmates' eyes nodding in tacit agreement. A discussion of the "militant" voices in some of the other writings we had read in the course ensued. Surely, I pointed out, some of these other writings have been just as, if not more, militant as the words in this introduction? Had they been offended by those also but failed to express their feelings about them? To my surprise, they said they were not offended by any of the Black American, Chicano or American Indian writings, but were hard-pressed to explain why when I asked for an explanation. A little further discussion revealed that they "understood" the anger expressed by the Black and Chicanos and they "empathized" with the frustrations and sorrow expressed by the American Indian. But the Asian Americans??

2 Then finally, one student said it for all of them: "It made me angry. *Their* anger made *me* angry, because I didn't even know the Asian Americans felt oppressed. I didn't expect their anger."

3 At this time I was involved in an academic due process procedure begun as a result of a grievance I had filed the previous semester against the administrators at my college. I had filed a grievance for violation of my rights as a teacher who had worked in the district for almost eleven years. My student's remark, "Their anger made me angry . . . I didn't expect their anger," explained for me the reactions of some of my own colleagues as well as the reactions of the administrators during those previous months. The grievance procedure was a time-consuming and emotionally draining process, but the basic principle was too important for me to ignore. That basic principle was that I, an individual teacher, do have certain rights which are given and my superiors cannot, should not, violate them with impunity. When this was pointed out to them, however, they responded with shocked surprise that I, of all people, would take them to task for violation of what was clearly written policy in our college district. They all seemed to exclaim, "We don't understand this; this is so uncharacteristic of her; she seemed such a nice person, so polite, so obedient, so non-troublemaking." What was even more surprising was once they were forced to acknowledge that I was determined to start the due process action, they assumed I was not doing it on my own. One of the administrators suggested someone must have pushed me into this, undoubtedly some of "those feminists" on our campus, he said wryly.

4 In this age when women are clearly making themselves visible on all fronts, I, an Asian American woman, am still functioning as a "front for those feminists" and therefore invisible. The realization of this sinks in slowly. Asian Americans as a whole

are finally coming to claim their own, demanding that they be included in the multi-cultural history of our country. I like to think, in spite of my administrator's myopia, that the most stereotyped minority of them all, the Asian American woman, is just now emerging to become part of that group. It took forever. Perhaps it is important to ask ourselves why it took so long. We should ask ourselves this question just when we think we are emerging as a viable minority in the fabric of our society. I should add to my student's words, "because I didn't even know they felt oppressed," that it took this long because we Asian American women have not admitted to ourselves that we *were* oppressed. We, the visible minority that is invisible.

5   I say this because until a few years ago I have been an Asian American woman working among non-Asians in an educational institution where most of the decision-makers were men[1]; an Asian American woman thriving under the smug illusion that I was *not* the stereotypic image of the Asian woman because I had a career teaching English in a community college. I did not think anything assertive was necessary to make my point. People who know me, I reasoned, the ones who count, know who I am and what I think. Thus, even when what I considered a veiled racist remark was made in a casual social setting, I would "let it go" because it was pointless to argue with people who didn't even know their remark was racist. I had supposed that I was practicing passive resistance while being stereotyped, but it was so passive no one noticed I was resisting; it was so much my expected role that it ultimately rendered me invisible.

6   My experience leads me to believe that contrary to what I thought, I had actually been contributing to my own stereotyping. Like the hero in Ralph Ellison's novel *The Invisible Man,* I had become invisible to white Americans, and it clung to me like a bad habit. Like most bad habits, this one crept up on me because I took it in minute doses like Mithradates' poison and my mind and body adapted so well to it I hardly noticed it was there.

7   For the past eleven years I have busied myself with the usual chores of an English teacher, a wife of a research chemist, and a mother of four rapidly growing children. I hadn't even done much to shatter this particular stereotype: the middle class woman happy to be bringing home the extra income and quietly fitting into the man's world of work. When the Asian American woman is lulled into believing that people perceive her as being different from other Asian women (the submissive, sub-servient, ready-to-please, easy-to-get-along-with Asian woman), she is kept comfort-ably content with the state of things. She becomes ineffectual in the milieu in which she moves. The seemingly apolitical middle class woman and the apolitical Asian woman constituted a double invisibility.

8   I had created an underground culture of survival for myself and had become in the eyes of others the person I was trying not to be. Because I was permitted to go to col-lege, permitted to take a stab at a career or two along the way, given "free choice" to marry and have a family, given a "choice" to eventually do both, I had assumed I was

[1] It is hoped this will change now that a black woman is Chancellor of our college district.

more or less free, not realizing that those who are free make and take choices; they do not choose from options proferred by "those out there."

9   I, personally, had not "emerged" until I was almost fifty years old. Apparently through a long conditioning process, I had learned how *not* to be seen for what I am. A long history of ineffectual activities had been, I realize now, initiation rites toward my eventual invisibility. The training begins in childhood; and for women and minorities, whatever is started in childhood is continued throughout their adult lives. I first recognized just how invisible I was in my first real confrontation with my parents a few years after the outbreak of World War II.

10   During the early years of the war, my older brother, Mike, and I left the concentration camp in Idaho to work and study at the University of Cincinnati. My parents came to Cincinnati soon after my father's release from Internment Camp (these were POW camps to which many of the Issei[2] men, leaders in their communities, were sent by the FBI), and worked as domestics in the suburbs. I did not see them too often because by this time I had met and was much influenced by a pacifist who was out on a "furlough" from a conscientious objectors' camp in Trenton, North Dakota. When my parents learned about my "boy friend" they were appalled and frightened. After all, this was the period when everyone in the country was expected to be one-hundred percent behind the war effort, and the Nisei[3] boys who had volunteered for the Armed Forces were out there fighting and dying to prove how American we really were. However, during interminable arguments with my father and overheard arguments between my parents, I was devastated to learn they were not so much concerned about my having become a pacifist, but they were more concerned about the possibility of my marrying one. They were understandably frightened (my father's prison years of course were still fresh on his mind) about repercussions on the rest of the family. In an attempt to make my father understand me, I argued that even if I didn't marry him, I'd still be a pacifist; but my father reassured me that it was "all right" for me to be a pacifist because as a Japanese national and a "girl" *it didn't make any difference to anyone.* In frustration I remember shouting, "But can't you see, *I'm* philosophically committed to the pacifist cause," but he dismissed this with "In my college days we used to call philosophy, foolosophy," and that was the end of that. When they were finally convinced I was not going to marry "my pacifist," the subject was dropped and we never discussed it again.

11   As if to confirm my father's assessment of the harmlessness of my opinions, my brother Mike, an American citizen, was suddenly expelled from the University of Cincinnati while I, "an enemy alien", was permitted to stay. We assumed that his stand as a pacifist, although he was classified a 4-F because of his health, contributed to his expulsion. We were told the Air Force was conducting sensitive wartime research on campus and requested his removal, but they apparently felt my presence on campus was not as threatening.

[2] Issei—Immigrant Japanese, living in the U.S.
[3] Nisei—Second generation Japanese, born in the U.S.

12   I left Cincinnati in 1945, hoping to leave behind this and other unpleasant memories gathered there during the war years, and plunged right into the politically active atmosphere at New York University where students, many of them returning veterans, were continuously promoting one cause or other by making speeches in Washington Square, passing out petitions, or staging demonstrations. On one occasion, I tagged along with a group of students who took a train to Albany to demonstrate on the steps of the State Capitol. I think I was the only Asian in this group of predominantly Jewish students from NYU. People who passed us were amused and shouted "Go home and grow up." I suppose Governor Dewey, who refused to see us, assumed we were a group of adolescents without a cause as most college students were considered to be during those days. It appears they weren't expecting any results from our demonstration. There were no newspersons, no security persons, no police. No one tried to stop us from doing what we were doing. We simply did "our thing" and went back to our studies until next time, and my father's words were again confirmed: it made no difference to anyone, being a young student demonstrator in peacetime, 1947.

13   Not only the young, but those who feel powerless over their own lives know what it is like not to make a difference on anyone or anything. The poor know it only too well, and we women have known it since we were little girls. The most insidious part of this conditioning process, I realize now, was that we have been trained not to expect a response in ways that mattered. We may be listened to and responded to with placating words and gestures, but our psychological mind set has already told us time and again that we were born into a ready-made world into which we must fit ourselves, and that many of us do it very well.

14   This mind set is the result of not believing that the political and social forces affecting our lives are determined by some person, or a group of persons, probably sitting behind a desk or around a conference table.

15   Just recently I read an article about "the remarkable track record of success" of the Nisei in the United States. One Nisei was quoted as saying he attributed our stamina and endurance to our ancestors whose characters had been shaped, he said, by their living in a country which has been constantly besieged by all manner of natural disasters, such as earthquakes and hurricanes. He said the Nisei has inherited a steely will, a will to endure and hence, to survive.

16   This evolutionary explanation disturbs me, because it equates the "act of God" (i.e., natural disasters) to the "act of man" (i.e., the war, the evacuation). The former is not within our power to alter, but the latter, I should think, is. By putting the "acts of God" on par with the acts of man, we shrug off personal responsibilities.

17   I have, for too long a period of time accepted the opinion of others (even though they were directly affecting my life) as if they were objective events totally out of my control. Because I separated such opinions from the persons who were making them, I accepted them the way I accepted natural disasters; and I endured them as inevitable. I have tried to cope with people whose points of view alarmed me in the same way that I had adjusted to natural phenomena, such as hurricanes, which plowed into my life from time to time. I would readjust my dismantled feelings in the

same way that we repaired the broken shutters after the storm. The Japanese have an all-purpose expression in their language for this attitude of resigned acceptance: "Shikataganai." "It can't be helped." "There's nothing I can do about it." It is said with the shrug of the shoulders and tone of finality, perhaps not unlike the "those-were-my-orders" tone that was used at the Nuremberg trials. With all the sociological studies that have been made about the causes of the evacuations of the Japanese Americans during World War II, we should know by now that "they" knew that the West Coast Japanese Americans would go without too much protest, and of course, "they" were right, for most of us (with the exception of those notable few), resigned to our fate, albeit bewildered and not willingly. We were not perceived by our government as responsive Americans; we were objects that happened to be standing in the path of the storm.

18   Perhaps this kind of acceptance is a way of coping with the "real" world. One stands against the wind for a time, and then succumbs eventually because there is no point to being stubborn against all odds. The wind will not respond to entreaties anyway, one reasons; one should have sense enough to know that. I'm not ready to accept this evolutionary reasoning. It is too rigid for me; I would like to think that my new awareness is going to make me more visible than ever, and to allow me to make some changes in the "man made disaster" I live in at the present time. Part of being visible is refusing to separate the actors from their actions, and demanding that they be responsible for them.

19   By now, riding along with the minorities' and women's movements, I think we are making a wedge into the main body of American life, but people are still looking right through and around us, assuming we are simply tagging along. Asian American women still remain in the background and we are heard but not really listened to. Like Musak, they think we are piped into the airwaves by someone else. We must remember that one of the most insidious ways of keeping women and minorities powerless is to let them only talk about harmless and inconsequential subjects, or let them speak freely and not listen to them with serious intent.

20   We need to raise our voices a little more, even as they say to us "This is so uncharacteristic of you." To finally recognize our own invisibility is to finally be on the path toward visibility. Invisibility is not a natural state for anyone.

WRITING ASSIGNMENTS

Analysis

1. Friedan's *The Feminine Mystique* is often credited with launching the modern women's movement. To what extent does her analysis reflect the experience of most American women? Who is left out?

2. Today, economic pressures make it unlikely that more than a small percentage of women will spend their lives as wives and mothers with no paying job. Yet a full generation after the women's movement, this lifestyle is the expressed goal of a significant percentage of young women. How would you account for this phenomenon?

3. Friedan says that the "alternative offered [to the housewife/mother role] was a choice that few women would contemplate." Why did the alternatives seem so limited and unattractive? Have things significantly changed since 1963?

4. Analyze the role that advertising, television, and the advice of experts played in developing the "feminine mystique" and in concealing the "problem that has no name."

5. Use Friedan's observations to respond to Lundberg and Farnham's analysis of mid-twentieth-century American mothers.

6. Steinem predicts that Women's Lib will lead to the decline of the exclusively male breadwinner role. What factors besides women's lib have led to this change?

7. Steinem says, "Married or not, for sexual reasons or social ones, most women still find it second nature to Uncle-Tom." What does she mean, and is she right?

8. Why does Steinem believe that Women's Lib might achieve a more peaceful society?

9. According to Yamada, why are Asian-Americans, especially Asian-American women, "invisible"?

10. Yamada's student said, "*Their* anger made *me* angry. . . . I didn't expect their anger." What are the stereotypes associated with Asian-American men and women, and how do they help to explain this student's attitude?

11. Compare the ways that the members of the Yamada family responded to internment during World War II. Why might internment have held different meanings for men and women?

12. What cultural values does the Japanese expression, "Shikataganai" reflect? How and why is Yamada resisting it?

Argument

1. Is the life of a middle-class housewife/mother as unfulfilling as Friedan says it is?

2. Steinem concludes, "If Women's Lib wins, perhaps we all do." Do you agree?

3. Steinem says, "Women don't want to exchange places with men." Do you agree?

4. Is Steinem's vision elitist? Define your terms and explain your answer.

5. Is Steinem's vision practical?

6. Explain why you believe that Asian-American men or women, or both, should or should not be considered an oppressed minority.

7. Yamada says, ". . . I had assumed I was more or less free, not realizing that those who are free make and take choices; they do not choose from options proferred by 'those out there.'" Do you agree with her definition of freedom?

Personal Writing and Writing from Research

1. Interview several women who were young adults in the 1950s and early 1960s to assess how their experiences compared with those described by Friedan. Report your findings in an essay or a series of profiles.

2. Use Friedan's 1963 observations to analyze Sylvia Plath's novel, *The Bell Jar* (published in 1971, but set in 1953), or Charlotte Perkins Gilman's 1892 story, "The Yellow Wallpaper."
3. Explain whether and why your life reflects the changes that Steinem predicted.
4. *Collaborative Project:* A generation has passed since Steinem's essay. Explain whether and why the changes that she predicted in one of the following areas did, in fact, generally occur: women's participation in and effect on government; the sexual division of labor; sexual politics; sex-role stereotyping in the home and family; child-rearing practices; school curricula and activities; marriage laws; divorce laws; access to abortion and birth control; differentials in compensation and the definition of compensable work; appearance of alternative lifestyles; men's health; religion; literature; manners and fashion.
5. Steinem uses the race-related term "Uncle-Tom" to describe woman's social role. Is this language accurate, effective, or offensive?
6. Yamada defines invisibility as feeling powerless over one's life and knowing what it is like to not make a difference for anyone or anything. Describe and explain your own experience with feeling invisible or powerless, or describe a situation where you were aware of another person's invisibility.

FEMINISM CHALLENGED

Understanding the Difference

Phyllis Schlafly

For more than 20 years, Phyllis Schlafly has been the most widely known conservative female critic of modern feminism. The wife of an attorney and the mother of six children, she is a Phi Beta Kappa graduate of Washington University in St. Louis and holds an MA in political science from Harvard. A prominent and extremely successful fund-raiser and campaigner for Republican Party candidates, she is the author of the 1964 best-seller, *A Choice Not an Echo*, and six other books. She has had her own radio program and newspaper column and has served on the Illinois Commission on the Status of Women. She is also a spokesperson in the "pro-life" and "family-values" movements. "Understanding the Difference" is excerpted from her 1977 book, *The Power of the Positive Woman*.

1   The first requirement for the acquisition of power by the Positive Woman is to understand the differences between men and women. Your outlook on life, your faith, your behavior, your potential for fulfillment, all are determined by the parameters of

your original premise. The Positive Woman starts with the assumption that the world is her oyster. She rejoices in the creative capability within her body and the power potential of her mind and spirit. She understands that men and women are different, and that those very differences provide the key to her success as a person and fulfillment as a woman.

2   The women's liberationist, on the other hand, is imprisoned by her own negative view of herself and of her place in the world around her. This view of women was most succinctly expressed in an advertisement designed by the principal women's liberationist organization, the National Organization for Women (NOW), and run in many magazines and newspapers and as spot announcements on many television stations. The advertisement showed a darling curlyheaded girl with the caption: "This healthy, normal baby has a handicap. She was born female."

3   This is the self-articulated dog-in-the-manger, chip-on-the-shoulder, fundamental dogma of the women's liberation movement. Someone—it is not clear who, perhaps God, perhaps the "Establishment," perhaps a conspiracy of male chauvinist pigs—dealt women a foul blow by making them female. It becomes necessary, therefore, for women to agitate and demonstrate and hurl demands on society in order to wrest from an oppressive male-dominated social structure the status that has been wrongfully denied to women through the centuries.

4   By its very nature, therefore, the women's liberation movement precipitates a series of conflict situations—in the legislatures, in the courts, in the schools, in industry—with man targeted as the enemy. Confrontation replaces cooperation as the watchword of all relationships. Women and men become adversaries instead of partners.

5   The second dogma of the women's liberationists is that, of all the injustices perpetrated upon women through the centuries, the most oppressive is the cruel fact that women have babies and men do not. Within the confines of the women's liberationist ideology, therefore, the abolition of this overriding inequality of women becomes the primary goal. This goal must be achieved at any and all costs—to the woman herself, to the baby, to the family, and to society. Women must be made equal to men in their ability *not* to become pregnant and *not* to be expected to care for babies they may bring into the world.

6   This is why women's liberationists are compulsively involved in the drive to make abortion and child-care centers for all women, regardless of religion or income, both socially acceptable and government-financed. Former Congresswoman Bella Abzug has defined the goal: "to enforce the constitutional right of females to terminate pregnancies that they do not wish to continue."

7   If man is targeted as the enemy, and the ultimate goal of women's liberation is independence from men and the avoidance of pregnancy and its consequences, then lesbianism is logically the highest form in the ritual of women's liberation. Many, such as Kate Millett, come to this conclusion, although many others do not.

8   The Positive Woman will never travel that dead-end road. It is self-evident to the Positive Woman that the female body with its baby-producing organs was not designed by a conspiracy of men but by the Divine Architect of the human race. Those

who think it is unfair that women have babies, whereas men cannot, will have to take up their complaint with God because no other power is capable of changing that fundamental fact. On some college campuses, I have been assured that other methods of reproduction will be developed. But most of us must deal with the real world rather than with the imagination of dreamers.

9   Another feature of the woman's natural role is the obvious fact that women can breast-feed babies and men cannot. This functional role was not imposed by conspiratorial males seeking to burden women with confining chores, but must be recognized as part of the plan of the Divine Architect for the survival of the human race through the centuries and in the countries that know no pasteurization of milk or sterilization of bottles.

10   The Positive Woman looks upon her femaleness and her fertility as part of her purpose, her potential, and her power. She rejoices that she has a capability for creativity that men can never have.

11   The third basic dogma of the women's liberation movement is that there is no difference between male and female except the sex organs, and that all those physical, cognitive, and emotional differences you *think* are there, are merely the result of centuries of restraints imposed by a male-dominated society and sex-stereotyped schooling. The role imposed on women is, by definition, inferior, according to the women's liberationists.

12   The Positive Woman knows that, while there are some physical competitions in which women are better (and can command more money) than men, including those that put a premium on grace and beauty, such as figure skating, the superior physical strength of males over females in competitions of strength, speed, and short-term endurance is beyond rational dispute.

13   In the Olympic Games, women not only cannot win any medals in competition with men, the gulf between them is so great that they cannot even qualify for the contests with men. No amount of training from infancy can enable women to throw the discus as far as men, or to match men in push-ups or in lifting weights. In track and field events, individual male records surpass those of women by 10 to 20 percent.

14   Female swimmers today are beating Johnny Weissmuller's records, but today's male swimmers are better still. Chris Evert can never win a tennis match against Jimmy Connors. If we removed lady's tees from golf courses, women would be out of the game. Putting women in football or wrestling matches can only be an exercise in laughs.

15   The Olympic Games, whose rules require strict verification to ascertain that no male enters a female contest and, with his masculine advantage, unfairly captures a woman's medal, formerly insisted on a visual inspection of the contestants' bodies. Science, however, has discovered that men and women are so innately different physically that their maleness/femaleness can be conclusively established by means of a simple skin test of fully clothed persons.

16   If there is *anyone* who should oppose enforced sex-equality, it is the women athletes. Babe Didrickson, who played and defeated some of the great male athletes of her time, is unique in the history of sports.[1]

17   If sex equality were enforced in professional sports, it would mean that men could enter the women's tournaments and win most of the money. Bobby Riggs has already threatened: "I think that men 55 years and over should be allowed to play women's tournaments—like the Virginia Slims. Everybody ought to know there's no sex after 55 anyway."

18   The Positive Woman remembers the essential validity of the old prayer: "Lord, give me the strength to change what I can change, the serenity to accept what I cannot change, and the wisdom to discern the difference." The women's liberationists are expending their time and energies erecting a make-believe world in which they hypothesize that *if* schooling were gender-free, and *if* the same money were spent on male and female sports programs, and *if* women were permitted to compete on equal terms, *then* they would prove themselves to be physically equal. Meanwhile, the Positive Woman has put the ineradicable physical differences into her mental computer, programmed her plan of action, and is already on the way to personal achievement.

19   Thus, while some militant women spend their time demanding more money for professional sports, ice skater Janet Lynn, a truly Positive Woman, quietly signed the most profitable financial contract in the history of women's athletics. It was not the strident demands of the women's liberationists that brought high prizes to women's tennis, but the discovery by sports promoters that beautiful female legs gracefully moving around the court made women's tennis a highly marketable television production to delight male audiences.

20   Many people thought that the remarkable filly named Ruffian would prove that a female race horse could compete equally with a male. Even with the handicap of extra weights placed on the male horse, the race was a disaster for the female. The gallant Ruffian gave her all in a noble effort to compete, but broke a leg in the race and, despite the immediate attention of top veterinarians, had to be put away.

21   Despite the claims of the women's liberation movement, there are countless physical differences between men and women. The female body is 50 to 60 percent water, the male 60 to 70 percent water, which explains why males can dilute alcohol better than women and delay its effect. The average woman is about 25 percent fatty tissue, while the male is 15 percent, making women more buoyant in water and able to swim with less effort. Males have a tendency to color blindness. Only 5 percent of persons who get gout are female. Boys are born bigger. Women live longer in most countries of the world, not only in the United States where we have a hard-driving competitive pace. Women excel in manual dexterity, verbal skills, and memory recall.

22   Arianna Stassinopoulos in her book *The Female Woman* has done a good job of spelling out the many specific physical differences that are so innate and so all-pervasive that

> even if Women's Lib was given a hundred, a thousand, ten thousand years in which to eradicate *all* the differences between the sexes, it would still be an impossible undertaking. . . .
> It is inconceivable that millions of years of evolutionary selection during a period of marked sexual division of labor have not left pronounced traces on the innate character of men and women. Aggressiveness, and mechanical and spatial skills, a sense of

direction, and physical strength—all masculine characteristics—are the qualities essential for a hunter; even food gatherers need these same qualities for defense and exploration. The prolonged period of dependence of human children, the difficulty of carrying the peculiarly heavy and inert human baby—a much heavier, clumsier burden than the monkey infant and much less able to cling on for safety—meant that women could not both look after their children and be hunters and explorers. Early humans learned to take advantage of this period of dependence to transmit rules, knowledge and skills to their offspring—women needed to develop verbal skills, a talent for personal relationships, and a predilection for nurturing going even beyond the maternal instinct.[2]

23   Does the physical advantage of men doom women to a life of servility and subservience? The Positive Woman knows that she has a complementary advantage which is at least as great—and, in the hands of a skillful woman, far greater. The Divine Architect who gave men a superior strength to lift weights also gave women a different kind of superior strength.

24   The women's liberationists and their dupes who try to tell each other that the sexual drive of men and women is really the same, and that it is only societal restraints that inhibit women from an equal desire, an equal enjoyment, and an equal freedom from the consequences, are doomed to frustration forever. It just isn't so, and pretending cannot make it so. The differences are not a woman's weakness but her strength.

25   Dr. Robert Collins, who has had ten years' experience in listening to and advising young women at a large eastern university, put his finger on the reason why casual "sexual activity" is such a cheat on women:

> A basic flaw in this new morality is the assumption that males and females are the same sexually. The simplicity of the male anatomy and its operation suggests that to a man, sex can be an activity apart from his whole being, a drive related to the organs themselves.
>
> In a woman, the complex internal organization, correlated with her other hormonal systems, indicates her sexuality must involve her total self. On the other hand, the man is orgasm-oriented with a drive that ignores most other aspects of the relationship. The woman is almost totally different. She is engulfed in romanticism and tries to find and express her total feelings for her partner.
>
> A study at a midwestern school shows that 80 percent of the women who had intercourse hoped to marry their partner. Only 12 percent of the men expected the same.
>
> Women say that soft, warm promises and tender touches are delightful, but that the act itself usually leads to a "Is that all there is to it?" reaction. . . .
>
> [A typical reaction is]: "It sure wasn't worth it. It was no fun at the time. I've been worried ever since. . . ."
>
> The new morality is a fad. It ignores history, it denies the physical and mental composition of human beings, it is intolerant, exploitative, and is oriented toward intercourse, not love.[3]

26   The new generation can brag all it wants about the new liberation of the new morality, but it is still the woman who is hurt the most. The new morality isn't just a

"fad"—it is a cheat and a thief. It robs the woman of her virtue, her youth, her beauty, and her love—for nothing, just nothing. It has produced a generation of young women searching for their identity, bored with sexual freedom, and despondent from the loneliness of living a life without commitment. They have abandoned the old commandments, but they can't find any new rules that work.

27   The Positive Woman recognizes the fact that, when it comes to sex, women are simply not the equal of men. The sexual drive of men is much stronger than that of women. That is how the human race was designed in order that it might perpetuate itself. The other side of the coin is that it is easier for women to control their sexual appetites. A Positive Woman cannot defeat a man in a wrestling or boxing match, but she can motivate him, inspire him, encourage him, teach him, restrain him, reward him, and have power over him that he can never achieve over her with all his muscle. How or whether a Positive Woman uses her power is determined solely by the way she alone defines her goals and develops her skills.

28   The differences between men and women are also emotional and psychological. Without woman's innate maternal instinct, the human race would have died out centuries ago. There is nothing so helpless in all earthly life as the newborn infant. It will die within hours if not cared for. Even in the most primitive, uneducated societies, women have always cared for their newborn babies. They didn't need any schooling to teach them how. They didn't need any welfare workers to tell them it is their social obligation. Even in societies to whom such concepts as "ought," "social responsibility," and "compassion for the helpless" were unknown, mothers cared for their new babies.

29   Why? Because caring for a baby serves the natural maternal need of a woman. Although not nearly so total as the baby's need, the woman's need is nonetheless real.

30   The overriding psychological need of a woman is to love something alive. A baby fulfills this need in the lives of most women. If a baby is not available to fill that need, women search for a baby-substitute. This is the reason why women have traditionally gone into teaching and nursing careers. They are doing what comes naturally to the female psyche. The schoolchild or the patient of any age provides an outlet for a woman to express her natural maternal need.

31   This maternal need in women is the reason why mothers whose children have grown up and flown from the nest are sometimes cut loose from their psychological moorings. The maternal need in women can show itself in love for grandchildren, nieces, nephews, or even neighbors' children. The maternal need in some women has even manifested itself in an extraordinary affection lavished on a dog, a cat, or a parakeet.

32   This is not to say that every woman must have a baby in order to be fulfilled. But it is to say that fulfillment for most women involves expressing their natural maternal urge by loving and caring for someone.

33   The women's liberation movement complains that traditional stereotyped roles assume that women are "passive" and that men are "aggressive." The anomaly is that a woman's most fundamental emotional need is not passive at all, but active. A woman naturally seeks to love affirmatively and to show that love in an active way by caring for the object of her affections.

34   The Positive Woman finds somebody on whom she can lavish her maternal love so that it doesn't well up inside her and cause psychological frustrations. Surely no woman is so isolated by geography or insulated by spirit that she cannot find someone worthy of her maternal love. All persons, men and women, gain by sharing something of themselves with their fellow humans, but women profit most of all because it is part of their very nature.

35   One of the strangest quirks of women's liberationists is their complaint that societal restraints prevent men from crying in public or showing their emotions, but permit women to do so, and that therefore we should "liberate" men to enable them, too, to cry in public. The public display of fear, sorrow, anger, and irritation reveals a lack of self-discipline that should be avoided by the Positive Woman just as much as by the Positive Man. Maternal love, however, is not a weakness but a manifestation of strength and service, and it should be nurtured by the Positive Woman.

36   Most women's organizations, recognizing the preference of most women to avoid hard-driving competition, handle the matter of succession of officers by the device of a nominating committee. This eliminates the unpleasantness and the tension of a competitive confrontation every year or two. Many women's organizations customarily use a prayer attributed to Mary, Queen of Scots, which is an excellent analysis by a woman of women's faults:

> Keep us, O God, from pettiness; let us be large in thought, in word, in deed. Let us be done with fault-finding and leave off self-seeking. . . . Grant that we may realize it is the little things that create differences, that in the big things of life we are at one.

37   Another silliness of the women's liberationists is their frenetic desire to force all women to accept the title *Ms* in place of *Miss* or *Mrs.* If Gloria Steinem and Betty Friedan want to call themselves *Ms* in order to conceal their marital status, their wishes should be respected.

38   But that doesn't satisfy the women's liberationists. They want all women to be compelled to use *Ms* whether they like it or not. The women's liberation movement has been waging a persistent campaign to browbeat the media into using *Ms* as the standard title for all women. The women's liberationists have already succeeding in getting the Department of Health, Education and Welfare to forbid schools and colleges from identifying women students as *Miss* or *Mrs.*[4]

39   All polls show that the majority of women do not care to be called *Ms.* A Roper poll indicated that 81 percent of the women questioned said they prefer *Miss* or *Mrs.* to *Ms.* Most married women feel they worked hard for the *r* in their names, and they don't care to be gratuitously deprived of it. Most single women don't care to have their name changed to an unfamiliar title that at best conveys overtones of feminist ideology and is polemical in meaning and at worst connotes misery instead of joy. Thus, Kate Smith, a very Positive Woman, proudly proclaimed on television that she is "Miss Kate Smith, not Ms." Like other Positive Women, she has been succeeding while negative women have been complaining.

40   Finally, women are different from men in dealing with the fundamentals of life itself. Men are philosophers, women are practical, and 'twas ever thus. Men may

philosophize about how life began and where we are heading; women are concerned about feeding the kids today. No woman would ever, as Karl Marx did, spend years reading political philosophy in the British Museum while her child starved to death. Women don't take naturally to a search for the intangible and the abstract. The Positive Woman knows who she is and where she is going, and she will reach her goal because the longest journey starts with a very practical first step. . . .

41 An effort to eliminate the differences by social engineering or legislative or constitutional tinkering cannot succeed, which is fortunate, but social relationships and spiritual values can be ruptured in the attempt. Thus the role reversals being forced upon high school students, under which guidance counselors urge reluctant girls to take "shop" and boys to take "home economics," further confuse a generation already unsure about its identity. They are as wrong as efforts to make a left-handed child right-handed.[5]

Notes

1. Babe Didrikson, a beautifully coordinated woman who excelled at every sport she tried, is considered by some to be the greatest all-around American athlete. Starting in track and field events, she won two gold medals in the 1932 Olympics. Turning to tennis, she gave champion Bill Tilden a good match. She would have won the big women's tennis tournaments such as Forest Hills, but in those days professionals were excluded. She was a star baseball and basketball player who once struck out the great Joe DiMaggio in Yankee Stadium.

Having conquered most other sports, the last one she learned was golf. Miss Didrikson quickly mastered this difficult game and won seventeen tournaments in a row. When she played in a charity exhibition golf match with the famous Babe Ruth, she bet him $50 a hole that she could outdrive him. Ruth, who could hit a golf ball much farther than his baseball home runs, quickly accepted. After four drives, Babe Ruth had lost $200 and he refused to bet any more. In 1943, Miss Didrikson entered the Phoenix Open Golf Tournament and won the qualifying medal with a sixty-seven, beating such great golfers as Ben Hogan, Sam Sneed, and Byron Nelson. Then the powers that ran the men's professional golf tournaments barred her from further play.

The dean of sportswriters, Grantland Rice, frequently said that Miss Didrikson could beat any man in the world in multisport competition that included such events as running, the high jump, the long jump, baseball, tennis, and golf.

Miss Didrikson was also an inspiration by the brave way she cheerfully accepted terminal cancer at age forty. Most people never knew that she won a dozen golf tournaments while playing with a colostomy.

2. Arianna Stassinopoulos, *The Female Woman* (New York: Random House, 1973), pp. 30–31.

3. *Chicago Tribune*, August 17, 1975.

4. HEW Regulation on Sex Discrimination in Schools and Colleges, effective July 18, 1975, # 86.21(c)(4).

5. The Minnesota Sex Bias Report was sent for comment to Dr. Rhoda L. Lorand, a nationally respected clinical psychologist and psychoanalyst in New York City. She stated bluntly that, if the program was adopted, the result would be "the promotion of lesbianism,

the downgrading of the institution of marriage, of motherhood, childrearing, the nuclear family, the advocacy of single parenthood and communal living, as well as contempt for all occupations and qualities traditionally recognized as feminine." She added:

> Putting pressure on boys and girls to behave like the opposite sex is placing them under a great strain because these pressures are at odds with biological endowment. Therapists have begun to note the confusion and unhappiness resulting from the blurring of gender-identity. Conflicting pressures between environmental and instinctual drives hinder the development of a firm sense of identity as a male or female (an intended goal of Women's Lib), lacking which the individual cannot acquire stability, self-esteem, or clear-cut goals.

> Moreover, it is taking all the joy and excitement out of life. Girls are made to feel ashamed of their longings to be courted and cherished, to be sexually attractive, to look forward to marriage, motherhood, and homemaking. Boys are made to feel ashamed of their chivalrous impulses. Feelings of protectiveness toward a girl and of manliness cause them to feel guilty and foolish, resulting in a retreat into passivity, while the girls end up unhappily trying to be sexual buddies of the boys. This unisex drive had its beginnings in the hippie movement and has been greatly intensified by all the publicity given by the communications media to the demands and accusations of the femininists (who really should be called masculinists, since they despise everything feminine).

Family Affairs

Maya Angelou

Born Marguerita Johnson in St. Louis in 1928, Angelou was raised by her grandmother in the small town of Stamps, Arkansas. An actor, musician, and writer, Angelou has toured the world with *Porgy and Bess,* composed scores for two screenplays, and written lyrics for Roberta Flack. She received Tony Award nominations in 1973 for her Broadway debut and in 1977 for her performance in *Roots.* Her poetry book, *Just Give Me a Cool Drink of Water 'fore I Diiie,* was nominated in 1972 for a Pulitzer Prize. She is also the recipient of a MacArthur Foundation award.

> You let down, from arched
> Windows,
> Over hand-cut stones of your
> Cathedrals, seas of golden hair.

> 5 While I, pulled by dusty braids,
> Left furrows in the
> Sands of African beaches.

Princes and commoners
Climbed over waves to reach
10 Your vaulted boudoirs,

As the sun, capriciously,
Struck silver fire from waiting
Chains, where I was bound.

My screams never reached
15 The rare tower where you
Lay, birthing masters for
My sons, and for my
Daughters, a swarm of
Unclean badgers, to consume
20 Their history.

Tired now of pedestal existence
For fear of flying
And vertigo, you descend
And step lightly over
25 My centuries of horror
And take my hand,

Smiling call me
Sister.

Sister, accept
30 That I must wait a
While. Allow an age
Of dust to fill
Ruts left on my
Beach in Africa.

black women and feminism

bell hooks

bell hooks is the pseudonym for Gloria Watkins. She was born in 1952, is a feminist writer and cultural critic, and teaches English and women's studies at Oberlin College. Her books include *And There We Wept,* poems; *Yearning: Race, Gender and Cultural Politics; A Woman's Mourning Song; Black Looks: Race and Representation; Breaking Bread: Insurgent Black Intellectual Life; Ain't I a*

Woman: Black Women and Feminism; Feminist Theory: From Margin to Center; and *Talking Back: Thinking Feminist, Thinking Black* (1989), from which "black women and feminism" is taken. Her column "Sisters of the Yam" appears monthly in *Zeta* magazine.

1   Toward the end of 1987 I spoke at Tufts University at an annual dinner for black women. My topic was "Black Women in Predominantly White Institutions." I was excited by the idea of talking with so many young black women but surprised when these women suggested that sexism was not a political issue of concern to black women, that the serious issue was racism. I've heard this response many times, yet somehow I did not expect that I would need to prove over and over that sexism ensures that many black females will be exploited and victimized. Confronted by these young black women to whom sexism was not important, I felt that feminism had failed to develop a politics that addresses black women. Particularly, I felt that black women active in black liberation struggles in the 1960s and early 1970s, who had spoken and written on sexism (remember the anthology *The Black Woman,* edited by Toni Cade Bambara?) had let our younger sisters down by not making more of a sustained political effort so that black women (and black people) would have greater understanding of the impact of sexist oppression on our lives.

2   When I began to share my own experiences of racism and sexism, pointing to incidents (particularly in relationships with black men), a veil was lifted. Suddenly the group acknowledged what had been previously denied—the ways sexism wounds us as black women. I had talked earlier about the way many black women students in predominantly white institutions keep silent in classes, stating emphatically that our progress in such places requires us to have a voice, to not remain silent. In the ensuing discussion, women commented on black fathers who had told their daughters "nobody wants a loud-talking black woman." The group expressed ambivalent feelings about speaking, particularly on political issues in classroom settings where they were often attacked or unsupported by other black women students.

3   Their earlier reluctance to acknowledge sexism reminded me of previous arguments with other groups of women about both the book and the film *The Color Purple.* Our discussions focused almost solely on whether portraying brutal sexist domination of a black female by a black male had any basis in reality. I was struck by the extent to which folks will go to argue that sexism in black communities has not promoted the abuse and subjugation of black women by black men. This fierce denial has its roots in the history of black people's response to racism and white supremacy. Traditionally it has been important for black people to assert that slavery, apartheid, and continued discrimination have not undermined the humanity of black people, that not only has the race been preserved but that the survival of black families and communities are the living testimony of our victory. To acknowledge then that our families and communities have been undermined by sexism would not only require an acknowledgement that racism is not the only form of domination and oppression that affects us as a people; it would mean critically challenging the assumption that

our survival as a people depends on creating a cultural climate in which black men can achieve manhood within paradigms constructed by white patriarchy.

4   Often the history of our struggle as black people is made synonymous with the efforts of black males to have patriarchal power and privilege. As one black woman college student put it, "In order to redeem the race we have to redeem black manhood." If such redemption means creating a society in which black men assume the stereotypical male role of provider and head of household, then sexism is seen not as destructive but as essential to the promotion and maintenance of the black family. Tragically, it has been our acceptance of this model that has prevented us from acknowledging that black sexist domination has *not* enhanced or enriched black family life. The seemingly positive aspects of the patriarchy (caretaker and provider) have been the most difficult for masses of black men to realize, and the negative aspects (maintaining control through psychological or physical violence) are practiced daily. Until black people redefine in a nonsexist revolutionary way the terms of our liberation, black women and men will always be confronted with the issue of whether supporting feminist efforts to end sexism is inimical to our interests as a people.

5   In her insightful essay, "Considering Feminism as a Model for Social Change," Sheila Radford-Hill makes the useful critique that black women producing feminist theory, myself included, focus more on the racism of white women within feminist movement, and on the importance of racial difference, than on the ways feminist struggle could strengthen and help black communities. In part, the direction of our work was shaped by the nature of our experience. Not only were there very few black women writing feminist theory, but most of us were not living in or working with black communities. The aim of *Ain't I A Woman* was not to focus on the racism of white women. Its primary purpose was to establish that sexism greatly determines the social status and experience of black women. I did not try to examine the ways that struggling to end sexism would benefit black people, but this is my current concern.

6   Many black women insist that they do not join the feminist movement because they cannot bond with white women who are racist. If one argues that there really are some white women who are resisting and challenging racism, who are genuinely committed to ending white supremacy, one is accused of being naive, of not acknowledging history. Most black women, rich and poor, have contact with white women, usually in work settings. In such settings black women cooperate with white women despite racism. Yet black women are reluctant to express solidarity with white feminists. Black women's consciousness is shaped by internalized racism and by reactionary white women's concerns as they are expressed in popular culture, such as daytime soap operas or in the world of white fashion and cosmetic products, which masses of black women consume without rejecting this racist propaganda and devaluing of black women.

7   Emulating white women or bonding with them in these "apolitical" areas is not consistently questioned or challenged. Yet I do not know a single black woman advocate of feminist politics who is not bombarded by ongoing interrogations by other

black people about linking with racist white women (as though we lack the political acumen to determine whether white women are racists, or when it is in our interest to act in solidarity with them).

8　At times, the insistence that feminism is really "a white female thing that has nothing to do with black women" masks black female rage towards white women, a rage rooted in the historical servant-served relationship where white women have used power to dominate, exploit, and oppress. Many black women share this animosity, and it is evoked again and again when white women attempt to assert control over us. This resistance to white female domination must be separated from a black female refusal to bond with white women engaged in feminist struggle. This refusal is often rooted as well in traditional sexist models: women learn to see one another as enemies, as threats, as competitors. Viewing white women as competitors for jobs, for companions, for valuation in a culture that only values select groups of women, often serves as a barrier to bonding, even in settings where radical white women are not acting in a dominating manner. In some settings it has become a way of one-upping white women for black women to trivialize feminism.

9　Black women must separate feminism as a political agenda from white women or we will never be able to focus on the issue of sexism as it affects black communities. Even though there are a few black women (I am one) who assert that we empower ourselves by using the term feminism, by addressing our concerns as black women as well as our concern with the welfare of the human community globally, we have had little impact. Small groups of black feminist theorists and activists who use the term "black feminism" (the Combahee River Collective is one example) have not had much success in organizing large groups of black women, or stimulating widespread interest in feminist movement. Their statement of purpose and plans for action focus exclusively on black women acknowledging the need for forms of separatism. Here the argument that black women do not collectively advocate feminism because of an unwillingness to bond with racist white women appears most problematic. Key concerns that serve as barriers to black women advocating feminist politics are heterosexism, the fear that one will be seen as betraying black men or promoting hatred of men and as a consequence becoming less desirable to male companions; homophobia (often I am told by black people that all feminists are lesbians); and deeply ingrained misogynist attitudes toward one another, perpetuating sexist thinking and sexist competition.

10　Recently I spoke with a number of black women about why they are not more involved in feminist thinking and feminist movement. Many of them talked about harsh treatment by other black women, about being socially ostracized or talked about in negative and contemptuous ways at all-female gatherings or at conferences on gender issues. A few people committed to feminist politics described times when they found support from white women and resistance from black women peers. A black woman scheduled on a panel arrived late and couldn't find a seat in the room. When she entered and had been standing for a while, I greeted her warmly from the podium and encouraged her to join me as there were seats in front. Not only did she choose to stand, during the break she said to me, "How dare you embarrass me by asking me to come up front." Her tone was quite hostile. I was disturbed that she saw this gesture as an attempt to embarrass her rather than as a gesture of recognition. This is not an isolated case. There are many occasions when we witness the failure of black women to trust one another, when we approach one another with suspicion.

11   Years ago I attended a small conference with about 20 black women. We were to organize a national conference on black feminism. We came from various positions, politics, and sexual preferences. A well-known black woman scholar at a prestigious institution, whose feminist thinking was not deemed appropriately advanced, was treated with contempt and hostility. It was a disturbing time. A number of the black women present had white women companions and lovers. Yet concerning the issue of whether white women should be allowed to attend the conference, they were adamant that it should be for black women only, that white women all too often try to control us. There was no space for constructive critical dialogue. How could they trust white women lovers to unlearn racism, to not be dominating, and yet in this setting act as though all white women were our enemies? The conference never happened. At least one black woman went away from this experience determined never to participate in an activity organized around black feminists or any other feminists. As a group we failed to create an atmosphere of solidarity. The only bonds established were along very traditional lines among the folks who were famous, who talked the loudest and the most, who were more politically correct. And there was no attempt to enable black women with different perspectives to come together.

12   It is our collective responsibility as individual black women committed to feminist movement to work at making space where black women who are just beginning to explore feminist issues can do so without fear of hostile treatment, quick judgments, dismissals, etc.

13   I find more black women than ever before are appearing on panels that focus on gender. Yet I have observed, and other black women thinkers have shared as well, that often these women see gender as a subject for discourse or for increased professional visibility, not for political action. Often professional black women with academic degrees are quite conservative politically. Their perspectives differ greatly from our foremothers who were politically astute, assertive, and radical in their work for social change.

14   Feminist praxis is greatly shaped by academic women and men. Since there are not many academic black women committed to radical politics, especially with a gender focus, there is no collective base in the academy for forging a feminist politics that addresses masses of black women. There is much more work by black women on gender and sexism emerging from scholars who do literary criticism and from creative fiction and drama writers than from women in history, sociology, and political science. While it does not negate commitment to radical politics, in literature it is much easier to separate academic work and political concerns. Concurrently, if black women academics are not committed to feminist ethics, to feminist consciousness-raising, they end up organizing conferences in which social interactions mirror sexist norms, including ways black women regard one another. For the uninitiated

coming to see and learn what feminism centered on black women might be like, this can be quite disillusioning.

15 Often in these settings the word "feminism" is evoked in negative terms, even though sexism and gender issues are discussed. I hear black women academics laying claim to the term "womanist" while rejecting "feminist." I do not think Alice Walker intended this term to deflect from feminist commitment, yet this is often how it is evoked. Walker defines womanist as black feminist or feminist of color. When I hear black women using the term womanist, it is in opposition to the term feminist; it is viewed as constituting something separate from feminist politics shaped by white women. For me, the term womanist is not sufficiently linked to a tradition of radical political commitment to struggle and change. What would a womanist politic look like? If it is a term for black feminist, then why do those who embrace it reject the other?

16 Radford-Hill makes the point:

> Not all black feminists practice or believe in black feminism. Many see black feminism as a vulgar detraction from the goal of female solidarity. Others of us, myself included, see black feminism as a necessary step toward ending racism and sexism, given the nature of gender oppression and the magnitude of society's resistance to racial justice.

17 I believe that women should think less in terms of feminism as an identity and more in terms of "advocating feminism"; to move from emphasis on personal lifestyle issues toward creating political paradigms and radical models of social change that emphasize collective as well as individual change. For this reason I do not call myself a black feminist. Black women must continue to insist on our right to participate in shaping feminist theory and practice that addresses our racial concerns as well as our feminist issues. Current feminist scholarship can be useful to black women in formulating critical analyses of gender issues about black people, particularly feminist work on parenting. (When I first read Dorothy Dinnerstein, it was interesting to think about her work in terms of black mother-son relationships.)

18 Black women need to construct a model of feminist theorizing and scholarship that is inclusive, that widens our options, that enhances our understanding of black experience and gender. Significantly, the most basic task confronting black feminists (irrespective of the terms we use to identify ourselves) is to educate one another and black people about sexism, about the ways resisting sexism can empower black women, a process which makes sharing feminist vision more difficult. Radford-Hill identifies "the crisis of black womanhood" as a serious problem that must be considered politically, asserting that "the extent to which black feminists can articulate and solve the crisis of black womanhood is the extent to which black women will undergo feminist transformation."

19 Black women must identify ways feminist thought and practice can aid in our process of self-recovery and share that knowledge with our sisters. This is the base on which to build political solidarity. When that grounding exists, black women will be fully engaged in feminist movement that transforms self, community, and society.

WRITING ASSIGNMENTS

Analysis

1. Trace the continuity and note the differences in the perspectives of Tocqueville, Roosevelt, Lundberg and Farnham, Schlafly, and Farrell.
2. Using the selections by Friedan and Steinem as representative of mainstream feminism, assess the tone and accuracy of Schlafly's characterization of the NOW advertisement and of women liberationists' attitudes toward men, motherhood, and sexual orientation.
3. Compare and contrast the views of Schlafly and Fausto-Sterling (Chapter 9) on women in sports. Which do you find more persuasive? Why?
4. Compare Schlafly's views on the differences between men and women to the perspectives offered by Barash, Gorman, Bem, or Friedl (Chapter 1).
5. How does Angelou's poem compare and contrast the history and personal experiences of women of European and African origin?
6. Explore the ways that the dominant culture's concepts of feminine beauty and of woman as wife-mother-homemaker ignore and devalue women of color and their history.
7. How does hooks characterize and explain African-American masculinity? Why does she reject the model of white manhood as a valid goal for black men?
8. Compare and contrast the perspectives of Angelou and hooks on the relationship between black and white women and on feminism.

Argument

1. In your opinion, is Schlafly's analysis of the differences in sexual drive and behavior between men and women correct?
2. Schlafly accuses the women's liberation movement of two "basic errors": "(1) that there are no emotional or cognitive differences between the sexes, and (2) that women should strive to be like men." Is Schlafly's characterization of the women's movement accurate? Draw evidence to support your answer from the selections in this chapter.
3. Do you agree with the characterizations of women and with the stance of the speaker in Angelou's "Family Affairs"? Why?
4. Do you agree with bell hooks that black women should participate in the feminist movement? Why? If so, how might they influence it?

Personal Writing and Writing from Research

1. Respond to Schlafly's conclusions: "An effort to eliminate the differences [between men and women] by social engineering or legislative or constitutional tinkering cannot succeed, but social relationships and spiritual values can be ruptured in the attempt. . . . They [these efforts] are as wrong as efforts to make a left-handed child right-handed."
2. In a personal essay, narrative, or poem, chronicle the history of women or men in your ethnic or racial group. Include images, like those chosen by Angelou,

through which the members of this group would recognize either their idealized or actual history.

3. *Collaborative Project:* Write a research paper on some specific aspect of the female African-American slave experience.
4. *Collaborative Project:* Analyze the way that stereotypes associated with African-American, Latin, Asian-American, or European men or women correlate with their social status and gender role.
5. Identify and report on the instances in recent history in which rape has been used as a political weapon of domination and repression.
6. The theme of women's silence, mentioned by both Yamada and hooks, recurs throughout this book. In a personal essay, reflect on the significance of lessons that men and women are taught about silence and voice.

MODERN MASCULINITIES

A New Vision of Masculinity

Cooper Thompson

Thompson founded Resources for Change, a Cambridge, Massachusetts, organization providing training on masculinity, sex roles, and homophobia. A member of the National Council of the National Organization for Changing Men and the coordinator of the Campaign to End Homophobia, he has conducted workshops on changing male socialization and has developed antisexist curricula for schools. "A New Vision of Masculinity" first appeared in 1985 in *Changing Men,* a journal dedicated to examining fundamental changes in men's lives.

1   I was once asked by a teacher in a suburban high school to give a guest presentation on male roles. She hoped that I might help her deal with four boys who exercised extraordinary control over the other boys in the class. Using ridicule and their status as physically imposing athletes, these four wrestlers had succeeded in stifling the participation of the other boys, who were reluctant to make comments in class discussions.

2   As a class we talked about the ways in which boys got status in that school and how they got put-down by others. I was told that the most humiliating putdown was being called a "fag." The list of behaviors which could elicit ridicule filled two large chalkboards, and it was detailed and comprehensive; I got the sense that a boy in this school had to conform to rigid, narrow standards of masculinity to avoid being called

a fag. I, too, felt this pressure and became very conscious of my mannerisms in front of the group. Partly from exasperation, I decided to test the seriousness of these assertions. Since one of the four boys had some streaks of pink in his shirt, and since he had told me that wearing pink was grounds for being called a fag, I told him that I thought he was a fag. Instead of laughing, he said, "I'm going to kill you."

3   Such is the stereotypic definition of strength that is associated with masculinity. But it is a very limited definition of strength, one based on dominance and control and acquired through the humiliation and degradation of others.

4   Contrast this with a view of strength offered by Pam McAllister in her introduction to *Reweaving the Web of Life:*

> The "Strength" card in my Tarot deck depicts, not a warrior going off to battle with his armor and his mighty sword, but a woman stroking a lion. The woman has not slain the lion nor maced it, not netted it, nor has she put on it a muzzle or a leash. And though the lion clearly has teeth and long sharp claws, the woman is not hiding, nor has she sought a protector, nor has she grown muscles. She doesn't appear to be talking to the lion, nor flattering it, nor tossing it fresh meat to distract its hungry jaws.
>
> The woman on the "Strength" card wears a flowing white dress and a garland of flowers. With one hand she cups the lion's jaws, with the other she caresses its nose. The lion on the card has big yellow eyes and a long red tongue curling out of its mouth. One paw is lifted and the mane falls in thick red curls across its broad torso. The woman. The lion. Together they depict strength.

5   This image of strength stands in direct contrast to the strength embodied in the actions of the four wrestlers. The collective strength of the woman and the lion is a strength unknown in a system of traditional male values. Other human qualities are equally foreign to a traditional conception of masculinity. In workshops I've offered on the male role stereotype, teachers and other school personnel easily generate lists of attitudes and behaviors which boys typically seem to not learn. Included in this list are being supportive and nurturant, accepting one's vulnerability and being able to ask for help, valuing women and "women's work," understanding and expressing emotions (except for anger), the ability to empathize with and empower other people, and learning to resolve conflict in non-aggressive, non-competitive ways.

LEARNING VIOLENCE

6   All of this should come as no surprise. Traditional definitions of masculinity include attributes such as independence, pride, resiliency, self-control, and physical strength. This is precisely the image of the Marlboro man, and to some extent, these are desirable attributes for boys and girls. But masculinity goes beyond these qualities to stress competitiveness, toughness, aggressiveness, and power. In this context, threats to one's status, however small, cannot be avoided or taken lightly. If a boy is called a fag, it means that he is perceived as weak or timid—and therefore not masculine enough for his peers. There is enormous pressure for him to fight back. Not being tough at these moments only proves the allegation.

7   Violence is learned not just as a way for boys to defend allegations that they are feminized, but as an effective, appropriate way for them to normally behave. In "The Civic Advocacy of Violence" Wayne Ewing clearly states:

> I used to think that we simply tolerated and permitted male abusiveness in our society. I have now come to understand rather, that we *advocate* physical violence. Violence is presented as effective. Violence is taught as the normal, appropriate and necessary behavior of power and control. Analyses which interweave advocacy of male violence with "SuperBowl Culture" have never been refuted. Civic expectations—translated into professionalism, financial commitments, city planning for recreational space, the raising of male children for competitive sport, the corporate ethics of business ownership of athletic teams, profiteering on entertainment—all result in the monument of the National Football League, symbol and reality at once of the advocacy of violence.

8   Ultimately, violence is the tool which maintains what I believe are the two most critical socializing forces in a boy's life: *homophobia,* the hatred of gay men (who are stereotyped as feminine) or those men believed to be gay, as well as the fear of being perceived as gay; and *misogyny,* the hatred of women. The two forces are targeted at different classes of victims, but they are really just the flip sides of the same coin. Homophobia is the hatred of feminine qualities in men while misogyny is the hatred of feminine qualities in women. The boy who is called a fag is the target of other boys' homophobia as well as the victim of his own homophobia. While the overt message is the absolute need to avoid being feminized, the implication is that females—and all that they traditionally represent—are contemptible. The United States Marines have a philosophy which conveniently combines homophobia and misogyny in the belief that "When you want to create a group of male killers, you kill 'the woman' in them."

9   The pressures of homophobia and misogyny in boys' lives have been poignantly demonstrated to me each time that I have repeated a simple yet provocative activity with students. I ask them to answer the question, "If you woke up tomorrow and discovered that you were the opposite sex from the one you are now, how would you and your life be different?" Girls consistently indicate that there are clear advantages to being a boy—from increased independence and career opportunities to decreased risks of physical and sexual assault—and eagerly answer the question. But boys often express disgust at this possibility and even refuse sometimes to answer the question. In her reports of a broadbased survey using this question, Alice Baumgartner reports the following responses as typical of boys: "If I were a girl, I'd be stupid and weak as a string;" "I would have to wear make-up, cook, be a mother, and yuckky stuff like that;" "I would have to hate snakes. Everything would be miserable;" "If I were a girl, I'd kill myself."

THE COSTS OF MASCULINITY

10   The costs associated with a traditional view of masculinity are enormous, and the damage occurs at both personal and societal levels. The belief that a boy should be

tough (aggressive, competitive, and daring) can create emotional pain for him. While a few boys experience short-term success for their toughness, there is little security in the long run. Instead, it leads to a series of challenges which few, if any, boys ultimately win. There is no security in being at the top when so many other boys are competing for the same status. Toughness also leads to increased chances of stress, physical injury, and even early death. It is considered manly to take extreme physical risks and voluntarily engage in combative, hostile activities.

11   The flip side of toughness—nurturance—is not a quality perceived as masculine and thus not valued. Because of this boys and men experience a greater emotional distance from other people and fewer opportunities to participate in meaningful interpersonal relationships. Studies consistently show that fathers spend very small amounts of time interacting with their children. In addition, men report that they seldom have intimate relationships with other men, reflecting their homophobia. They are afraid of getting too close and don't know how to take down the walls that they have built between themselves.

12   As boys grow older and accept adult roles, the larger social costs of masculinity clearly emerge. Most women experience male resistance to an expansion of women's roles; one of the assumptions of traditional masculinity is the belief that women should be subordinate to men. The consequence is that men are often not willing to accept females as equal, competent partners in personal and professional settings. Whether the setting is a sexual relationship, the family, the streets, or the battlefield, men are continuously engaged in efforts to dominate. Statistics on child abuse consistently indicate that the vast majority of abusers are men, and that there is no "typical" abuser. Rape may be the fastest growing crime in the United States. And it is men, regardless of nationality, who provoke and sustain war. In short, traditional masculinity is life threatening.

NEW SOCIALIZATION FOR BOYS

13   Masculinity, like many other human traits, is determined by both biological and environmental factors. While some believe that biological factors are significant in shaping some masculine behavior, there is undeniable evidence that cultural and environmental factors are strong enough to override biological impulses. What is it, then, that we should be teaching boys about being a man in a modern world?

- Boys must learn to accept their vulnerability, learn to express a range of emotions such as fear and sadness, and learn to ask for help and support in appropriate situations.
- Boys must learn to be gentle, nurturant, cooperative, and communicative, and in particular, learn non-violent means of resolving conflicts.
- Boys must learn to accept those attitudes and behaviors which have traditionally been labeled feminine as necessary for full human development—thereby reducing homophobia and misogyny. This is tantamount to teaching boys to love other boys and girls.

14   Certain qualities like courage, physical strength, and independence, which are traditionally associated with masculinity, are indeed positive qualities for males, provided that they are not manifested in obsessive ways nor used to exploit or dominate others. It is not necessary to completely disregard or unlearn what is traditionally called masculine. I believe, however, that the three areas above are crucial for developing a broader view of masculinity, one which is healthier for all life.

15   These three areas are equally crucial for reducing aggressive, violent behavior among boys and men. Males must learn to cherish life for the sake of their *own* wholeness as human beings, not just *for* their children, friends, and lovers. If males were more nurturant, they would be less likely to hurt those they love.

16   Leonard Eron, writing in the *American Psychologist,* puts the issue of unlearning aggression and learning nurturance in clear-cut terms:

> Socialization is crucial in determining levels of aggression. No matter how aggression is measured or observed, as a group males always score higher than females. But this is not true for all girls. There are some girls who seem to have been socialized like boys who are just as aggressive as boys. Just as some females can learn to be aggressive, so males can learn *not* to be aggressive. If we want to reduce the level of aggression in society, we should also discourage boys from aggression very early on in life and reward them too for other behaviors; in other words, we should socialize boys more like girls, and they should be encouraged to develop socially positive qualities such as tenderness, cooperation, and aesthetic appreciation. The level of individual aggression in society will be reduced only when male adolescents and young adults, as a result of socialization, subscribe to the same standards of behavior as have been traditionally encouraged for women.

17   Where will this change in socialization occur? In his first few years, much of a boy's learning about masculinity comes from the influences of parents, siblings and images of masculinity such as those found on television. Massive efforts will be needed to make changes here. But at older ages, school curriculum and the school environment provide powerful reinforcing images of traditional masculinity. This reinforcement occurs through a variety of channels, including curriculum content, role modeling, and extracurricular activities, especially competitive sports.

18   School athletics are a microcosm of the socialization of male values. While participation in competitive activities can be enjoyable and healthy, it too easily becomes a lesson in the need for toughness, invulnerability, and dominance. Athletes learn to ignore their own injuries and pain and instead try to injure and inflict pain on others in their attempts to win, regardless of the cost to themselves or their opponents. Yet the lessons learned in athletics are believed to be vital for full and complete masculine development, and as a model for problem-solving in other areas of life.

19   In addition to encouraging traditional male values, schools provide too few experiences in nurturance, cooperation, negotiation, non-violent conflict resolution, and strategies for empathizing with and empowering others. Schools should become places where boys have the opportunity to learn these skills; clearly, they won't learn them on the street, from peers, or on television.

SETTING NEW EXAMPLES

20 Despite the pressure on men to display their masculinity in traditional ways, there are examples of men and boys who are changing. "Fathering" is one example of a positive change. In recent years, there has been a popular emphasis on child-care activities, with men becoming more involved in providing care to children, both professionally and as fathers. This is a clear shift from the more traditional view that child rearing should be delegated to women and is not an appropriate activity for men.

21 For all of the male resistance it has generated, the Women's Liberation Movement has at least provided a stimulus for some men to accept women as equal partners in most areas of life. These are the men who have chosen to learn and grow from women's experiences and together with women are creating new norms for relationships. Popular literature and research on male sex roles are expanding, reflecting a wider interest in masculinity. Weekly news magazines such as *Time* and *Newsweek* have run major stories on the "new masculinity," suggesting that positive changes are taking place in the home and in the workplace. Small groups of men scattered around the country have organized against pornography, battering and sexual assault. Finally, there is the National Organization for Changing Men which has a pro-feminist, pro-gay, pro-"new man" agenda, and its ranks are slowly growing.

22 In schools where I have worked with teachers, they report that years of efforts to enhance educational opportunities for girls have also had some positive effects on boys. The boys seem more tolerant of girls' participation in co-ed sports activities and in traditionally male shops and courses. They seem to have a greater respect for the accomplishments of women through women's contributions to literature and history. Among elementary school-aged males, the expression of vulnerable feelings is gaining acceptance. In general, however, there has been far too little attention paid to redirecting male role development.

BOYS WILL BE BOYS

23 I think back to the four wrestlers and the stifling culture of masculinity in which they live. If schools were to radically alter this culture and substitute for it a new vision of masculinity, what would that look like? In this environment, boys would express a full range of behaviors and emotions without fear of being chastised. They would be permitted and encouraged to cry, to be afraid, to show joy, and to express love in a gentle fashion. Extreme concern for career goals would be replaced by a consideration of one's need for recreation, health, and meaningful work. Older boys would be encouraged to tutor and play with younger students. Moreover, boys would receive as much recognition for artistic talents as they do for athletics, and, in general, they would value leisure-time, recreational activities as highly as competitive sports.

24 In a system where maleness and femaleness were equally valued, boys might no longer feel that they have to "prove" themselves to other boys; they would simply accept the worth of each person and value those differences. Boys would realize that it

is permissible to admit failure. In addition, they would seek out opportunities to learn from girls and women. Emotional support would become commonplace, and it would no longer be seen as just the role of the female to provide the support. Relationships between boys and girls would no longer be based on limited roles, but instead would become expressions of two individuals learning from and supporting one another. Relationships between boys would reflect their care for one another rather than their mutual fear and distrust.

25   Aggressive styles of resolving conflicts would be the exception rather than the norm. Girls would feel welcome in activities dominated by boys, knowing that they were safe from the threat of being sexually harassed. Boys would no longer boast of beating up another boy or of how much they "got off" of a girl the night before. In fact, the boys would be as outraged as the girls at rape or other violent crimes in the community. Finally, boys would become active in efforts to stop nuclear proliferation and all other forms of military violence, following the examples set by activist women.

26   The development of a new conception of masculinity based on this vision is an ambitious task, but one which is essential for the health and safety of both men and women. The survival of our society may rest on the degree to which we are able to teach men to cherish life.

We Should Embrace Traditional Masculinity

Warren Farrell

A founder of the men's pro-feminist movement, Farrell served on the board of NOW, the National Organization for Women, until 1974. Gloria Steinem praised his 1975 book, *The Liberated Man*. But his work as a therapist, particularly with men and men's groups, caused him to shift from liberal pro-feminism to the advocacy of men's rights. His articles in *Transitions* and his 1987 book, *Why Men Are the Way They Are*, reflect his new perspective, as does his membership on the board of Men's Rights Incorporated and, since 1990, on the board of the National Congress for Men. He now denies that men are privileged and holds that women have been more successful at removing the restrictions that gender roles place on both sexes. Excerpted from *Why Men Are the Way They Are*, "We Should Embrace Traditional Masculinity" was published in *To Be a Man*.

1   Every virtue, taken to the extreme, becomes a vice. For the past twenty years I have critiqued traditional masculinity because masculinity has been taken to the extreme.

And taken to the extreme it creates anxiety, homicide, rape, war, and suicide; not taken to the extreme it has many virtues not to be tossed out with the bathwater.

2   Praise of men is an endangered species. But the good about men is not. And when something good is being endangered it needs special attention. And so, for a rare moment in recent history, here is special attention to what's good about male socialization. . . .

GIVING/GENEROSITY

3   Why do we think of women as giving of themselves and men as giving gifts? Because women's socialization teaches direct giving—as listening nurturers, cooks of men's meals, and doing more of his wash than he does of hers. He may give by working in a coal mine and contracting black lung so his child can attend college as he never could, but his giving is done at the mine—where we don't see it. The result of his giving is a check. With women's giving we appreciate more than the result, we appreciate the process: we see her cook the meal, serve it, and usually clean it up. We don't see him wading through water in a dark and damp mine shaft, or driving a truck at 2 A.M. on his fourth cup of coffee, behind schedule in traffic and with no time to nap. We see him at home withdrawing from the coffee.

4   He may spend much of his life earning money to finance a home his wife fell in love with, but we don't think of him as giving when he's away from home nearly as much as we think of her as giving when she cleans up his dishes.

5   Sometimes a man's giving is reflexive and role-based, such as when he reflexively picks up a tab at a restaurant. We forget this is also giving: fifty dollars for dinner and drinks may represent a day's work in after-tax income. Theater tickets, gas, and babysitters are another day's work. We don't think of his picking up these tabs as being as giving as when a woman spends two days preparing a special meal for him. Both forms of giving are role-based; hers are just more direct. . . .

FAIRNESS

6   The best thing emerging from sports, games, work rules, winning, and losing is fairness. Not necessarily honesty—fairness. In Little League, when I trapped a ball in my glove just after a bounce, the umpire credited me with catching a fly. I volunteered to the umpire that I hadn't. The umpire, embarrassed, changed the decision. The angry coach bawled me out. The other coach bawled out my coach for bawling me out. They disagreed on honesty. But neither would have disagreed with the fairness of a neutral umpire making the decision.

7   Male socialization teaches the value of a careful system of rules, within which anyone can work to gain advantage, and some of which can be gotten around (with possible consequences). Once mastered, the rules give everyone a much more equal chance than they would have had without the rules. To men, mastering these rules feels like survival—survival of themselves and their family. A lifetime of practicing these rules gives many men a sixth sense for fairness. Groups of men and women who have disregarded these rules as "too male" or "too establishment," as did the

Students for a Democratic Society in the sixties and seventies, soon evolve into back-stabbing elites which self-destruct.

MALE ACTION

NURTURING

8 Carl wasn't great at expressing feeling. And he didn't understand fully that sometimes Cindy just needed a listening ear. His way of supporting her was to volunteer to help Cindy with the problem that was making her upset. For Carl, taking Cindy seriously meant taking Cindy's problem seriously, and taking Cindy's problem seriously meant trying to find a solution. To him this was an act of love. Anything less, like just standing around when she was hurting, was an act of cruelty. "If Cindy's bleeding," he'd say, "find a solution. . . . Don't just stand there with the sickening supportive smile on your face while the woman I love is bleeding to death!" *Solutions are male nurturance. . . .*

LEADERSHIP

9 Accusations that "men have the power" have appeared more frequently in the past decade and a half than appreciation for the billions of hours sacrificed by men to give themselves the leadership training to get that power. Or the benefits of the leadership itself. For example, few articles explain how male socialization has trained millions of leaders to lead thousands of businesses that are now providing millions of women with opportunities for leadership that might not exist were it not for male leadership.

OUTRAGEOUSNESS

10 While women are socialized to get male attention by being "good girls" or not offending male egos, men are being socialized to get female attention by standing out. One way a man can stand out is to be outrageous. The best part of outrageousness is the barriers it breaks to allow all of us more freedom to experiment with discovering more of ourselves. The Beatles' hair, considered outrageous at the time, permitted a generation to experiment with their hair; Elvis the Pelvis allowed a generation to experiment with their sexual selves; the Wright Brothers were told it was scientifically impossible to fly—and suicidal to try; and Salvador Dali, Picasso, and Copernicus looked at the world in ways considered outrageous in their time; in retrospect, we can see that they freed us to live in a way we could not have dreamed of before.

MALE PSYCHOLOGY

TO KEEP EMOTIONS UNDER CONTROL

11 Although in relationships this tight lid leads to a "male volcano" after months of repressed emotions, the flip side is our dependence on this male trait in crisis situa-

tions. Dirk recalls a head-on collision. "Five cars crashed. There was glass and blood everywhere. Four of us guys ran from car to car, following the screams and preparing tourniquets. We stopped two cars to recruit passengers to redirect traffic, called the police, and removed a woman and her son from a car that burst into flames a minute later."

12   The newspapers reported the accident. But no headlines read, "Men Control Their Emotions in Order to Save Lives of Women and Children." They ran a picture—not of four men standing next to the women and children they saved, but of the five cars that collided.

EGO STRENGTH

13   When women reevaluate what goes wrong in a relationship the unspoken assumption is that this takes ego strength. When men compete fiercely to be number one, we see it as a reflection of their fragile egos (which it can be) and call it strategizing, *rather than recognizing the ego strength required to conduct a self-reevaluation immediately after a loss*. A man needs to ask, "What did *I* do wrong?" And then, when he finds the answer, rather than credit himself with his introspection, he must focus immediately on correcting it before the next game. . . .

TO EXPRESS ANGER

14   "One minute we were shouting and calling each other names. A minute later we were concentrating on the next play." The male tendency to take sports seriously combined with the willingness to express feelings intensely leads many adult men to say, "I lose my temper for a minute, then it's done with." The positive side of male anger is the quick, intense release of emotions, with the subsequent calm that follows the storm. If the intensity is understood, and not exacerbated, grudges are rarely held. The intensity, like all powerful energy, can be harnessed—and channeled into powerful lovemaking. . . .

MALE STRENGTH

TO SAVE HER LIFE AT THE RISK OF HIS OWN

15   I described in the introduction [of my book] how my younger brother Wayne died in an avalanche as he ventured ahead to check out a dangerous area alone rather than have his woman friend share the risk or do it herself. No news account of his death discussed this as an example of men's willingness to forfeit their lives for the women they love. We read of accounts of women lifting automobiles to save the life of a child, but not to save the life of a husband. Frequently, a woman who hears about this difference gets defensive even though she says she wants to appreciate men more.

16   There is nothing to be defensive about. It is not a statement that men are better. Members of each sex do what they are socialized to do both to give themselves the

feeling of being part of a whole and to deviate a bit to feel like an individual. This makes both sexes equal—with different programming. A man's dying for a woman he loves doesn't make him better at all, but part of his socialization leaves him vulnerable. My brother was quite vulnerable.

TO GIVE UP HIS LIFE FOR HIS BELIEFS

17   Some men give up their lives at war because they believe in their country; others do it because if they cannot be a hero they'd rather not live; others do it to support families. Others risk their lives in war so that if they live, they will earn enough money and status to "earn" a wife. Men with different class or ethnic backgrounds do the same in the CIA, FBI, State Department, and Mafia; their beliefs or their willingness to support their families are as important as their entire existence.

18   For these men, these are not empty words. While the worst part of this is an extraordinary statement of male insecurity and compensation for powerlessness, the best part is the extraordinary conviction men have for their beliefs and their families. It is a statement (within their value system) of the importance of values, responsibility, and quality of life: theirs and their family's. . . .

MALE RESPONSIBILITIES

SELF-SUFFICIENCY

19   We don't call men "career men," because the word *career* is built into the word *man*. Self-sufficiency is built into masculinity. . . .

20   Male socialization is an overdose in self-sufficiency. There are no fairy tales of a princess on a white horse finding a male Sleeping Beauty and sweeping him off to a castle; no fairy tales glorifying a man who is not self-sufficient. When the going gets tough, he doesn't talk it through, he gets going.

21   How do these fairy tales translate into reality? Liberation has been defined as giving women the "right to choose": to choose the option of being at home or being at work. *Men do not learn they have the right to choose to be at home. That would imply someone else would have to take care of him at home.* A man doesn't learn to expect that. He learns, instead, "The world doesn't owe you a living." Self-sufficiency implies *earning* rights. The right to choose, he learns, comes from choosing, for example, to take a job that pays a lot so he has more choices when he is away from the job. As a result of a man's training to take care of himself, millions of women have been freer to look at their own values—and to criticize men—than they would be if they had to support them. . . .

RISK TAKING

22   The male socialization to take risks on the playing field prepares a man to take risks investing in stocks, businesses, and conglomerates. To invest in his career with years

of training, and then extra training. A plastic surgeon may have risked from age five to thirty-five as a student or a part-time student, underpaid and overworked, in order, during the second half of his life, to be able to earn a half million dollars a year. . . .

23   On numerous levels, male socialization teaches men to risk a lot and be willing to fail a lot—and all for the hope of being rewarded a lot. (Conversely, if he doesn't risk, he doesn't expect the rewards.) If he survives, he will then be able to provide a security for his wife and children that he never had for himself. . . .

TO DEVELOP IDENTITY

24   The pressure on men to be more than self-sufficient, which forced them to take risks and self-start, to sort out their values quickly, to learn how and when to challenge authority, and to invent, resulted, at best, in the development of *identity*. Identity arises out of seeing both how we fit in and how we don't fit in—but especially how we don't fit in. The foundation of society is here before we arrive and after we pass. Identity is discovering our uniqueness in that continuity. As we take risks, and challenge what exists, the friction between ourselves and society makes all the boundaries clearer. Which is how we develop identity, and why the best parts of male socialization are helpful in developing identity. Of course, most men sell a good portion of their identity out to institutions just as most women sell out to a man. But the part of a man true to the values he has sorted out still challenges, still takes risks, still benefits from the development of identity. . . .

RESPONSIBILITY

25   Male socialization is a recipe book of taking responsibility. From the responsibility of getting a job at age fourteen so he can pay for his first date's food and tickets, to performing adequately within view of the girl he wants to ask out to increase his chances of acceptance, to actually asking his first date out, to arranging for his parents to drive, then, in later years, to borrowing the car, then driving himself, then taking initiatives—all of these are responsibility. . . .

26   My study of male-female language-pattern differences reflects the male training to take responsibility. Men are much less likely to use phrases like "This happened to me," and much more likely to use phrases like "I did this."

WHAT MALES CAN DO

SENSE OF EFFICACY

27   In the process of learning to take risks, men get especially strong training in learning what is and what is not effective—a sense of efficacy. In the process of trying a wide variety of jobs, we learn what we are effective at. We are socialized with a different attitude toward lost investments—as experiences that fine-tune us to the questions

that we must ask to prevent the next loss. We see the loss as an investment in investing. Tinkering for hours under a hood teaches him by trial and error how to be effective with a car (I said teaches him—it hasn't taught me!).

28   Once again, this is reflected in male-female language differences. Men are much less likely to say, "Maybe we can get Bill to do that," and much more likely to say, "Maybe if I try. . . ."

DOING RATHER THAN COMPLAINING

29   To become effective, men learn to make the unarticulated distinction between two types of complaining: "I'm helpless" versus "This is the complaint, now here's the solution." Men are not tolerant enough of other men complaining, "I'm helpless." But the best part of this intolerance is the pressure it exerts on a man to get rid of the problem that created the complaint.

PUSHING THE LIMITS OF ONE'S TALENTS

30   Doing may be better than complaining, but doing is not enough. A man's pressure to earn as much as he can with his talents means a constant pushing of the limits of each and every talent to discover which one can support him best. When people hear "pushing the limits of one's talents" they think of talents as raw capability; they feel that job advancement involves an expansion of talents and an application of talents toward an appropriate job and frequent promotions. Successful people learn that pushing the limits of one's talents also means balancing the politics of everyone else's egos while making themselves shine; balancing facade with personal integrity; and selling themselves repeatedly without appearing as if they're selling. The struggle to master the complex politics of advancement is the real pushing of the limits of one's talents.

31   The recent focus on discrimination has made us feel that the formula for success is qualifications plus lack of discrimination. That one-two approach has limited our appreciation of the extraordinary subtlety and range of talents required for advancement.

MALE FLEXIBILITY

SENSE OF HUMOR

32   Whether it's Woody Allen's ability to laugh at the schlemiel in himself or George Carlin's ability to laugh at masculinity itself, one of the best things that emerges from men's training to see life as a game is the ability to laugh both at our own roles in the game and at the game itself. Even the most traditional and serious of male systems are mocked, such as Bill Murray in *Stripes* mocking the military. It is difficult to find movies similarly mocking the traditional female role—for example, a movie mocking motherhood. . . .

CHANGE WITHOUT BLAME

33 Although men have made fewer changes than women, what changes they have made—as in fathering—have occurred without movements that blamed women. Fifteen years ago, few men were sensitive to orgasms or clitorises. Few had heard of the ERA. Few fathers-to-be joined their wives in the delivery room, in the preparation for the birth of their child. But soon, men had changed in all these ways.

34 The changes that occurred happened without attacking women with equal-but-opposite rhetoric, such as "Women hold a monopoly of power over the child," or "Women have a fragile mothering ego perpetuated by a quiet matriarchy that sends men into the field to die while women conspire to sleep in warm beds at home." Nor did men respond to blame by labeling it psychological abuse.

35 When we hear the phrase "the battle between the sexes," there is an unspoken assumption that both sexes have been blaming equally. The battle, though, could easily be called "the female attack on men," not "the male attack on women." There is a distinction between responding to blame and initiating it. Men have changed less, but they have also blamed less.

Wake-Up Call

Robert Reich

A political economist, Robert Reich was a member of the faculty of Harvard's John F. Kennedy School of Government before becoming secretary of labor in the Clinton administration. A Rhodes scholar and graduate of Yale Law School, he held positions in the Ford and Carter administrations. His books include *Minding America's Business* (with Ira Magaziner) (1982), *The Next American Frontier* (1983), *New Deals: The Chrysler Revival and the American System* (1985), *Tales of a New America* (1987), *The Power of Public Ideas* (1988), and *The Work of Nations* (1991). His "Wake-Up Call" appeared in the October 1989 issue of *Ms.* magazine.

1 "Lost by four votes," she said simply. "I'll be home soon." I must have looked shaken as I put down the phone. Our precocious six-year-old, who had been eying me, summed up the situation: "They fired Mommy, didn't they?"

2 Sexism had always been something of an abstraction to me. It might show up in corporate bureaucracies or working-class communities where Rambo still reigned. But surely no such noxious bias would be found in our overwhelmingly liberal, intellectual university community.

3 Yet a string of white males had been voted into tenured professorships just before my wife's candidacy. Most had not written as much, nor inspired the same praise

from specialists around the nation. None of their writings had been subjected to the detailed scrutiny—footnote by footnote—given her latest manuscript. Not one of the male candidates had aroused the degree of anger and bitterness that characterized her tenure review.

4   Why? I knew most of the men who had voted against her. Most were thoughtful, intelligent men who had traveled and read widely, and held positions of responsibility and trust. Gradually I came to understand that they were applying their standard of scholarship as impartially as they knew how. Yet their standard assumed that she had had the same formative intellectual experience as they, and had come to view the modes and purposes of scholarship as they do.

5   Through the years my wife had helped me to see the gender biases of these assumptions. Her experiences and understandings, and those of other women scholars, have been shaped by the irrefutable reality of gender. The values and perspectives she brings to bear on the world—and in particular the world of ideas—are different because she has experienced the world differently. In fact, it is the very uniqueness of her female perspective that animates her scholarship, that gives it its originality and intellectual bite.

6   Presumably the men who supported her had been able to imagine the life of the mind from a different perspective than their own. The majority of men on her faculty voted to grant her tenure. They had been able and willing to expand their standard—not to compromise or to reduce it, but to broaden it—to include a woman's way of knowing. I suspect that those who did not, did not care to try.

7   And why would they not have cared to try? Apart from the few diehards, they were kindly, tolerant men. But perhaps they did not feel that she had invited them to try. Early on, her closest friends on the faculty were a group of young professors who took delight in challenging the sacred cows of prevailing scholarship. Her early articles openly proclaimed a feminist perspective. She had not played at being a good daughter to the older and more traditional men on the faculty, giggling at their jokes and massaging their egos. Nor had she pretended to be one of them, speaking loudly and talking tough. They had no category for her, and to that extent she had made them uncomfortable. So when it came time for them to see the world from her perspective, they chose not to.

8   Since the vote she has remained strong, and as certain of the worth of her scholarship as before. But the experience has shaken me. It has made me wary of my own limited perspective—the countless ways in which I fail to understand my female colleagues and students, and their ways of knowing the world.

9   I have begun to notice small things. A recruiter for a large company calls to ask about a student who is being considered for a job. "Does she plan to have a family?" he inquires, innocently enough. "Is she really, er, serious about a career?" It is not the first time such a question has been put to me about a female student, but it is the first time I hear it clearly, for what it is.

10   A male colleague is critical of a young woman assistant professor: "She's not assertive enough in the classroom," he confides. "She's too anxious to please—doesn't

know her own mind." Then later, another colleague about the same young woman: "She's so whiny. I find her very abrasive." It is possible, of course, that she is both diffident and abrasive. But I can't help wondering if these characterizations more accurately reflect how my two colleagues feel about women in general—their mothers, wives, girlfriends—than about this particular woman.

11   At a board meeting of a small foundation on which I serve, the lone woman director tries to express doubts about a pending decision. At first several loquacious men in the group won't give her a chance to speak. When finally she begins to voice her concern she is repeatedly interrupted. She perseveres, and eventually states her objection. But her concern goes unaddressed in the remainder of the meeting as if she had never raised it. It seems to me that this isn't the first time she was ignored, but it is the first time I noticed.

12   In my class I present a complex management problem. An organization is rife with dissension. I ask: what steps should the manager take to improve the situation? The answers of my male students are filled with words like "strategy," "conflict," "interests," "claims," "trade-offs," and "rights." My female students use words like "resolution," "relationship," "cooperation," and "loyalty." Have their vocabularies and approach to problems always been somewhat different, or am I listening now as never before?

13   The vice president of a corporation that I advise tells me he can't implement one of my recommendations, although he agrees with it. "I have no authority," he explains. "It's not my turf." Later the same day, his assistant vice president tells me that the recommendation can be implemented easily. "It's not formally within our responsibility," she says off-handedly. "But we'll just make some suggestions here and there, at the right time, to the right folks, and it'll get done." Is the male vice president especially mindful of formal lines of authority and his female assistant especially casual, or do they exemplify differences in how men and women in general approach questions of leadership?

14   If being a "feminist" means noticing these sorts of things, then I became a feminist the day my wife was denied tenure. But what is my responsibility, as a male feminist, beyond merely noticing? At the least to remind corporate recruiters that they shouldn't be asking about whether prospective female employees want to have a family; to warn male colleagues about subtle possibilities of sexual bias in their evaluation of female colleagues; to help ensure that women are listened to within otherwise all-male meetings; to support my women students in the classroom; and to give explicit legitimacy to differences in the perceptions and leadership styles of men and women. In other words, just as I seek to educate myself, I must also help educate other men.

15   This is no small task. The day after the vote on my wife's tenure, I phoned one of her opponents—an old curmudgeon, as arrogant as he is smart. Without the slightest sense of the irony lying in the epithet I chose to hurl at him, I called him a son of a bitch.

My Life in the Military Closet

José Zuniga

José Zuniga's personal essay appeared in the *New York Times Magazine* on July 11, 1993, when the United States was involved in a bitter debate over official policy on homosexuals in the military. A former Army sergeant and the Sixth Army's Soldier of the Year, he is now a gay rights activist.

1 Lieut. Gen. Glynn C. Mallory Jr., commander of the Sixth Army and one of the Pentagon's star tacticians during the Persian Gulf war, stood not more than three feet from me, addressing a crowd at the noncommissioned officers' club on the Presidio military base of San Francisco. From time to time he paused from his speech to scan the several pale blue index cards onto which my military career had been abbreviated. Unbeknown to him, Mallory had long been my mentor. When I was assigned to the First Cavalry Division at Fort Hood, Tex., Mallory had commanded the nearby rival Second Armored Division. I had heard and admired his many speeches on the qualities of a good soldier: loyalty, resolve, physical and ethical fitness. Now, on a breezy day in March 1993, Mallory would reward me as an exemplar of just those values.

2 As I stood at rigid attention, the three-star general eloquently extolled the accomplishments of a 23-year-old Army sergeant.

3 "You can be justifiably proud of this distinction, and I know you will continue to serve with the same dedication that prompted your selection as the Soldier of the Year," Mallory said, facing the audience. As he pinned a fifth Army Commendation Medal on my freshly pressed uniform, he whispered, "I'm damned proud to serve with you, son."

4 Barely a week earlier, Mallory sat with me and several colleagues in a conference room watching a CNN report on homosexuals in the military. "Fags," he snorted, did not belong in "this man's Army."

5 The words rang in my ears as Mallory pinned the award on me. I had kept my mouth shut then, and I did so now; ambition trumped my anger. I continued to smolder, knowing what I alone between us knew: I was one of the "fags" who did not belong.

6 I entered boot camp in September 1989. As I and 20 or so nervous recruits jumped off the bus at the training center in Fort Bliss, Tex., a tyrannical drill sergeant herded us to the quadrangle. We ran to keep up with his angry directions; we flinched as he barked insults and introduced us to "his Army." His vocal cords strained as he assaulted our virility.

7 "I'm going to make men out of you little faggots," he screamed, ordering us to drop and do more push-ups than seemed physically possible. "You little pansies aren't fit to spit-shine my boots! When I'm done with you mama's boys you'll be real soldiers!"

8   Although the sergeant intended his message for the group as a whole, his barbs were clearly aimed at one recruit in particular. The unfortunate target of this attack, a farm boy now squirming in formation, wore his naïveté like a neon sign. His innocence became the weakness on which the drill sergeant fed. "Come on, grandma!" the drill sergeant would repeatedly snarl at the recruit, even though the young man would often outperform many of us.

9   In every formation and at every occasion the recruit was singled out as the weak link due to some undefinable characteristic the drill sergeant directly attributed to homosexuality. Whether the young man was in fact gay I do not know, nor did facts seem to matter. The drill sergeant seized on his plight as an opportunity to build esprit de corps, and the rest of the group dutifully focused our hatred and venom on him. We would bond by purging one of our own.

10   The strategy achieved the desired effect. Three weeks into basic training the recruit was discharged for "failure to adapt." His dream of one day becoming an Army doctor, a goal he had promised his parents he would accomplish, was dashed because he had been randomly selected to symbolize everything the sergeant sought to extinguish in the rest of us. As for us, we simply redoubled our efforts not to fall behind.

11   The incident marked my first encounter with an inherent contradiction in military psychology. The Army requires fellow soldiers to form close bonds founded on caring and concern, yet it forbids them from caring for one another too much. Thus, slapping each other on the butt with a wet towel is an acceptable gesture only if a "fag" joke follows to defuse it. From buttocks-grabbing to sexually laden double entendres, the aura of homoeroticism is ever-present. Yet even as the Army promotes certain of what can only be called gay values, it teaches its recruits to hate what it is teaching. The message is confusing to say the least.

12   On graduation day we lined up in alphabetical order (a feat we had come to master) behind the ramshackle auditorium that served as the post's movie house and recreation center. We had learned to rely on one another, to share close quarters with men we never imagined we would even speak to, to think of each other as brothers— for in battle, the drill sergeant had reiterated, it was on our shoulders that responsibility for our buddies' lives would rest. As I walked across the highly buffed hardwood stage floor and shook the drill sergeant's hand, I could not help thinking of the lamb whose career we had sacrificed to learn that lesson. I was well on my way to becoming "all I could be."

13   I didn't know I was gay when I entered the Army. At the time, I had a girlfriend, whom I met when I was 19. Cheryl was gregarious and social, I was taciturn and shy; after a few dates we became fast friends. My main interests, however, were professional, and my aspirations were largely military. Two of my great-grandfathers were war heroes, one a Spanish officer under Maximilian (Napoleon's chosen emperor of Mexico in 1864), and the other a Zapatista in the Mexican revolution of 1910. My four grandfathers also had served in the Spanish and Mexican Armies, and my father had been a military officer as well. I knew that I, too, would become a soldier.

14   The military life also appealed to an ingrained desire for regimen. Born into a traditional Roman Catholic family, I attended church every Sunday and during days of holy obligation, and I served as an altar boy whenever one of the regulars called in sick. I studied the Catholic doctrine in Bible school and eventually attended parochial schools in East Chicago. Yet amid the strictures of home life I found time for the traditional pursuits of an average American boy: playing baseball, missing curfew, dating girls.

15   After boot camp I was assigned to Fort Hood, where I worked first as an ambulance driver, then as editor of the First Cavalry Division newspaper. It was there that I met Andrea V. She was a top-notch supply technician with a trait rare among Army supply clerks: an intense desire to help fellow soldiers through any bind. She was also gay, the first homosexual I had met in the military. Everyone in the company had heard about her lesbianism. Because of her generosity, we chose to overlook it.

16   That state of affairs ended, however, with the arrival of a gung-ho staff sergeant. He was a welcome addition to our unit: he brought field experience, enthusiasm and intelligence. He also brought a voracious sexual appetite and a legacy of sexual-harassment complaints to prove it.

17   What seemed at first to be a platonic friendship between Andrea and the sergeant soon erupted into one of the most talked-about scandals on the post: she had agreed to have sex with him, it was viciously rumored, in order to prove her femininity. When she refused to continue the sexual relationship, the irate sergeant taunted her for being a lesbian. To safeguard our own reputations, the rest of us joined in, mocking the sergeant's involvement with a known "dyke."

18   We stood by as the sergeant selectively enforced Army policy to preserve his sense of manhood. Thus it came as no surprise when, three weeks later, Andrea was expelled from the military with "homosexual" stamped on her record. In watching her life fall into havoc, however, I became aware of an inner conflict of my own—a conflict that, given the message of Andrea's discharge, I preferred not to acknowledge.

19   During my assignment to Fort Hood, I struck a bond with a certain soldier. Ours was the classic military friendship: car-pooling to and from work, sharing a six-pack on a Friday night. Together we helped one another adjust to the rigors of military life. We served together for six months in Texas before deploying with the First Cavalry Division to the Persian Gulf in September.

20   We worked together, well behind the front lines: I as a military journalist, editing one of three tabloid newspapers published by the Army during the Persian Gulf conflict, he as a radio technician. The climate was inhospitable, and the stress of the situation was tremendous. My friend and I spent most of our time together, and our friendship intensified. We shared our fears, we shared our mail during times when one of us received none, we shared every facet of our lives. He talked about his girlfriend in Texas; I talked about mine.

21   Cheryl, meanwhile, wrote constantly to boost my spirits and remind me of the happy life that awaited me upon my return to the States. I longed for the security she promised. One night, from a telephone deep in the Saudi desert, I proposed.

22   With the impending start of the ground war I volunteered for reassignment as a combat medic on the front line; my friend stayed behind. Living conditions on the front were brutal—filthy clothes, cold food, news blackouts and "whore's baths," in which we rinsed ourselves off with frigid water. I craved companionship. Through some feat of technological wizardry, my friend contacted me by radio to share, long-distance, in my misery. I began to feel a closeness to this man that I could never imagine feeling for anyone else, a closeness so seemingly unnatural that it frightened me.

23   I don't know if my friend ever realized the depth of my affection for him. Back in Texas, I tested him in code, trying discreetly to draw him out, aware all the while that he could turn me in if I went too far. A native Californian, he confessed to having seen and heard it all, and he would casually mention gay friends. Was he trying to tell me something? Yet other times he would adopt a mocking lisp and effeminate body language. Even if he did feel the same as I did, I rationalized, he would never admit it, for fear of reprisal. I never did learn if he was gay; looking back, I am almost certain he was not. A month after my marriage, he was reassigned.

24   I refused to believe I might really be gay, both because it so clashed with my stereotypes of gay people and, I suppose, because the consequences to what was shaping up as a very promising Army career would have been devastating. Instead I returned to editing the First Cavalry newspaper and immersed myself in work. And I dedicated myself to making my new marriage succeed; I sought refuge in the glossy photo of my wife that sat on my desk. But with the marriage as a cover, I was suddenly free to introspect, and certain doubts quietly gathered force.

25   One night, obviously depressed, I went out drinking with a good friend, a female officer. Paradoxically, in the Army, drinking with a woman is not considered unusual, since military life effectively reduces everyone, men and women alike, to the same hypertrophied sex. My friend asked me what was wrong. I had heard she was a lesbian and, taking the risk, confided that I thought I might be gay. She insisted that I drive with her that night to a gay bar in Austin.

26   The bar was loud and crowded; strobe lights flashed as we tossed back drink after drink, not caring that first call was at 5 A.M. for a three-mile run around the post. Standing in a corner of the bar I looked around me at a crowd of patrons, including a few muscular young men in tell-tale military haircuts, who all dressed like me, talked like me and did not throw themselves at me in the manner of the predators described in my Army buddies' gay jokes.

27   This enlightening experience came to a crashing halt, though, when someone came running into the bar, screaming for all the military types to run to the back room. Within seconds several of us were whisked into a liquor stockroom, the slam of a heavy dead bolt and our breathing the only sounds echoing through the room. Probably military police coming to check if any Army queers were here, my lesbian friend intimated. After a few minutes we were let out; the coast was clear.

28   "There is no safe house in which the C.I.D. [Criminal Investigation Division] or military police can't reach us," she said squarely. "They're out there taking down license-plate numbers right now."

29   In that moment the term "coming out of the closet" became clear in all its literal meaning, and with it came an urge to exit. I drove home, desperate to share my pain with my wife, but I found her sleeping and could not bear to wake her.

30   Gradually, secretly, I pursued a new set of friends. Finding them posed little problem: once I made one gay friend, I soon met the majority of gays and lesbians at the installation. For homosexuals in the military, such networks are critical, as they provide mutual support and defense against the various indignities and humiliations of daily life.

31   One afternoon several of us listened in amazement as a friend, Marc S., described a nightmare interrogation he had recently endured. Two days earlier his lover, a Medical Service Corps officer, had been hauled in for questioning by the C.I.D. In exchange for an honorable discharge, the lover had agreed to provide military authorities with details of his relationship with Marc. Shortly thereafter Marc had been pulled aside for questioning and presented with a similar bargain: he, too, could depart with an honorable discharge if he gave the C.I.D. a list of all his gay and lesbian friends.

32   "This is not a threat," he tearfully recalled the softer of the two agents saying after reading Marc his Miranda rights. "But if you don't cooperate we'll have to expand the investigation."

33   Marc resisted the Army's scare tactics, but already word had spread and made him a pariah among his friends. He had anticipated that reaction from his straight friends, but he didn't realize his gay friends also would run for cover. He became afraid to venture out, knowing he was being watched. He feared for us, urging us not to associate with him and risk our careers. So we, his best friends, stayed away.

34   Marc's refusal to cooperate only spurred the C.I.D.'s efforts to snare other offenders in its net. His discharge was delayed two months while an extensive investigation was conducted, but in the end Marc, like thousands of homosexuals before him, was discharged and branded with a mark on his papers that will stigmatize him forever. We witnessed from afar the slow death of his career, afraid even to send a note of sympathy.

35   Six months after my return from the Persian Gulf, Cheryl and I moved from Killeen, Tex., a military town with nothing to offer but pawn shops, liquor stores and strip joints, to San Francisco. Outwardly, our social life in Killeen adhered to the conventions of married coupledom: we attended neighborhood picnics and traveled to nearby Belton Lake for organized marital retreats. Because we lived off-post, few people knew how little time Cheryl and I actually spent together. That changed with my reassignment to the Presidio. The expense of living in San Francisco forced us to move into military housing. As much as the arrangement helped our finances, it increased the tension developing between us.

36   I was treated well at the Presidio; my combat record as a journalist and the Combat Medical Badge I proudly wore on my uniform set me apart from other soldiers assigned there, many of whom were either first-time recruits or seasoned officers awaiting retirement. As I had in the past, I buried myself in work, convinced that by doing so I could avoid my moral dilemma and carry on with my married life. But the strategy didn't work. I realized, reluctantly, that I could no longer hide from someone

I loved as much as I loved Cheryl. One night after dinner I confessed that I thought I might be gay. She responded with a melancholy smile. "I know."

37   In early 1992 Cheryl and I separated. She returned to Ohio and I again immersed myself in work. But I maintained the facade of a happily married heterosexual: the wedding photo remained on my desk, and I lied about Cheryl's whereabouts, making excuses when she could not attend social functions. I constructed a life of duplicity to dispel any rumor that might arise.

38   In the weeks before being named Sixth Army Soldier of the Year, I watched with admiration as Petty Officer Keith Meinhold, Lieut. (j.g.) Tracy Thorne, Col. Margarethe Cammermeyer and several other brave military men and women came out and challenged the ban against homosexuals in the military. Though in some ways my homosexuality was still abstract, my fear of being discovered, and my shame from that fear, was not. I struggled with the thought of also coming out, but I was painfully aware of the consequences.

39   Two weeks after the award, I watched a production of David Drake's one-man play, "The Night Larry Kramer Kissed Me," with a group of civilian gay friends I had met in San Francisco. A monologue in the play presented a portrait of a society in which diversity is a cherished value, and my silence began to eat at me. In the audience that night was Elizabeth Birch, the head of litigation for Apple Computer and a chairwoman of the National Gay and Lesbian Task Force board. After the play a mutual friend introduced us. I told her I thought I might be ready to come out and asked for her help.

40   After several meetings with the task force, a plan was devised. They would present me as the surprise speaker at an event being organized for the weekend of the Gay and Lesbian March on Washington. My coming out clearly would be a public relations coup for homosexuals fighting the military prohibitions, but the task force wanted to be sure I was prepared to sacrifice my career. I assured them that I was. Once we had a plan we quickly realized how easily it could be foiled. I had already arranged for military leave for that weekend: if anyone in my command caught wind of my impending disclosure, I could be given a "lawful order" to remain on base, and thereby sequestered from the press. Fearing that the task-force phone lines might be tapped, my attorney, James Kennedy, a former Army prosecutor, advised code names; I became Luke, he became Obi-Wan Kenobi—and General Mallory became Darth Vader. Our code was successful, as was the public relations assault: the task force arranged for more than 20 embargoed interviews to take place before my official coming out.

41   I signed out on leave the morning of April 23 and flew to Washington that afternoon. As I left the plane at Dulles Airport I realized that that would be my last night as a public servant with a private life; thereafter I would become a public figure famous for my expulsion into the civilian world. I can't remember much of what happened during my speech, only what seemed like hours of applause, followed by an inner feeling of sheer terror. The next morning I marched with the veterans' contingent in the 1993 March on Washington. I was now a part of the gay, lesbian and bisexual military family, fighting for the right to serve openly and with dignity, joining arms with Meinhold, Thorne, Cammermeyer and the others.

42   Immediately upon my return to San Francisco I was isolated from my peers and assigned to live in an empty building with a private bathroom and shower; the privacy of the other soldiers with whom I had shared a community shower, it seemed, was now compromised. I was not allowed to return to my job as a journalist, and I was reassigned to answer telephones in a supply stockroom. I was advised to check in twice a day with my unit so that the command could keep a tight rein on my activities. And I was forced to endure an hourlong sermon from a chaplain, once friendly, who now asked me to define morality and compared homosexuality to bestiality and child pornography. I was relieved to learn I would receive an honorable discharge.

43   My trials, however, did not end there. In the days that followed, I was accused of wearing an unauthorized medal during the Washington ceremony (an award that had been posted in my record, although the Army insists the medal had only been recommended and approved) and stripped of my noncommissioned-officer status. But the Army's retaliatory action ultimately backfired; the local press learned of it and elevated me to martyr status. I followed the news in bewilderment, as almost overnight I was transformed into a celebrity activist. Soon I was out on the streets, ready to assume my new role as a symbol and outspoken critic in the fight for gay civil rights.

44   I have since thought a great deal about what homosexuals are fighting for. We have never asked the military to lead the way in social change; we simply ask that the military catch up with modern society. The issue at stake is not whether gay service members exist or even perform well—I think my case, among others, proves that we not only exist but also excel. Rather, the question is whether heterosexual service members can tolerate the presence of their gay colleagues without resorting to violence or falling to pieces. To ban homosexuals from the military out of fear that acknowledging them would damage morale is a disingenuous attempt to blame the messenger for the message.

45   And the truth is that if the ban were lifted today, homosexuals in the military, already conservative by nature, would continue their lives of discretion, pursuing excellence but without fear of investigation and sanctioned hatred. Intolerance will not disappear overnight, and few gay soldiers would be willing to risk the abuse, both overt and subtle, that disclosure would bring. Nevertheless, for the Government to place a stamp of approval on discrimination of any sort is to make a mockery of the very values it asks its citizens to uphold and its military to defend.

46   I am on a national speaking tour now, and while my new role is sometimes thrilling, it has not come without personal cost. Shortly after my announcement, I spoke with my father, who told me that he loved me. Several weeks later I came across an article in a Texas paper where I had worked many years before. The article was a profile of my life, and it said that my father had disowned me. Stunned, I called the editor of the article, my former boss, and asked how the reporter could have stated as fact something that plainly was not true. The editor told me the paper had contacted my father. "He told our reporter that he had no son named José."

47   Has all this attention been worth losing my career, and more important, my family? I wonder, sometimes. But I remember a story a 72-year-old veteran, a combat medic in the Second World War and later an Army general, told me not long ago. For

more than a week in November 1944, he and his platoon had borne the brunt of a German offensive. At last, relief arrived in the form of a company-size unit of infantrymen, but with it came word that his lover, a rifleman in another battalion, had been mortally wounded in a firefight a week earlier.

48   "You know what allowed me to pick up my weapon and go on?" the veteran asked me. "The realization that the man who wields the hammer is the one who drives the nails. I vowed someday to make a difference in Roy's memory." Now a gay rights activist in Florida, the veteran urged me to continue the battle, not only for future generations of gay, lesbian and bisexual service members but also in the memory of the thousands who sacrificed their lives for what they believed was right and just.

49   I have strived to fulfill that duty. One night recently, I went to a gay dance club in a town where I was speaking. I needed to forget the loneliness of the road and my disappointment at not seeing more people my age actively fighting for gay rights. At the club I caught sight of two young lovers holding each other in a corner of the dance floor. Their crew cuts gave them away as military. As the night wore on, the two approached me and introduced themselves.

50   "We're both in basic training here, José," said the 18-year-old with a shy smile. "We saw you on CNN when you came out." His lover added, his eyes shifting from mine to his partner's: "Thanks for doing what you did. It took a lot of guts." As they walked back onto the dance floor to rejoin their friends.

51   I wondered what would happen to these airmen. What could I do to insure that the opportunity to excel was not stolen from them? When will the day come when qualified and dedicated service members are allowed to serve without having to deny their identity and their love? Soon, my heart told me. But not without a fight.

WRITING ASSIGNMENTS

Analysis

1. Explain Thompson's analysis of the role of homophobia and misogyny in the definition and formation of traditional masculinity. Supplement his examples with illustrations drawn from your own experience and observation.

2. Drawing on Thompson and Farrell and your own values, compare and contrast the advantages and disadvantages to men of one of the following aspects of traditional masculinity: dominance, competitiveness, strength, aggressiveness, independence, self-reliance, resiliency, self-control, or power.

3. Describe a visual image—comparable to McAllister's evocation of the "Strength" card in the Tarot deck—for courage, self-control, resiliency, or independence, and interpret it.

4. Reich asserts the existence of a valuable "female perspective." In an essay, assess whether his examples persuasively illustrate and explain this perspective.

5. In an essay, explain how Thompson's critique or Farrell's defense of traditional masculinity helps to explain Zuniga's descriptions of and experiences in military life.

Argument

1. Thompson says, "The survival of our society may rest on the degree to which we are able to teach men to cherish life." Do you agree with him that a world governed by men with a new conception of masculinity and by women would inevitably be less violent and more nurturing and cooperative?
2. Do Schlafly, defender of traditional femininity, and Farrell, defender of traditional masculinity, basically agree or disagree in their assessment of traditional gender roles?
3. Farrell argues by analogy and illustration, noting, for example, the sacrifice of a coal miner, the nonconformity of the Beatles or Elvis Presley, and the self-control of the men who saved lives in a traffic accident. How well do these illustrations and analogies support the points he makes? Is his reasoning logical and persuasive? Select several examples for analysis.
4. Farrell says, ". . . there is an unspoken assumption that both sexes have been blaming equally. The battle, though, could easily be called 'the female attack on men,' not 'the male attack on women.' There is a distinction between responding to blame and initiating it. Men have changed less, but they have also blamed less." Explain why you agree or disagree with these statements.
5. Based on evidence provided in Zuniga's account and other pertinent information, should openly gay people be allowed to serve in the military? Why?

Personal Writing and Writing from Research

1. Gathering evidence from personal interviews, observations of popular culture, and library research, write a research paper detailing and analyzing homosexual stereotypes.
2. *Collaborative Project:* Thompson notes the ways that language shapes, reflects, and reinforces traditional gender differences and roles. In a research paper, analyze expressions, sayings, and slang terms drawn from your own research that illustrate this function of language.
3. Answer Thompson's question: "If you woke up tomorrow and discovered that you were the opposite sex from the one you are now, how would you and your life be different?"
4. Explain which perspective you find the most appealing: Thompson's, Farrell's, or Reich's.
5. Observe and take notes on a situation involving a problem to be solved or a disagreement to be resolved, focusing on the behavior of the male and female participants. Based on the evidence provided by this one situation, explain whether Thompson's, Farrell's, or Reich's characterizations of male and female behavior are most accurate and insightful.
6. Explore how you, like Zuniga, handled discovering something about yourself which you could neither deny nor change.

THE FAMILY

Ozzie, Ricky, David, and Harriet Nelson shortly after "The Ozzie and Harriet" show first aired on TV in 1952.

For most of us today, the family—whatever form it takes—continues to be a refuge from the struggles, inequities, and inevitable disappointments of our public lives. At different stages of our lives, we also depend on it for material support.

In the family of our childhood, which is our first school, we learn who we are. Its lessons leave an enduring imprint, for we learn them when we are inexperienced and vulnerable. Our family teaches us the meaning and expression of love, the personal qualities and skills we should develop, and the values by which we should live. As our first society, it teaches us the nature of power and how to relate to others. These lessons are mediated by the gender roles that adults model and consciously and unconsciously impose on children. Even before we understand the biological distinction between male and female, we have already absorbed lessons in the meaning of masculinity and femininity.

In "A Cultural Earthquake," Arlene Skolnick explains the recent changes in family life and gender roles in terms of long-term economic, demographic, political, and cultural trends. She argues that these external factors will continue to alter the family and the roles its members play.

The next four selections explore the experiences of members in traditional families where masculine and feminine roles are clearly defined and largely accepted. In John McCluskey, Jr.'s "Forty in the Shade," a divorced African-American father is both proud of and haunted by his patriarchal heritage.

Evoking an alternative but still traditional model of father-son relationships, Native-American poet Simon Ortiz celebrates his father's gentleness and love in "My Father's Song."

Hisaye Yamamoto's "Seventeen Syllables" examines gender roles, the generation gap, and the gulf between Japanese-born parents and their American-born child in a pre-World War II farm family.

In "Discarded," David Sherwood recalls how his brother's "difference" led to rejection. In these four selections, the family's authority figures accept and, at least initially, enforce traditional concepts of masculinity and femininity.

In contrast, the parents and children in the final three selections challenge traditional gender roles, but they find no easy alternatives. These are families and individuals in transition. In David Michael Kaplan's "Doe Season," the father defends his daughter's presence on an otherwise all-male hunting trip.

In Bel Kaufman's "Sunday in the Park," a confrontation between one set of parents and another father uncovers discomfiting feelings and raises questions for the couple.

Finally, Jan Clausen's "Daddy" explores the consequences of divorce, remarriage, and homosexual parenting on a young daughter.

All of these selections confirm that the family is the first crucible in which we forge our identity, including our concepts of masculinity and femininity. Whether children imitate, reject, or redefine the models they see at home, they cannot escape their influence any more than the family itself can escape the influence of society at large. Increased awareness of how our family experiences shape us may persuade us to affirm traditional models or lead us to redefine family structure and gender roles in ways more responsive to our needs.

A Cultural Earthquake

Arlene Skolnick

Arlene Skolnick grew up in a family in which it was assumed that a woman's place was in the home. But when she married in 1954 at age 21, she did not settle into domesticity. Instead, she pursued a PhD in psychology at Yale.

In 1962, she and her husband moved to Berkeley, California, where he began teaching in the university's sociology department and she joined the Institute for Human Development. In 1969, they collaborated on a *Family in Transition*. During that period of social upheaval, she was amazed to discover how little had been written about changes in the family: "Existing sociology was based on the notion that the 1950s style, traditional, stereotyped family was a timeless entity built into biology and society." Her work since then, which has taken her away from psychology and into family sociology, has been directed at correcting that misconception. She has written a textbook on marriage, *The Intimate Environment* (1987), and another book, *Embattled Paradise* (1991), from which "A Cultural Earthquake" is taken.

Journal Topics: (1) Describe how your favorite television programs model family life and gender roles. How have these programs influenced you? (2) Explain how one of the following has affected your family's life or the life of a close friend: the shift from a manufacturing to a service economy, the need to take responsibility for an aging grandparent, the desire of a family member to change the role he or she formerly played in the family.

As You Read: (1) Skolnick describes the *Ozzie and Harriet* family, from the 1950s television series, as "cheerful, well-off, white [and] suburban." A traditional nuclear family, it includes two married people of the opposite sex and their children. According to Skolnick, how does this TV program model masculine and feminine gender roles? (2) How does Skolnick account for the mass appeal of this television family to the many Americans whose daily lives and values differed from those depicted on this television show? (3) What political and social changes does Skolnick identify in the late 1960s and 1970s that undermine this "sentimental model"?

[We] also need, as much as anything else, language adequate to the times we live in. We need to see how we live now and we can only see with words and images which leave us no escape into nostalgia for another time and place.

—Michael Ignatieff
The Needs of Strangers

1   In 1962, *Look* magazine invited a number of scholars, scientists, and political leaders to predict what America would be like twenty-five years into the future. Most of the forecasters saw the America of 1987 as streamlined, clean, orderly, prosperous—a high-tech world of 500-mile-an-hour jet-powered carplanes and automated kitchens that would cook meals and clean up in minutes. Along with predictions of such technological wonders were several descriptions of family life.

2   "Linda (the wife)," described a profile of a typical family, "runs her home with extreme good taste and manages her children with serene authority. But she does not try to run or manage her husband." Another article imagined a mother's calendar on a typical day: "Clothes disposer repairman here. Shop: Buy baked ham pills, scotch and soda capsules. Pay radar bill. Have the Whites and Hammonds over for capsules. Take Bob's jet to hangar for grease job. Go to hypnotist for headache therapy."

3   Looking backward from the future these writers were trying to describe, we learn more about the "structure of feelings" of that era—its distinctive mindset—than about the realities of our own. Their boundless faith in science and technology, and in a future that promised more of everything, now seems quaint. They imagined that the technology of 1987 would transform the material landscape of everyday life, but the future family they saw was unchanged, as if preserved in a time capsule.

4   Although the calendar indicated that the 1960s had begun, 1962 was still part of the era historians have called the American celebration, the American high, the proud decades—the years when America's victory in World War II thrust the nation into an era of unprecedented prosperity and power in the world. The *Look* piece was among the last of a string of similar books and articles. In 1955, the editors of *Fortune* magazine had published "The Fabulous Future: America in 1980." The distinguished contributors to that article also predicted a stable, even, more uniformly prosperous and nearly classless America.

5   It seemed as if the nation had reached a final stage of historical development, that it was a "completed society." The stability and legitimacy of major institutions went largely unquestioned. "All the problems are solved," complained a college editor in 1957; there seemed to be little to write about. The only possible improvements would be those wrought by the kinds of technological wizardry described by the writers in *Look*. "Pockets of poverty" and other difficulties remained to be mopped up, but major social change—"the kind that is painful and agonizing and that forces individuals and generations into a sense of radical disjunction between traditional ways and contemporary realities—would henceforth be confined to developing nations, like Tunisia."

6   The central symbol of the nearly perfected America of the 1950s was the suburban family. Suburbia meant more than physical comfort; it embodied a long-held American

dream of a happy, secure family life. The leading television situation comedies of the time—"Father Knows Best," "Leave It to Beaver," "The Adventures of Ozzie and Harriet"—portrayed cheerful, well-off, white suburban families, "orderly lives lived without major trauma or disturbance."

7   Television images, then as now, did not portray the way most Americans actually lived. These were idealized families in idealized settings, successfully masquerading as "normal," "healthy," "typical," "average." Years later, Billy Gray, the actor who played Bud in "Father Knows Best," said he felt "ashamed" he had ever had anything to do with the show. It was all "totally false," he said, and had caused many Americans to feel inadequate, because they thought that was the way life was supposed to be and that their own lives failed to measure up.

8   Contrary to the homogeneous, idealized family portrayed in the sit-coms, the most distinctive feature of American family life has always been its diversity. Searching for the "normal American family" in the late 1950s, one researcher found "the most astonishing variance in its structure and function." Families differed by income, by social class, by ethnicity and religion, by neighborhood and region, by number of members, by relations with kin, by patterns of authority and affection, by life-style, by the balance of happiness and unhappiness.

9   Yet, those smiling television families incarnated a symbolism deeply rooted in American culture; anthropologists have shown that this "sentimental model" defines family life even for those whose daily lives and cultural traditions differ radically from it. Further, television's families did reflect a set of social trends affecting a sizable chunk of the population. The young adults of the time were rushing into marriage at a younger age than any other generation in American history, and producing a record crop of babies. With the mass migration to the suburbs, for the first time a majority of families joined the homeowner class.

10   To many social scientists as well as TV producers, America was "a middle class society in which some people were simply more middle class than others." Sociological theorists saw the suburban family as the most highly developed version of a timeless social unit. The nuclear family, wrote one anthropologist, was "a biological phenomenon—as rooted in organs and physiological structures as insect societies."

11   Little wonder, then, that the writers of the *Look* article projected Ozzie and Harriet's family unchanged into a stable, streamlined future. In 1962 there seemed no reason to doubt that the next twenty-five years would continue to bring social stability and economic progress. No one predicted assassinations, urban riots, student protests, a lost war, economic stagnation. Least likely of all was the prospect of revolutionary change in the most intimate aspects of American life—the family, sexual mores, the roles of women and men.

12   Ten years after the "American high" had reached its peak, the hopes and expectations of the 1950s lay in ruins. Instead of the social stability that had been expected, the two decades that followed were among the most turbulent periods of American history, comparable only to the Civil War era. To a greater extent than in any earlier period, the upheaval was as much about cultural and sexual standards as public issues.

13   Between 1965 and 1975, the land of togetherness became the land of swinging singles, open marriage, creative divorce, encounter groups, communes, alternative lifestyles, women's liberation, the Woodstock Nation, and "the greening of America." A land where teenage girls wore girdles even to gym class became a land of miniskirts, braless ness, topless bathing suits, and nude beaches.

14   Middle-class norms that once seemed carved in stone were crumbling away. In the 1950s, observes the anthropologist Lionel Tiger, there was a "broad embargo on visual and aural information about virtually anything between people's legs. Movies could not depict two humans in the same bed unless one acrobat maintained a foot on the floor." A leading director got into trouble with censors for using the word *virgin* in a movie; homosexuality, out-of-wedlock childbearing, and abortion were dark and dirty secrets.

15   But by the early 1970s, sexual mores had been transformed. Abortion became legal; four-letter words became a staple of Hollywood films; homosexuals came out of the closet, marched in the streets, and ran for political office; unwed girls and women began to keep their babies; unwed middle-class couples openly moved in together, a practice known in its formerly nonrespectable days among the lower class as "shacking up." During the same years, apart from these and other changes in morality, the leading statistical indicators of family life were revealing equally dramatic departures from the trends of the 1950s: skyrocketing divorce rates, a surge of women into the workplace, rising rates of single motherhood, and so on. The solid American family of Mom, Dad, and the kids was becoming fragmented into a bewildering array of lifestyles. It was as if, said the president of the Population Association of America, an "earthquake had shuddered through the American family."

16   By the late 1970s, the mood of the country had shifted once again. A decade of revolt and liberation had spawned an inevitable backlash. The passion for change and experiment had burned itself out. But apart from social and cultural change, the decade was marked by a series of events that undid the assumptions about progress, prosperity, and American power in the world that had dominated both the 1950s and the 1960s.

17   After Watergate, Vietnam, energy crises, inflation, and economic stagnation, nostalgia settled like a haze on American political and cultural life. Instead of looking forward to the automated utopia of a "fabulous future," Americans hungered for the stability, order, and tradition of a lost golden age. But even as the image of a Norman Rockwell America became a cultural ideal and "old-fashioned" became a term of high praise, a deepening sense of decay, disintegration, and crisis hung over the present. Somehow, the family seemed to be at the center of it all, or at least it supplied us with a language for talking about the feeling that things were falling apart. In his now-notorious "malaise" speech, President Carter captured the national mood. Supposedly addressing the energy crisis, he lamented that "in a nation that was proud of hard work, strong families, close-knit communities and faith in God, too many of us now tend to worship self-indulgence and consumption."

18   The election of 1980 marked a turning of the cultural as well as the political tides. A "new politics of old values" swept Ronald Reagan into the presidency. The "liberated,"

"greened" America of the 1960s and 1970s had become a land of sexual fear, television evangelists, and antidrug and antipornography crusades. Underneath it all was a profound, collective yearning for enduring emotional bonds and a fear that the social fabric had become dangerously frayed. Reagan came to power promising to restore all that had been lost since "the proud decades": American might abroad, the traditional family at home.

19   Despite the nostalgia for traditional moral codes and family values that dominated the culture and political rhetoric of the Reagan era, social reality did not turn back. The intact nuclear family may have returned to the top of the television charts—"The Cosby Show" and "Family Ties" supplying the same rewards as "Father Knows Best" and "Ozzie and Harriet"—but the celebration of traditional family values masked the radical changes that had taken place in family life and household economics. By the end of the 1980s it was clear that the New Right's dream of restoring the family forms, affluence, and dominance of the 1950s "American high" had failed.

WHAT HAPPENED TO THE AMERICAN FAMILY?

20   . . . Looking in detail at the family in specific times and places, historians have located no golden age of family harmony and stability. Every family pattern, it seems, has its own costs and benefits, its own tensions and internal contradictions, its own concerns about the gap between ideal and real.

21   One recent survey notes that Americans have been worrying about the family for over three hundred years: "Within decades of the Puritans' arrival in Massachusetts Bay Colony, Puritan jeremiads were already decrying the increasing fragility of marriage, the growing selfishness and irresponsibility of parents and the increasing rebelliousness of children." The "crisis of the family," it seems, is a national tradition, and not just in America: historians of the family in other countries have made much the same discovery. The facts, as opposed to fantasies, about pre-twentieth-century family life portray not a world we have lost but one we have in many ways escaped—a world of high mortality rates and rampant disease, in which vast numbers of people barely subsisted.

22   Nor were the 1950s the golden age of family life. It was in part the tensions and discontents simmering underneath the seemingly bland surface of life in that decade that fueled the cultural revolts of the 1960s. And the social critics of the time denounced the suburbs and the suburban family as fiercely as their later counterparts denounced narcissism and individualism, blaming them for "many of the country's real and alleged ills, from destroying its farmland to emasculating its husbands."

23   In any event, the family patterns of the baby-boom era were a response to the historical circumstances of that particular period. Further, in evaluating the changes that took place since the 1960s, it is important to realize that the 1950s family was not as traditional as most people assume it to have been. In fact, the decade stands out as an unusual one for twentieth-century family life, whose historical trends have been falling birth rates, rising divorce rates, and later ages of marriage. The family

patterns of the 1950s are as much in need of explanation as are the departures from them that have occurred since then.

24   But realizing that there never was a golden past we can return to only makes it more difficult to assess the sense of strain and crisis that change has brought. The sheer speed of the changes has been disorienting, leaving all of us with a sense of loss and bewilderment. Those most committed to the traditional order have seen their deeply held values and assumptions swept away; those who hoped that change would repair an unjust social system have seen those hopes frustrated.

25   Women have gained the freedom both to have children and to pursue careers, but society and institutions have not adapted to a world where women are in the workplace to stay. Large numbers of women have lost the economic security of traditional lifelong marriage, without the earning capacity to support themselves and their children. Men have felt the ground shift under their own definitions of male roles as woman have challenged traditional notions of gender; men have lost the legitimacy, if not the reality, of their traditional domination over women. . . .

26   Nevertheless, the lure of nostalgia blinds us to the facts of social change and impedes us from coming to grips with the problems created by that change. . . .

SOURCES OF SOCIAL TRANSFORMATION

27   The changes in larger society, as well as their reverberations in the family, call into question basic assumptions about the nature of American society, its family arrangements, and Americans themselves. A "cultural struggle" ensues as people debate the meaning of change. One of these periods of cultural upheaval occurred in the early decades of the nineteenth century; a second occurred in the decades just before and after the turn of the twentieth century. For the last thirty years, we have been living through another such wave of social change.

28   Three related structural changes seem to have set the current cycle of family change in motion: first, the shift into a "postindustrial" information and service economy; second, a demographic revolution that not only created mass longevity but reshaped the individual and family life course, creating life stages and circumstances unknown to earlier generations; third, a process I call "psychological gentrification," which involves an introspective approach to experience, a greater sense of one's own individuality and subjectivity, a concern with self-fulfillment and self-development. This is the change misdiagnosed as narcissism.

THE POSTINDUSTRIAL REVOLUTION

29   To most Americans, the "traditional" family consists of a breadwinner-father and a mother who stays home to care for the children and the household. When New Right politicians and preachers speak of the biblical, Christian, or Judeo-Christian family, this is the family pattern they have in mind. Yet in historical and international perspective, the breadwinner/housewife form of family is, as the sociologist Kingsley

Davis observes, an uncommon and short-lived arrangement—an "aberration that arose in a particular stage of development and tends to recur in countries now undergoing development."

30   The breadwinner family is actually the first form of the modern family, associated with the early stages of the Industrial Revolution. For most of human history, work was a household enterprise in which all family members took part. The shift of the workplace from the home that came with industry had a profound effect on gender as well as parent and child roles.

31   If the early stages of modernization helped to create the breadwinner/housewife family, the later stages helped to undo it. Davis has tracked the rise and fall of the breadwinner system in the United States and other countries at various stages of industrialism. With the onset of industrialization, the new family pattern develops slowly, eventually reaching a climax in which few wives are employed, then declines as a steadily growing number of married women find white-collar jobs as file clerks, secretaries, teachers, and the like. In America, the breadwinner system peaked in 1890.

32   Since 1945 the United States, along with other highly advanced societies, has been shifting from a goods-producing to a service-producing economy, from the factory to the office, from blue-collar work to white-collar work. The term "postindustrial society" is often used to describe this shift. Yet, as a number of writers have suggested, the changes seem more a continuation of industrial society—a high-tech era based on an increasingly complex division of labor, the further application of science and technology to increase productivity. If the steam engine, the steel plant, and the automobile assembly line symbolize the old order, the computer, VCR, satellite broadcasting, CAT scanners, and genetic engineering symbolize the new. One could also argue that the invention of the typewriter marks the onset of the postindustrial era, symbolizing the beginning of the service and information economy and the coming feminization of the work force.

33   The historical shift of women into the workplace has been going on for a century, but did not reach a critical mass until the 1970s. The long-term impact of postindustrialism on family life was magnified by the effects of inflation. The shift in the economy was reducing the number of high-paying blue-collar jobs for auto and steel workers, and creating a demand for the low-paying pink-collar jobs like typist and file clerk. Also, since the mid-1960s, the costs of food, housing, education, and other goods and services have risen faster than the average male breadwinner's income. Despite their lower pay, married women's contributions to the family income became critical to maintaining living standards in both middle- and working-class families.

34   It was this quiet revolution of women's steady march into the workplace that set the stage for the feminist revival of the 1970s. There is no evidence that feminist ideas led the mass of married women to work in the first place. Nevertheless, the impact of both the feminist movement and the new realities of working women has shifted the cultural ideal of marriage in a more egalitarian or symmetrical direction. At the moment, we are in a painful period of "cultural lag" or "stalled revolution." Women have changed, but social arrangements—and men—have not kept pace.

35   The postindustrial shift of women into the workplace has led to other changes in family life: it has increased the "opportunity costs" of pregnancy and child rearing—that is, the money lost when women leave their jobs to bear and raise children—fostering lower fertility rates. There is also some evidence that the increasing employment of women makes divorce more likely, by reducing a woman's dependence on her husband's income, making it easier for her to leave an unhappy marriage.

36   Finally, the shift to a service and information economy has had effects on family life besides those linked to gender. For young people, the coming of the postindustrial society has made adolescence and the transition to adulthood more complex and problematic, exacerbating a dilemma that arose in the nineteenth century with the decline of the family economy. A greater amount of schooling is now necessary not only to maintain middle-class status but even to find jobs in the manufacturing sector. Until the 1970s, there was a supply of moderately well-paying jobs that did not require a high school diploma. High school graduates could find an array of decent jobs open to them. More schooling was necessary for a middle-class career, but there were alternative paths to making a living.

37   The high-tech postindustrial economy has changed all that. Today all roads to a successful livelihood lead through the classroom. Recent decades have seen a plummeting demand for unskilled labor and a sharp decline in the kind of well-paying blue-collar job that used to form the backbone of the American economy. A young working-class man who in the 1950s could have found an unskilled job paying enough to support a family now faces radically curtailed economic prospects. These vast changes in the economy led to shifts in family behavior that paralleled those due to cultural change—later marriage, lower fertility, women flooding into the workplace. For many people, these choices reflected economic pressures, not new values.

THE LIFE-COURSE REVOLUTION

38 The breadwinner/housewife family was a response not only to nineteenth-century working conditions but to nineteenth-century demographic circumstances. Because people lived shorter lives and had more children, a woman could expect to live her entire life with children in the home. Today, the average woman can expect to live more than thirty-three years after her last child has left the house. The traditional nuclear unit of parents and small children exists for only a small proportion of the life of an individual or a family. Shifts in the length and patterning of the life course have made the conditions of modern existence unimaginably different from those that existed only a century ago.

39 Nostalgic images of family stability in past times typically leave out the terrible facts of high mortality rates in infancy and early adulthood. Before the twentieth century, death was as much a hovering presence in the home as divorce is today. While the death of a baby or small child was almost a typical experience of parents down to the early decades of the twentieth century, the loss of a father or mother was also a common event of childhood and adolescence. The biography of almost any Victorian conveys the vulnerability of even the upper classes to untimely death.

40   In historical perspective, these changes have been remarkably sudden. Only in the twentieth century could a majority of people expect to live out the normal life course of growing up, marrying, having children, and surviving with one's spouse until age fifty. The changes in life chances between the 1920s and the 1950s have been as rapid as in the years between 1880 and 1920.

41   In advanced societies today, death strikes few youngsters and few adults between their twenties and fifties. Couples in enduring marriages will spend most of their married life together without having young children in the home. The shrinking of the active parental phase of the life course is also one of the reasons women have entered the work force in increasing numbers since the 1950s. Domesticity is not enough to fill a life span of almost eighty years. Little wonder then that marriage has become more of a personal and sexual relationship than it was in the past.

42   The emergence of old age as an expectable part of the life course is, as Ronald Blyth points out, one of the essential ways we differ from our ancestors; today's elders are among the first generations in which the mass of the population, not just the hardy few, survive long enough to experience the aging process, that "destruction of the physical self" so familiar to us now. People over eighty-five are the fastest-growing age group today. But for much of old age, people are not *old* in the traditional sense but healthy and active.

43   Our lives have become not just longer but more complicated. Stages of life that scarcely existed a hundred years ago have become part of the average person's experience: adolescence, middle age, empty nest, retirement. Also, in recent years, the life course has grown more fluid; people experience more transitions than earlier generations did, not just because of rising divorce rates but because of changes in the workplace. In an age of rapidly changing technology and market conditions, few employees can count on being "organization" men or women the way people did in the 1950s.

44   Ironically, the demographic and social changes that lengthened and reshaped the life course were desired themselves, yet are responsible for some of the major problems besetting family life today. Before mass longevity, the aged were not a problem population because there were so few of them. Mixed-up adolescents were rare when adult work began in childhood and formal education ended, if it ever began, in grade school. Identity was not a problem when a person's place in society was decided at birth. In the past, middle-aged men and women were not sandwiched between the needs of their adolescent children and their aging parents; nor when life expectancy was forty-nine or fifty did they have to confront the issue of what to do with the rest of their lives. Even though the "woman question" was an issue during most of the nineteenth century, women then did not confront the reality that the active phase of mothering would usually involve only a small portion of their lives.

45   All of this possibility for change created new sources of stress. Transitions can be problematic periods in which both individual identities and family relations have to be redefined and renegotiated. The emergence of a focus on the self and the idea of development as applied to adults is not just a fantasy of pop psychology. The popularity of books like Gail Sheehy's *Passages* reflects genuine changes in the structure of

individual experience across the life course. The emergence of a heightened sense of self is a natural by-product of this more complicated life course.

PSYCHOLOGICAL GENTRIFICATION

46 The third major transformation is in part a product of the changes in the nature of work and in the shape of the life course. But it is also a product of other social and cultural changes, especially rising levels of education and increases in the standard of living and leisure time. In the past, few jobs required learning or personal development. Working hours were long—about fifty-three hours a week at the turn of the century—and there was little time for leisure or extended vacations. Thus men's lives were dominated by the job; women's, by domesticity.

47 The affluent, postindustrial society of the postwar era involved more than an increase in living standards. Despite persisting inequality, the decades since the end of World War II were years of remarkable progress for masses of Americans. The democratization that began in the 1940s when the G.I. Bill opened up educational opportunity and the possibilities of home ownership eventually led to "the democratization of personhood"—the opportunity for large numbers of ordinary people to "take themselves seriously . . . to make a sustained project of the ordinary self."

48 At a time when jeremiads about the decline of the American mind appear on the best-seller lists, it is easy to forget that during the post-war decades higher education became a reality for the first time to millions of Americans. In 1940 only 15 percent of young people between eighteen and twenty-two went to college; a college education was one of those rarely crossed boundaries separating the upper middle class from those below them. By the middle of the 1960s nearly half of young Americans went to college. By the end of the decade the number of college students was four times what it had been in the 1940s.

49 The explosion of education was due not only to the demand of a new middle class for what it saw as key to success for its children; it was also due to the need of a postindustrial economy for a more educated work force. However pragmatic and instrumental the motivation for increased education, rising educational levels have had a profound influence on American culture. Middle-class Americans became, as the sociologist Todd Gitlin observes, "cultural omnivores," traveling abroad, going to concerts, museums, and theaters, joining book clubs, in growing numbers. Everyday life in America has become "internationalized," as Americans became more familiar with and appreciative of other cultures. "We have grown from a nation of meat-and-potato eaters to a nation of sushi samplers," observes Walter Mead, "and we like it that way."

50 Another result of this increasing cosmopolitanism is that avant-garde ideas that had once shocked the bourgeoisie in earlier generations, from cubist painting to bohemian sexual mores to Freudian psychology, diffused to college students in the 1960s and then to the middle-class masses in the 1970s. This diffusion can be clearly seen in the comparison of the results of national surveys conducted in 1957 and 1976 by the University of Michigan's Institute of Social Research. Aimed at assessing the

state of American mental health, the studies delved into a wide range of questions concerning satisfactions and dissatisfactions with self, family relations, and work.

51 Comparisons of the two surveys reveal striking insights into the recent changes in American culture. In *The Inner American,* Joseph Veroff, Elizabeth Douvan, and Richard Kulka suggest that a "psychological revolution" took place between 1957 and 1976. Over the course of two decades, Americans had become more introspective, more attentive to inner experience, more willing to admit to marital and personal problems than in the past, and yet more satisfied with their marriages. Above all, they became more attentive to the emotional quality of relationships, not just in the family but at work as well. Increasingly, people wanted friendly, warm relationships at work and intimacy and closeness in the family.

52 Paradoxically, the new emphasis on warmth and intimacy can place new burdens on family relationships and create discontents that didn't exist when family life was a matter of conformity to social roles and rituals. But the results of this study, carried out at the height of the so-called Me Decade, show no evidence that we have become a nation of narcissistic, unattached individuals. Family ties were shown to be even more important than in the past, especially for men. Despite high divorce rates and a willingness to admit marital problems, the study found an overwhelming preference for being married, and many more men and women were happy about their marriages than they had been in 1957.

53 The Michigan studies provide clear documentation for the process of psychological gentrification. The habit of introspection, the psychological approach to life and preoccupation with warmth and intimacy was not new in the 1970s. In the 1950s, however, it was found almost exclusively among the most highly educated. Twenty years later this way of looking at the self and the world had become "common coin."

CONCLUSION

54 As a result of all the changes I discussed in this chapter, the realities of life in late-twentieth-century America and other advanced societies are unlike those faced by any earlier generation. No other people ever lived longer or healthier lives, or exercised so much choice about life's central dramas: work, marriage, parenthood. Many of the troubles and anxieties confronting the American family today arise out of benefits few of us would undo if we could—lower mortality rates, reliable birth control, mass education, the democratization of American life.

55 The metaphor of an earthquake, often invoked to describe the social and cultural upheavals of the 1960s and 1970s, turns out to be a fairly good model of what actually did happen during those years. No other natural cataclysm—hurricanes, tornadoes, floods—strikes less randomly than earthquakes; they occur at fairly regular intervals, along clearly detectable fault lines.

56 The seismic forces at work in the social and cultural earthquake were, on the one side, locked-in cultural norms about family structure, gender roles, and sexuality

and, on the other, a set of long-term changes that include the demographic, economic, and structural trends I have discussed. For example, the sexual revolution of the 1960s was also a product of a long trend away from Victorian sexual restrictions; premarital sex had been increasing gradually since the early decades of the twentieth century. As a result of these trends, social reality was increasingly at odds with the prevailing assumptions that "all brides are virgins, all marriages are first marriages, all wives are housewives."

57   The reality of everyday experience was at odds not only with the rigidity of middle-class norms but also with the cultural images of family happiness that were supposed to result from holding on to those norms. All during the silent 1950s, these discontents were simmering below the surface. In the 1960s and 1970s the upheavals of the Vietnam War and racial tensions called established cultural norms into question. Pressure continued to build up along the fault line, the trends reaching what the sociologist Jessie Bernard calls "tipping points." Behavior that had formerly been practiced only by a minority approached, or became, majority behavior. In a time of political turbulence, the two sides of the fault line jolted apart. We are still digging out the rubble, but there is no way of going back to where we were before.

WRITING ASSIGNMENTS

Analysis

1. Skolnick uses one metaphor, "embattled paradise," to characterize the family, and another, "a cultural earthquake," to describe its recent history. Explain the connotations of these metaphors and assess their relevance to the information contained in her essay.
2. Skolnick begins her essay by recalling the 1962 *Look* magazine article that predicted what America would look like 25 years later. Assess the effectiveness of this lead-in. How does this historical anecdote draw the reader into the essay? What themes does it introduce?
3. Explain what Skolnick means when she says, "If the steam engine, the steel plant, and the automobile assembly line symbolize the old order, the computer, VCR, satellite broadcasting, CAT scanners, and genetic engineering symbolize the new."
4. *Collaborative Project:* Survey adults who came of age during the 1960s or 1970s, and compare their views then and now on any of the following: the sexual revolution, divorce, women's liberation, homosexuality, homosexual rights, single-parent families, or abortion. What do they think Americans have gained and lost?
5. Apply Skolnick's comments about "psychological gentrification" to the attitudes toward gender roles and family relations of Andy's father in "Doe Season," the child's parents in "Daddy," or Larry's parents in "Sunday in the Park."

Argument

1. *Collaborative Project:* Write the transcript of a debate in which these are the two positions: (1) The increase in teen pregnancies, divorce, and single-parent, often-poor families illustrates moral decay in modern America; and (2) These factors are best explained by economic and social changes.
2. Skolnick quotes one anthropologist as saying that the nuclear family was "a biological phenomenon—as rooted in organs and physiological structures as insect societies." Use the selections in Chapters 1 and 2 to support or refute the biological basis of the nuclear family.

Personal Writing and Writing from Research

1. Skolnick says, ". . . the impact of both the feminist movement and the new realities of working women has shifted the cultural ideal of marriage in a more egalitarian or symmetrical direction. At the moment, we are in a painful period of 'cultural lag' or 'stalled revolution.' Women have changed, but social arrangements—and men—have not kept pace." As a collaborative project using library research and interviews, evaluate Skolnick's generalizations in terms of one of the following issues:

   - men's and women's respective goals in marriage and criteria for selecting a spouse,
   - the division of labor in the home, including child care,
   - adjustments in the workplace to accommodate workers with family responsibilities,
   - compensation for women and men in the same fields, and for men and women in comparable fields that have traditionally been sex-stereotyped, such as nursing, teaching, fire and police work, construction, the trades, and engineering.

2. *Collaborative Project:* Focusing on several prime-time, long-running programs, construct one or more portraits of American family life today.
3. Interview several of your contemporaries about their assessment of contemporary American family life. Move from this general topic to their personal experiences and then to their hopes and plans for the future. Use the evidence you have gathered to write a paper confirming or denying the cultural and structural changes described by Skolnick.
4. Select one of the three structural changes in American society that Skolnick identifies and write a paper describing how it has affected your family and your own expectations.
5. Select one of the following historical developments mentioned in Skolnick's essay to investigate further: changes in the college-going population, the changing nature of work and workers, the "democratization of culture," and the changing nature of leisure in America. Have these developments affected men and women differently?

Forty in the Shade

John McCluskey, Jr.

Born in Middletown, Ohio, in 1944, John McCluskey, Jr., received a BA from Harvard and an MA in creative writing from Stanford. A professor of African-American literature at Indiana University in Bloomington, McCluskey is praised for his sense of history and strong feeling for black cultural traditions. He believes that the African-American cultural experience has been a heroic one that has nurtured the individual and the group. A critic, essayist, editor, and fiction writer, McCluskey published his first novel, *Look What They Done to My Song,* in 1974. "Forty in the Shade" comes from his second novel, *Mr. America's Last Season Blues* (1983).

Journal Topics: (1) Profile one or more of your ancestors whom you regard as a role model. What skills and personal qualities did this person possess? Are you and this role model the same sex? (2) How do the challenges that you face differ from those your same-sex parent or grandparents faced?

As You Read: (1) Identify the qualities that define manhood in the Americus family. (2) Compare the role that men and women play in the several generations of this family. (3) Describe how Roscoe Jr. differs from his forefathers and how his world differs from theirs. (4) How does the issue of race contribute to the challenges faced by the men in the Americus family?

The loves and lives of the daddies of daddies of daddies. New blood in those extensions as they drive through their lives. On his fortieth birthday, Roscoe Sr., had walked into the kitchen, pushed his hat far back on his head, relit a stub of a cigar, and spoke to his four sons gathered restlessly at the kitchen table.

"Cut that playing out now." Then he had settled back in a chair, stroking his belly upward. That was the signal. Roscoe Jr., stopped cuffing his brothers on the sides of their heads. Irwin snatched a wandering marble from under the table and straightened up.

"You boys young now. Or at least you pretend you young. But I know you got sense. You lived in this house long enough for you to have good sense. So believe me when I tell you that you only as young as you feel. A lot of folks say that, but only a few live by it. You can do anything you want if you decide to. Anything, that is, except act too mannish and cross me and your mama. Especially your mama. If you cross me, you'll get stripes across your butts, just a whippin. But if you cross your mama, you in for a stone beatin. You'll look worse than a zebra. But I'm not here to scare you this day, just here to tell you that I feel like a million dollars, and when y'all get to be forty years old just remember what your old man was like on this day. And that he announced that he would never die."

Looks were traded all around. Except that it was afternoon and he was home with the family, he looked OK. There was no madness burning brightly in the eyes, no nervous high-voltage wringing of the hands. These were the only cues the boys knew, picked up from watching Mr. Otis Sparks whom everyone called crazy. Sparks was a man who walked the back alleys at night, crying, groaning, chanting to himself. Nutty as a fruitcake, neighbors had whispered about him. But, no, there was nothing like that about their father. And he said that he would live forever!

5   They shrugged and watched him go tenderly among his gifts. The can of cheap cigars was Emmanuel's idea. The shirts in brilliant geometric designs were Irwin's. Irwin would be a whiz with triangles and trigonometry. The checkered ties to balance the shirts were Chris's gift, Irwin was just a kid after all. Roscoe Sr., would wear those shirts and those ties, not together, however, but wear them just the same, for he would rather risk the teases of gin-drinking poker players than the disappointment of his sons.

And after the thank-yous and the bearhugs, the older boys would notice him slipping two fingers of bourbon into his tea. That afternoon, forty in the shade of his kitchen, he would sip from the cup, lean dangerously back in the chair, and tell them what they had heard only a few times before. About family and blood and time. About how the family was so tight and never took any mess from anything or anybody. He would lead them through the maze of family history, the broken line of steel mills, of stinking slaughterhouses, and the Ohio River, of Georgia pine forests. The end was the beginning, and a huge man and a town in Georgia—Georgia where the root ends were warmed at the fiery core. Of family of blood of time.

BUT, DADDY

And it was 1834, that end which was the beginning, and the lie of Major Riley. No one knew where the "major" part came from except, perhaps, that the old man was continually waiting around for a war to prove his courage. Such a war would never come, at least enough for him to recognize the daily struggles of men as war. The man died in 1859, mad, wrestling death in a shameful way, much like an old hound, its throat slashed, yet still closing in on a cornered raccoon.

But in 1834 his tall slave Caesar, the best blacksmith in south-central Georgia, bought his freedom. Was given a note from the courage-keeping major. "Return this boy to me." Caesar couldn't read, and thought the scribbling was sure enough freedom papers, a sign of mutual honor among men. He started north on a useless swaybacked horse that the major sold him. Only once did he bother to show that note. That one time was almost his undoing. He showed it to a kind-faced bank clerk who was riding out to a plantation to confirm some figures. The man greeted Caesar and summoned enough nerve to ask for the freedom paper. He read it, then rode down the road a piece with Caesar. When they came upon three paterollers, he turned Caesar over to them. Caesar was only five miles from Riley's plantation and somehow hoping that the North, the Ohio River, would be just over the next ridge. Tennessee as an acre, Kentucky as a backyard of his new life.

The three men led him back to the Major, the long-gone clerk done read them the note because they couldn't read either. They were grizzled men in tatters, "dirt-eaters" they used to call them. Well, they rode back a couple miles before Caesar took and slapped away the rifle of one of the men, slammed a right to the face of another man, crushing bone, and urged the broken-down horse toward the trees. A ball whizzed past his head. Another. He dug his heels into that horse's ribs. They got to the woods, crossed a stream, then headed for thicker cover. Whatever that horse was, he seemed to take to the forest, wasn't scared of the darkness and the trees, whatsoever. Caesar slapped that horse on, and they followed the stream away from Riley's plantation. Yells, curses, screams behind them. Were they a mile away from the paterollers? Were the men just at his ear? He didn't bother to look back, just pushing that horse on, knowing that it would fall out sooner or later from being so tired and from surprise that it could run so fast.

10   And away, away he rode, not knowing where except that it was away from the plantations. He rode for what seemed like hours until that horse slowed down and stopped. Caesar cursed and kicked that horse, then realized that it had done the best it could do. It needed rest. "Can you see him now, boys? Can you see him in those strange woods on foot?"

Roscoe Sr., had stood, his hat cocked well over one eye by then, fists raised. Then he removed his hat and ran his thumb across his forehead. From the front of the house came their mother's humming, the insistent hum that's never noticed until it stops. The boys didn't dare move, didn't dare speak.

"You must see him lead that horse out of the woods and look across a road to a big field of cotton. There must have been a dozen or so folk in the field, and every once in a while one of them would straighten up and half-scream, half-chant his way through a song. Like young Job who screamed like a woman and called that singing. Then down the road came a wagon. The driver was sitting up there with his head down, shoulders rocking slowly to the corner of his mouth, a large floppy hat draped low, shadowing his eyes. Caesar greeted the man, scaring him half to death. The driver looked around to see if the overseer was around.

"What do you want?" that driver must have asked.

"I want somebody to write a note for me." As he fanned flies, he explained all to the driver, trusting him. The man glanced again to the woods, to the broken-down horse nibbling brush at the wood's edge, to the big man standing in front of the wagon. Then he scratched his throat.

15   "Only person I know can write is back there about a mile. Name is Ola. But you better not try to see her. She in the house." He must have explained that the owner of the plantation was away, but that the head overseer was around. "You wait here off the road, back up in the piney woods. I'll take you to her."

"How long will that be?" Caesar asked. Any second now he expected the white trash to come busting out of those woods.

"I don't know. Just do like I say if you want me to help you."

Why should he trust that man he had never seen before? Just because they were the same color? He was never going back to Riley's plantation. Never. He faded into the trees, looking behind, around him, searching out sound, then watched the road. Again, the screamchant from the field.

And it seemed like hours before that wagon came back along the road, moving just as slow as it did before. Looking straight ahead as the wagon came up, the driver said, "Climb in back there and get under that blanket. And keep still if you don't want one hundred lashes."

20 "To hell with lashes," I can hear Caesar saying. "I take lashes off no man."

"Just hush up and get in back." Caesar could hear the man talking as that wagon started moving. He told Caesar about three men who stopped him three miles down the road. They asked him whether he had seen a big man on an ugly gray horse. The driver said that he had and pointed off in another direction. They lit out, not even bothering to thank him.

"Their horses looked a little tired. We don't have much time. They might come back trying to find me."

Yet Caesar still wondered at his faith. Suppose this man driving the wagon had told them otherwise? Suppose they were waiting up the road to take him in? They'd give the driver a new coat for his treason. You often trusted those you suffered with, but then only a few of those could be trusted with your life. The wagon slowed, picked up speed, slowed again. Either the man or the horse couldn't make up its mind. Why was it taking so long? Caesar kept an eye out, watched the brownish red road snake from under the wagon and away. The wagon pulled inside a gate, then stopped. He heard voices.

"Stay here and don't move, son. I'm bringing Ola for you."

25 The afternoon sun baked him under the scratchy cover. Flies discovered the smell of his sweat from the small opening he kept in order to breathe. Flies as traitors, the enemy that sun. And he waited, not moving, just the fingers still propping the cover to keep the air coming in, though it was as if a hand had been clapped over his nose and mouth. Then footsteps, a woman's voice shushed quiet.

"I got somebody here who can write. Tell her what you want. Just stay like you is."

Caesar could see only the gray cotton skirt draped over thin hips, an elbow with dry skin at the joint.

"Sho is hot, Cle," the voice said. Then she asked Caesar what he wanted her to write. He told her, watching her arm move. "Not so fast." She wrote on, the old man talking to himself about the weather, about fishing. Then several pieces of paper dropped past the opening. She pushed two pieces under the cover and picked up the others.

"Clumsy, ain't I?" she giggled.

30 "Thank you, girl. We'll see you later."

The gray dress moved away. Caesar heard the man climb in the wagon. They were moving again, turning in a circle.

"You going back to your horse and them piney woods now. Ola gave you two papers. You might lose one. You never know."

They moved on the bumpy road, and Caesar tried to make out the writing. He couldn't read, only judge script. But it was too dark to judge. He pushed the paper into the light.

"Put that paper back in! The woods got eyes, that cotton field got eyes. Them crows can spread secrets just as sure as I'm sitting here. Ain't you lived long enough to know that?"

35   Then soon the wagon stopped. "There's yo' hoss yonder. He should be good and rested by now. There's something for him in this here bucket. When you finish with the bucket leave it by the big bush over there. Walk back in the woods and wait until dark. Ain't too long now 'fore dark. Then y'all start north. Them po' trash will probably stop somewhere and get drunk come dark. You follow the north star, son. Just follow the star."

A HOME, WHERE?

Then Chris had shifted, Emmanuel shifted. The name, Daddy. Tell us about the name.

Sons, we here as testimony of Caesar's faith in the old man and his courage getting through woods at night. South Georgia was evil in them days, the devil's playground. If I could find you boys another word for it, I would tell it to you. But evil is the best I can do now 'cause your Mama in the next room half-listenin' and she don't want me introducin' y'all to cuss words . . .

His mind was on the North. On Canada and the snow. Somebody probably told him about cutting east to Savannah and catching a ship bound for Philadelphia or someplace like that. But Caesar was not excited about getting out on anybody's ocean, so he took his chances on land. Chance those paterollers, those mountains in Tennessee, past those caves in Kentucky that could hide a hundred bears, past those Indians in Ohio who caught and boiled runaway slaves for stew—that's what they used to tell them in those days, you know. He knew the dangers, though not the vastness of the land. Can you ride with him awhile?

Two days after he left the plantation with his new papers, he stopped just above a small town and rested under some big ol' pine trees. They probably smelled like turpentine. By now those things like slave catchers and Indians didn't bother him. Now it was his name that bothered him. He had told himself that he would take the Major's last name whenever he went free. That was before the Major tried to trick him back into slavery. No, he'd never call himself Riley.

40   He lay beneath that tree thinking, must have. It was nice there and he rested and the horse rested, and he knew that somewhere he would have to leave that horse and get another one. Gotta leave the best of your helpers sometimes. That town was quiet and peaceful, and somewhere he heard a bell ringing. He must have thought again about the North. If he had to stay in the woods, would there be plenty of fish in the creeks, plenty rabbits in the woods just like down there?

He decided just like that to take the name of that town because of that peaceful moment, nothing else. Somehow with the name he could always remember that moment of peace while struggling to get away. Americus was the name of the town. Americus was the name he took. Caesar Americus. (Years later somebody would tell him how the town got its name. It was named after the richest, powerfulest, and drunkest man around. The man used to claim that he was "a merry ole cuss" and so named his town after his ways. Some white folks got strange ways of makin' jokes, sons.)

He never told how he got from central Georgia. And to me that was always the part I wanted to hear about. Did he go west to the Mississippi and catch a boat going up past Memphis, St. Louis, and Cairo, Illinois? Did he get in with a free black family riding North in a wagon? We don't know, except three months later this warm-weather man done crossed the Ohio River and is working in Cincinnati. It was October and turning cold already. The first chill made him give up thinking about Canada for a while.

He worked on the river. After all, it wasn't the ocean and you could always see the other side. You could make a lot of money working the river. In those days, river rats was what they called the men working on the barges. And he soon became the heart of legends as something of an imitator. Could solo at the head of crews doing them Irish songs. Out-Irish the Irish, he could. Could do the same with the German language, too. Plus he could out-drink them red-faced Germans who came to Cincinnati with their beer recipes and would make whole fortunes on beer, then later on sausages and hams. And he stayed on in that town which on warm evenings grew to stink of river and a little further up among its hills to smell of slaughtered cows and pigs.

In 1842 Caesar opened a bar on the levee, a bar which became the prime target of threats and hisses from the local chapter of the Colored Women's Temperance Society. A window was once broken by an enraged woman screaming about the evils of drink. She called Caesar the devil's helper and a scoundrel who gave the race a bad name. She aimed a rock at the shingle with his name over the door, NORTH STAR CAFE, C. AMERICUS, ESQ., PROPRIETOR. Missed. Then the others joined in the screaming, looking around for rocks. Caesar pleaded with them. Told them they were taking food from the mouths of his young wife and baby sons. He promised a healthy donation to the society, to close at a decent hour, to allow no man to drink himself into a blind stupor. He told them he would even take the "bones" from the fists of the river rats. All this he told them, hating himself for having to say it. All this to save his North Star Café, a testimony to faith.

BUT, DADDY, WHERE IS HOME IN THIS STRANGE LAND?

45   The bar would be passed down, battle-tried, standing squat there near the alley in Bucktown. From Caesar's oldest son Stewart to Stewart's oldest son Asbury to his second son Leo because Asbury's oldest, Theodore, my Daddy, had died in France in 1918. It stopped with Uncle Leo, who wasn't too interested in running a café. The

family café died out until I come up here and opened up my little place over the B & O tracks. But it ain't good enough yet to call a real café in the way the family used to have. One of these days it will be.

But let me get back to Caesar. The business was his life, though he raised big strapping sons who worked the river. One went clear to Oberlin to hear the great Frederick Douglass and shake his hand. There were the two who fought for the Union, the same two who begged their father, fifty-year-old Caesar, to stay at the café and keep it open. Folks would need that kind of place to talk, lean back in their chairs, back into their lives. Although he could still floor a bull with one punch, they thought him too old to do anything else. He resigned himself to an uneasy peace of sheltering countless frightened families who crossed over from Kentucky, content to feed them hot meals and let the men sample his homemade whiskey.

He kept the bar open for blue-suited men who would limp in, their pants baggy, thinning in the seat and at the knees, and coats too tight. An army of men. They would sit long into the winter nights, and they would talk of battles along hills and rivers named after Indians. The men pointed to scars and said that they never wanted to see war again. When Caesar died, these same scarred men rode through the night to make one of the largest funerals ever held in Cincinnati.

Let me tell y'all right quick about the end of the North Star Café in that town. It was 1918, a little before the war ended. Leo, bless his soul, wasn't too good a manager. He thought the bar could run itself on its past history, I guess. So when he saw it was about to go under, he sold it to an Irishman named Gilligan. Didn't check with none of the family, just up and sold the place. Well, I was mad at him for that, stayed mad at him for that, stayed mad at him for years. I hung around town working in the stockyards and in a foundry for five or six years before I came up here. Heard that the steel and paper mills were hiring like crazy. When I got up here, I walked into the rolling mill office, and the man gave me a shovel and asked me if I could start that day. Worked long hours and made real good money, too. Then later on I fell in with a man named Herschel Evans, and old Herschel had him a truck. On weekends we'd drive down to the coal mines, right along the Ohio River below Portsmouth. We'd leave before the sun came up, get down there, and load that truck skyhigh with coal, buy some large jars of moonshine, and bring all that back here. We'd sell the coal and moonshine in one day, try to get some sleep, and then be back in the mill the next day. By and by I had enough money so that I could open me up an after-hours joint. Right where it is now at the B & O overpass. All these years I've wanted to buy another place, but it's never worked out that way. The depression came along and stopped everything. Settled over this town like a mean and suffocating fog.

It took until after the war for me to really recover. Started fish fries on Friday nights and chicken fries on Saturdays. Your mama did most of the cooking. They were fighting to get in here then, so many of them. I painted the windows black out of respect for the church folk and had to pay a little side-money to Officer Starkey to keep them quiet downtown at police headquarters. There were four of y'all already. Bedrooms had to be added on and the kitchen needed new plumbing. Well, it got so we kept it open four nights a week.

AND DADDY WHAT MORE, EVEN NOW FROM BEYOND DEATH, WHAT MORE?

50 And still what more of the birth, of work, of death of the fathers? The deaths were quick. Caesar died in the café, a loud laugh going to a rattling cough. He fell to the floor behind the bar. Steward died just as suddenly, while breaking up an argument between two teamsters. Asbury died of pneumonia, the result of working in the rain while helping to put up a YMCA building. Dazed from gas, Theodore stepped on a mine in central France. But Roscoe Sr.'s death was the cruelest of all.

By his fiftieth birthday, Roscoe Sr., the Old Man, as the boys had begun to call him, could afford to drive a red Buick Dynaflow. He wore another dark hat, greying already along the brim, cocked to one side of his large head. There was always a half-smoked cigar in one corner of his mouth. On that fiftieth birthday he leaned back on a chair in the bright kitchen as he had done ten years before.

"Sons, gather close to you the ones you love and protect them if you can." That before the history.

Strange about the murderers of giants in this world—the thinness of their rage, their unforgivable isolation. It was snaggatoothed Jake Mays who did it. Few folks respected Mays and it wasn't just because of his weakness. A weak man can be tolerated and even loved by some. But Mays's weakness willed ugliness. He'd smack a woman or a child for show, but he never touched a man who insulted him.

It started, if it is ever clear when anything starts, when Mays lost his first ten fights as a child, when his father looked at him in pity, frowning at his fistless son. Or was it simply the day after the night Jake lost one hundred dollars in an American Legion crap game? That morning he was on his way to Robinson's Café for a cup of coffee. To tease the new big-legged waitress, maybe, and let any stray smile from her soothe his sense of hurt. Tyrone was playing touch football in the street with a gang of other boys. Quarterback for one of the teams, Tyrone faded back, as he had heard Otto Graham do, and fired a long pass to one of his men. The ball missed the outstretched arms of the receiver by a few yards and hit slow-moving Jake square in the face. The players leaned on fences, cars, on each other, snickering. Looked at Mays's hurt face and laughed some more. Tyrone ran to gather the ball and mumbled something about being sorry. But it was those grins and laughs that Mays saw and heard. He limped closer to Tyrone and smacked him hard. Once. No one moved. Then, as Mays moved away, Tyrone searched for a rock, a pop bottle, to throw. Whatever he found and threw missed. Mays turned around, stared at the boy, then walked on more quickly, looking back twice.

55 When Roscoe heard about it, he walked out of the house. He found Mays at Robinson's, hunched over coffee. He called Mays outside, and without a word he whipped Mays like a child. The few people in the café crowded in the door to watch, the slaps sounding like dull shots. Then Roscoe let him drop to the pavement, bleeding from a busted lip.

"Don't ever touch one of my boys again. Nobody touches my sons except me." Then he turned and walked away, wiping his hands as if he had touched something filthy.

But there is even a pride in cowardice, a desperate and nervous pride. Near dawn, with a knife and slipping up on the Old Man as he was closing up, Mays found a desperate strength to strike once, twice. Surprised at what he had done, he covered his opened mouth with both hands and ran. Another man, rushing to catch a hand in the last poker game, found Roscoe near the door trying to crawl inside. The knife lay only a few feet away. This man cried his way to a phone and called an ambulance. Then he called Roscoe's home. The sons beat the ambulance there. Beat the 6:30 freight train that rumbled past every morning, heading south, shaking the old blackeyed building.

By the time of the funeral it was decided between Roscoe and Emmanuel that they would have to catch Mays, that he would have to die. He already had a four-day head-start. The question was who. Roscoe Jr., was finishing his freshman year at Ohio State, and the boys argued that he should go back to school. When Earline overheard them, she tried to stop such talk. After all, there was a law, and to harm the worthless Mays would be two crimes committed. They told her that justice was a sometime thing if you didn't perform it yourself.

And Emmanuel packed a bag after talking with old Silas, a man who roomed in the same house with Mays. Silas, with the all-seeing eye, said Mays was in Chicago. Emmanuel left without saying good-bye to anyone, and by the next morning he was winding through Indiana, feeding a quart of oil to his old Ford every three hundred miles, a revolver resting beneath the front seat. No one heard from him for a month. And no one expected Emmanuel to return without Mays. Emmanuel, the quiet one who sang in the church choir and rarely had fights while growing up. But when he did fight he hurt others so badly. Didn't know where to stop, this Emmanuel, whose intensity silenced the agitators and forced them to look around for someone to stop these few fights.

60   Then the scribbled letters started coming and kept coming, one about every other month for the next three years. At first Earline would read the letters silently, then refold them. She hid them away, and all they knew were the names of the towns. "Your brother is in Battle Creek, Wyoming, now." After she died a letter mysteriously came to Baby Sister once a year. Baby Sister also found the earlier ones and shared them with Roscoe and any other brother who happened to visit her. All those tortured letters with no return addresses.

One letter said he had missed Mays by three days in St. Paul, Minnesota. When a letter came from Lincoln, Nebraska, the brothers figured Mays's time was up. In a place like that Mays should stick out like a rabbit against the snow. But then the letters came from Denver, Salt Lake City, Cheyenne, Denver again. Places Roscoe had never been, could barely imagine except as towns where cowboys shot up bars on Saturday nights.

Earline went to work in a container plant and raised her children. She was too old to start factory work, but they needed the money. Factory work paid much better than domestic work. A sympathetic foreman understood and gave her the lightest job on the line. The boys helped her run the after-hours club on weekends. Baby Sister ran the house.

Earline had talked less and less about Emmanuel before she died, as she talked less and less about the law and justice. Her husband had died at the hands of a miserable and lonely man, and no matter how senseless and enraging the fact, nothing would ever bring the big man back home. Emmanuel would come back one day, and she had hoped to live to see that day. She hoped that when he did return he could still smile, that he could live again, that everything in his life had not been wasted.

OLD MAN, WHERE IS THE FAITH IN THE NOW OF OUR PASTS?

On the morning of his fortieth birthday, Roscoe Jr., stopped his car in front of the house where until two months ago he had lived. As if on cue, his two daughters rushed to the car, appearing as if they wanted to turn, but were held in check by that shadow behind the front door. Roscoe waved to the shadow of his wife, then opened the door for his children.

65   "Give me a little of that good sugar," he begged them. "Thataway, thataway." Then he pulled them down and announced that he was taking them to the zoo. They clapped their hands, did mean shimmies in their gratitude. Real showboats, his girls. Real class. They presented him with a boldly striped silk tie, and he made a mighty fuss over it. Then he let them roll the window down partially, but not too much, he scolded, because once they would get on the expressway, the wind might just reach in and pull them out.

"Then we could fly?" asked Grace, the daughter with Roscoe's mouth and forehead.

Mayisha giggled. "The way you eat, Grace, you'd be too heavy to fly." Mayisha, with her mother's face, who would be very tall. Roscoe remembered the slouch of her shoulders as she walked to the car. Teach a tall woman to keep high her head and shoulders. Teach her to move like a natural queen. He would teach her not to deny nature's gift of elegant motions. Ever. It only made for stunted beauty.

The girls talked of approaching summer, of swimming lessons they looked forward to, of Bible school they wanted to avoid. Roscoe was relieved that they were still too young for boys. What would he do then? What will he do then? What will he do now? All that he knew for sure was that he was taking his two daughters out for a summer's day and nothing else—the bar, the insatiable Everjean, spiteful Charlotte—nothing else mattered.

Grace curled up next to him. "Daddy, when are we going to King's Point like you promised?"

70   "How come you're asking Daddy?" Mayisha asked. "You're scared of all the rides anyway."

"Well, let's just see how things turn out today, huh? Today is the zoo."

And the zoo was a hot round of cages with Roscoe coaxing the girls back to see the lions twice. Cotton candy, peanuts, and popcorn. He loved the zoo as much as they did. Zoos and circuses had always been weaknesses of his. Some people remembered cities by the weather or money made or lost there, by lovers. Roscoe remembered places by the food, the bars, and most important, the zoos. There were Washington and Cleveland and St. Louis and San Diego and the Bronx, good zoos in all those places. As he watched the lions for the second time, the girls fidgeted and hummed songs. He considered other places, other times.

Once into a time the air was much chillier, no leaves on the trees. For seven hours he held his wife's hands in the labor room of a hospital. Her lips dry, her eyes frequently opening in the stunned surprise of the cycle of pain. Roscoe held her hands and tried to think of the greatest pain he had known. The twisted knee in the Michigan game? The cracked rib much earlier in high school? None of the bumps, few of the smashes of bone against his muscle gave him pain great beyond the moment. Few caused hours of agony. As he looked at his wife he was a little embarrassed that there was a mystery about her pain that he could never know. Was it a ripple of pain moving wavelike across her belly? A sharp stab? Later in the waiting room after she had been wheeled into delivery, he studied the afternoon. Outside it was partly sunny with the temperature near freezing. He could hear the steady rhythm of a heavy wire against the flagpole in front of the hospital. The traffic flowed in the fitful movement of his luck. It would be a boy this time, he knew. A big healthy fat-cheeked baby boy to carry the family name. Then he thought again to the pain, though his wife would be numbed from her stomach down. Again, to the pain he could only guess at.

"Daddy, how come we can't do this every day?"

75 Grace. It was Grace talking through her mouthful of popcorn. Grace that afternoon, too.

"You'd like the zoo every day, Grace?" asked Roscoe, reaching to retie a ribbon around her hair.

"Well, not zoos all the time. Maybe parks, yeah, parks. Or swimming? Mama doesn't like to swim."

"Maybe your mama gets a little tired sometime working around the house. You have to understand that."

"I understand," she said, taking another fistful of popcorn. "But I still like the parks and swimming and stuff like that."

80 He and Charlotte had agreed not to get back at one another through the girls, not to use them as weapons. They would tell them that, even though they were separated, they still loved each other and the girls very very much. The children would nod helplessly and they wouldn't understand. They could not understand what their parents could not understand.

"Hey, girl, you almost finished with that popcorn? Let's go back to the bears."

Mayisha had been quietly watching the morning crowd, the Cub Scout troops, the elderly folk with small bags of peanuts. Mayisha, the serene wise one. She'd be a painter, photographer, taking in all in the way she does. Roscoe knew that he'd screen the boys so roughly that only the most intelligent, the most aggressive would trouble themselves for her. After all, she wouldn't want to be bothered with idle chatter about clothes, cars, and dances. No, not his Mayisha.

With Roscoe holding his daughters' hands, they moved off through the bright afternoon. The times with his daughters were the best times. The lady days. Going home, he told them the funny animal stories his grandmother had once told him. One day he would tell them the family history.

Then in the speckled shade of an old maple tree in front of the house, Roscoe's ladies stepped grandly from the car. A finger lowered a slat in the front window venetian blinds. He was ready for the stare coming over it from the cool dark of the house he once called home. The stare of those last days, the last nights that he slept on the couch. The girls lingered at the curb. After the hugs and kisses, they stood there wanting more, expecting more, needing more. But there was only his smile.

85   "Will we see you tomorrow, daddy?"

"I can't promise tomorrow, but I can promise you Saturday. Where do you want to go?"

"Fun Park, can we Daddy, huh? I want to try the roller coaster this time."

Roscoe nodded and waved. "Take care of your pretty selves. And your mother."

He pulled off from the shadow of the old tree and down the quiet street into the gloom of memory. Stared into the mirror.

90   "Well, Old Man, what do you think now? Am I less of a man because I didn't go inside and hold the woman I've loved for seven of the last twelve years?"

Then he caught himself, as he noticed Mrs. Patterson pausing to watch him from among her daffodils. He smiled at the elderly woman who once brought them spice cakes. Waved, this man Americus, this former husband, football and wrestling star—waved and drove to the other side of town.

WRITING ASSIGNMENTS

Analysis

1. Does the story celebrate Roscoe Jr.'s patriarchal heritage as unambivalently as he does? Explain Roscoe Jr.'s views, but also provide an alternative assessment of Caesar and Roscoe Sr. If you share Roscoe Jr.'s enthusiasm, do you believe that the model his forefathers set is still worth emulating today?

2. Rewrite this multigenerational saga from Earline's perspective. Take account of these details: (a) "When Earline overheard them, she tried to stop such talk. After all, there was a law, and to harm the worthless Mays would be two crimes committed." (b) "She hoped that when he [Emmanuel] did return he could still smile, that he could live again, that everything in his life had not been wasted."

3. Explain the rhetorical effect of beginning the story with Roscoe Sr.'s 40th birthday and ending it with Roscoe Jr.'s.

4. Compare and contrast the father-daughter relationships in "Forty in the Shade," "Seventeen Syllables," and "Doe Season."

5. How does the history of the Americus family illustrate Skolnick's analysis of the effects on the family of the post-Industrial Revolution?

Argument

1. Imagine you are a 40-year-old Emmanuel who has never found Mays and now plans to come home. Write a letter to Roscoe Jr. in which you either defend or

regret the years spent seeking to avenge your father's murder. Your self-justification should take into account your sense of family traditions and manly values.

2. Use the story of the Americus family to argue that children, particularly boys, either do or do not need the active involvement on a father figure in their lives.

3. Who is the better male role model, Larry's father in "Sunday in the Park" or Roscoe Sr. in "Forty in the Shade"?

4. Defend or oppose the efficacy and justice of occasional violence, drawing your illustrations from "Forty in the Shade," "Seventeen Syllables," and "Sunday in the Park."

Personal Writing and Writing from Research

1. There are many storytellers in "Forty in the Shade," beginning with Caesar, who tells his story to the driver to gain an ally in his escape. How is storytelling used to inculcate values, motivate action, and explain experience? Write an essay explaining the function of storytelling in the Americus family and in your own. Include stories from your own family to illustrate your points.

2. Research the laws and customs governing slave family life before Emancipation, and then compare the views of several social historians and sociologists on the long-term effects of these laws and customs on African-American families.

My Father's Song

Simon J. Ortiz

Poet and short-story writer Simon Ortiz (b. 1941) is an Acoma Pueblo Indian. He was born in Albuquerque, New Mexico, and educated in Bureau of Indian Affairs schools. After Army service, he attended the University of New Mexico and the University of Iowa. He has taught at several universities and edits the *Rough Rock News,* a Native-American publication. His books include *Naked in the Wind* (1970), *The Good Journey* (1977), *Howbah Indians* (1977), *Fight Back: For the Sake of the People* (1980), *A Poem Is a Journey* (1981), and *From Sand Creek* (1982). "My Father's Song" appeared in *Going for the Rain* (1976).

Journal Topics: Write a brief physical description of your father or of a man who played an important role in your childhood. Then briefly describe your memory of an event that characterizes this man for you.

As You Read: Although the speaker repeatedly refers to his father's voice, his songs, and him "saying things," the father actually says very little in the poem. What message does the father communicate, and by what means? What can you infer about the relationship between this father and son?

Wanting to say things,
I miss my father tonight.
His voice, the slight catch,
the depth from his thin chest,
5   the tremble of emotion
in something he has just said
to his son, his song:

We planted corn one Spring at Acu—
we planted several times
10 but this one particular time
I remember the soft damp sand
in my hand.

My father had stopped at one point
to show me an overturned furrow;
15 the plowshare had unearthed
the burrow nest of a mouse
in the soft moist sand.

Very gently, he scooped tiny pink animals
into the palm of his hand
20 and told me to touch them.
We took them to the edge
of the field and put them in the shade
of a sand moist clod.

I remember the very softness
25 of cool and warm sand and tiny alive mice
and my father saying things.

Seventeen Syllables

Hisaye Yamamoto

Born of immigrant parents in 1921 in Redondo Beach, California, Yamamoto began writing as a teenager. During World War II, she was interned for three years in Poston, Arizona. After the war, despite anti-Japanese sentiment, she gained national recognition for her writing. In 1986, she received the American Book Award for Lifetime Achievement from the Before Columbus Foundation. "Seventeen Syllables" was written in 1949 and appears in *Seventeen Syllables and Other Stories* (1988).

Journal Topics: (1) Write the dialogue (what *could* have been said) for an emotionally loaded scene in which, at the time, either you or another member of your family did not directly communicate your thoughts and feelings. (2) If you plan to marry or are already married, describe any apprehensions you have about fulfilling the role of husband or wife. Also describe any apprehensions you may have about what your spouse might expect of you. (3) What has your family taught you about the merits and disadvantages of expressing feelings of which they may not approve?

As You Read: (1) Compare Mr. Hayashi's and Rosie's responses to Mrs. Hayashi's poetry writing. How does Mrs. Hayashi handle their reactions? (2) List as many reasons as you can find in the story to explain Mr. Hayashi's feelings about his wife's writing. (3) Are Mr. Hayashi's violent explosion and Mrs. Hayashi's verbal explosion comparable? (4) Why does her mother implore Rosie, "Promise me you will never marry!"? Explain the phases of Rosie's response. (5) What is the significance of the number 17? (6) Why does Mrs. Hayashi temporarily withhold the "embrace and consoling hand" that the crying Rosie expects at the story's conclusion?

The first Rosie knew that her mother had taken to writing poems was one evening when she finished one and read it aloud for her daughter's approval. It was about cats, and Rosie pretended to understand it thoroughly and appreciate it no end, partly because she hesitated to disillusion her mother about the quantity and quality of Japanese she had learned in all the years now that she had been going to Japanese school every Saturday (and Wednesday, too, in the summer). Even so, her mother must have been skeptical about the depth of Rosie's understanding, because she explained afterwards about the kind of poem she was trying to write.

See, Rosie, she said, it was a *haiku,* a poem in which she must pack all her meaning into seventeen syllables only, which were divided into three lines of five, seven, and five syllables. In the one she had just read, she had tried to capture the charm of a kitten, as well as comment on the superstition that owning a cat of three colors meant good luck.

"Yes, yes, I understand. How utterly lovely," Rosie said, and her mother, either satisfied or seeing through the deception and resigned, went back to composing.

The truth was that Rosie was lazy; English lay ready on the tongue but Japanese had to be searched for and examined, and even then put forth tentatively (probably to meet with laughter). It was so much easier to say yes, yes, even when one meant no, no. Besides, this was what was in her mind to say: I was looking through one of your magazines from Japan last night, Mother, and towards the back I found some *haiku* in English that delighted me. There was one that made me giggle off and on until I fell asleep—

It is morning, and lo!
I lie awake, comme il faut,
sighing for some dough.

5   Now, how to reach her mother, how to communicate the melancholy song? Rosie knew formal Japanese by fits and starts, her mother had even less English, no French. It was much more possible to say yes, yes.

It developed that her mother was writing the *haiku* for a daily newspaper, the *Mainichi Shimbun,* that was published in San Francisco. Los Angeles, to be sure, was closer to the farming community in which the Hayashi family lived and several Japanese vernaculars were printed there, but Rosie's parents said they preferred the tone of the northern paper. Once a week, the *Mainichi* would have a section devoted to *haiku,* and her mother became an extravagant contributor, taking for herself the blossoming pen name, Ume Hanazono.

So Rosie and her father lived for awhile with two women, her mother and Ume Hanazono. Her mother (Tome Hayashi by name) kept house, cooked, washed, and, along with her husband and the Carrascos, the Mexican family hired for the harvest, did her ample share of picking tomatoes out in the sweltering fields and boxing them in tidy strata in the cool packing shed. Ume Hanazono, who came to life after the dinner dishes were done, was an earnest, muttering stranger who often neglected speaking when spoken to and stayed busy at the parlor table as late as midnight scribbling with pencil on scratch paper or carefully copying characters on good paper with her fat, pale green Parker.

The new interest had some repercussions on the household routine. Before, Rosie had been accustomed to her parents and herself taking their hot baths early and going to bed almost immediately afterwards, unless her parents challenged each other to a game of flower cards or unless company dropped in. Now if her father wanted to play cards, he had to resort to solitaire (at which he always cheated fearlessly), and if a group of friends came over, it was bound to contain someone who was also writing *haiku,* and the small assemblage would be split in two, her father entertaining the non-literary members and her mother comparing ecstatic notes with the visiting poet.

If they went out, it was more of the same thing. But Ume Hanazono's life span, even for a poet's, was very brief—perhaps three months at most.

10   One night they went over to see the Hayano family in the neighboring town to the west, an adventure both painful and attractive to Rosie. It was attractive because there were four Hayano girls, all lovely and each one named after a season of the year (Haru, Natsu, Aki, Fuyu), painful because something had been wrong with Mrs. Hayano ever since the birth of her first child. Rosie would sometimes watch Mrs. Hayano, reputed to have been the belle of her native village, making her way about a room, stooped, slowly shuffling, violently trembling (*always* trembling), and she would be reminded that this woman, in this same condition, had carried and given issue to three babies. She would look wonderingly at Mr. Hayano, handsome, tall, and strong, and she would look at her four pretty friends. But it was not a matter she could come to any decision about.

On this visit, however, Mrs. Hayano sat all evening in the rocker, as motionless and unobtrusive as it was possible for her to be, and Rosie found the greater part of the evening practically anaesthetic. Too, Rosie spent most of it in the girls' room, because Haru, the garrulous one, said almost as soon as the bows and other greetings were over, "Oh, you must see my new coat!"

It was a pale plaid of grey, sand, and blue, with an enormous collar, and Rosie, seeing nothing special in it, said, "Gee, how nice."

"Nice?" said Haru, indignantly. "Is that all you can say about it? It's gorgeous! And so cheap, too. Only seventeen-ninety-eight, because it was a sale. The saleslady said it was twenty-five dollars regular."

"Gee," said Rosie. Natsu, who never said much and when she said anything said it shyly, fingered the coat covetously and Haru pulled it away.

15   "Mine," she said, putting it on. She minced in the aisle between the two large beds and smiled happily. "Let's see how your mother likes it."

She broke into the front room and the adult conversation and went to stand in front of Rosie's mother, while the rest watched from the door. Rosie's mother was properly envious. "May I inherit it when you're through with it?"

Haru, pleased, giggled and said yes, she could, but Natsu reminded gravely from the door, "You promised me, Haru."

Everyone laughed but Natsu, who shamefacedly retreated into the bedroom. Haru came in laughing, taking off the coat. "We were only kidding, Natsu," she said. "Here, you try it on now."

After Natsu buttoned herself into the coat, inspected herself solemnly in the bureau mirror, and reluctantly shed it, Rosie, Aki, and Fuyu got their turns, and Fuyu, who was eight, drowned in it while her sisters and Rosie doubled up in amusement. They all went into the front room later, because Haru's mother quaveringly called to her to fix the tea and rice cakes and open a can of sliced peaches for everybody. Rosie noticed that her mother and Mr. Hayano were talking together at the little table— they were discussing a *haiku* that Mr. Hayano was planning to send to the *Mainichi*, while her father was sitting at one end of the sofa looking through a copy of *Life*, the new picture magazine. Occasionally, her father would comment on a photograph, holding it toward Mrs. Hayano and speaking to her as he always did—loudly, as though he thought someone such as she must surely be at least a trifle deaf also.

20   The five girls had their refreshments at the kitchen table, and it was while Rosie was showing the sisters her trick of swallowing peach slices without chewing (she chased each slippery crescent down with a swig of tea) that her father brought his empty teacup and untouched saucer to the sink and said, "Come on, Rosie, we're going home now."

"Already?" asked Rosie.

"Work tomorrow," he said.

He sounded irritated, and Rosie, puzzled, gulped one last yellow slice and stood up to go, while the sisters began protesting, as was their wont.

"We have to get up at five-thirty," he told them, going into the front room quickly, so that they did not have their usual chance to hang onto his hands and plead for an extension of time.

25   Rosie, following, saw that her mother and Mr. Hayano were sipping tea and still talking together, while Mrs. Hayano concentrated, quivering, on raising the handle-less Japanese cup to her lips with both her hands and lowering it back to her lap. Her father, saying nothing, went out the door, onto the bright porch, and down the steps. Her mother looked up and asked, "Where is he going?"

"Where is he going?" Rosie said. "He said we were going home now."

Going home?" Her mother looked with embarrassment at Mr. Hayano and his absorbed wife and then forced a smile. "He must be tired," she said.

Haru was not giving up yet. "May Rosie stay overnight?" she asked, and Natsu, Aki, and Fuyu came to reinforce their sister's plea by helping her make a circle around Rosie's mother. Rosie, for once having no desire to stay, was relieved when her mother, apologizing to the perturbed Mr. and Mrs. Hayano for her father's abruptness at the same time, managed to shake her head no at the quartet, kindly but adamant, so that they broke their circle and let her go.

Rosie's father looked ahead into the windshield as the two joined him. "I'm sorry," her mother said. "You must be tired." Her father, stepping on the starter, said nothing. "You know how I get when it's *haiku*," she continued, "I forget what time it is." He only grunted.

30   As they rode homeward silently. Rosie, sitting between, felt a rush of hate for both—for her mother for begging, for her father for denying her mother. I wish this old Ford would crash, right now, she thought, then immediately, no, no, I wish my father would laugh, but it was too late: already the vision had passed through her mind of the green pick-up crumpled in the dark against one of the mighty eucalyptus trees they were just riding past, of the three contorted, bleeding bodies, one of them hers.

Rosie ran between two patches of tomatoes, her heart working more rambunctiously than she had ever known it to. How lucky it was that Aunt Taka and Uncle Gimpachi had come tonight, though, how very lucky. Otherwise she might not have really kept her half-promise to meet Jesus Carrasco. Jesus was going to be a senior in September at the same school she went to, and his parents were the ones helping with the tomatoes this year. She and Jesus, who hardly remembered seeing each other at Cleveland High where there were so many other people and two whole grades between them, had become great friends this summer—he always had a joke for her when he periodically drove the loaded pick-up up from the fields to the shed where she was usually sorting while her mother and father did the packing, and they laughed a great deal together over infinitesimal repartee during the afternoon break for chilled watermelon or ice cream in the shade of the shed.

What she enjoyed most was racing him to see which could finish picking a double row first. He, who could work faster, would tease her by slowing down until she thought she would surely pass him this time, then speeding up furiously to leave her several sprawling vines behind. Once he had made her screech hideously by crossing over, while her back was turned, to place atop the tomatoes in her green-stained bucket a truly monstrous, pale green worm (it had looked more like an infant snake). And it was when they had finished a contest this morning, after she had pantingly pointed a green finger at the immature tomatoes evident in the lugs at the end of his row and he had returned the accusation (with justice), that he had startlingly brought up the matter of their possibly meeting outside the range of both their parents' dubious eyes.

"What for?" she had asked.

"I've got a secret I want to tell you," he said.

35 "Tell me now," she demanded.

"It won't be ready till tonight," he said.

She laughed. "Tell me tomorrow then."

"It'll be gone tomorrow," he threatened.

"Well, for seven hakes, what is it?" she had asked, more than twice, and when he had suggested that the packing shed would be an appropriate place to find out, she had cautiously answered maybe. She had not been certain she was going to keep the appointment until the arrival of mother's sister and her husband. Their coming seemed a sort of signal of permission, of grace, and she had definitely made up her mind to lie and leave as she was bowing them welcome.

40 So as soon as everyone appeared settled back for the evening, she announced loudly that she was going to the privy outside. "I'm going to the *benjo!*" and slipped out the door. And now that she was actually on her way, her heart pumped in such an undisciplined way that she could hear it with her ears. It's because I'm running, she told herself, slowing to a walk. The shed was up ahead, one more patch away, in the middle of the fields. Its bulk, looming in the dimness, took on a sinisterness that was funny when Rosie reminded herself that it was only a wooden frame with a canvas roof and three canvas walls that made a slapping noise on breezy days.

Jesus was sitting on the narrow plank that was the sorting platform and she went around to the other side and jumped backwards to seat herself on the rim of a packing stand. "Well, tell me," she said without greeting, thinking her voice sounded reassuringly familiar.

"I saw you coming out the door," Jesus said. "I heard you running part of the way, too."

"Uh-huh," Rosie said. "Now tell me the secret."

"I was afraid you wouldn't come," he said.

45   Rosie delved around on the chicken-wire bottom of the stall for number two tomatoes, ripe, which she was sitting beside, and came up with a left-over that felt edible.
She bit into it and began sucking out the pulp and seeds. "I'm here," she pointed out.

"Rosie, are you sorry you came?"

"Sorry? What for?" she said. "You said you were going to tell me something."

"I will, I will," Jesus said, but his voice contained disappointment, and Rosie fleet-
ingly felt the older of the two, realizing a brand-new power which vanished without
category under her recognition.

"I have to go back in a minute," she said. "My aunt and uncle are here from Win-
tersburg. I told them I was going to the privy."

50   Jesus laughed. "You funny thing," he said. "You slay me!"

"Just because you have a bathroom *inside*," Rosie said. "Come on, tell me."

Chuckling, Jesus came around to lean on the stand facing her. They still could not
see each other very clearly, but Rosie noticed that Jesus became very sober again as
he took the hollow tomato from her hand and dropped it back into the stall. When he
took hold of her empty hand, she could find no words to protest; her vocabulary had
become distressingly constricted and she thought desperately that all that remained
intact now was yes and no and oh, and even these few sounds would not easily out.
Thus, kissed by Jesus, Rosie fell for the first time entirely victim to a helplessness de-
lectable beyond speech. But the terrible, beautiful sensation lasted no more than a
second, and the reality of Jesus' lips and tongue and teeth and hands made her pull
away with such strength that she nearly tumbled.

Rosie stopped running as she approached the lights from the windows of home.
How long since she had left? She could not guess, but gasping yet, she went to the
privy in back and locked herself in. Her own breathing deafened her in the dark, close
space, and she sat and waited until she could hear at last the nightly calling of the
frogs and crickets. Even then, all she could think to say was oh, my, and the pressure
of Jesus' face against her face would not leave.

No one had missed her in the parlor, however, and Rosie walked in and through
quickly, announcing that she was next going to take a bath. "Your father's in the
bathhouse," her mother said, and Rosie, in her room, recalled that she had not seen
him when she entered. There had been only Aunt Taka and Uncle Gimpachi with her
mother at the table, drinking tea. She got her robe and straw sandals and crossed the
parlor again to go outside. Her mother was telling them about the *haiku* competition
in the *Mainichi* and the poem she had entered.

55   Rosie met her father coming out of the bathhouse. "Are you through, Father?" she
asked. "I was going to ask you to scrub my back."

"Scrub your own back," he said shortly, going toward the main house.

"What have I done now?" she yelled after him. She suddenly felt like doing a lot of
yelling. But he did not answer, and she went into the bathhouse. Turning on the dangling light, she removed her denims and T-shirt and threw them in the big carton for
dirty clothes standing next to the washing machine. Her other things she took with

her into the bath compartment to wash after her bath. After she had scooped a basin of hot water from the square wooden tub, she sat on the grey cement of the floor and soaped herself at exaggerated leisure, singing "Red Sails in the Sunset" at the top of her voice and using da-da-da where she suspected her words. Then, standing up, still singing, for she was possessed by the notion that any attempt now to analyze would result in spoilage and she believed that the larger her volume the less she would be able to hear herself think, she obtained more hot water and poured it on until she was free of lather. Only then did she allow herself to step into the steaming vat, one leg first, then the remainder of her body inch by inch until the water no longer stung and she could move around at will.

She took a long time soaking, afterwards remembering to go around outside to stoke the embers of the tin-lined fireplace beneath the tub and to throw on a few more sticks so that the water might keep its heat for her mother, and when she finally returned to the parlor, she found her mother still talking *haiku* with her aunt and uncle, the three of them on another round of tea. Her father was nowhere in sight.

At Japanese school the next day (Wednesday, it was), Rosie was grave and giddy by turns. Preoccupied at her desk in the row for students on Book Eight, she made up for it at recess by performing wild mimicry for the benefit of her friend Chizuko. She held her nose and whined a witticism or two in what she considered was the manner of Fred Allen; she assumed intoxication and a British accent to go over the climax of the Rudy Vallee recording of the pub conversation about William Ewart Gladstone; she was the child Shirley Temple piping, "On the Good Ship Lollipop"; she was the gentleman soprano of the Four Inkspots trilling, "If I Didn't Care." And she felt reasonably satisfied when Chizuko wept and gasped, "Oh, Rosie, you ought to be in the movies!"

60   Her father came after her at noon, bringing her sandwiches of minced ham and two nectarines to eat while she rode, so that she could pitch right into the sorting when they got home. The lugs were piling up, he said, and the ripe tomatoes in them would probably have to be taken to the cannery tomorrow if they were not ready for the produce haulers tonight. "This heat's not doing them any good. And we've got no time for a break today."

It *was* hot, probably the hottest day of the year, and Rosie's blouse stuck damply to her back even under the protection of the canvas. But she worked as efficiently as a flawless machine and kept the stalls heaped, with one part of her mind listening in to the parental murmuring about the heat and the tomatoes and with another part planning the exact words she would say to Jesus when he drove up with the first load of the afternoon. But when at last she saw that the pick-up was coming, her hands went berserk and the tomatoes started falling in the wrong stalls, and her father said, "Hey, hey! Rosie, watch what you're doing!"

"Well, I have to go to the *benjo*," she said, hiding panic.

"Go in the weeds over there," he said, only half-joking.

"Oh, Father!" she protested.

65   "Oh, go on home," her mother said. "We'll make out for awhile."

In the privy Rosie peered through a knothole toward the fields, watching as much as she could of Jesus. Happily she thought she saw him look in the direction of the house from time to time before he finished unloading and went back toward the patch where his mother and father worked. As she was heading for the shed, a very presentable black car purred up the dirt driveway to the house and its driver motioned to her. Was this the Hayashi home, he wanted to know. She nodded. Was she a Hayashi? Yes, she said, thinking that he was a good-looking man. He got out of the car with a huge, flat package and she saw that he warmly wore a business suit. "I have something here for your mother then," he said, in a more elegant Japanese than she was used to.

She told him where her mother was and he came along with her, patting his face with an immaculate white handkerchief and saying something about the coolness of San Francisco. To her surprised mother and father, he bowed and introduced himself as, among other things, the *haiku* editor of the *Mainichi Shimbun,* saying that since he had been coming as far as Los Angeles anyway, he had decided to bring her the first prize she had won in the recent contest.

"First prize?" her mother echoed, believing and not believing, pleased and overwhelmed. Handed the package with a bow, she bobbed her head up and down numerous times to express her utter gratitude.

"It is nothing much," he added, "but I hope it will serve as a token of our great appreciation for your contributions and our great admiration of your considerable talent."

70   "I am not worthy," she said, falling easily into his style. "It is I who should make some sign of my humble thanks for being permitted to contribute."

"No, no, to the contrary," he said, bowing again.

But Rosie's mother insisted, and then saying that she knew she was being unorthodox, she asked if she might open the package because her curiosity was so great. Certainly she might. In fact, he would like her reaction to it, for personally, it was one of his favorite *Hiroshiges.*

Rosie thought it was a pleasant picture, which looked to have been sketched with delicate quickness. There were pink clouds, containing some graceful calligraphy, and a sea that was a pale blue except at the edges, containing four sampans with indications of people in them. Pines edged the water and on the far-off beach there was a cluster of thatched huts towered over by pine-dotted mountains of grey and blue. The frame was scalloped and gilt.

After Rosie's mother pronounced it without peer and somewhat prodded her father into nodding agreement, she said Mr. Kuroda must at least have a cup of tea after coming all this way, and although Mr. Kuroda did not want to impose, he soon agreed that a cup of tea would be refreshing and went along with her to the house, carrying the picture for her.

75   "Ha, your mother's crazy!" Rosie's father said, and Rosie laughed uneasily as she resumed judgment on the tomatoes. She had emptied six lugs when he broke into an imaginary conversation with Jesus to tell her to go and remind her mother of the tomatoes, and she went slowly.

Mr. Kuroda was in his shirtsleeves expounding some *haiku* theory as he munched a rice cake, and her mother was rapt. Abashed in the great man's presence, Rosie stood next to her mother's chair until her mother looked up inquiringly, and then she started to whisper the message, but her mother pushed her gently away and reproached, "You are not being very polite to our guest."

"Father says the tomatoes . . ." Rosie said aloud, smiling foolishly.

"Tell him I shall only be a minute," her mother said, speaking the language of Mr. Kuroda.

When Rosie carried the reply to her father, he did not seem to hear and she said again, "Mother says she'll be back in a minute."

80   "All right, all right," he nodded, and they worked again in silence. But suddenly, her father uttered an incredible noise, exactly like the cork of a bottle popping, and the next Rosie knew, he was stalking angrily toward the house, almost running in fact, and she chased after him crying, "Father! Father! What are you going to do?"

He stopped long enough to order her back to the shed. "Never mind!" he shouted. "Get on with the sorting!"

And from the place in the fields where she stood, frightened and vacillating, Rosie saw her father enter the house. Soon Mr. Kuroda came out alone, putting on his coat. Mr. Kuroda got into his car and backed out down the driveway onto the highway. Next her father emerged, also alone, something in his arms (it was the picture, she realized), and, going over to the bathhouse woodpile, he threw the picture on the ground and picked up the axe. Smashing the picture, glass and all (she heard the explosion faintly), he reached over for the kerosene that was used to encourage the bath fire and poured it over the wreckage. I am dreaming, Rosie said to herself, I am dreaming, but her father, having made sure that his act of cremation was irrevocable, was even then returning to the fields.

Rosie ran past him and toward the house. What had become of her mother? She burst into the parlor and found her mother at the back window watching the dying fire. They watched together until there remained only a feeble smoke under the blazing sun. Her mother was very calm.

"Do you know why I married your father?" she said without turning.

85   "No," said Rosie. It was the most frightening question she had ever been called upon to answer. Don't tell me now, she wanted to say, tell me tomorrow, tell me next week, don't tell me today. But she knew she would be told now, that the telling would combine with the other violence of the hot afternoon to level her life, her world to the very ground.

It was like a story out of the magazines illustrated in sepia, which she had consumed so greedily for a period until the information had somehow reached her that those wretchedly unhappy autobiographies, offered to her as the testimonials of living men and women, were largely inventions: Her mother, at nineteen, had come to America and married her father as an alternative to suicide.

At eighteen she had been in love with the first son of one of the well-to-do families in her village. The two had met whenever and wherever they could, secretly, because it would not have done for his family to see him favor her—her father had no money;

he was a drunkard and a gambler besides. She had learned she was with child; an excellent match had already been arranged for her lover. Despised by her family, she had given premature birth to a stillborn son, who would be seventeen now. Her family did not turn her out, but she could no longer project herself in any direction without refreshing in them the memory of her indiscretion. She wrote to Aunt Taka, her favorite sister in America, threatening to kill herself if Aunt Taka would not send for her. Aunt Taka hastily arranged a marriage with a young man of whom she knew, but lately arrived from Japan, a young man of simple mind, it was said, but of kindly heart. The young man was never told why his unseen betrothed was so eager to hasten the day of meeting.

The story was told perfectly, with neither groping for words nor untoward passion. It was as though her mother had memorized it by heart, reciting it to herself so many times over that its nagging vileness had long since gone.

"I had a brother then?" Rosie asked, for this was what seemed to matter now; she would think about the other later, she assured herself, pushing back the illumination which threatened all that darkness that had hitherto been merely mysterious or even glamorous. "A half brother?"

90   "Yes."

"I would have liked a brother," she said.

Suddenly, her mother knelt on the floor and took her by the wrists. "Rosie," she said urgently, "Promise me you will never marry!" Shocked more by the request than the revelation, Rosie stared at her mother's face. Jesus, Jesus, she called silently, not certain whether she was invoking the help of the son of the Carrascos or of God, until there returned sweetly the memory of Jesus' hand, how it had touched her and where. Still her mother waited for an answer, holding her wrists so tightly that her hands were going numb. She tried to pull free. Promise, her mother whispered fiercely, promise. Yes, yes, I promise, Rosie said. But for an instant she turned away, and her mother, hearing the familiar glib agreement, released her. Oh, you, you, you, her eyes and twisted mouth said, you fool. Rosie, covering her face, began at last to cry, and the embrace and consoling hand came much later than she expected.

WRITING ASSIGNMENTS

Analysis

1. Assuming the role of teen counselor, write a letter to Rosie in which you explain how differences in country of birth and native language contribute to the generation gap between her and her parents. Do these factors influence Rosie's relationship with her mother and father in the same ways?

2. How would a family sociologist, such as Arlene Skolnick, characterize the Hayashi family in terms of how it fulfills the description of the "institutional" family or the "sentimental" family?

3. In her essay, "Double-Telling: Intertextual Silence in Hisaye Yamamoto's Fiction," literary scholar King-Kok Cheung defines two Japanese cultural values:

gaman and *enryo*. *Gaman* refers to the suppression of emotion and anger and to a dogged perseverance; *enryo* refers to reserve, reticence, modesty, indirection, and the avoidance of confrontation. Japanese culture imposes these values on both men and women. Compare and contrast the way these values affect Mr. Hayashi and Mrs. Hayashi.
4. Identify a scene in the story when the characters suppress their feelings and conceal them from others. Rewrite that scene in dialogue, having the characters express themselves fully and directly.
5. How does having Rosie narrate the story influence its tone and meaning?

Argument

1. Rewrite the essential events of this story in the form of a letter from Mr. Hayashi to a friend, explaining his feelings and justifying his actions.
2. Is "Seventeen Syllables" more Rosie's story or her mother's?

Personal Writing and Writing from Research

1. Research the history of Japanese immigration to the United States, with particular emphasis on how policies affected family life. Do your findings help explain the relationship of Mr. and Mrs. Hayashi?
2. Interview students in your school or members of your class to discover whether a generation gap exists between them and their parents, or between their parents and grandparents. What are the factors contributing to this generation gap? Compare Rosie's experiences to those of your peers.

Discarded

David Sherwood

"Discarded" first appeared in the "About Men" column in the *New York Times Sunday Magazine*. This column was introduced in 1983 as a forum to reflect the as-yet-uncharted changes in American men since the women's movement began. It is in some sense intended to be a counterpart to the column called "Hers," which first appeared daily in the *Times* and now alternates with "About Men" on Sunday. At first, the *Times* solicited essays from well-known writers, but soon most contributors were amateurs. According to *Times* editors, more than half of the essays submitted to the column concern men's thinking about their fathers.

Journal Topics: (1) Describe how your high-school peers treated a boy or girl whose mannerisms and behavior deviated from what the group considered appropriately masculine or feminine. (2) Describe the basis of your parents' disapproval of some interest, personality trait, or physical characteristic of yours or of your siblings. How did you or your sibling react to their disapproval?

As You Read: (1) List the details in Sherwood's description of his father that suggest why the father would reject an "effeminate" son. (2) What changes in David's life explain his oscillations between accepting and rejecting Andy? (3) How do the descriptions of the adult David and Andy correlate with stereotypes of heterosexual and gay males?

1   My younger brother, Andy, lives in Paris and I in Hartford. Neither of us ever has any money to speak of, so we hardly get to see each other or even to talk on the phone. We keep in touch by sending letters back and forth across the Atlantic.

2   Judging by the letters, I think of Andy as a fine, fine writer. But lately, he has been writing a book, and, based on the chapters he's sent me, I'd say that publishers won't be encouraging. Andy's book is about our small family and, most especially, Andy's unhappy childhood some forty years ago. What happens, I think, is that as Andy writes about his childhood, he sort of becomes again the child he once was—a child having a hard time of it. The change he undergoes changes his writing for the worse.

3   Andy was a boy whose father seemed to show him next to no sign of love or respect. "Next to no" will allow for signals of affection and esteem perhaps apparent at the time, but of which we have no recollection. We had the same father, but he was not the same with the two of us. He was all I could ever have wished for, but he never took a shine to Andy.

4   Andy liked to try on women's clothes; he would draw picture after picture of plume-hatted hoop-skirted women; his favorite playmates were girls; his gestures were effeminate. It was all beyond endurance for our father, who, aside from being the schoolteacher to whom a Class of 1945 yearbook was dedicated, was a graceful athlete, a deadpan poker player and a man who had a way with the ladies. His small son's achievements—good comportment, words spelled right—were, so far as one could tell, scant source of pleasure to him. Our father had a wry sense of humor and a quicksilver laugh, but he seemed to lose his light touch in my brother's presence. Altogether then, Andy found little to assure him that he was in any way precious to his father. When we were still kids, our father, barely forty, died.

5   We'd been raised in Delaware, on a boarding school's campus, among people we'd known forever: teachers, support staff, their wives and children. Nobody there made an issue of Andy. But once our father died, we moved to Wilmington so our mother could find work. And in the Wilmington of 1945, among my new seventh-grade pals, Andy seemed suddenly exotic. What had bothered my father about him now bothered me. So I was glad we were enrolled in separate schools, glad that Andy was away at piano lessons when my friends dropped by, glad not to have to introduce him or even have them see him. I remember once meeting a boy who'd just transferred to my school from Andy's. The name Sherwood registered with him right off. "You got a fairy named Andy for a brother?" he asked.

6   I kept Andy at more than arm's length for years thereafter. But once I'd become the father of a boy myself, we became brothers again. What happened, I think, was two things. Andy liked being Uncle Andy. It gave him a valued mainstream credential. And I, living a humdrummish life, found myself now pleased to tell friends about this gay brother of mine who lived in New York, as he did then, with an illustrator of medical textbooks and relaxed at restaurants like Max's Kansas City. In those days I wished to seem more interesting than I knew myself to be. Acknowledging Andy and visiting him was a way to do it. More than that, I'd be in his living room watching him amusing my son, and I'd feel shame for having never been an older brother to him. One day, I called up two of his former friends and threatened to rip their place up if they didn't quickly return to Andy some furniture they owed him money for. It was the first favor I'd ever done him.

7   Andy's adult life, in my eyes, has been one of accomplishment. He tutors private pupils in voice and piano; he once taught harpsichord; he has sung countertenor with chamber groups, and these are not his primary endeavors. Mostly, he teaches English to French adults whose tuitions are paid by their employers. The head of his school, he wrote in 1981, "has told me I'm her best teacher. She's been putting me with new students who've come to test the school out for their companies, so that, if they like it, more will follow. I, then, have to create the most favorable impression, a sort of . . . seduction. . . ."

8   My brother, in fact, has fashioned for himself a life that leans often on the seducer's art. Apart from his classroom role, he is a photographer whose prints are, once in a while, exhibited and sold in galleries, and he must coax from acquaintances who pose for him a certain moroseness of expression that flavors his photographs and causes the public and an occasional magazine or museum to buy them. Engaged in the 1960s for anonymous bit parts in opera—no singing, no dancing—Andy was reproved sometimes for diverting attention from the principals. "Mr. Rudel at the New York City Opera," he said, "told me everyone was watching me in *The Flaming Angel* instead of the heroine. Mr. Bing at the Met told me the same thing in *Andrea Chenier*."

9   "I turn many fewer heads than I used to," he now writes. "A friend and I have a pastime we call 'Existing,' which consists of guessing if a stranger is aware of us, and if so, of which one, or whether we obviously don't 'exist' and are looked through, not at." These strangers, by whom Andy and his friend define their "existence," are boys and men first seen from afar, then from up close as they pass one another on the sidewalk. "When we do get a glance," he adds, "it is usually for Patrice, who is 15 years younger."

10   Andy can handle the increasing absence of glances from strangers. But he is encumbered by having never seduced an affectionate glance from our father. I want to believe that, had our father lived longer, he'd have made his peace with Andy. Their love of music and language, their storytelling skills, their parallel teaching careers—there is common ground there now. But I also know, as a father of five, how tough it is to look with new eyes upon a child who baffles you, disappoints you.

11   Andy will live out his years not knowing how things might have worked out between them. Each draft of his book that arrives shows how punishing his recollec-
tions are, how infirm they make him, and how hard it is to get out from under the
shadow of a father who hasn't loved you.

WRITING ASSIGNMENTS

Analysis

1. Describe and explain the evolution of David's feelings for Andy.
2. What is the significance of David's "first favor" for Andy? What does this gesture say about David's concept of brotherhood and masculinity, and about his
   attitude toward Andy?
3. In a letter, Andy writes, "I, then, have to create the most favorable impression, a sort of . . . seduction. . . ." David continues the seduction metaphor,
   "My brother, in fact, has fashioned for himself a life that leans often on the seducer's art." What are the thematic implications of the repeated use of the
   seduction metaphor and of David's use of "fashioned" and "leans" in the sentence above?
4. *Collaborative Project:* Write several letters that Andy/Andrea from "Doe Season" and Andy from "Discarded" might exchange in which they compare and
   evaluate the way their fathers shaped their gender-role behavior.

Argument

1. Drawing on "Discarded," "Doe Season," and your own observations or experiences, take a position on whether effeminate males or mannish females face
   more social rejection.
2. "Discarded" illustrates how easy it is to see someone exclusively in terms of
   one facet of that person. Just as Andy's father can see Andy only in terms of
   his sexual orientation, so people sometimes see others only in terms of their
   ethnic origin, gender, religion, politics, etc. In a letter to the editor of a major
   metropolitan daily newspaper, take a stand on whether such stereotyping is
   inevitable. If you believe it is not, suggest ways to overcome it.
3. David believes that Andy has been permanently damaged by their father's rejection. In a speech intended for high-school students about the consequences of parental disapproval, take a position on whether these effects are
   permanent. Use Andy as an illustration, but also supplement his story with
   others based on your reading, interviews, and personal experience.
4. Which has been a greater problem for Andy—his homosexuality or his father's
   and brother's reaction to his homosexuality?

Personal Writing and Writing from Research

1. Write a research paper describing several stereotypes based on national origin, ethnic identity, race, religion, class, occupation, or sexual orientation, and

include the historical background for each of them, how the stereotypes have evolved, and the consequences to those so stereotyped.

2. Compare your experience with Andy's as the object of rejection based on something about yourself over which you had no control. Or, compare your experience with David's as the one whose rejection of someone else evolves into acceptance, and explain that evolution.

3. Write a research paper describing cultures that honor individuals whose sexual orientation or gender-role behavior deviates from traditional American norms of masculinity and femininity.

Doe Season

David Michael Kaplan

Before publication in *Comfort* (1987), Kaplan's first collection, "Doe Season" was selected for *Best American Short Stories of 1985*. The stories in *Comfort* focus on difficult family relationships, primarily from the point of view of young women. Critics have noted the influence of the magic realist school on Kaplan's work. One reviewer says Kaplan's stories "focus on the extraordinary moments of recognition in ordinary lives. He is at his best suggesting how such moments may alter, for the better or worse, our relationship with those to whom we are most deeply bound—children, parents, lovers—in love and guilt."

Journal Topics: (1) Describe your attitudes toward or experiences with hunting. (2) What role has hunting played in human history? How is hunting related to masculinity? (3) Write about a childhood outing or event you shared with an adult family member that left an indelible mark on you because it shaped your sense of identity.

As You Read: (1) Record the thoughts and words of Andy, her father, Mac, and Charlie Spoon that reveal their assumptions about gender roles. How do Andy's father's attitudes differ from those of Charlie Spoon and Mac? (2) What skills and personality traits must Andy display in order to be accepted by the male hunters? (3) Why does Andy become angry at the deer? Why does she shoot it?

They were always the same woods, she thought sleepily as they drove through the early morning darkness—deep and immense, covered with yesterday's snowfall, which had frozen overnight. They were the same woods that lay behind her house, *and they stretch all the way to here,* she thought, *for miles and miles, longer than I could walk in a day, or a week even, but they are still the same woods.* The thought made her feel good: it was like thinking of God; it was like thinking of the space between here and the moon; it was like thinking of all the foreign countries from her geography book where even now, Andy knew, people were going to bed, while they—she and her father and Charlie Spoon and Mac, Charlie's eleven-year-old son—were driving deeper into the Pennsylvania countryside, to go hunting.

They had risen long before dawn. Her mother, yawning and not trying to hide her sleepiness, cooked them eggs and French toast. Her father smoked a cigarette and flicked ashes into his saucer while Andy listened, wondering *Why doesn't he come?* and *Won't he ever come?* until at last a car pulled into the graveled drive and honked. "That will be Charlie Spoon," her father said; he always said "Charlie Spoon," even though his real name was Spreun, because Charlie was, in a sense, shaped like a spoon, with a large head and a narrow waist and chest.

Andy's mother kissed her and her father and said, "Well, have a good time" and "Be careful." Soon they were outside in the bitter dark, loading gear by the back-porch light, their breath steaming. The woods behind the house were then only a black streak against the wash of night.

Andy dozed in the car and woke to find that it was half light. Mac—also sleeping—had slid against her. She pushed him away and looked out the window. Her breath clouded the glass, and she was cold; the car's heater didn't work right. They were riding over gentle hills, the woods on both sides now—the same woods, she knew, because she had been watching the whole way, even while she slept. They had been in her dreams, and she had never lost sight of them.

5   Charlie Spoon was driving. "I don't understand why she's coming," he said to her father. "How old is she anyway—eight?"

"Nine," her father replied. "She's small for her age."

"So—nine. What's the difference? She'll just add to the noise and get tired besides."

"No, she won't," her father said, "She can walk me to death. And she'll bring good luck, you'll see. Animals—I don't know how she does it, but they come right up to her. We go walking in the woods, and we'll spot more raccoons and possums and such than I ever see when I'm alone."

Charlie grunted.

10   "Besides, she's not a bad little shot, even if she doesn't hunt yet. She shoots the .22 real good."

"Popgun," Charlie said, and snorted. "And target shooting ain't deer hunting."

"Well, she's not gonna be shooting anyway, Charlie," her father said. "Don't worry. She'll be no bother."

"I still don't know why she's coming," Charlie said.

"Because she wants to, and I want her to. Just like you and Mac. No difference."

15   Charlie turned onto a side road and after a mile or so slowed down. "That's it!" he cried. He stopped, backed up, and entered a narrow dirt road almost hidden by trees. Five hundred yards down, the road ran parallel to a fenced-in field. Charlie parked in a cleared area deeply rutted by frozen tractor tracks. The gate was locked. *In the spring,* Andy thought, *there will be cows here, and a dog that chases them,* but now the field was unmarked and bare.

"This is it," Charlie Spoon declared. "Me and Mac was up here just two weeks ago, scouting it out, and there's deer. Mac saw the tracks."

"That's right," Mac said.

"Well, we'll just see about that," her father said, putting on his gloves. He turned to Andy. "How you doing, honeybun?"

"Just fine," she said.

20   Andy shivered and stamped as they unloaded: first the rifles, which they unsheathed and checked, sliding the bolts, sighting through scopes, adjusting the slings; then the gear, their food and tents and sleeping bags and stove stored in four backpacks—three big ones for Charlie Spoon and her father and Mac, and a day pack for her.

"That's about your size," Mac said, to tease her.

She reddened and said, "Mac, I can carry a pack big as yours any day." He laughed and pressed his knee against the back of hers, so that her leg buckled. "Cut it out," she said. She wanted to make an iceball and throw it at him, but she knew that her father and Charlie were anxious to get going, and she didn't want to displease them.

Mac slid under the gate, and they handed the packs over to him. Then they slid under and began walking across the field toward the same woods that ran all the way back to her home, where even now her mother was probably rising again to wash their breakfast dishes and make herself a fresh pot of coffee. *She is there, and we are here:* the thought satisfied Andy. There was no place else she would rather be.

Mac came up beside her. "Over there's Canada," he said, nodding toward the woods.

25   "Huh!" she said. "Not likely."

"I don't mean *right* over there. I mean farther up north. You think I'm dumb?"

Dumb as your father, she thought.

"Look at that," Mac said, pointing to a piece of cow dung lying on a spot scraped bare of snow. "A frozen meadow muffin." He picked it up and sailed it at her. "Catch!"

"Mac!" she yelled. His laugh was as gawky as he was. She walked faster. He seemed different today somehow, bundled in his yellow-and-black-checkered coat, a rifle in hand, his silly floppy hat not quite covering his ears. They all seemed different as she watched them trudge through the snow—Mac and her father and Charlie Spoon— bigger, maybe, as if the cold landscape enlarged rather than diminished them, so that they, the only figures in that landscape, took on size and meaning just by being there. If they weren't there, everything would be quieter, and the woods would be the same as before. *But they are here,* Andy thought, looking behind her at the boot prints in the snow, *and I am too, and so it's all different.*

30   "We'll go down to the cut where we found those deer tracks," Charlie said as they entered the woods. "Maybe we'll get lucky and get a late one coming through."

The woods descended into a gully. The snow was softer and deeper here, so that often Andy sank to her knees. Charlie and Mac worked the top of the gully while she and her father walked along the base some thirty yards behind them. "If they miss the first shot, we'll get the second," her father said, and she nodded as if she had known this all the time. She listened to the crunch of their boots, their breathing, and the drumming of a distant woodpecker. And the crackling. In winter the woods crackled as if everything were straining, ready to snap like dried chicken bones.

We are hunting, Andy thought. The cold air burned her nostrils.

They stopped to make lunch by a rock outcropping that protected them from the wind. Her father heated the bean soup her mother had made for them, and they ate it with bread already stiff from the cold. He and Charlie took a few pulls from a flask of Jim Beam while she scoured the plates with snow and repacked them. Then they all had coffee with sugar and powdered milk, and her father poured her a cup too. "We won't tell your momma," he said, and Mac laughed. Andy held the cup the way her father did, not by the handle but around the rim. The coffee tasted smoky. She felt a little queasy, but she drank it all.

Charlie Spoon picked his teeth with a fingernail. "Now, you might've noticed one thing," he said.

35   "What's that?" her father asked.

"You might've noticed you don't hear no rifles. That's because there ain't no other hunters here. We've got the whole damn woods to ourselves. Now, I ask you—do I know how to find 'em?"

"We haven't seen deer yet, neither."

"Oh, we will," Charlie said, "but not for a while now." He leaned back against the rock. "Deer're sleeping, resting up for the evening feed."

"I seen a deer behind our house once, and it was afternoon," Andy said.

40   "Yeah, honey, but that was *before* deer season," Charlie said, grinning. "They know something now. They're smart that way."

"That's right," Mac said.

Andy looked at her father—had she said something stupid?

"Well, Charlie," he said, "if they know so much, how come so many get themselves shot?"

"Them's the ones that don't *believe* what they know," Charlie replied. The men laughed. Andy hesitated, and then laughed with them.

45   They moved on, as much to keep warm as to find a deer. The wind became even stronger. Blowing through the treetops, it sounded like the ocean, and once Andy thought she could smell salt air. But that was impossible; the ocean was *hundreds* of miles away, farther than Canada even. She and her parents had gone last summer to stay for a week at a motel on the New Jersey shore. That was the first time she'd seen the ocean, and it frightened her. It was huge and empty, yet always moving. Everything lay hidden. If you walked in it, you couldn't see how deep it was or what might be below; if you swam, something could pull you under and you'd never be seen again. Its musky, rank smell made her think of things dying. Her mother had floated beyond the breakers, calling to her to come in, but Andy wouldn't go farther than a few feet into the surf. Her mother swam and splashed with animal-like delight while her father, smiling shyly, held his white arms above the waist-deep water as if afraid to get them wet. Once a comber rolled over and sent them both tossing, and when her mother tried to stand up, the surf receding behind, Andy saw that her mother's swimsuit top had come off, so that her breasts swayed free, her nipples like two dark eyes. Embarrassed, Andy looked around: except for two women under a yellow umbrella farther up, the beach was empty. Her mother stood up unsteadily, regained her footing. Taking what seemed the longest time, she calmly refixed her

top. Andy lay on the beach towel and closed her eyes. The sound of the surf made her head ache.

And now it was winter; the sky was already dimming, not just with the absence of light but with a mist that clung to the hunters' faces like cobwebs. They made camp early. Andy was chilled. When she stood still, she kept wiggling her toes to make sure they were there. Her father rubbed her arms and held her to him briefly, and that felt better. She unpacked the food while the others put up the tents.

"How about rounding us up some firewood, Mac?" Charlie asked.

"I'll do it," Andy said. Charlie looked at her thoughtfully and then handed her the canvas carrier.

There wasn't much wood on the ground, so it took her a while to get a good load. She was about a hundred yards from camp, near a cluster of high, lichen-covered boulders, when she saw through a crack in the rock a buck and two does walking gingerly, almost daintily, through the alder trees. She tried to hush her breathing as they passed not more than twenty yards away. There was nothing she could do. If she yelled, they'd be gone; by the time she got back to camp, they'd be gone. The buck stopped, nostrils quivering tail up and alert. He looked directly at her. Still she didn't move, not one muscle. He was a beautiful buck, the color of late-turned maple leaves. Unafraid, he lowered his tail, and he and his does silently merged into the trees. Andy walked back to camp and dropped the firewood.

50 "I saw three deer," she said. "A buck and two does."

"Where?" Charlie Spoon cried, looking behind her as if they might have followed her into camp.

"In the woods yonder. They're gone now."

"Well, hell!" Charlie banged his coffee cup against his knee.

"Didn't I say she could find animals?" her father said, grinning.

55 "Too late to go after them," Charlie muttered. "It'll be dark in a quarter hour. Damn!"

"Damn," Mac echoed.

"They just walk right up to her," her father said.

"Well, leastwise this proves there's deer here." Charlie began snapping long branches into shorter ones. "You know, I think I'll stick with you," he told Andy, "since you're so good at finding deer and all. How'd that be?"

"Okay, I guess," Andy murmured. She hoped he was kidding; no way did she want to hunt with Charlie Spoon. Still, she was pleased he had said it.

60 Her father and Charlie took one tent, she and Mac the other. When they were in their sleeping bags, Mac said in the darkness, "I bet you really didn't see no deer, did you?"

She sighed. "I did, Mac. Why would I lie?"

"How big was the buck?"

"Four point. I counted."

Mac snorted.

65 "You just believe what you want, Mac," she said testily.

"Too bad it ain't buck season," he said. "Well, I got to go pee."

"So pee."

She heard him turn in his bag. "You ever see it?" he asked.

"It? What's 'it'?"

70   "It. A pecker."

"Sure," she lied.

"Whose? Your father's?" ·

She was uncomfortable. "No," she said.

"Well, whose then?"

75   "Oh I don't know! Leave me be, why don't you?"

"Didn't see a deer, didn't see a pecker," Mac said teasingly.

She didn't answer right away. Then she said, "My cousin Lewis. I saw his."

"Well, how old's he?"

"One and a half."

80   "Ha! A baby! A baby's is like a little worm. It ain't a real one at all."

If he says he'll show me his, she thought, *I'll kick him. I'll just get out of my bag and kick him.*

"I went hunting with my daddy and Versh and Danny Simmons last year in buck season," Mac said, "and we got ourselves one. And we hogdressed the thing. You know what that is, don't you?"

"No," she said. She was confused. What was he talking about now?

"That's when you cut him open and take out all his guts, so the meat don't spoil. Makes him lighter to pack out, too."

85   She tried to imagine what the deer's guts might look like, pulled from the gaping hole. "What do you do with them?" she said. "The guts?"

"Oh, you just leave 'em for the bears."

She ran her finger like a knife blade along her belly.

"When we left them on the ground," Mac said, "they smoked. Like they were cooking."

"Huh," she said.

90   "They cut off the deer's pecker, too, you know."

Andy imagined Lewis's pecker and shuddered. "Mac, you're disgusting."

He laughed. "Well, I gotta go pee." She heard him rustle out of his bag. "Broo!" he cried, flapping his arms. "It's cold!"

He makes so much noise, she thought, *just noise and more noise.*

Her father woke them before first light. He warned them to talk softly and said that they were going to the place where Andy had seen the deer, to try to cut them off on their way back from their night feeding. Andy couldn't shake off her sleep. Stuffing her sleeping bag into its sack seemed to take an hour, and tying her boots was the strangest thing she'd ever done. Charlie Spoon made hot chocolate and oatmeal with raisins. Andy closed her eyes and, between beats of her heart, listened to the breathing of the forest. *When I open my eyes, it will be lighter,* she decided. But when she did, it was still just as dark, except for the swaths of their flashlights and the hissing blue flame of the stove. *There has to be just one moment when it all changes from dark to light,* Andy thought. She had missed it yesterday, in the car; today she would watch more closely.

95   But when she remembered again, it was already first light and they had moved to the rocks by the deer trail and had set up shooting positions—Mac and Charlie Spoon on the up-trail side, she and her father behind them, some six feet up on a ledge. The day became brighter, the sun piercing the tall pines, raking the hunters, yet providing little warmth. Andy now smelled alder and pine and the slightly rotten odor of rock lichen. She rubbed her hand over the stone and considered that it must be very old, had probably been here before the giant pines, *before anyone was in these woods at all.* A chipmunk sniffed on a nearby branch. She aimed an imaginary rifle and pressed the trigger. The chipmunk froze, then scurried away. Her legs were cramping on the narrow ledge. Her father seemed to doze, one hand in his parka, the other cupped lightly around the rifle. She could smell his scent of old wool and leather. His cheeks were speckled with gray-black whiskers, and he worked his jaws slightly, as if chewing a small piece of gum.

Please let us get a deer, she prayed.

A branch snapped on the other side of the rock face. Her father's hand stiffened on the rifle, startling her—*He hasn't been sleeping at all,* she marveled—and then his jaw relaxed, as did the lines around his eyes, and she heard Charlie Spoon call, "Yo, don't shoot, it's us." He and Mac appeared from around the rock. They stopped beneath the ledge. Charlie solemnly crossed his arms.

"I don't believe we're gonna get any deer here," he said drily.

Andy's father lowered his rifle to Charlie and jumped down from the ledge. Then he reached up for Andy. She dropped into his arms and he set her gently on the ground.

100   Mac sidled up to her. "I knew you didn't see no deer," he said.

"Just because they don't come when you want 'em to don't mean she didn't see them," her father said.

Still, she felt bad. Her telling about the deer had caused them to spend the morning there, cold and expectant, with nothing to show for it.

They tramped through the woods for another two hours, not caring much about noise. Mac found some deer tracks, and they argued about how old they were. They split up for a while and then rejoined at an old logging road that deer might use, and followed it. The road crossed a stream, which had mostly frozen over but in a few spots still caught leaves and twigs in an icy swirl. They forded it by jumping from rock to rock. The road narrowed after that, and the woods thickened.

They stopped for lunch, heating up Charlie's wife's corn chowder. Andy's father cut squares of applesauce cake with his hunting knife and handed them to her and Mac, who ate his almost daintily. Andy could faintly taste knife oil on the cake. She was tired. She stretched her leg; the muscle that had cramped on the rock still ached.

105   "Might as well relax," her father said, as if reading her thoughts. "We won't find deer till suppertime."

Charlie Spoon leaned back against his pack and folded his hands across his stomach. "Well, even if we don't get a deer," he said expansively, "it's still great to be out here, breathe some fresh air, clomp around a bit. Get away from the house and the old lady." He winked at Mac, who looked away.

"That's what the woods are all about, anyway," Charlie said. "It's where the women don't want to go." He bowed his head toward Andy. "With your exception, of course, little lady." He helped himself to another piece of applesauce cake.

"She ain't a woman," Mac said.

"Well, she damn well's gonna be," Charlie said. He grinned at her. "Or will you? You're half a boy anyway. You go by a boy's name. What's your real name? Andrea, ain't it?"

110 "That's right," she said. She hoped that if she didn't look at him, Charlie would stop.

"Well, which do you like? Andy or Andrea?"

"Don't matter," she mumbled. "Either."

"She's always been Andy to me," her father said.

Charlie Spoon was still grinning. "So what are you gonna be, Andrea? A boy or a girl?"

115 "I'm a girl," she said.

"But you want to go hunting and fishing and everything, huh?"

"She can do whatever she likes," her father said.

"Hell, you might as well have just had a boy and be done with it!" Charlie exclaimed.

"That's funny," her father said, and chuckled. "That's just what her momma tells me."

120 They were looking at her, and she wanted to get away from them all, even her father, who chose to joke with them.

"I'm going to walk a bit," she said.

She heard them laughing as she walked down the logging trail. She flapped her arms; she whistled. *I don't care how much noise I make,* she thought. Two grouse flew from the underbrush, startling here. A little farther down, the trail ended in a clearing that enlarged into a frozen meadow; beyond it the woods began again. A few moldering posts were all that was left of a fence that had once enclosed the field. The low afternoon sunlight reflected brightly off the snow, so that Andy's eyes hurt. She squinted hard. A gust of wind blew across the field, stinging her face. And then, as if it had been waiting for her, the doe emerged from the trees opposite and stepped cautiously into the field. Andy watched: it stopped and stood quietly for what seemed a long time and then ambled across. It stopped again about seventy yards away and began to browse in a patch of sugar grass uncovered by the wind. Carefully, slowly, never taking her eyes from the doe, Andy walked backward, trying to step into the boot prints she'd already made. When she was far enough back into the woods, she turned and walked faster, her heart racing. *Please let it stay,* she prayed.

"There's doe in the field yonder," she told them.

They got their rifles and hurried down the trail.

125 "No use," her father said. "We're making too much noise any way you look at it."

"At least we got us the wind in our favor," Charlie Spoon said, breathing heavily.

But the doe was still there, grazing.

"Good Lord," Charlie whispered. He looked at her father. "Well, whose shot?"

"Andy spotted it," her father said in a low voice. "Let her shoot it."

130 "What!" Charlie's eyes widened.

Andy couldn't believe what her father had just said. She'd only shot tin cans and targets; she'd never even fired her father's .30-.30, and she'd never killed anything.

"I can't," she whispered.

"That's right, she can't," Charlie Spoon insisted. "She's not old enough and she don't have a license even if she was!"

"Well, who's to tell?" her father said in a low voice. "Nobody's going to know but us." He looked at her. "Do you want to shoot it, punkin?"

135 *Why doesn't it hear us?* she wondered. *Why doesn't it run away?* "I don't know," she said.

"Well, I'm sure as hell gonna shoot it," Charlie said. Her father grasped Charlie's rifle barrel and held it. His voice was steady.

"Andy's a good shot. It's her deer. She found it, not you. You'd still be sitting on your ass back in camp." He turned to her again. "Now—do you want to shoot it, Andy? Yes or no."

He was looking at her; they were all looking at her. Suddenly she was angry at the deer, who refused to hear them, who wouldn't run away even when it could. "I'll shoot it," she said. Charlie turned away in disgust.

She lay on the ground and pressed the rifle stock against her shoulder bone. The snow was cold through her parka; she smelled oil and wax and damp earth. She pulled off one glove with her teeth. "It sights just like the .22," her father said gently. "Cartridge's already chambered." As she had done so many times before, she sighted down the scope; now the doe was in the reticle. She moved the barrel until the cross hairs lined up. Her father was breathing beside her.

140 "Aim where the chest and legs meet, or a little above, punkin," he was saying calmly. "That's the killing shot."

But now, seeing it in the scope, Andy was hesitant. Her finger weakened on the trigger. Still, she nodded at what her father said and sighted again, the cross hairs lining up in exactly the same spot—the doe had hardly moved, its brownish-gray body outlined starkly against the blue-backed snow. *It doesn't know,* Andy thought. *It just doesn't know.* And as she looked, deer and snow and faraway trees flattened within the circular frame to become like a picture on a calendar, not real, and she felt calm, as if she had been dreaming everything—the day, the deer, the hunt itself. And she, finger on trigger, was only a part of that dream.

"Shoot!" Charlie hissed.

Through the scope she saw the deer look up, ears high and straining.

Charlie groaned, and just as he did, and just at the moment when Andy knew— *knew*—the doe would bound away, as if she could feel its haunches tensing and gathering power, she pulled the trigger. Later she would think, *I felt the recoil, I smelled the smoke, but I don't remember pulling the trigger.* Through the scope the deer seemed to shrink into itself, and then slowly knelt, hind legs first, head raised as if to cry out. It trembled, still straining to keep its head high, as if that alone would save it; failing, it collapsed, shuddered, and lay still.

145   "Whoee!" Mac cried.

"One shot! One shot!" her father yelled, clapping her on the back. Charlie Spoon was shaking his head and smiling dumbly.

"I told you she was a great little shot!" her father said. "I told you!" Mac danced and clapped his hands. She was dazed, not quite understanding what had happened. And then they were crossing the field toward the fallen doe, she walking dreamlike, the men laughing and joking, released now from the tension of silence and anticipation. Suddenly Mac pointed and cried out, "Look at that!"

The doe was rising, legs unsteady. They stared at it, unable to comprehend, and in that moment the doe regained its feet and looked at them, as if it too were trying to understand. Her father whistled softly. Charlie Spoon unslung his rifle and raised it to his shoulder, but the doe was already bounding away. His hurried shot missed, and the deer disappeared into the woods.

"Damn, damn, damn," he moaned.

150   "I don't believe it," her father said. "That deer was dead."

"Dead, hell!" Charlie yelled. "It was gutshot, that's all. Stunned and gutshot. Clean shot, my ass!"

What have I done? Andy thought.

Her father slung his rifle over his shoulder. "Well, let's go. It can't get too far."

"Hell, I've seen deer run ten miles gutshot," Charlie said. He waved his arms. "We may never find her."

155   As they crossed the field, Mac came up to her and said in a low voice, "Gutshot a deer, you'll go to hell."

"Shut up, Mac," she said, her voice cracking. It was a terrible thing she had done, she knew. She couldn't bear to think of the doe in pain and frightened. *Please let it die,* she prayed.

But though they searched all the last hour of daylight, so that they had to recross the field and go up the logging trail in a twilight made even deeper by thick, smoky clouds, they didn't find the doe. They lost its trail almost immediately in the dense stands of alderberry and larch.

"I am cold, and I am tired," Charlie Spoon declared. "And if you ask me, that deer's in another county already."

"No one's asking you, Charlie," her father said.

160   They had a supper of hard salami and ham, bread, and the rest of the applesauce cake. It seemed a bother to heat the coffee, so they had cold chocolate instead. Everyone turned in early.

"We'll find it in the morning, honeybun," her father said, as she went to her tent.

"I don't like to think of it suffering." She was almost in tears.

"It's dead already, punkin. Don't even think about it." He kissed her, his breath sour and his beard rough against her cheek.

Andy was sure she wouldn't get to sleep; the image of the doe falling, falling, then rising again, repeated itself whenever she closed her eyes. Then she heard an owl hoot and realized that it had awakened her, so she must have been asleep after all. She hoped the owl would hush, but instead it hooted louder. She wished her father or Charlie Spoon would wake up and do something about it, but no one moved in the other tent, and suddenly she was afraid that they had all decamped, wanting nothing more to do with her. She whispered, "Mac, Mac," to the sleeping bag where he should be, but no one answered. She tried to find the flashlight she always kept by her side, but couldn't, and she cried in panic, "Mac, are you there?" He mumbled something, and immediately she felt foolish and hoped he wouldn't reply.

165   When she awoke again, everything had changed. The owl was gone, the woods were still, and she sensed light, blue and pale, light where before there had been none. *The moon must have come out,* she thought. And it was warm, too, warmer than it should have been. She got out of her sleeping bag and took off her parka—it was that warm. Mac was asleep, wheezing like an old man. She unzipped the tent and stepped outside.

The woods were more beautiful than she had ever seen them. The moon made everything ice-rimmed glimmer with a crystallized, immanent light, while underneath that ice the branches of trees were as stark as skeletons. She heard a crunching in the snow, the one sound in all that silence, and there, walking down the logging trail into their camp, was the doe. Its body, like everything around her, was silvered with frost and moonlight. It walked past the tent where her father and Charlie Spoon were sleeping and stopped no more than six feet from her. Andy saw that she had shot it, yes, had shot it cleanly, just where she thought she had, the wound a jagged, bloody hole in the doe's chest.

A heart shot, she thought.

The doe stepped closer, so that Andy, if she wished, could have reached out and touched it. It looked at her as if expecting her to do this, and so she did, running her hand, slowly at first, along the rough, matted fur, then down to the edge of the wound, where she stopped. The doe stood still. Hesitantly, Andy felt the edge of the wound. The torn flesh was sticky and warm. The wound parted under her touch. And then, almost without her knowing it, her fingers were within, probing, yet still the doe didn't move. Andy pressed deeper, through flesh and muscle and sinew, until her whole hand and more was inside the wound and she had found the doe's heart, warm and beating. She cupped it gently in her hand. *Alive,* she marveled. *Alive.*

The heart quickened under her touch, becoming warmer and warmer until it was hot enough to burn. Andy tried to remove her hand, but the wound closed about it and held her fast. Her hand was burning. She cried out in agony, sure they would all hear and come help, but they didn't. And then her hand pulled free, followed by a steaming rush of blood, more blood than she ever could have imagined—it covered her hand and arm, and she saw to her horror that her hand was steaming. She moaned and fell to her knees and plunged her hand into the snow. The doe looked at her gently and then turned and walked back up the trail.

170   In the morning, when she woke, Andy could still smell the blood, but she felt no pain. She looked at her hand. Even though it appeared unscathed, it felt weak and withered. She couldn't move it freely and was afraid the others would notice. *I will*

hide it in my jacket pocket, she decided, *so nobody can see.* She ate the oatmeal that her father cooked and stayed apart from them all. No one spoke to her, and that suited her. A light snow began to fall. It was the last day of their hunting trip. She wanted to be home.

Her father dumped the dregs of his coffee. "Well, let's go look for her," he said.

Again they crossed the field. Andy lagged behind. She averted her eyes from the spot where the doe had fallen, already filling up with snow. Mac and Charlie entered the woods first, followed by her father. Andy remained in the field and considered the smear of gray sky, the nearby flock of crows pecking at unyielding stubble. *I will stay here,* she thought, *and not move for a long while.* But now someone—Mac—was yelling. Her father appeared at the woods' edge and waved for her to come. She ran and pushed through a brake of alderberry and larch. The thick underbrush scratched her face. For a moment she felt lost and looked wildly about. Then, where the brush thinned, she saw them standing quietly in the falling snow. They were staring down at the dead doe. A film covered its upturned eye, and its body was lightly dusted with snow.

"I told you she wouldn't get too far," Andy's father said triumphantly. "We must've just missed her yesterday. Too blind to see."

"We're just damn lucky no animal got to her last night," Charlie muttered.

175   Her father lifted the doe's foreleg. The wound was blood-clotted, brown, and caked like frozen mud. "Clean shot," he said to Charlie. He grinned. "My little girl."

Then he pulled out his knife, the blade gray as the morning. Mac whispered to Andy, "Now watch this," while Charlie Spoon lifted the doe from behind by its forelegs so that its head rested between his knees, its underside exposed. Her father's knife sliced thickly from chest to belly to crotch, and Andy was running from them, back to the field and across, scattering the crows who cawed and circled angrily. And now they were all calling to her—Charlie Spoon and Mac and her father—crying *Andy, Andy* (but that wasn't her name, she would no longer be called that); yet louder than any of them was the wind blowing through the treetops, like the ocean where her mother floated in green water, also calling *Come in, come in,* while all around her roared the mocking of the terrible, now inevitable, sea.

WRITING ASSIGNMENTS

Analysis

1. "Doe Season" employs a number of archetypes (universal symbols, patterns, and themes) that evoke deep, sometimes unconscious, responses in the reader. How do archetypes of the hunt, blood, the woods, and the ocean contribute to and expand the significance of these particular characters and events?
2. Compare and contrast the paragraph about Andy's first visit to the ocean with the story's last paragraph.
3. Trace and explain the evolution of Andy's relationship with her father.
4. Identify and explain details that foreshadow the story's conclusion.
5. Explain the thematic significance of Andy's surrealistic dream about the doe.

6. Why is the story titled "Doe Season"?
7. Compare and contrast images of the feminine in "Doe Season" and "Daddy," or images of the masculine in "Doe Season" and "Sunday in the Park."
8. Why is Andy, inexperienced and a girl, a more successful hunter than the males?

Argument

1. In response to Charlie Spoon's needling, Andy's father says, "She [Andy] can do whatever she likes." Does the story prove him right?
2. Does the story reinforce false stereotypes about masculinity and femininity? Is it sexist?
3. Write a profile of Andy's father in which you argue that he is or is not a "liberated" man.
4. Use "Doe Season" as evidence to refute or support the position taken in one or more of the readings in Chapter 1 on the biological and/or cultural origin of gender roles.
5. Is this story just as much about growing up as about gender?

Personal Writing and Writing from Research

1. Write an essay or story about a turning-point experience in your relationship with your mother or father.
2. *Collaborative Project:* Compare the role of a shared interest in helping to define relationships with a parent, friend, or colleague.
3. Either individually or as a group, research myths associated with hunting and relate them to images of men as providers and protectors.
4. Either individually or as a group, research initiation rituals associated with hunting and relate them to gender roles.
5. How are images of nature related to images of femaleness?

Sunday in the Park

Bel Kaufman

Born in Berlin, Germany, and raised in Russia, Bel Kaufman came to the United States at age 12. She is the granddaughter of Yiddish humorist Sholom Aleichem. After earning a BA from Hunter College and an MA from Columbia University, she taught in New York City high schools for 20 years before becoming a professor of English in 1964 at the Borough of Manhattan Community College. A novelist and contributor to *Esquire, Saturday Review,* and the *New York Times,* she also writes lyrics for musicals. She is best known for her 1965 novel, *Up the Down Staircase,* which a *Time* writer called "easily the most popular novel about U.S. public schools in history." "Sunday in the Park" won the National Education Association/P.E.N. 1983 short-story contest.

Journal Topics: (1) Describe an incident from your childhood in which aggressive behavior required a response. What was your role? (2) What childhood lessons did you learn from your family about dealing with violence? (3) Do boys and girls react differently to aggressive behavior? If so, why?

As You Read: (1) List the physical characteristics, such as body language, diction, and attitudes, by which the author differentiates the two fathers. (2) Why are Larry's parents angry at Larry and at each other after the confrontation with Joe's father? (3) Is there any suggestion of class difference between the two families?

It was still warm in the late-afternoon sun, and the city noises came muffled through the trees in the park. She put her book down on the bench, removed her sunglasses, and sighed contentedly. Morton was reading the *Times Magazine* section, one arm flung around her shoulder; their three-year-old son, Larry, was playing in the sandbox: a faint breeze fanned her hair softly against her cheek. It was five-thirty of a Sunday afternoon, and the small playground, tucked away in a corner of the park, was all but deserted. The swings and seesaws stood motionless and abandoned, the slides were empty, and only in the sandbox two little boys squatted diligently side by side. *How good this is,* she thought, and almost smiled at her sense of well-being. They must go out in the sun more often; Morton was so city-pale, cooped up all week inside the gray factorylike university. She squeezed his arm affectionately and glanced at Larry, delighting in the pointed little face frowning in concentration over the tunnel he was digging. The other boy suddenly stood up and with a quick, deliberate swing of his chubby arm threw a spadeful of sand at Larry. It just missed his head. Larry continued digging; the boy remained standing, shovel raised, stolid and impassive.

"No, no, little boy." She shook her finger at him, her eyes searching for the child's mother or nurse. "We mustn't throw sand. It may get in someone's eyes and hurt. We must play nicely in the nice sandbox." The boy looked at her in unblinking expectancy. He was about Larry's age but perhaps ten pounds heavier, a husky little boy with none of Larry's quickness and sensitivity in his face. Where was his mother? The only other people left in the playground were two women and a little girl on roller skates leaving now through the gate, and a man on a bench a few feet away. He was a big man, and he seemed to be taking up the whole bench as he held the Sunday comics close to his face. She supposed he was the child's father. He did not look up from his comics, but spat once deftly out of the corner of his mouth. She turned her eyes away.

At that moment, as swiftly as before, the fat little boy threw another spadeful of sand at Larry. This time some of it landed on his hair and forehead. Larry looked up at his mother, his mouth tentative; her expression would tell him whether to cry or not.

Her first instinct was to rush to her son, brush the sand out his hair, and punish the other child, but she controlled it. She always said that she wanted Larry to learn to fight his own battles.

5   "Don't *do* that, little boy," she said sharply, leaning forward on the bench. "You mustn't throw sand!"

The man on the bench moved his mouth as if to spit again, but instead he spoke. He did not look at her, but at the boy only.

"You go right ahead, Joe," he said loudly. "Throw all you want. This here is a *public* sandbox."

She felt a sudden weakness in her knees as she glanced at Morton. He had become aware of what was happening. He put his *Times* down carefully on his lap and turned his fine, lean face toward the man, smiling the shy, apologetic smile he might have offered a student in pointing out an error in his thinking. When he spoke to the man, it was with his usual reasonableness.

"You're quite right," he said pleasantly, "but just because this is a public place. . . ."

10   The man lowered his funnies and looked at Morton. He looked at him from head to foot, slowly and deliberately. "Yeah?" His insolent voice was edged with menace. "My kid's got just as good right here as yours, and if he feels like throwing sand, he'll throw it, and if you don't like, you can take your kid the hell out of here."

The children were listening, their eyes and mouths wide open, their spades forgotten in small fists. She noticed the muscle in Morton's jaw tighten. He was rarely angry, he seldom lost his temper. She was suffused with tenderness for her husband and an impotent rage against the man for involving him in a situation so alien and so distasteful to him.

"Now, just a minute," Morton said courteously, "you must realize. . . ."

"Aw, shut up," said the man.

Her heart began to pound. Morton half rose; the *Times* slid to the ground. Slowly the other man stood up. He took a couple of steps toward Morton, then stopped. He flexed his great arms, waiting. She pressed her trembling knees together. Would there be violence, fighting? How dreadful, how incredible. . . . She must do something, stop time, call for help. She wanted to put her hand on her husband's sleeve, to pull him down, but for some reason she didn't.

15   Morton adjusted his glasses. He was very pale. "This is ridiculous," he said unevenly. "I must ask you. . . ."

"Oh, yeah?" said the man. He stood with his legs spread apart, rocking a little, looking at Morton with utter scorn. "You and who else?"

For a moment the two men looked at each other nakedly. Then Morton turned his back on the man and said quietly, "Come on, let's get out of here." He walked awkwardly, almost limping with self-consciousness, to the sandbox. He stooped and lifted Larry and his shovel out.

At once Larry came to life; his face lost its rapt expression and he began to kick and cry. "I don't *want* to go home. I want to play better. I don't *want* any supper, I don't *like* supper . . ." It became a chant as they walked, pulling their child between them, his feet dragging on the ground. In order to get to the exit gate they had to pass the bench where the man sat sprawling again. She was careful not to look at him. With all the dignity she could summon, she pulled Larry's sandy, perspiring little hand, while Morton pulled the other. Slowly and with head high she walked with her husband and child out of the playground.

Her first feeling was one of relief that a fight had been avoided, that no one was hurt. Yet beneath it there was a layer of something else, something heavy and inescapable. She sensed that it was more than just an unpleasant incident, more than defeat of reason by force. She felt dimly it had something to do with her and Morton, something acutely personal, familiar, and important.

20   Suddenly, Morton spoke. "It wouldn't have proved anything."

"What?" she asked.

"A fight. It wouldn't have proved anything beyond the fact that he's bigger than I am."

"Of course," she said.

"The only possible outcome," he continued reasonably, "would have been—what? My glasses broken, perhaps a tooth or two replaced, a couple of days' work missed—and for what? For justice? For truth?"

25   "Of course," she repeated. She quickened her step. She wanted only to get home and to busy herself with her familiar tasks; perhaps then the feeling, glued like heavy plaster on her heart, would be gone. *Of all the stupid, despicable bullies,* she thought, pulling harder on Larry's hand. The child was still crying. Always before she had felt a tender pity for his defenseless little body, the frail arms, the narrow shoulders with sharp, winglike shoulder blades, the thin and unsure legs, but now her mouth tightened in resentment.

"Stop crying," she said sharply. "I'm ashamed of you!" She felt as if all three of them were tracking mud along the street. The child cried louder.

If there had been an issue involved, she thought, *if there had been something to fight for. . . . But what else could he possibly have done? Allow himself to be beaten? Attempt to educate the man? Call a policeman? "Officer, there's a man in the park who won't stop his child from throwing sand on mine. . . ."* The whole thing was as silly as that, and not worth thinking about.

"Can't you keep him quiet, for Pete's sake?" Morton asked irritably.

"What do you suppose I've been trying to do?" she said.

30   Larry pulled back, dragging his feet.

"If you can't discipline this child, I will," Morton snapped, making a move toward the boy.

But her voice stopped him. She was shocked to hear it, thin and cold and penetrating with contempt. "Indeed?" she heard herself say, "You and who else?"

WRITING ASSIGNMENTS

Analysis

1. Describe the masculine stereotypes personified by the two fathers and compare them to images of masculinity in "Forty in the Shade."

2. Identify evidence of class difference between the two families and suggest how this difference affected all three parents' behavior.

3. What do his parents' reactions to Larry's crying reveal about their feelings at that moment? In what sense does Larry become their scapegoat?

4. How does descriptive language indicate changes in the woman's attitude toward her son and husband?
5. What are the rhetorical effect and thematic significance of having the woman repeat the taunt by Joe's father, ". . . You and who else?"
6. Retell the story from the perspective of one of the fathers.
7. Explain the effect of telling the story from Larry's mother's point of view. What is the significance of identifying her only as "she"?
8. Compare and contrast the characters' attempts to redefine gender roles in "Doe Season" and "Sunday in the Park."

Argument

1. Agree or disagree with this statement: There will always be bullies, and the only way to stop a bully is to answer force with force. Support your position by referring to specific historical and current events, or to examples from books, plays, and movies.
2. You overhear someone saying, "Women say they like gentle men, but they really prefer a fighter." Do you agree? Use evidence, where relevant, from "Forty in the Shade," "Sunday in the Park," and "A Cultural Earthquake" to support your position.

Personal Writing and Writing from Research

1. As a close friend of either Larry's mother or father, what would you say to help your friend understand the other spouse's behavior during the events described in "Sunday in the Park"?
2. The mother says, "She sensed that it was more than just an unpleasant incident, more than defeat of reason by force." In a personal essay, analyze a comparably self-revealing and unsettling event in your life.
3. Prepare a research report on alternatives to violence in responding to aggressive behavior. Illustrate your findings with historical examples.
4. *Collaborative Project:* Compile an annotated list of American films, grouped by decade, that confront the issue of how to respond to violence. Characterize the kinds of responses that are modeled and endorsed. Are there trends or patterns? Is there a correlation between the values depicted in the movies and what was happening in the United States at the time the movies were made?

Daddy

Jan Clausen

Jan Clausen (b. 1950) lives in New York, where she is active in feminist and lesbian political groups. She founded the magazine *Conditions* in 1977 and was its editor for five years. She writes poetry, fiction, and criticism. Her books include *Waking at the Bottom of* the Dark (1979), *Mother, Sister, Daughter, Lover* (1980), and *Sinking Stealing* (1985).

Journal Topics: (1) What are your views of homosexual parents? (2) What are some of the ways that divorce affects a child's relationship with parents?

As You Read: (1) Compare the deliberate and unintentional modeling of feminine identity given to the little girl by members of both households. (2) What evidence do you find that the parents are competing for the child's loyalty and that economics plays a part in that competition? (3) Why does the child cry and vomit while she talks with her mother about moving to her father's when at the opening of the story she says, "I like Daddy's best." (4) What evidence, if any, does the story provide that the mother's lesbianism has affected her daughter?

I like my Daddy's best. It has more rooms. Mommy just has an apartment and you have to go upstairs. The bathroom is in my room. Daddy has two bathrooms. He owns the whole house. Mommy used to live there when I was a little baby. Before they got divorced. That means not married anymore. You get married when you love each other.

Mommy loves me. Daddy says I'm his favorite girl in the whole world, sugar. He always calls me sugar. We like to go to a restaurant for breakfast. Sometimes we go there for dinner if he has to work in the city. I went to his office lots of times. He has books there. You go way up in the elevator. Sometimes I feel like I'm going to throw up. But I don't. Then you see the river. There's no one there except Daddy and me. Sometimes Ellen comes.

My Mommy works. She goes to meetings. First I have to go to school and then daycare. You can make noise at daycare. At school you have to be quiet or you get punished. But I didn't ever get punished. Mommy helps me with my homework. Sometimes we read a book together. Daddy asks me add and take away. He says sugar you're so smart you can be anything you want to be when you grow up. A doctor or lawyer or a professor or anything. My Daddy's a lawyer. I don't know if I'll get married.

Daddy said maybe next year I can go to a different school where they have lots of things to play with. You can paint and go on trips and they have nice books. The kids make so much noise in my class. Some of them talk Spanish and the boys are bad. I got a star for doing my homework right.

5   My Daddy takes me on Sunday. Sometimes I sleep there if Mommy goes away. I have to be good. Daddy says he'll get me something when we go shopping if I behave. I have to take a bath before I go and brush my hair. Daddy says he likes little girls that smell nice and clean. Sometimes Ellen lets me try her perfume. Once she let me put some powder on my face and some blue stuff on my eyes. That's eye shadow. But I had to wash my face before I went home. Mommy doesn't wear makeup. Or Carolyn. They said it looks silly.

Once in the summer I stayed at my Daddy's for a whole week. Ellen was there. She helped take care of me. You're so helpless David she said. She laughed. We all laughed. I had fun. We went to Coney Island. During the week I just call my Daddy two times because he works hard. Sometimes if he goes on a trip he can't see me. Daddy and Ellen went on a trip to Florida. They had to fly in an airplane. They sent me a postcard every day. You could go swimming in the winter there. Mommy and me went to the country but the car broke.

Sometimes Carolyn stays overnight. We only have two beds. She has to sleep in the same bed with Mommy. When I wake up I get in bed with them. We all hug each other. Carolyn and Mommy kiss each other all the time. But they aren't married. Only a man and a woman can get married. When they want to have a baby the man's penis gets bigger and he puts it in the woman's vagina. It feels good to touch your vagina. Me and Veronica did it in the bathtub. When the baby comes out the doctor has to cut the Mommy's vagina with some scissors. Mommy showed me a picture in her book.

I saw Daddy's penis before. Mommy has hair on her vagina. She has hair on her legs and Carolyn has lots of hair on her legs like a man. Ellen doesn't. Mommy said maybe Ellen does have hair on her legs but she shaves it. Sometimes I forget and call Carolyn Ellen. She gets mad. Sometimes I forget and call Mommy Daddy. I have a cat called Meatball at Mommy's but sometimes I forget and call Meatball Max instead. That's Daddy's dog.

Daddy is all Jewish. So is Ellen. Mommy is only part Jewish. But Daddy said I could be Jewish if I want. You can't have Christmas if you're Jewish. Mommy and me had a little Christmas tree. Carolyn came. We made cookies. I had Chanukah at my Daddy's. He gave me a doll named Samantha that talks and a skateboard and green pants and a yellow top. He says when I learn to tell time he'll get me a watch.

10   I wish Mommy would get me a TV. I just have a little one. Sometimes it gets broken. Daddy has a color TV at his house. It has a thing with buttons you push to change the program. Mommy said I watch too much TV. I said if you get me a new TV I promise I'll only watch two programs every day. Mommy said we're not going to just throw things away and get a new one every year. I told her Andrea has a color TV in her house and Veronica has a nice big TV in her room that you can see good. Mommy said I'm not getting a TV and that's all. Mommy made me feel bad. I started crying. Mommy said go to your room you're spoiling my dinner. I said *asshole* to Mommy. That's a curse. Sometimes my Mommy says a curse to me. I cried and cried.

Mommy said get in your room. She spanked me and said now get in your room. I ran in my room and closed the door. Mommy hurts my feelings. She won't let me watch TV. She always goes to a meeting and I have to stay with the baby sitter. I don't say a curse to my Daddy. My Daddy isn't mean to me. I screamed and screamed for my Daddy and Mrs. Taylor next door got mad and banged on the wall.

Mommy said go in the other room and call him then. Daddy said you sound like you've been crying. What's the matter, sugar. Nothing I said. Daddy doesn't like me to cry. He says crying is for little babies. I can't stand to see a woman cry, sugar, he says. Then I laugh and he tells me blow my nose. What are we going to do on Sunday I said. Oh that's a surprise Daddy said. Is it going somewhere I said. Yes we're going somewhere but that's not the real surprise Daddy said. Is it a present I said. Daddy said just wait and see, what did you do in school today. Daddy always asks what did I do in school. I told him the teacher had to punish Carlos. Daddy said listen isn't it about your bedtime. I have work to do. Ellen says hi. Blow me a goodnight kiss.

I hugged my Mommy. She hugged me back. She said she was sorry she got mad. But don't beg for things. A new TV is expensive. We don't need it. Mommy always says it's too expensive. I said I wish you were married to the President. Then we could live in the White House. I saw a picture in school. You could have anything you want. They don't have cockroaches.

The President is a good man. He helps people. George Washington was the President. Veronica gave me a doll of his wife at my birthday. It has a long dress. Mommy said he was mean to Indians and Black people. But we studied about him in school and he wasn't. They had voted once. You could vote for Ford or Carter. My Daddy voted for Carter. I'm glad my Daddy voted for who won. My Mommy didn't vote.

15   Mommy doesn't like things. She doesn't like the President and she doesn't like Mary Hartman like my Daddy. I told her to get Charmin toilet paper like they have on TV because it's so soft to squeeze. She said that's a rip-off. She only takes me to McDonald's once every month. I got a Ronald McDonald cup to drink my milk. She said that's a gimmick. I like milk. Milk is a natural. I told Mommy that and she got mad. I said you don't like anything Mommy. She said I like lots of things. I like plants. I like to play basketball. I like sleeping late on Sunday mornings. I like to eat. I like books. I like women. I like you.

Do you like men I said. I don't like most men very much Mommy said. Some men are okay. My Daddy likes women I said. Does he Mommy said.

I asked my Daddy does he like women. He said extremely. Some of my favorite people are woman he said. Like you. And Ellen. Why do you ask. I said I don't know, Daddy said do you like men. I love you Daddy I said. I bet she gets that you know where Ellen said.

On Sunday we had breakfast at my Daddy's house. We had pancakes. Daddy makes them. He puts on his cook's hat. Then we went shopping. Then we went to a movie of Cinderella. Ellen came too. Then we went to a restaurant. I had ice cream with chocolate. Ellen and Daddy held each other's hand. Daddy said now I'm going to tell you the surprise. Ellen and I are getting married. How does that sound, sugar. Ellen said for god's sake David give her a little time to react.

Daddy said I can be in the wedding. He said Ellen will wear a pretty dress and he will break a glass. He did that when he and Mommy got married too. Then Ellen will have the same name as Mommy and Daddy and me and I can call her Mommy too if I want. I won't have to see my Daddy just on Sunday because Ellen will be there to help take care of me. She only works in the morning. It will be like a real family with a Mommy and Daddy and a kid. But I can't say that part because Daddy said it's supposed to still be a secret.

20   I didn't feel good when Daddy brought me home. I felt like I had to throw up. Mommy held my hand. I lay down on the bed and she brought Meatball to play with

me. She asked what did I do with Daddy today. She always asks me that. I told her we saw Cinderella. It was okay. She rode in a pumpkin. Some parts were boring. The Prince loved her. Daddy and Ellen are going to get married.

I started crying. I cried hard. Then I had to throw up. It got on the rug. Mommy got the washcloth. She brought my pajamas. She hugged me. She said I love you. She said it won't be so different when Daddy and Ellen are married. You like Ellen don't you.

I love you Mommy, I love you, I love you I said. Why don't you like my Daddy. I love my Daddy.

I don't dislike your father Mommy said. We don't have much in common that's all. I'm happy living here just with you. You're special to me and you're special to your Daddy. You see him every week.

I cried and cried. I love you Mommy. I love you and Daddy both the same. And I love Ellen because she's going to be my Mommy too. I'll miss you. I'll miss you so much when I live there. I'll cry. I'm going to have a big sunny room and Daddy said he'll paint it and I can pick a color. I'm going to have a new kitty so I won't miss Meatball. Next year I can go to that nice school and Ellen might have a baby. It would be a brother or a sister. Daddy's going to get me a bicycle. I can take anything there I want. I'll just leave a few toys here for when I come to visit you on Sunday.

WRITING ASSIGNMENTS

Analysis

1. Explain the effect of telling this story through a young child's perspective.
2. *Collaborative Project:* Have each member of your group write the events of this story from either Ellen's, Daddy's, Mommy's, or Carolyn's point of view.
3. Compare and contrast the feminine role models presented in the mother's and father's households.
4. Write a profile of the mother that covers everything except her sexual orientation.
5. How do differences in economic status between the mother's and father's households affect the child?

Argument

1. You have been asked to evaluate this child's home environment, because the child's father is seeking custody and the mother has refused to give it up. Write a recommendation to the court based on your view of what is best for the child.
2. Do you approve of the way the parents in this story handle their differences and communicate their opinions about each other to their child? If you disapprove, include advice to the parents in your essay.
3. Does a person's sexual orientation have any bearing on his or her ability to be a good parent?

Personal Writing and Writing from Research

1. Analyze your feelings about this mother's lesbianism.
2. Research the laws on child custody and child support. How have they changed over the last 50 years?
3. Analyze one element of popular culture directed at children (fairy tales, television, advertising, toys) to assess how it models feminine behavior.
4. Using both personal interviews and library research, survey homosexual men and women about their attitudes toward raising a child.

CHAPTER 4

COMING OF AGE

SYLVIA   by Nicole Hollander

Cinderella's foot slid easily into the glass slipper.

"Now we can live happily ever after."

"Actually, Prince,"

said Cinderella, "I usually wear Birkenstocks, that is, if I'm not planning to walk, in which case I'd wear something that ties up the front with good arch support. Let me show you my shoes," she said gaily, taking the glassy-eyed Prince by the hand and leading him to her closet.

SOMEDAY MY PRINCE WILL COME...

Starting in adolescence, we "come of age." We develop an adult body and sexual drive. While realigning our relationship with our family, we develop and demonstrate the skills and values we will use to make our way and gain social acceptance. For most Americans, this is a tumultuous time because, given our diverse and mobile society, we face as many challenges as opportunities, and both can be confusing.

A larger world calls. While some of us try to preserve our traditional way of life and our place in it, most of us move beyond our first home and family and seek to establish our independence. If we feel trapped by pressures to conform to the customs and values of home, neighborhood, or community, we may rebel. At times we may look back, uneasy about ruptured bonds and uncertain of our course. Simultaneously anxious and defiant, we continue trying to resolve the tension between our individual and social identities.

Increasingly, we seek the company and approval of our peers. Sexual maturity arouses longings that thrill, obsess, confuse, and may even embarrass us. Self-absorbed, we reassess ourselves constantly and seek reassurance from others.

As we explore that larger social world, we take stock of it. What does it offer? What does it demand? What are the rules? How does it define success, and what do we need to thrive in love, at work, and in our community? What are the rites of passage from childhood to adult status? How do we want to fit in?

While we try to answer these questions, we realize that in many ways society is also taking stock of us. Thus, the answers to these questions will depend in part on each individual's temperament and the prevailing values of our culture. But they are also influenced by our class, ethnicity, and gender.

In "The Fragile Sex," Michael D'Antonio analyzes the biological, cultural, and personal factors that turn all too many boys into problems for themselves and others. Somewhat removed from mainstream culture, the Native-American brothers in Louise Erdrich's "The Red Convertible" come of age on the reservation, suspended between two cultures. Then, in "she being Brand," a poem that also calls on the symbolism of the automobile, e. e. cummings fuses two American rites of passage: driving a car and sexual initiation.

In "'Some Day My Prince Will Come': Female Acculturation Through the Fairy Tale," Marcia Lieberman examines the rites of passage and the social roles laid out for girls in traditional fairy tales. Jeanne Desy's "The Princess Who Stood on Her Own Two Feet" updates and transforms that traditional message.

For Maya Angelou in "A Job on the Streetcars," World War II San Francisco is no fairy tale. Tasks associated with work and prejudice rather than with romantic love mark her coming of age. In "Growing," Helena Maria Viramonte depicts a Chicana teetering on the verge of adulthood. And in "Hanging Fire," poet Audre Lorde expresses the isolation and anxiety of adolescence.

Finally, in an excerpt from her novel, *Family Affairs,* Sue Miller captures many of the moods and expressions of emerging male and female sexuality.

The Fragile Sex

Michael D'Antonio

Michael D'Antonio, a professional writer, says he is "interested in how thinking, ideas, beliefs, and values affect social conditions, especially the lives of regular citizens, rather than the great historical figures." His curiosity has led to his writing a number of books about intriguing aspects of modern American life, including *Fall from Grace* (1987) about the Christian Right, *Heaven on Earth: Dispatches from America's Spiritual Frontier* (1992) about the New Age movement, and *Atomic Harvest* (1993) about the secret history of a nuclear weapons complex. "The Fragile Sex," which first appeared in the *Los Angeles Times Magazine* on Sunday, Dec. 4, 1994, is part of a book now in progress, *Devouring the Young: Parents and Children in an Era of Self-Interest.*

Journal Topics: (1) Describe your memories of how disruptive children, ages 12–15 years old, were treated in school. Were such children more likely to be boys or girls? (2) How necessary is a father figure to a child's development? Do boys have a greater need than girls for a father figure? (3) Based on your experience, do boys' and girls' academic aptitudes differ? If so, how?

As You Read: (1) What evidence does this reading provide about brain differences in boys and girls? How do these differences affect behavior? (2) Why are boys more likely to experience academic difficulty and get into trouble than girls? (3) What are the advantages and disadvantages to society of traditional masculinity?

1 With straight brown hair, blue eyes and a broad smile, Ryan Arnold had always been able to clunk into a room wearing huge sneakers and a floppy T-shirt and charm almost anyone. But last year when he turned 12, his temperament shifted. His grades plummeted, he started smoking and he took long bike trips along the railroad tracks, past the old factories and warehouses in Martinez, a small town near Walnut Creek [California].

2 Patricia Arnold, who had chosen to rear him alone, was shocked. "He had always been my little buddy; so good," she recalls. "I had a 20-year plan in mind for how his life would go, and this kind of behavior wasn't in the blueprint. I was scared of him."

3 It didn't take long for Ryan's teachers to suggest that he might be emotionally disturbed. His grandfather offered to pay for anything that might straighten the boy out: doctors, medicine, even a psychiatric group home. "We knew there was something seriously wrong with him," says Arnold. "I wanted an explanation, a diagnosis, and I became passionate about finding one."

4   A psychologist found Ryan to have mild emotional and learning difficulties. He became one of an increasing number of American boys—more than 1.7 million in all—
who have been declared emotionally disturbed or educationally disabled. This is a
particularly male problem, and just one aspect of a crisis that frightens parents and
anyone else who deals with boys. Emotionally disturbed boys outnumber girls nearly
4 to 1. For learning disabilities, the ratio is more than 2 to 1. Boys clog the court system, fill juvenile detention centers and threaten public safety. Juvenile arrests for violent crimes—which almost always involve males—increased by 50% between 1987
and 1991. The murder rate for teens—victims are almost all male—is up 104% from
20 years ago, and last year, nearly 7,000 boys between ages 15 and 24 were killed. The
American boy has become so frightening that many states are moving to lower the
age when criminal defendants can be tried as adults.

5   Experts across the nation are struggling to explain what is happening. In a spate of
new books, they offer competing explanations—from absent fathers to the evils of
technology—to account for the troubled state of American boys. Altogether, the research suggests that today's boys—deeply distressed and tragically misunderstood—
may be victims of their own biology and society's confusion about masculinity.

6   "This is a complex issue because there are several things going on that are all
true," says Dr. Judith Rapoport, chief of the child psychiatry branch at the National
Institute of Mental Health. Rapoport uses magnetic resonance imaging to map the
brains of developing children and hunt for neurological factors that make boys different from girls. The MRIs can show brain damage, differences in the size of parts of
the brain and even differences in the neurological connections called synapses. Based
on what is known, Rapoport says, "it's clear that boy's brains may be more vulnerable,
and they do get these [psychiatric] diseases more often."

7   Biology's influence may be significant, but Rapoport also suspects there's a
strong social component to the troubled-boy phenomenon. Sometimes a boy like
Ryan Arnold isn't sick. Sometimes he is just going through a difficult adolescence
at a time when society looks askance at all male aggression. "We have to ask if society is more intolerant about males and more ready to label them as medical cases,"
says Rapoport. It is possible, she adds, that aggression and other masculine traits—
including many that were once admired—have been so "pathologized" that today
Tom Sawyer would be labeled as disturbed.

8   Our changing attitude toward boys can be seen in the way young males are portrayed in the media and discussed in everyday conversation. Bad men and boys are increasingly the staples of television talk shows. And, of course, the news is full of male
rapists and murderers. Boys are portrayed as the drug pushers in public service announcements. They are the danger lurking on city streets. Even the simple phrase
"boys will be boys" carries a more ominous meaning now since it's the title of a recent book about male violence. All this evidence suggests that, to some degree, society believes that boys are, by definition, bad. In some cases, when the experts send
boys to treatment and special education, they may be acting out of fear and anti-boy
prejudice.

9   "Males are now regarded as 'The Problem' and people look at boys as if their masculinity is something to be cured, or overcome," says David Blankenhorn, author of

"Fatherless America," which will be published next year by Basic Books, and president of the private Institute for American Values of New York, which conducts research and analysis of family issues. He argues that many boys are being victimized by adult standards that are heavily freighted with feminist politics. "This is especially true in schools," he adds. "Schools are institutions run by women in which women and girls are seen as disadvantaged and boys are seen as a toxic problem. In school, the goal of getting girls to achieve is wonderful. The goal for boys is making them behave."

0 While some boys are no doubt misunderstood, it is clear that a great number are truly troubled. One measure of this distress is that juvenile suicide, always more common among boys, peaked in 1977, and the rate is still more than three times what it was in 1960. Boys are the subject of broad research by social scientists looking at the ways that parents, schools and other institutions may be failing them. In the meantime, hard science has begun to focus on the difference in male and female brains. Once a neglected area, the comparative study of the brain has been energized by new technology and a cadre of scientists willing to say that sex differences are real. Some researchers are so impressed by what they are learning that they suggest it may be biologically impossible for many boys to meet the modern standard of behavior. In such cases, they say, boys may be penalized simply for being boys.

1 Research scientist Laura Allen begins her study of the brain in autopsy labs at hospitals throughout Southern California. A UCLA neuroanatomist, she collects brain tissue samples from cadavers and returns to her lab to continue her studies on gender differences. During the past decade, Allen has contributed substantially to a growing body of knowledge about brain function. "It used to be accepted that men and women process information the same way. We now know that is not true," she says. "The entire brain is different at a very subtle level, at least."

2 In the 1980s, Allen's research confirmed that a critical part of the brain responsible for passing information from one hemisphere to the other—the corpus callosum—is larger in females. Two other parts of the brain that perform a similar function, she discovered, are also larger in women. Other researchers have shown that boys' brains mature more slowly, especially the frontal lobes, which handle many social and cognitive functions. Scientists generally agree that high levels of the male hormone testosterone, which are necessary to transform a fetus into a boy, are causing the difference.

3 Allen's colleague, neuroendocrinologist Roger Gorski, has pioneered research showing how hormones affect mammalian brains, especially the parts that control sexual activity. Gorski has used hormone injections to induce female rats to behave like rutting males, and to make males behave like receptive females in heat. In normal rats, natural levels of male and female hormones create substantial structural differences in the part of the brain that controls sexual behavior. "Since sex and aggression are very, very close," notes Gorski, "these differences may have an impact beyond sex."

4 The effect of biology on intellectual functioning has been widely noted. Several studies have shown that scores on certain tests of mental abilities go up and down

depending on the levels of hormones in a subject's body. Likewise, little girls with elevated testosterone levels are more likely to choose the toys that boys prefer: sports cars, trucks and Lincoln Logs. But the differences extend beyond hormones to the actual functioning of the brain. Scientists have discovered, for example, that women use more of their brain in the task of spelling than men.

15   The research, and her own experience with her son and daughter, have convinced Allen that biology is perhaps the central factor in the problems of boys. "I have a little boy in kindergarten," she says. "My son is a good little boy, but he cannot be expected to be just like a well-behaved little girl. Boys need parents to be a lot more understanding."

16   Allen is not alone in her assessment. Laboratories across the country are uncovering neurological clues to boys' behavior problems. These discoveries suggest that some boys are not to blame if they cannot meet our rising expectations of civility. "We actually know quite a bit about the brain and these behavioral disturbances," says neuropsychologist Ruben Gur, who leads a brain study team at the University of Pennsylvania. "Anyone in science who doesn't know this must be sleeping."

17   For example, psychologists and educators have long known that girls excel at communication and social skills. Boys have been observed to be more aggressive and physical. Girls tend to be more cooperative and reflective. Many parents would likely agree with these generalities. Now there's emerging evidence that the stereotypical behavior is caused by differences in the brain, differences that Gur and others have documented with magnetic resonance imaging.

18   The MRI pictures and post-mortem studies show some intriguing variations. Females seem to have more gray matter, the active brain cells that perform thinking. The rate of blood flow in the female brain is faster, adds Gur, and the electrical activity in women's brains also seems to be quicker. Also, females tend to activate both sides of their brain for a given type of problem, he says, while males tend to be "lateralized" thinkers, restricting activity to one side or the other. "Stated simply," says Gur, "women run hotter and are more revved-up." He theorizes that this extra activity makes it easier for women to score high on tests of communication and social skills. Women, for example, are much better at identifying the emotions a person shows in a photograph. Men, with their ability to concentrate activity in one side of the brain, dominate fields such as mathematics, which require this kind of thinking. "It's all in the way we are wired," Gur says.

19   Different wiring may also explain why boys are far more likely to have learning and behavior problems. It turns out that baby boys are more vulnerable to minor brain damage—during birth or because of later injury—than girls. Scientists guess that this is because higher levels of testosterone make the male brain less resilient. Testosterone may also delay the development of certain spheres of the brain critical to social skills and communication. If these areas are injured, boys are less able to heal or adapt.

20   It may be these tiny injuries that cause the most common brain disorder found in boys—Attention Deficit Disorder, which can manifest itself in the form of failure at school, aggression and even criminal behavior. "A child like this becomes frustrated,

associates learning with failure and becomes aggressive," Gur says. "They are not simply bad boys. It's not that easy. They might have ADD and act out in frustration."

21 The diagnosis of ADD (formerly called hyperactivity) involves as much art as science. Doctors and therapists tend to look for a variety of behavior problems, among them fidgeting, distraction, impulsiveness and excessive talking. All can get a boy into a lot of trouble at school. But they don't necessarily mean that he is emotionally disturbed or a social deviant. In fact, the act of labeling a child disturbed or disabled may do more harm than good.

22 "These kids are identified as problems in most schools often by the second grade," notes psychiatrist John Ratey, who is also a Harvard assistant professor of psychiatry. "This happens quickly because schools today emphasize cooperative learning and social skills. But these kids can't do it. They are identified as a problem and then everybody treats them differently. Teachers aren't the same with the kids who aren't so nice. Parents with children in these schools try to avoid having their kids placed in the same classroom." Often, these seemingly unruly children are reprimanded, counseled and punished. Their trouble may be linked to a male tendency toward ADD and other brain-based problems. If it is ADD, the stimulant Ritalin may be enough to quiet a boy down and keep him on track in school. Teachers and school administrators are often the first to recommend Ritalin, and some districts have even gone to court to argue that a child be given the medicine by his parents. Sometimes children are treated with talking therapy, other stimulants, or anti-depressive drugs.

23 In the past few years, as scientific findings about brain development and gender have reached a wider audience, more and more children are being treated, notes Ratey. He ought to know. As author of *Driven to Distraction*, a widely praised new book on attention deficit, Ratey has helped put ADD in the vernacular. "ADD has become the diagnosis of the decade," he says. "It's the Prozac of the '90s; everybody's interested in it." Ratey and other specialists report a growing number of children and adults coming to them for treatment—drugs and/or psychotherapy—and finding relief after years of struggling with problems apparently caused by undiagnosed ADD. Though Ritalin is not without side effects (those include loss of appetite, sleep disturbances and reports of slowed growth rates when used for long periods), it's been widely embraced by parents and counselors. One measure of its popularity: the U.S. drug industry's production of Ritalin has risen 300% since 1990.

24 Yet Ratey suspects that many cases of ADD are still undiagnosed and many boys misunderstood. "ADD is not the only cause of boys' problems," he adds, "but it's a very important factor, and once it's diagnosed and treated, the change can be dramatic."

25 The diagnosis of a mild attention deficit for Ryan Arnold was not severe enough to merit drug therapy. Instead, he was counseled for one hour each week, and his mother established a more ordered routine at home. A few months later, Ryan's school performance improved. But he remains aggressive, unpredictable and fidgety.

26 In Martinez, on a Sunday afternoon when he would rather be outside with his friends, Ryan is more than a little impatient when his mother invites him to sit and chat. He arrives in the room pushing his trail bike and dressed in baggy blue striped

shorts and a huge gray T-shirt. He leans the bike against a wall and looks out the window at the street before sitting down and squirming in his chair.

27   "Excuse me, sir. I don't mean to be rude. But is this going to take long?"

28   Ryan struggles through a few minutes of conversation. In one breath he angrily criticizes a therapist he has seen.

29   "I hate Don," he says. His mother cuts him off with an urgently whispered "Ryan!"

30   A moment later, Ryan offers to massage his mother's sore neck. He recalls enjoying school until fourth grade, when he began to feel bored and restless. "Right now baseball is my life. My teachers say they don't understand me. I don't know why they are baffled. I'm just trying to be myself. Can I go now?"

31   When Ryan again looks anxiously out the window, his mother dismisses him so that he can join a friend waiting on the sidewalk. After he's gone, Patricia Arnold says she does not believe that ADD is the real cause of her son's troubles. One of Ryan's therapists, Don Elium, has suggested that the boy suffers from a lack of firm guidance and male role models. Boys need to be around men who can show them how to contain and control their naturally aggressive impulses, says Elium. This makes sense to Arnold, who first learned about this theory in Elium's book, *Raising a Son*. Elium, a marriage, child and family counselor, teaches psychology at John F. Kennedy University in Orinda, near Oakland.

32   Elium would say it's not only difficult but also dangerous for a boy to be raised outside the company of men. However, with single-mother households increasing and divorce splitting half of all marriages, legions of boys are coming of age today without a constant male role model. At the same time, boyish behavior that was once considered normal—aggression, defiance, mischievousness, risk-taking—is gradually being redefined as pathological. If boys are in trouble, says Elium, it's because too many men have abandoned their sons, and adults in general are failing to help boys meet a social standard that requires them to be more cooperative.

33   "Many women, feminists especially, are afraid that masculinity will run wild and become life-threatening," adds Jeanne Elium, Elium's wife and coauthor of *Raising a Son*. "Many mothers are afraid of the aggressiveness in boys. Our son began staring me down when he was about 3 years old. I thought, 'Oh, my God, what do I do now?' I didn't understand him."

34   The Eliums believe that many mothers and teachers don't understand the natural assertiveness in boys. However, they are often responsible for teaching them to be more sensitive and considerate. This is necessary, so that boys can be successful, but this civilizing process must be done with great care. Too often, they say, boys are made to feel inferior or even disturbed. This notion that males are bad is reinforced by a stream of feminist thought that argues that women are natural peacemakers while male aggression—in the form of patriarchy—is the main source of war, pollution, poverty, virtually every kind of suffering in the world.

35   "Good feminism helps boys with feelings and relationships, but harsh views about boys being awful creatures and jokes about testosterone poisoning hurt rather than help," argues Priscilla Vail, a New York educator and author of books on child development. "Bad feminism has eroded our willingness to respect differences in males

and females. Boys do need something different than girls. And if we start diagnosing every boy who throws a rock through the window, we're in trouble."

36   "Boys take apart things, they crash around a room, they seem more out of control," says Don Elium. The Eliums prize the energy of boys who may seem overly rambunctious. They describe that energy as a natural, exciting and potentially creative force. The problem is, "boys are often made to feel ashamed that they can't act more like girls, ashamed of being boys," says Don Elium. "But if you try to kill these impulses rather than mold them, you create boys that are either murderous or suicidal."

37   He suggests that boys be given more outlets for their impulses. In school this might mean longer recesses, to let boys burn off steam. Teachers must also understand the difficulties boys have with such tasks as reading, sitting still and working cooperatively. Some teachers do try to accommodate boys, for instance, by touching them often to calm them down, or letting a hyperactive boy stand in the back of a classroom when he can no longer sit still. At home, Elium hopes that fathers will play a stronger role in their sons' lives, showing them that male assertiveness doesn't have to devolve into brutish behavior. Single mothers can also help their sons with this task. But the key, according to the Eliums, is found in male role models.

38   The vision of a world in which boys have access to the time and attention of male role models is appealing, yet, say some critics, it's fraught with real-world complexities that make it practically impossible to realize. "There are not a lot of wonderful men out there," says New York family therapist Olga Silverstein, "and the fact is, a lot of women have to raise sons alone. They have no choice. To say they must have men to help is ridiculous."

39   Silverstein helped bring feminist concepts to the family therapy movement in the '70s, and according to the theories she puts forward in her book *The Courage to Raise Good Men,* with the disappearance of men from their lives, boys need more attention from their mothers. "Mothers have abandoned their sons because they think they can't raise them well, or they will turn them into sissies if they maintain a close relationship. But if mothers pull away, then who is the boy left with? No one. He raises himself, and we are seeing the results."

40   Boys get into trouble mainly because they don't know how to relate to other people, argues Silverstein. Mothers who want to create strong and self-sufficient sons fail to become attached to them in an emotional relationship that teaches them empathy for other human beings. Without empathy, says Silverstein, "we wind up with boys who are shooting each other."

41   Silverstein's book describes how parents, especially mothers, have trained their sons to be highly competitive and self-absorbed. These mothers, eager to prevent their sons from becoming "Mama's boys," push them away at an early age. "Why would we be surprised, then, that boys turn out to be more violent and that men have abandoned the family? We train them to do that, and it works."

42   Instead of leaving a boy alone, or handing him off to a macho-man father figure, Silverstein advises mothers to bond with their sons and maintain a respectful but close relationship into adulthood.

43ᵉ   Patti Kubasek and her son Chris discovered the value of this kind of relationship last year. At the time, 14-year-old Chris was sliding into truancy and gang activity in the months that followed his father's death from cancer. His grades fell, he got into fights at school and he was caught with a knife. He also began hanging around with suburban gangbangers in Martinez.

44   "My mom and I would fight twice a day. Everything she did drove me nuts," recalls Chris, a blond-haired boy who is so tall that an easy chair barely contains his arms and legs. "I wasn't exactly nice to anyone."

45   After her husband died, she and Chris had "talked a lot about his father," Kubasek says. "He took me from one room of the house to another, stopping to talk about him in each room." But in her grief, Kubasek had thrown herself into work and the pursuit of a college degree, abandoning her relationship with her son. Trying to renew it, she read books about mothers and sons and brought Chris to a therapist. They started to talk and she realized how sad her son had been.

46   As Chris began to see that his mother was serious about trying to restore their relationship, he gradually calmed down. Over time, and with the intervention of his mother and counselors, he left his gang friends. Now he's thriving again at school.

47   Chris says his mother's openness was all-important in his decision to restore his life. "When she showed me how much she really cared," he says, "it really made a difference."

48   A close mother-son relationship will produce a man who understands others, controls his aggressive impulses and communicates successfully, says Silverstein. This kind of boy will be as different in his outlook on life as today's girls are different from their grandmothers. "We have broken the gender barrier when it comes to girls and careers. They feel comfortable at work and at home. Now we have to let boys back into the family emotionally. That's what they need. To say that they can't be helped because of their nature is a great rationalization. I refuse to accept it, because if you do, there is no hope for the future."

49   The help of at least one parent is vital when all of society is conspiring to turn boys into brutes, adds Angela Phillips, who fears that men are in danger of becoming the "rogue elephants" of the human race, admitted to family life for the purpose of mating only. Phillips, who specializes in writing about children and family relationships, agrees with Silverstein when it comes to boys who have been emotionally abandoned and have no secure attachment to their families. But she goes one step further. "Lessons in violence, indifference and separation are provided every day for every male child," Phillips argues in *The Trouble With Boys*. "Learning them is part of learning to survive as a boy."

50   Indeed, a boy who is not deemed sufficiently aggressive, who likes beautiful, soft or cuddly toys, may be considered effeminate and referred for counseling by his parents. In contrast, the femininity of a female child is rarely questioned. "A girl can dress up as a fairy princess or wears sneakers and jeans and no one will worry about her femininity."

51   It should be no wonder that boys are troubled when their natural aggression runs up against modern standards of behavior. Surviving as a boy may get more difficult as

the post-industrial world becomes more complex and brawn becomes a devalued asset. Where once a man who had trouble communicating could make a good wage in a steel mill, writes Phillips, he is now frustrated because the mills are closed and he has no aptitude for high-tech work. Some boys look at these men and, rightly or wrongly, conclude that the world no longer holds a place for them. Phillips argues that poor males who lack communication skills naturally seek an identity in the culture of street violence, where strength is still valued.

52   The sense of failure "is reinforced by the level of information they need to process and the high stress levels in modern life," observes Charlotte Tomaino, who runs a group practice in New York called Neuropsychological Services of Westchester. Tomaino, who has treated hundreds of patients with brain-related disorders, says society's rules about acceptable behavior and the skills required to succeed are changing too fast for some boys to keep up.

53   "It's like survival of the fittest, only the fittest will be the people who have good impulse control, can orchestrate events, organize things and focus their attention," says Tomaino. All these skills appear to be located in the frontal lobe of the brain, which develops much more slowly in boys, according to some researchers. This could mean that boys are being judged by a standard that is harder and harder for them to reach, she says. "Twenty years ago, no one had to do many of the things we must now do with technology and communication," she says. "Our institutions are more complex and difficult. I'm concerned that we're going to have many more of these boys in the future."

54   The partisans in the struggle to understand boys can each point to children who have been helped by one approach or another. Psychotherapists can offer up patients who improve with a variety of interventions, from better fathering to behavior modification therapy. At the same time, neuroscientists note that many boys with ADD improve when their brains are dosed with chemicals, though they've not yet found chemical solutions for the wide range of disorders facing children and young men.

55   While they may disagree about the cause and treatment, none of the various schools of research would argue with the notion that boys are in a kind of crisis, and that their emotional and educational disabilities burden families and communities. Many of those who research and treat boys' problems are beginning to see the appeal of an approach that takes into consideration both the nature of the boy child and the way we nurture them.

56   Even an ardent "hard" scientist, such as Laura Allen, acknowledges that the way a boy is raised can overcome certain genetic tendencies. "In a study at Berkeley they followed boys who were given lots of attention in the first 18 months and those who were not," she notes. Years later, the boys who were given more affection scored higher on IQ tests. These findings seem to refute those who look at IQ and other measures of cognition and declare that biology is destiny.

57   "Boys seem to benefit from more one-on-one attention," says Allen. "I think the affection may change the sex hormone level in the brain, which then affects brain development." On the other hand, boys also seem to be more damaged by problems

within a family, especially divorce, at least in the short run. Allen even wonders if boys may be more vulnerable to the loss of parental attention inherent with day care. "I worry about day care because infants need a lot of cuddling to develop and I'm not sure you can get that kind of nurturing by paying for it," she says.

58   Despite the scientific advances, the complexity of human behavior makes the diagnosis of and treatment of emotional problems difficult. "You can't just treat all these kids with Ritalin and then, because they slow down, declare that that was the problem all along," says Paul McHugh, chairman of the psychiatry department at Johns Hopkins Medical School in Baltimore. "Ritalin will slow almost any kid down. And a lot of kids who supposedly have neurologically based ADD can't sit still in school but they can watch TV for two hours. That tells me that we're too impressed by our biological discoveries and using them to explain things without taking into account other factors."

59   McHugh insists that how boys are treated has a much greater effect on their behavior than brain structure. "Boys have a genetic influence to be aggressive. But if you raise them a certain way, that will assert itself as leadership or entrepreneurial skill. If he is raised in another environment that is not as nurturing, he may become violent. That is why broken families have more of these problems. It's harder for them to provide the right environment."

60   A parent who is aware of a boy's special needs can help him from an early age. Steve Brooks, a single father of a boy named Brandon, recognized that his son needed help when he seemed unable to conform to the rules of the preschool he attended in the San Francisco Bay Area. "I got constant phone calls from school saying he was unruly and he couldn't concentrate."

61   Brandon was dramatically different from his sister, Tarren, who had experienced little trouble adjusting to school and excelled at working cooperatively. "Tarren was eager to please and knew how to do it," recalls Brooks. "Brandon didn't have a clue."

62   Although he wasn't found to have ADD, Brandon exhibited many of the traits and behaviors typical of boys who are. He dismantled anything that came apart, including his own toys. He spoke out of turn, fought with other children and raced around.

63   "He sometimes would have rages and literally throw things around," Brooks says. "It was hard for anyone, teachers included, to have enough patience to deal with him."

64   During the past year, at the suggestion of his school principal, Brandon received special education classes. He got extra attention from his father. Both have helped him learn how to focus on specific tasks, such as schoolwork, and taught him how to interact with other children. Now 7, Brandon seems to be thriving. But he is still a bundle of aggressive energy.

65   On a recent Sunday morning he scampered in and out of his home half a dozen times in 15 minutes. Dressed in shorts and a T-shirt, he was a blur of activity, just like the Tasmanian devil on his shirt. "We're building a house out there," he said to his dad, his voice filled with excitement. "You should see it." The house, made of cardboard, was one of the many projects Brandon would tackle this weekend. None would exhaust his energy.

66   "People expect a level of behavior from kids that is more civilized, more gentle," says Brooks. "I'm trying to give Brandon outlets for his energy while teaching him what's expected." He takes his son on long hikes and extended camping trips. He'll do almost anything to help his son learn the modern survival skills of self-control. Along the way, says Brooks, he has come to admire the depth of his son's energy.

67   "I have to say I appreciate him, and I appreciate male power more in general," he concludes. "But Brandon has to live in the modern world, and he was running the risk of being stigmatized by his behavior. I had to save him from a lot of problems in the future."

WRITING ASSIGNMENTS

Analysis

1. Why is the reading's title both surprising and appropriate?
2. How does this reading define natural masculinity? Is this definition accurate?
3. What biological factors, cultural trends, and personal experiences put boys at risk? Are these contributing factors interrelated? Are they all equally important?
4. Identify and explain the various suggestions offered to help boys. Which do you consider most useful? Why?
5. Define and illustrate the expression, "Boys will be boys."
6. How do the problems of boys depicted in two of this chapter's readings ("The Red Convertible" and the excerpt from *Family Pictures*) illustrate the cultural and social issues discussed in "The Fragile Sex"?

Argument

1. "Males are now regarded as 'The Problem' and people look at boys as if their masculinity is something to be cured, or overcome," according to David Blankenhorn. Is there a reaction against traditional masculinity in American society today? If so, what causes it? Is this reaction justified?
2. Do boys need male role models? Why?
3. Does modern American life offer too few opportunities for the exercise of traditional masculinity? Why? What opportunities do exist?

Personal Writing and Writing from Research

1. Draw on your personal experiences to illustrate or refute the claim that schools are too quick to identify boys as problems.
2. Write a research paper on Attention Deficit Disorder (ADD).
3. Investigate the history, use, and results of the use of the drug Ritalin.
4. Conduct further research on the work of one of the experts cited in this reading.
5. Write a research paper on the experience of boys in school. You may want to consult Myra and David Sadker's *Failing at Fairness* (1994), which contains a chapter and extensive bibliography on this topic.

The Red Convertible

Louise Erdrich

Born in 1954 of German and Chippewa Indian descent, Louise Erdrich grew up in North Dakota as a member of the Turtle Mountain Band of Chippewa. She graduated in 1976 from Dartmouth College, where she received many prizes for her fiction and poetry, including the American Academy of Poets Prize. In 1979, she received an MA in creative writing from Johns Hopkins University. She has been an editor of the Boston Indian Council newspaper, *The Circle.* In 1984, a collection of her poetry, *Jacklight,* was published, and her first novel, *Love Medicine,* won the National Book Critics Circle Award. She has continued the *Love Medicine* series in *The Beet Queen* (1986) and *Tracks* (1988). She and her husband, Michael Dorris, a professor of Native-American studies at Dartmouth College, wrote *The Crown of Columbus* (1992). Her most recent novel is *Bingo Palace.*

Journal Topics: (1) Describe what getting your driver's license or driving your first car meant to you. (2) Describe your first job and its significance to you and to others. (3) Describe your relationship with a sibling of the same sex.

As You Read: (1) What does the red convertible symbolize for Lyman and Henry Lamartine? (2) How does non-Native American culture influence the lives of these Chippewa brothers? (3) How does Lyman's coming of age differ from Henry's?

I was the first one to drive a convertible on my reservation. And of course it was red, a red Olds. I owned that car along with my brother Henry Junior. We owned it together until his boots filled with water on a windy night and he bought out my share. Now Henry owns the whole car, and his youngest brother Lyman (that's myself), Lyman walks everywhere he goes.

How did I earn enough money to buy my share in the first place? My own talent was I could always make money. I had a touch for it, unusual in a Chippewa. From the first I was different that way, and everyone recognized it. I was the only kid they let in the American Legion Hall to shine shoes, for example, and one Christmas I sold spiritual bouquets for the mission door to door. The nuns let me keep a percentage. Once I started, it seemed the more money I made the easier the money came. Everyone encouraged it. When I was fifteen I got a job washing dishes at the Joliet Café, and that was where my first big break happened.

It wasn't long before I was promoted to bussing tables, and then the short-order cook quit and I was hired to take her place. No sooner than you know it I was managing the Joliet. The rest is history. I went on managing. I soon became part owner, and of course there was no stopping me then. It wasn't long before the whole thing was mine.

After I'd owned the Joliet for one year, it blew over in the worst tornado ever seen around here. The whole operation was smashed to bits. A total loss. The fryalator was up in a tree, the grill torn in half like it was paper. I was only sixteen. I had it all in my mother's name, and I lost it quick, but before I lost it I had every one of my relatives, and their relatives, to dinner, and I also bought that red Olds I mentioned, along with Henry.

5   The first time we saw it! I'll tell you when we first saw it. We had gotten a ride up to Winnipeg, and both of us had money. Don't ask me why, because we never mentioned a car or anything, we just had all our money. Mine was cash, a big bankroll from the Joliet's insurance. Henry had two checks—a week's extra pay for being laid off, and his regular check from the Jewel Bearing Plant.

We were walking down Portage anyway, seeing the sights, when we saw it. There it was, parked, large as life. Really as *if* it was alive. I thought of the word *repose*, because the car wasn't simply stopped, parked, or whatever. That car reposed, calm and gleaming, a FOR SALE sign in its left front window. Then, before we had thought it over at all, the car belonged to us and our pockets were empty. We had just enough money for gas back home.

We went places in that car, me and Henry. We took off driving all one whole summer. We started off toward the Little Knife River and Mandaree in Fort Berthold and then we found ourselves down in Wakpala somehow, and then suddenly we were over in Montana on the Rocky Boys, and yet the summer was not even half over. Some people hang on to details when they travel, but we didn't let them bother us and just lived our everyday lives here to there.

I do remember this one place with willows. I remember I laid under those trees and it was comfortable. So comfortable. The branches bent down all around me like a tent or a stable. And quiet, it was quiet, even though there was a powwow close enough so I could see it going on. The air was not too still, not too windy either. When the dust rises up and hangs in the air around the dancers like that, I feel good. Henry was asleep with his arms thrown wide. Later on, he woke up and we started driving again. We were somewhere in Montana, or maybe on the Blood Reserve—it could have been anywhere. Anyway it was where we met the girl.

All her hair was in buns around her ears, that's the first thing I noticed about her. She was posed alongside the road with her arm out, so we stopped. That girl was short, so short her lumber shirt looked comical on her, like a nightgown. She had jeans on and fancy moccasins and she carried a little suitcase.

10   "Hop on in," says Henry. So she climbs in between us.

"We'll take you home," I says. "Where do you live?"

"Chicken," she says.

"Where the hell's that?" I ask her.

"Alaska."

15   "Okay," says Henry, and we drive.

We got up there and never wanted to leave. The sun doesn't truly set there in summer, and the night is more a soft dusk. You might doze off, sometimes, but before you know it you're up again, like an animal in nature. You never feel like you have to sleep hard or put away the world. And things would grow up there. One day just dirt or moss, the next day flowers and long grass. The girl's name was Susy. Her family really took to us. They fed us and put us up. We had our own tent to live in by their house, and the kids would be in and out of there all day and night. They couldn't get over me and Henry being brothers, we looked so different. We told them we knew we had the same mother, anyway.

One night Susy came in to visit us. We sat around in the tent talking of this thing and that. The season was changing. It was getting darker by that time, and the cold was even getting just a little mean. I told her it was time for us to go. She stood up on a chair.

"You never seen my hair," Susy said.

That was true. She was standing on a chair, but still, when she unclipped her buns the hair reached all the way to the ground. Our eyes opened. You couldn't tell how much hair she had when it was rolled up so neatly. Then my brother Henry did something funny. He went up to the chair and said, "Jump on my shoulders." So she did that, and her hair reached down past his waist, and he started twirling, this way and that, so her hair was flung out from side to side.

20   "I always wondered what it was like to have long pretty hair," Henry says. Well we laughed. It was a funny sight, the way he did it. The next morning we got up and took leave of those people.

On to greener pastures, as they say. It was down through Spokane and across Idaho then Montana and very soon we were racing the weather right along under the Canadian border through Columbus, Des Lacs, and then we were in Bottineau County and soon home. We'd made most of the trip, that summer, without putting up the car hood at all. We got home just in time, it turned out, for the army to remember Henry had signed up to join it.

I don't wonder that the army was so glad to get my brother that they turned him into a Marine. He was built like a brick outhouse anyway. We liked to tease him that they really wanted him for his Indian nose. He had a nose big and sharp as a hatchet, like the nose on Red Tomahawk, the Indian who killed Sitting Bull, whose profile is on signs all along the North Dakota highways. Henry went off to training camp, came home once during Christmas, then the next thing you know we got an overseas letter from him. It was 1970, and he said he was stationed up in the northern hill country. Whereabouts I did not know. He wasn't such a hot letter writer, and only got off two before the enemy caught him. I could never keep it straight, which direction those good Vietnam soldiers were from.

I wrote him back several times, even though I didn't know if those letters would get through. I kept him informed all about the car. Most of the time I had it up on blocks in the yard or half taken apart, because that long trip did a hard job on it under the hood.

I always had good luck with numbers, and never worried about the draft myself. I never even had to think about what my number was. But Henry was never lucky in the same way as me. It was at least three years before Henry came home. By then I guess the whole war was solved in the government's mind, but for him it would keep on going. In those years I'd put his car into almost perfect shape. I always thought of it as his car while he was gone, even though when he left he said, "Now it's yours," and threw me his key.

25 "Thanks for the extra key," I'd say. "I'll put it up in your drawer just in case I need it." He laughed.

When he came home, though, Henry was very different, and I'll say this, the change was no good. You could hardly expect him to change for the better, I know. But he was quiet, so quiet, and never comfortable sitting still anywhere but always up and moving around. I thought back to times we'd sat still for whole afternoons, never moving a muscle, just shifting our weight along the ground, talking to whoever sat with us, watching things. He'd always had a joke, then, too, and now you couldn't get him to laugh, or when he did it was more the sound of a man choking, a sound that stopped up the throats of other people around him. They got to leaving him alone most of the time, and I didn't blame them. It was a fact: Henry was jumpy and mean.

I'd bought a color TV set for my mom and the rest of us while Henry was away. Money still came very easy. I was sorry I'd ever bought it though, because of Henry. I was also sorry I'd bought color, because with black-and-white the pictures seem older and farther away. But what are you going to do? He sat in front of it, watching it, and that was the only time he was completely still. But it was the kind of stillness that you see in a rabbit when it freezes and before it will bolt. He was not easy. He sat in his chair gripping the armrests with all his might, as if the chair itself was moving at a high speed and if he let go at all he would rocket forward and maybe crash right through the set.

Once I was in the room watching TV with Henry and I heard his teeth click at something. I looked over, and he'd bitten through his lip. Blood was going down his chin. I tell you right then I wanted to smash that tube to pieces. I went over to it but Henry must have known what I was up to. He rushed from his chair and shoved me out of the way, against the wall. I told myself he didn't know what he was doing.

My mom came in, turned the set off real quiet, and told us she had made something for supper. So we went and sat down. There was still blood going down Henry's chin, but he didn't notice it and no one said anything, even though every time he took a bit of his bread his blood fell onto it until he was eating his own blood mixed in with the food.

30 While Henry was not around we talked about what was going to happen to him. There were no Indian doctors on the reservation, and my mom was afraid of trusting Old Man Pillager because he courted her long ago and was jealous of her husbands. He might take revenge through her son. We were afraid that if we brought Henry to a regular hospital they would keep him.

"They don't fix them in those places," Mom said; "they just give them drugs."

"We wouldn't get him there in the first place," I agreed, "so let's just forget about it."

Then I thought about the car.

Henry had not even looked at the car since he'd gotten home, though like I said, it was in tip-top condition and ready to drive. I thought the car might bring the old Henry back somehow. So I bided my time and waited for my chance to interest him in the vehicle.

35   One night Henry was off somewhere, I took myself a hammer. I went out to that car and I did a number on its underside. Whacked it up. Bent the tail pipe double. Ripped the muffler loose. By the time I was done with the car it looked worse than any typical Indian car that has been driven all its life on reservation roads, which they always say are like government promises—full of holes. It just about hurt me, I'll tell you that! I threw dirt in the carburetor and I ripped all the electric tape off the seats. I made it look just as beat up as I could. Then I sat back and waited for Henry to find it.

Still, it took him over a month. That was all right, because it was just getting warm enough, not melting, but warm enough to work outside.

"Lyman," he says, walking in one day, "that red car looks like shit."

"Well it's old," I says. "You got to expect that."

"No way!" says Henry. "That car's a classic! But you went and ran the piss right out of it, Lyman, and you know it don't deserve that. I kept that car in A-one shape. You don't remember. You're too young. But when I left, that car was running like a watch. Now I don't even know if I can get it to start again, let alone get it anywhere near its old condition."

40   "Well you try," I said, like I was getting mad, "but I say it's a piece of junk."

Then I walked out before he could realize I knew he'd strung together more than six words at once.

After that I thought he'd freeze himself to death working on that car. He was out there all day, and at night he rigged up a little lamp, ran a cord out the window, and had himself some light to see by while he worked. He was better than he had been before, but that's still not saying much. It was easier for him to do the things the rest of us did. He ate more slowly and didn't jump up and down during the meal to get this or that or look out the window. I put my hand in the back of the TV set, I admit, and fiddled around with it good, so that it was almost impossible now to get a clear picture. He didn't look at it very often anyway. He was always out with that car or going off to get parts for it. By the time it was really melting outside, he had it fixed.

I had been feeling down in the dumps about Henry around this time. We had always been together before. Henry and Lyman. But he was such a loner now that I didn't know how to take it. So I jumped at the chance one day when Henry seemed friendly. It's not that he smiled or anything. He just said, "Let's take that old shitbox for a spin." Just the way he said it made me think he could be coming around.

We went out to the car. It was spring. The sun was shining very bright. My only sister, Bonita, who was just eleven years old, came out and made us stand together for a picture. Henry leaned his elbow on the red car's windshield, and he took his other arm and put it over my shoulder, very carefully, as though it was heavy for him to lift and he didn't want to bring the weight down all at once.

45   "Smile," Bonita said, and he did.

That picture, I never look at it anymore. A few months ago, I don't know why, I got his picture out and tacked it on the wall. I felt good about Henry at the time, close to him. I felt good having his picture on the wall, until one night when I was looking at television. I was a little drunk and stoned. I looked up at the wall and Henry was staring at me. I don't know what it was, but his smile had changed, or maybe it was gone. All I know is I couldn't stay in the same room with that picture. I was shaking. I got up, closed the door, and went into the kitchen. A little later my friend Ray came over and we both went back into that room. We put the picture in a brown bag, folded the bag over and over tightly, then put it way back in a closet.

I still see that picture now, as if it tugs at me, whenever I pass that closet door. The picture is very clear in my mind. It was so sunny that day Henry had to squint against the glare. Or maybe the camera Bonita held flashed like a mirror, blinding him, before she snapped the picture. My face is right out in the sun, big and round. But he might have drawn back, because the shadows on his face are deep as holes. There are two shadows curved like little hooks around the ends of his smile, as if to frame it and try to keep it there—that one, first smile that looked like it might have hurt his face. He has his field jacket on and the worn-in clothes he'd come back in and kept wearing ever since. After Bonita took the picture, she went into the house and we got into the car. There was a full cooler in the trunk. We started off, east, toward Pembina and the Red River because Henry said he wanted to see the high water.

The trip over there was beautiful. When everything starts changing, drying up, clearing off, you feel like your whole life is starting. Henry felt it, too. The top was down and the car hummed like a top. He'd really put it back in shape, even the tape on the seats was very carefully put down and glued back in layers. It's not that he smiled again or even joked, but his face looked to me as if it was clear, more peaceful. It looked as though he wasn't thinking of anything in particular except the bare fields and windbreaks and houses we were passing.

The river was high and full of winter trash when he got there. The sun was still out, but it was colder by the river. There were still little clumps of dirty snow here and there on the banks. The water hadn't gone over the banks yet, but it would, you could tell. It was just at its limit, hard swollen glossy like an old gray scar. We made ourselves a fire, and we sat down and watched the current go. As I watched it I felt something squeezing inside me and tightening and trying to let go all at the same time. I knew I was not just feeling it myself; I knew I was feeling what Henry was going through at that moment. Except that I couldn't stand it, the closing and opening. I jumped to my feet. I took Henry by the shoulders and I started shaking him. "Wake up," I says, "wake up, wake up, wake up!" I didn't know what had come over me. I sat down beside him again.

50   His face was totally white and hard. Then it broke, like stones break all of a sudden when water boils up inside them.

"I know it," he says. "I know it. I can't help it. It's no use."

We start talking. He said he knew what I'd done with the car. It was obvious it had been whacked out of shape and not just neglected. He said he wanted to give the car to me for good now, it was no use. He said he'd fixed it just to give it back and I should take it.

"No way," I says, "I don't want it."

"That's okay," he says, "you take it."

55   "I don't want it, though," I says back to him, and then to emphasize, just to emphasize, you understand, I touch his shoulder. He slaps my hand off.

"Take that car," he says.

"No," I say, "make me," I say, and then he grabs my jacket and rips the arm loose. That jacket is a class act, suede with tags and zippers. I push Henry backwards, off the log. He jumps up and bowls me over. We go down in a clinch and come up swinging hard, for all we're worth, with our fists. He socks my jaw so hard I feel like it swings loose. Then I'm at his ribcage and land a good one under his chin so his head snaps back. He's dazzled. He looks at me and I look at him and then his eyes are full of tears and blood and at first I think he's crying. But no, he's laughing. "Ha! Ha!" he says. "Ha! Ha! Take good care of it."

"Okay," I says, "okay, no problem. Ha! Ha!"

I can't help it, and I start laughing, too. My face feels fat and strange, and after a while I get a beer from the cooler in the trunk, and when I hand it to Henry he takes his shirt and wipes my germs off. "Hoof-and-mouth disease," he says. For some reason this cracks me up, and so we're really laughing for a while, and then we drink all the rest of the beers one by one and throw them in the river and see how far, how fast, the current takes them before they fill up and sink.

60   "You want to go on back?" I ask after a while. "Maybe we could snag a couple nice Kashpaw girls."

He says nothing. But I can tell his mood is turning again.

"They're all crazy, the girls up here, every damn one of them."

"You're crazy too," I say, to jolly him up. "Crazy Lamartine boys!"

He looks as though he will take this wrong at first. His face twists, then clears, and he jumps up on his feet. "That's right!" he says. "Crazier 'n hell. Crazy Indians!"

65   I think it's the old Henry again. He throws off his jacket and starts swinging his legs out from the knees like a fancy dancer. He's down doing something between a grouse dance and a bunny hop, no kind of dance I ever saw before, but neither has anyone else on all this green growing earth. He's wild. He wants to pitch whoopee! He's up and at me and all over. All this time I'm laughing so hard, so hard my belly is getting tied up in a knot.

"Got to cool me off!" he shouts all of a sudden. Then he runs over to the river and jumps in.

There's boards and other things in the current. It's so high. No sound comes from the river after the splash he makes, so I run right over. I look around. It's getting dark. I see he's halfway across the water already, and I know he didn't swim there but the current took him. It's far. I hear his voice, though, very clearly across it.

"My boots are filling," he says.

He says this in a normal voice, like he just noticed and he doesn't know what to think of it. Then he's gone. A branch comes by. Another branch. And I go in.

70   By the time I get out of the river, off the snag I pulled myself onto, the sun is down. I walk back to the car, turn on the high beams, and drive it up the bank. I put it in first gear and then I take my foot off the clutch. I get out, close the door, and watch it plow softly into the water. The headlights reach in as they go down, searching, still lighted even after the water swirls over the back end. I wait. The wires short out. It is all finally dark. And then there is only the water, the sound of it going and running and going and running and running.

WRITING ASSIGNMENTS

Analysis

1. Identify and evaluate the ways that non-Native American culture affects the lives of the Lamartine brothers.
2. What role do competition and violence play in the lives of Lyman and Henry Lamartine?
3. How do the coming-of-age experiences and circumstances of the Lamartine brothers differ?
4. How do you explain the timing and method of Lyman's disposal of the red convertible?
5. What cultural attitudes and environmental circumstances explain why no one talks much about or seeks outside help for Henry's problems?
6. Why does Erdrich switch to the present tense to narrate the events on the Red River?

Argument

1. Are Henry Lamartine and inner-city youth both social outsiders and victims of mainstream society's violence? Explain your answer.

Personal Writing and Writing from Research

1. *Collaborative Project:* Describe post-war traumatic stress syndrome and trace its long-term effects on Vietnam War veterans.
2. Research Native-American participation in the Vietnam War.
3. Compare a youthful trip you took with the Lamartine brothers' automotive odyssey to Alaska.

she being Brand

e. e. cummings

Poet, painter, novelist, and playwright, e. e. cummings (1894–1962) is considered among the most stylistically innovative of twentieth-century poets. He invented words, combined common words to create a new synthesis, revised grammatical and linguistic rules, and experimented with poems as visual objects on the page. One critic says that cummings juggled and distorted conventional language in order to jar the reader into examining experiences with fresh eyes. Much of his poetry celebrates familiar nineteenth-century themes such as the individual, the natural over the man-made order, intuition, and imagination. He also satirizes the mass mind, commercialism, and conformity.

Journal Topics: (1) Describe your first experience driving a standard transmission automobile. (2) Describe your first sexual experience.

As You Read: (1) Describe the speaker in this poem. Who is the "she" in the poem? (2) What experience(s) does the poem describe? (3) Is this poem funny? Why? (4) How do the irregular lines, nonstandard punctuation, and other verbal experiments contribute to the poem's themes?

she being Brand

-new; and you
know consequently a
little stiff i was
5 careful of her and(having

thoroughly oiled the universal
joint tested my gas felt of
her radiator made sure her springs were O.

K.)i went right to it flooded-the-carburetor cranked her

10 up, slipped the
clutch(and then somehow got into reverse she
kicked what
the hell)next
minute i was back in neutral tried and

15 again slo-wly;bare,ly nudg.   ing(my

lev-er Right-
oh and her gears being in
A 1 shape passed
from low through
20 second-in-to-high like
greased lightning just as we turned the corner of Divinity

avenue i touched the accelerator and give

her the juice, good
                                    it
25 was the first ride and believe i we was
happy to see how nice she acted right up to
the last minute coming back down by the Public
Gardens i slammed on
the

30 internalexpanding
&
externalcontracting
brakes Bothatonce and

brought allofher tremB
35 -ling
to a:dead.

stand-
;Still)

WRITING ASSIGNMENTS

Analysis

1. Trace and explain cummings's use of ambiguity to evoke two important coming-of-age experiences.
2. In either prose or verse, rewrite cummings's poem from "her" point of view.
3. Compare and contrast the role of the automobile in the coming-of-age experiences in "she being Brand," "The Red Convertible," and the excerpt from *Family Pictures*.
4. Analyze cummings's use of puns to develop his themes.

Argument

1. Is the poem more a celebration of youthful adventures or a witty criticism of American popular culture and values?

Personal Writing and Writing from Research

1. Analyze e. e. cummings's handling in other poems of the effects of modern technology on human relationships.
2. *Collaborative Project:* Trace the connection between sex and automobiles in selected contemporary advertisements, music, and movies.

Some Day My Prince Will Come
Female Acculturation through the Fairy Tale

Marcia K. Lieberman

"Some Day My Prince Will Come" first appeared in *College English, 34,* (1972) and has been frequently anthologized since. It is part of a critical reconsideration of traditional children's literature that has gained momentum since the women's movement beginning in the 1960s.

Journal Topics: (1) Name your favorite childhood fairy tale, and explain why it was your favorite. (2) Reflect on whether there are any similarities between your favorite heroine or hero and yourself, as you are or as you wish to be.

As You Read: (1) List the principal traits of the fairy tale heroine. (2) Describe recurring fairy-tale plot lines. (3) Explain the connection between the heroine's personal qualities and her social role. (4) How do heroines and heroes in fairy tales differ?

1   Generations of children have read the popular fairy books, and in doing so may have absorbed far more from them than merely the outlines of the various stories. What is the precise effect that the story of "Snow White and the Seven Dwarfs" has upon a child? Not only do children find out what happens to the various princes and princesses, wood-cutters, witches, and children of their favorite tales, but they also learn behavioral and associational patterns, value systems, and how to predict the consequences of specific acts or circumstances. Among other things, these tales present a picture of sexual roles, behavior, and psychology, and a way of predicting outcome or fate according to sex, which is important because of the intense interest that

children take in "endings"; they always want to know how things will "turn out." A close examination of the treatment of girls and women in fairy tales reveals certain patterns which are keenly interesting not only in themselves, but also as material which has undoubtedly played a major contribution in forming the sexual role concept of children, and in suggesting to them the limitations that are imposed by sex upon a person's chances of success in various endeavors. It is now being questioned whether those traits that have been characterized as feminine have a biological or a cultural basis: discarding the assumptions of the past, we are asking what is inherent in our nature, and what has become ours through the gentle but forcible process of acculturation. Many feminists accept nothing as a "given" about the nature of female personality; nearly all the work on that vast subject is yet to be done. In considering the possibility that gender has a cultural character and origin we need to examine the primary channels of acculturation. Millions of women must surely have formed their psycho-sexual self-concepts, and their ideas of what they could or could not accomplish, what sort of behavior would be rewarded, and of the nature of reward itself, in part from their favorite fairy tales. These stories have been made the repositories of the dreams, hopes, and fantasies of generations of girls. . . .

2   Certain premises and patterns emerge at once, of which only the stereotyped figures of the wicked step-mother has received much general notice. The beauty contest is a constant and primary device in many of the stories. Where there are several daughters in a family, or several unrelated girls in a story, the prettiest is invariably singled out and designated for reward, or first for punishment and later for reward. Beautiful girls are never ignored; they may be oppressed at first by wicked figures, as the jealous Queen persecutes Snow White, but ultimately they are chosen for reward. Two fundamental conventions are associated here: the special destiny of the youngest child when there are several children in a family (this holds true for youngest brothers as well as for youngest sisters, as long as the siblings are of the same sex), and the focus on beauty as a girl's most valuable asset, perhaps her only valuable asset. Good-temper and meekness are so regularly associated with beauty, and ill-temper with ugliness, that this in itself must influence children's expectations. The most famous example of this associational pattern occurs in "Cinderella," with the opposition of the ugly, cruel, bad-tempered older sisters to the younger, beautiful, sweet Cinderella, but in *The Blue Fairy Book* it also occurs in many other stories, such as "Beauty and the Beast" and "Toads and Diamonds." Even when there is no series of sisters (in "Snow-White and Rose-Red" both girls are beautiful and sweet) the beautiful single daughter is nearly always noted for her docility, gentleness and good temper.

3   This pattern, and the concomitant one of reward distribution, probably acts to promote jealousy and divisiveness among girls. The stories reflect an intensely competitive spirit: they are frequently about contests, for which there can be only one winner because there is only one prize. Girls win the prize if they are the fairest of them all; boys win if they are bold, active, and lucky. If a child identifies with the beauty, she may learn to be suspicious of ugly girls, who are portrayed as cruel, sly,

and unscrupulous in these stories; if she identifies with the plain girls, she may learn to be suspicious and jealous of pretty girls, beauty being a gift of fate, not something that can be attained. There are no examples of a cross-pattern, that is, of plain but good-tempered girls. It is a psychological truth that as children, and as women, girls fear homeliness (even attractive girls are frequently convinced that they are plain), and this fear is a major source of anxiety, diffidence, and convictions of inadequacy and inferiority among women. It is probably also a source of envy and discord among them. Girls may be predisposed to imagine that there is a link between the lovable face and the lovable character, and to fear, if plain themselves, that they will also prove to be unpleasant, thus using the patterns to set up self-fulfilling prophecies.

4   The immediate and predictable result of being beautiful is being chosen, this word having profound importance to a girl. The beautiful girl does not have to *do* anything to merit being chosen; she does not have to show pluck, resourcefulness, or wit; she is chosen because she is beautiful. Prince Hyacinth chooses the Dear Little Princess for his bride from among the portraits of many princesses that are shown to him because she is the prettiest; the bear chooses the beautiful youngest daughter in "East of the Sun & West of the Moon"; at least twenty kings compete to win Bellissima in "The Yellow Dwarf"; the prince who penetrates the jungle of thorns and briars to find the Sleeping Beauty does so because he had heard about her loveliness; Cinderella instantly captivates her prince during a ball that amounts to a beauty contest; the old king in "The White Cat" says he will designate as his heir whichever of his sons brings home the loveliest princess, thereby creating a beauty contest as a hurdle to inheriting his crown; the prince in "The Water-Lily or The Gold-Spinners" rescues and marries the youngest and fairest of the three enslaved maidens; the King falls in love with Goldilocks because of her beauty; the enchanted sheep dies for love of the beautiful Miranda in "The Wonderful Sheep"; Prince Darling pursues Celia because she is beautiful; the young king in "Trusty John" demands the Princess of the Golden Roof for her beauty, and so on. This is a principal factor contributing to the passivity of most of the females in these stories (even those few heroines who are given some sort of active role are usually passive in another part of the story). Since the heroines are chosen for their beauty *(en soi)*, not for anything they do *(pour soi)*, they seem to exist passively until they are seen by the hero, or described to him. They wait, are chosen, and are rewarded.

5   Marriage is the fulcrum and major event of nearly every fairy tale; it is the reward for girls, or sometimes their punishment. (This is almost equally true for boys, although the boy who wins the hand of the princess gets power as well as a pretty wife, because the princess is often part of a package deal including half or all of a kingdom). While it would be futile and anachronistic to suppose that these tales could or should have depicted alternate options or rewards for heroines or heroes, we must still observe that marriage dominates them, and note what they show as leading to marriage, and as resulting from it. Poor boys play an active role in winning kingdoms and princesses; Espen Cinderlad, the despised and youngest of the three brothers in so many Norwegian folk tales, wins the Princess on the Glass Hill by riding up

a veritable hill of glass. Poor girls are chosen by princes because they have been seen by them.

6   Marriage is associated with getting rich: it will be seen that the reward basis in fairy and folk tales is overwhelmingly mercenary. Good, poor, and pretty girls always win rich and handsome princes, never merely handsome, good, but poor men. (If the heroine or hero is already rich, she or he may marry someone of equal rank and wealth, as in "The White Cat," "Trusty John," "The Sleeping Beauty," etc.; if poor, she or he marries someone richer.) Since girls are chosen for their beauty, it is easy for a child to infer that beauty leads to wealth, that being chosen means getting rich. Beauty has an obviously commercial advantage even in stories in which marriage appears to be a punishment rather than a reward: "Bluebeard," in which the suitor is wealthy though ugly, and the stories in which a girl is wooed by a beast, such as "Beauty and the Beast," "East of the Sun & West of the Moon," and "The Black Bull of Norroway."

7   The bear in "East of the Sun & West of the Moon" promises to enrich the whole family of a poor husbandman if they will give him the beautiful youngest daughter. Although the girl at first refuses to go, her beauty is seen as the family's sole asset, and she is sold, like a commodity, to the bear (the family does not know that he is a prince under an enchantment). "Beauty and the Beast" is similar to this part of "East of the Sun," and the Snow-White of "Snow-White and Rose-Red" also becomes rich upon marrying an enchanted prince who had been a bear. Cinderella may be the best-known story of this type.

8   Apart from the princesses who are served out as prizes in competitions (to the lad who can ride up a glass hill, or slay a giant, or answer three riddles, or bring back some rarity), won by lucky fellows like Espen Cinderlad, a few girls in *The Blue Fairy Book* find themselves chosen as brides for mercantile reasons, such as the girl in "Toads and Diamonds" who was rewarded by a fairy so that flowers and jewels dropped from her mouth whenever she spoke. In "Rumpelstiltzkin," the little dwarf helps the poor miller's daughter to spin straw into gold for three successive nights, so that the King thinks to himself, "'She's only a miller's daughter, it's true . . . but I couldn't find a richer wife if I were to search the whole world over,'" consequently making her his queen. The system of rewards in fairy tales, then, equates these three factors: being beautiful, being chosen, and getting rich. . . .

9   An examination of the best-known stories shows that active resourceful girls are in fact rare; most of the heroines are passive, submissive, and helpless. In the story of "Hansel and Gretel" it is true that Gretel pushes the witch into the oven; Hansel is locked up in the stable, where the witch has been fattening him. At the beginning of the story, however, when the children overhear their parents' plan to lose them in the forest, we read that "Gretel wept bitterly and spoke to Hansel: 'Now it's all up with us.' 'No, no, Gretel,' said Hansel, 'don't fret yourself, I'll be able to find a way of escape, no fear.'" It is Hansel who devises the plan of gathering pebbles and dropping them on the path as they are led into the forest. "Later in the dark forest, Gretel began to cry, and said: 'How are we ever to get out of the wood?' But Hansel comforted her. 'Wait a bit,'

he said, 'till the moon is up, and then we'll find our way sure enough.' And when the full moon had risen he took his sister by the hand and followed the pebbles, which shone like new threepenny bits, and showed them the path."

10   After they get home, they overhear their parents scheming to lose them again. Gretel weeps again, and again Hansel consoles her. Gretel does perform the decisive action at the end, but for the first half of the story she is the frightened little sister, looking to her brother for comfort and help.

11   Even so, Gretel is one of the most active of the girls, but her company is small. The heroines of the very similar "East of the Sun" and 'The Black Bull of Norroway" are initially passive, but then undertake difficult quests when they lose their men. The heroine of "East of the Sun" succumbs to curiosity (the common trap for women: this story is derived from the myth of Cupid and Psyche), and attempts to look at her bear-lover during the night, and the second heroine forgets to remain motionless while her bull-lover fights with the devil (good girls sit still). The lovers disappear when their commands are broken. The girls travel to the ends of the earth seeking them, but they cannot make themselves seen or recognized by their men until the last moment. The Master-maid, in a story whose conclusion resembles these other two, is concealed in a backroom of a giant's house. A prince, looking for adventure, comes to serve the giant, who gives him tasks that are impossible to accomplish. The Master-maid knows the giant's secrets and tells the prince how to do the impossible chores. She knows what to do, but does not act herself. When the giant tells her to kill the prince, she helps the prince to run away, escaping with him. Without her advice the escape would be impossible, yet apparently she had never attempted to run away herself, but had been waiting in the back room for the prince-escort to show up.

12   Most of the heroines in *The Blue Fairy Book,* however, are entirely passive, submissive, and helpless. This is most obviously true of the Sleeping Beauty, who lies asleep, in the ultimate state of passivity, waiting for a brave prince to awaken and save her. (She is like the Snow White of "Snow White and the Seven Dwarfs," who lies in a death-like sleep, her beauty being visible through her glass coffin, until a prince comes along and falls in love with her.) When the prince does penetrate the tangle of thorns and brambles, enters the castle, finds her chamber, and awakens her, the princess opens her eyes and says, "'Is it you, my Prince? You have waited a long while.'" This is not the end of the story, although it is the most famous part. The Sleeping Beauty, who was, while enchanted, the archetype of the passive, waiting beauty, retains this character in the second part, when she is awake. She marries the prince, and has two children who look savory to her mother-in-law, an Ogress with a taste for human flesh. While her son is away on a hunting trip the Ogress Queen orders the cook to kill and serve for dinner first one child and then the other. The cook hides the children, serving first a roast lamb and then a kid, instead. When the Ogress demands that her daughter-in-law be killed next, the cook tells her the Queen-mother's orders. The young Queen folds up at once: "'Do it; do it' (said she, stretching out her neck). 'Execute your orders, and then I shall go and see my children . . . whom I so much and so tenderly loved.'" The compassionate cook, however, decides

to hide her too, and the young King returns in time to save them all from the Ogress' wrath and impending disaster.

13   Cinderella plays as passive a role in her story. After leaving her slipper at the ball she has nothing more to do but stay home and wait. The prince has commanded that the slipper be carried to every house in the kingdom, and that it be tried on the foot of every woman. Cinderella can remain quietly at home; the prince's servant will come to her house and will discover her identity. Cinderella's male counterpart, Espen Cinderlad, the hero of a great many Norwegian folk tales, plays a very different role. Although he is the youngest of the three brothers, as Cinderella is the youngest sister, he is a Cinderlad by choice. His brothers may ridicule and despise him, but no one forces him to sit by the fire and poke in the ashes all day; he elects to do so. All the while, he knows that he is the cleverest of the three, and eventually he leaves the fireside and wins a princess and half a kingdom by undertaking some adventure or winning a contest.

14   The Princess on the Glass Hill is the prototype of female passivity. The whole story is in the title; the Princess has been perched somehow on top of a glass hill, and thus made virtually inaccessible. There she sits, a waiting prize for whatever man can ride a horse up the glassy slope. So many of the heroines of fairy stories, including the well-known Rapunzel, are locked up in towers, locked into a magic sleep, imprisoned by giants, or otherwise enslaved, and waiting to be rescued by a passing prince, that the helpless, imprisoned maiden is the quintessential heroine of the fairy tale.

15   In the interesting story of "The Goose-Girl," an old Queen sends off her beautiful daughter, accompanied by a maid, to be married to a distant prince. The Queen gives her daughter a rag stained with three drops of her own blood. During the journey the maid brusquely refuses to bring the Princess a drink of water, saying "I don't mean to be your servant any longer." The intimidated Princess only murmurs, "Oh! heaven, what am I to do?" This continues, the maid growing ruder, the Princess meeker, until she loses the rag, whereupon the maid rejoices, knowing that she now has full power over the girl, "for in losing the drops of blood the Princess had become weak and powerless." The maid commands the Princess to change clothes and horses with her, and never to speak to anyone about what has happened. The possession of the rag had assured the Princess' social status; without it she becomes *déclassée,* and while her behavior was no less meek and docile before losing the rag than afterwards, there is no formal role reversal until she loses it. Upon their arrival the maid presents herself as the Prince's bride, while the Princess is given the job of goose-girl. At length, due solely to the intervention of others, the secret is discovered, the maid killed, and the goose-girl married to the Prince.

16   The heroine of "Felicia and the Pot of Pinks" is equally submissive to ill-treatment. After their father's death, her brother forbids her to sit on his chairs:

> Felicia, who was very gentle, said nothing, but stood up crying quietly; while Bruno, for that was her brother's name, sat comfortably by the fire. Presently, when supper-time came, Bruno had a delicious egg, and he threw the shell to Felicia, saying:
> "There, that is all I can give you; if you don't like it, go out and catch frogs; there are

plenty of them in the marsh close by." Felicia did not answer but she cried more bitterly than ever, and went away to her own little room.

17   The underlying associational pattern of these stories links the figures of the victimized girl and the interesting girl; it is always the interesting girl, the special girl, who is in trouble. It needs to be asked whether a child's absorption of the associational patterns found in these myths and legends may not sensitize the personality, rendering it susceptible to melodramatic self-conceptions and expectations. Because victimized girls like Felicia, the Goose-girl, and Cinderella are invariably rescued and rewarded, indeed glorified, children learn that suffering goodness can afford to remain meek, and need not and perhaps should not strive to defend itself, for if it did so perhaps the fairy godmother would not turn up for once, to set things right at the end. Moreover, the special thrill of persecution, bordering at once upon self-pity and self-righteousness, would have to be surrendered. Submissive, meek, passive female behavior is suggested and rewarded by the action of these stories.

18   Many of the girls are not merely passive, however; they are frequently victims and even martyrs as well. The Cinderella story is not simply a rags-to-riches tale. Cinderella is no Horatio Alger; her name is partly synonymous with female martyrdom. Her ugly older sisters, who are jealous of her beauty, keep her dressed in rags and hidden at home. They order her to do all the meanest housework. Cinderella bears this ill-treatment meekly: she is the patient sufferer, an object of pity. When the older sisters go off to the ball she bursts into tears; it is only the sound of her weeping that arouses her fairy godmother. Ultimately, her loneliness and her suffering are sentimentalized and become an integral part of the glamor. "Cinderella" and the other stories of this type show children that the girl who is singled out for rejection and bad treatment, and who submits to her lot, weeping but never running away, has a special compensatory destiny awaiting her. One of the pleasures provided by these stories is that the child-reader is free to indulge in pity, to be sorry for the heroine. The girl in tears is invariably the heroine; that is one of the ways the child can identify the heroine, for no one mistakenly feels sorry for the ugly older sisters, or for any of the villains or villainesses. When these characters suffer, they are only receiving their "just deserts." The child who dreams of being a Cinderella dreams perforce not only of being chosen and elevated by a prince, but also of being a glamorous sufferer or victim. What these stories convey is that women in distress are interesting. Fairy stories provide children with a concentrated early introduction to the archetype of the suffering heroine. . . .

19   The girl who marries Blue Beard is a prime example of the helpless damsel-victim, desperately waiting for a rescuer. She knows that her husband will not hesitate to murder her, because she has seen the corpses of his other murdered wives in the forbidden closet. The enraged Blue Beard announces that he will cut off her head; he gives her fifteen minutes to say her prayers, after which he bellows for her so loudly that the house trembles:

> The distressed wife came down, and threw herself at his feet, all in tears, with her hair about her shoulders.

"This signifies nothing." said Blue Beard: "you must die": then, taking hold of her hair with one hand, and lifting up the sword with the other, he was going to take off her head. The poor lady, turning about to him, and looking at him with dying eyes, desired him to afford her one little moment to recollect herself.

"No, no," said he, "recommend thyself to God," and was just about to strike. . . .

20   "At this very instant," as the story continues, her brothers rush in and save her.

21   It is worth noticing that the one Greek legend that Lang included in *The Blue Fairy Book* is the Perseus story, which Lang entitled "The Terrible Head." It features two utterly helpless women, the first being Danae, who is put into a chest with her infant son, Perseus, and thrown out to sea, to drown or starve or drift away. Fortunately the chest comes to land, and Danae and her baby are saved. At the conclusion of the story, as the grown-up Perseus is flying home with the Gorgon's head, he looks down and sees "a beautiful girl chained to a stake at the high-water mark of the sea. The girl was so frightened or so tired that she was only prevented from falling by the iron chain about her waist, and there she hung, as if she were dead." Perseus learns that she has been left there as a sacrifice to a sea-monster, he cuts her free, kills the monster, and carries her off as his bride.

22   Few other rescues are as dramatic as that of Blue Beard's wife or of Andromeda, but the device of the rescue itself is constantly used. The sexes of the rescuer and the person in danger are almost as constantly predictable, men come along to rescue women who are in danger of death, or are enslaved, imprisoned, abused, or plunged into an enchanted sleep which resembles death. Two well-known stories that were not included in *The Blue Fairy Book,* "Snow White and the Seven Dwarfs" and "Rapunzel," are notable examples of this type: Snow-White is saved from a sleep which everyone assumes is death by the arrival of a handsome prince; Rapunzel, locked up in a tower by a cruel witch, is found and initially rescued by her prince.

23   Whatever the condition of younger women in fairy tales, . . . the older women in the tales are often more active and powerful than men. It is true that some older women in fairy tales have power, but of what kind? In order to understand the meaning of women's power in fairy tales, we must examine the nature, the value, and the use of their power.

24   There are only a few powerful good women in *The Blue Fairy Book,* and they are nearly all fairies: the tiny, jolly, ugly old fairy in "Prince Hyacinth," the stately fairies in "Prince Darling," "Toads and Diamonds," and "Felicia," and of course Cinderella's fairy godmother. They are rarely on the scene; they only appear in order to save young people in distress, and then they're off again. These good fairies have gender only in a technical sense; to children, they probably appear as women only in the sense that dwarfs and wizards appear as men. They are not human beings, they are asexual, and many of them are old. They are not examples of powerful women with whom children can identify as role models; they do not provide meaningful alternatives to the stereotype of the younger, passive heroine. A girl may hope to become a princess, but can she ever become a fairy?

25   Powerful, bad, older women appear to outnumber powerful, good ones. A certain number of these are also not fully human; they are fairies, witches, trolls, or

Ogresses. It is generally implied that such females are wicked because of their race: thus the young king in "The Sleeping Beauty" fears his mother while he loves her, "for she was of the race of the Ogres, and the King (his father) would never have married her had it not been for her vast riches; it was even whispered about the Court that she had Ogreish inclinations, and that, whenever she saw little children passing by, she had all the difficulty in the world to avoid falling upon them." Either extra-human race or extreme ugliness is often associated with female wickedness, and in such a way as to suggest that they explain the wickedness. The evil Fairy of the Desert in "The Yellow Dwarf" is described as a "tall old woman, whose ugliness was even more surprising than her extreme old age." The sheep-king in "The Wonderful Sheep" tells Miranda that he was transformed into a sheep by a fairy "'whom I had known as long as I could remember, and whose ugliness had always horrified me.'" The bear-prince in "East of the Sun" is under a spell cast by a troll-hag, and the fairy who considers herself slighted by the Sleeping Beauty's parents is described as being old: the original illustration for Lang's book shows her to be an ugly old crone, whereas the other fairies are young and lovely.

26   In the case of wicked but human women, it is also implied that being ill-favored is corollary to being ill-natured, as with Cinderella's step-mother and step-sisters. Cinderella is pretty and sweet, like her dead mother. The step-mother is proud and haughty, and her two daughters by her former husband are like her, so that their ill-temper appears to be genetic, or at least transmitted by the mother. The circumstances in "Toads and Diamonds" are similar: the old widow has two daughters, of whom the eldest resembles her mother "in face and humour. . . . They were both so disagreeable and so proud that there was no living with them. The youngest, who was the very picture of her father for courtesy and sweetness of temper, was withal one of the most beautiful girls ever seen."

27   Powerful good women are nearly always fairies, and they are remote: they come only when desperately needed. Whether human or extra-human, those women who are either partially or thoroughly evil are generally shown as active, ambitious, strong-willed and, most often, ugly. They are jealous of any woman more beautiful than they, which is not surprising in view of the power deriving from beauty in fairy tales. In "Cinderella" the domineering step-mother and step-sisters contrast with the passive heroine. The odious step-mother wants power, and successfully makes her will prevail in the house; we are told that Cinderella bore her ill-treatment patiently, "and dared not tell her father, who would have rattled her off; for his wife governed him entirely." The wicked maid in "The Goose-Girl" is not described as being either fair or ugly (except that the Princess appears to be fairer than the maid at the end), but like the other female villains she is jealous of beauty and greedy for wealth. She decides to usurp the Princess' place, and being evil she is also strong and determined, and initially successful. Being powerful is mainly associated with being unwomanly.

28   The moral value of activity thus becomes sex-linked. The boy who sets out to seek his fortune, like Dick Whittington, Jack the Giant-Killer, or Espen Cinderlad, is a stock figure and, provided that he has a kind heart, is assured of success. What is

praiseworthy in males, however, is rejected in females; the counterpart of the energetic, aspiring boy is the scheming, ambitious woman. Some heroines show a kind of strength in their ability to endure, but they do not actively seek to change their lot. (The only exceptions to this rule are in the stories that appear to derive from the myth of Cupid and Psyche: "East of the Sun" and "The Black Bull of Norroway," in which the heroines seek their lost lovers. We may speculate whether the pre-Christian origin of these stories diminishes the stress placed on female passivity and acceptance, but this is purely conjectural.) We can remark that these stories reflect a bias against the active, ambitious, "pushy" woman, and have probably also served to instill this bias in young readers. They establish a dichotomy between those women who are gentle, passive, and fair, and those who are active, wicked, and ugly. Women who are powerful and good are never human; those women who are human, and who have power or seek it, are nearly always portrayed as repulsive.

29   While character depiction in fairy tales is, to be sure, meagre, and we can usually group characters according to temperamental type (beautiful and sweet, or ugly and evil), there are a couple of girls who are not portrayed as being either perfectly admirable or as wicked. The princesses in "The Yellow Dwarf," "Goldilocks," and "Trusty John" are described as being spoiled, vain, and wilful: the problem is that they refuse to marry anyone. The Queen in "The Yellow Dwarf" expostulates with her daughter:

> "Bellissima," she said, "I do wish you would not be so proud. What makes you despise all these nice kings? I wish you to marry one of them, and you do not try to please me."
>
> "I am so happy," Bellissima answered: "do leave me in peace, madam. I don't want to care for anyone."
>
> "But you would be very happy with any of these princes," said the Queen, "and I shall be very angry if you fall in love with anyone who is not worthy of you."
>
> But the Princess thought so much of herself that she did not consider any one of her lovers clever or handsome enough for her; and her mother, who was getting really angry at her determination not to be married, began to wish that she had not allowed her to have her own way so much.

30   Princess Goldilocks similarly refuses to consider marriage, although she is not as adamant as Bellissima. The princess in the Grimms' story, "King Thrushbeard," which is not included in this collection, behaves like Bellissima; her angry father declares that he will give her to the very next comer, whatever his rank: the next man to enter the castle being a beggar, the king marries his daughter to him. The princess suffers poverty with her beggar-husband, until he reveals himself as one of the suitor kings she had rejected. Bellissima is punished more severely; indeed, her story is remarkable because it is one of the rare examples outside of H. C. Andersen of a story with a sad ending. Because Bellissima had refused to marry, she is forced by a train of circumstances to promise to marry the ugly Yellow Dwarf. She tries to avoid this fate by consenting to wed one of her suitors at last, but the dwarf intervenes at the wedding. Ultimately the dwarf kills the suitor, whom Bellissima had come to love, and she dies of a broken heart. A kind mermaid transforms the ill-fated lovers into two palm trees.

31   These princesses are portrayed as reprehensible because they refuse to marry; hence, they are considered "stuck-up," as children would say. The alternate construction, that they wished to preserve their freedom and their identity, is denied or disallowed (although Bellissima had said to her mother, "'I am so happy, do leave me in peace, madam.'") There is a sense of triumph when a wilful princess submits or is forced to submit to a husband.

32   *The Blue Fairy Book* is filled with weddings, but it shows little of married life. It contains thirty stories in which marriage is a component, but eighteen of these stories literally end with the wedding. Most of the other twelve show so little of the marital life of the hero or heroine that technically they too may be said to end with marriage. Only a few of the stories show any part of the married life of young people, or even of old ones. The Sleeping Beauty is a totally passive wife and mother, and Blue Beard's wife, like the Sleeping Beauty, depends on a man to rescue her. Whereas the Sleeping Beauty is menaced by her mother-in-law who, being an Ogress, is only half-human, Blue Beard's wife is endangered by *being* the wife of her ferocious husband. (Her error may be ascribed to her having an independent sense of curiosity, or to rash disobedience.) This widely-known story established a potent myth in which a helpless woman violates her husband's arbitrary command and then is subject to his savage, implacable fury. It is fully the counterpoise of the other stock marital situation containing a scheming, overbearing wife and a timid, hen-pecked husband, as in "Cinderella"; moreover, whereas the domineering wife is always implicitly regarded as abhorrent, the helpless, threatened, passive wife is uncritically viewed and thus implicitly approved of. As Andromeda, Blue Beard's wife, or the imperiled Pauline, her function is to provide us with a couple of thrills of a more or less sadistic tincture.

33   The other peculiar aspect of the depiction of marriage in these stories is that nearly all the young heroes and heroines are the children of widows or widowers; only five of the thirty-seven stories in the book contain a set of parents: these include "The Sleeping Beauty," in which the parents leave the castle when the hundred-year enchantment begins, and the two similar tales of "Little Thumb" and "Hansel and Gretel," in both of which the parents decide to get rid of their children because they are too poor to feed them. (In "Little Thumb" the husband persuades his reluctant wife, and in "Hansel and Gretel" the wife persuades her reluctant husband.) Cinderella has two parents, but the only one who plays a part in the story is her stepmother. In general, the young people of these stories are described as having only one parent, or none. Although marriage is such a constant event in the stories, and is central to their reward system, few marriages are indeed shown in fairy tales. Like the White Queen's rule, there's jam tomorrow and jam yesterday, but never jam today. The stories can be described as being preoccupied with marriage without portraying it; as a real condition, it's nearly always off-stage.

34   In effect, these stories focus upon courtship, which is magnified into the most important and exciting part of a girl's life, brief though courtship is, because it is the part of her life in which she most counts as a person herself. After marriage she ceases to be wooed, her consent is no longer sought, she derives her status from her

husband, and her personal identity is thus snuffed out. When fairy tales show courtship as exciting, and conclude with marriage, and the vague statement that "they lived happily ever after," children may develop a deep-seated desire always to be courted, since marriage is literally the end of the story.

35   The controversy about what is biologically determined and what is learned has just begun. These are the questions now being asked, and not yet answered: to what extent is passivity a biological attribute of females; to what extent is it culturally determined? Perhaps it will be argued that these stories show archetypal female behavior, but one may wonder to what extent they reflect female attributes, or to what extent they serve as training manuals for girls? If one argued that the characteristically passive behavior of female characters in fairy stories is a reflection of an attribute inherent in female personality, would one also argue, as consistency would require, that the mercantile reward system of fairy stories reflects values that are inherent in human nature? We must consider the possibility that the classical attributes of "femininity" found in these stories are in fact imprinted in children and reinforced by the stories themselves. Analyses of the influence of the most popular children's literature may give us an insight into some of the origins of psycho-sexual identity.

WRITING ASSIGNMENTS

Analysis

1. What role does beauty, or its absence, play in the lives of fairy-tale females?
2. Lieberman says that in fairy tales, girls can be intensely competitive, but also passive, docile, and patient. Explain this paradox. With whom and for what do they compete? In what circumstances are they passive, docile, and patient?
3. Compare and contrast the personal attributes and life experiences of fairy-tale heroes with the qualities and experiences that construct American masculinity.

Argument

1. Rewrite a traditional fairy tale from the perspective of its villain so as to give it an interpretation favorable, or at least more sympathetic, to the villain.
2. Demonstrate how the traditional attributes of fairy-tale heroes or heroines are, or are not, relevant and valuable today.
3. Defend fairy tales for their ability to comfort and empower children in an often violent and hostile world. Refer to specific tales to support your position.

Personal Writing and Writing from Research

1. *Collaborative Project:* Trace the portrayal of one of these fairy-tale heroines and her social role over time, across cultures, and in different media: Cinderella, Little Red Riding Hood, Sleeping Beauty, Snow White, Gretel, Beauty of "Beauty and the Beast."
2. Explain how a favorite fairy tale or tales helped to shape your self-image and expectations.

3. Analyze a selection of fairy tale heroes to determine how they might acculturate boys.

4. Survey and report on contemporary literature for children that presents alternatives to the sexual stereotyping of traditional fairy tales.

5. *Collaborative Project:* After reading Bruno Bettelheim's *The Uses of Enchantment: The Meaning and Importance of Fairy Tales,* compare his and Lieberman's views on the effect of fairy tales on children.

The Princess Who Stood on Her Own Two Feet

Jeanne Desy

This story first appeared in *Stories for Free Children* (1982) and was published in 1986 in a bilingual (Spanish/English) picture-book edition. It is among a growing body of literature for children that transforms the traditional elements of fairy tales to reflect the major changes in gender roles and social institutions since the 1960s.

Journal Topics: (1) Briefly describe yourself, listing the personal traits and skills with which you are most and least satisfied. (2) Write about a romantic relationship in which either you or your lover tried to transform the other.

As You Read: (1) Note the presence of conventional fairy-tale characters and elements and their unconventional treatment. (2) Characterize the story's tone and locate the stylistic elements that create it.

A long time ago in a kingdom by the sea there lived a Princess tall and bright as a sunflower. Whatever the royal tutors taught her, she mastered with ease. She could tally the royal treasure on her gold and silver abacus, and charm even the Wizard with her enchantments. In short, she had every gift but love, for in all the kingdom there was no suitable match for her.

So she played the zither and designed great tapestries and trained her finches to eat from her hand, for she had a way with animals.

Yet she was bored and lonely, as princesses often are, being a breed apart. Seeing her situation, the Wizard came to see her one day, a strange and elegant creature trotting along at his heels. The Princess clapped her hands in delight, for she loved anything odd.

"What is it?" she cried. The Wizard grimaced.

5   "Who knows?" he said. "It's supposed to be something enchanted. I got it through the mail." The Royal Wizard looked a little shamefaced. It was not the first time he had been taken in by mail-order promises.

"It won't turn into anything else," he explained. "It just is what it is."

"But what is it?"

"They call it a dog," the Wizard said. "An Afghan hound."

Since in this kingdom dogs had never been seen, the Princess was quite delighted. When she brushed the silky, golden dog, she secretly thought it looked rather like her, with its thin aristocratic features and delicate nose. Actually, the Wizard had thought so too, but you can never be sure what a Princess will take as an insult. In any case, the Princess and the dog became constant companions. It followed her on her morning rides and slept at the foot of her bed every night. When she talked, it watched her so attentively that she often thought it understood.

10   Still, a dog is a dog and not a Prince, and the Princess longed to marry. Often she sat at her window in the high tower, her embroidery idle in her aristocratic hands, and gazed down the road, dreaming of a handsome prince in flashing armor.

One summer day word came that the Prince of a neighboring kingdom wished to discuss an alliance. The royal maids confided that he was dashing and princely, and the Princess's heart leaped with joy. Eagerly she awaited the betrothal feast.

When the Prince entered the great banquet hall and cast his dark, romantic gaze upon her, the Princess nearly swooned in her chair. She sat shyly while everyone toasted the Prince and the golden Princess and peace forever between the two kingdoms. The dog watched quietly from its accustomed place at her feet.

After many leisurely courses, the great feast ended, and the troubadors began to play. The Prince and Princess listened to the lyrical songs honoring their love, and she let him hold her hand under the table—an act noted with triumphant approval by the King and Queen. The Princess was filled with happiness that such a man would love her.

At last the troubadors swung into a waltz, and it was time for the Prince and Princess to lead the dance. Her heart bursting with joy, the Princess rose to take his arm. But as she rose to her feet, a great shadow darkened the Prince's face, and he stared at her as if stricken.

15   "What is it?" she cried. But the Prince would not speak, and dashed from the hall.

For a long time the Princess studied her mirror that night, wondering what the Prince had seen.

"If you could talk," she said to the dog, "you could tell me, I know it," for the animal's eyes were bright and intelligent. "What did I do wrong?"

The dog, in fact, could talk; it's just that nobody had ever asked him anything before.

"You didn't do anything," he said. "It's your height."

20   "My height?" The Princess was more astonished by what the dog said than the fact that he said it. As an amateur wizard, she had heard of talking animals.

"But I am a Princess!" she wailed. "I'm supposed to be tall." For in her kingdom, all the royal family was tall, and the Princess the tallest of all, and she had thought that was the way things were supposed to be.

The dog privately marveled at her naïveté, and explained that in the world outside this kingdom, men liked to be taller than their wives.

"But why?" asked the Princess.

The dog struggled to explain. "They think if they're not, they can't . . . train falcons as well. Or something." Now that he thought for a moment, he didn't know either.

25   "It's my legs," she muttered. "When we were sitting down, everything was fine. It's these darn long legs." The dog cocked his head. He thought she had nice legs, and he was in a position to know. The Princess strode to the bell pull and summoned the Wizard.

"Okay," she said when he arrived. "I know the truth."

"Who told you?" the Wizard asked. Somebody was in for a bit of a stay in irons.

"The dog." The Wizard sighed. In fact, he had *known* the creature was enchanted.

"It's my height." she continued bitterly. The Wizard nodded. "I want you to make me shorter," she said. "A foot shorter, at least. Now."

30   Using all his persuasive powers, which were considerable, the Wizard explained to her that he could not possibly do that. "Fatter," he said, "yes. Thinner, yes. Turn you into a raven, maybe. But shorter, no. I cannot make you even an inch shorter, my dear."

The Princess was inconsolable.

Seeing her sorrow, the King sent his emissary to the neighboring kingdom with some very attractive offers. Finally the neighboring King and Queen agreed to persuade the Prince to give the match another chance. The Queen spoke to him grandly of chivalry and honor, and the King spoke to him privately of certain gambling debts.

In due course he arrived at the castle, where the Princess had taken to her canopied bed. They had a lovely romantic talk, with him at the bedside holding her hand, and the nobility, of course, standing respectfully at the foot of the bed, as such things are done. In truth, he found the Princess quite lovely when she was sitting or lying down.

"Come on," he said, "let's get some fresh air. We'll go riding." He had in mind a certain dragon in these parts, against whom he might display his talents. And so the Prince strode and the Princess slouched to the stables.

35   On a horse, as in a chair, the Princess was no taller than he, so they cantered along happily. Seeing an attractive hedge ahead, the Prince urged his mount into a gallop and sailed the hedge proudly. He turned to see her appreciation, only to find the Princess doing the same, and holding her seat quite gracefully. Truthfully, he felt like leaving again.

"Didn't anyone ever tell you," he said coldly, "that ladies ride side saddle?" Well, of course they had, but the Princess always thought that that was a silly, unbalanced position that took all the fun out of riding. Now she apologized prettily and swung her legs around.

At length the Prince hurdled another fence, even more dashingly than before, and turned to see the Princess attempting to do the same thing. But riding sidesaddle, she did not have a sure seat, and tumbled to the ground.

"Girls shouldn't jump," the Prince told the air, as he helped her up.

But on her feet, she was again a head taller than he. She saw the dim displeasure in his eyes. Then, with truly royal impulsiveness, she made a decision to sacrifice for love. She crumpled to the ground.

40   "My legs," she said, "I can't stand." The Prince swelled with pride, picked her up, and carried her back to the castle.

There the Royal Physician, the Wizard, and even the Witch examined her legs, with the nobility in attendance.

She was given infusions and teas and herbs and packs, but nothing worked. She simply could not stand.

"When there is nothing wrong but foolishness," the Witch muttered, "you can't fix it." And she left. She had no patience with lovesickness.

The prince lingered on day after day, as a guest of the King, while the Princess grew well and happy, although she did not stand. Carried to the window seat, she would sit happily and watch him stride around the room, describing his chivalric exploits, and she would sigh with contentment. The loss of the use of her legs seemed a small price to pay for such a man. The dog observed her without comment.

45   Since she was often idle now, the Princess practised witty and amusing sayings. She meant only to please the Prince, but he turned on her after one particularly subtle and clever remark and said sharply, "Haven't you ever heard that women should be seen and not heard?"

The Princess sank into thought. She didn't quite understand the saying, but she sensed that it was somehow like her tallness. For just as he preferred her sitting, not standing, he seemed more pleased when she listened, and more remote when she talked.

The next day when the Prince came to her chambers he found the royal entourage gathered around her bed.

"What's the matter?" he asked. They told him the Princess could not speak, not for herbs or infusions or magic spells. And the Prince sat by the bed and held her hand and spoke to her gently, and she was given a slate to write her desires. All went well for several days. But the Prince was not a great reader, so she put the slate aside, and made conversation with only her eyes and her smile. The Prince told her daily how lovely she was, and then he occupied himself with princely pastimes. Much of the time her only companion was the dog.

One morning the Prince came to see her before he went hunting. His eyes fixed with disgust on the dog, who lay comfortably over her feet.

50   "Really," the Prince said, "sometimes you surprise me." He went to strike the dog from the bed, but the Princess stayed his hand. He looked at her in amazement.

That night the Princess lay sleepless in the moonlight, and at last, hearing the castle fall silent, and knowing that nobody would catch her talking, she whispered to the dog. "I don't know what I would do without you."

"You'd better get used to the idea," said the dog. "The Prince doesn't like me."

"He will never take you away." The Princess hugged the dog fiercely. The dog looked at her skeptically and gave a little doggy cough.

"He took everything else away," he said.

55   "No," she said. "I did that. I made myself . . . someone he could love."

"I love you, too," the dog said.

"Of course you do." She scratched his ears.

"And," said the dog, "I loved you *then*." The Princess lay a long time thinking before she finally slept.

The next morning the Prince strode in more handsome and dashing than ever, although oddly enough, the Princess could have sworn he was getting shorter.

60   As he leaned down to kiss her, his smile disappeared. She frowned a question at him: What's the matter?

"You've still *got* that thing," he said, pointing to the dog. The Princess grabbed her slate.

"He is all I have," she wrote hastily. The lady-in-waiting read it to the Prince.

"You have *me*," the Prince said, his chin high, "I believe you love that smelly thing more than you love me." He strode (he never walked any other way) to the door.

"I *was* going to talk to you about the wedding feast," he said, as he left. "But now, never mind!"

65   The Princess wept softly and copiously, and the dog licked a tear from her trembling hand.

"What does he *want?*" she asked the dog.

"Roast dog for the wedding feast, I'd imagine," he said. The Princess cried out in horror.

"Oh, not literally," the dog said. "But it follows." And he would say no more.

At last the Princess called the Wizard and wrote on her slate what the dog had said. The Wizard sighed. How awkward. Talking animals were always so frank. He hemmed and hawed until the Princess glared to remind him that Wizards are paid by royalty to advise and interpret—not to sigh.

70   "All right," he said at last. "Things always come in threes. Everything."

The Princess looked at him blankly.

"Wishes always come in threes," the Wizard said. "And sacrifices, too. So far, you've given up walking. You've given up speech. One more to go."

"Why does he want me to give up the dog?" she wrote.

The Wizard looked sorrowfully at her from under his bushy brows.

75   "Because you love it," he said.

"But that takes nothing from him!" she scribbled. The Wizard smiled, thinking that the same thing could be said of her height and her speech.

"If you could convince him of that, my dear," he said, "you would be more skilled in magic than I."

When he was gone, the Princess reached for her cards and cast her own fortune, muttering to herself. The dog watched bright-eyed as the wands of growth were covered by the swords of discord. When the ace of swords fell, the Princess gasped. The dog put a delicate paw on the card.

"You poor dumb thing," she said, for it is hard to think of a dog any other way, whether it talks or not. "You don't understand. That is death on a horse. Death to my love."

80   "His banner is the white rose," said the dog, looking at the card intently. "He is also rebirth." They heard the Prince's striding step outside the door.

"Quick," the Princess said. "Under the bed." The dog's large brown eyes spoke volumes, but he flattened and slid under the bed. And the Prince's visit was surprisingly jolly.

After some time the Prince looked around with imitation surprise. "Something's missing," he said. "I know. It's that creature of yours. You know, I think I was allergic to it. I feel much better now that it's gone." He thumped his chest to show how clear it was. The Princess grabbed her slate, wrote furiously, and thrust it at the Royal Physician.

"'He loved me,'" the Royal Physician read aloud.

"Not as I love you," the Prince said earnestly. The Princess gestured impatiently for the reading to continue.

85   "That's not all she wrote," the Royal Physician said. "It says, 'The dog loved me *then.*'"

When everyone was gone, the dog crept out to find the Princess installed at her window seat thinking furiously.

"If I am to keep you," she said to him, "we shall have to disenchant you with the spells book." The dog smiled, or seemed to. She cast dice, she drew pentagrams, she crossed rowan twigs and chanted every incantation in the index. Nothing worked. The dog was still a dog, silken, elegant, and seeming to grin in the heat. Finally the Princess clapped shut the last book and sank back.

"Nothing works," she said. "I don't know what we shall do. Meanwhile, when you hear anyone coming, hide in the cupboard or beneath the bed."

"You're putting off the inevitable," the dog told her sadly.

90   "I'll think of something," she said. But she couldn't.

At last it was the eve of her wedding day. While the rest of the castle buzzed with excitement, the Princess sat mute in her despair.

"I can't give you up and I can't take you!" she wailed. And the dog saw that she was feeling grave pain.

"Sometimes," the dog said, looking beyond her shoulder, "sometimes one must give up everything for love." The Princess's lip trembled and she looked away.

"What will I *do?*" she cried again. The dog did not answer. She turned toward him and then fell to her knees in shock, for the dog lay motionless on the floor. For hours she sat weeping at his side, holding his lifeless paw.

95   At last she went to her cupboard and took out her wedding dress, which was of the softest whitest velvet. She wrapped the dog in its folds and picked him up gently.

Through the halls of the castle the Princess walked, and the nobility and chambermaids and royal bishops stopped in their busy preparations to watch her, for the Princess had not walked now for many months. To their astonished faces she said, "I am going to bury the one who really loved me."

On the steps of the castle she met the Prince, who was just dismounting and calling out jovial hearty things to his companions. So surprised was he to see her walking that he lost his footing and tumbled to the ground. She paused briefly to look down at him, held the dog closer to her body, and walked on. The Prince got up and went after her.

"What's going on here?" he asked. "What are you doing? Isn't that your wedding dress?" She turned so he could see the dog's head where it nestled in her left arm.

"I thought you got rid of that thing weeks ago," the Prince said. It was difficult for him to find an emotion suitable to this complex situation. He tried feeling hurt.

100 "What you call 'this thing,'" the Princess said, "died to spare me pain. And I intend to bury him with honor." The Prince only half-heard her, for he was struck by another realization.

"You're talking!"

"Yes," She smiled.

Looking down at him, she said, "I'm talking. The better to tell you good-bye. So good-bye." And off she went. She could stride too, when she wanted to.

"Well, my dear," the Queen said that night, when the Princess appeared in the throne room. "You've made a proper mess of things. We have alliances to think of. I'm sure you're aware of the very complex negotiations you have quite ruined. Your duty as a Princess . . ."

105 "It is not necessarily my duty to sacrifice everything," the Princess interrupted. "And I have other duties: a Princess says what she thinks. A Princess stands on her own two feet. A Princess stands tall. And she does not betray those who love her." Her royal parents did not reply. But they seemed to ponder her words.

The Princess lay awake that night for many hours. She was tired from the day's exertions, for she let no other hand dig the dog's grave or fill it but she could not sleep without slippers and stole through the silent castle out to the gravesite. There she mused upon love, and what she had given for love, and what the dog had given.

"How foolish we are," she said aloud. "For a stupid Prince I let my wise companion die."

At last the Princess dried her tears on her hem and stirred herself to examine the white rose she had planted on the dog's grave. She watered it again with her little silver watering can. It looked as though it would live.

As she slipped to the castle through the ornamental gardens, she heard a quiet jingling near the gate. On the bridge there was silhouetted a horseman. The delicate silver bridles of his horse sparkled in the moonlight. She could see by his crested shield that he must be nobility, perhaps a Prince. Well, there was many an empty room in the castle tonight, with the wedding feast canceled and all the guests gone home. She approached the rider.

110 He was quite an attractive fellow, thin with silky golden hair. She smiled up at him, admiring his lean and elegant hand on the reins.

"Where have you come from?" she asked.

He looked puzzled. "Truthfully," he replied. "I can't remember. I know I have traveled a long dark road, but that is all I know." He gave an odd little cough.

The Princess looked past him, where the road was bright in the moonlight.

"I see," she said slowly. "And what is your banner?" For she could not quite decipher it waving above him. He moved it down. A white rose on a black background.

115   "Death," she breathed.

"No, no." he said, smiling. "Rebirth. And for that, a death is sometimes necessary." He dismounted and bent to kiss the Princess's hand. She breathed a tiny prayer as he straightened up, but it was not answered. Indeed, he was several inches shorter than she was. The Princess straightened her spine.

"It is a pleasure to look up to a proud and beautiful lady," the young Prince said, and his large brown eyes spoke volumes. The Princess blushed.

"We're still holding hands," she said foolishly. The elegant Prince smiled, and kept hold of her hand, and they went toward the castle.

In the shadows the Wizard watched them benignly until they were out of sight. Then he turned to the fluffy black cat at his feet.

120   "Well, Mirabelle," he said. "One never knows the ways of enchantments." The cat left off from licking one shoulder for a moment and regarded him, but said nothing. Mirabelle never had been much of a conversationalist.

"Ah, well." the Wizard said. "I gather from all this—I shall make a note—that sometimes one must sacrifice for love."

Mirabelle looked intently at the Wizard. "On the other hand," the cat said at last, "sometimes one must *refuse* to sacrifice."

"Worth saying," said the Wizard approvingly. "And true. True." And then, because he had a weakness for talking animals, he took Mirabelle home for an extra dish of cream.

WRITING ASSIGNMENTS

Analysis

1. Use Lieberman's analysis to explain the significance of the changes that the prince requires in the princess.
2. Characterize the story's tone, illustrating your analysis with examples, and explain how the tone reinforces the theme.
3. Compare and contrast this princess with the traditional fairy-tale heroine.

Argument

1. Which is the more accurate "lesson" of this story: the Wizard's ". . . sometimes one must sacrifice for love," or Mirabelle's "sometimes one must *refuse* to sacrifice"?
2. Is the princess a liberated woman?
3. Is this story unfair to men?

Personal Writing and Writing from Research

1. *Collaborative Project:* Analyze the way that this story and other contemporary fairy tales, including their feature-film adaptations, transform the elements of traditional fairy tales.

2. Do Desy's princess and the stars of contemporary popular culture indicate that our cultural ideals are changing?
3. *Collaborative Project:* Analyze the lyrics of several contemporary love songs to determine whether their portrayal of masculinity and femininity conforms to or deviates from traditional gender roles.

A Job on the Streetcars

Maya Angelou

Born Marguerita Johnson in St. Louis in 1928, Maya Angelou was raised by her grandmother in the small town of Stamps, Arkansas. An actress, musician, and writer, Angelou has toured the world with *Porgy and Bess,* composed scores for two screenplays, and written lyrics for Roberta Flack. She received Tony Award nominations in 1973 for her Broadway debut and in 1977 for her performance in *Roots.* Her poetry book, *Just Give Me a Cool Drink of Water 'fore I Diiie,* was nominated in 1972 for a Pulitzer Prize. She is also the recipient of a MacArthur Foundation award. Angelou has traced her life and times through five volumes of autobiography. "A Job on the Streetcars" comes from one of those volumes, *I Know Why the Caged Bird Sings* (1970). She has said, "I am feminist, I am black, I am a human being. The three are inseparable."

Journal Topics: (1) Describe your first job and assess its importance in your life. (2) If you have ever been the victim of discrimination, describe the circumstances and your response. Would you handle the situation differently today?

As You Read: (1) Characterize the relationship between Angelou and her mother. What qualities does the mother possess and encourage in her daughter? What role does the mother play in Angelou's getting and keeping her job on the streetcars? (2) Why does Angelou persist? How does the experience change her? (3) How does Angelou characterize the realities and challenges of youth?

Later, my room had all the cheeriness of a dungeon and the appeal of a tomb. It was going to be impossible to stay there, but leaving held no attraction for me, either. Running away from home would be anticlimactic after Mexico, and a dull story after my month in the car lot. But the need for change bulldozed a road down the center of my mind.

I had it. The answer came to me with the suddenness of a collision. I would go to work. Mother wouldn't be difficult to convince; after all, in school I was a year ahead of my grade and Mother was a firm believer in self-sufficiency. In fact, she'd be pleased to think that I had that much gumption, that much of her in my character. (She liked to speak of herself as the original "do-it-yourself girl.")

Once I had settled on getting a job, all that remained was to decide which kind of job I was most fitted for. My intellectual pride had kept me from selecting typing, shorthand or filing as subjects in school, so office work was ruled out. War plants and shipyards demanded birth certificates, and mine would reveal me to be fifteen, and ineligible for work. So the well-paying defense jobs were also out. Women had replaced men on the streetcars as conductors and motormen, and the thought of sailing up and down the hills of San Francisco in a dark-blue uniform, with a money changer at my belt, caught my fancy.

Mother was as easy as I had anticipated. The world was moving so fast, so much money was being made, so many people were dying in Guam, and Germany, that hordes of strangers became good friends overnight. Life was cheap and death entirely free. How could she have the time to think about my academic career?

5   To her question of what I planned to do, I replied that I would get a job on the streetcars. She rejected the proposal with: "They don't accept colored people on the streetcars."

I would like to claim an immediate fury which was followed by the noble determination to break the restricting tradition. But the truth is, my first reaction was one of disappointment. I'd pictured myself, dressed in a neat blue serge suit, my money changer swinging jauntily at my waist, and a cheery smile for the passengers which would make their own work day brighter.

From disappointment, I gradually ascended the emotional ladder to haughty indignation, and finally to that state of stubbornness where the mind is locked like the jaws of an enraged bulldog.

I would go to work on the streetcars and wear a blue serge suit. Mother gave me her support with one of her usual terse asides, "That's what you want to do? Then nothing beats a trial but a failure. Give it everything you've got. I've told you many times, 'Can't do is like Don't Care.' Neither of them have a home."

Translated, that meant there was nothing a person can't do, and there should be nothing a human being didn't care about. It was the most positive encouragement I could have hoped for.

10   In the offices of the Market Street Railway Company the receptionist seemed as surprised to see me there as I was surprised to find the interior dingy and the décor drab. Somehow I had expected waxed surfaces and carpeted floors. If I had met no resistance, I might have decided against working for such a poor-mouth-looking concern. As it was, I explained that I had come to see about a job. She asked, was I sent by an agency, and when I replied that I was not, she told me they were only accepting applicants from agencies.

The classified pages of the morning papers had listed advertisements for motorettes and conductorettes and I reminded her of that. She gave me a face full of astonishment that my suspicious nature would not accept.

"I am applying for the job listed in this morning's *Chronicle* and I'd like to be presented to your personnel manager." While I spoke in supercilious accents, and looked at the room as if I had an oil well in my own backyard, my armpits were being pricked by millions of hot pointed needles. She saw her escape and dived into it.

"He's out. He's out for the day. You might call tomorrow and if he's in, I'm sure you can see him." Then she swiveled her chair around on its rusty screws and with that I was supposed to be dismissed.

"May I ask his name?"

15   She half turned, acting surprised to find me still there.

"His name? Whose name?"

"Your personnel manager."

We were firmly joined in the hypocrisy to play out the scene.

"The personnel manager? Oh, he's Mr. Cooper, but I'm not sure you'll find him here tomorrow. He's . . . Oh, but you can try."

20   "Thank you."

"You're welcome."

And I was out of the musty room and into the even mustier lobby. In the street I saw the receptionist and myself going faithfully through paces that were stale with familiarity, although I had never encountered that kind of situation before and, probably, neither had she. We were like actors who, knowing the play by heart, were still able to cry afresh over the old tragedies and laugh spontaneously at the comic situations.

The miserable little encounter had nothing to do with me, the me of me, any more than it had to do with that silly clerk. The incident was a recurring dream, concocted years before by stupid whites and it eternally came back to haunt us all. The secretary and I were like Hamlet and Laertes in the final scene, where, because of harm done by one ancestor to another, we were bound to duel to the death. Also because the play must end somewhere.

I went further than forgiving the clerk, I accepted her as a fellow victim of the same puppeteer.

25   On the streetcar, I put my fare into the box and the conductorette looked at me with the usual hard eyes of white contempt. "Move into the car, please move on in the car." She patted her money changer.

Her Southern nasal accent sliced my meditation and I looked deep into my thoughts. All lies, all comfortable lies. The receptionist was not innocent and neither was I. The whole charade we had played out in that crummy waiting room had directly to do with me, Black, and her, white.

I wouldn't move into the streetcar but stood on the ledge over the conductor, glaring. My mind shouted so energetically that the announcement made my veins stand out, and my mouth tighten into a prune.

I WOULD HAVE THE JOB. I WOULD BE A CONDUCTORETTE AND SLING A FULL MONEY CHANGER FROM MY BELT. I WOULD.

The next three weeks were a honeycomb of determination with apertures for the days to go in and out. The Negro organizations to whom I appealed for support bounced me back and forth like a shuttlecock on a badminton court. Why did I insist on that particular job? Openings were going begging that paid nearly twice the money. The minor officials with whom I was able to win an audience thought me mad. Possibly I was.

30   Downtown San Francisco became alien and cold, and the streets I had loved in a personal familiarity were unknown lanes that twisted with malicious intent. Old buildings, whose gray rococo facades housed my memories of the Forty-Niners, and Diamond Lil, Robert Service, Sutter and Jack London, were then imposing structures viciously joined to keep me out. My trips to the streetcar office were of the frequency of a person on salary. The struggle expanded. I was no longer in conflict only with the Market Street Railway but with the marble lobby of the building which housed its offices, and elevators and their operators.

During this period of strain Mother and I began our first steps on the long path toward mutual adult admiration. She never asked for reports and I didn't offer any details. But every morning she made breakfast, gave me carfare and lunch money, as if I were going to work. She comprehended the perversity of life, that in the struggle lies the joy. That I was no glory seeker was obvious to her, and that I had to exhaust every possibility before giving in was also clear.

On my way out of the house one morning she said, "Life is going to give you just what you put in it. Put your whole heart in everything you do, and pray, then you can wait." Another time she reminded me that "God helps those who help themselves." She had a store of aphorisms which she dished out as the occasion demanded. Strangely, as bored as I was with clichés, her inflection gave them something new, and set me thinking for a little while at least. Later when asked how I got my job, I was never able to say exactly. I only knew that one day, which was tiresomely like all the others before it, I sat in the Railway office, ostensibly waiting to be interviewed. The receptionist called me to her desk and shuffled a bundle of papers to me. They were job application forms. She said they had to be filled in triplicate. I had little time to wonder if I had won or not, for the standard questions reminded me of the necessity for dexterous lying. How old was I? List my previous jobs, starting from the last held and go backward to the first. How much money did I earn, and why did I leave the position? Give two references (not relatives).

Sitting at a side table my mind and I wove a cat's ladder of neat truths and total lies. I kept my face blank (an old art) and wrote quickly the fable of Marguerite Johnson, aged nineteen, former companion and driver for Mrs. Annie Henderson (a White Lady) in Stamps, Arkansas.

I was given blood tests, aptitude tests, physical coordination tests, and Rorschachs, then on a blissful day I was hired as the first Negro on the San Francisco streetcars.

35   Mother gave me the money to have my blue serge suit tailored, and I learned to fill out work cards, operate the money changer and punch transfers. The time crowded together and at an End of Days I was swinging on the back of the rackety trolley, smiling sweetly and persuading my charges to "step forward in the car, please."

For one whole semester the street cars and I shimmied up and scooted down the sheer hills of San Francisco. I lost some of my need for the Black ghetto's shielding-sponge quality, as I clanged and cleared my way down Market Street, with its honky-tonk homes for homeless sailors, past the quiet retreat of Golden Gate Park and along closed undwelled-in-looking dwellings of the Sunset District.

My work shifts were split so haphazardly that it was easy to believe that my superiors had chosen them maliciously. Upon mentioning my suspicions to Mother, she said, "Don't worry about it. You ask for what you want, and you pay for what you get. And I'm going to show you that it ain't no trouble when you pack double."

She stayed awake to drive me out of the car barn at four thirty in the mornings, or to pick me up when I was relieved just before dawn. Her awareness of life's perils convinced her that while I would be safe on the public conveyances, she "wasn't about to trust a taxi driver with her baby."

When the spring classes began, I resumed my commitment with formal education. I was so much wiser and older, so much more independent, with a bank account and clothes that I had bought for myself, that I was sure that I had learned and earned the magic formula which would make me a part of the gay life my contemporaries led.

40   Not a bit of it. Within weeks, I realized that my schoolmates and I were on paths moving dramatically away from each other. They were concerned and excited over the approaching football games, but I had in my immediate past raced a car down a dark and foreign Mexican mountain. They concentrated great interest on who was worthy of being student body president, and when the metal bands would be removed from their teeth, while I remembered sleeping for a month in a wrecked automobile and conducting a streetcar in the uneven hours of the morning.

Without willing it, I had gone from being ignorant of being ignorant to being aware of being aware. And the worst part of my awareness was that I didn't know what I was aware of. I knew I knew very little, but I was certain that the things I had yet to learn wouldn't be taught to me at George Washington High School.

I began to cut classes, to walk in Golden Gate Park or wander along the shiny counter of the Emporium Department Store. When Mother discovered that I was playing truant, she told me that if I didn't want to go to school one day, if there were no tests being held, and if my school work was up to standard, all I had to do was tell her and I could stay home. She said that she didn't want some white woman calling her up to tell her something about her child that she didn't know. And she didn't want to be put in the position of lying to a white woman because I wasn't woman enough to speak up. That put an end to my truancy, but nothing appeared to lighten the long gloomy day that going to school became.

To be left alone on the tightrope of youthful unknowing is to experience the excruciating beauty of full freedom and the threat of eternal indecision. Few, if any, survive their teens. Most surrender to the vague but murderous pressure of adult conformity. It becomes easier to die and avoid conflicts than to maintain a constant battle with the superior forces of maturity.

Until recently each generation found it more expedient to plead guilty to the charge of being young and ignorant, easier to take the punishment meted out by the older generation (which had itself confessed to the same crime short years before). The command to grow up at once was more bearable than the faceless horror of wavering purpose, which was youth.

45   The bright hours when the young rebelled against the descending sun had to give way to twenty-four-hour periods called "days" that were named as well as numbered.

The Black female is assaulted in her tender years by all those common forces of nature at the same time that she is caught in the tripartite crossfire of masculine prejudice, white illogical hate and Black lack of power.

The fact that the adult American Negro female emerges a formidable character is often met with amazement, distaste and even belligerence. It is seldom accepted as an inevitable outcome of the struggle won by survivors and deserves respect if not enthusiastic acceptance.

WRITING ASSIGNMENTS

Analysis

1. Explain the change in attitude reflected in the main character's sequential responses to being turned away: first, "I went further than forgiving the clerk, I accepted her as a fellow victim of the same puppeteer," and, second, "The receptionist was not innocent and neither was I. The whole charade we had played out in that crummy waiting room had directly to do with me, Black, and her, white."
2. Compare and contrast the main character's personal traits and goals to those of the princess in "The Princess Who Stood on Her Own Two Feet," the traditional heroine of fairy tales, or the traditional hero of fairy tales.
3. Angelou writes, "Without willing it, I had gone from being ignorant of being ignorant to being aware of being aware." What does she mean?
4. Explain the significance of the story's setting: San Francisco during World War II.

Argument

1. Characterize and evaluate the girl's tactics. Was she too aggressive, or not aggressive enough?
2. On balance, was getting and keeping this job worth the time and trouble it cost?
3. Angelou says, "It becomes easier to die and avoid conflicts than to maintain a constant battle with the superior forces of maturity." What does "superior" mean in this context? Do you agree with this characterization of the relationship between youth and maturity?

Personal Writing and Writing from Research

1. Use one of the following as the basis of a personal essay:

   - "To be left on the tightrope of youthful unknowing is to experience the excruciating beauty of full freedom and the threat of eternal indecision."
   - "Few, if any, survive their teens. Most surrender to the vague but murderous pressure of adult conformity."

2. *Collaborative Project:* Write a research paper on the post-Civil War, *organized* activities of African-American women to achieve political, economic, and social goals. (See Josephine St. Pierre Ruffin's speech in Chapter 2.)

Growing

Helena Maria Viramontes

Helena Maria Viramontes was born in East Los Angeles in 1954. She currently lives in Los Angeles, where she has been the coordinator of the Los Angeles Latino Writers Association, literary editor of *XismeArte Magazine,* and winner of several literary awards, including the University of California, Irvine, Chicano Literary Contest. "Growing" comes from *The Moths and Other Stories* (1985).

Journal Topics: (1) What rules did your family establish for you when you became a teen-ager and wanted to go out with your friends? (2) Did the rules for you differ from those for your opposite-sex sibling? If so, how were these differences explained?

As You Read: (1) How does the story define and inculcate men's and women's roles? (2) Are there any settings where the distinctions between male and female are suspended? (3) How do Naomi's ethnicity and social class help to define her gender role?

The two walked down First Street hand in reluctant hand. The smaller one wore a thick, red sweater which had a desperately loose button that swung like a pendulum. She carried her crayons, humming "Jesus loves little boys and girls" to the speeding echo of the Saturday morning traffic, and was totally oblivious to her older sister's wrath.

"My eye!" Naomi ground out the words from between her teeth. She turned to her youngest sister who seemed unconcerned and quite delighted at the prospect of another adventure. "Chaperone," she said with great disdain. "My EYE!" Lucía was chosen by Apá to be Naomi's chaperone. Infuriated, Naomi dragged her along impatiently, pulling and jerking at almost every step. She was 14, almost 15, the idea of having to be watched by a young snot like Lucía was insulting to her maturity. She flicked her hair over her shoulder. "Goddammit," she murmured, making sure that the words were soft enough so that both God and Lucía could not hear them.

There seemed to be no way out of the custom. Her arguments were always the same and always turned into pleas. This morning was no different. Amá, Naomi said, exasperated but determined not to cower out of this one, Amá, the United States is different. Here girls don't need chaperones. Parents trust their daughters. As usual

Amá turned to the kitchen sink or the ice box, shrugged her shoulders and said: "You have to ask your father." Naomi's nostrils flexed in fury as she pleaded, but, Amá, it's embarrassing. I'm too old for that. I am an adult. And as usual, Apá felt different, and in his house she had absolutely no other choice but to drag Lucía to a sock hop or church carnival or anywhere Apá was sure a social interaction was inevitable and Lucía came along as a spy, a gnat, a pain in the neck.

Well, Naomi debated with herself, it wasn't Lucía's fault, really. She suddenly felt sympathy for the humming little girl who scrambled to keep up with her as they crossed the freeway overpass. She stopped and tugged Lucía's shorts up, and although her shoelaces were tied, Naomi retied them. No, it wasn't her fault after all, Naomi thought, and she patted her sister's soft light brown almost blondish hair; it was Apá's. She slowed her pace as they continued their journey to Jorge's house. It was Apá who refused to trust her and she could not understand what she had done to make him so distrustful. TÚ ERES MUJER, he thundered like a great voice above the heavens, and that was the end of any argument, any question, because he said those words not as a truth, but as a verdict, and she could almost see the clouds parting, the thunderbolts breaking the tranquility of her sex. Naomi tightened her grasp with the thought, shaking her head in disbelief.

5   "So what's wrong with being a mujer," she asked herself out loud.

"Wait up. Wait," Lucía said, rushing behind her.

"Well, would you hurry. Would you?" Naomi reconsidered: Lucía did have some fault in the matter after all, and she became irritated at once at Lucía's smile and the way her chaperone had of taking and holding her hand. As they passed El Gallo, Lucía began fussing, hanging on to her older sister's waist for reassurance.

"Stop it. Would you stop it?" She unglued her sister's grasp and continued pulling her along. "What's wrong with you?" she asked Lucía. I'll tell you what's wrong with you, she thought, as they waited at the corner of an intersection for the light to change: You have a big mouth. That's it. If it wasn't for Lucía's willingness to tattle, she would not have been grounded for three months. Three months, twelve Saturday nights and two church bazaars later, Naomi still hadn't forgiven her youngest sister. When they crossed the street, a homely young man with a face full of acne honked at her tight purple pedal pushers. The two were startled by the honk.

"Go to hell," she yelled at the man in the blue and white Chevy. She indignantly continued her walk.

10   "Don't be mad, my little baby," he said, his car crawling across the street, then speeding off leaving tracks on the pavement. "You make me ache," he yelled, and he was gone.

"GO TO HELL, goddamn you!" she screamed at the top of her lungs forgetting for a moment that Lucía told everything to Apá. What a big mouth her youngest sister had, for chrissakes. Three months.

Naomi stewed in anger when she thought of the Salesian Carnival and how she first met a Letterman Senior whose eyes, she remembered with a soft smile, sparkled like crystals of brown sugar. She sighed deeply as she recalled the excitement she experienced when she first became aware that he was following them from booth to booth. Joe's hair was greased back and his dimples were deep. When he finally handed her a stuffed rabbit he had won pitching dimes, she knew she wanted him.

As they continued walking, Lucía waved to the Fruit Man. He slipped off his teeth and again, she was bewildered.

"Would you hurry up!" Naomi told Lucía as she told her that same night at the carnival. Joe walked beside them and he took out a whole roll of tickets, trying to convince her to leave her youngest sister on the ferris wheel. "You could watch her from behind the gym," he had told her, and his eyes smiled pleasure. "Come on," he said, "have a little fun." They waited in the ferris wheel line of people.

15   "Stay on the ride," she finally instructed Lucía, making sure her sweater was buttoned. "And when it stops again, just give the man another ticket, okay?" Lucía said okay, excited at the prospect of heights and dips and her stomach wheezing in between. After Naomi saw her go up for the first time, she waved to her, then slipped away into the darkness and joined the other hungry couples behind the gym. Occasionally, she would open her eyes to see the lights of the ferris wheel spinning in the air with dizzy speed.

When Naomi returned to the ferris wheel, her hair undone, her lips still tingling from his newly stubbled cheeks, Lucía walked off and vomited. She vomited the popcorn, a hot dog, some chocolate raisins, and a candied apple and all Naomi knew was that she was definitely in trouble.

"It was the ferris wheel," Lucía said to Apá. "The wheel going like this over and over again." She circled her arms in the air and vomited again at the thought of it.

"Where was your sister?" Apá had asked, his voice raising.

"I don't know," Lucía replied, and Naomi knew she had just committed a major offense, and Joe would never wait until her prison sentence was completed.

20   "Owwww," Lucía said. "You're pulling too hard."

"You're a slow poke, that's why," Naomi snarled back. They crossed the street and passed the rows of junk yards and the shells of cars which looked like abandoned skull heads. They passed Señora Núñez's neat, wooden house and Naomi saw her peeking through the curtains of her window. They passed the Tú y Yo, the one room dirt pit of a liquor store where the men bought their beers and sat outside on the curb drinking quietly. When they reached Fourth Street, Naomi spotted the neighborhood kids playing stickball with a broomstick and a ball. Naomi recognized them right away and Tina waved to her from the pitcher's mound.

"Wanna play?" Lourdes yelled from center field. "Come on, have some fun."

"Can't," Naomi replied. "I can't." Kids, kids, she thought. My, my. It wasn't more than a few years ago that she played baseball with Eloy and the rest of them. But she was in high school now, too old now, and it was unbecoming of her. She was an adult.

"I'm tired," Lucía said. "I wanna ice cream."

25   "You got money?"

"No."

"Then shut up." Lucía sat on the curb, hot and tired, and began removing her sweater. Naomi decided to sit down next to her for a few minutes and watch the game. Anyway, she wasn't really that much in a hurry to get to Jorge's. A few minutes wouldn't make much difference to someone who spent most of his time listening to the radio.

She counted them by names. They were all there. Fifteen of them and their ages varied just as much as their clothes. They dressed in an assortment of colors, and looked like confetti thrown out in the street. Pants, skirts, shorts were always too big and had to be tugged up constantly, and shirt sleeves rolled and unrolled, or socks colorfully mismatched with shoes that did not fit. But the way they dressed presented no obstacle for scoring or yelling foul and she enjoyed the abandonment with which they played. She knew that the only decision these kids made was what to play next, and for a moment she wished to return to those days.

Chano's team was up. The teams were oddly numbered. Chano had nine on his team because everybody wanted to be on a winning team. It was an unwritten law of stickball that anyone who wanted to play joined in on whatever team they preferred. Tina's team had the family faithful 6. Of course numbers determined nothing. Naomi remembered once playing with Eloy and three of her cousins against ten players, and still winning by three points.

30   Chano was at bat and everybody fanned out far and wide. He was a power hitter and Tina's team prepared for him. They could not afford a homerun now because Piri was on second, legs apart, waiting to rush home and score. And Piri wanted to score at all costs. It was important for him because his father sat outside the liquor store with a couple of his uncles and a couple of malt liquors watching the game.

"Steal the base," his father yelled. "Run, menso." But Piri hesitated. He was too afraid to take the risk. Tina pitched and Chano swung, missed, strike one.

"Batter, batter, swing," Naomi yelled from the curb. She stood to watch the action better.

"I wanna ice cream," Lucía said.

"Come on Chano," Piri yelled, bending his knees and resting his hands on them like a true baseball player. He spat, clapped his hands. "Come on."

35   "Ah, shut up, sissy." This came from Lourdes, Tina's younger sister. Naomi smiled at the rivals. "Can't you see you're making the pitcher nervous?" She pushed him hard between the shoulder blades, then returned to her position in the outfield, holding her hand over her eyes to shield them from the sun. "Strike the batter out," she screamed at the top of her lungs. "Come on, strike the menso out!" Tina delivered another pitch, but not before going through the motions of a professional preparing for the perfect pitch. Naomi knew she was a much better pitcher than Tina. Strike two. Maybe not. Lourdes let out such a cry of joy that Piri's father called her a dog.

Chano was angry now, nervous and upset. He put his bat down, spat in his hands and rubbed them together, wiped the sides of his jeans, kicked the dirt for perfect footing.

"Get on with the game," Naomi shouted impatiently. Chano tested his swing. He swung so hard that he caused Juan, Tina's brother and devoted catcher, to jump back.

"Hey, baboso, watch out." Juan said. "You almost hit my coco." And he pointed to his forehead.

"Well, don't be so stupid," Chano replied, positioning himself once again. "Next time back off when I come to bat."

40   "Baboso," Juan repeated.

"Say it to my face," Chano said, breaking his stance and turning to Juan. "Say it again so I can break this bat over your head."

"Ah, come on," Kiki, the shortshop yelled, "I gotta go home pretty soon."

"Let up," Tina demanded.

"Shut up, marrana," Piri said, turning to his father to make sure he heard. "Tinasana, cola de marrana. Tinasana cola de marrana." Tina became so infuriated that she threw the ball directly at his stomach. Piri folded over in pain.

45   "No! No!" Sylvia yelled. "Don't get off the base or she'll tag you out."

"It's a trick," Miguel yelled from behind home plate.

"That's what you get!" This came from Lourdes. Piri did not move, and although Naomi felt sorry for him, she giggled at the scene just the same.

"I heard the ice cream man," Lucía said.

"You're all right, Tina." Naomi yelled, laughing. "You're A-O-K." And with that compliment, Tina took a bow for her performance until everyone began shouting and booing. Tina was prepared. She pitched and Chano made the connection quick, hard, the ball rising high and flying over Piri's, Lourdes', Naomi's and Lucía's head and landing inside the Chinese Cemetery.

50   "DON'T JUST STAND THERE!!" Tina screamed to Lourdes. "Go get it, stupid." After Lourdes broke out of her trance, she ran to the tall, chain link fence which surrounded the cemetery, jumped on it with great urgency and crawled up like a scrambling spider. When she jumped over the top of the fence, her dress tore with a rip roar.

"We saw your calzones, we saw your calzones," Lucía sang.

"Go! Lourdes, go!" Naomi jumped up and down in excitement, feeling like a player who so much wanted to help her team win, but was benched on the sidelines for good. The kids blended into one huge noise, like an untuned orchestra, screaming and shouting, Get the ball, Run in, Piri. Go Lourdes, Go. Throw the ball. Chano pick up your feetthrowtheballrunrunrunthrow the ball. "THROW the ball to me!!" Naomi waved and waved her arms. She was no longer concerned with her age, her menstruations, her breasts that bounced with every jump. All she wanted was an out at home plate. To hell with being benched. "Throw it to me," she yelled.

In the meantime, Lourdes searched frantically for the ball, tip-toeing across the graves saying, excuse me, please excuse me, excuse me, until she found the ball peacefully buried behind a huge gray marble stone, and she yelled to no one in particular, CATCH IT, SOMEONE CATCH IT. She threw the ball up and over the fence and it landed near Lucía. Lucía was about to reach for it when Naomi picked it off the ground and threw it straight to Tina. Tina caught the ball, dropped it, picked it up, and was about to throw it to Juan at homeplate, when she realized that Juan had picked up the homeplate and run, zigzagging across the street while Piri and Chano ran after him. Chano was a much faster runner, but Piri insisted that he be the first to touch the base.

"I gotta touch it first," he kept repeating between pants. "I gotta."

55   The kids on both teams grew wild with anger and encouragement. Seeing an opportunity, Tina ran as fast as her stocky legs could take her. Because Chano slowed down to let Piri touch the base first, Tina was able to reach him, and with one quick blow, she thundered OUT! She made one last desperate throw to Juan so that he could tag Piri out, but she threw it so hard that it struck Piri right in the back of his head, and the blow forced him to stumble just within reach of Juan and homeplate.

"You're out!!" Tina said, out of breath. "O-U-T, out."

"No fair!" Piri immediately screamed. "NO FAIR!!" He stomped his feet in rage. "You marrana, you marrana."

"Don't be such a baby. Take it like a man," Piri's father said as he opened another malt liquor with a can opener. But Piri continued stomping and screaming until his shouts were buried by the honk of an oncoming car and the kids obediently opened up like a zipper to let the car pass.

Naomi felt like a victor. She had helped once again. Delighted, she giggled, laughed, laughed harder, suppressed her laughter into chuckles, then laughed again. Lucía sat quietly, to her surprise, and her eyes were heavy with sleep. She wiped them, looked at Naomi. "Vamos," Naomi said, offering her hand. By the end of the block, she lifted Lucía and laid her head on her shoulder. As Lucía fell asleep, Naomi wondered why things were always so complicated once you became older. Funny how the old want to be young and the young want to be old. She was guilty of that. Now that she was older, her obligations became heavier both at home and at school. There were too many expectations, and no one instructed her on how to fulfill them, and wasn't it crazy? She cradled Lucía gently, kissed her cheek. They were almost at Jorge's now, and reading to him was just one more thing she dreaded, and one more thing she had no control over: it was another one of Apá's thunderous commands.

60   When she was Lucía's age, she hunted for lizards and played stickball with her cousins. When her body began to bleed at twelve, Eloy saw her in a different light. Under the house, he sucked her swelling nipples and became jealous when she spoke to other boys. He no longer wanted to throw rocks at the cars on the freeway with her and she began to act differently because everyone began treating her differently and wasn't it crazy? She could no longer be herself and her father could no longer trust her, because she was a woman. Jorge's gate hung on a hinge and she was almost afraid it would fall off when she opened it. She felt Lucía's warm, deep breath on her neck and it tickled her.

"Tomorrow," she whispered lovingly to her sister, as she entered the yard, "tomorrow I'll buy you all the ice creams you want."

WRITING ASSIGNMENTS

Analysis

1. Assess the respective influences of biology and culture on the gender roles of the characters in "Growing." How do these influences intersect?

2. Use Lieberman's analysis to explain the gender-related attitudes and behavior of selected characters in "Growing."
3. Explain the role of sports in the lives of boys and girls in "Growing."
4. Explain the metaphoric significance of Naomi's feeling "benched on the sidelines for good," and then later saying, "To hell with being benched."
5. What are the connotations for Naomi's father of the word *mujer*?

Argument

1. As her high-school counselor, advise Naomi about how and why she should either conform to or resist the role that her community expects her to play.
2. In a letter from her father to Naomi, explain a father's role and what it means to be a woman.

Personal Writing and Writing from Research

1. Interview students from differing cultural backgrounds about customs relating to the status and expected behavior of boys and girls on reaching puberty. Have these customs changed over two or three generations? If so, how and why?
2. *Collaborative Project:* Do a cross-cultural comparison of coming-of-age rituals.

Hanging Fire

Audre Lorde

Born in New York to West Indian parents, Audre Lorde (1934–1992) was a poet, novelist, essayist, lesbian, feminist, and activist. She was educated at the University of Mexico, Columbia University, and Hunter College, where she became a professor of English. Her published works include *The First Cities, Undersong* (1968); *Cables to Rage* (1970); *From a Land Where Other People Live* (1973), which was nominated for the 1974 National Book Award; *New York Head Shop and Museum* (1975); *The Cancer Journals* (1980), which charts her struggle against the breast cancer that eventually killed her; *Chosen Poems: Old and New* (1982); the autobiographical novel *Zami: A New Spelling of My Name* (1982); the essay collection *Sister Outside;* and *Our Dead Behind Us* (1986). Her essays, collected in *Sister Outside* (1984) and *A Burst of Light* (1988), include discussion of the relationship of poetry to politics and the erotic. "Hanging Fire" appeared in *The Black Unicorn* (1978).

Journal Topics: (1) Recall your state of mind, your concerns, and your feelings at age 14 and describe them. (2) Describe your relationship with one of your parents during your adolescence.

As You Read: (1) What details in the poem reveal the speaker's gender? What, if any, details of the poem reflect the experience of a typical 14-year-old boy or girl? (2) How do the poem's organization and punctuation support the speaker's mood and the poem's theme?

I am fourteen
and my skin has betrayed me
the boy I cannot live without
still sucks his thumb
5 in secret
how come my knees are
always so ashy
what if I die
before morning
10 and momma's in the bedroom
with the door closed.

I have to learn how to dance
in time for the next party
my room is too small for me
15 suppose I die before graduation
they will sing sad melodies
but finally
tell the truth about me
There is nothing I want to do
20 and too much
that has to be done
and momma's in the bedroom
with the door closed.

Nobody even stops to think
25 about my side of it
I should have been on Math Team
my marks were better than his
why do I have to be
the one
30 wearing braces
I have nothing to wear tomorrow
will I live long enough
to grow up
and momma's in the bedroom
35 with the door closed.

Family Pictures

Sue Miller

Sue Miller's work includes *The Good Mother,* a novel, and *Inventing the Abbotts,* a collection of stories. This selection is excerpted from *Family Pictures* (1990). Her most recent novel, *For Love,* was published in 1993.

Journal Topics: Write about your participation in a group activity that you later regretted. Why did you go along? Or write about your decision not to participate, and explain the consequences of your decision. How did either of these incidents affect your self-image and your standing in the group?

As You Read: (1) What role does Tucker play in the group? How do the other boys feel about him? (2) Who is responsible for what happens? (3) Why do the individuals behave as they do?

Mack told his mother he didn't know what time he'd be home, and went up the street to Al's house. Together they walked through the rain down Fifty-seventh Street to Steinway's. Tucker Franklin was meeting them there. They didn't much like Tucker—not even girls liked him, although he might have been the best-looking boy in class. But his clothes were too expensive, he smiled too much: he was slimy. Still, he was one of the few boys who had his own car, so they went out with him a lot.

Mack's friends were all sixteen or seventeen. They all had their licenses. Sometimes on Saturday nights all they did was drive, carloads of them. They drove all over the city. Someone would have heard of a place downtown where they had good fried shrimp to take out. They'd drive there, pass the greasy cartons and the little cups of hot sauce back and forth in the car. Someone else heard that if you went down by the planetarium parking lot and just walked around, you could watch people doing it in their cars. You could tell which ones to look at, too, because the cars rocked a little with the fucking motion. They drove to girls' houses, to parties they heard about in South Shore or the North Side. Someone knew about a place that sold beer with no ID, a bar in the ghetto that served anyone. They crashed slumber parties, they dropped in where someone's girlfriend was baby-sitting. They had music on the radio, they yelled out the windows at girls walking in threes and fours, at other cars full of boys.

They were all good boys. They were all applying to college. They were all on teams, they made A's and B's, they sometimes had girlfriends. But what they liked to do most of all on Saturday night was drive around. When Mack was dating Sharon Fine, he had missed it. He had felt left out when Al or Terry or Soletski had talked about what they'd done without him.

Tonight they sat for a long time in the booths by the windows at Steinway's, drinking Cokes and waiting for someone good to walk by. But the steady drizzle meant there wasn't much life on the street. A group of three girls came in and sat with them awhile, pushed into a tangled, exciting intimacy because the booth was meant for only four people. But they were pre-freshmen, too young, and when they asked the boys to come to a party they knew about, the boys were suddenly contemptuous and mean to them, and they left.

5   Finally they went with Tucker to a party in South Shore; but they didn't stay long. Too many girls they didn't know. They stopped on the way back at a drive-in on Stony Island for hamburgers and French fries. Then they dropped into the Tropical Hut to see if anyone they knew was there, but the witch in pancake makeup who ran the place gave them a hard time. "Are you going to order anything, boys?" she asked about twenty times. "If you're not going to order anything, you'll have to leave."

Now it was nearly eleven. There was nothing to do. Mack felt the kind of restlessness that once or twice recently had gotten him into a fight. They were driving along the Midway—the wide grassy band dividing Hyde Park from Woodlawn—on the wrong side, the Woodlawn side, when Tucker remembered that Kathy Wood lived over here. They made noises, crude remarks. Mack held his fists in front of his chest and said in falsetto, "Kathy Wood. You bet she would!"

Kathy Wood had huge breasts. She wore tight sweaters so that everyone could see them. But even though everyone talked about her—about her tits—no one ever asked her out. She wasn't pretty, she wore too much makeup, she was too quiet, and her breasts were too big, freakishly big. It would be like taking out a spass. You wouldn't do it.

Now Tucker was saying she had a crush on him, that she had written him a note a couple of weeks earlier. He said he bet he could get her to show them her tits. A dollar each.

They sat in the car while Tucker ran up the long, glistening walk and rang her bell. After a moment, the door opened and he disappeared. He was gone awhile, and they got restless. Terry needed to pee. Mack began a narrative describing what was happening between Tucker and Kathy, in a syrupy French accent borrowed from Charles Boyer. Terry got out of the car, finally, and disappeared around the side of Kathy's house.

10   When the door opened, Mack stopped talking. He watched Tucker come back down the walk. Tucker was smiling. They rolled down the windows and looked out into the light rain at him.

He leaned against the car. "C'mon," he said. "I think this will work out. She's alone."

This, it turned out, was not quite the case. She was babysitting for a younger sister, who was asleep upstairs, and when they all came stomping in—wiping the wet off their feet with clumsy thuds, talking loudly—she was nervous, she kept telling them to keep it quiet. She led them downstairs through the regular part of the basement—a washer and dryer, stacks of paint cans, a huge cast-iron furnace like the one Mack tended at home—to a rec room with one fluorescent bulb floating in a metal reflector above the Ping-Pong table. The other half of the room slid away into darkness.

Mack was restless and excited. Something was going to happen! He began to sort through a stack of forty-fives in the darkest corner of the room, squinting over each label, pretending not to listen to Tucker working on Kathy. ("Listen, we all talk about you all the time. No joke. Half the guys in the junior class are crazy to take you out. I'm not kidding.")

Mack put on a few records. Soletski and Terry had started to play Ping-Pong. Al began hitting a punching bag in rhythm to the music. There was enough noise so that you couldn't really hear Tucker except when a record stopped. He was sitting next to Kathy on the couch, talking to her earnestly and sincerely. Abruptly, though, he came over to Mack. He remembered he might have some beers in the trunk, and he asked Mack if he'd go out and check. "I'd go myself, but . . ." He gestured behind him. "You know."

15   "Your servant, your humble servant," Mack said, backing away toward the door and bowing to Tucker over and over.

It was black and wet outside. The rain had softened, and the air smelled clean. For a moment Mack had the impulse to leave, just to walk home alone in the wet spring night. He stood for a long time under the little overhang by the front door, thinking about it. Then he walked out to Tucker's car. Rolled into corners of the trunk, just as Tucker thought, were seven Black Labels. Mack gathered them up awkwardly and slammed the trunk shut on the empty, echoing street. He felt around in the glove compartment and found a church key. He went back into the house, down to the ugly basement.

Tucker was dancing with Kathy now, his hands working her back. She seemed lost in pleasure, but when she saw Mack hand the first beer can to Al, she jerked away from Tucker. "Oh, my God!" she said. "Oh, you guys! God, you've got to remember to take the cans with you when you go. Oh, if my parents thought I'd been drinking . . . Oh, my God." Mack saw that she wasn't wearing the layer of makeup she usually had on in school. It made her look younger, more normal. He turned away from her and gave a can to Soletski.

Tucker had followed her. He folded his arms around her again, talking all the while. "What do you think we are, idiots? No one will ever know. Don't worry about it. C'mon. No one's leaving anything behind."

They danced some more. When the record stopped, Mack put another one on quickly. He selected a stack of them, all slow ones. After three or four songs, Tucker and Kathy stayed locked together even on the breaks while the next record dropped. Mack was watching from the couch, sipping his tepid beer slowly. Tucker's hands had begun to slide up and down Kathy's sides, along her waist and breasts. Mack had a little hard-on, watching. In the break after "You Belong to Me," before the next record dropped, he could hear Tucker asking Kathy to unhook her bra. "I just want to feel you without this thing," he said. His hand was resting on her tight blue sweater where the strip of her bra cut visibly into the flesh of her back. "C'mon. I mean, what will it hurt? I won't try to touch them, I promise. I just want to feel you."

20   She seemed to be objecting, but coyly, flirtatiously; and then the music started up again. When Kathy had her back to Mack, Tucker grinned at him over her shoulder. But his lips never stopped moving by her ear.

All the boys were grinning now. They didn't meet each other's eyes, and everyone was busy doing something, but they were all grinning. And each time the record stopped, there was a frozen kind of attentiveness in the air while they tried to hear Tucker's murmuring voice.

Tucker and Kathy had been dancing for half an hour or so, when suddenly he said loudly, "How bout cutting that light, you guys?"

Kathy was smiling, her eyes shut.

She'd agreed to something! Mack felt a pitiless contempt for her. He got up and reached for the light pull.

25   But Soletski was playing Ping-Pong with Al now, and he said he wanted to go to twenty-one. Mack didn't want to seem too eager anyway, and so he sat back down and waited through two more records. They all listened to the music, to the *pock* of the ball, and smiled crazily at each other. Finally it was Soletski who turned the light off. He came and sat next to Mack on the couch.

It still wasn't completely dark. The door to the other part of the basement was open, and there was a bare bulb lighting that space. A strange parallelogram of light fell into the rec room. Mack could see Tucker and Kathy, but not Al, who was somewhere in the back of the room, in the dark. Terry had come over to the couch now too. Tucker slowly moved Kathy to just outside the slice of light. After a few minutes, she reached up behind her—her elbows looked like wings—and fumbling through her sweater, she unhooked her bra. Tucker's hands lifted to her sides, pulled at the sweater from there, trying to release her breasts. Finally you could see the *boing* of one as it flopped out under the soft wool, even bigger than it was in the bra. Tucker said "Oh!" so loudly you could hear him over the music. He flattened Kathy against his chest and arched against her.

On the couch they all sat, staring. Tucker danced with her a long while. Mack changed the stack twice. In the end Tucker had stopped moving his feet. He was just swaying. He had Kathy turned with her side to them. They could all see his busy hands sliding along the covered breast. Mack could hear Tucker talking, telling her how good she felt. Mack wanted to touch himself, but he was embarrassed to. The music stopped and started, over and over, and they all watched Tucker's hand, and the band of white skin that slowly widened between her pants and her sweater.

Kathy was holding tight around Tucker's neck now. Her hips moved slowly against him. Tucker's hand slid under the edge of the sweater. They watched her gut suck in, heard her inhale. His hand moved up. You could see it under the sweater resting on her breast, squeezing, letting go. Mack tried to imagine what it must feel like. Sharon Fine hadn't let him go this far. Tucker's hand was moving faster now; it was as though he were milking her tit. The sweater had pushed up on his arm, and Mack saw glimpses of the breast, huge and fat and white—bluish, almost—sliding around under his fingers.

Then Tucker just pushed the sweater up—he just did it!—and there it was. Mack stared at the nipple. Tucker's hand came back to it, quickly, but very gently now. He was letting them see. Soletski made a noise, and then the music stopped again. They could hear Tucker's voice, muffled behind her arms. "C'mon, sure. Let me look." She murmured. "Oh, please. C'mon. I know they're so great. Just let me look." But she was holding tight, as though she'd never let go.

30   Mack was frantically adding two or three records to the stack, starting the machine all over, looking back and forth as much as he could at Tucker's fingers and the fat white thing pushing out between them.

When the music set them in motion, Tucker's fingers began again. He pulled the nipple out, made it longer. "Jesus!" Terry whispered. It was as though Tucker heard this. He began doing stunts. He held the nipple at them, wiggled it back and forth, poked his finger far into its pinkish tip. He pretended to squirt it in their direction. They couldn't believe it. Mack ached. He could feel Soletski or Terry moving, the rhythm of the couch. Tucker was really talking now: "Oh, come on. Yeah. Yeah. Come on. Just let us look. These guys too. They're my friends. They want to see. Nah. No one'll tell. Just for one second."

And then her head pulled back, she turned to the three of them on the couch. She actually sort of smiled at them, as though she were a person, as though they might be expected to like her. Then, as she buried her head against Tucker's shoulder, she turned her body away from him, open to them. One of Tucker's hands held her head down on his shoulder, the other moved across her exposed chest, lifted both breasts.

Suddenly she spun back against him, embraced him again. Tucker began kissing her, holding her butt and nearly lifting her up as he jerked into her. Her breasts squished flat. Mack couldn't see them anymore. He realized that his mouth was open, his throat dry. Then there was no music, and he could hear the breathing in the room.

After a few moments Tucker straightened up a little, pulled her sweater down. He lifted his hands and loosened her arms from around his neck. He stepped away from her, into the light.

35   She squinted at him and then looked over to the couch. It was as though she had just waked from a nap; it reminded Mack of his sisters. Her eyes were puffy, her hair frazzled. Her sweater was ruckled strangely above her breasts, on account of the pushed-up bra.

"Well, ah," Tucker said. His voice was loud and casual. "I guess we better go now." He was backing up.

"You don't have to," she said. "My parents won't be home till real late."

"Yeah, but I have a—uh—" He looked at his watch. "A twelve-thirty curfew."

The guys on the couch were getting up. They edged ahead of Tucker to the open door. Al emerged from the darkness. No one was talking but Tucker. "I'd like to stay. I'd really like to, Kathy. But—" He spread his hands. "I got this curfew." His grin was dopey, helpless.

40   Mack was at the door. He looked back once at Kathy's face in the funny light. Ahead of him he heard Soletski and Terry running up the stairs. They were starting to laugh. Al pushed from behind him and followed them. As Mack started up, Tucker

was coming out the rec room door, almost walking backward. Kathy followed him. Tucker was close to laughter; Mack could hear it in his voice.

"But listen," he was saying. "I'll see you in school Monday, right?"

Mack was nearly running now too, but he stopped at the top of the stairs to look down once more. Kathy's face was lifted up at them; she understood now what had happened. If they stayed they could watch her cry. Tucker was actually pushing past Mack, his voice cracking. "Thanks a lot," he said, he brayed, and snorts of laughter erupted from him as he ran for the front door, open to the wet black night.

Mack was the last one out. He ran too, but not fast enough. Before he was outside he could hear her crying start in the basement, an involuntary sharp wail, as though she were in pain, as though she had burned herself.

In the car they were noisy—laughing, talking about her boobs, about how bitchin' cool Tucker was. Mack got in and they peeled out, the tires squealing. He looked back at the open front door. For a moment he felt bad that he hadn't shut it behind him. It wasn't a safe neighborhood, and she might not come up from the basement for a while.

45 The radio was on; they were all talking at once. Everyone got his wallet out, and they began an elaborate, laughing exchange of ones, fives, to pay Tucker off. "Want to know the best part?" Tucker asked as they drove down Fifty-ninth Street. "The best part is, *we left the beer cans!*" They were hysterical, Mack too, laughing, whumping each other till they cried.

Tucker did have a curfew, it turned out. He dropped Mack and Al at Blackstone, and they walked home, hardly speaking, suddenly. The water-weighted air floated in garish clouds under the high streetlamps. No one else was on the street.

"Did you feel sorry for her?" Mack asked after a minute. Al was his best friend.

"Kind of. Not right then. But afterward. Tucker is . . ." His voice trailed off.

"Yeah," Mack said. "He's an asshole. But we did it too—you know what I mean?"

50 "Well, it's not the same, though," Al said.

"I don't know. We watched, didn't we? Maybe we're worse, actually. We paid him money to do it for us."

"Yeah, but it's not." Al was shaking his head. "It's not the same." They were almost at Harper Avenue.

"Well, maybe not," Mack said. "Listen, are you hungry or anything? Want to go back to the Tropical Hut?"

"Nah," Al said. "What? Are you?"

55 "I don't know," Mack said. "I just don't feel like . . ." He raised his shoulders. "I don't know. You're not hungry?"

"No. And I got to get home anyway. There's not enough time. My deadline's one. We'd barely get there and I'd have to . . ."

"Yeah," Mack said.

"I would otherwise."

"Yeah," Mack said, and raised his hand slightly at his hip as he turned into the square.

60   Al stood watching him for a few seconds. Then he called out, "It's not the same, Mack." Mack kept walking.

The houses were dark around the square, except for the Graysons' porch light. There was a glow from the rear of Mack's house, though. The kitchen. Mack went down the side walk to the backyard to see who was awake.

His mother, alone tonight, was sitting at the table, reading under the wall lamp. The light over her head made her dark hair look white. Next to her, cigarette smoke rose straight, then cirrussed in some little wind. She was wearing her old red bathrobe. She was utterly still, as she never was during the day. Mack felt like a spy, as though he were seeing something private, something it was wrong to look at. This was how she looked when she thought she was alone, when she thought no one was watching her. She turned a page, reached for the cigarette and pulled on it, sat in the cloud she released.

All of a sudden her head lifted, she swung it to look at the kitchen doorway. She must hear something, Mack thought. Then, after a few seconds, she slowly turned to the window: she was staring straight out to where he stood in the side yard, though he was sure she couldn't see him. But Mack felt as though they were looking right into each others hearts, as though there were no glass between them. Mack felt somehow that she'd been watching him with this deep gaze all night, that she had known, had always known, what he was doing. Without blaming him, she saw who he was, how he was. His throat ached.

Her head bent down again. In a moment she turned the page. Some part of him wanted to call out to her.

65   He backed up slowly, his eyes steady on her still form. He stopped when he touched the fence. For a minute he stood leaning against it. He felt a sense of desperation, of trapped yearning for something nameless, something he couldn't have guessed at. Then he turned and climbed the fence, dropped silently onto the weedy embankment, and scrambled up.

It was a different world up here, with strange bluish lights high overhead. His childhood was full of myths about this world. About live rails, attempted suicides. Maimings. There were ten or twelve sets of tracks going north and south on the wide rise. Mack walked south for a while, not looking at the dark houses, at the familiar backyards of the street. He picked up a couple of rocks. He threw one across the shiny rails, trying to skip it over them as though they were still water.

Behind him, far away, he heard a train. He turned and saw the distant headlight growing larger three tracks over. He stepped back, out of the way, to the edge of the embankment. The wild metal shriek came closer, screamed down at him. It was probably the last of the scheduled commuter trains from downtown, the noisiest of the trains that ran past their house.

Suddenly it was there. The wind of its passing slapped against Mack; the noise was all around him. The wide yellow squares of light flipped by, dizzyingly fast. He saw one set of head and shoulders in the first car through the glass; none in the second. His arm was cocked. As the last car screamed past, he threw it forward with all his strength, and the stone rocketed into the glass, splintering it, multiplying light into the car.

WRITING ASSIGNMENTS

Analysis

1. What are the symbols of masculinity for the boys in this story, and how do they combine to create a hierarchy among the boys?
2. How do details of the story's setting underscore its gender-related themes?
3. Identify your audience, and retell the story from either Tucker's or Kathy Wood's point of view.
4. What does the brief exchange between Mack and Al just before they part reveal about their values, feelings, and relationship?
5. How might the presence of Mack's mother at the beginning and end of the story affect Mack's feelings about the evening's events?
6. Explore the symbolic role of cars in this story, "The Red Convertible," "Growing," and "she being Brand."
7. Compare and contrast Tucker's and Kathy Wood's motives and expectations.

Argument

1. Characterize the interaction between Kathy Wood and the boys. Is she assaulted, victimized, date-raped, used, or acting as a consenting participant?
2. Use the events of this story to confirm or refute Lieberman's generalizations about feminine socialization.
3. Is this story more about male-male competition or male-female sex?

Personal Writing and Writing from Research

1. Does the double standard still exist? Do you think it should?
2. *Collaborative Project:* Do males in a group behave differently toward females from the way they would behave as individuals? Consider settings such as military units, teams, fraternities, and others. If so, why?
3. If you were Kathy Wood's friend, what would you tell her?

EDUCATION

By the early 1990s, more than 14 million students were enrolled in undergraduate and graduate programs in more than 3,600 American colleges and universities. Who are they? What do they expect from their education? What do they study? How are they taught? What is the relationship between students and their schools, or between society and higher education generally? The answers to these questions have changed over time and continue to change.

In an excerpt from "Expansion and Contraction: A History of Women in American Higher Education," Patricia Albjerg Graham tells us that the model for higher education was once the small liberal arts college. These colleges were often a pleasant backwater where a privileged, mostly white, male elite acquired culture—a body of knowledge and a set of experiences—from a marginalized, almost monastic class of scholars. During the late nineteenth century, there occurred a proliferation of different kinds of schools to serve a diversified student population that included a limited number of women and African Americans. This diversity then gave way to a new model, the modern research university. Graham shows that these dramatic changes have affected men and women in very different ways.

The next selection, a collection of historical documents by leaders in education, chronicles aspects of the debate over the education of women and African Americans. Although most of the selections are a century old, they address issues of enduring concern, often from perspectives still current today.

Perhaps surprisingly, the educational establishment has generally resisted change. In "The Expert: Images of Knowledge," Mark Gerzon uses his own experiences at Harvard as a springboard to explore and criticize what he believes to be the persistently conservative and patriarchal values of higher education's most elite institutions.

Responding to criticism, some scholars have attempted to transform established disciplines, and others are pioneering new fields. Ethnic and women's studies developed in part in response to the civil rights and women's movements of the 1960s and 1970s. In "Scholarly Studies of Men," Harry Brod, a philosopher and men's studies scholar, argues the case for including men's studies in the curriculum.

Student demographics continue to change. Beginning in 1979, female students outnumbered male students at both the undergraduate and graduate levels, although women are more likely than men to be part-time students. But statistics that reflect improved access for women to higher education may tell an incomplete story. In "Test Drive," Myra and David Sadker challenge the standardized tests that are the gatekeepers at all levels of education.

In "The Classroom Climate: Still a Chilly One for Women," Bernice Resnick Sandler describes the different teaching styles and learning environments—and their consequences—experienced by male and female students in classrooms from elementary school to the graduate level. Her findings add fuel to the debate about the relative merits of co-ed and single-sex education and about the most effective learning environments for other nondominant groups besides women.

Marge Piercy's poem, "Unlearning to Not Speak" expresses one woman's reclaiming of the voice that her educational experiences stifled.

Finally, in "College Men: Gender Roles in Transition," sociologist Mirra Komarovsky again sounds the theme of qualified change, this time as it applies to how students' attitudes about gender roles affect their educational expectations and behavior.

Expansion and Exclusion
A History of Women in American Higher Education

Patricia Albjerg Graham

The dean of Harvard University's School of Education for 10 years, Patricia Albjerg Graham now is the Charles Warren Professor of the History of American Education at Harvard and president of the Spencer Foundation. She served as the director of the National Institute of Education in the Carter administration. Her book, *S.O.S.: Sustain Our Schools,* spells out how families, government, higher education, and business should participate in education in order to save our schools.

"Expansion and Exclusion: A History of Women in American Higher Education," which was published in *Signs* (Summer 1978, Vol. 3, No. 4), shows how changes in higher education have mirrored changes in our social structure, institutions, and cultural values. Higher education has generally been a conservative institution, reacting to and often resisting, rather than initiating, change.

Journal Topics: (1) Describe the role that higher education has played in your family's history. (2) Explain whether your gender has influenced your own or your family's educational expectations of you. (3) Provide your personal definitions of "a good school" or "an educated person."

As You Read: (1) What role did higher education play in mainstream American life before the second half of the nineteenth century? (2) Describe the two monolithic models that have dominated American higher education at different times in our history, except for the period 1875–1925. (3) How did prevailing ideas about femininity affect the role of women in higher education? (4) Why did men benefit more than women from the post-1925 changes in higher education? (5) Identify contemporary social trends that may once again transform higher education.

1   Explanations of the historical role of women in higher education in the United States between the mid-nineteenth and the mid-twentieth centuries rest upon understanding a series of related changes in both education and the status of women. In

my essay I will analyze three major shifts in higher education: (1) Its movement out of the eddies and tributaries of American life into the mainstream of activity, (2) its transformation from the domain of the few to the domain of the many, and (3) the evolution of its organizational ideal from an early monolithic model through a period of diversity to a later monolithic form quite different from the first. Interacting with these were two changes that concerned women: (1) a transition of the canons of "true womanhood" or of the "ideal of true womanhood," given in the prescriptive literature of the period, from religious and social ideals to secular and social ones (this submitted women to new, more complex pressures that thwarted their professional ambitions and development); and (2) a dramatic increase in the proportion of women the prescriptive literature affected, or a universalization of social norms.

2   The opportunities for highly educated women were greater at the end of the nineteenth century than they were in the mid-twentieth century. Such an assertion clearly challenges the traditional American optimism about the existence of a progressive improvement in opportunities for all segments of American society. However, the democratization of higher education which occurred in the early and middle years of the twentieth century did not cut across sex lines with equal effects. Men benefited from it much more than women.

I

3   In the late nineteenth century, faculty members of American colleges and universities still perceived themselves and their calling as outside the mainstream of American values and mores. Not all the priestly vows of poverty, chastity, and obedience were expected of professors, but the first was required, and considerable respect for the latter two was expected as well. Professional salaries were low, and a standard of genteel poverty prevailed in most college communities. The exceptions occurred at the prestigious institutions, where faculty members were sometimes scions of families of independent means. Everywhere, however, an academic career somehow seemed suitable for a child who could not adjust to the "real" world of business. . . .

4   That colleges were separate from the mainstream of American life can be easily seen in the smallness of their size throughout the nineteenth century. In 1870 the student population included just over 1 percent of the traditional college age group.[1] Indeed, from the founding of Harvard in 1636 until as late as the end of World War II, college attendance was a rarity. The proportion of the age group attending college increased steadily, but slowly, after 1870, at the rate of 1 percentage point a decade, until 1920, when it jumped to 8 percent.[2] . . .

---

[1] U.S. Department of Health, Education, and Welfare, National Center for Education Statistics, *Digest of Education Statistics* (Washington, D.C.: Government Printing Office, 1973), p. 75, table 89.
   [2] Ibid.

5   During the last part of the nineteenth century, the characteristics of higher education in America began to change. Higher education, like many other facets of public life, was beginning to become a system. During these years an important shift took place in the very definition of an "educated man": In the early part of the century, he had knowledge of the classics, however it might be obtained (private study, tutors, travel, college education); by the end of the century, the educated man was seen as a person who had attended college. A goal—knowledge of the classics—was increasingly replaced by a process—studying at a college. Formal education thus began to play an ever-increasing role in American life, but its recipients were still set apart by the scarcity of their numbers.

6   The organizational forms and ideological commitments of prestigious colleges in America also underwent a period of rapid change in the last quarter of the nineteenth century. Before the Civil War, the liberal arts college for men possessed a prescribed curriculum and embodied the monolithic ideal of classical education. In the late nineteenth century, this ideal was increasingly abandoned for a variety of educational institutions, based on differing organizational principles and directed toward differing educational goals. For a brief period, from approximately 1875 to 1925, a strikingly heterogeneous array of acceptable and praiseworthy institutions existed in America. This coincided with a crucial period in the history of women in America and aided their advancement. For approximately fifty years, a competitive tension reigned among the various types of higher educational institutions in America. This was followed by the reemergence of a monolith, the research university, which quickly became a new ideal type. This new monolith differed markedly from the old one of fifty years before. If the old had defined itself in terms of the classics, the early twentieth-century monolith defined itself in terms of graduate research. However, the periods in which the two monoliths triumphed were similar in one characteristic: A single standard of higher education received public sanction and acclaim. A direct result was that institutions traditionally based on other standards had to choose between emulating the now almost universal model or resign themselves to providing alternatives without widespread public and professional support. An indirect result was that those categories of people, particularly women, who had not earlier won secure places for themselves in society and were now continuing to try to do so, faced a dwindling number of accepted educational pathways. This loss of variety was more serious for women as a group than men. . . .

7   The overwhelming concern with scholarship, with the primacy of the institutional responsibility for generating rather than transmitting knowledge, was a direct outgrowth of the efforts of Charles William Eliot at Harvard and others to broaden the college curriculum. The move away from a prescribed curriculum that was taught by a faculty concerned more with students than with subjects led to the development of an elective system in which faculty members taught a limited number of courses, all of them in their "specialty." Such a shift meant that the faculty members had to have such specialties, which became increasingly narrow over the years. A mid-nineteenth-century professor might have thought of himself as a professor of

the classics; his successor was a classicist; his successor concerned himself only with ancient Greek; his successor became a specialist in the early plays of Aeschylus. His successor, expert in Aeschylus's use of the metaphor, is unemployed.

8   Despite the growth of community colleges in this period, the degree to which higher education forms a pyramid with the values of research universities at the pinnacle dominating the structure is striking. All institutions discuss the need to give weight to three criteria in considering faculty for promotion (scholarship, teaching, and service), but there is little doubt anywhere that the prestige (although not necessarily the appointment) rests heavily on the first. My point is not that more good scholarship is being done by faculty members now than in the past, although that is probably true, but rather that research, preferably published and widely recognized, occupies a universal prestige and dominates other useful faculty qualities in a way that it did not in an earlier era. The institutions which have led in establishing this new value system and whose practices and institutional priorities have been widely emulated by other institutions are the old universities of the East, such as Harvard, Yale, Princeton, and Columbia, as well as the newer ones to the West, Chicago, Berkeley, and Stanford. In terms of prestige, though not necessarily in terms of remuneration or other matters, the Ivies have set the standard. . . .

9   Gradually in the pre-World War II years and increasingly in the fifties and sixties, faculties, particularly those in universities, also came to believe that they had a responsible role in government or in the private sector. Even more important, their services were sought by government and industry, a phenomenon that rarely happened in earlier years. The faculties now tended to think of themselves as men of affairs, not as part of a remote alternative culture. . . . By the fifties and sixties, . . . successful professors were expected to be familiar with the routines of the market place, whether through outside grants for research or through consultantships in Washington or elsewhere. . . .

II

10   Though these changes in the colleges and universities occurred without particular concern for their effects on women, the initial consequences have been substantial. Unlike men, who were never barred from attending college on account of their sex, women were unable to enroll in any college until Oberlin permitted them entrance in 1837, ostensibly to provide ministers with intelligent, cultivated, and thoroughly schooled wives. When the shortage of male students during the Civil War made institutions willing to consider tuition-paying women as well, they became 21 percent of the total undergraduate enrollment by 1870. This figure included the students in the newly established women's colleges that began to sprout up and down the eastern seaboard as independent schools, chiefly in safe bucolic locations, or occasionally, as "coordinate colleges" adjacent to established men's colleges that refused to admit women students (Radcliffe at Harvard, Barnard at Columbia, and Evelyn at

Princeton). By 1880 women constituted 32 percent of the undergraduate student body; by 1910 almost 40 percent. A decade later, 1919–20, women were 47 percent of the undergraduate enrollment, nearly as much as their proportion in the population.[3]

11   The decade of the twenties was critical for educated women. During that ten-year period, women achieved their highest proportion of the undergraduate population, of doctoral recipients, and of faculty members. A record 32.5 percent of college presidents, professors, and instructors were women when the decade closed in 1930.[4] That success was reflected in other professions as well. During this period, women constituted nearly 45 percent of the professional work force, a share that began declining in 1930 and reached a low point in 1960.[5] Further, from 1870 to 1930, the proportion of women in the professions was twice as high as that in the work force. By the end of the thirties, the proportion of all undergraduate women was declining, although the proportion of women receiving the A.B. was still rising slightly, and the drop had begun in the proportion of women receiving the doctorate.[6] If the percentage of women on faculties remained at the 1930 level, this was but a reflection of the professional training taken by women in the teens, twenties, and thirties who were still teaching in 1940.[7]

12   The women who came to maturity in the years before and immediately after World War I are probably the ones who benefited most from the flexibility of choice of the teens and early twenties. Writing in 1938, Marjorie Nicolson, who was born in 1894 and received her B.A. in 1914 from the University of Michigan, described her compatriots:

> We of the pre-war generation used to pride ourselves sentimentally on being the "lost generation," used to think that because war cut across the stable path on which our feet were set we were an unfortunate generation. But as I look back upon the records, I find myself wondering whether our generation was not the only generation of women which ever really found itself. We came late enough to escape the self-consciousness and belligerence of the pioneers, to take education and training for granted. We came early enough to take equally for granted professional positions in which we could make full use of our training. This was our double glory. Positions were everywhere open to us; it never occurred to us at that time that we were taken only because men were not available. . . . The millenium had come; it did not occur to us that life could be different. Within a decade shades of the prison house began to close, not upon the growing boy, but upon the emancipated girls.[8]

---

[3] Ibid., p. 84, table 100.

[4] A jump in 1880 had brought the proportion of women faculty to 32 percent, but the numbers of faculty were then so small and so ill defined that the proportion is probably a statistical anomaly (ibid., and Rudolph C. Blitz, "Women in the Professions, 1870–1970," *Monthly Labor Review* 97, no. 5 [May 1974]: 37).

[5] Blitz, p. 34.

[6] Ibid.

[7] U.S. Department of Health, Education, and Welfare, p. 84, table 100.

[8] Marjorie Nicolson, "The Rights and Privileges Pertaining Thereto," *Journal of the American Association of University Women* 31, no. 3 (April 1938): 136.

13   Yet, even before the decline began, all was not rosy for professional women. There was no glorious past when women professionals were ever treated equally with men. The most prestigious institutions never considered women for regular faculty positions until well after World War II. When Alice Hamilton joined the Harvard Medical School faculty in 1919 as an assistant professor (at the age of 50), with an international reputation as the leading figure in industrial toxicology, she was told that a condition of her appointment was that she must not march in the commencement procession. When women did join the faculties of institutions which would hire them, they were paid less than men. A study of fifty land-grant institutions revealed in 1927–28 that median salaries for women faculty were $860 less than for men. The higher the woman faculty member's rank, the greater the difference between her salary and that of men in corresponding posts. Women instructors received 96.6 percent of men instructors' salaries; women professors, 86.5 percent of that of men professors; women deans, 77.6 percent of that of men deans.[9] The years of the mid-twentieth century brought a decline for women's participation in an academic life whose past was itself hardly halcyon (see table 1).

14   The complex explanation for the limited and diminished role that highly educated women have played in American society and in the professions in the middle years of the twentieth century lies principally in the interrelationship of several major factors. First, college was not substantially at variance with society's expectations for men. If male attendance was not conventional, it was still consistent with nineteenth- and early twentieth-century expectations that men should prepare themselves in some way to support themselves and their families successfully as adults.[10] Gradually, college attendance became more typical for men, particularly if they were white. However, since society had quite different expectations for women, the new rationale for college attendance did not apply to them. Barbara Welter has described the quintessential female traits in the prescriptive literature for women from 1820–60, views that lingered on later in the century, as piety, purity, submissiveness, and domesticity.[11] Being an undergraduate with the independence it implied, the opportunities it afforded for subsequent employment, and the threats to purity and piety that the campus provided violated these canons. By virtue of the smallness of the original undergraduate body, this group of men and women became an elite in the classical sense of that term, a group set apart from the mass of society and potentially exempt from its strictures. As Rose Coser and others have noted, "Where the

[9] Editorial, "Women in our Economy," *Journal of the American Association of University Women* 31, no. 3 (April 1938): 171.

[10] Robert McCaughey has observed in his study of the Barnard College faculty that "men have been able to maximize the opportunities of academic prosperity, while women have been able to minimize the disadvantages of academic adversity" ("A Statistical Profile of the Barnard College Faculty, 1900–1974," mimeographed [New York: Department of History, Barnard College, Columbia University, 1975], p. 16).

[11] Barbara Welter, "The Cult of True Womanhood: 1820–1860," *American Quarterly* 18 (Summer 1966): 151–74. For a regional revision, see Julie Ray Jeffrey, "Women in the Southern Farmers' Alliance," *Feminist Studies* 3, no. 3 (Winter 1975): 72–91.

TABLE 1

Year Ending	Under-graduate Students in Age Group 18–21* (%)	Women as Under-graduates* (%)	Women with Bachelor's or First Professional Degree (%)	Women as Doctorates† (%)	Women as Faculty (%)
1870	1.68‡	21‡	15	0	12
1880	2.72‡	32‡	19	6	36
1890	2.99	35‡	17	1	20
1900	3.91	35‡	19	6	20
1910	4.99	39‡	25	11	20
1920	7.88	47‡	34	15	26
1930	11.89	43‡	40	18	27
1940	14.49	40	41	13	28
1950	26.94	31	24	10	25
1960	31.27	36	35	10	22
1970	43.73	41	41	13	25
1971	45.19	42	42	14	22§
1972	45.89	42	42	16	22§
1973	45.41	43	42	18	23§
1974	41.35	45	42	19	24§
1975	42.34	45	43	21	24‖
1976	43.55	45	44	23	24‖

Sources—U.S. Department of Health, Education, and Welfare, National Center for Education Statistics. *Digest of Education Statistics, 1976* (Washington D.C.: Government Printing Office, 1976), and *Projections of Education Statistics to 1984–85* (Washington D.C.: Government Printing Office, 1977: and estimates of the National Center for Education Studies.

* Figures for undergraduate students are degree credit and prior to 1974 include students enrolled for the first professional degrees.

† Percentages should be viewed with care since the annual total of doctoral degrees conferred in 1890 and before was less than 150.

‡ U.S. Department of Health, Education, and Welfare, National Center for Education Statistics. *Digest of Education Statistics, 1973* (Washington D.C.: Government Printing Office, 1973), p. 75, tables 89, 100.

§ Data are estimated and represent full-time faculty only.

‖ Data represent full-time faculty only.

position of women is securely subordinate, a few exceptional achievers do not threaten the system and their achievement gains salience over their womanhood."[12] This was the case for undergraduate women until the base of undergraduates began to broaden in the middle years of the twentieth century.[13]

[12] Rose Coser, review of *Changing Women in Changing Society, Science* 182, no. 411 (November 2, 1973): 471.

[13] Among the many studies which would enhance our knowledge of higher education would be one comparing the social class origins of men and women as undergraduates and faculty over the

15   Next, except for the Roman Catholic men's colleges, the Ivy League institutions have persistently been the most resistant to admission of women, as undergraduates, graduate students, or faculty. Yale and Princeton accepted their first women undergraduates in 1969. The first woman to be appointed to a tenured professorship at Harvard was Cecilia Payne-Gaposhkin, an astronomer, in 1956; at Yale, Mary Wright in Chinese history in 1959; at Princeton, Suzanne Keller, a sociologist, in 1969; and at Columbia, Marjorie Nicolson in English in 1941.

16   The current absence of women from the faculties of the major research-oriented institutions is well-documented. Although women constitute currently 24 percent of the college and university faculties across the nation, they make up a much smaller percentage of the faculties of the most prestigious institutions, particularly in the tenured ranks. The proportion of women in the arts and sciences faculties at Harvard is 3 percent; at Yale, 1.6 percent; at Princeton, 1 percent; at Stanford, 5 percent; at Berkeley, 5.6 percent; at Chicago, 5 percent; and at Columbia, 5 percent.[14] The point, of course, is that if these institutions became the models for higher education, then their practice of excluding women as students and markedly limiting their role on faculties and in administration was broadly noticed throughout the remaining institutions.

17   Though other institutions could not afford the financial luxury of limiting their undergraduates to men only, it was easy enough to follow the lead of prestigious institutions in selecting predominantly male faculties and administrations. At the faculty level, the differences between women's opportunities and men's have been most noticeable. If, as Richard Lester has told us, the merit system was working in faculty hiring (despite the absence of Jews from most faculties until the forties or Catholics from many philosophy and religion departments until later than that), the absence of women simply meant that they did not stack up against men at the best places.[15] An institution that was trying to move up the prestige ladder, then, was well advised to recognize this fact and treat its own faculty women accordingly. After World War II, several of the women's colleges made a deliberate effort to increase the number of men on their faculties, presumably in the hope that this was a sign of improved quality, or at least, status.

18   The reasoning, of course, became circular. If research was the way, and nearly the only way, to achieve recognition in academe, then access to the research facilities and to the time and money to utilize them, was essential. Increasingly in the last twenty-five years, the model of the solitary researcher poring over an Icelandic saga in the privacy of his or her study (an undertaking that requires much diligence but not

---

last century. I suspect, but as yet cannot document, that women students and faculty came from a higher social class than men, a finding borne out by Robert McCaughey in his previously cited study of the Barnard faculty from 1870–1970. Certainly, current data on undergraduates reveal that fewer bright daughters of poor families attend college than similarly gifted sons. If that is the case generally, it reaffirms my principal point about the greater difficulty of a middle- or lower-class girl emancipating herself from the expectations of domesticity in adult life.

   [14] These figures were compiled by administrators at the named institutions and supplied to the author in the spring of 1976.

   [15] Richard A. Lester, *Antibias Regulation of Universities: Faculty Problems and Their Solutions* (New York: McGraw-Hill Book Co., 1974).

much financial outlay for materials) has been replaced by that of a team working together on a common project with outside funds. This, particularly true in the physical and natural sciences, has even begun to permeate the social sciences. The major
universities, with the best facilities for such research, are often most knowledgeable
about outside sources of money. Furthermore, in these institutions, teaching loads
typically have been less strenuous and more oriented toward the research interests of
the faculty. Finally, these are the places that abound with graduate students, that indispensable, inexpensive, and often inventive supporting staff for researchers. Persons of either sex find it extremely difficult to do major research when isolated from
proper facilities and from an environment that supports such endeavors.

19   In an earlier era, when teaching skills were more highly prized and when concern
for students seemed more important, it was not such a disadvantage for women faculty to be concentrated in institutions which do not make major contributions to research. Women's "natural" talents seemed to make it appropriate for them to focus
their energies in the instructional and nurturing activities that characterized the
revered professors of past generations but that are now less important as a source of
respect. Typically, women have also faithfully responded to the committee assignments that are time consuming, often dull, and sometimes necessary. Service there
represents loyalty to the institution, another virtue not highly regarded today. Men
who have been dedicated teachers, concerned advisers to students, and dutiful committee members have suffered the same professional disadvantages as the women
who have performed these tasks.

20   Finally, shifts in the expectations of society for women and of women for themselves occurred during the twentieth century. A principal change in the years from
1920 to 1960 has been toward a uniform standard by which all women would be
judged. The attitudes toward women are indicative of a general development in
America toward a common cultural standard. The roots of such efforts lie undoubtedly in the Americanization campaigns of the early years of the century that reached
their flowering during the years of World War I. By the late 1920s and 1930s, that
common cultural standard was emerging. Class differences were being minimized as
both the lower and upper classes gravitated toward the attitudes and beliefs associated with the middle class. Regionalism played less of a role; accents, except for
southern ones, began to disappear from American speech. Even ethnic differences
were reduced as Jews anglicized their names and Slavs and Scandinavians dropped
syllables and unwieldy consonants from theirs.

21   The peak of this cultural homogenization probably came about during World War
II when the common experience of military service, much more widespread for
American men than World War I had been, brought together Irish-Americans from
Boston and Hoosier Protestants. Even the traditional distinctions between officers
and enlisted men and their distinct social class origins blurred during World War II
under the pressure of mass mobilization. By 1950 listening to network radio was a
national experience for Americans. Comparable adventures on television were approaching. The proportion of the rural population was dropping steadily, having
fallen below 50 percent in 1920. In short, by 1970 nearly 90 percent of Americans

lived in an urban setting, whether it was town, suburb, or city.[16] Information reached them via national magazines, networks, and wire services. Big purveyors of information were getting larger; the small ones were dropping by the wayside. The homogenization of American culture had become so noticeable that by the early fifties Will Herberg and others were arguing for cultural pluralism as an antidote to the monotony of American life.[17] Such a call won few listeners in that decade, and not until the sixties did it find adherents.

22   The feminine ideal—as opposed to the feminist one—that won such wide support in the early and middle years of the twentieth century was a constellation of virtues: youth, appearance, acquiescence, and domesticity. Every woman was supposed to enhance her youth and her appearance and foster her natural predilection for acquiescence and domesticity. The parallel between these qualities and those previously noted as the female virtues a century earlier (piety, purity, submissiveness, and domesticity) is remarkable and points to the legitimacy in many minds of the persistence of these qualities as natural or "divinely right." Yet, piety was not important for the secular twentieth-century woman. Neither was purity, particularly after the availability of effective contraception. For many Americans, the fabled emancipation of women in the twentieth century amounted to a rejection of those two nineteenth-century virtues and adoption of the twentieth-century one: acquiescence. Finally, the eternal theme of domesticity recurred. The American woman of the mid-twentieth century was to appear young, beautiful, and ardent on demand. She was also to find happiness in her home. Many found that combination difficult.

23   Unlike the nineteenth century's prescriptive behavior for women, the twentieth century's was not in conflict with college attendance. In fact, undergraduate study was either consistent with or irrelevant to it. To be an undergraduate became proper youthful behavior for a young woman, whose appearance was not harmed by such a step. The posture of any student should be acquiescent, not assertive. In addition, college was frequently considered the ideal place to meet the one with whom the domestic life would be shared. A woman reporter on the *New York Times* described the college girl in 1962: "After four years of studying everything from ancient art to modern psychology, the average college girl views her future through a wedding band. Despite compelling evidence that she will be working at 35, by choice or necessity, today's 21-year-old woman has difficulty looking beyond the ceremonies of her own marriage and her babies' christenings."[18] College had begun to play the role that high school had in the lives of women at the turn of the century, for many simply a pleasant interlude on the way to growing up.

24   Graduate school, however, was a different matter. For most women, the psychological and financial factors considered in that decision were much more serious than

---

[16] U.S. Bureau of the Census, *Statistical Abstracts of the United States: 1974,* 95th ed. (Washington, D.C.: Government Printing Office, 1974), p. 20, table 20.

[17] Will Herberg, *Protestant Catholic Jew* (Garden City, N.Y.: Doubleday & Co., 1956).

[18] Marilyn Bender, "College Girl Often Sees No Future But Marriage," *New York Times* (March 26, 1962).

those for college, because graduate school was still seen as a prelude to the professions. The twentieth-century female virtues were seriously at odds with a career. It is difficult to imagine anything more hostile to professionalism than eroticism. Professionalism supposedly implies a commitment to rationality and rigorous objective standards. Eroticism, with its component of sensuality, is the antithesis of such rationality. If a woman were to be truly a woman in contemporary America, she had to have some qualities that qualified as erotic. The possession of those characteristics so necessary to her definition as a woman denied her professionalism. While it is not a bad thing for a man to be sexy or good-looking, those qualities are not as essential to his self-definition. For him to fail to be assertive or for him to place the responsibilities of his home and family over those of his job, however, would lead many to question his professional commitment. Yet these were precisely the expectations for women.

25   For women, then, graduate school and, even more, completion of it with the ritual of one's thesis "defense" (a nonacquiescent act certainly), placed strains on women's self-perceptions and so on society's perceptions of them. The attempted resolutions of these dilemmas varied. One common manner of handling the confusion was to adopt that final, stalwart feminine virtue, domesticity, by marrying and having children. Women graduate students began to marry, a tremendous change from an earlier era when 75 percent of the women who earned Ph.D's between 1875 and 1924 remained spinsters.[19] Such efforts to harmonize domestic responsibilities and those of the profession were sometimes difficult, but they represented the movement, which increased during the sixties, of women seeking full participation in society and referring less to their legitimate "spheres."

26   With piety and purity gone as laudable feminine qualities, another complication for some women graduate students appeared: a distinctive involvement with her professor. This encounter was sexual, either implicitly or explicitly. Probably over 90 percent of graduate school professors are men, most of whom find women attractive intellectually and, potentially, in other realms as well. For most professors, undoubtedly, the potentiality does not become an actuality. However, the proportion of women graduate students who encounter professors whose interest in them transcends the academic is high. Most women find this attention flattering but confusing, since the woman is never clear (and sometimes this is an ambiguity she compounds by her own actions) whether the interest displayed in her is a reflection of her scholarly promise or of something else. As yet, social scientists have not formally attempted to assess this factor's effect on women graduate students, but informal discussions about it among women who have been in graduate school do occur. There are no direct parallels for male graduate students, except perhaps for homosexual involvements. These, too, have not been reported in the otherwise abundant social science literature, but their absence from the literature does not confirm their absence from life.

[19] William H. Chafe, *The American Woman* (New York: Oxford University Press, 1972), p. 100.

27   Such complications, those of the variance between the expectations for women and the professional commitment required for completion of graduate school, are reflected in the substantially reduced proportion of women receiving doctorates in the forties and the fifties. From more than 15 percent of the doctoral recipients in the early thirties, women fell to below 10 percent in the fifties (see table 1). A study conducted by the American Historical Association of a small number of leading coeducational liberal arts college history departments showed a decline of women full professors of history from 16 percent to 0 percent in 1970.[20] In 1974, only Barnard, Wellesley, and Radcliffe, of the Seven Sisters Colleges, had women presidents, although Smith has now joined the group with the first woman president in its history, and Vassar with its second. The most recent figures from the National Center for Education Statistics reveal that, despite affirmative action programs, a decline is still evident at the senior faculty positions. The percentage of women full professors and associate professors fell between 1974 and 1975, while salary disparities between male and female professors grew.[21] The women of the forties and fifties absorbed the new values and withdrew from the professional arena. They married at very high rates at more youthful ages and had lots of babies. The birth rate reached its peak in 1957, at which time the average age for first marriage for women was just over 20. To marry young and to have several children was to insure following some of the canons of femininity. It also made it very difficult to combine a meaningful personal life with a productive professional one.

28   In the last several years, many women, seeming to recognize this difficulty, have taken steps to avoid it. The rate of women receiving doctorates has grown substantially since 1970, more than a percent per year, an increase unique in the last century.[22] The birth rate has fallen; the marriage age has risen; the divorce rate has increased. Women are speaking openly about their legitimate search for meaningful work, a search that a decade or two ago was often cloaked with such self-abnegating phrases as, "I'm only looking for a little something part time to help out a bit," or, more proudly, "I need work to put my husband through medical school." Although her own standards are less clear, the educated woman of the mid-seventies is less inclined to admit allegiance to the female virtues of the past several decades.

29   Conceivably, the monolithic ideal of the research university may also be breaking up under the pressure of new demands for higher education. In many quarters, concerns for "lifelong education" are being enthusiastically expressed. Previously, adult education programs were geared to housewives returning to school or preparing to reenter the work force. Now, however, colleges and universities may be amending their definitions to include all adults as a major part of the student body. Should this be so, opportunities for flexibility in scheduling and career, heretofore a hallmark of

---

[20] American Historical Association, "Report of the Ad Hoc Committee on the Status of Women in the Historical Profession" (Washington, D.C.: American Historical Association, 1973).

[21] Reported in *Higher Education and National Affairs* 25, no. 4 (January 30, 1976): 1. While this article was at press, Bryn Mawr and Mt. Holyoke also appointed women presidents.

[22] Betty M. Vetter, "Women, Men, and the Doctorate," *Science* 187, no. 4174 (January 31, 1975): 301.

the life of the professional woman, may come to characterize that of the professional man as well. This may bring with it the chance to meld significant commitments to both work and family, however that family may be defined. Continuing education may then prove to be another example of innovation in which programs originally designed for women are seen to benefit men as well and thereby are permitted to enter the academic mainstream. Should my guesses about the future prove true, and it is not at all clear that they will, the educational diversity that benefited women in the late nineteenth century may reappear to do so again in the late twentieth.

WRITING ASSIGNMENTS

Analysis

1. Define the shifts in higher education between the mid-nineteenth century and the mid-twentieth century and explain why they affected men and women differently.
2. What expectations and goals do contemporary students have of a college education? Consider how students' class, ethnicity, and gender might affect their expectations and goals.
3. How has the emphasis on scholarship (preferably published research) rather than on teaching and service affected both faculty and students? Has this emphasis historically affected men and women differently?
4. According to Graham, what is the feminine ideal and how have its prescriptions influenced women's experiences in higher education?

Argument

1. On balance, is the emphasis on research, especially on published research, good or bad for higher education? You may wish to focus on the impact of this emphasis on students, on faculty, on the institution as a whole, or on society generally.
2. Has the effort to diversify the student body and faculty—that is, increase the number of women and persons from minority groups—improved your school? Be sure to define your standards for improvement.
3. Do affirmative action efforts to increase the number of women and minority students and faculty in higher education put people who are not members of "underrepresented groups" at a disadvantage?
4. Writing in 1978, Graham concludes by saying, ". . . the educational diversity that benefited women in the late nineteenth century may reappear to do so again in the late twentieth." In your opinion, to what extent, if at all, has this benefit been realized?

Personal Writing and Writing from Research

1. Trace and explain changes at your college over a defined period in one or more of the following: composition of the student body or faculty, curriculum,

graduation requirements, the school's status and reputation, the role of research, revenue sources, and the school's relationship to the surrounding community or to society.

2. Reflect on how the definition of an "educated person" has evolved, and offer your own definition.
3. Historically, how has the ideal education for men and women differed?
4. *Collaborative Project:* Trace the history of some facet of women's higher education. Consider topics such as the history of women's participation as students, faculty, and administrators; the development and purposes of colleges for women students; the representation of women students and faculty in different academic disciplines; the development of women's studies and women's history; and women's athletic programs.
5. Write a research paper on the role that gender has played in the academic careers of women faculty at your school. Base your paper primarily on interviews with women faculty.
6. Write a profile of a female pioneer in higher education such as M. Carey Thomas, Cecelia Payne-Gaposhkin, Alice Hamilton, Marjorie Nicolson, or Johnetta Cole.
7. Profile women leaders in higher education today.
8. Trace the development of black colleges in America. How and why does their history parallel or differ from the history of higher education for women?

A Sampling of Historical Documents Concerning Education

These documents reflect two parallel debates that raged most heatedly in the final quarter of the nineteenth century and in the opening years of the twentieth century, but which continue to smolder today. The first debate concerns the education of women; the second, the education of African Americans.

Journal Topics: (1) Should women's education differ from men's? Why? (2) What do you believe are the advantages or disadvantages of single-sex education or coeducation? (3) What do you believe are the advantages or disadvantages of black colleges? (4) Describe what you know about women's colleges or black colleges.

As You Read: (1) How do these writers' ideas about education for women or African Americans reflect their basic assumptions about the differences, natural or acquired, between men and women or among several races? (2) To what extent are the educational histories of women and African Americans similar or different?

Sex in Education

Edward H. Clarke, MD

Edward Clarke MD, one-time professor and member of the board of the Harvard Medical School, was invited in 1872 to address the New England Women's Club in Boston on the relation of sex to education, because he had deplored the bodily removal of women from medical classes in Philadelphia. Instead of the liberal sentiments that his listeners expected, he stunned his audience by arguing that higher education was destroying the health and reproductive capacities of young women. One year later, he expanded his ideas into a book, *Sex in Education; or, a Fair Chance for Girls,* from which this excerpt is taken. Immensely successful, the first edition sold out in one week and went through 17 editions in 13 years. Despite criticism, Clarke's ideas remained popular and influential for years to come.

Miss D_____ entered Vassar College at the age of fourteen. Up to that age, she had been a healthy girl, judged by the standard of American girls. Her parents were apparently strong enough to yield her a fair dower of force. The catamenial function first showed signs of activity in her Sophomore Year, when she was fifteen years old. Its appearance at this age is confirmatory evidence of the normal state of her health at that period of her college career. Its commencement was normal, without pain or excess. She performed all her college duties regularly and steadily. She studied, recited, stood at the blackboard, walked, and went through her gymnastic exercises, from the beginning to the end of the term, just as boys do. Her account of her regimen there was so nearly that of a boy's regimen, that it would puzzle a physiologist to determine, from the account alone, whether the subject of it was male or female. She was an average scholar, who maintained a fair position in her class, not one of the anxious sort, that are ambitious of leading all the rest. Her first warning was fainting away, while exercising in the gymnasium, at a time when she should have been comparatively quiet, both mentally and physically. This warning was repeated several times, under the same circumstances. Finally she was compelled to renounce gymnastic exercises altogether. In her Junior Year, the organism's periodical function began to be performed with pain, moderate at first, but more and more severe with each returning month. When between seventeen and eighteen years old, dysmenorrhœa was established as the order of that function. Coincident with the appearance of pain, there was a diminution of excretion; and, as the former increased, the latter became more marked. In other respects she was well; and, in all respects, she appeared to be well to her companions and to the faculty of the college. She graduated before nineteen, with fair honors and a poor physique. The year succeeding her graduation was one of steadily-advancing invalidism. She was tortured for two or three days out of every month; and, for two or three days after each season of torture, was weak and miserable, so that about one sixth or fifth of her time was consumed in this way. The excretion from the blood, which had been gradually lessening, after a time substantially stopped, though a periodical effort to keep it up was made. She now suffered from what is called amenorrhœa. At the same time she became pale, hysterical, nervous in the ordinary sense, and almost constantly complained of headache. Physicians were applied to for aid: drugs were administered; travelling, with consequent change of air and scene, was undertaken; and all with little apparent avail. After this experience, she was brought to Boston for advice, when the writer first saw her, and learned all these details. She presented no evidence of local uterine congestion, inflammation, ulceration, or displacement. The evidence was altogether in favor of an arrest of the development of the reproductive apparatus, at a stage when the development was nearly complete. Confirmatory proof of such an arrest was found in examining her breast, where the milliner had supplied the organs Nature should have grown. It is unnecessary for our present purpose to detail what treatment was advised. It is sufficient to say, that she probably never will become physically what she would have been had her education been physiologically guided.

This case needs very little comment: its teachings are obvious. Miss D_____ went to college in good physical condition. During the four years of her college life, her parents and the college faculty required her to get what is popularly called an education. Nature required her, during the same period, to build and put in working-order a large and complicated reproductive mechanism, a matter that is popularly ignored,—shoved out of sight like a disgrace. She naturally obeyed the requirements of the faculty, which she could see, rather than the requirements of the mechanism within her, that she could not see. Subjected to the college regimen, she worked four years in getting a liberal education. Her way of work was sustained and continuous, and out of harmony with the rhythmical periodicity of the female organization. The stream of vital and constructive force evolved within her was turned steadily to the brain, and away from the ovaries and their accessories. The result of this sort of education was, that these last-mentioned organs, deprived of sufficient opportunity and nutriment, first began to perform their functions with pain, a warning of error that was unheeded; then, to cease to grow; next, to set up once a month a grumbling torture that made life miserable; and lastly, the brain and the whole nervous system, disturbed, in obedience to the law, that, if one member suffers, all the members suffer, became neuralgic and hysterical. And so Miss D_____ spent the few years next succeeding her graduation in conflict with dysmenorrhœa, headache, neuralgia, and hysteria. Her parents marvelled at her ill-health; and she furnished another text for the often-repeated sermon on the delicacy of American girls. . . .

Address to the Students at the Opening of the Academic Year 1899–1900

M. Carey Thomas

M. Carey Thomas, president of Bryn Mawr College, sought to create a women's college that treated women as the intellectual equals of men. She dispensed with the domestic services required of students at most women's colleges and discouraged students from thinking that it was a woman's destiny to marry and have children. She also introduced entrance examinations tougher than those of male colleges, very high academic standards, and a curriculum like that at the most elite men's colleges.

1   It is always my custom to welcome the students at the beginning of each academic year. I regretted very much that I was compelled to be absent on the first day, the opening of the fifteenth year of the college, but I was, I think, well employed in assisting to welcome the new President of Wellesley College. Indeed the speechmaking at Wellesley was so interesting in many ways that I shall refer to it again in a few moments and shall make some of the views on women's education there put forth the text of what I wish to speak to you about after I have given out the necessary announcements. . . .

2   . . . This year for the first time we can begin to test the experiment of older and younger students, graduates and seniors and juniors and freshmen living together in each of our halls of residence in nearly equal proportions, instead of being massed in halls by classes. . . . [In this] mutual association will, we hope, be fashioned and perfected the type of Bryn Mawr women which will, we hope, become as well known and universally admired a type as the Oxford and Cambridge man or as the graduate of the great English public schools. No such type can possibly be created except by a residence college and unless carefully divided like Oxford and Cambridge into resident halls a very large college loses the power to mould its students in external ways. There used to be, but at present we might almost say there is not a type of Harvard man, and it is much lamented by old Harvard men and Harvard professors. Princeton still preserves a type, but the Cornell, Hopkins, Columbia, University of Pennsylvania, Michigan men are as different as the homes from which they come or as the homes or boarding houses in which they live, and this great lack is so strongly felt that there is a great modern movement in men's education to return to the dormitory system. President Eliot in his address of welcome to President Hazard said that as men's colleges in this country had failed as schools of manners it was left to women's colleges to lead the way in showing how youth of both sexes could be taken by the hundred and be given the bearing and manners of gentlemen and gentlewomen. He then proceeded to say that manners as such were of vastly more importance to women than men. Whether this is true or not, and in the old fashioned

matrimonial market which President Eliot was probably referring to, where a man exchanges dollars for a woman's social charm, it is true, it is certainly true that for both men and women success of every kind in after life depends greatly on gentle breeding. Doctors, lawyers, teachers, philanthropists, social leaders, everything in life in which men and women are associated together is aided or retarded by good breeding. Such breeding can best be learned at home, but in a large community like this there will always be those whose student homes are better schools of manners than the homes of other students, and living together as we do the highest standards should prevail. We all have an opportunity to correct provincialisms, uncouth pronunciations, to get rid of expressions that no person of culture could possibly use. . . .

3   I am so infinitely proud of the standard of good conduct here wherever I go I am met by unknown friends that you the students of the college have made for me. Your system of self government is the fullest system known; it preceded all other self government systems in colleges in this country. Bryn Mawr is the only college in the world where a student has never been disciplined for offences of conduct apart from the strictly academic offences of unfairness in examinations. I appeal to the student body assembled to maintain this standard, to raise it higher. I sometimes wonder if you know how people regard the Bryn Mawr standards and how [much] lies in your hands by some rough hoyden horse play or brutal practical joking. Manners do, as President Eliot says, matter immensely and if the Bryn Mawr woman could add to scholarship and character gentle breeding and could join high standards of behavior and usages of culture and gentle observances to high standards of scholarship we should have the type we are seeking to create.

4   President Carter of Williams in answering to the toast "The ideal New England college", said that he wondered sometimes if the ideal women's college in flooding with the light of learning the women within its walls could also look after the sweetness, whether sweet sixteen at entering would be sweet sixteen at graduation. Emphatically no. Sweet sixteen has the charm of childhood and ignorance that will shortly be relegated to the harems of the east.

5   President Eliot also said (you see that there were many doctrinaire utterances about women, for when do men gathered together on the platform of a women's college resist the attempt to shove, usually out of its path, the resistless force they see before them, which we call the higher education of women) President Eliot said that the president and faculty of a women's college had no guide from the past, that the great tradition of learning existing from the time of the Egyptians to the present existed only for men and that this vast body of inherited tradition was of no service in women's education, that women's colleges simply imitated men when they used the same educational methods instead of inventing new ones of their own and that furthermore it would indeed be strange if women's intellects were not at least as unlike men's as their bodies. This is the old argument of the rural deans over again who came up from all the country villages of England to vote against Oxford and Cambridge giving women the same degrees as men when they had done the same work and would not be worthy of a serious reply had it not been thrown deliberately by the president of one of the greatest of American universities as a gauntlet in the face of

an immense audience, most of whom were directly interested in the education of women students. It only shows us that as progressive as one may be in education or other things there may be in our minds some dark spot of mediaevalism, and clearly in President Eliot's otherwise luminous intelligence women's education is this dark spot. He might as well have told the president of Wellesley to invent a new Christian religion for Wellesley and new symphonies or operas, a new Beethoven and Wagner, new statues and pictures, a new Phidias and a new Titian, new tennis, new gold, a new way to swim, skate and run, new food, and new drink. It would be easier to do all this than to create for women a new science of geography, a new Greek Tragedies, new Chemistry, new philosophies, in short, a new intellectual heavens and earth. President Taylor of Vassar in talking over this remark afterward said to me—and I think he would not object to my quoting it to you, as he told me he had often said it, that during all the years he had been educating women he had been trying to find some difference between their intellects and men's and that whenever he thought he could put his finger on a difference he found that the accuracy of his observation was overturned by future classes of students. He thought he had found but one difference, a difference of habit of life, the difference implied by women's willingness to work more hours over a difficult problem or a difficult passage of translation, whereas a man would see that a change of occupation was the proper thing and would return to attack the difficult subject after several hours of relaxation and fresh air, a woman would pore over it until she had lost her power of thinking freshly. This he accounted for by the different conditions of women's life and the fact that a woman's work in the household is never finished. I think that I may add one more difference to that suggested by President Taylor; it is this: as yet college women are not as ready to accept criticism, they are not used to the take and give of life. They have been more sheltered, less criticised and more praised. Often in teaching women professors have to be more careful then in teaching men, as honest criticism depresses students unduly.

6   Professor Palmer, of Harvard, whose remarks are always sane and to the point, said in answering the toast, "The Ideal College Woman", as having married Wellesley's former president and holding the post, as he said, of husband of the college, that if the difference between the minds of men and women is so great, it is strange that under the free elective system women did not overwhelmingly elect certain courses: French and German, for example, instead of Greek and Latin, Art and Music instead of Mathematics, and that undoubtedly if the difference existed it ought to manifest itself in this way. In point of fact you will find by comparing the favourite studies at men's and women's colleges that the same waves of interest seem to sweep over both. In certain periods of the years modern languages are given the preference over classical languages. In certain other years History and Political Economy draw the most students. Furthermore it is strange if the intellectual training for men is not fit for women that we see in women's as in men's students [sic] such a steady growth in intellectual honesty, in clear thinking, in reasonableness, in scientific habit of thinking.

7   When I was in Aix-les-Bains this summer taking the cure for sciatica, my books gave out and as I could not do serious reading during a great deal of the time I had to

supply myself with the only available literature, modern French novels. In reading these novels I was very much struck with the different type of women the Anglo-Saxon race has evolved by the wider opportunities given to women of the Anglo-Saxon race. Much of the interest and tragedy of these novels turned on the doubt and distrust felt by the French husband of his wife, of his fear that she was deceiving him and that her love for him had stopped. Instead of asking her a frank question and receiving a frank reply the whole miserable drama of suspicion and jealousy and watching and spying unfolded itself. He did not ask her a question because he knew that she would deceive him. Thus, however unworthy of love and confidence women are men will love them and it is correspondingly true of women's love for men. The world is made so and the happiness of the home depends upon love and confidence between men and women. I thought as I read these novels how impossible it would be for such relations to exist between the collegebred woman and her husband. I should like to read to you a poem written by a great writer of English prose as embodying this new type of woman which we are, I hope, moulding and fashioning at Bryn Mawr College. I will close by reading Stevenson's verses: "To My Wife":

> "Trusty, dusky, vivid, true,
> With eyes of gold and bramble-dew,
> Steel-true and blade-straight,
> The great artificer
> Made my mate.

> "Honour, anger, valour, fire;
> A love that life could never tire,
>   Death quench or evil stir,
> The mighty master
>   Gave to her.

> "Teacher, tender, comrade, wife,
> A fellow-farer true through life,
>   Heart-whole and soul-free
> The august father
>   Gave to me."

The Atlanta Exposition Address

Booker T. Washington

Booker T. Washington (1856–1915) was born a slave. In 1872, he enrolled at Hampton Institute and paid his way by working there as a janitor. After teaching and further study, he was chosen to lead Tuskegee Normal and Industrial School in Alabama. Over the next 34 years, he built Tuskegee from an impoverished school to a major, 1,500-student institution that focused on technical training and applied sciences. Although a champion of African-American education, he accepted a doctrine of social separatism of the races that, in many ways, mirrored the doctrine of separate spheres for men and women. "The Atlanta Exposition Address" was delivered in 1895 to a white audience.

1   One-third of the population of the South is of the Negro race. No enterprise seeking the material, civil, or moral welfare of this section can disregard this element of our population and reach the highest success. I but convey to you, Mr. President and Directors, the sentiment of the masses of my race when I say that in no way have the value and manhood of the American Negro been more fittingly and generously recognized than by the managers of this magnificent Exposition at every stage of its progress. It is a recognition that will do more to cement the friendship of the two races than any occurrence since the dawn of our freedom.

2   Not only this, but the opportunity here afforded will awaken among us a new era of industrial progress. Ignorant and inexperienced, it is not strange that in the first years of our new life we began at the top instead of at the bottom; that a seat in Congress or the State Legislature was more sought than real estate or industrial skill; that the political convention or stump speaking had more attractions than starting a dairy farm or truck garden.

3   A ship lost at sea for many days suddenly sighted a friendly vessel. From the mast of the unfortunate vessel was seen a signal: "Water, water, we die of thirst." The answer from the friendly vessel at once came back, "Cast down your bucket where you are." A second time the signal, "Water, water, send us water," ran up from the distressed vessel and was answered, "Cast down your bucket where you are." And a third and fourth signal for water was answered "Cast down your bucket where you are." The captain of the distressed vessel, at last heeding the injunction, cast down his bucket and it came up full of fresh, sparkling water from the mouth of the Amazon River.

4   To those of my race who depend on bettering their condition in a foreign land, or who underestimate the importance of cultivating friendly relations with the Southern white man who is their next-door neighbor, I would say, Cast down your bucket where you are; cast it down in making friends, in every manly way, of the people of all races by whom we are surrounded. Cast it down in agriculture, mechanics, in commerce, in domestic service, and in the professions. And in this connection it is well to bear in mind that whatever other sins the South may be called upon to bear, when it comes to business pure and simple, it is in the South that the Negro is given a man's chance in the commercial world, and in nothing is this Exposition more eloquent than in emphasizing this chance. Our greatest danger is that, in the great leap from slavery to freedom, we may overlook the fact that the masses of us are to live by the productions of our hands and fail to keep in mind that we shall prosper in the proportion as we learn to dignify and glorify common labor, and put brains and skill into the common occupations of life: shall prosper in proportion as we learn to draw the line between the superficial and the substantial, the ornamental gewgaws of life and

the useful. No race can prosper till it learns that there is as much dignity in tilling a field as in writing a poem. It is at the bottom of life we must begin, and not at the top. Nor should we permit our grievances to overshadow our opportunities.

5   To those of the white race who look to the incoming of those of foreign birth and strange tongue and habits for the prosperity of the South, were I permitted I would repeat what I say to my own race, "Cast down your bucket where you are." Cast it down among the 8,000,000 Negroes whose habits you know, whose fidelity and love you have tested in days when to have proved treacherous meant the ruin of your fire-sides. Cast down your bucket among these people who have, without strikes and labor wars, tilled your fields, cleared your forests, builded your railroads and cities, and brought forth treasures from the bowels of the earth and helped make possible this magnificent representation of the progress of the South. Casting down your bucket among my people, helping and encouraging them as you are doing on these grounds, and, with education of head, hand and heart, you will find that they will buy your surplus land, make blossom the waste places in your fields, and run your factories.

6   While doing this, you can be sure in the future, as in the past, that you and your families will be surrounded by the most patient, faithful, law-abiding, and unresentful people that the world has seen. As we have proved our loyalty to you in the past, in nursing your children, watching by the sick-bed of your mothers and fathers, and often following them with tear-dimmed eyes to their graves, so in the future, in our humble way, we shall stand by you with a devotion that no foreigner can approach, ready to lay down our lives, if need be, in defense of yours: interlacing our industrial, commercial, civil, and religious life with yours in a way that shall make the interests of both races one. In all things that are purely social we can be as separate as the fingers, yet one as the hand in all things essential to mutual progress.

7   There is no defense or security for any of us except in the highest intelligence and development of all. If anywhere there are efforts tending to curtail the fullest growth of the Negro, let these efforts be turned into stimulating, encouraging and making him the most useful and intelligent citizen. Effort or means so invested will pay a thousand per cent interest. These efforts will be twice blessed—"blessing him that gives and him that takes."

8   There is no escape, through law of man or God, from the inevitable:

> The laws of changeless justice bind
> Oppressor with oppressed,
> And close as sin and suffering joined
> We march to fate abreast.

9   Nearly sixteen million hands will aid you in pulling the load upward, or they will pull against you the load downward. We shall constitute one-third and more of the ignorance and crime of the South, or one-third its intelligence and progress; we shall contribute one-third to the business and industrial prosperity of the South, or we shall prove a veritable body of death, stagnating, depressing, retarding every effort to advance the body politic.

10   Gentlemen of the Exposition: As we present to you our humble effort at an exhibition of our progress, you must not expect over much. Starting thirty years ago with ownership here and there in a few quilts and pumpkins and chickens (gathered from miscellaneous sources), remember: the path that has led us from these to the invention and production of agricultural implements, buggies, steam engines, newspapers, books, statuary, carving, paintings, the management of drugstores and banks, has not been trodden without contact with thorns and thistles. While we take pride in what we exhibit as a result of our independent efforts, we do not for a moment forget that our part in this exhibition would fall far short of your expectations but for the constant help that has come to our educational life, not only from the Southern states, but especially from Northern philanthropists who have made their gifts a constant stream of blessing and encouragement.

11   The wisest among my race understand that the agitation of questions of social equality is the extremest folly, and that progress in the enjoyment of all the privileges that will come to us must be the result of severe and constant struggle rather than of artificial forcing. No race that has anything to contribute to the markets of the world is long in any degree ostracized. It is important and right that all privileges of the law be ours, but it is vastly more important that we be prepared for the exercise of those privileges. The opportunity to earn a dollar in a factory just now is worth infinitely more than the opportunity to spend a dollar in an opera house.

12   In conclusion, may I repeat that nothing in thirty years has given us more hope and encouragement and drawn us so near to you of the white race as this opportunity offered by the Exposition; and here bending, as it were, over the altar that represents the results of the struggles of your race and mine, both starting practically empty-handed three decades ago, I pledge that, in your effort to work out the great and intricate problem which God has laid at the doors of the South, you shall have at all times the patient, sympathetic help of my race. Only let this be constantly in mind that, while from representations in these buildings of the product of field, of forest, of mine, of factory, letters and art, much good will come—yet far above and beyond material benefits, will be that higher good, that let us pray God will come, in a blotting out of sectional differences and racial animosities and suspicions, in a determination to administer absolute justice, in a willing obedience among all classes to the mandates of law. This, coupled with material prosperity, will bring into our beloved South a new heaven and a new earth.

Reply to Booker T. Washington

John Hope

John Hope (1968–1936) delivered his rebuttal to Booker T. Washington before a black debating society in Washington, DC. A graduate of Worcester Academy in Massachusetts and Brown University, he became a professor of classics and sciences at Roger Williams

University in Nashville, Tennessee. He was one of the founders of the Niagara Movement, which preceded the National Association for the Advancement of Colored People. In 1906, he became the first black president of Atlanta Baptist College (Morehouse College), and in 1929, the president of Atlanta University.

If we are not striving for equality, in heaven's name for what are we living? I regard it as cowardly and dishonest for any of our colored men to tell white people or colored people that we are not struggling for equality. If money, education, and honesty will not bring to me as much privilege, as much equality as they bring to any American citizen, then they are to me a curse, and not a blessing. God forbid that we should get the implements with which to fashion our freedom, and then be too lazy or pusillanimous to fashion it. Let us not fool ourselves nor be fooled by others. If we cannot do what other freemen do, then we are not free. Yes, my friends, I want equality. Nothing less. I want all that my God-given powers will enable me to get, then why not equality? Now, catch your breath, for I am going to use an adjective: I am going to say we demand social equality. In this Republic we shall be less than freemen, if we have a whit less than that which thrift, education, and honor afford other freemen. If equality, political, economic, and social, is the boon of other men in this great country of ours, then equality, political, economic, and social, is what we demand. Why build a wall to keep me out? I am no wild beast, nor am I an unclean thing.

Rise, Brothers! Come let us possess this land. Never say: "Let well enough alone." Cease to console yourselves with adages that numb the moral sense. Be discontented. Be dissatisfied. "Sweat and grunt" under present conditions. Be as restless as the tempestuous billows on the boundless sea. Let your discontent break mountain-high against the wall of prejudice, and swamp it to the very foundation. Then we shall not have to plead for justice nor on bended knee crave mercy; for we shall be men. Then and not until then will liberty in its highest sense be the boast of our Republic.

The Talented Tenth *and* Advice to a Black Schoolgirl

W. E. B. Du Bois

W. E. B. Du Bois (1868–1963) was the most influential black intellectual in the first half of the twentieth century. Born in Massachusetts, he was educated at Fisk University and was the first black to earn a PhD from Harvard. In his most famous book, *The Souls of Black Folk,* he prophesied, "The problem of the Twentieth Century is the problem of the color line." He was a founder of the National Association for the Advancement of Colored People. Challenging Booker T. Washington in *The Negro Problem* (1903), Du Bois argued for an education that would lift blacks from poverty to equality. He urged that "the talented tenth" be educated for leadership. In 1905, at the request of a white high-school teacher, Du Bois wrote to a black female student who was "very bright" but refused to study because she would "never have a chance to use her knowledge."

THE TALENTED TENTH

1   The Negro race, like all races, is going to be saved by its exceptional men. The problem of education, then, among Negroes must first of all deal with the Talented Tenth; it is the problem of developing the Best of this race that they may guide the Mass away from the contamination and death of the Worst, in their own and other races. Now the training of men is a difficult and intricate task. Its technique is a matter for educational experts, but its object is for the vision of seers. If we make money the object of man-training, we shall develop money-makers but not necessarily men; if we make technical skill the object of education, we may possess artisans but not, in nature, men. Men we shall have only as we make manhood the object of the work of the schools—intelligence, broad sympathy, knowledge of the world that was and is, and of the relation of men to it—this is the curriculum of that Higher Education which must underlie true life. . . . From the very first it has been the educated and intelligent of the Negro people that have led and elevated the mass, and the sole obstacles that nullified and retarded their efforts were slavery and race prejudice; for what is slavery but the legalized survival of the unfit and the nullification of the work of natural internal leadership? . . .

2   It is the fashion of today to . . . say that with freedom Negro leadership should have begun at the plow and not in the Senate—a foolish and mischievous lie; two hundred and fifty years that black serf toiled at the plow and yet that toiling was in vain till the Senate passed the war amendments; and two hundred and fifty years more the half-free serf of today may toil at his plow, but unless he have political rights and righteously guarded civic status, he will still remain the poverty-stricken and ignorant plaything of rascals, that he now is. This all sane men know even if they dare not say it. . . .

3   How then shall the leaders of a struggling people be trained and the hands of the risen few strengthened? There can be but one answer: The best and most capable of their youth must be schooled in the colleges and universities of the land. We will not quarrel as to just what the university of the Negro should teach or how it should teach it—I willingly admit that each soul and each race-soul needs its own peculiar curriculum. But this is true: A university is a human invention for the transmission of knowledge and culture from generation to generation, through the training of quick minds and pure hearts, and for this work no other human invention will suffice, not even trade and industrial schools.

4   All men cannot go to college but some men must; every isolated group or nation must have its yeast, must have for the talented few centers of training where men

are not so mystified and befuddled by the hard and necessary toil of earning a living, as to have no aims higher than their bellies, and no God greater than Gold. This is true training, and thus in the beginning were the favored sons of the freedmen trained. . . . Where ought they to have begun to build? At the bottom, of course, quibbles the mole with his eyes in the earth. Aye! truly at the bottom, at the very bottom; at the bottom of knowledge, down in the very depths of knowledge there where the roots of justice strike into the lowest soil of Truth. And so they did begin; they founded colleges, and up from the colleges shot normal schools, and out from the normal schools went teachers, and around the normal teachers clustered other teachers to teach the public schools; the college trained in Greek and Latin and mathematics, 2,000 men; and these men trained full 50,000 others in morals and manners, and they in turn taught thrift and the alphabet to nine millions of men, who today hold $300,000,000 of property. It was a miracle—the most wonderful peace-battle of the nineteenth century, and yet today men smile at it, and in fine superiority tell us that it was all a strange mistake; that a proper way to found a system of education is first to gather the children and buy them spelling books and hoes; afterward men may look about for teachers, if haply they may find them; or again they would teach men Work, but as for Life—why, what has Work to do with Life, they ask vacantly. . . .

5   The college-bred Negro . . . is, as he ought to be, the group leader, the man who sets the ideals of the community where he lives, directs its thoughts, and heads its social movements. It need hardly be argued that the Negro people need social leadership more than most groups; that they have no traditions to fall back upon, no long-established customs, no strong family ties, no well-defined social classes. All these things must be slowly and painfully evolved. The preacher was, even before the war, the group leader of the Negroes, and the church their greatest social institution. Naturally this preacher was ignorant and often immoral, and the problem of replacing the older type by better educated men has been a difficult one. Both by direct work and by direct influence on other preachers, and on congregations, the college-bred preacher has an opportunity for reformatory work and moral inspiration, the value of which cannot be overestimated.

6   It has, however, been in the furnishing of teachers that the Negro college has found its peculiar function. Few persons realize how vast a work, how mighty a revolution has been thus accomplished. To furnish five millions and more of ignorant people with teachers of their own race and blood, in one generation, was not only a very difficult undertaking, but a very important one, in that it placed before the eyes of almost every Negro child an attainable ideal. It brought the masses of the blacks in contact with modern civilization, made black men the leaders of their communities and trainers of the new generation. In this work college-bred Negroes were first teachers, and then teachers of teachers. And here it is that the broad culture of college work has been of peculiar value. Knowledge of life and its wider meaning has been the point of Negroes' deepest ignorance, and the sending out of teachers whose training has not been simply for breadwinning, but also for human culture, has been of inestimable value in the training of these men. . . .

7   The main question, so far as the Southern Negro is concerned, is: What, under the present circumstance, must a system of education do in order to raise the Negro as quickly as possible in the scale of civilization? The answer to this question seems to me clear: It must strengthen the Negro's character, increase his knowledge, and teach him to earn a living. Now it goes without saying, that it is hard to do all these things simultaneously or suddenly, and that at the same time it will not do to give all the attention to one and neglect the others; we could give black boys trades, but that alone will not civilize a race of ex-slaves; we might simply increase their knowledge of the world, but this would not necessarily make them wish to use this knowledge honestly; we might seek to strengthen character and purpose, but to what end if this people have nothing to eat or to wear? . . . Schoolhouses do not teach themselves—piles of brick and mortar and machinery do not send out *men*. It is the trained, living human soul, cultivated and strengthened by long study and thought, that breathes the real breath of life into boys and girls and makes them human, whether they be black or white, Greek, Russian, or American. . . .

8   I would not deny, or for a moment seem to deny, the paramount necessity of teaching the Negro to work, and to work steadily and skillfully; or seem to depreciate in the slightest degree the important part industrial schools must play in the accomplishment of these ends, but I *do* say, and insist upon it, that it is industrialism drunk with its vision of success to imagine that its work can be accomplished without providing for the training of broadly cultured men and women to teach its own teachers, and to teach the teachers of the public schools. . . .

9   I am an earnest advocate of manual training and trade teaching for black boys, and for white boys, too. I believe that next to the founding of Negro colleges the most valuable addition to Negro education since the war has been industrial training for black boys. Nevertheless, I insist that the object of all true education is not to make men carpenters, it is to make carpenters men; there are two means of making the carpenter a man, each equally important; the first is to give the group and community in which he works liberally trained teachers and leaders to teach him and his family what life means; the second is to give him sufficient intelligence and technical skill to make him an efficient workman; the first object demands the Negro college and college-bred men—not a quantity of such colleges, but a few of excellent quality; not too many college-bred men, but enough to leaven the lump, to inspire the masses, to raise the Talented Tenth to leadership; the second object demands a good system of common schools, well-taught, conveniently located, and properly equipped. . . .

10   Men of America, the problem is plain before you. Here is a race transplanted through the criminal foolishness of your fathers. Whether you like it or not the millions are here, and here they will remain. If you do not lift them up, they will pull you down. Education and work are the levers to uplift a people. Work alone will not do it unless inspired by the right ideals and guided by intelligence. Education must not simply teach work—it must teach Life. The Talented Tenth of the Negro race must be made leaders of thought and missionaries of culture among their people. No others can do this work and Negro colleges must train men for it. The Negro race, like all other races, is going to be saved by its exceptional men.

ADVICE TO A BLACK SCHOOLGIRL

I wonder if you will let a stranger say a word to you about yourself? I have heard that you are a young woman of some ability but that you are neglecting your school work because you have become hopeless of trying to do anything in the world. I am very sorry for this. How any human being whose wonderful fortune it is to live in the 20th century should under ordinarily fair advantages despair of life is almost unbelievable. And if in addition to this that person is, as I am, of Negro lineage with all the hopes and yearnings of hundreds of millions of human souls dependent in some degree on her striving, then her bitterness amounts to crime.

There are in the U.S. today tens of thousands of colored girls who would be happy beyond measure to have the chance of educating themselves that you are neglecting. If you train yourself as you easily can, there are wonderful chances of usefulness before you: you can join the ranks of 15,000 Negro women teachers, of hundreds of nurses and physicians, of the growing number of clerks and stenographers, and above all of the host of homemakers. Ignorance is a cure for nothing. Get the very best training possible & the doors of opportunity will fly open before you as they are flying before thousands of your fellows. On the other hand every time a colored person neglects an opportunity, it makes it more difficult for others of the race to get such an opportunity. Do you want to cut off the chances of the boys and girls of tomorrow?

WRITING ASSIGNMENTS

Analysis

1. First describe Dr. Edward H. Clarke's explanation for Miss D_____'s physical deterioration while in college, then suggest an alternative.
2. Compare and contrast the content and purposes of education for African Americans as envisioned by Booker T. Washington, on the one hand, and John Hope and W. E. B. Du Bois, on the other.
3. How might differences in personal history contribute to the philosophical differences between Booker T. Washington, on the one hand, and John Hope and W. E. B. Du Bois, on the other?
4. How did the obstacles encountered by women seeking higher education compare to those facing African Americans in the nineteenth and early twentieth centuries?

Argument

1. Is the public well-served by having a diversity of schools based on ideals as different as those expressed by these historical figures and described by Graham in the chapter's opening selection?
2. Is there a justification today for single-sex or single-race education?

Personal Writing and Writing from Research

1. To what extent are ideas like those of Edward H. Clarke or Booker T. Washington expressed in discussions of education today? Why?
2. Trace the history of Bryn Mawr, Tuskegee Institute, or any other current or former single-sex or single-race school. How and why have the school's goals, curriculum, student body, and stature changed since the late 1800s?
3. Survey the role of either women's single-sex colleges or black colleges in higher education today.

The Expert
Images of Knowledge

Mark Gerzon

Mark Gerzon is a graduate of Harvard University, which has historically enjoyed a reputation for excellence. Its celebrated faculty members not only are scholars, but often are leaders in government, business, the sciences, technology, and the arts. For most of its history, Harvard only admitted mostly white, affluent men. While the makeup of its student body has changed dramatically in the last several decades, Harvard continues to attract the most sought-after students. But despite Harvard's stature, Gerzon argues that the educational elitism epitomized by Harvard continues to have detrimental consequences for students, for society, and for knowledge itself. His own experiences provide the springboard for his critical portrait of "the expert," one of the five archetypes of American masculinity that he describes in his 1982 book, *A Choice of Heroes.*

Journal Topics: (1) Explore your own assumptions, if any, about the differences between male and female areas of expertise. (2) Reflect on whether the content of your education and your role models have reinforced or challenged the concepts of male intellectual superiority and expertise. (3) How, if at all, have your own educational choices been influenced by your gender?

As You Read: (1) How does Gerzon link traditional masculinity and the concept of "the expert"? (2) How does this linkage influence what male students choose to study and their approach to learning? (3) How does this linkage affect our culture's view of female intellectual ability? (4) What evidence does Gerzon provide for a historical bias in favor of male intellectual superiority? (5) How has education mirrored and reinforced that bias?

Let it not be said, wherever there is energy or creative genius, "she has a masculine mind."

—Margaret Fuller, *Women in the Nineteenth Century,* 1845

Why is thinking something women never do?
Why is logic never even tried?

—Professor Henry Higgins in *My Fair Lady*

1   Several years ago, when I first started writing about masculinity, I considered it simply a subject that I intended to study. I began by reading American history and assumed that, with enough research, the pieces would fall into place. It was simply a question of supporting my argument with the relevant facts. If I had written such a book, I might indeed have known something about masculinity. But I would have learned nothing about myself.

2   Life intervened. I was asked to help create, and later to edit, a global newspaper called *WorldPaper.* It was a challenge that required all my energy and enthusiasm and took me from Cairo to Colombo, Bogotá to Beijing. Foolishly, I tried for a few months to work on this book during nights and weekends. It quickly became clear that I was losing touch with my children and my wife. That I was trying to write a book about the meaning of manhood only made it worse. How could I write about men's changing values at the price of betraying my own?

3   It hurt to abandon the book, but I had no choice. For three years, I thought the only work I was doing on it was to read an occasional book and to clip relevant articles. But I now realize that I was doing the most important work of all. I was learning that the subject was part of me. If I merely gathered information, reviewed the literature, organized my facts, and wrote down my findings, I would have been only another specialist who knew everything about his subject except his own stake in it.

4   Even after I realized the intimate connection between myself and my subject, I still tried to avoid exploring myself. I had illusions about my own masculinity that I did not want to give up, questions about my own behavior that I did not want to ask, and episodes in my own childhood I did not want to remember. The early drafts of this book are a study in self-evasion.

5   My difficulties, I think, reveal a common masculine dilemma. I was so eager to do my job—that is, to write this book—that I tried to avoid self-exploration. My subject was something "out there," an intellectual wilderness I had to master. It was too frightening to see that the uncharted terrain was inside me.

6   Why did I put the subject so far from my self? When did I begin to treat my emotions as if they were a liability rather than an asset to my intellect? What led me to divide myself into a part that knows and another part that feels? How had I learned to approach learning this way?

7   I was trying to answer these questions without success when my wife, Shelley, and I were asked to lead a workshop for high school teachers. Our job was to tell the teachers, who taught courses in family living and child development, about current

research and teaching methods concerning sex roles. After spending several evenings planning the workshop, Shelley and I thought we were well prepared.

8   As soon as we walked into the university seminar room, we realized that we had overlooked one obvious fact: of more than two dozen teachers, not one was male. And we learned, after taking a quick poll, that many of them did not have a single male student in their courses.

9   It dawned on me that older women were teaching younger women about changes in sex roles. The situation was so extreme that one teacher, whose course included an exercise in making a marriage contract, asked girls to play the role of husbands. She had no choice: the potential husbands were not there to play themselves. They were across the hall in their calculus or economics classes.

10   "If you can't get young men in your classes, you'll only reach half of the people who need to learn about this," I commented. "Why don't they take the courses you offer?"

11   "The problem is guidance counselors and parents," one teacher from a big urban high school replied. "They tell the boys not to waste time on these fluff courses. To get into college, they're better off taking math and physics, or even English. Not Family Living."

12   "At our school," said a teacher from a small private school, "we call the course Personal Survival. We try to teach some of the skills needed to live satisfying adult lives. But we have the same problem: boys won't take it. They want to take courses that will look better on their records."

13   In high school, I was just like them. I would not have been caught dead in Family Living. It was a mushy course for people with nothing better to do—in other words, girls. When I graduated, my mind was crammed full of facts: grammatical, historical, mathematical. I needed them to get high college board scores. I had never once been asked to study family structures, the pressures on marriage and the reasons for divorce, child rearing and child development, sexuality—or masculinity. These were not considered a necessary part of a young man's education.

14   College, unfortunately, often only reinforces this one-dimensional education. As a Harvard student in the sixties, I automatically considered myself an independent critical thinker. My classmates and I had no intention of mindlessly accepting tradition. We held that nothing was safe from our scrutiny. Certainly not Harvard. We questioned its relations with the Defense Department, admissions policies, dress codes, financial investments, community relations, racial biases, and everything else. Or so we thought.

15   As it turned out, I overlooked one issue entirely. I never once wondered why all of my professors were men. I never once considered the implications of being educated at a university that, even a decade later, had a tenured faculty with only 3 percent women.

16   At the height of the student movement, I wrote a book about the generation gap, published my senior year. I claimed to be writing about youth's dissent, and in some areas I did so thoughtfully. But as the book's opening paragraph revealed, my awareness of women's experience as something different from my own was almost

nonexistent. I wrote that I intended to describe the white, middle-class "generation of young people who were born after the Second World War." In the next phrase, however, I unconsciously switched to "young men." The book touches on women's experience only in the sections dealing with sex and marriage—that is, only when it mattered to men.

17 Today, the masculine mentality of the book is painfully apparent. I assumed that men were at the center of social change, women at the periphery. In retrospect, it is remarkable that no one criticized this shortcoming. The book won recognition from the American Library Association and was praised in newspapers throughout the country; I appeared on the *Today Show* and scores of other talk shows. And no one ever asked me what happened to the half of my generation that was not born male.

18 I suppose that I was no worse—and no better—than other men. That is why I remained so unaware of my intellectual prejudice against women. It fit. Like so many of my classmates, I arrived in Cambridge with the inbred notion that women were less intellectually motivated, if not less gifted, than we were. I was welcomed by an institution of higher learning that did not permit more than a handful of women to teach. I studied subjects in which men were always the professors and women, at best, section leaders or subordinate instructors. I assumed that women were less high-powered intellectually; certainly they seemed less ambitious and perhaps less capable. This assumption was never challenged during four years of Harvard's expensive tutelage.

19 When I recently returned to what paradoxically is called my alma mater, I was struck by the difference a decade can make. For the young men who study in those ivy-covered halls, such obtuseness is no longer possible. The Harvard man—and the intellectual style he represents—is being scrutinized. It made me think anew about the old one-liner: "You can always tell a Harvard man, but you can't tell him much." The humor seemed hollow.

20 "Harvard makes me so damn angry," a member of the interdepartmental Women Students' Coalition told me. "Harvard has an image of intellectual excellence and an image of femininity. The two are incompatible. The intellectual should be confident, aggressive, competitive. The woman should be supportive, helpful, accommodating. If you are a woman intellectual, the contradiction can be excruciating." She felt that men believe the true intellectual is always supposed to have an answer, to be in control. He was never supposed to say in wide-eyed amazement: "Wow, I never thought of that" or "I'm really confused about this." To do so was to admit ignorance and uncertainty. It was to appear vulnerable. For a Harvard man, this was bad form. He was always supposed to appear well informed even when he was not.

21 If you investigate any particular incident—from a professor's sexual harassment of a female student to the failure of a department to offer tenure to a qualified woman candidate—disputes quickly ensue. The accused professor will say the student acted seductively; the department chairman will say the rejected candidate had a difficult personality.

22 What is incontestable, however, are the numbers. In October 1980, the Women's Equity Action League (WEAL) filed a complaint against the Kennedy School of Government at Harvard with the Department of Labor's Office of Federal Contract

Compliance. The school's dean excused himself with the plea that the school had made every effort at compliance. But he could not deny the numbers. At the time the WEAL brief was filed, the school's faculty consisted of forty-four men and three women.

23 It is no coincidence that the target was the Kennedy School. Its offices are filled with former and would-be political insiders with far-reaching influence in all the halls of power. The presence of women is inversely related to proximity to power. The number of women declines as one travels up the academic pyramid. Today there are more women than men undergraduates in America's colleges. But men vastly outnumber women among junior faculty. The disproportion is even greater among senior faculty. And at the apex, among the deans of colleges and the heads of departments, women are rarely seen.

24 A few years ago, Harvard established the Women's Studies Committee. It encouraged faculty members to pay greater attention in their courses to issues pertaining to women. But, as is the custom, the chairman of the committee is a tenured faculty member (that is, male). When I asked the committee's coordinator whether she thought it would make much progress, she sighed. "It's going to be slow. Let's face it," she said. "Most white male faculty members, trained in their disciplines anywhere from fifteen to thirty years ago, are not interested in issues dealing with the study of women. And they are not about to become interested, either."

25 I wish I could have taken those "white male faculty members" to my tenth reunion last year. They would have been amazed at their former students' discussions. We who had been taught so much about economics and law, who were so well versed in literature and science, who had made names for ourselves in politics and the media, who were now at other schools and universities teaching the next generation—we talked more than anything else about our relations with women. We talked about how unprepared we were to start families, to be fathers as well as workers, to adapt to lovers or wives who were feminists. We talked about how much we had to learn as men, and how much we wished that we had started sooner.

26 Perhaps the most successful of my classmates is a lawyer in a prestigious New York firm. Everyone marveled at his quick rise in his profession. His brilliance is undisputed. Pitted against lawyers with twice his experience, he came out on top. But when I saw him, his inner sadness was so intense that it could not be concealed by his hearty handshake and greeting. He was in the midst of a divorce. He felt helpless. He had wanted his marriage to work "with all his heart," he told me, but his wife was inexplicably dissatisfied. She complained that he was distant, unresponsive, unreachable.

27 "She said to me, 'I can't live with a man who lives only in his head,'" he told me bitterly. "Now what the hell does that mean? We make love. We talk. We go out to dinner. What is she after?"

28 The attempt to consign women to intellectual inferiority is nothing new. It is at least as old as Aristotle. "The author of nature," wrote the father of Western logic, "gave man strength of body and intrepidity of mind to enable him to face great hardships, and to woman was given a weak and delicate constitution, accompanied by natural softness and modest timidity, which fit her for a sedentary life."

29   How did Aristotle know this? He knew it because he was an Expert.

30   At his best, the Expert pursues the truth—the fabled *veritas*. But at other times the Expert uses his mind to pursue power: power over nature and all its creatures, power over women and other men. Whoever knows more has power. In a technological world, the power of the mind is vital. Knowledge then is a weapon, a political tool. Those who have access to it have power; those who do not are powerless.

31   Unlike the true seeker of knowledge, the Expert is often more concerned with protecting his power than with establishing the truth. When others disagree, he tends to dismiss them as emotional or irrational. He will say that they do not have the facts or that they are biased. His attitude is condescending. His mind is powerful. It has made him indispensable. He is the Expert; he knows more.

32   "No person of the feminine sex has ever produced an original scientific work," wrote Auguste de Candolle, one of the first historians of science, in 1885. Woman's poor performance did not result from lack of opportunity. It was caused by the peculiarities of her mind, which "takes pleasure in ideas that are readily seized by a kind of intuition" and to which "the slow method of observation and calculation by which truth is surely arrived at are not pleasing." Woman's mind is also flawed by its "feeble independence of opinion" and its "horror of doubt." She is endowed with a "reasoning faculty less intense than in man." And so Candolle concluded: "These reasons are more than sufficient to explain the position of woman in scientific pursuits."

33   For centuries the Expert proceeded to defend his biases as objective fact. For decades scientists (that is, white middle-class men) measured the cranium, that exquisite casement of the human brain. After establishing that modern man had a larger brain than primitive man, they began to test other hypotheses. They struggled to establish scientifically that the white race had larger brains than the black, that men had larger brains than women. They assumed that bigger meant better.

34   They were impressed by the size of the zoologist Cuvier's brain (1830 grams), the novelist Turgenev's (2012 grams), and those of other intellectual giants. But they were shocked when more weighty brains (2269 and 2800 grams, respectively) were discovered that belonged to a retarded London newsboy and to an epileptic idiot.

35   The Expert revised the hypothesis. If women are not inferior because they have smaller brains, then they are inferior because they have *different* brains. Armed with their cranium counters, the men of science discovered that the frontal lobe—the region of the brain that performs higher intellectual processes—was more pronounced in men. This "proof" of male intellectual superiority was eventually discredited.

36   The search for differences in the brain continues today. Neurobiologists are now fairly certain that sex differences are caused by the action of hormones during embryonic development. It has long been known that an adult female rat, given male sex hormones soon after birth, will not exhibit typical mating behavior, nor will she ovulate. Similarly, an adult male rat that is castrated early in life will not act like a male even if it is later injected with testosterone, the male sex hormone. With photographs showing the differences between male and female rat brains, specialists now debate whether the differences are parallel in humans.

37   Assume that the differences exist. Assume, for example, that there are indeed sex differences in the distribution of synaptic connections of nerve cells in the preoptic area of the brain. Or assume, as does Julian Jaynes, that "mental abilities in women are spread over both the left and right hemispheres" and that "psychological functions in women are not localized into one or the other hemisphere of the brain to the same degree as men." Does that make women less or more intelligent than men? Does it render women more or less capable of making a scientific discovery or of running an organization?

38   The Expert's brilliance, and his blindness, is the paradox of our time. He has created a technological society, a society that has used technical knowledge to create wealth and power of unprecedented proportion. The Expert's technology has transformed every aspect of life: farming, medicine, business, communication, education, even the family. The Expert's domain is the growing knowledge industry, or what the economist John Kenneth Galbraith has called the "technostructure." It is the Expert's intellect, not his physical strength or courage, that makes him a hero. His frontier is knowledge; his weapon is data. His goal is to possess information and skills that are invaluable and that he can use to benefit himself, his employer, and, if possible, his society. His knowledge is essential to creating a livable future.

39   If the Expert used his talents to offer a unique part of himself to the world, it should not matter whether a woman does also. But if a man also uses his intellectual talents in order to make himself feel manly, then he will feel threatened if a woman has similar pursuits. Whether it is the scientist in his laboratory or the novelist at his typewriter (or, as we shall see, the minister in his pulpit), it should not matter if a woman is entitled to perform the same task. It should not matter, but it does.

40   From Aristotle onward, the Expert has considered the second sex to have a second-class intellect. In the past, the Expert often blamed the inferior performance of women's minds on their mysterious bodies. No one spoke with more authority about the ramifications of women's "weak and delicate" bodies than American doctors. In the nineteenth century, they seemed obsessed by a woman's body. The more they learned about the unique anatomical features in its hidden hollows, the more power they attributed to them.

41   According to a learned professor addressing an American medical society in 1870, it seemed that "the Almighty, in creating the female sex, had taken the uterus and built up woman around it." To cure women of their ailments—from backaches to nervous exhaustion to unruliness—physicians would probe the sexual interior. While denigrating midwives for their superstitious and folkloric methods, medical doctors would leech the uterus, inject it, cauterize it. It was a new frontier.

42   By 1906, one knowledgeable gynecological surgeon estimated that one hundred fifty thousand women in America had been separated from their ovaries by the surgeon's knife. The ovariotomy, boasted one of its staunch advocates, made the patient more "tractable, orderly, industrious and cleanly." In the Expert's informed judgment, this was how woman should behave.

43   Dr. J. Marion Sims was praised by his male peers as "the architect of the vagina." He was cited as one of "the three men who in the history of all times had done most

for their fellow men." His disciples called him the father of gynecology. He invented the speculum and, he says, "saw everything as no man had ever seen it before . . . I felt like an explorer in medicine who first views a new and important territory." Although he admitted that he "hated . . . investigating the organs of the female pelvis," Dr. Sims nevertheless chose to specialize in them.

44   According to the Expert, the uterus was the mind's worst enemy. Shortly after the Civil War, Dr. Edward H. Clarke of Harvard argued that higher education in "masculine" subjects (including science) would cause women's uteruses to atrophy. Such scholars were convinced that if women tried to use their brains as men did, they would destroy their femininity.

45   Even in the twentieth century, studies were conducted that "confirmed" the incompatibility of women and higher education. One such study showed that less than a third of female college graduates married compared to 80 percent of women in general. The renowned psychologist G. Stanley Hall found the educated woman to be the "very apotheosis of selfishness." By developing her brain rather than her uterus, she has "taken up and utilized in her own life all that was meant for her descendants."

46   "Beware!" warned one of these self-appointed Experts. "Science pronounces that the woman who studies is lost!" When the gifted writer Charlotte Perkins Gilman collapsed with a nervous disorder, she sought out the greatest nerve specialist in the country. His prescription: "Live as domestic a life as possible . . . And never touch pen, brush, or pencil as long as you live." Leave creativity to men, implied his patriarchal prescription, and be a housewife.

47   Had the Expert been more self-confident, and therefore more modest, he could have developed medical science quite differently. Instead of displacing midwives, for example, the Expert could have trained them to deliver babies. But doctors, proud of their new skills and new status, were not interested in sharing them with the women who traditionally assisted in childbirth. Instead, they emphasized that they, as professional men, were alone qualified to bring new children into the world. And they succeeded. In New York City, shortly after the turn of the century, three thousand midwives were still at work. By 1914, half of them were gone. By World War II, there were just over two hundred; by 1957, only two; and in 1963, the last midwife retired. The Expert had won: he alone was in charge of a woman's body. Unable to bear children himself, the Expert achieved the next best thing: power over those who could.

48   The antipathy toward women of these early medical scientists is still shared by much of the male scientific community, although it is expressed more subtly now. In James Watson's extraordinary account of the discovery of DNA, *The Double Helix,* only one woman is prominent among the scores of British and American scientists portrayed in its pages. Although Rosalind Franklin played a central role in this exciting scientific drama, Watson could speak of her only with derision. Listening to her lecture on her X-ray analysis of DNA, he talked of her "nervous style" and her lack of "warmth and frivolity." He wondered "how she would look if she took off her glasses and did something novel with her hair." It is the classic double bind: if she is not pretty, she is dismissed as unfeminine; if she is pretty, she is treated as a sex object. She could not be both feminine and a scholar.

49 ·   Only after Franklin's early death did Watson recognize how unfair he had been. He realized "years too late the struggles that the intelligent woman faces to be accepted by a scientific world which often regards women as mere diversions from serious thinking. Rosalind's exemplary courage and integrity were apparent to all when, knowing she was mortally ill, she did not complain but continued working on a high level until a few weeks before her death." With this posthumous praise, the Expert belatedly acknowledged that a woman, too, contributed to discovering the genetic code.

50   Now women scientists work in every area of research. But their distribution is peculiar: the highest percentage are in biological research; the next highest in chemical; and the lowest, in the physical sciences. As one biochemist put it: "The closer the work is to living organic process, the more women there seem to be." ...

51   If the hard sciences are dominated by men, one might guess that the softest sciences would be women's domain. Indeed, social sciences such as anthropology, psychology, and sociology—which involve the study of real human beings, their emotions and social bonds—are now studied and taught by many women. It is in these disciplines, not surprisingly, that so many feminists have found their professional homes. But the roots of social science, like science itself, are deeply rooted in sexual bias. Many of the seminal works of Western philosophy and social science are burdened with the Expert's distorted view of masculinity and femininity.

52   "What is truth to woman?" asked Friedrich Nietzsche. "From the beginning nothing has been more alien, repugnant and hostile to woman than truth—her great art is the lie." Woman's striving for equality, according to the author of *Beyond Good and Evil* and other landmarks of Western philosophy, is a sign of decadence, not progress. She should not become man's equal; she should fear man. For the woman who "unlearns fear surrenders her most womanly instincts."

53   *Woman is fearful; man intrepid.*

54   "The fundamental fault of the female character," wrote Arthur Schopenhauer, "is that it has no sense of justice ... women are defective in the powers of reasoning and deliberation."

55   *Woman is inferior; man, superior.*

56   "Woman's sensibility is rudimentary rather than highly developed," explained Émile Durkheim, whose works are respectfully studied in introductory sociology courses. "Society is less necessary to her because she is less impregnated with sociability ... very simple social forms satisfy all her needs. Man, on the contrary, needs others ... he is a more complex social being."

57   *Woman is simple; man, complex.*

58   "If there was nothing else to do but love ... woman would be supreme," concluded Auguste Comte, sometimes called the father of sociology. "But we have above everything else to think and to act ... therefore man takes the command ... woman's life is essentially domestic, public life being confined to men."

59   *Woman is emotional; man, decisive.*

60   Yes, according to the Expert, the intellect is clearly a masculine gift. Women are creatures of myth and superstition. When the Expert finally turned to the study of the human mind itself, he brought these deeply entrenched biases with him.

THE EXPERT • 329

61   Failing to substantiate men's supremacy through biology, the Expert turned to psychology. Women tend toward hysteria (from the Greek *hystera,* womb). By contrast, men are gifted with the creative intellectual force of life, our capacity for seminal thought, our *logos spermatikos.* It was with such logic that the premier and predominantly male science of the mind, psychoanalysis, began to study the predominantly female problem of hysteria.

62   The founder of psychoanalysis, Sigmund Freud, believed that "human beings consist of men and women and that this distinction is the most significant one that exists." He was careful not to let his profession seem biased, saying merely that "women are different beings—we will not say lesser, rather the opposite—from men." But in his revelations of his personal life, he threw self-restraint to the winds. Writing of his own courtship, he admitted, "If, for instance, I imagined my gentle girl as a competitor, it would end in my telling her, as I did seventeen months ago, that I am fond of her and implore her to withdraw from the strife into the calm uncompetitive activity of my home."

63   Some of his followers excuse Freud for his views on women by pointing out that he was only reflecting his time. But they underestimate their mentor's critical faculties. In fact, Freud was specifically opposed to women's equality and made a point of expressing this view. For instance, although he praised John Stuart Mill, the author of *On the Subjugation of Women,* as "perhaps the man of the century who best managed to free himself from the domination of customary prejudices," he took particular exception to Mill's views on women. The founder of psychoanalysis did not merely reflect his era's prejudices against women. He forthrightly endorsed them.

64   Feminists are now unsparing in their criticism of Freud. "Psychoanalysis," said one, "is a child of the hysterical woman." At least in one sense she was right. Modern psychiatry is a tool primarily in the hands of men and is used primarily on women. Almost nine out of ten of the American Psychiatric Association's twenty-five thousand members are men; two thirds of their patients are women. It all fits perfectly the traditional paradigm: men are Experts; women are not.

65   But the era of complacency is being challenged. "Is it possible that the issues raised around women cut deeper into American psychiatry than even racism and homosexuality?" asked Dr. Alan Stone, then president of the APA, in an address to its 1980 convention. "That the questions raised in connection with women touch our personal as well as our professional identity?" Later, speaking privately with a reporter, Stone said the answer to both questions was yes. "I believe psychiatrists, the majority of them, are still deeply convinced that a lot of the problems they see are the results of bad mothering," he continued. "A lot are deeply concerned that the women's movement attacks the traditional role of women that is central to mothering. That set of convictions runs deeper than many are willing to admit."

66   The arrogance of the Expert is not limited to science, whether soft or hard. If men had tried to bar women from science alone, they might have succeeded. They could have fooled women into believing that the study of man's universe was men's work, and that women should deal with the finer, more feminine pursuits of art, literature, and theater. But the Expert was not so gracious. He wanted to be in charge of those

fields, too. When the French Academy, founded in 1635, recently voted on whether or not to accept a distinguished writer as its first woman member, one man who voted nay explained: "A woman as a woman has simply no place in the academy. Of course, I have a great deal of admiration for her work. But it is like putting a dove in a rabbit hutch. Adding one inhabitant like that makes the place overpopulated." This illustrious French scholar willingly resorted to barnyard logic in order to keep a woman from sharing his honors. The Expert wants to keep women not only out of science, but out of any creative expression that leads to fame—or power.

67   Consider, for instance, art. Surely in the world of color and form we can expect to find creative women at work. Surely there we should find these fair creatures, so aesthetically aware, so attuned to color, so patient with detail, so habituated to confinement in the home, so endowed with leisure. Nothing seems more natural than the delicate hand of a woman, poised with brush in hand before an easel. Yet where in the museums of the world, where in the grand illustrated volumes of art history, are the women? Did they not exist, or have they been lost? They were caught, in Germaine Greer's phrase, in an "obstacle race." Until the nineteenth century, almost all women painters were related to men painters. It is their male relation whose paintings hang in the museums, whose names are indexed in the expensive art books.

68   Instead of compassion for the special obstacles faced by women artists and writers, the Expert tends to question their fitness. When Norman Mailer describes the novel as the "Great Bitch" and proceeds to list three dozen male writers who have "had a piece of her," his insecurity is obvious. His need to place himself above women becomes transparent when he gratuitously adds: "One cannot speak of a woman as having a piece of the Bitch." By reducing the writing of novels to screwing bitches, Mailer claims the creative act for men only. It is as if he feels compelled to eliminate half his competition in order to enhance his own claim to fame.

69   So the Expert claimed the arts as well as the sciences for himself. . . .

70   Even more striking, however, is how the Expert appointed himself the supreme authority on raising children. In the age of expertise, men assiduously avoided caring for children. That was women's work. Only men who were somehow unfit to do real work would allow themselves to be engaged in child care. In generation after generation, men left the care of young children to women while they went off to be Frontiersmen, Breadwinners, and Soldiers. Yet it was men who took the lead in the study of child development.

71   We must give the Expert credit. He is bold. Regardless of his ignorance, he is always ready to claim omniscience. "If a man wishes to raise the best grain or vegetables . . . all admit that he must study the conditions under which alone such things are possible," observed one turn-of-the-century male expert on child rearing. "But instinct and maternal love are too often assumed to be a sufficient guide for a mother."

72   What is needed, concluded the Expert, is a rational, systematic, scientific approach—devised, naturally, by men. It must be foolproof, because children will still be raised by women, not laboratories. "The home we have with us—inevitably and

inexorably with us," lamented John B. Watson, one of the early behaviorists, in his 1920s opus *The Psychological Care of the Infant and Child.* "Even though it is proven unsuccessful, we shall always have it. The behaviorist has to accept the home and make the best of it."

73   The slur is unmistakable. If only the (male) scientist rather than the mother could shape the family environment, children would develop into happier and finer human beings. No brilliant scientist stepped forward, however, to provide that care. While claiming superiority even in this, the most maternal sphere, men did not venture into it themselves. The Expert wants only to provide the theory; he will leave its practice to women.

74   In one of history's finer ironies, many men now find themselves with equal, if not sole, responsibility for their children's upbringing. Many of us are suddenly being thrust into the mother's role. On the sidelines, we were such experts. Thrown into the fray, our bravura disappears. The hero in Robert Miner's novel *Mother's Day,* for example, develops ulcers as soon as he takes over the responsibility for his two children. "Labor pains, perhaps, for mothers of my gender," he muses. Even the most mundane tasks, like carting kids with lunchboxes off to school, drives him crazy. For all our vaunted intelligence, we find ourselves incompetent to care for children. Like the father played by Dustin Hoffman in *Kramer vs. Kramer,* suddenly we are incapable of even making scrambled eggs.

75   That is one reason why the Expert wants to keep his distance from children: they do not reinforce his illusions about himself. He wants everyone to be enchanted by the power of his mind, the breadth of his knowledge. But children are unimpressed by lofty mental acrobatics. They want to be with people who care for them, who will enter their world. The Expert cannot. He is too busy being smarter, older, stronger, or more important. He cannot be with children because he has lost touch with the child in himself.

76   The Expert's knowledge about children has reached almost godlike proportions in the current abortion debate. No man in Washington has ever had an abortion or been pregnant. No man has experienced a baby growing within him that he did not want or could not care for. Yet when bills deciding who can or cannot have abortions are written, debated, and passed in Congress, the actors are virtually all men. Calling themselves pro-life, they are, once again, playing the Expert. They will decide at what moment life begins. They will discover the instant of the soul's inception. They will decide which women should give birth and which should not. They will be masters of the womb.

77   When the Expert leaps to the defense of the unborn, he tells himself that his motives are rooted in fatherly love. Indeed, he portrays himself as the savior of the helpless child-to-be, nobly pitting himself against the irresponsible mother and the amoral abortionist. But if the Expert's concern were truly for the child's welfare, why would his concern end so abruptly as soon as the child is born? Why would he cut welfare payments to poverty-stricken families, thus jeopardizing a child's health? Why would he allow infant formula to be promoted aggressively in the Third World,

causing widespread disease and death? Why would he slash school lunch programs, which are the only hot meal of the day for many poor children? And why, finally, would he undercut young women's access to birth control, without which unwanted pregnancies are inevitable? . . .

WRITING ASSIGNMENTS

Analysis

1. According to Gerzon, how do the values of traditional masculinity influence how male students learn and what they choose to study?
2. Gerzon quotes a member of Harvard's interdepartmental Women Students' Coalition as saying, "Harvard has an image of intellectual excellence and an image of femininity. The two are incompatible." Does this attitude exist at your school? Why? Among whom? How is it expressed? How is it challenged?
3. Define an "intellectual" and illustrate your definition with specific examples.
4. According to Gerzon, how has the assumption of male intellectual superiority affected the development of specific professions and academic disciplines?

Argument

1. Gerzon observes, "The presence of women is inversely related to proximity to power. The number of women declines as one travels up the academic pyramid." He argues that this situation reflects a pervasive cultural bias in favor of men and a specific cultural assumption of male intellectual superiority. Explain why you agree or disagree with his analysis.
2. Does Gerzon's analysis of why so few women occupy positions of power apply to other historically marginalized groups as well? Might other factors than "cultural bias" partially explain why women and members of minority groups remain largely excluded from power?
3. Gerzon describes himself as a typical product of an elite school: a successful male. Despite Harvard's prestige, why does he judge his education to have been "one-dimensional" and therefore inadequate? Do you agree with him?
4. Are Gerzon's assertions about the male educational experience generally accurate, or do they primarily reflect the experience of white middle- or upper-middle-class men?

Personal Writing and Writing from Research

1. *Collaborative Project:* Expanding on the data Gerzon provides, write a research paper tracing the history of attitudes concerning the differences between male and female intellectual ability.
2. Survey the coverage in popular literature (trade books and magazines) in recent years of one or more specific biological differences in male and female brains and the possible implications of such differences. How does this research influence the debate over male and female intellectual abilities? If

possible, assess how accurately the popular accounts reflect the scientific findings as they were reported in scholarly journals or books.

3. In a research paper based primarily on an examination of television, magazine, and newspaper advertisements, assess whether the role of the masculine "expert" remains influential in American popular culture.

4. Trace the changes in curriculum, course content, and canonical readings in one academic discipline during the last 30 years.

Scholarly Studies of Men
The New Field Is an Essential Complement to Women's Studies

Harry Brod

Since 1982, Harry Brod has held a joint appointment in the Program for the Study of Women and Men in Society and the Department of Philosophy at the University of Southern California. He is the editor of *The Making of Masculinities: The New Men's Studies* (1987). A frequent lecturer and men's movement activist, he has been a national spokesperson for the National Organization for Changing Men. "Scholarly Studies of Men" appeared in *The Chronicle of Higher Education* in March 1990.

Journal Topics: (1) Briefly describe what you know, have heard, or assume about "men's studies." (2) How might men's studies be related to or differ from the men's movement or men's rights? (3) What might be the relationship between men's studies and women's studies? (4) What might be the benefits or drawbacks of having a men's studies program on your campus?

As You Read: (1) To what audience is Brod's argument most directly addressed? What objections does he anticipate and respond to? (2) According to Brod, what is the value of men's studies to men, to women, and to scholarship generally?

1   In something of a turn of the tables, scholars in women's studies are having to decide what to do about a new field that is emerging in academe. The new kid asking to enter the club is "men's studies."

2   For some feminist scholars, the phenomenon seems either preposterous or dangerous, or more likely both. After all, the traditional curriculum that women's studies sought to reform was, in essence, men's studies. Other feminists, however, believe that the new field of men's studies is really a welcome extension of feminism's intellectual

insights into hitherto male terrain. I believe that the field of men's studies is not only compatible with women's studies, but also an essential complement.

3   Men's studies begin by accepting as valid feminism's critique of traditional scholarship for its androcentric bias in generalizing from men to all human beings. The field adds the perspective that this bias not only excludes women and/or judges them to be deficient, but also ignores whatever may be specific to men *as men,* rather than as generic humans. The field also invokes feminist concepts that "gender" is not natural difference, but constructed power, to argue that the multiple forms of masculinities and femininities need to be re-examined.

4   The field of men's studies, for most of us anyway, thus is rooted in a feminist commitment to challenge existing concepts of gender. The debate within our still-nascent field over that commitment, however, has made some feminists skeptical about our entire enterprise. They see in the call for a new "gender studies" focused on both men and women the possibility that women's priorities and standpoints will again be subsumed and ignored under generic labels. Other feminists, though, find that the idea of a broadly conceived "gender studies," in which "gender" describes power and not just difference, does reflect the underlying conceptualization of their field. We should recognize, however, that the meaning of terms is still in flux. At my own institution, for example, our current solution is to develop a program in "Women's and Gender Studies."

5   Feminists' legitimate fear of once again having women's discourse subordinated to men's should not blind us to the very real and much-needed intellectual project that the field of men's studies is undertaking. To simplify a more extended argument, I believe the field is an essential complement to women's studies because neither gender ultimately can be studied in isolation. Gender is, itself, a relational concept: Masculinities and femininities are not isolated "roles," but contested relationships.

6   But it does not follow from my argument for men's studies as an intellectual enterprise that the field must be established in any particular form in academic institutions. Such decisions should be made by women in women's studies. And any efforts to divert resources from women's studies to men's studies must be resisted; funds for the new men's studies must come from the old.

7   The new field has important implications for scholarship. For example, many explanations of the "gender gap" in political voting patterns have failed to see that it takes two to make a gap. Having noted the appearance of a "gap," social scientists have rushed to explain the changes in women that have produced it. Yet some of the evidence shows that the gap was produced more by a shift in men's than in women's political identification and voting patterns. By trying to understand the mutability and diversity of masculinities, men's studies avoid the pitfall of associating change only with women while assuming male constancy—a sexist bias.

8   By pointedly taking up the question of power relations among men in addition to those between the sexes, the new field also allows for a more differentiated conception of patriarchy. For the power of the real and symbolic father is not simply that of male over female, but also that of heterosexual over homosexual, one generation over

another, and other constellations of authority. The field forces us to ask, Why does society privilege some men over others, even as it gives all men power over women? Why do so many of our founding myths contain fathers willing to kill their sons—the violence committed and permitted by Abraham against Isaac, Laius against Oedipus, the Christian God the Father against Jesus?

9   Further, the field of men's studies is not simply calling for sensitivity to diversity, though it surely does that, but also tries to apply an understanding of difference gained from radical feminism to men, arguing that sexuality is as socially constructed as identity. The field therefore is also forging special links to gay studies.

10   Two current phenomena show the need for men's studies to transcend a white, middle-class origin and orientation: the large number of suicides among Vietnam-era veterans and the huge number of college-age black men in prison rather than in college. When we speak of men's issues, there really is more to consider than the existential anxieties of middle-aged, middle-class executives and fathers, popular media treatments notwithstanding.

11   A final example from my own experience highlights the way feminism has helped me to ask new questions about men. I have noticed in recent years that many of the female political activists I know have devoted increasing attention to women's issues, for example moving from the peace movement to the women's peace movement or from environmentalism to the fusion of ecological and feminist concerns called ecofeminism.

12   At first, I simply contrasted this to the conventional wisdom that people become more conservative, *i.e.,* more "mature," with age. But I also recalled that the women's movement has been said to differ from others precisely because its members tend to become more radical as they age; it took only brief reflection to identify the conventional dictum as a male norm. Accordingly, I then asked myself what it was about women's lives that made them different. As I was coming up with various plausible answers I suddenly caught myself. I realized that I was committing the usual error of looking only to women to explain difference. In fact, as I started to see, if one believes as I do that there is validity in various radical social critiques, then the women's pattern should be the norm, as life experiences increasingly validate early perceptions of biased treatment of certain groups. Thus the question should not be, "What happens to women to radicalize them?" but rather "What happens to men to deradicalize them?" That question, more for men's studies than for women's studies, can open up fruitful areas of inquiry.

13   Indeed, I believe that any strategy for fundamental feminist transformation requires a more informed understanding of men. By exposing and demystifying the culture of male dominance from the inside out, the field of men's studies offers both women and subordinated men the empowerment such knowledge brings.

14   By elucidating the many and varied prices of male power—the drawbacks and limitations of traditional roles—the field helps motivate men to make common cause with feminist struggles, though not, it must be said, on the basis of any simple cost-benefit analysis, since the price men pay still purchases more than it pays for.

15   The field of men's studies, then, emerges not as some counterweight or corrective to women's studies, but as the extension and radicalization of women's studies. For it is the adoption of thoroughly women-centered perspectives, taking women as norm rather than "other," that helps us ask new questions about men.

WRITING ASSIGNMENTS

Analysis

1. Identify and explain the intellectual assumptions and positions on which men's studies, as described by Brod, are based.
2. Explain why "taking up the question of power relations among men in addition to those between the sexes" expands our understanding not only of patriarchy, but also of the diversity among men and of various masculinities.
3. Brod says, "For it is the adoption of thoroughly women-centered perspectives, taking women as norm rather than as 'other,' that helps us ask new questions about men." What does it mean to take men or women as the "norm"? Explain how doing either might affect our perspective on work, on health issues, on law, or on sexuality.
4. Define the audience that Brod addresses, identify the objections that he anticipates, and explain why he addresses his argument to this audience.
5. What is the value of men's studies to men, to women, or to scholarship generally?

Argument

1. Explain why you agree or disagree with Brod that men's studies are an essential complement to women's studies.
2. Take a position on whether a men's studies program like the one envisioned by Brod would or would not appeal to male undergraduates.

Personal Writing and Writing from Research

1. Develop a research topic on men after consulting *The Making of Masculinities,* edited by Brod. This anthology contains articles on men's history, biology, work, play, relationships, and images in literature.
2. In a personal essay, explore the extent to which your world view is "woman-centered" or "man-centered," and explain the consequences of your perspective.

Test Drive

Myra and David Sadker

Professors at The American University in Washington, DC, Myra and David Sadker have been involved in training programs to combat sexism and sexual harassment throughout the United States and overseas. They have directed many federal equity grants and written more than 75 articles and 6 books including *Failing at Fairness: How America's Schools Cheat Girls* (1994), from which "Test Drive" is taken.

Journal Topics: (1) Describe your experiences preparing for, taking, or receiving your scores for either the SAT or ACT. (2) What do you think these and other standardized tests measure? (3) Do you believe these tests are accurate and fair?

As You Read: (1) Why are these tests important to students, their families, schools, and society? (2) What are the consistent patterns in test scores? (3) Why does the origin of the SAT contribute to doubts about the fairness and accuracy of standardized tests?

1   From middle school to medical school, girls and women face a testing gender gap that denies them the best educational programs and prizes. Lower test scores block females in disproportionate numbers from the finest colleges and the most prestigious graduate schools and professions. This gender gap is especially startling because of the early advantage girls hold, but around middle school their scores begin a steady decline. It is one of the costliest falls suffered in education, yet few people notice. Females are the only group in America to begin school testing ahead and leave having fallen behind. That this dive has received so little national attention is a powerful reminder of the persistence and pervasiveness of sexism in school.

2   The only test where the female drop-off has received publicity is the Scholastic Aptitude Test (SAT), recently renamed the Scholastic Assessment Test, which is required for admission to most colleges. On this critical exam, boys typically receive scores that are 50 to 60 points higher. In fact, this gender gap is so predictable it has become an accepted feature of the educational landscape. Few people talk about the SAT gender gap; fewer still are angry or upset. We cannot help but wonder if the reaction would be different if females were in the SAT driver's seat, and males watched as their college choices vanished in a trail of dust left by high-scoring young women.

3   As we investigated these testing troubles, we discovered it is far more than an SAT issue. Critical tests at every level of education short-circuit girls and women. The more we researched, the more concerned we became. We were surprised by what we found, but unlocking the information was not easy.

4   When we requested male and female scores from the companies that produce America's tests, we struck a bureaucratic wall. While a few companies were cooperative, others demanded detailed, written explanations of our intentions. We felt as if we were violating some official government secrets act. Some companies claimed they kept no record of test scores by gender, while others stated flat out that they had the information but would not release it. The persistence of our graduate students, who tenaciously refused to be put off by outright refusal or evasive answers, and the cooperation of organizations such as FairTest in Cambridge, Massachusetts, were critical to uncovering the information presented in this chapter.

REVERSAL OF FORTUNE

5   Five-year-old Jessica came home from kindergarten smiling broadly, eager to share her latest achievements. Her mother, an attorney, was curious:

6   "What did you do in school today?"

7   "I learned to bubble."

8   "You blew bubbles? Did you have fun?"

9   "I didn't blow bubbles. I bubbled. I practiced filling in the little test bubbles with my pencil. You know, not going outside the lines and coloring in the whole bubble."

10   Jessica attends a school in Washington, D.C., but her lesson could have been in almost any school in America. The typical student, in Jessica's terms, bubbles three times every year. Some students undergo as many as twelve standardized tests annually, and each year more states require still more tests—enough to support a billion-dollar-a-year industry.

11   When standardized test scores from schools around the country are collected and analyzed, they provide a national picture of American education, one that brings into focus academic success and failure. This school portrait reveals the extraordinary reversal of fortune experienced by many girls and women as their initially promising test scores falter and tumble.

12   Among the nation's many test "photographers," one of the best known is the National Assessment of Educational Progress. Often called the "Nation's Report Card," the NAEP has been taking academic snapshots of America's students since 1969. Funded by the federal government, the National Assessment tests nine-, thirteen-, and seventeen-year-olds in several different subjects. Unlike the SAT exam, which develops academic pictures of only the college-bound, the National Assessment offers information on a sample of all students during elementary, middle, and senior high school. It is through this and other national tests that we learn how well girls begin their school careers and what happens with each year's promotion to a new grade.

13   Girls begin school looking like the favored sex. They outperform boys on almost every measure. Most people are aware of their verbal advantage and their reading and writing skills. Fewer realize that in these early years girls also surpass boys on math and social studies tests; in fact, they surpass boys on every standardized test in every academic area except science, where boys hold a slight advantage. If tests offer the

nation a school photograph, they depict elementary school girls as capable and looking toward a promising future.[1]

14   Female test scores begin to descend around middle school when the girls are overtaken by the boys. Girls' test scores continue their downward slide throughout the rest of their education. In science, the small lead enjoyed by elementary school boys widens in middle school and is further expanded in high school. The longer girls stay in school, the further behind they fall, especially in the critical areas of mathematics and science.[2]

15   The National Assessment of Educational Progress displays a familiar school picture, one with a commonly accepted gender divide: boys overtaking girls in math and increasing their superiority in science, and girls maintaining an advantage in reading and writing.[3] But not all tests draw this widely accepted division. In fact, the most important tests paint a much more depressing portrait.

16   In October of their junior year, college-bound students take a scaled-down version of the SAT called the Preliminary Scholastic Assessment Test, or PSAT. This test also gives students an opportunity to win college scholarships. The results of the PSAT are used to select winners of the prestigious National Merit Scholarships, and many states and colleges also use PSAT scores in awarding scholarships of their own. For example, a student from Maryland who scores well on the PSAT will find tuition to any Maryland college or university reduced by $3,000. So high scores on this test can be both a boost for a student's self-esteem and an economic windfall.

17   Modeled on the SAT, the PSAT serves as an early indicator of the winners and losers in the great SAT contest soon to follow. The test is similar to the SAT, with both math and verbal questions, but it is much shorter. Timing is vital for success on both the PSAT and the SAT. Students have only a minute or less to spend on each question. They must move quickly to attain a strong score.

18   The PSAT is the first national peek into the future. For girls it is a frightening preview. Boys score so much higher than girls on the PSAT that two out of three Merit semifinalists are male. PSAT results are like a fire bell in the night, and the developer of the test, the Educational Testing Service (ETS), knows it. ETS tackles this disturbing problem head-on; it rigs the scoring in an attempt to reduce the gender gap. ETS counts the PSAT verbal score twice and the math score only once. By giving twice the weight to verbal performance, traditionally an area of female strength, ETS officially recognizes the impact of gender-based scoring differences. All this effort still does not result in equal male and female performance. While eighteen thousand boys reach the highest PSAT categories, only eight thousand girls attain them.

19   Doubling verbal scores reduces but does not eliminate the gender gap because boys outscore girls on *both* the verbal and the math sections of the PSAT. Without this adjustment, the dramatic male lead in mathematics would create an even greater difference. But the PSAT is only the opening act. The main event—the SAT—is only a few months away.[4]

20   Handicappers would have to spot girls about 60 points to make the SAT an even bet. Most Americans are not surprised to learn that males typically outscore females by approximately 50 points on the math section. The fact that boys also surpass girls

on the verbal section is less well known. Actually, males' verbal SAT scores add another 8, 10, or 12 points to their overall testing lead. In the public mind the smaller male lead on the verbal section has become misconstrued as a female advantage. It's not. The SAT is a clean male sweep, one for which the lower-scoring girls pay dearly.

21   The SAT is one of life's memorable markers. Twenty or thirty years after the SAT scores arrive in the mail and the envelope is opened, people recall the wave of pain or joy or bewilderment the information brought. Test scores label students, put a value on intellect, classify brain power, expose the unseeable—just how smart someone really is or isn't. Most believe these test scores are a truer reflection of their real intelligence than report card grades.

22   Boys looking into the SAT mirror see in it an image bigger than life. Girls see less than is really there. After taking the SAT, they may wonder if their excellent school grades were given for hard work rather than real intelligence. Or perhaps their higher grades were only the teacher's "thank you" for their quiet, cooperative behavior. After all, report card grades are just the teacher's opinion. The SAT, on the other hand, is objective, scientific, national. Girls are persuaded by the impressive SAT printout that compares them to a million of their peers that the scores are tangible proof of their worst fear: They really aren't as smart as they had hoped. They begin to think that maybe they don't deserve to get into that selective college after all.

23   The SATs send an even more devastating message to minority girls. With the exception of Asian-American test takers, minority students do not perform as well on the SATs as white students, a fact as well known as it is troubling. Less well known is that within each racial or ethnic group, minority girls consistently score behind minority boys. For example, girls whose families are originally from Asia, Mexico, or Puerto Rico score approximately 50 points lower than boys from these areas. Girls of Latin American origin face the largest gap on the SAT: Boys score an average of 62 points higher. For Native Americans the gender gap is 46 points, and for African-Americans the gap is narrowest at 19 points. Regardless of ethnic or racial background, all American girls share a common bond: a gender gap in test performance that leaves them behind the boys.

24   Although the SAT receives the most publicity, it is not the only college admission test. In many areas, especially the Midwest, more than a million students take the American College Testing Program, the ACT. This test is described not as an aptitude measure but as an assessment of academic achievement. It evaluates students in four areas: English, mathematics, the natural sciences, and reading. To create questions directly measuring what students learn in school, ACT test makers analyze textbooks and interview teachers. Since girls attain better grades in class work, many anticipate that they should achieve similar success on the ACT.

25   Girls do perform better on the ACT than on the SAT. They score almost a full point higher than boys on the English section of the ACT, but on the rest of the test, boys are ahead, from a small lead in reading to more than one full point on both the math and science sections. Even on a test designed to mirror school learning, boys' composite scores are higher and the gender gap persists.

26   While almost college-bound students engage in an academic duel with either the SAT or the ACT, a smaller group confronts an additional challenge, the achievement

tests. Unlike the SATs, these one-hour, multiple-choice exams gauge not general aptitude but academic accomplishment in more than a dozen subject areas, from mathematics to science, from foreign language to history. The most selective colleges and universities require students to take three achievement tests along with the SAT. One would expect that girls would do better on these tests, which, like the ACT, are based on class work. They don't.

27   The achievement tests are a male landslide. In 1992 boys registered higher scores on eleven of the fourteen achievement tests. Girls performed better on only three. While boys typically overshadowed girls by more than 30 points, the girls averaged only 4 points higher on the three tests. In 1992 the largest gender gap was in physics (62 points), but the year before it had been in European history (60 points). In fact, males led in almost all fields: the sciences, social sciences, math, and even most languages. Boys averaged 46 points higher in chemistry and 33 points higher in biology. On the two math achievement tests, the size of the gender gap was consistent: 37 points in Math I and 38 points in Math II. In American history the gap was 25 points; in Latin, 28; in French, 12; in Hebrew, 8; and in Spanish, 3. Girls were in the driver's seat on only three tests: German (3 points), English composition (3 points), and literature (6 points).

28   When the achievement test results arrived in our office, we began recording the scores and graphing the gender gap. One of our graduate students, a young woman from England, watched with growing amazement as the bar graph emerged. Soon a cluster of graduate students, all female, gathered to watch as the size of each gender gap was recorded. "This is unbelievable," whispered one. The others nodded silently, at last realizing why their own scores had not lived up to expectations. The size of the gender gap on achievement tests was shocking new information even to students studying for graduate and doctoral degrees.

29   After students are admitted to colleges, the importance of tests is not diminished. College and university women realize that standardized tests hold the key—or shut the door—to graduate programs, professional schools, future careers, and economic prospects. In these times of runaway college grade inflation, graduate schools have learned to accept extraordinarily high grade point averages with a great deal of skepticism, relying on standardized tests to assist graduate admission and scholarship decisions.

30   The test most often required for entrance to graduate and doctoral programs is the Graduate Record Examination, or GRE, an older sibling of the SAT and one that bears a remarkable family resemblance. The GRE has three sections: verbal, quantitative, and analytical. As in the SAT, 200 is the lowest possible score and 800 is perfect. And as in the SAT, on all sections women score lower than men.

31   As test takers grow older, the gender gap grows wider. In 1987–88, the last year the Educational Testing Service published information on GRE scores, males scored a jolting 80 points higher than females on the quantitative math section, a substantially larger advantage than they enjoyed on the SATs. Men scored 21 points higher than women on the verbal section and 26 points higher on the analytical section. Although the SAT gender gap is substantial, the 127-point male lead on the GRE is larger still. And as on the SAT, there are performance differences among racial and

ethnic groups. As of 1988 most minorities continued to score below the GRE average, a gap ranging from 200 to more than 500 points. The one exception was Asian-Pacific Americans; their total score was only slightly below the average, but their math score was the highest of any group. Within each of these racial and ethnic groups, males continued to outperform females. For whites, Native Americans, as well as students from Mexican and Puerto Rican backgrounds, males enjoyed more than a 100-point advantage. Smaller gender gaps were registered by African-Americans (79 points) and Asian-Pacific Americans (59 points).

32   The size of the gender gap on the GREs was a shock, and it made us even more curious to see the scores on the GRE subject area tests. Like the SAT achievements, the GRE offers in-depth assessments in subjects from sociology to engineering, from geology to literature, and these tests are required for admission to many graduate programs. Did the gender gap on the SAT achievements reappear in the GRE subject fields, or perhaps even increase? We can only speculate. Although we made several requests, we were not allowed to see these scores.

33   Persuading testing companies to release scores posed a constant challenge. The last reported results for the basic GRE were in 1988, and we therefore requested more recent scores for this exam. After repeated phone calls, we were finally allowed to listen over the phone to a summary of more recent GRE test scores but only if we agreed not to publish them. We are honor-bound not to print what we heard, but the information we received did not make us optimistic about options for women.

34   Standardized tests are also crucial in the competitive race for access to professional schools, including law, medicine, and business. Only a few points on these tests can mean the difference between acceptance and rejection, scholarships and a future of debt. These professional tests differ in content and approach, but they share a common thread: Women score lower than men on all of them.

35   As law has become a popular professional choice, college graduates flock in increasing numbers to testing sites for the Law School Admission Test (LSAT). The LSAT measures logical and analytical reasoning, reading comprehension, and writing. Although there is no separate math section, there is a gender gap. The LSAT has been scored on a scale from 10 to 48. In 1991 men averaged 33.3 and women 32.4, typical of the modest but persistent male advantage on this exam. Like so many standardized tests, the LSAT is out of step with the grades that men and women receive in college. A man with a C average in college registered a 29 on the LSAT, while a woman with the same C average attained only 25.7. A man with an A− grade point average typically scored 38.8, while the A− woman's score was 37.1. At every level, when women and men earned the same grade point average, the female applicant to law school had her chances diminished by a lower LSAT score.

36   During the past decade, business schools have also seen a hefty increase in applications. The Graduate Management Admission Test (GMAT) is used in admission decisions by almost a thousand graduate business schools. The GMAT includes reading comprehension, English usage, and math problems, and it reports scores on a scale ranging from 200 to 800, with 500 the average. In 1991 women were below the midpoint, averaging 477, while men were above, at 504.

37   The most challenging graduate-level exam is the Medical College Admission Test (MCAT), which runs from 8:30 A.M. to 5:00 P.M. The $140 admission fee buys 221 questions in verbal reasoning, physical sciences, biological sciences, and writing skills. Although most of the questions are multiple choice, two thirty-minute essays are also required. On a scale ranging from 3 to 45, the typical female score is 22.5 while the average male score is more than 24. In the fight for limited medical school openings, especially at the most prestigious schools, each point is critical. The MCAT, the LSAT, and in fact the vast majority of these tests act as unseen trip wires, making women stumble just as they are about to cross the threshold into America's elite and lucrative professions.

38   While writing this chapter, we often found ourselves wishing there was a Consumer's Guide to Tests, one that would inform the public about the gender gap. There isn't, but it is possible to make some comparisons. To do this we obtained the last year of available test scores (1987–88 for the GREs, 1991 and 1992 for all others) and converted these scores into percentages. Comparing these percentages enables us to measure the size of the gender gap on each test. Women who apply to graduate and doctoral programs using the GRE face the greatest test obstacle, while women applying to optometry school score only slightly below male applicants. Women striving for admission to America's most advanced or competitive graduate and professional programs continue to be harmed by the gender gap in standardized testing. In many ways it is gifted girls and women who are hurt the most.

VISIBLE CEILING

39   The test ceiling first materializes in preadolescence when talented girls compete for a limited number of openings in special summer programs for the gifted. Tests are often the tollgate to these elite programs. In New Jersey's selective summer enrichment program in science and social science, PSAT scores determine who will be admitted and who will be denied. It is not unusual to have sixty-five boys but only thirty-five girls chosen to participate. Johns Hopkins University's prestigious Center for Talented Youth (CTY) selects participants based on SAT scores earned by fifth, sixth, and seventh graders. At every level more males than females pass the admission test. In 1992 a total of 5,882 males but only 4,612 females qualified. Ironically, many of these programs offer classes on how to improve test scores, lessons that high-scoring boys have already mastered.[5]

40   But if failure brings penalty, success is suspect. When girls are admitted to elite programs and schools, their achievement is questioned, trivialized, and dismissed. One girl who was accepted to a top magnet high school for math and science confided: "When I got in here, the parents of boys who didn't make it were very upset with me. They said, 'You got in because you were part of a quota. They had to have a certain number of girls so they took you.'"

41   When scholarships are awarded, girls are once again sent the message they don't belong, this time with a price tag attached. More than one hundred scholarship

programs rely on standardized tests to select recipients. Few are more prestigious than the National Merit Scholarship Program, which awards over eighty-five hundred college scholarships based on PSAT scores. There is a temptation to rename these winning students National Magnet Scholars since they attract interest and dollars from so many colleges.

42   Although we already knew that girls do less well on both the PSAT and the SAT, we were interested in learning how many girls were admitted to the magic circle of National Merit Semifinalists. The National Merit Corporation in Evanston was pleased to tell us that more than fifteen thousand students annually make the semifinalist round, and about half of them win scholarships. We learned that the National Merit Board awards two thousand of these scholarships, and the rest come from corporate and college sponsors. What we did not learn was how many girls qualified. When we asked how many girls and boys were identified as semifinalists, we were transferred to another office. Then another office. Then a third office. Finally, the public information office told us that they didn't have that information, but we persisted. After all, every test contains a box that the student checks to indicate male or female; in the stressful world of standardized testing, this may be one of the few questions most students answer with confidence.

43   "Don't you ask students to indicate their gender?" we asked.

44   "Well, yes," the information officer responded, "but we don't use that information. The College Board does in New York. Perhaps they can help you."

45   The College Board, awash in statistics, was also stumped by our question. "We really aren't equipped to do research here. All that information is in Princeton at the Educational Testing Service."

46   The people at ETS were friendly and acknowledged that they did have gender information: "Colleges buy our mailing lists to send out recruitment information. They ask for the sex of each applicant so that they can properly address their recruitment letters. But we really don't track how well males and females do in qualifying for the National Merit awards. We do publish the names of the finalists, so you could count how many males and females there are."

47   "But there are over fifteen thousand names each year. That's a lot to count."

48   "Yes, I know. And some of the foreign names are difficult to sort out. Sorry."

49   Our next call was to FairTest, the Cambridge, Massachusetts, organization that tracks test statistics, numbers that seem to elude the test makers.

50   "You were rubberwalled," said Bob Schaffer of FairTest. "They redirect your calls from one place to another, bouncing you from office to office until you tire out and give up. Of course they have that information. They just hide it. I have the numbers here. Last year girls did the best in a long time, with about thirty-seven percent becoming semifinalists. Typically, boys win at least sixty percent of the semifinalist slots. There're always a few percent unaccounted for. They have that information, they just run you into walls made of rubber instead of stone."[6]

51   High test scores unlock scholarship dollars at 85 percent of the private colleges and nearly 90 percent of public institutions, and they can result in state grants as well. In Wisconsin, for example, scores on the SAT or ACT exams as well as grade

point averages are used to select All-State Academic Scholars. More than a hundred students receive $1,500 scholarships each year based on their grades and test scores. Even with grades thrown into the mix, the majority of Wisconsin winners, from 60 percent to 65 percent, are male. Actually, the inequity is really more extreme than it appears since boys make up only 35 percent to 40 percent of the students nominated by teachers for these awards. FairTest and others charge that such results, which are not atypical, prove test bias.[7] Not everyone is ready to blame the exams, but as more people learn about the inequitable distribution of scholarship dollars, opposition is growing to the practice of using standardized tests to decide who will win awards. New York State is a case in point.

52   New York offers an impressive twenty-six thousand academic scholarships each year. In 1988, using SAT and ACT scores, New York awarded 72 percent of its Empire State Scholarships and 57 percent of its Regents Scholarships to boys. The American Civil Liberties Union and others charged that this method of awarding scholarships was discriminatory, and federal judge John Walker agreed, writing: "SAT scores capture a student's academic achievement no more than a student's yearbook photograph captures the full image of her experiences in high school."[8] This decision legally limiting the use of standardized tests for scholarship awards is likely to spark other court cases in other states. While the legal process runs its course, boys will continue to garner the lion's share of scholarships, and girls will continue to lose out.

53   Scholarship dollars provide a tangible ledger sheet of the cost paid by girls and women because of the gender gap in standardized tests.[9] Less tangible but perhaps even more damaging is the psychological price. Low scores are mentally locked away, rarely revealed. A woman in one of our graduate courses finally gained enough confidence in her academic ability to share her SAT secret with her classmates:

> I took the PSAT when I was a sophomore in high school. I scored a 710 combined. My parents had always been proud of how bright I was—until those scores arrived. They never thought I was smart again.
>
> I remember I had a date that weekend with a boy I really liked. He asked me what I got on the PSAT. I told him 710, and he said, "That's great! What did you get on the math?" I was so humiliated, I made up a score.

54   Poor test performance can be hidden from others but not from the test takers themselves. A low score is a lifelong brand, a never-ending reminder of intellectual weakness; it is a stop sign, quietly directing students away from prestigious programs and demanding careers and steering them instead on a path of lower expectations and fewer choices. It is a path more likely to be traveled by gifted and competent women.

55   Students who remember SAT scores with the greatest pain are the girls at the top of the class. A high school girl with an A+ grade point average typically scores 83 points lower than a boy with an A+ average. The more talented and competent the girl, the greater the gender gap. Perhaps that is why test results hit smart girls like a bombshell. Lower-than-expected scores direct girls away from the highly selective colleges, and later on they are an obstacle to elite graduate and professional schools.

56   Donna, a woman who attended one of our workshops in New England, wrote about her experience with tests and how this rerouting process takes place:

> Ever since I can remember, I wanted to be a lawyer. In high school I joined the prelaw club, and in college I was president of the law and government society. I worked hard in college, and my grades were very good. I felt so lucky. Half my friends didn't know what they wanted to be, while I felt I always knew.
>
> But deep down I had a fear. My SAT scores were not good, and by my second semester in college I had already started to worry about the LSATs.
>
> I first took the LSAT as a junior. It was a disaster. I convinced myself that my score would rise when I retook the test as a senior, but I was still very nervous. I pulled out all the stops. I took dozens of practice tests as well as the Stanley Kaplan preparation program, and I studied all the time. But it wasn't like my courses in college where if I worked hard enough I could succeed. The more I studied, the more terrified I became. On the day of the test I was the first one there, more than an hour early. That only made it worse. I went to the ladies' room, looked in the mirror, and realized I had rushed so much I hadn't even washed all the shampoo out of my hair. That was a bad sign.
>
> My LSATs never improved. My grades were good enough to get me into law school, but my LSAT was bad enough to keep me out of the top schools and eventually the top jobs. The LSAT didn't stop me from becoming a lawyer—I wanted it too much. But I know the test slowed me down and hurt my career. I work as hard as it takes, and I'm sure I could compete with the best students in the best law schools. I just never had the chance.

57   Like Donna, many women have personal stories of how tests altered their lives. They are bewildered and sometimes resentful. When they went through school, they did what good girls were supposed to: They followed the rules, were conscientious about their studies, finished their homework, and received good grades. Then the standardized test score knocked the wind out of their plans. They attended less prestigious schools, abandoned hopes for a scholarship, decided against further education, and even gave up career goals completely.[10]

INVISIBLE SCORES

58 Despite the enormous cost of the testing gender gap, most people don't even know it exists. The *USA Today* headline on August 27, 1992, read: SAT SCORES SHOW SIGNS OF RECOVERY, a story echoed in hundreds of the nation's newspapers. The upbeat accounts reported that the average SAT verbal score had increased 1 point since 1991, while the average math score had improved 2 points. Optimistic news stories portrayed the 3-point gain as a milestone on the road to educational recovery. Local papers touted neighborhood high schools' SAT averages as if they were sports scores. Most articles lamented the continuing poor performance of minority students, and a few even turned to the past, recalling that between 1969 and 1991 SAT scores nationally had tumbled 60 points. The 1992 upturn, a modest 3 points, might signal the end of this national embarrassment.

59   The source of these stories was a twenty-one-page news release issued by the sponsors of the SAT. In this news release were analyses of scoring differences between urban and rural, and majority and minority students; there was no discussion of the gender gap.[11] But tucked in the end of the report was a chart of male and female scores which revealed that since 1969 boys' scores had dropped a substantial 50 points while girls' scores had skidded a whopping 65. The chart also disclosed that in 1992 girls trailed boys by 52 points. This information was not picked up by the media, however; the gender gap was a nonstory in newspapers across the country.

60   Hidden from public view, this gender gap has evolved into a major educational mystery. Girls enter school with a standardized testing advantage, yet their lead mysteriously vanishes. Girls are winners on report cards and later on college transcripts, yet the boys attain higher scores on the standardized tests. Why the contradiction?

DESIGNING TESTS

61   "The tests are biased!" critics charge, an accusation fueled by the somewhat shady history of test development. Standardized tests were not widely used until World War I, when the army found itself inundated with new recruits. To sort and categorize this immense number of soldiers, the army turned to the new profession of psychology and produced the Army Mental Test. This test was destined to play an important role in college admissions because in a few short years it was reborn as the nation's first SAT.

62   It was not college that motivated the army to measure intelligence but the need to match soldiers with appropriate jobs. Unfortunately, the Army Mental Test was so culturally biased that upper- or middle-class white, native-born Americans won all the intelligence points—and all the good jobs. The passage of time has made these questions as alien to us today as they must have appeared to the immigrants who tried unsuccessfully to answer them seventy-five years ago.[12]

The Percheron is a kind of	goat	horse
	cow	sheep
"There's a reason" is an "ad" for a	drink	revolver
	flour	cleanser
The number of a Kaffir's legs is	two	four
	six	eight
The Pierce Arrow car is made in	Buffalo	Detroit
	Toledo	Flint
Five hundred is played with	rackets	pins
	cards	dice

63   Test results confirmed the popular prejudice of the day: Certain races and groups were bright, and others were less intelligent. In fact, the father of the Army Mental

Test, Carl Campbell Brigham, believed that Americans of Nordic ancestry were genetically brighter than others and as one traveled south through Europe, intelligence levels dropped off. According to Brigham, by the time Africa was reached, the intellectual gene pool had just about run dry. Brigham's insights extended to Jews, whose intelligence he concluded was highly exaggerated. He viewed the arrival of Africans as "the most sinister development in the history of the continent." Brigham wrote, "The really important steps are those looking toward the prevention of the continued propagation of defective strains in the present population."[13]

64   After the war, Brigham took his views to Princeton where he became a professor. He might never have been heard from again if it had not been for the trouble at Columbia University. Early in the century almost half of the students attending public school in New York City were children of immigrants, many of them Eastern European Jews. By 1915 a substantial portion of those students had found their way to the door of Columbia University, and the Ivy League school felt besieged, trapped by its own geography. The dean feared that the refugee scholars might frighten away Columbia's typical undergraduates—polished students from "homes of refinement." Could heaven rescue Columbia from this alien threat?

65   Heaven sent a savior in the form of a new admissions test, a more effective filter to weed out immigrants. Reenter Professor Brigham of Princeton, who fashioned the Scholastic Aptitude Test from his experience developing the culturally biased Army Mental test. Not surprisingly, immigrant applicants performed miserably on the SAT, and far fewer were admitted to Columbia. As the "old" Columbia reemerged, Harvard, Yale, Princeton, and others also came to rely on the new test for "discriminating" admissions. Although the College Board and the Educational Testing Service are quick to disown the prejudices of their founder, today's test critics use this history of prejudice to fuel their contemporary suspicions and concerns.

66   The Educational Testing Service maintains that today's SAT is a far cry from the past and in fact helps colleges evaluate applicants more fairly. Since high schools across the country differ in difficulty, SATs are needed to unmask school inequalities. They offer colleges a common yardstick to measure applicants and help to determine if an A average at one school is equivalent to an A average at another. The SATs also give some students (those with a low grade point average) a second chance to show they can do college work. Used this way, the test can be viewed as a force for fairness.

67   But critics claim that the ghost of Professor Brigham still haunts the exam. While today's SATs have eliminated the blatant discrimination of the past, the charge is that subtle bias endures. After all, the primary purpose of the SAT is to predict how well high school applicants will perform in college courses, a task the test does not do very well. Each year the SAT misleads with an optimistic forecast of future male performance in college and an underprediction of the grades to be earned by women. As we have seen, high school boys and girls receiving the same grades in the same courses do not have the same SAT scores. The female scores are typically 30 to 40 points lower. In short, the SAT overpredicts the college performance of male high school students while the potential of high school females is underestimated and devalued.

68   Critics blame sophisticated test biases for this underprediction.[14] For example, boys answer more questions correctly when these include male characters; girls achieve more on questions with female characters or an equal number of males and females. While many SAT questions do not include people, those that do are more likely to represent the male world. For example, a recent group of SAT reading comprehension questions mentioned forty-two men but only three women. One of the three was anthropologist Margaret Mead, whose research was criticized throughout the passage.

69   Even themes and topics can be more "male friendly," and this affects scores, as the reaction of a gifted high school girl shows:

> On the PSAT, the question that was supposed to be easiest on the analogies was a comparison between football and a gridiron. I had no idea what a gridiron was. It shook me that this was supposed to be the easiest question, and I had trouble concentrating on the rest of the test.

70   Males excel not only on questions dealing with sports but also on test items about measurement, money, science, dates, and wars. Girls surpass boys when the questions concern personal relationships, aesthetics, civil rights, women's rights, abstract concepts, and topics traditionally thought to interest women. For example, on recent SAT exams, boys were more successful on analogies about finance and war—choice (C) in the first question and (B) in the second:[15]

Dividends : Stockholders
    (A) investments : corporations
    (B) purchases : customers
    (C) royalties : authors
    (D) taxes : workers
    (E) mortgages : homeowners
Mercenary : Soldier
    (A) censor : author
    (B) hack : writer
    (C) agent : performer
    (D) fraud : artist
    (E) critic : soldier

71   But girls scored better when the questions related to aesthetics—choice (D) in the first question and (B) in the second:

Pendant : Jewelry
    (A) frame : picture
    (B) cue : drama
    (C) violin : music
    (D) mobile : structure
    (E) poetry : prose

Sheen: (Select the antonym)
    (A) uneven in length
    (B) dull finish
    (C) strong flavor
    (D) narrow margin
    (E) simple shape

72   Phyllis Rosser, a leading SAT critic, is convinced that the road to scoring equality is paved with questions that avoid gender imbalance. She says, "Standardized tests would be much fairer if items girls do poorly on were eliminated or revised. If boys were scoring lower, they would waste no time rewriting the test."[16] Most test developers claim they are already hard at work filtering out questions likely to be friendlier to one gender than the other. But critics claim that more male items penetrate this filter and remain on the exam.[17] And some educators and test designers reject the whole idea of rewriting questions to expunge themes or references related to gender. Marcia Linn of Berkeley warns that the process of purging offensive words and themes could reduce questions to the lowest common context, one of bland and neutered words and people.[18]

73   While critics and test makers debate the problem of bias in question content, some studies show that even if the words are right, the format is wrong. The very approach and design of standardized tests favors males. Boys do better on multiple choice questions, the kind used on standardized tests. But girls perform best on essay questions, more difficult and time-consuming to grade and rarely found on these exams. Also, boys perform better in the beat-the-clock pressure cooker created by timed tests such as the SAT, while girls are more likely to succeed when the test is not timed.[19]

74   At the center of all this controversy, test producers maintain that their exams are fair, accurate, and improving. ETS is revising the SAT, but critics who have seen revision samples say there is far more similarity than difference. The major change in the verbal section is the replacement of antonym questions with more sentence completions and reading passages. On the math section more than 80 percent of the items will be identical, but there will be some opportunity for students to write in their own answers instead of always selecting from multiple choice options. FairTest calls the planned alterations "trivial."[20] In fact, the clearest change may be in name only. Dropping "aptitude" because the term implies innate, unchanging ability, the exam's new name is Scholastic Assessment Test. The one-hour achievement tests are also being renamed "SAT-II." The only change in those tests is a more frequently administered writing component in the English composition test.

75   Overall, even the ETS doubts that improved tests will dramatically alter the gender gap because the gap is not a function of the test but a function of the different educational experiences boys and girls receive. For example, boys still take more high school mathematics and science courses, and this imbalance contributes to higher male test scores. More girls than boys now take college admission tests, which means that less-qualified girls are now taking the test and lowering the average score of all females. And virtually every test company has a review panel to expunge biased words

and problems. ETS suggests that the lower female scores are not a sign of test unfairness but rather the signal of a real educational problem. From the point of view of ETS, test critics are misguided; they are attacking the messenger because they do not like the message.[21]

GRADE INFLATION

76 While girls are behind boys on standardized tests that measure achievement, females are ahead when it comes to report card grades. This paradox is one of education's most persistent puzzles. In our search for answers, one of our visits was to a Virginia high school.

"Do you think there is any favoritism in the way teachers evaluate and grade boys and girls?" we ask the students.

This question hits a raw nerve, and several boys are ready to tell their stories. A seventeen-year-old senior says: "In my organic chemistry class, the girls are definitely graded easier than the boys. Last week the teacher returned a lab report with low grades, and some girls were upset and practically in tears. He let them go back and redo it again, and they got the points back. When boys get mad, they get confrontational. I would never have been able to get those points back from my organic chemistry teacher. I think that teachers will bend and cater to the sensitivities of females."

"I agree," another male student says, getting into the discussion. "I think that boys get more attention in class, but they also get checked more closely. When a male and a female student slack off, grading is tougher on the guy."

A tenth-grade Asian-American girl says, "I have found that teachers will help girls and tell them the answer. If boys don't know the answer, they will be made to solve it themselves."

Ben, sitting in the back row, raises his hand, then says: "That's right. It happened again last week in calculus. I was working on a problem, and I asked the teacher for help. He said, 'You can handle this. Figure it out yourself.' Then a girl asked for help on the same problem. The teacher went over to her desk, took her pencil, set up the problem for her, started the computations, and then let her do the last step. And I was still sitting there trying to figure it out."

"That made you angry?"

"I was burned. I struggled with that problem and never did get the right answer. And that girl not only got help but she got credit for getting it right. She ended up with a higher grade."

"Who got the better education," we ask, "you or that girl?"

Ben looks startled. This is a new angle on his story, and he takes his time thinking about it. A little less sure but still concerned that he is a victim, Ben responds, "Maybe I did end up learning more about how to do the problem—but my grade sure didn't show it."

77 Ben still felt the injustice in his situation, but now he had a new view of the problem: The higher grade awarded to the girl had a price tag, and the teacher's favoritism may not have been a favor after all. As the short-circuited student, the one who had the work done for her instead of doing it herself, she learned less.

78   School counselors and teachers are familiar with the classroom compromises made by girls. A former high school mathematics teacher and college counselor at a prestigious all-girls school outside Washington, D.C., reported that in 1992 twenty-one of the sixty-seven seniors at her school received National Merit recognition. This is the largest percentage of test success enjoyed by girls in any high school in America.

79   "Looking at the entering scores of those students, you would not anticipate that one in three would graduate with national honors," she said. "They entered as good students, but they graduated as the best. The difference is that we don't trade passivity for good grades. We expect our students to take calculus and physics and computer science. We expect them to participate actively in class discussion, to take tough courses, and to do well."

80   But this school is the exception. Most teachers face classes filled with both boys and girls vying for the teacher's attention. In the whirlwind pace of classroom interaction, the good behavior of girls can be a lifesaver tossed to the teacher. Without their active cooperation, classroom dynamics might spin out of control. Many teachers share this fear, and they often return the favor by giving well-behaved girls special consideration. Researchers report that teachers evaluate cooperative girls as more intelligent than others, and they give them higher report card grades. While many boys have discovered the secret to higher standardized test scores, good girls have broken the code for better classroom grades.[22]

81   Good grades for good behavior is a compromise worked out in the earliest school years. Linda Grant observed elementary school teachers in midwestern and southern classrooms. Over the course of several years she concentrated on how teachers evaluated girls, and she found they measured female students by blending good behavior with academic achievement. Here's what the teachers in her study said about their high-achieving white female students—the ones they rewarded with the best grades.

> I knew about an hour after the year began that [Clarissa] was going to be a top student. She does everything neatly and on time and obeys the rules and sets a good example. She reads beautifully, gets along with everybody.

> I have no doubt that [Sheila] will stay in [gifted track classes]. She's always careful and cooperative. She works very hard and is equally strong in reading and math. Pleasant. All the students like her. All the teachers, too.

82   But Audra was a different story. Although compliance and competence were still connected, it was not a positive association:

> All I can say is that it's good we're living in an era of women's lib. She wants to be a broncobuster, can you imagine that? She wears jeans all the time—always too big—and her hair's a mess. I don't think I could get a comb through it even if she would stand still long enough for me to try. I just don't know what will become of her. On top of everything else, she never seems to listen to what I say.[23]

83   Author and teacher Raphaela Best has suggested that many girls enter school socialized for docility. Elementary teachers rely on that cadre of dependable female citizens to orient new students, handle chores, and even help the teacher manage discipline problems. "If they talk," one teacher instructed her newly assigned female

monitor, "give them one warning, then send them back to their desks."[24] One of our graduate students remembered being sent to the back of the room to sit with the misbehaving boys. "I was devastated," she said, "until the teacher explained that this wasn't for punishment but to quiet the bad boys." In many classrooms female students are made exemplars of appropriate academic and social behavior. And when report cards are sent home, girls are rewarded for their meritorious service.

THE BUBBLE BURSTS

84   "She gets unbelievable grades," the proud parents exclaimed, unaware that the A's may be most unbelievable to the girl receiving them. When grades and standardized test scores diverge and part company, girls reject the validity of grades, which are likely to be higher, and believe test scores, which are likely to be lower, as the true measure of intelligence.

85   Self-doubt afflicts even the most intellectually talented young women. Karen Arnold studied students graduating at the top of their class. For the past decade she has tracked high school valedictorians and salutatorians, forty-six women and thirty-five men selected from schools throughout Illinois. When these students graduated, they reported equal estimations of their own intelligence. But by their sophomore year of college the women had lowered their opinions of their own intellect while the men had not. By the time these top students were college seniors, not a single female valedictorian still thought her intelligence was "far above average" even though most were planning to enter graduate and professional schools. But 23 percent of the male valedictorians still put themselves in this top category. Although the women continued to earn high grades in college—slightly higher than the men, in fact—they saw themselves as less competent.[25]

86   Fewer women than men in this valedictorian study found their way into prestigious professions. In increasing numbers they abandoned careers in science, mathematics, and medicine. A decade of interviews reveals that even top-graded high school women harbor deep-rooted questions about their intellectual ability, and this uncertainty affects their future.

87   These academic superstars did not lower their self-assessments and aspirations until college, but many girls hesitate and falter much earlier. When Lyn Mikel Brown and Carol Gilligan interviewed girls at the Laurel School, they discovered that as early as age ten, female students were questioning themselves and relinquishing their opinions.[26] At about the same age that Brown and Gilligan were hearing the "I don't know" refrain in interviews, the National Assessment of Educational Progress exam in science was recording the very same female response. Unlike most multiple choice tests where students must select the one correct response from several possibilities, this test also offered the unusual opportunity of choosing "I don't know." Filling in the oval for "I don't know" was the only obviously incorrect choice. After all, a lucky guess gave students full credit while "I don't know" was hopeless, equivalent to raising a white flag and surrendering. Girls more than boys selected "I don't know" and abandoned any chance of getting credit for the question. Although the

process for responding was a bit different on this test, the outcome was the same: Girls scored lower than boys.[27]

88   Only a few short years before the National Assessments, there is not even a hint of the dive girls are about to take. Female students sail into elementary school with great expectations. Their scores on standardized tests confirm their confidence. Like Jessica at the beginning of this chapter, young girls are pleased at their ability to "bubble," and they are even more satisfied with the test results bubbles bring. But by upper-elementary school, standardized tests, especially in math and science, may find Jessica choosing incorrect responses or neatly filling in the bubble for "I don't know."

89   Bubbles usually ascend, but as girls grow older, their test bubbles pull them down, lowering their self-esteem and educational horizons. When Jessica sets off for college, she will take more than her suitcase and stereo; she will also carry with her the extra burden of self-doubt.

Notes

1. Mullis, Ina V. S., et al, *Trends in Academic Progress.* Prepared by the Educational Testing Service for the National Center for Educational Statistics, Office of Educational Research and Improvement, U.S. Department of Education, Washington, DC, November 1991.

Hafner, Anne, et al. *National Education Longitudinal Study of 1988: A Profile of the American Eighth Grader.* Washington, DC: National Center for Educational Statistics, Office of Educational Research and Improvement, U.S. Department of Education, June 1990.

Mullis, Ina V. S., John A. Dossey, Eugene H. Owen, and Gary Phillips, *The State of Mathematics Achievement: Executive Summary.* Washington, DC: National Center for Educational Statistics, Office of Educational Research and Improvement, U.S. Department of Education, June 1991.

Jones, Lee R., et al. *The 1990 Science Report Card: NAEP's Assessment of Fourth, Eighth and Twelfth Graders.* Prepared by the Educational Testing Service for the National Center for Educational Statistics, Office of Educational Research and Improvement, U.S. Department of Education, Washington, DC, March 1992.

2. Zoller, Uri, and David Ben-Chaim. "Gender Differences in Examination-Type Preferences, Test Anxiety and Academic Achievement in College Science Education—A Case Study," *Science Education* 74:6 (April 1990), pp. 597–608.

Hueftle, S. J., Steven Rakow, and W. W. Welch. *Images of Science.* Minneapolis: Science Assessment and Research Project, University of Minnesota, 1983.

Zimmerer, L. K., and S. M. Bennett. "Gender Differences in the California Statewide Assessment of Attitudes and Achievement in Science." Paper presented at the American Educational Research Association, Washington, DC, April 1987.

Linn, Marcia C., and J. S. Hyde. "Gender, Mathematics and Science." *Educational Researcher* 18:8 (1989), pp. 17–19, 21–22.

Howe, A. C., and W. Doody. "Spatial Visualization and Sex-Related Differences in Science Achievement," *Science Education* 73:6 (1989), pp. 703–9.

3. Wilt, Elizabeth A., Stephen B. Dunbar, and H. D. Hoover. "A Multivariate Perspective on Sex Differences in Achievement and Later Performance Among Adolescents." Paper

presented at the American Educational Research Association, Chicago, Illinois, March 20, 1991.

Kimball, Meredith M. "A New Perspective on Women's Math Achievement," *Psychological Bulletin* 105:2 (1989), pp. 198–214.

4. Test data used in this chapter were obtained from reports, tables, news releases, and studies issued by the test publishers. The Educational Testing Service in Princeton, NJ, provided numerous reports and statistics related to the PSAT, SAT, Achievement tests, GRE, and GMAT. While the GRE data provided were from 1987–88, all other data reflected 1991 and 1992 test administrations. The ACT data were derived from a variety of profile and normative reports for 1990 and 1991 issued by American College Testing in Iowa City, Iowa.

Professional organizations and schools often contract with testing services to develop and administer their admissions tests. For example, the Medical College Admission Test (MCAT) is developed by ACT in Iowa City. For each of these admissions tests, the professional association responsible was contacted first and usually provided the information and statistics for this chapter. These organizations included but were not limited to the Association of American Medical Colleges, Dental Admissions Testing Program, Optometry Admissions Testing Program, Graduate Management Admission Council, and the Law School Data Assembly Service.

The Psychological Corporation in San Antonio, Texas, was asked to provide data on numerous tests they administer. They provided data only on the Miller Analogies Test. It should be noted that on this test, women had a higher mean score than men. However, none of the data concerning other tests distributed by the Psychological Corporation was provided. Since all of their tests cannot be evaluated equally, none of the tests, including the Miller Analogies Test, was included in this chapter.

A good summary of test data and legal rights is provided in Connor, Katherine, and Ellen J. Vargyas, "The Legal Implications of Gender Bias in Standardized Testing," *Berkeley Women's Law Journal* 7 (1992), pp. 13–89.

5. Rosser, Phyllis, and the National Center for Fair and Open Testing. *Sex Bias in College Admissions Tests: Why Women Lose Out.* Cambridge, MA: FairTest, 1989.

Personal correspondence from William C. Gustin, coordinator, Center for Talented Youth (CTY), The Johns Hopkins University, October 27, 1992.

6. Telephone conversation with Bob Schaffer at FairTest, September 30, 1992.

7. Rosser, Phyllis. *The SAT Gender Gap: Identifying the Causes.* Washington, DC: Center for Women Policy Studies, 1989.

8. Quoted in Glaberson, William, "U.S. Court Says Awards Based on S.A.T.s Are Unfair to Girls," *The New York Times* (February 4, 1989), pp. 1, 50.

9. Dorsher, Mike. "Are Biased Tests Hurting Girls?" *The Wall Street Journal* (September 17, 1992).

Davidoff, Judith. "Are Girls Getting Cheated?" *Isthmus* (September 3, 1992), p. 6.

Reid, Alexander. "Ruling Seen Changing How Scholarships Are Won," *The Boston Globe* 35:1 (February 10, 1989).

10. Rosser, Phyllis. "Gender and Testing." Paper commissioned by the National Commission on Testing and Public Policy, Graduate School of Education, University of California at Berkeley, 1989.

11. "College Board Reports Rise in SAT Scores for Class of 1992, but Many Urban, Rural and Minority Students Being Left Behind," College Board News Release (August 27, 1992).

12. Owen, David. *None of the Above: Behind the Myth of Scholastic Aptitude.* Boston: Houghton Mifflin, 1985, pp. 181, 183.

Hoffman, Banesh. *The Tyranny of Testing.* New York: Crowell-Collier, 1962.

13. Crouse, James, and Dale Trusheim. *The Case Against the SAT.* Chicago: University of Chicago Press, 1988, pp. 19, 23.

14. Bridgeman, Brent, and Cathy Wendler. *Prediction of Grades in College Mathematical Courses as a Component of SAT-M Placement Validity.* New York: College Entrance Examination Board (February 1990).

McCornack, R., and M. McLeod. "Gender Bias in the Prediction of College Course Performance," *Journal of Educational Measurement* 25:4 (1988), pp. 321–32.

Wainer, Howard, and Linda Steinberg. "Sex Differences in Performance on the Mathematics Section of the Scholastic Aptitude Test: A Bidirectional Validity Study." Princeton, NJ: Educational Testing Service, 1990.

Horner, Blair, and Joe Sammons with FairTest staff. *Rolling Loaded Dice: Use of the Scholastic Aptitude Test (SAT) for Higher Education Admissions in New York State.* New York: Public Interest Research Group, 1989.

15. Items from the PSAT and SAT are taken from Rosser, *The SAT Gender Gap: Identifying the Causes,* pp. 141–42.

16. Telephone interview with Phyllis Rosser, September 1992.

17. Eckstrom, Ruth B., Marlaine E. Lockheed, and Thomas F. Donlon. "Sex Differences and Sex Bias in Test Content," *Educational Horizons* 58:1 (Fall 1979), pp. 47–52.

Becker, Betsy Jane. "Item Characteristics and Gender Differences on the SAT-M for Mathematically Able Youths," *American Educational Research Journal* 27:1 (Spring 1990), pp. 65–87.

Loewen, James, Phyllis Rosser, and J. Katzman. "Gender Bias in SAT Items." Paper presented at the Annual Meeting of the American Educational Research Association, New Orleans, Louisiana, April 5–9, 1988.

Chipman, Susan. "Word Problems Where Test Bias Creeps In." Paper presented at the Annual Meeting of the American Educational Research Association, New Orleans, Louisiana, April 5–9, 1988.

Pearlman, M. "Trends in Women's Total Score and Item Performance on Verbal Measures." Paper presented at the Annual Meeting of the American Educational Research Association, Washington, DC, April 1987.

Zwick, Rebecca, and Erickan Kadriye. "Analysis of Differential Item Functioning in the NAEP History Assessment," *Journal of Educational Measurement* 26:1 (Spring 1989), pp. 55–66.

Wendler, Cathy L. W., and Sydell T. Carlton. "An Examination of SAT Verbal Items for Differential Performance by Women and Men: An Exploratory Study." Paper presented at the American Educational Research Association, Washington, DC, April 1987.

Sappington, John, Chris Larsen, James Martin, and Kari Murphy. "Sex Differences in Math Problem Solving as a Function of Gender-Specific Item Content," *Educational and Psychological Measurement* 51 (1991), pp. 1041–48.

Murphy, Laura, and Steven Ross. "Protagonist Gender as a Design Variable in Adapting Mathematics Story Problems to Learner Interests," *Educational Technology Research and Development* 38:3 (1990), pp. 27–37.

18. Linn, Marcia C. "Gender Differences in Educational Achievement." Unpublished paper based on research funded by the National Science Foundation, grant MDR-88-50552 and grant MDR-89-54753.

19. Mazzeo, John, Alicia P. Schmitt, and Carole A. Bleistein. "Do Women Perform Better, Relative to Men, on Constructed-Response Tests or Multiple-Choice Tests? Evidence from the Advanced Placement Examinations." Paper presented at the Annual Meeting of the National Council of Measurement in Education, Chicago, Illinois, April 1991.

Gallagher, Shelagh, and Edward S. Johnson. "The Effect of Time Limits on Performance of Mental Rotations by Gifted Adolescents," *Gifted Child Quarterly* 36:1 (Winter 1992), pp. 19–22.

20. "Trivial Changes Highlight 'New SAT,'" *FairTest Examiner* 7:1 (Winter 92–93), pp. 1, 4–5.

Jordan, Mary. "SAT Changes Name, but It Won't Score 1,600 with Critics," *The Washington Post* (March 27, 1993), p. A7.

21. Kubota, Mel, and Anne Connell. "On Diversity and the SAT," *The College Board Review* 162 (Winter 1991–92), pp. 6–17.

College Entrance Examination Board. *College-Bound Seniors: 1989 Profile of SAT and Achievement Test Takers.* New York: College Entrance Examination Board, 1989.

College Entrance Examination Board. *Guidelines on the Uses of College Board Test Scores and Related Data.* New York: College Entrance Examination Board, March 1988.

Cameron, Robert G. "Issues in Testing Bias," *College and University* 64:3 (Spring 1989), pp. 269–79.

College Entrance Examination Board. *1988–89 ATP Guide for High Schools and Colleges.* New York: College Entrance Examination Board, 1988.

22. Gold, Dolores, Gail Crombie, and Sally Noble. "Relations Between Teachers' Judgments of Girls' and Boys' Compliance and Intellectual Competence," *Sex Roles* 16:7–8 (April 1987), pp. 351–58.

Kornblau, B. "The Teachable Pupil Survey: A Technique for Assessing Teacher's Perceptions of Pupil Attributes," *Psychology in the Schools* 19 (1982), pp. 170–74.

23. Grant, Linda. "Race and the Schooling of Young Girls." In Wrigley, Julia (ed.), *Education and Gender Equality.* London: Falmer Press, 1992, pp. 91–114.

24. Best, Raphaela. *We've All Got Scars: What Boys and Girls Learn in Elementary School.* Bloomington, IN: Indiana University Press, 1983, p. 90.

25. Arnold, Karen D. "The Illinois Valedictorian Project: Academically Talented Women Ten Years After High School Graduation." Paper presented at the Annual Meeting of the American Educational Research Association, San Francisco, California, April 24, 1992.

Arnold, Karen. "Values and Vocations: The Career Aspirations of Academically Gifted Females in the First Five Years After High School." Paper presented at the Annual Meeting of the American Educational Research Association, Washington, DC, April 24, 1987.

Arnold, Karen, and Terry Denny. "The Lives of Academic Achievers: The Career Aspirations of Male and Female High School Valedictorians and Salutatorians." Paper presented at the Annual Meeting of the American Educational Research Association, Chicago, Illinois, April 1985.

26. Brown, Lyn Mikel, and Carol Gilligan. *Meeting at the Crossroads.* Cambridge, MA: Harvard University Press, 1992.

27. Linn, Marcia, et al. "Gender Differences in National Assessment of Educational Progress Science Items: What Does 'I Don't Know' Really Mean?" *Journal of Research in Science Teaching* 24:3 (1987), pp. 267–78.

WRITING ASSIGNMENTS

Analysis

1. After reading this selection, analyze the title's multiple meanings. What is a "test drive" and how is it analogous to the relationship between students and higher education? Who is the driver, and what is the vehicle being driven? Also, how do the standardized tests themselves *drive* the educational system?
2. Analyze how the authors' word choice in the reading's first section establishes a tone of alarm and underscores their claim: "That this dive [in female test scores] has received so little national attention is a powerful reminder of the persistence and pervasiveness of sexism in school." Is their diction appropriate, or is it perhaps unfairly or at least prematurely loaded?
3. How are standardized tests used?
4. What generalizations could be drawn about male and female intellectual ability and academic performance based solely on the evidence of standardized test scores?
5. How might the content and format of standardized tests give males an advantage?
6. Proponents of standardized tests claim that they accurately predict academic performance. Why then do females earn higher grades than males who outperform them on standardized tests?
7. How might differences in female and male educational experiences help explain differences in test scores?

Argument

1. Are standardized tests necessarily unfair because males as a group consistently earn higher scores than females as a group? Or, because certain ethnic or racial groups earn higher scores than others? How does evidence provided in this article about standardized testing's history and current practices affect your response?
2. Are the alleged problems with standardized tests serious enough to justify discontinuing their use?
3. What is the legitimate role for standardized tests in our current educational system?
4. Should standardized tests be changed? How?
5. Does the evidence in this reading support the authors' claim? (See Analysis, question 2.)
6. Is the practice of taking behavior into account when assigning grades necessarily bad? Whom does it help? Whom does it harm? You may want to consider D'Antonio's "The Fragile Sex" (Chapter 4) and Sandler's "The Classroom Climate: Still a Chilly One for Women" (next) before you respond.

Personal Writing and Writing from Research

1. Analyze your own experiences with standardized tests and scores in light of the information provided in this reading.
2. Under the heading "Grade Inflation," the authors suggest that teachers reward girls with higher grades for their generally more passive and docile behavior. Reflecting on your personal experience, explain whether, at what educational levels, and in which kinds of classes or courses this practice occurs. If it occurs, what are its consequences?
3. *Collaborative Project:* Trace the history of and controversies surrounding standardized testing, giving particular attention to the connection between the tests and issues of race, ethnicity, and gender. You may want to consider the highly controversial book *The Bell Curve* (1994).

The Classroom Climate
Still a Chilly One for Women

Bernice Resnick Sandler

Bernice Resnick Sandler directs the Project on the Status and Education of Women for the Association of American Colleges, the oldest national program dealing with equity for women in academe. Under her direction, the project issued the first paper on campus sexual harassment and the first comprehensive paper on how men and women are treated differently on campus. She also played a major role in the passage and development of Title IX. This article was published in *Educating Men and Women Together: Coeducation in a Changing World* (1987), an anthology edited by Carol Lasser.

In 1992, the American Association of University Women published a study, "How Schools Shortchange Girls," which concludes that the findings reported by Sandler persist in American education.

Journal Topics: (1) In your opinion, what are the advantages and/or disadvantages of single-sex education for female students? (2) For male students? (3) Does your opinion change depending on the level of education: primary, secondary, or post-secondary? (4) If you have ever noticed a difference in the way male and female students are treated in class, describe what you've observed.

As You Read: (1) Do Sandler's findings surprise you? Do you think they are more likely to reflect the classroom environment in science, math, humanities, business, or arts classes? If so, why? (2) How might Sandler's beginning with "overt" rather than the "subtle" differences in the way male and female students are treated influence the reader's reaction to her findings?

1   Although many overt barriers have fallen during the last decade so that the door to higher education is now open for women, there are many subtle barriers that still remain—barriers that may be almost invisible to both students and faculty. Indeed, both students and faculty may be completely unaware that anything different is occurring. Yet faculty—men and women alike—often inadvertently treat men and women students *differently* and thereby subtly undermine women's confidence in their academic ability, lower their academic and occupational aspirations, inhibit their learning, and generally lower their self-esteem.

2   My study of these barriers and this differential treatment grew out of my own personal experiences. A few years ago I attended a seminar for executives at the Aspen Institute in Colorado. There were nineteen people there, four of us female; it was the largest number of women they had ever had. After a few days, I began to realize that the women were getting interrupted quite a bit. I did not want to appear paranoid, so I asked the other women whether or not they had noticed the interruptions. They agreed with my observation. But because of my training in research, and because I wanted to be absolutely sure, I made a table showing the number of male interruptors, male interruptees, female interruptors and female interruptees. The next morning I did not participate but merely observed the seminar and collected data. It turned out that the remaining three women had approximately *double* the number of interruptions compared to the remaining fifteen men. There was also a difference in the kind of interruption for men and women. The interruptions of the men's discourse were really a continuation or development of their comments, such as, "What you are saying is that Confucius and Marx were not very far apart." The interruptions of the women's comments were of a very different nature; they tended to be trivial and unrelated to the women's comments. For example, one woman's husband, a reporter for *The New York Times,* was attending the conference as a spouse. One interruption of her speech consisted of, "Well, what do you think [your husband] would say about that?" This interruption subtly or not so subtly communicated to her that what she had said was not quite as worthwhile as what other people (the men) had said.

3   I showed my table to the two male co-leaders after the session and tried to convey the information as pleasantly as possible, without a confrontation and with a smile. The men denied the accuracy of my data and insisted I had surely misunderstood; but the next morning there were *no* interruptions of any kind for the women. In other words, the behavior—interrupting—was changeable. To me this meant it was time to write a paper on the subject with the hope of changing other people's behavior.

4   Under a grant from the Fund for the Improvement of Post-Secondary Education (FIPSE), our Project on the Status and Education of Women began to examine our own extensive files and the literature about differential behavior, and to identify how men and women students are treated differently. We gradually came to realize that

many of the so-called problems of women may indeed be related *in part* to how they are treated in the classroom.[1] Let me list some of these problems.

5   • Women are seen as passive and may often act that way.
6   • Women do not participate in class as much as men.
7   • Despite an increase in the number of women in fields such as medicine and law, most women still major in the traditionally female fields, which perpetuate sex segregation in the workplace and perpetuate the occupational ghetto where women earn less money.
8   • Some women experience a decline in their academic aspirations during their college years.

9   We looked at two kinds of behaviors: how women are singled out and treated differently, and how women are ignored.

10   The behaviors I describe and explore are not limited to men. Often women faculty engage in the same behaviors. Even faculty who are most concerned about discrimination may inadvertently and unknowingly treat men and women differently.

11   These behaviors do not happen in every class, nor do they happen all the time, but they happen often enough so that they constitute a pattern. This pattern of behavior dampens women's ambition, lessens their classroom participation, and attacks their self-confidence, so that women's leadership potential is diminished.

12   To begin with, some behaviors are not subtle at all; there are obvious overt behaviors that are often disparaging. Indeed, we were surprised to find out that there was still a lot of overtly discriminatory behavior in college classrooms.

13   Overt discriminatory comments on the part of faculty are not only still surprisingly prevalent but these comments are also often intentional; perhaps those teachers who engage in them are unaware of their potential to do real harm. Such comments may occur not only in individual student-teacher exchanges, but also in classrooms, office consultations, academic advising situations, and other learning contexts.[2] Further, there are some indications that overtly sexist verbal behavior on the part of faculty may be most concentrated in those fields and institutions where women are relative newcomers, and that it often increases in both intensity and effect at the graduate level. All of the quotations and examples below are real. All of these examples were culled from recent reports and research, all from within the last few years.

> In other classes they hear women described as "fat housewives," "dumb blondes," as physically "dirty," as "broads," "chicks," or "dames," depending on the age of the speaker.[3]

> Class time is taken up by some professors with dirty jokes which . . . often happen to be derogatory to women (i.e., referring to a woman by a part of her anatomy, portraying women in jokes as simple-minded or teases, showing women as part of the "decoration" on a slide.)[4]

14   The invidious nature of such comments can perhaps best be understood by comparing them to similar racial remarks. Few, if any, professors would now make disparaging

comments about a black's "seriousness of purpose" or "academic commitment," or use racist humor as a classroom device. In order to experience the derogatory nature of such comments, the reader may wish to substitute the word "black," or any other minority, in the examples that follow. Here are some categories into which such comments fall:

15 • *Comments that disparage women in general,* such as habitual references to "busy-body middle-aged women," statements to the effect that "women are no good at anything," or the description of a class constituted solely of women as a "goddam chicken pen."[5]

16 • *Comments that disparage women's intellectual ability,* such as belittling women's competencies in spatial concepts or math, or making statements in class discussion such as, "Well, you girls probably found this boring," or "You women wouldn't understand this feeling. . . ."[6]

17 • *Comments that disparage women's seriousness or academic commitment* or both, such as, "I know you're competent, and your thesis advisor knows you're competent. The question in our minds is, are you really serious about what you're doing?" or "You're so cute. I can't see you as a professor of anything."[7]

18 • *Comments that divert discussion of a woman student's work toward a discussion of her physical attributes or appearance,* such as cutting a student off in mid-sentence to praise her attractiveness, or suggesting that a student's sweater "looks big enough for both of us." Although such comments may seem harmless to some professors, and may even be made with the aim of complimenting the student, they often make women uncomfortable because essentially private matters related primarily to the sex of the student are made to take precedence over the exchange of ideas and information. As one student noted, "I have yet to hear a professor comment on the daily appearance of a male colleague. I have yet to go through a week without some comment pertaining to my appearance."

19 • *Comments that refer to males as "men" but to females as "girls" or "gals," rather than "women."* This non-parallel terminology implies that women are viewed as similar to children and as less serious and as less capable than men.

20 • *Comments that rely on sexist humor as a classroom device,* either "innocently" to "spice up a dull subject" or with the conscious or unconscious motive of making women feel uncomfortable. Sexist humor can range from the blatantly sexual, such as a physics lecture in which the effects of a vacuum are shown by changes in the size of a crudely drawn woman's "boobs," or the depiction of women in anatomy teaching slides in *Playboy* centerfold poses, to jokes about dating and about women students waiting to be called by men. Such behavior relies on a certain bad taste (usually depicting women in a sexual context that is typically derogatory) in order to create a lively atmosphere in class.[8]

21 Although they admit awareness of sex-stereotyping language, many professors often justify their continued use of these labels. Frequently they joke about their

continued male chauvinism, as though their admission serves as an exoneration for a continuation of sexism.

22   Sexual harassment can also have a devastating effect on some women's participation in the classroom and elsewhere.[9] Women have been known to drop or to avoid courses, to change majors, and even to change schools or drop out as a result of sexual harassment. Even when the effect of this behavior is less drastic, sexual harassment, like other overt remarks, tells a woman that she is viewed in *sexual* terms rather than as an individual capable of scholastic and professional achievement; it tells a woman that she is *not* viewed as an individual learner, but as a woman, who like "all women" is of limited intellectual ability, operating out of her appropriate "sphere" and likely to fail.

23   The subtle behaviors are of a different order. Often neither the professor nor the student may notice that anything special has occurred. Singly, these behaviors may have little effect. But when they occur repeatedly, they give a subtle but powerful message to women: they are not as worthwhile as men nor are they expected to participate fully in class, in college, or in life at large.

24   The Project on the Status and Education of Women identified close to thirty different kinds of subtle behaviors that give women this kind of message.[10] Here are some examples:

25   • Faculty make more eye contact with men than with women, so that individual men students are more likely to feel recognized and encouraged to participate in class. After reading our report, one female instructor discovered that when she asked a question, she looked only at her male students, as if only men students were expected to respond.

26   • Professors are more likely to nod and gesture in response to men's comments and questions than to women's.

27   • Faculty often assume a position of attentiveness such as leaning forward when men are talking. When women talk, faculty may be inattentive, looking at the clock or shuffling papers.

28   • Professors may group students according to sex, especially in a way that implies that women students are not as competent as men or do not have equal status with men. Some laboratory teachers insist that there be no all-women laboratory teams because "women can't handle the equipment on their own." Others may group the women together "so that they can help each other," or so that they "don't delay the men."

29   • Professors may give men detailed instructions about how to complete a particular problem or lab assignment in the expectation they will eventually succeed on their own, but may actually do the assignment for women—or allow them to fail with less instruction.

30   • Despite the popular notion that in everyday situations women talk more than men, studies[11] show that in formal groups containing men and women,

men talk more often than women;
men talk for longer periods and take more turns at speaking;

men exert more control over the topic of conversation;

men interrupt women much more frequently than women interrupt men; and, as I had noticed at Aspen,

men's interruptions of women more often introduce trivial or inappropriately personal comments that bring the woman's discussion to an end or change its focus.

31   Not only do men talk more, but what men say often carries more weight. A suggestion made by a man is more likely to be listened to, credited to him, developed in further discussion, and adopted by a group than the same suggestion made by a woman. The difficulty in "being heard" or "having their comments taken seriously" has often been noted by women in professional peer groups and is strikingly similar to those cited by some women college students.

32   Teachers themselves may inadvertently reinforce women students' "invisibility," or communicate different expectations for women than for men students. Faculty behaviors that can have this effect include but are not limited to the following:[12]

33   • *Ignoring women students while recognizing men students, even when women clearly volunteer to participate in class.* This pattern may lead individual women students to feel invisible.

34   • *Calling directly on men students but not on women students.* Male faculty, especially, may tend to call directly on men students significantly more often than on women students, possibly because faculty unconsciously presume men will have more of value to say or will be more eager to speak up. Sometimes, however, faculty may wish to "protect" women students from the "embarrassment" they assume women may feel about speaking in class and thus simply discount them as participants.

35   • *Calling men students by name more often than women students.* Sometimes faculty are surprised to discover that they know the names of proportionately more men than women students in their classes. Calling a student by name reinforces the student's sense of being recognized as an individual. Students of both sexes should be addressed similarly, last names for both or first names for both. Calling men by last name but women by first name implies that women are not on a par with men as adults or as future professionals.

36   • *Addressing the class as if no women were present.* Asking a question with "Suppose your wife . . ." or "When you were a boy . . ." discounts women students as potential contributors.

37   • *"Coaching" men but not women students in working toward a fuller answer by probing for additional elaboration or explanation.* Faculty are more likely to ask men students, for example, "What do you mean by that?"

38   • *Waiting longer for men than for women to answer a question before going on to another student.* Studies at the elementary school level indicate that teachers tend to give brighter students more time to formulate a response. Thus, interrupting women, giving women less time to answer a question, may subtly

communicate that women are not expected to know the answer. Men's silence after a question may be more likely to be perceived as the result of reflection or the effort to formulate an answer, whereas women's silence is attributed to "shyness" or lack of a suitable response.

39   • *Asking women students lower-order questions that require factual answers while asking men higher-order questions that demand personal evaluation and critical thinking.* Such a pattern presumes, and subtly communicates to women students, that they may not be capable of independent thought.

40   • *Responding more extensively to men's comments than to women's comments.* This pattern may be exacerbated because men students may also be more likely to pay more attention to and pick up on each other's comments, but to overlook those made by women. Thus, male students may receive far more reinforcement than women for intellectual participation.

41   • *Crediting men's comments to their "author,"* "As Bill pointed out . . ." but not giving authorship to women's comments.

42   • *Using classroom examples that reflect stereotyped ideas about men's and women's social and professional roles,* as when the scientist, doctor, or accountant is always "he," while the lab assistant, patient, or secretary is always "she."

43   • *Using the generic "he" or "man" to represent both men and women.* Often when a professor is criticized for using the generic "he" or "man" the professor will label the issue trivial. It makes one wonder: if the issue is indeed trivial, why is it so difficult for professors and others to change it?

44   Why should these behaviors occur? Many behaviors, of course, originate long before students reach the college classroom, some perhaps as early as the cradle. Parents treat male and female babies very differently. For example, they let baby boys cry longer than girls before picking them up. Parents talk more to girls, and then when girls exhibit more verbal behavior, we say this is inborn.

45   Two major hypotheses may explain the differential treatment. One is differential expectations and perceptions. If we expect girls and women to be passive and dependent and not interested in math or science, we may well set up self-fulfilling prophecies. Second, and perhaps underlying the differential expectations and perceptions, is the devaluation of what is female. Throughout our society, what women do has been seen as less valuable than what men do.

46   There have been numerous experiments in which two groups of subjects rate such items as articles, works of art, and resumés.[13] The name of the authors are changed for each group; those items ascribed to women for the first group are ascribed to men for the second group; and those items ascribed to men for the first group are ascribed to women in the second group. The results of these experiments are singularly consistent: if people believe a woman created the item, they rank it lower than if they believe a male created it. Both men and women consistently devalue those items ascribed to females. Studies of how women's success is viewed show a similar pattern: men's success is attributed to talent; women's success is attributed to luck.

47   Even when men and women act similarly, their behavior is viewed differently. He is "assertive"; she is "aggressive" or "hostile." He "lost his cool," implying it was an aberration; she's "emotional" or "menopausal." Thus, her behavior is devalued, even when it is the same as his.

48   So those who believe, perhaps without even knowing it, that women are not as intellectual, not as capable, not as serious as men, may simply ignore women, treat them differently, or view them as peripheral to the classroom, to the college, and to life itself. The classroom is chilly for women because of these behaviors. Add to this the low number of women faculty and the lack of attention to women in the curriculum itself, and indeed one can see that women and men in the same classroom have very different experiences.

49   These behaviors are not limited only to the classroom. The Project on the Status and Education of Women has published an article examining behaviors that occur outside of the classroom—in housing, student services, and all extracurricular activities.[14] We are also planning a report on the climate for women faculty and administrators, in which we will explore how they too are treated differently.

50   What can we do about the chilly classroom right now? The project's report addresses institutional or public solutions to the problem and includes approximately 100 recommendations for faculty, administrators, and students.[15] These recommendations fall into four categories:

1. How to increase awareness of the issues;
2. How to institutionalize solutions, such as issuing a policy statement, or incorporating climate issues into faculty and student evaluations and grievance procedures;
3. How to provide direct help to faculty, such as holding workshops or incorporating climate issues into faculty development programs;
4. How to show support, such as providing funds for institutional research or issuing memos from the president or dean about climate issues.

51   As overt discrimination disappears, we become increasingly aware of its subtle forms and the less obvious barriers to women's development. We also become increasingly aware of the different ways in which men and women view discrimination. Men are more likely to acknowledge and understand overt, intentional discrimination. When overt barriers are dismantled, as when a department chair no longer excludes women from his department, many men assume that the problem of discrimination is thereby solved.

52   Many women, on the other hand, view discrimination as being more than just the formal overt barriers. They see a whole host of subtle behaviors that have a discriminatory impact. For example, women may view social behavior, such as male faculty always having lunch together, as having a discriminatory effect because women thereby are excluded from informal sources of information and the subsequent opportunity to learn more about their profession. Thus, many men tend to overstate the progress that has been made, and many women tend to *understate* the progress; that

is, men think in terms of how far we have come, and women think in terms of how far we have to go.

53   The subtle barriers—like those that occur in the classroom—will not be eradicated easily, particularly because they occur not only in college classrooms but also in the ordinary relations between men and women. These barriers are the product of perhaps thousands of years of history, and it will take more than our lifetime—perhaps several generations—to eradicate them completely.

54   Let me close with something that is characteristic of the new mood of women, a "quotation" from a tablet that was discovered, you understand, by an all-woman team of archaeologists, assisted by women staff and women students:

> And they shall beat their pots and pans into printing presses,
> And weave their cloth into protest banners.
> Nations of women shall lift up their voices with nations of other women.
> Neither shall they accept discrimination anymore.[16]

55   Now this may sound apocryphal but I suspect it may yet prove to come from the Book of Prophets. For what women are learning is the politics of change. The campus, the nation, the world will never again be the same.

Notes

1. The results of this research have been published as a pamphlet. See Roberta M. Hall and Bernice R. Sandler, *The Classroom Climate: A Chilly One for Women?* (Washington, DC: Project on the Status and Education of Women, Association of American Colleges, 1982).

2. For further exploration of these issues see Roberta M. Hall and Bernice R. Sandler, *Out of the Classroom: A Chilly Campus Climate for Women?* (Washington, DC: Project on the Status and Education of Women, Association of American Colleges, 1984).

3. Hall and Sandler, *Classroom Climate,* p. 5.

4. Ibid.

5. Ibid., p. 6.

6. Ibid.

7. Ibid.

8. Ibid.

9. See, for example, *Sexual Harassment: A Hidden Issue* (Washington, DC: Project on the Status and Education of Women, Association of American Colleges, 1978).

10. For a fuller description of these behaviors, see Hall and Sandler, *Classroom Climate,* and Hall and Sandler, *Out of the Classroom.*

11. Hall and Sandler, *Classroom Climate,* p. 8.

12. See note 10.

13. For an overview and discussion, see Veronica F. Nieva and Barbara A. Gutek, "Sex Effects on Evaluation," *The Academy of Management Review* 5 (1980): 267–76.

14. See Hall and Sandler, *Out of the Classroom.*

15. Hall and Sandler, *Classroom Climate,* pp. 13–17.

16. From a poster by Mary Chagnon, n.d.

WRITING ASSIGNMENTS

Analysis

1. In an essay directed to teachers, briefly describe the "pattern of behavior [that] dampens women's ambition, lessens their classroom participation, and attacks their self-confidence, so that women's leadership potential is diminished," and explain how this behavior causes these effects.
2. Explain why, according to Sandler, these behaviors occur. Do the findings reported by Komarovsky in the following selection suggest additional reasons for the "chilly climate" that Sandler says women students experience?
3. Why do many women, according to Sandler, believe that subtle discriminatory behavior is just as damaging as, but harder to eradicate than, overtly discriminatory behavior?
4. How do the different treatments of male and female students reflect traditional gender roles?

Argument

1. Is Sandler correct in saying that overt disparaging comments are no longer made, or tolerated if made, about members of other groups besides women? Explain your position and provide evidence to support it.
2. Explain why you agree or disagree with Sandler's estimate of the effects on women of the subtle and overt gender-linked behaviors that she describes.
3. Are males, particularly white males, objects of discrimination in the classroom today? Explain and illustrate your answer.
4. Do other groups of students—immigrants, members of minority groups, significantly older students—also receive "different" and damaging treatment in the classroom? Explain and illustrate your answer.
5. Is Sandler's article a persuasive argument in favor of the benefits of single-sex education for women? For men? If so, at what level: primary, secondary, post-secondary?

Personal Writing and Writing from Research

1. Describe an incident of gender, age, class, racial, or ethnic discrimination in the classroom, and explain its effect on you.
2. *Collaborative Project:* Observe several meetings of a few classes that your group has selected in order to monitor both overt and subtle examples of gender or other kinds of discrimination. If you find these behaviors, classify them and include your findings in a written report in which you also suggest ways to correct the problems you have documented.

Unlearning to Not Speak

Marge Piercy

Born in 1936 in a predominantly black Detroit neighborhood, Piercy is the daughter of working-class Jewish parents. She attended Northwestern University on a scholarship and earned an MA, an experience she describes in the novel *Braided Lives* (1982). A political activist, she participated in the civil rights, anti-Vietnam War, and feminist movements. She is a prolific writer of fiction and poetry. "Unlearning to Not Speak" is taken from *Circles on the Water: Selected Poems* (1982).

Journal Topics: Recall if at any time during your education you perceived that boys and girls were treated differently. Briefly describe those experiences.

As You Read: (1) How did the speaker in this poem learn not to speak? (2) How are the experiences and feelings described in this poem related to the findings reported by Sandler?

Blizzards of paper
in slow motion
sift through her.
In nightmares she suddenly recalls
5   a class she signed up for
but forgot to attend.
Now it is too late.
Now it is time for finals:
losers will be shot.
10   Phrases of men who lectured her
drift and rustle in piles:
Why don't you speak up?
Why are you shouting?
You have the wrong answer,
15   wrong line, wrong face.
They tell her she is womb-man,
babymachine, mirror image, toy,
earth mother and penis-poor,
a dish of synthetic strawberry icecream
20   rapidly melting.
She grunts to a halt.
She must learn again to speak
starting with I
starting with We

25 starting as the infant does
with her own true hunger
and pleasure
and rage.

College Men
Gender Roles in Transition

Mirra Komarovsky

Mirra Komarovsky received her PhD from Columbia University and was chairperson of the Sociology Department of Barnard College for 17 years. Her books include *Women in the Modern World, The Unemployed Man and His Family* (1940), *Blue Collar Marriage* (1967), *Dilemmas of Masculinity: A Study of College Youth* (1976), and *Women in College: Shaping New Feminine Identities* (1985)—a longitudinal study of a sample of women undergraduates over four years of college. She is a past president of the American Sociological Society. "College Men: Gender Roles in Transition" was published in *Educating Men and Women Together* (1987).

Journal Topics: (1) If you have ever felt intimidated by another student's intelligence or mastery of a subject, describe that experience. Were your feelings at all related to your gender or to the gender of the other person? (2) Have you ever "played dumb"? If so, why? (3) Do you think that female and male students handle themselves differently when they don't understand or disagree with a teacher, or when they disagree with a grade they've received? If so, explain how and why.

As You Read: (1) How is student ambivalence about masculinity and femininity manifested in both classroom and out-of-classroom behavior? (2) How do these student-life inconsistencies reflect confusion about masculinity and femininity in future family and work roles? (3) Do the behavior and attitudes described by Komarovsky exist among students of all ethnic groups and classes?

1 Feminine and masculine social roles in contemporary society present a crazy quilt of contradictions. The ideal images of femininity and masculinity, the division of labor between the sexes in the world of work, in the family, and in other institutional sectors, and the ideologies that support them reflect massive inconsistencies. These inconsistencies are caused by the familiar lead-lag pattern of social change, that is, by rapid changes in some and resistances to change in other related elements of the social system.

2   I shall document this thesis, drawing largely upon my study of college seniors in an Ivy League men's college, published in 1976, *Dilemmas of Masculinity: A Study of College Youth.*[1] Supplementary evidence of masculine role strains is included in my book, *Women in College: Shaping New Feminine Identities,* published in 1985.[2]

3   One caveat is in order. I have chosen to highlight the current strains in gender roles. This purpose accounts for a certain one-sidedness of the portrayal and a neglect of some positive changes that have taken place in intersexual relationships.

4   As I look at the current scene from a perspective of the past several decades, I see tremendous changes in some attitudes of undergraduates and no change in others, with the result that ambivalences, intrapsychic and interpersonal conflicts, and anomie (in the sense of new situations as yet undefined by social norms) are rife.

5   The male seniors of my 1976 study generally expressed a wish for an intellectually rewarding relationship with a woman. Men's ideal woman today is a far cry from the legendary dumb blonde. To be sure, what some men meant by intellectual rapport was having an appreciative listener: "I wouldn't go out with a girl who wasn't quick and perceptive enough to catch an intellectual subtlety," remarked one young senior. But a more typical attitude was expressed by another youth: "I am looking for an intelligent girl who has opinions on politics, social problems—someone I could talk to about things guys talk about."[3]

6   Despite this typical attitude, a sizeable minority, about one-third of the sample, reported that intellectual insecurity vis-à-vis female friends did constitute for them a source of some stress. The following excerpts from interviews illustrate the views of this troubled third:

7   "I may be a little frightened of a man who is superior to me in some field of knowledge, but if a girl knows more than I do, I resent her." Again, another commented: "I enjoy talking to more intelligent girls, but I have no desire for a deep relationship with them. I guess I still believe that the man should be more intelligent." And still another senior reported: "Once I was seeing a philosophy major, and we got along quite well. We shared a similar outlook on life, and while we had some divergent opinions, I seemed better able to document my position. One day, by chance, I heard her discussing with another girl an aspect of Kant that just the night before she described to me as obscure and confusing. But now she was explaining it to a girl so clearly and matter-of-factly that I felt sort of hurt and foolish. Perhaps it was immature of me to react this way."[4]

8   Some men were caught in a double bind. They valued originality and intelligence in female as well as male associates, but they could not relinquish the internalized norm that as men they should enjoy an edge of superiority over women. One senior remarked about his current girlfriend: "I am beginning to feel that she is not bright enough. She never says anything that would make me sit up and say, 'Ah, that's interesting!' I want a girl who has some defined crystal of her own personality and does not merely echo my thoughts." He recently met a girl who fascinated him with her quick and perceptive intelligence but this new girl made him feel "nervous and humble."[5]

9   Occasionally a man intellectually committed to egalitarian ideals experienced guilt. As one put it: "Tugging at my conscience is the thought that I am really most comfortable in situations where my fragile sense of security is not threatened by a woman."[6]

10   A similar mix of newer egalitarian and traditional attitudes was revealed with respect to the question: "Are some majors or occupational choices considered unfeminine?" The majority of male seniors in my 1976 study expressed acceptance of pioneering choices on the part of their female friends. One youth remarked that he would be flattered to date a career-oriented woman, adding: "A girl so dedicated to her work must think an awful lot of you if she wants to spend time with you."[7]

11   But again, there were some voices from the past. A pre-law student confessed: "When I went to take the law boards, I was shocked to see all those girls. I didn't think I would feel that way, but I did. Any girl has to be pretty smart and aggressive to go into this field, and it is a threat to the security of all men in the legal profession."[8]

12   Another student, having declared his full support for equal opportunities for women in the occupational world, added a qualification: "A woman should not be in a position of firing an employee. It is an unpleasant thing to do. Besides, it is unfair to the man. He may be a very poor employer, but he is still a human being, and it may be just compounding his unhappiness to be fired by a woman."[9]

13   Some observers might argue that in our competitive society comparative rating, rivalry, and envy are also unavoidable in male-to-male relationships. But there remains an important difference—the normative expectation that in certain specified spheres, although not all, a male must enjoy an extra margin of superiority over a woman. This expectation runs counter to some newer values which modern men also accept.

14   Such inconsistencies are often unconscious. One liberal senior exclaimed passionately: "There are no unfeminine majors—I admire a coed who is pre-law or pre-med. More power to her." But the same senior in another part of the interview was asked to illustrate what he felt was unfeminine behavior. Well, he answered, contrasting "guys" and "girls," he was turned off by a girl who was too concerned about grades. If a pre-med guy goes to see a professor about a C in chemistry, he doesn't like it, but he understands the guy's anxiety about getting into medical school; however, in a girl he finds such grade-consciousness positively obnoxious. There were other illustrations of sanctioning new goals for women but condemning the means necessary to realize such goals. For example, what male students saw as an acceptable degree of assertiveness in a male student club director, and what they even admired as effective leadership, was occasionally perceived as abrasive and aggressive in a female director.[10]

15   Nowhere are such unconscious ambivalences more striking than in the attitudes of the seniors toward their future wives' occupational roles. The ethos on the campus of this study clearly demanded a liberal attitude toward working wives. But the interviews revealed that the images of the full-time homemaker and a career wife each contained both attractive and repellent traits.

16   Deprecating remarks about housewifery were not uncommon, even among men with traditional views of women's roles. A conservative senior declared, "A woman who works is more interesting than a housewife." "If I were a woman," remarked another senior, "I would want a career. It must be boring sitting around the house doing the same thing day in, day out. I don't have much respect for the type of woman whom I see doing the detergent commercials on TV."[11]

17   But the low esteem attached by some of the men to full-time homemaking coexisted with other sentiments and convictions which required just such a pattern for one's wife. For example, asked about the disadvantages of being a woman, one senior replied, "Life ends at 40. The woman raised her children, and all that remains is garden clubs and that sort of thing—unless, of course, she has a profession." In another part of the interview, this young man explained that he enjoyed shyness in a girl and detested aggressive and ambitious women. He could never be attracted to a career woman. It is no exaggeration to conclude that this man could not countenance in a woman who was to be his wife the very qualities that he himself felt were necessary for a fulfilling middle age—for any woman.[12]

18   An articulate senior illustrates my thesis vividly: "I would not want to marry a woman whose only goal is to become a housewife. This type of woman would not have enough bounce and zest in her. I don't think a girl has much imagination if she just wants to settle down and raise a family from the very beginning. Moreover, I want an independent girl, one who has her own interests and does not always have to depend on me for stimulation and diversion. However, when we both agree to have children, my wife must be the one to raise them. She'll have to forfeit her freedom for the children. I believe that, when a woman wants a child, she must also accept the full responsibility of child care."[13]

19   To sum up, male attitudes toward working wives included the following contradictions: recognition of the right of an able woman to a career of her choice; admiration for women who measure up in terms of the dominant values of our society; a sense of both the lure and also the threat that such women present; a low valuation attached to housewifery, but the conviction that there is no substitute for the mother's care of young children; and the deeply internalized norm of male occupational superiority pitted against the principle of equal opportunity irrespective of sex.

20   Such ambivalences on the part of college men tend to exacerbate role conflicts in women. The latter sense that even the men who pay lip service to the creativity of child rearing and domesticity reserve their admiration (if occasionally tinged with ambivalence) for women achievers outside the home.

21   If men really believed that the rearing of children is more difficult, creative, and significant than writing books or managing corporations, they would demand more of a hand in it too. How telling of our operative values is a report published in *The New York Times* in 1981 citing two male nursery school teachers who in new encounters described themselves as "school" rather than nursery school teachers.

22   I have stressed masculine ambivalences. But my 1985 study of women undergraduates reveals that they are caught up in role confusion which in turn creates problems for their male associates. To pick out a random illustration, some women were

emotionally attracted to macho men who "took charge of things," but such men were not likely to satisfy their equally strong expectations for egalitarian rather than traditional female-male relationships.

23   What of the future?

24   I cannot conceive of a utopian society in which human beings could be completely free of painful dilemmas, incompatible goals, regret, jealousy, or frustrations. The problems I have just illustrated do not fall, in my opinion, into the category of those intrinsic to the human condition. I consider the difficulties I have cited as social problems, that is, potentially remediable difficulties stemming from the lead-lag character of social change.

25   To illustrate this point, I turn to my recent study, in which female freshmen filled out an adjective checklist for "My Ideal Man." They frequently checked such expressive attributes as sensitive, warm, affectionate, and the like. In one case, a boyfriend, looking over the checked qualities, exclaimed, "But you are describing a woman, not a man. What you want is a sister."[14]

26   This young man, and to an extent all of us, are in trouble because we are caught on the horns of a false dilemma—not having the imagination to realize that there is a third option. The only alternative that came to the young man's mind when traditional gender roles were challenged was simple reversal. I could almost hear him say: "If I am not the one to tell her, 'rely on me, I'll be brave and strong,' must I then say, 'I'll rely on you?' If the husband is not going to be the mainstay, the leader, the dominant partner—will the wife then be the boss? If women are not to be reared to be loving, warm, supportive, will they be hard, competitive and aggressive?"

27   But are courage and warmth, achievement and compassion, moral strength and sensitivity, self-confidence and capacity to love, doing and being—are these antithetical qualities to be neatly allocated to each sex? Must we not, instead, try to rear both little boys and little girls to be warm *and* strong, creative *and* sensitive, able to accept responsibility for themselves and for others? Ideally these are the attributes which, in various degrees, might be combined in all human beings, played out at different times and in different situations.

28   Models of egalitarian sexual relationships, especially in marriage, were simply not available in reality or in literature on a scale to shape the imagination of these students, or free them of the false dilemma of power. A clearer insight into the possibility of complementary strengths and weaknesses within a marriage was shown, in an earlier study, by a twenty-eight-year-old taxi driver with nine years of schooling. Asked who was the boss in his family, he answered: "It is hard to say. We go to pieces differently. She's like a powerful engine that shakes itself to pieces. I'm likely to run down. I make her calm down and she makes me stick together."[15]

29   We need to present to both men and women more vivid models of egalitarian relationships between the sexes in order to replace the traditional ones so deeply etched in social consciousness. But the agenda for needed reforms is far broader and more radical than consciousness-raising. In order to translate pious egalitarian pronouncements about wider and more equal options for men and women into a new reality, we shall have to reorganize several institutions in a far more profound way, in my opinion, than

would be necessary, for example, to solve the problems of the black minority in the United States. For example, we Americans are vociferous about the sanctity and centrality of the family, even as we grant every other major institution a prior claim to pursue its interest without the slightest concession to family welfare. The public takes it for granted that the industrial time clock is not to be tampered with, no matter what the consequences are for children and families. A recent survey of many top American companies showed that only about one-third offer some flexible work hours, only 4 percent have policies aimed to help the spouse of a relocating employee to find a job, and only 19 percent offer monetary support for child-care facilities.[16]

30   Strong social movements are necessary to mediate between intolerable conditions and social remedies. What better proof is needed than a comparison of public nurseries in Britain and Sweden, provided in a study by Mary Ruggie? The unprecedented increase in paid employment of mothers with young children in Britain failed to generate enlightened policies with regard to nursery school. By contrast, in Sweden the coalition of government, business, and labor resulted in the commitment of the state to cope with the consequences of the entry of women into the labor force.[17]

31   The social reorganization to be brought about by political and social movements and public policies is too complex a subject to be treated in this discussion. The necessary radical changes will take time. There is no gainsaying the pessimistic short-range outlook, for reasons obvious to us all. But the long-range outlook is a different story.

32   The demographic, economic, and cultural trends that are changing the status of women are not likely to be reversed. Even in an irrational society fraught with vested interests and fearful resistance to new values, there does exist a strain toward consistency. In a society such as ours, in which the proportion of married women in the labor force exceeds 50 percent, in which over half of college freshmen are women, in which the fertility rate stands at a low 1.9 children per woman, in such a society the persistence of traditional sex roles will continue to cause such stress and contradictions as to generate, I believe, over the long run, an irresistible pressure for necessary social reorganization in the direction of sex equality. Our society must become one in which neither sex is the "second sex."

Notes

1. Mirra Komarovsky, *Dilemmas of Masculinity: A Study of College Youth* (New York: W. W. Norton, 1976).

2. Mirra Komarovsky, *Women in College: Shaping New Feminine Identities* (New York: Basic Books, 1985).

3. Komarovsky, *Masculinity,* p. 47.

4. Ibid., p. 49.

5. Ibid., p. 50.

6. Ibid., p. 131.

7. Ibid., p. 25.

8. Ibid., p. 26.

9. Ibid., p. 36.
10. Ibid., p. 27.
11. Ibid., p. 35.
12. Idem.
13. Ibid., p. 38.
14. Komarovsky, *Women*, p. 245.
15. Mirra Komarovsky, *Blue Collar Marriage* (New York: Random House/Vintage Books, 1967), p. 179.
16. Komarovsky, *Women*, pp. 317–18.
17. Mary Ruggie, *The State and Working Women* (Princeton, NJ: Princeton University Press, 1984).

WRITING ASSIGNMENTS

Analysis

1. Explain what Komarovsky means by "a crazy quilt of contradictions" and "massive inconsistencies" in contemporary feminine and masculine social roles. Provide additional examples from your own observations and experiences.
2. Define and illustrate the "lead-lag" pattern of social change, which, according to Komarovsky, explains these inconsistencies in gender roles. You may illustrate this pattern by examples from other areas of social change, such as race relations or attitudes toward homosexuality.
3. How do conflicting attitudes about gender roles among both men and women contribute to duplicitous behavior (for example, a young woman's "playing dumb")?
4. Explain how conflicting attitudes about gender roles among the students whom Komarovsky studied influence their choice of major and career. Are these effects still evident today?
5. Explain how traditional expectations of feminine behavior cause behavior that is acceptable, even admired, in men to be judged negatively in women. What are the consequences of this double-standard for career choices, on-the-job behavior, marriage, and family life?
6. How do young women's conflicting expectations of masculine behavior create problems for men in personal relationships, family life, and at work?
7. Explain what Komarovsky means when she says, "We are caught on the horns of a false dilemma—not having the imagination to realize that there is a third option."
8. Describe the changes needed in other social institutions if family welfare is to be protected and egalitarian relationships promoted.

Argument

1. Komarovsky's findings of "massive inconsistencies" in feminine and masculine social roles are based on her 1976 research on men and her 1985 research on women. Do inconsistencies persist today?

2. Are Komarovsky's findings not generally applicable because her research only focused on students at Ivy League colleges?
3. Take a position on whether "complementary," "egalitarian relationships between the sexes" are possible and/or desirable.
4. Explain why you agree or disagree with Komarovsky's belief that "over the long run, [there is] an irresistible pressure for necessary social reorganization in the direction of sex equality."

Personal Writing and Writing from Research

1. Komarovsky alludes to the prevalence of "ambivalences, intrapsychic and interpersonal conflicts, and anomie in the sense of new situations as yet undefined by social norms" concerning gender roles and relations among undergraduates. Explain whether you and your peers experience this confusion, and provide examples to illustrate your position.
2. *Collaborative Project:* Interview male and female students about some of the attitudes and expectations covered by Komarovsky's research. Report your findings and compare them to hers.
3. *Collaborative Project:* Compare and contrast social policies that support egalitarian relationships and family welfare in the United States with several other developed countries.

LOVE AND MARRIAGE

We worship romantic love. And why not? Romantic love convinces us that we are special and understood, and it gives us a sense of oneness with another, which helps us overcome our existential isolation. Romantic love inspires rapture, devotion, and tenderness. It engenders an expansiveness of spirit, transforms our vision of the world and ourselves, and comforts us. It can be splendid, magical, and sometimes heroic.

But romantic love can also be terrifying. It undermines our self-control and reduces our independence. It makes us vulnerable. This vulnerability can spark possessiveness and jealousy, even violence. Whether such love appears suddenly or grows gradually, its future is uncertain. We want it to endure, to be everlasting. Often it is not.

Even the words we use to describe romantic love reveal our misgivings about its risks. We "fall in love," as if into an abyss, and are then "starry-eyed," "head-over-heels," and "dazed." Lovers are "mad for" or "crazy about" each other. These expressions reflect the disorientation and transformations that even happy lovers experience. Unrequited lovers are "lovesick," and those who lose love are "broken-hearted."

The first segment of this chapter examines the nature of romantic love, our conceptions about it, how we express it, and its effect on us. In "Feminine and Masculine Love," sociologist Francesca M. Cancian looks first at how men and women express love and then at the various ways our society interprets and values those expressions. In an excerpt from her book *You Just Don't Understand,* Deborah Tannen, a linguistics professor, defines two clashing communication styles, which she claims originate in different male and female psychological needs.

Next, the husband and wife in Amy Tan's story "Rice Husband" have different emotional needs, which their communication styles reflect and aggravate. The title of Raymond Carver's short story, "What We Talk About When We Talk About Love," promises insights into the nature of love. His four speaking characters claim some expertise based on past and present experiences with and observations of love. But despite their strong opinions, their conversation resolves little.

Intense, powerful, and volatile, love's beginnings are an emotional and private affair. But love's power to unsettle us, to change us, even—when accompanied by sex—to produce children, leads both individuals and society to try to contain or channel love. Enter marriage.

In earlier times, marriage was primarily a practical institution, arranged by families and based on dynastic, property, status, and survival considerations. Love may have been a desirable outcome, but was not a precondition to or necessary ingredient of marriage. But over the last 200 years, our culture has adopted a romanticized view of marriage, grounded on three assumptions: that marriage partners are freely chosen, that the decision to marry is based on love, and that romantic love endures within marriage.

Today, in a public ceremony performed before civil or religious authority, usually in the presence of a community of family and friends, men and women take the vows that legalize and institutionalize their commitment. The marriage commitment links private romantic passion with social responsibilities and with the ongoing, mundane need to provide shelter, food, and care. Fulfilling both our romantic and practical expectations of marriage has often proven difficult.

The next segment explores many facets of marriage in America. Alice Walker's story "Roselily" reminds us that lovers do not always marry and that people often have mixed motives for marrying, love not necessarily among them. In "The Marriage Gap," Charisse Jones analyzes the many reasons why people do not marry. Her interview subjects confirm the social and personal significance of marriage even as they lament its decline in the African-American community. Although Jones focuses on a particular community, she raises issues that concern us all.

Excerpts from "Perspectives on Marriage," a manual used in Roman Catholic premarriage counseling, spotlight the practical decisions and emotional adjustments that couples will face in their attempt to balance love with children, work, and the concerns of daily life.

In "Can a Woman Be Liberated and Married?" Caryl Rivers analyzes the foundation, challenges, and rewards of her own modern marriage. Finally, in "Here Comes the Groom," Andrew Sullivan, in his appeal for legalized marriage for homosexuals, also affirms the importance of marriage.

Feminine and Masculine Love

Francesca M. Cancian

Francesca M. Cancian is a PhD and has been a professor of sociology at the University of California, Irvine, since 1976. Her publications include *What Are Norms? A Study of Belief and Action in a Mayan Community* (1975) and *Love in America* (1987), from which "Feminine and Masculine Love" is taken.

In analyzing love and how we think about love, Cancian criticizes many contemporary psychologists and sociologists for their too-"feminine" conception of love. She proposes a new definition of love that combines self-development, usually associated with "masculine" independence, and commitment, usually associated with "feminine" expressiveness and nurturing.

Journal Topics: (1) What are the signs that show a couple love each other? (2) Do men and women express love differently? If so, how? (3) Are men or women more loving? Why? (4) Briefly describe a loving relationship between two adults you know well.

As You Read: (1) What does Cancian mean by a "feminine" conception of love? (2) By a "masculine" conception of love? (3) Does Cancian believe that women are "superior" to men in love?

1   Most Americans have an incomplete, feminine conception of love. We identify love with emotional expression and talking about feelings, aspects of love that women prefer and in which women tend to be more skilled than men. We often ignore the instrumental and physical aspects of love that men prefer, such as providing help, sharing activities, and sex. . . .

2   Our feminine conception of love exaggerates the difference between men's and women's ability to love, and their need for love. It reinforces men's power advantage, and encourages women to overspecialize in relationships, while men overspecialize in work. . . .

DEFINITIONS OF LOVE

3   "Love is active, doing something for your good even if it bothers me" says a fundamentalist Christian. "Love is sharing, the real sharing of feelings" says a divorced secretary who is in love again. In Ancient Greece, the ideal love was the adoration of a man for a beautiful young boy who was his lover. In the thirteenth century, the exemplar of love was the chaste devotion of a knight for another man's wife. In Puritan New England, love between husband and wife was the ideal, and in Victorian times, the asexual devotion of a mother for her child seemed the essence of love.

4   What is a useful definition of enduring love in the contemporary United States? On what grounds can I reject the feminine definition of love in favor of a broader, androgynous definition that includes the masculine style of love? One guideline for a definition comes from the prototypes of enduring love—the relations between committed lovers, husband and wife, parent and child. These relationships combine practical assistance with physical and emotional closeness. Studies of attachment between infants and their mothers emphasize the importance of being protected and fed as well as being touched and held. In marriage, according to most family sociologists, both practical help and affection are part of enduring love, or "the affection we feel for those with whom our lives are deeply intertwined." Our own informal observations often point in the same direction: if we consider the relationships that are the prototypes of enduring love, it seems that love is a combination of instrumental and expressive qualities.

5   Historical studies provide a second guideline for defining love. In pre-capitalist America, . . . love was a complex whole that included feelings and working together. Then love was split into feminine and masculine fragments by the separation of the home and the workplace. This historical analysis suggests that affection, material help, and routine cooperation are all part of love.

6   Consistent with these guidelines, my working definition of enduring love between adults is: a relationship where a small number of people both (1) express affection, acceptance, and other positive feelings to each other, and (2) provide each other with care and practical assistance. Love also includes (3) commitment—an intention to maintain the affection and the assistance for a long time, despite difficulties; and

(4) specialness—giving the loved person priority over others. The concept of love in all contemporary adult relationships—with a spouse, friend, relative, or lover—seems to emphasize these four qualities. Enduring sexual love for people who live together also includes sexual intimacy and physical affection, as well as cooperation in the routine tasks of daily life. Finally, the new images of love add the qualities of promoting each other's self-development, and communicating and understanding each other's personal feelings and experiences. My focus is on enduring sexual love between men and women. I will for the sake of simplicity refer to it as "love," and use the terms "attachments" and "close relationships" more broadly, to include relations with friends, relatives, and lovers.

7   In contrast to this broad definition of love, a narrower, feminized definition dominates both contemporary scholarship and public opinion. Most scholars who study love or close friendship focus on qualities that are stereotypically feminine, especially talking about feelings. For example, Abraham Maslow defines love as "a feeling of tenderness and affection with great enjoyment, happiness, satisfaction, elation and even ecstasy." Among healthy individuals, "there is a growing intimacy and honesty and self-expression." Studies of friendship usually distinguish close friends from acquaintances on the basis of how much personal information is disclosed, and research on married couples and lovers emphasizes communication and self-disclosure. Thus, a study of older couples identifies love as a "basic need" in marriage, along with personality fulfillment, respect, communication, finding meaning, and integrating past experience. Love is measured by four questions about feelings: for example, whether one's spouse expresses "a feeling of being emotionally close to me." Providing practical help, money, or sex are not considered to be among the basic needs satisfied by marriage. A recent book on marital love by Lillian Rubin also emphasizes emotional expression. She focuses on intimacy, which she defines as "reciprocal expression of feeling and thought, not out of fear or dependent need, but out of a wish to know another's inner life and be able to share one's own." Intimacy is distinct from nurturance or caretaking, she argues, and men are usually unable to be intimate.

8   Among the general public also, love is defined primarily as expressing feelings and verbal disclosure, not as instrumental help, especially among the more affluent. Recent surveys show that most people identify "open, honest communications" as the most important quality of a love relationship, while a contemporary dictionary defines love as "strong affection for another arising out of kinship or personal ties" and as attraction based on sexual desire, affection, and tenderness.

9   These contemporary definitions of love clearly emphasize qualities that are seen as feminine in our culture. A study of gender roles in 1968 found that warmth, expressiveness, and talkativeness were seen as appropriate for females, and not males. In 1978 the core features of gender stereotypes were unchanged although fewer qualities were seen as appropriate for only one sex. Expressing tender feelings, being gentle and very aware of the feelings of others were still ideal qualities for women and not men. The desirable qualities for men and not women included being very independent, unemotional, and interested in sex. Thus sexuality is the only "masculine"

component in popular definitions of love. Both scholars and the general public continue to use a feminized definition of love.

FEMINISTS ON LOVE AND GENDER

10 In the nineteenth century, the feminization of love was part of the ideology of separate spheres that polarized gender roles. In the fifties, sociologists, like Talcott Parsons, defending gender differentiation in the nuclear family, emphasized the "natural" division between expressive wives and instrumental husbands. Today it is feminist scholars like Nancy Chodorow and Carol Gilligan who are among the most influential defenders of feminine love. Although their purpose is to attack our system of gender roles, their theories partly reinforce this system by arguing that women are loving and connected to others while men are separate.

11 Nancy Chodorow's psychoanalytic theory has been especially influential. Her argument—in greatly simplified form—is that as infants, both boys and girls have a strong identification and intimate attachment with their mothers. Since boys grow up to be men, they must repress this early identification and in the process they repress their capacity for intimacy. Girls retain their early identification since they will grow up to be women like their mothers, and throughout their lives females see themselves as connected to others. As a result of this process, Chodorow argues, "girls come to define and experience themselves as continuous with others; . . . boys come to define themselves as more separate and distinct." This theory implies that love is feminine—women are more open to love than men and this gender difference will remain as long as women are the primary caretakers of infants.

12 Several scholars have used Chodorow's theory to develop the idea that love and attachment are fundamental aspects of women's personality, but not men's. Carol Gilligan's influential book on female personality development asserts that women define their identity "by a standard of responsibility and care." The predominant female image is "a network of connection, a web of relationships that is sustained by a process of communication." In contrast, males favor a "hierarchical ordering, with its imagery of winning and losing and the potential for violence which it contains." "Although the world of the self that men describe at times includes 'people' and 'deep attachments,' no particular person or relationship is mentioned . . . Thus the male 'I' is defined in separation . . ." Lillian Rubin's recent books make a similar argument. These works imply that women will be loving and men will be separate as long as infants are raised by women.

13 On the other hand, feminist historians and psychologists like Mary Ryan and Jean Baker Miller have developed an incisive criticism of the feminized perspective on love. They argue that the type of love in which women specialize is distorted and partial, because it is split off from productivity and power—qualities associated with the masculine role and the public sphere. Mary Ryan's work shows how love became women's responsibility in the nineteenth century, and the conception of love shifted

towards emphasizing tenderness, powerlessness, and the expression of emotion. Jean Baker Miller argues that women's ways of loving—their need to be attached to a man and to serve others—result from women's powerlessness. A better way of loving would integrate power with women's style of love. Ryan and Miller emphasize the flexibility of gender roles and the inadequacy of a concept of love that includes only the feminine half of human qualities. In contrast, Chodorow emphasizes the rigidity of gender differences after childhood, and defines love in terms of feminine qualities. The two theoretical approaches are not as inconsistent as my simplified sketches suggest, and many scholars combine them. However, they have different empirical implications. Chodorow's approach, but not Ryan's, implies that women are much more loving than men.

EVIDENCE ON WOMEN'S "SUPERIORITY" IN LOVE

14   A large number of studies show that women are more interested and more skilled in love than men. However, most of these studies are biased measures based on feminine styles of loving, such as verbal self-disclosure, emotional expression, and willingness to report that one has close relationships. When less biased measures are used, such as how often people see their friends and relatives, the differences between women and men are often small.

15   Women have a greater number of close relationships than men. At all stages of the life cycle, women see their relatives more often. Men and women report closer relations with their mothers than their fathers, and are generally closer to female kin. Thus an average Yale man in the seventies talked about himself more with his mother than his father, and was more satisfied with his relation with his mother. His most frequent grievance with his father was that he gave too little of himself and was cold and uninvolved; his grievance with his mother was that she gave too much of herself and was alternately overprotective and punitive. A recent national survey concludes that "men in our society appear to find close interpersonal relations with their children problematic."

16   Throughout their lives, women are more likely to have a confidant—a person to whom they disclose personal experiences and feelings. Girls prefer to be with one friend or a small group, while boys usually play competitive games in large groups. Men usually get together with friends for sports or other activities, while women explicitly meet to talk and be together.

17   Many men are very isolated, given their weak ties with their family and kin. Among blue-collar couples interviewed in 1950, 64% of the husbands had no confidants besides their spouses, compared with 24% of the wives. The predominantly upper-middle-class men interviewed by Daniel Levinson in the seventies were no less isolated. He concluded that "close friendship with a man or a woman is rarely experienced by American men." Most men apparently have no loving relationships besides their wives or lovers, and given the estrangement that often occurs in marriage, many men must have no loving relationships at all.

18   Several psychologists have suggested that there is a natural reversal of these specialized roles in middle age, as men become more concerned with relationships and women turn towards independence and achievement; but there is little evidence, as far as I know, showing that men's relationships become more numerous or more intimate after middle age, and some evidence to the contrary.

19   Women are also more skilled than men in talking about relationships. Women disclose more about personal experiences than men and are expected to disclose more. Men who deviate and talk a lot about their personal experience are defined as too feminine and poorly adjusted. Women value talking about feelings and relationships, whether they are working class or middle class. Working-class wives prefer to talk about themselves, their close relationships with family and friends, and their homes, while their husbands prefer to talk about cars, sports, work and politics. The same gender-specific preferences are expressed by college students.

20   Men do talk more about one area of personal experience—their victories and achievements; but talking about success is associated with being powerful, not intimate. Women say more about their fears and disappointments, and it is sharing one's weaknesses that usually is interpreted as a sign of intimacy. Women are also more accepting of the expression of intense feelings, including love, sadness, and fear, and more skilled in interpreting other people's emotions.

21   Finally, in their leisure time women are drawn to love and human entanglements, while men are drawn to competition with other men. Women prefer watching the emotional struggles on daytime soap operas or, if they are more educated, the highbrow soap operas on educational channels. Most men like to watch competitive and often aggressive sports. Reading tastes show the same pattern. Women read novels about love, while men's magazines feature stories about adventure and encounters with death by groups of men.

22   However, this evidence on women's greater involvement and skill in love is not as strong as it appears. Part of the reason that men seem so much less loving than women is that men's behavior is measured with a feminine ruler. Most research considers only the kinds of loving behavior that are associated with the feminine role, such as talking about personal troubles, and rarely compares women and men on masculine qualities such as giving practical help or being interested in sexual intercourse.

23   When less biased measures are used, the behavior of men and women is often quite similar. For example, in a careful study of kinship relations among young adults in a southern city, Bert Adams found that women were much more likely than men to say that their parents and relatives were very important in their lives (58% of women and 37% of men). In actual contact with relatives there were much smaller differences (88% of women and 81% of men whose parents lived in the city saw them weekly). He concludes that "differences between males and females in relations with parents are discernible primarily in the subjective sphere; contact frequencies are quite similar."

24   The differences between the sexes are often small even when biased measures are used. For example, Marjorie Lowenthal and Clayton Haven reported the widely quoted finding that elderly women were more likely than men to have a friend with

whom they could talk about their personal troubles—clearly a measure of a traditionally feminine behavior. The figures revealed that 81% of the married women and 74% of the married men had a confidant—not a sizable difference. On the other hand, whatever the measure, virtually all studies find that women are more involved in close relationships than men, even if the difference is small.

25   In sum, women are moderately superior to men in love—they have more close relationships and care more about them, and they also seem to be more skilled at love, especially those aspects of love that involve expressing feelings and being vulnerable. But this does not mean that men are separate and unconcerned with close relationships. When national surveys ask people what is most important in their lives, women tend to put family bonds first while men put family bonds first or second, along with work. For both sexes, love is very important.

EVIDENCE ON THE MASCULINE STYLE OF LOVE

26   Men tend to have a distinctive style of love that focuses on practical help, shared physical activities, spending time together, and sex. The major elements of the masculine style of love emerge in Margaret Reedy's study of 102 upper-middle-class couples in the late seventies. She showed individuals statements describing aspects of love and asked them to rate how well the statements described their marriages. On the whole, husband and wife had similar views of their marriage, but several sex differences emerged. Giving practical help and spending time together were more important to men. They were more likely to give high ratings to statements like: "When she needs help I help her" and "She would rather spend her time with me than with anyone else." Men also described themselves as more sexually attracted, and endorsed such statements as: "I get physically excited and aroused just thinking about her." In addition, emotional security was less important to men than women, and men were less likely to describe the relationship as secure, safe, and comforting. Several hundred young, highly educated couples studied in the late seventies showed a similar pattern. The husbands gave greater emphasis to feeling responsible for their partner's well-being and putting their spouse's needs first, as well as to spending time together. The wives gave greater importance to emotional involvement and verbal self-disclosure, but also were more concerned than the men about maintaining their separate activities and their independence.

27   The different significance of practical help to men and women was demonstrated by seven couples who recorded their own interactions for several days. They noted how pleasant their relations were and also counted how often their spouse did a helpful chore, like cooking a good meal or repairing a faucet, and how often they expressed acceptance or affection. The social scientists doing the study used a feminized definition of love. They labeled practical help as "instrumental behavior" and expressing acceptance as "affectionate behaviour," thereby denying the affectionate aspect of practical help. The wives seemed to be using the same scheme; they thought their marital relations were pleasant that day if their husbands had directed

a lot of affectionate behaviour to them, regardless of their positive instrumental behavior. But the husbands' enjoyment of their marital relations depended on their wives' instrumental actions, not their affection. One husband, when told by the researchers to increase his affectionate behavior towards his wife, decided to wash her car, and was surprised when neither his wife nor the researchers accepted that as an "affectionate" act.

28   The masculine perspective is clearly expressed by a working-class husband discussing his wife's complaints about his lack of communication: "What does she want? Proof? She's got it, hasn't she? Would I be knocking myself out to get things for her—like to keep up this house—if I didn't love her? Why does a man do things like that if not because he loves his wife and kids? I swear, I can't figure what she wants." But his wife, who has a feminine orientation to love, says: "It is not enough that he supports us and takes care of us. I appreciate that, but I want him to share things with me. I need for him to tell me his feelings." Many working-class women agree with men that a man's job is something he does out of love for his family. But middle-class women and social scientists rarely recognize men's practical help as a form of love. Indeed, for upper-middle-class men whose jobs offer a great deal of intrinsic gratification, the belief that "I'm doing it for my family" seems somewhat self-serving.

29   Similar differences in men's and women's styles of love emerge in relationships between two persons of the same sex. Compared with homosexual men, lesbians are more likely to have stable relationships; they place a higher value on tenderness and verbal self-disclosure and engage in sex less frequently. In friendships also, men value sharing activities, while women emphasize confiding their troubles and establishing a supportive emotional attachment. Thus men specialize in certain kinds of loving activities, but except for sex these activities are usually not recognized as love.

30   The relation between sex and love is unclear. Men separate sex and love more than women, but sexual intercourse seems to be the most meaningful way of giving and receiving love for many men. A 29-year-old carpenter who has been married for three years said that after sex, "I feel so close to her and the kids. We feel like a real family then. I don't talk to her very often, I guess, but somehow I feel we have really communicated after we have made love."

31   Because sexual intimacy is the only "masculine" way of expressing love that is culturally recognized in our society, the recent trend towards viewing sex as a way for men and women to mutually express intimacy is an important challenge to the feminization of love. However, the connection between sexuality and love has been weakened both by defining sex as a form of casual recreation, and by emphasizing rape and incest, and viewing male sexuality as a way that men dominate and punish women.

32   A final, somewhat surprising feature of men's style of love is that men have a more romantic attitude toward their partner than women. Men were more likely to select statements like "we are perfect for each other," in Reedy's study. In a survey of college students, 65% of the men, but only 24% of the women said they would not marry someone that they were not in love with, even if the person had all the other qualities they desired. The usual sociological explanation for men's romanticism is that women are more dependent on men for money and status; therefore women are more

realistic or mercenary. However, the hypothesis of mercenary wives is inconsistent with women's greater concern about self-disclosure and emotional intimacy. Perhaps men are more romantic because they are less responsible for "working on" the emotional aspects of the relationship, and therefore see love as magically and perfectly present or absent. Women in contrast, may assume that love varies and depends on their own efforts.

33   Except for romanticism, men's style of love fits the masculine role of being the powerful provider. The qualities judged most important in being a man, according to a large national survey, are being a good provider, having strong views about what is right and wrong, and being concerned with a woman's sexual satisfaction—qualities that are emphasized in the masculine style of love.

POWER AND STYLES OF LOVE

34 It is striking how the differences between men's and women's style of love reinforce the power of men over women. Men's style of love involves giving women important resources that men control and women believe they need, and ignoring the resources that women control and men need. Thus men's dependency on women remains covert and repressed, while women's dependency on men is overt and exaggerated; and it is overt dependency that affects power, according to social exchange theory. The feminine gender role intensifies this power differential by encouraging women to think they have a great need for men's love and protection, as feminists have pointed out. In fact, evidence on the high death rates of unmarried men implies that men need love at least as much as women.

35   Sexual relations can also reinforce male dominance insofar as the man takes the initiative and intercourse is defined either as him "taking" his pleasure or being skilled at "giving" her pleasure, in either case giving him control. The man's power advantage is further strengthened if the couple assumes that the man's needs can be filled by any attractive woman, while her sexual needs can only be filled by the man she loves.

36   In contrast, women's preferred ways of loving involve admitting dependency and sharing or losing control. The intimate talk about personal troubles that appeals to women requires a mutual vulnerability, a willingness to see oneself as weak and in need of support. The intense emotionality that is supposed to characterize women also seems inconsistent with being in control. Finally, the feminine style of love emphasizes reciprocal, equal exchange of confidences and emotional support, and not the unequal exchange that leads to power over another. It is true that a woman, like a man, can gain power by providing her partner with understanding, sex, cooked meals, or other valued services, and motherly nurturance and care can slide over into controlling the other person. But a woman's potential power over a man is usually undercut because the services she provides are devalued and his need for them is denied. The couple may even see these services as her duty or as her response to his requests and demands.

37   Men's power advantage over women will decline if they adopt an androgynous style of love and become more expressive, vulnerable, and openly dependent, while becoming more androgynous will increase women's power. Therefore, men probably resist a change towards androgynous love more than women. The hostility of many men towards the human potential movement and talking about their feelings may be part of this resistance; they may sense that if they become more aware of their feelings of dependency and their need for care, their power over women will diminish.

38   In sum, men are not as uninvolved and unskilled in love as the feminine perspective suggests. There is a distinctive masculine style of love focused on help, shared activities, and sex, but it is usually ignored by scholars and the general public. Recognizing it would undercut our traditional gender roles, which are based on identifying women with expressive love and weakness and men with competent achievement and power.

THE COSTS OF FEMINIZED LOVE

39   The feminization of love intensifies the apparent differences between women and men in several ways. Firstly, defining love as expressive leads to a false opposition between women's love and men's work. It obscures the loving aspect of the male provider role and the competent, active component of women's love. A major way that women are loving is by actively caring for others and doing physical, productive (but unpaid) work for their families. Nurturing children or a husband consists largely of instrumental acts like preparing meals, washing clothes, or providing care during illness. But because of our focus on the expressive side of love, the work of caring for another person is either ignored or is redefined as expressing feelings; doing is redefined as being. Thus, from the feminized perspective on love, child care is a subtle communication of attitudes, not work or an instrumental form of love. A wife washing her husband's shirt is seen as expressing feelings, while a husband washing his wife's car is seen as doing a job.

40   The feminization of love also lowers the status of women and reinforces the power difference between the sexes. Our culture tends to glorify achievement, while emotional expression is disparaged as sentimental, foolish, and unrelated to the serious business of the real world. Defining love as purely expressive demeans women, since love is in their sphere. It also leads men to see love as "sissy" or humiliating behavior that threatens their status, something they should avoid. Finally, love is devalued by being restricted to the sphere of women. Studies of the prestige of occupations show that jobs lose status once they become women's work.

41   Psychological theories of human development illustrate the simultaneous devaluation of women and love. In these theories, a healthy person develops from a dependent child to an autonomous adult, and the upper-middle-class male is taken as the ideal. Self-development is equated with masculine independence, as Carol Gilligan has shown, and women who emphasize attachment are judged to be developmentally retarded.

42   The pervasiveness of this perspective was documented in a study of mental health professionals who were asked to describe mental health, femininity, and masculinity. They associated both mental health and masculinity with independence, rationality, and dominance. In contrast, qualities such as tact, gentleness, or awareness of the feelings of others were associated with femininity and not with mental health.

43   The feminization of love also legitimates impersonal, exploitative relations in the workplace and among men. It is part of the ideology of separate spheres that reserves love and personal relationships for women and the home. Men, in this ideology, should be judged by their instrumental and economic achievements. For example, Daniel Levinson's conception of development for a man centers on the Dream of glorious achievement in his occupation. Attachments are subservient to the goals of becoming an autonomous person and attaining the Dream; if relationships impede progress towards the Dream, they must be renounced. Thus a man who has not progressed towards his Dream by mid life should break out of his established way of life by "leaving his wife, quitting his job, or moving to another region." This concept of self-development not only discourages men from close relationships; it also defines men without challenging careers (which means most men) as failures, and implies that if a man is poor, it is because he has failed in his personal development.

44   The feminization of love contributes to overspecialization and unequal power between the sexes, implying that women need love and marriage much more than men and are much more skilled at love. Women are encouraged to become overinvolved in attachments, while men become overinvolved in work. The cost of this overspecialization is sometimes a matter of life or death.

WRITING ASSIGNMENTS

Analysis

1. Compare and contrast what Cancian calls the feminine and masculine conceptions of love.
2. How is the feminine conception of love related to the sexual division of labor in nineteenth-century America?
3. Explain how accepting either the masculine or the feminine definition of love leads to distorted interpretations and biased evaluations of both men's and women's behavior.
4. Explain how the feminization of love lowers the status of women and reinforces the power difference between the sexes.
5. How does Cancian's analysis of love help to explain the differences in attitudes and the misunderstandings between the characters in Carver's "What We Talk About When We Talk About Love" and Tan's "Rice Husband"?
6. How do Cancian's definitions of love correlate with Tannen's theories about male and female primary needs and differing communication styles?

Argument

1. Does Cancian's working definition of love encompass "being in love" or romantic love? If it doesn't, is her definition inadequate?
2. Will increased women's equality and power lead to new concepts of love?
3. Do women benefit from a more androgynous conception of love, such as the one offered by Cancian? Do men?
4. Do you agree with Cancian's observations about the differences between men's and women's communication skills and styles?
5. Does Caryl Rivers's marriage, described in "Can a Woman Be Liberated and Married?" fulfill Cancian's working, androgynous definition of love?
6. Are men or women more romantic? Why?

Personal Writing and Writing from Research

1. Compare and contrast Cancian's working definition of love with your own.
2. What is the relationship, if any, between love and sex? Do men's and women's answers to this question generally differ? Why?
3. Cancian refers to several historical redefinitions of love. In a research paper, explain the courtly or chivalric conception of love in medieval times, or the Victorian glorification of the mother-child relationship.
4. Cancian critically refers to Abraham Maslow, Lillian Rubin, Nancy Chodorow, and Carol Gilligan as defenders of a feminine conception of love. Read, analyze, and evaluate the discussion of love, or of gender differences in love, in either Maslow's *Motivation and Personality* (1970), Rubin's *Intimate Strangers* (1983), Chodorow's *The Reproduction of Mothering* (1978), or Gilligan's *In a Different Voice* (1982).

You Just Don't Understand

Deborah Tannen

A professor of linguistics at Georgetown University, Deborah Tannen is a PhD and has written, in addition to scholarly publications, two books for the general public, *That's Not What I Meant! How Conversational Style Makes or Breaks Your Relations with Others* (1986) and *You Just Don't Understand* (1990), from which this selection is excerpted.

In analyzing communication, Tannen distinguishes between messages—the informational content of communication—and "metamessages"—the "information about the relations among the people involved, and their attitudes toward what they are saying or doing and the people they are saying or doing it to." She argues that misunderstandings arise from the way we respond to these metamessages.

Journal Topics: (1) Describe a time when you shared a problem with a friend or lover and were either comforted or upset by his or her response. What about the response caused your feelings? (2) How do you feel when your boyfriend or girlfriend makes plans for a time you would normally spend together without checking with you? (3) How do you feel when your boyfriend or girlfriend expects you to check with him or her before you make plans?

As You Read: (1) How does a primary need for connection affect a person's communication style? How does a need for independence affect it? (2) Explain how these different needs can create misunderstandings. (3) How does Tannen connect these differences to gender?

INTIMACY AND INDEPENDENCE

1 *Intimacy* is key in a world of connection where individuals negotiate complex networks of friendship, minimize differences, try to reach consensus, and avoid the appearance of superiority, which would highlight differences. In a world of status, *independence* is key, because a primary means of establishing status is to tell others what to do, and taking orders is a marker of low status. Though all humans need both intimacy and independence, women tend to focus on the first and men on the second. It is as if their lifeblood ran in different directions.

2 These differences can give women and men differing views of the same situation, as they did in the case of a couple I will call Linda and Josh. When Josh's old high-school chum called him at work and announced he'd be in town on business the following month, Josh invited him to stay for the weekend. That evening he informed Linda that they were going to have a houseguest, and that he and his chum would go out together the first night to shoot the breeze like old times. Linda was upset. She was going to be away on business the week before, and the Friday night when Josh would be out with his chum would be her first night home. But what upset her the most was that Josh had made these plans on his own and informed her of them, rather than discussing them with her before extending the invitation.

3 Linda would never make plans, for a weekend or an evening, without first checking with Josh. She can't understand why he doesn't show her the same courtesy and consideration that she shows him. But when she protests, Josh says, "I can't say to my friend, 'I have to ask my wife for permission'!"

4 To Josh, checking with his wife means seeking permission, which implies that he is not independent, not free to act on his own. It would make him feel like a child or an underling. To Linda, checking with her husband has nothing to do with permission. She assumes that spouses discuss their plans with each other because their lives are intertwined, so the actions of one have consequences for the other. Not only does Linda not mind telling someone, "I have to check with Josh"; quite the contrary—she likes it. It makes her feel good to know and show that she is involved with someone, that her life is bound up with someone else's.

5   Linda and Josh both felt more upset by this incident, and others like it, than seemed warranted, because it cut to the core of their primary concerns. Linda was hurt because she sensed a failure of closeness in their relationship: He didn't care about her as much as she cared about him. And he was hurt because he felt she was trying to control him and limit his freedom.

6   A similar conflict exists between Louise and Howie, another couple, about spending money. Louise would never buy anything costing more than a hundred dollars without discussing it with Howie, but he goes out and buys whatever he wants and feels they can afford, like a table saw or a new power mower. Louise is disturbed, not because she disapproves of the purchases, but because she feels he is acting as if she were not in the picture.

7   Many women feel it is natural to consult with their partners at every turn, while many men automatically make more decisions without consulting their partners. This may reflect a broad difference in conceptions of decision making. Women expect decisions to be discussed first and made by consensus. They appreciate the discussion itself as evidence of involvement and communication. But many men feel oppressed by lengthy discussions about what they see as minor decisions, and they feel hemmed in if they can't just act without talking first. When women try to initiate a freewheeling discussion by asking, "What do you think?" men often think they are being asked to decide. . . .

ASYMMETRIES: WOMEN AND MEN TALKING AT CROSS-PURPOSES

8 Eve had a lump removed from her breast. Shortly after the operation, talking to her sister, she said that she found it upsetting to have been cut into, and that looking at the stitches was distressing because they left a seam that had changed the contour of her breast. Her sister said, "I know. When I had my operation I felt the same way." Eve made the same observation to her friend Karen, who said, "I know. It's like your body has been violated." But when she told her husband, Mark, how she felt, he said, "You can have plastic surgery to cover up the scar and restore the shape of your breast."

9   Eve had been comforted by her sister and her friend, but she was not comforted by Mark's comment. Quite the contrary, it upset her more. Not only didn't she hear what she wanted, that he understood her feelings, but, far worse, she felt he was asking her to undergo more surgery just when she was telling him how much this operation had upset her. "I'm not having any more surgery!" she protested. "I'm sorry you don't like the way it looks." Mark was hurt and puzzled. "I don't care," he protested. "It doesn't bother me at all." She asked, "Then why are you telling me to have plastic surgery?" He answered, "Because you were saying *you* were upset about the way it looked."

10   Eve felt like a heel: Mark had been wonderfully supportive and concerned throughout her surgery. How could she snap at him because of what he said—"just words"—

when what he had done was unassailable? And yet she had perceived in his words metamessages that cut to the core of their relationship. It was self-evident to him that his comment was a reaction to her complaint, but she heard it as an independent complaint of his. He thought he was reassuring her that she needn't feel bad about her scar because there was something she could *do* about it. She heard his suggestion that she do something about the scar as evidence that *he* was bothered by it. Furthermore, whereas she wanted reassurance that it was normal to feel bad in her situation, his telling her that the problem could easily be fixed implied she had no right to feel bad about it.

11   Eve wanted the gift of understanding, but Mark gave her the gift of advice. He was taking the role of problem solver, whereas she simply wanted confirmation for her feelings.

12   A similar misunderstanding arose between a husband and wife following a car accident in which she had been seriously injured. Because she hated being in the hospital, the wife asked to come home early. But once home, she suffered pain from having to move around more. Her husband said, "Why didn't you stay in the hospital where you would have been more comfortable?" This hurt her because it seemed to imply that he did not want her home. She didn't think of his suggestion that she should have stayed in the hospital as a response to her complaints about the pain she was suffering; she thought of it as an independent expression of his preference not to have her at home.

"THEY'RE MY TROUBLES—NOT YOURS"

13   If women are often frustrated because men do not respond to their troubles by offering matching troubles, men are often frustrated because women do. Some men not only take no comfort in such a response, they take offense. For example, a woman told me that when her companion talks about a personal concern—for example, his feelings about growing older—she responds, "I know how you feel; I feel the same way." To her surprise and chagrin, he gets annoyed; he feels she is trying to take something away from him by denying the uniqueness of his experience.

14   A similar miscommunication was responsible for the following interchange, which began as a conversation and ended as an argument:

> HE: I'm really tired. I didn't sleep well last night.
> SHE: I didn't sleep well either. I never do.
> HE: Why are you trying to belittle me?
> SHE: I'm not! I'm just trying to show that I understand!

15   This woman was not only hurt by her husband's reaction; she was mystified by it. How could he think she was belittling him? By "belittle me," he meant "belittle my experience." He was filtering her attempts to establish connection through his concern with preserving independence and avoiding being put down.

"I'LL FIX IT FOR YOU"

16 Women and men are both often frustrated by the other's way of responding to their expression of troubles. And they are further hurt by the other's frustration. If women resent men's tendency to offer solutions to problems, men complain about women's refusal to take action to solve the problems they complain about. Since many men see themselves as problem solvers, a complaint or a trouble is a challenge to their ability to think of a solution, just as a woman presenting a broken bicycle or stalling car poses a challenge to their ingenuity in fixing it. But whereas many women appreciate help in fixing mechanical equipment, few are inclined to appreciate help in "fixing" emotional troubles. . . .

17   Trying to solve a problem or fix a trouble focuses on the message level of talk. But for most women who habitually report problems at work or in friendships, the message is not the main point of complaining. It's the metamessage that counts: Telling about a problem is a bid for an expression of understanding ("I know how you feel") or a similar complaint ("I felt the same way when something similar happened to me"). In other words, troubles talk is intended to reinforce rapport by sending the metamessage "We're the same; you're not alone." Women are frustrated when they not only don't get this reinforcement but, quite the opposite, feel distanced by the advice, which seems to send the metamessage "We're not the same. You have the problems; I have the solutions."

18   Furthermore, mutual understanding is symmetrical, and this symmetry contributes to a sense of community. But giving advice is asymmetrical. It frames the advice giver as more knowledgeable, more reasonable, more in control—in a word, one-up. And this contributes to the distancing effect. . . .

MATCHING TROUBLES

19 The very different way that women respond to the telling of troubles is dramatized in a short story, "New Haven," by Alice Mattison. Eleanor tells Patsy that she has fallen in love with a married man. Patsy responds by first displaying understanding and then offering a matching revelation about a similar experience:

> "Well," says Patsy. "I know how you feel."
> "You do?"
> "In a way, I do. Well, I should tell you. I've been sleeping with a married man for
> two years."

20 Patsy then tells Eleanor about her affair and how she feels about it. After they discuss Patsy's affair, however, Patsy says:

> "But you were telling me about this man and I cut you off. I'm sorry. See? I'm getting self-centered."
> "It's OK." But she is pleased again.

The conversation then returns to Eleanor's incipient affair. Thus Patsy responds first by confirming Eleanor's feelings and matching her experience, reinforcing their similarity, and then by encouraging Eleanor to tell more. Within the frame of Patsy's similar predicament, the potential asymmetry inherent in revealing personal problems is avoided, and the friendship is brought into balance.

21   What made Eleanor's conversation with Patsy so pleasing to Eleanor was that they shared a sense of how to talk about troubles, and this reinforced their friendship. Though Eleanor raised the matter of her affair, she did not elaborate on it until Patsy pressed her to do so. In another story by the same author, "The Knitting," a woman named Beth is staying with her sister in order to visit her sister's daughter Stephanie in a psychiatric hospital. While there, Beth receives a disturbing telephone call from her boyfriend, Alec. Having been thus reminded of her troubles, she wants to talk about them, but she refrains, because her sister doesn't ask. She feels required, instead, to focus on her sister's problem, the reason for her visit:

> She'd like to talk about her muted half-quarrels with Alec of the last weeks, but her sister does not ask about the phone call. Then Beth thinks they should talk about Stephanie.

The women in these stories are balancing a delicate system by which troubles talk is used to confirm their feelings and create a sense of community.

22   When women confront men's ways of talking to them, they judge them by the standards of women's conversational styles. Women show concern by following up someone else's statement of trouble by questioning her about it. When men change the subject, women think they are showing a lack of sympathy—a failure of intimacy. But the failure to ask probing questions could just as well be a way of respecting the other's need for independence. When Eleanor tells Patsy that she is in love with Peter, Patsy asks, "Are you sleeping with him?" This exploration of Eleanor's topic could well strike many men—and some women—as intrusive, though Eleanor takes it as a show of interest that nourishes their friendship.

23   Women tend to show understanding of another woman's feelings. When men try to reassure women by telling them that their situation is not so bleak, the women hear their feelings being belittled or discounted. Again, they encounter a failure of intimacy just when they were bidding to reinforce it. Trying to trigger a symmetrical communication, they end up in an asymmetrical one.

WRITING ASSIGNMENTS

Analysis

1. Define "metamessages" and explain how they can lead individuals to interpret the same words in very different ways. Illustrate your explanation with examples from Tannen and from your own observations and experiences of communication between two people who love each other.

2. Assuming Tannen's theories about communication styles are correct, explain why most women are more concerned with connection and intimacy, and most men with status and independence.
3. Use Tannen's theories about gender-based communication styles and gender-linked differences in primary needs to explain the interactions between the characters in "What We Talk About When We Talk About Love" or "Rice Husband."

Argument

1. Do you agree with Tannen that most men are more concerned with status and independence, and most women with connection and intimacy?
2. Are the differences in communication style more a reflection of gender or of power differences? That is, are more-powerful women more likely to use a communication style that emphasizes independence and status, and less-powerful men, a style that emphasizes connection and intimacy?
3. Does a person's communication style change depending on the context and company? Why?
4. Is it possible to change one's communication style? What factors would facilitate or interfere with such a change?
5. Do Tannen's theories reflect a bias in favor of what Cancian calls a feminine conception of love?
6. Do the men in Tannen's anecdotes illustrate what Cancian calls a masculine conception of love and/or a primary need for independence and status?

Personal Writing and Writing from Research

1. Do Tannen's theories and observations apply to you? Describe, illustrate, and explain your communication style.
2. Experiment with either the "status" or "connection" communication style, whichever is *not* your customary one, and evaluate the consequences.
3. *Collaborative Project:* Test Tannen's theories by carefully observing and listening to extended conversations between males and females and between two people of different status (employer-employee, teacher-student, parent-child). Report and evaluate your findings.
4. Tannen conducted her research in the United States. Research communication styles in another culture or cultures and compare your findings to Tannen's. Or observe communication styles in various American subcultures in order to evaluate Tannen's theories.

Rice Husband

Amy Tan

Amy Tan was born in California in 1952, two-and-a-half years after her parents immigrated to the United States. Her parents hoped she would become a neurosurgeon by profession and a concert pianist by avocation, but instead she earned a master's degree in linguistics and became a consultant to programs for disabled children, and later a free-lance writer. Visiting China for the first time in 1987, she found it was just as her mother had said: "As soon as my feet touched China, I became Chinese."

"Rice Husband" comes from *The Joy Luck Club* (1989), a collection of interrelated stories about four Chinese women and their American-born daughters. Her second book, *The Kitchen God's Wife* (1991), tells the story of the events in China before and during World War II that led to the protagonist's immigration to the United States.

Journal Topics: (1) How do you handle the question of who pays for what with a roommate, a business acquaintance, a friend, a lover? (2) In a marriage, how do you think that finances and assets should be handled? Why?

As You Read: (1) Explain the origin and rationale for the way that Harold and Lena handle their finances. (2) What bothers Lena about this arrangement? (3) Is the arrangement fair? What does "fairness" mean in this context? (4) How does money relate to power and love in their relationship? (5) How does the handling of money relate to Harold and Lena's respective self-esteem?

LENA ST. CLAIR

To this day, I believe my mother has the mysterious ability to see things before they happen. She has a Chinese saying for what she knows. *Chunwang chihan:* If the lips are gone, the teeth will be cold. Which means, I suppose, one thing is always the result of another.

But she does not predict when earthquakes will come, or how the stock market will do. She sees only bad things that affect our family. And she knows what causes them. But now she laments that she never did anything to stop them.

One time when I was growing up in San Francisco, she looked at the way our new apartment sat too steeply on the hill. She said the new baby in her womb would fall out dead, and it did.

When a plumbing and bathroom fixtures store opened up across the street from our bank, my mother said the bank would soon have all its money drained away. And one month later, an officer of the bank was arrested for embezzlement.

5 And just after my father died last year, she said she knew this would happen. Because a philodendron plant my father had given her had withered and died, despite the fact that she watered it faithfully. She said the plant had damaged its roots and no water could get to it. The autopsy report she later received showed my father had had ninety-percent blockage of the arteries before he died of a heart attack at the age of seventy-four. My father was not Chinese like my mother, but English-Irish American, who enjoyed his five slices of bacon and three eggs sunny-side up every morning.

I remember this ability of my mother's, because now she is visiting my husband and me in the house we just bought in Woodside. And I wonder what she will see.

Harold and I were lucky to find this place, which is near the summit of Highway 9, then a left-right-left down three forks of unmarked dirt roads, unmarked because the residents always tear down the signs to keep out salesmen, developers, and city inspectors. We are only a forty-minute drive to my mother's apartment in San Francisco. This became a sixty-minute ordeal coming back from San Francisco, when my mother was with us in the car. After we got to the two-lane winding road to the summit, she touched her hand gently to Harold's shoulder and softly said, "Ai, tire squealing." And then a little later, "Too much tear and wear on car."

Harold had smiled and slowed down, but I could see his hands were clenched on the steering wheel of the Jaguar, as he glanced nervously in his rearview mirror at the line of impatient cars that was growing by the minute. And I was secretly glad to watch his discomfort. He was always the one who tailgated old ladies in their Buicks, honking his horn and revvying the engine as if he would run them over unless they pulled over.

And at the same time, I hated myself for being mean-spirited, for thinking Harold deserved this torment. Yet I couldn't help myself. I was mad at Harold and he was exasperated with me. That morning, before we picked my mother up, he had said, "You should pay for the exterminators, because Mirugai is your cat and so they're *your* fleas. It's only fair."

10 None of our friends could ever believe we fight over something as stupid as fleas, but they would also never believe that our problems are much, much deeper than that, so deep I don't even know where bottom is.

And now that my mother is here—she is staying for a week, or until the electricians are done rewiring her building in San Francisco—we have to pretend nothing is the matter.

Meanwhile she asks over and over again why we had to pay so much for a renovated barn and a mildew-lined pool on four acres of land, two of which are covered with redwood trees and poison oak. Actually she doesn't really ask, she just says, "Aii, so much money, so much," as we show her different parts of the house and land. And her laments always compel Harold to explain to my mother in simple terms: "Well, you see, it's the details that cost so much. Like this wood floor. It's hand-bleached. And the walls here, this marbleized effect, it's hand-sponged. It's really worth it."

And my mother nods and agrees: "Bleach and sponge cost so much."

During our brief tour of the house, she's already found the flaws. She says the slant of the floor makes her feel as if she is "running down." She thinks the guest room where she will be staying—which is really a former hayloft shaped by a sloped roof—has "two lopsides." She sees spiders in high corners and even fleas jumping up in the air—pah! pah! pah!—like little spatters of hot oil. My mother knows, underneath all the fancy details that cost so much, this house is still a barn.

15   She can see all this. And it annoys me that all she sees are the bad parts. But then I look around and everything she's said is true. And this convinces me she can see what else is going on, between Harold and me. She knows what's going to happen to us. Because I remember something else she saw when I was eight years old.

My mother had looked in my rice bowl and told me I would marry a bad man.

"Aii, Lena," she had said after that dinner so many years ago, "your future husband have one pock mark for every rice you not finish."

She put my bowl down. "I once know a pock-mark man. Mean man, bad man."

And I thought of a mean neighbor boy who had tiny pits in his cheeks, and it was true, those marks were the size of rice grains. This boy was about twelve and his name was Arnold.

20   Arnold would shoot rubber bands at my legs whenever I walked past his building on my way home from school, and one time he ran over my doll with his bicycle, crushing her legs below the knees. I didn't want this cruel boy to be my future husband. So I picked up that cold bowl of rice and scraped the last few grains into my mouth, then smiled at my mother, confident my future husband would be not Arnold but someone whose face was as smooth as the porcelain in my now clean bowl.

But my mother sighed. "Yesterday, you not finish rice either." I thought of those unfinished mouthfuls of rice, and then the grains that lined my bowl the day before, and the day before that. By the minute, my eight-year-old heart grew more and more terror-stricken over the growing possibility that my future husband was fated to be this mean boy, Arnold. And thanks to my poor eating habits, his hideous face would eventually resemble the craters of the moon.

This would have been a funny incident to remember from my childhood, but it is actually a memory I recall from time to time with a mixture of nausea and remorse. My loathing for Arnold had grown to such a point that I eventually found a way to make him die. I let one thing result from another. Of course, all of it could have been just loosely connected coincidences. And whether that's true or not, I know the *intention* was there. Because when I want something to happen—or not happen—I begin to look at all events and all things as relevant, an opportunity to take or avoid.

I found the opportunity. The same week my mother told me about the rice bowl and my future husband, I saw a shocking film at Sunday school. I remember the teacher had dimmed the lights so that all we could see were silhouettes of one another. Then the teacher looked at us, a roomful of squirmy, well-fed Chinese-

American children, and she said, "This film will show you why you should give tithings to God, to do God's work."

She said, "I want you to think about a nickel's worth of candy money, or however much you eat each week—your Good and Plentys, your Necco wafers, your jujubes— and compare that to what you are about to see. And I also want you to think about what your true blessings in life really are."

25   And then she set the film projector clattering away. The film showed missionaries in Africa and India. These good souls worked with people whose legs were swollen to the size of tree trunks, whose numb limbs had become as twisted as jungle vines. But the most terrible of the afflictions were men and women with leprosy. Their faces were covered with every kind of misery I could imagine: pits and pustules, cracks and bumps, and fissures that I was sure erupted with the same vehemence as snails writhing in a bed of salt. If my mother had been in the room, she would have told me these poor people were victims of future husbands and wives who had failed to eat *platefuls* of food.

After seeing this film, I did a terrible thing. I saw what I had to do so I would not have to marry Arnold. I began to leave more rice in my bowl. And then I extended my prodigal ways beyond Chinese food. I did not finish my creamed corn, broccoli, Rice Krispies, or peanut butter sandwiches. And once, when I bit into a candy bar and saw how lumpy it was, how full of secret dark spots and creamy goo, I sacrificed that as well.

I considered that probably nothing would happen to Arnold, that he might not get leprosy, move to Africa and die. And this somehow balanced the dark possibility that he might.

He didn't die right away. In fact, it was some five years later, by which time I had become quite thin. I had stopped eating, not because of Arnold, whom I had long forgotten, but to be fashionably anorexic like all the other thirteen-year-old girls who were dieting and finding other ways to suffer as teenagers. I was sitting at the breakfast table, waiting for my mother to finish packing a sack lunch which I always promptly threw away as soon as I rounded the corner. My father was eating with his fingers, dabbing the ends of his bacon into the egg yolks with one hand, while holding the newspaper with the other.

"Oh my, listen to this," he said, still dabbing. And that's when he announced that Arnold Reisman, a boy who lived in our old neighborhood in Oakland, had died of complications from measles. He had just been accepted to Cal State Hayward and was planning to become a podiatrist.

30   "'Doctors were at first baffled by the disease, which they report is extremely rare and generally attacks children between the ages of ten and twenty, months to years after they have contracted the measles virus,'" read my father. "'The boy had had a mild case of the measles when he was twelve, reported his mother. Problems this year were first noticed when the boy developed motor coordination problems and mental lethargy which increased until he fell into a coma. The boy, age seventeen, never regained consciousness.'

"Didn't you know that boy?" asked my father, and I stood there mute.

"This is shame," said my mother, looking at me. "This is terrible shame."

And I thought she could see through me and that she knew I was the one who had caused Arnold to die. I was terrified.

That night, in my room, I gorged myself. I had stolen a half-gallon of strawberry ice cream from the freezer, and I forced spoonful after spoonful down my throat. And later, for several hours after that, I sat hunched on the fire escape landing outside my bedroom, retching back into the ice cream container. And I remember wondering why it was that eating something good could make me feel so terrible, while vomiting something terrible could make me feel so good.

35   The thought that I could have caused Arnold's death is not so ridiculous. Perhaps he *was* destined to be my husband. Because I think to myself, even today, how can the world in all its chaos come up with so many coincidences, so many similarities and exact opposites? Why did Arnold single me out for his rubber band torture? How is it that he contracted measles the same year I began consciously to hate him? And why did I think of Arnold in the first place—when my mother looked in my rice bowl—and then come to hate him so much? Isn't hate merely the result of wounded love?

And even when I can finally dismiss all of this as ridiculous, I still feel that somehow, for the most part, we deserve what we get. I didn't get Arnold. I got Harold.

Harold and I work at the same architectural firm, Livotny & Associates. Only Harold Livotny is a partner and I am an associate. We met eight years ago, before he started Livotny & Associates. I was twenty-eight, a project assistant, and he was thirty-four. We both worked in the restaurant design and development division of Harned Kelley & Davis.

We started seeing each other for working lunches, to talk about the projects, and we would always split the tab right in half, even though I usually ordered only a salad because I have this tendency to gain weight easily. Later, when we started meeting secretly for dinner, we still divided the bill.

And we just continued that way, everything right down the middle. If anything, I encouraged it. Sometimes I insisted on paying for the whole thing: meal, drinks, and tip. And it really didn't bother me.

40   "Lena, you're really extraordinary," Harold said after six months of dinners, five months of post-prandial lovemaking, and one week of timid and silly love confessions. We were lying in bed, between new purple sheets I had just bought for him. His old set of white sheets was stained in revealing places, not very romantic.

And he nuzzled my neck and whispered, "I don't think I've ever met another woman, who's so together . . ."—and I remember feeling a hiccup of fear upon hearing the words "another woman," because I could imagine dozens, hundreds of adoring women eager to buy Harold breakfast, lunch, and dinner to feel the pleasure of his breath on their skin.

Then he bit my neck and said in a rush, "Nor anyone who's as soft and squishy and lovable as you are."

And with that, I swooned inside, caught off balance by this latest revelation of love, wondering how such a remarkable person as Harold could think I was extraordinary.

Now that I'm angry at Harold, it's hard to remember what was so remarkable about him. And I know they're there, the good qualities, because I wasn't that stupid to fall in love with him, to marry him. All I can remember is how awfully lucky I felt, and consequently how worried I was that all this undeserved good fortune would someday slip away. When I fantasized about moving in with him, I also dredged up my deepest fears: that he would tell me I smelled bad, that I had terrible bathroom habits, that my taste in music and television was appalling. I worried that Harold would someday get a new prescription for his glasses and he'd put them on one morning, look me up and down, and say, "Why, gosh, you aren't the girl I thought you were, are you?"

45   And I think that feeling of fear never left me, that I would be caught someday, exposed as a sham of a woman. But recently, a friend of mine, Rose, who's in therapy now because her marriage has already fallen apart, told me those kinds of thoughts are commonplace in women like us.

"At first I thought it was because I was raised with all this Chinese humility," Rose said. "Or that maybe it was because when you're Chinese you're supposed to accept everything, flow with the Tao and not make waves. But my therapist said, Why do you blame your culture, your ethnicity? And I remembered reading an article about baby boomers, how we expect the best and when we get it we worry that maybe we should have expected more, because it's all diminishing returns after a certain age."

And after my talk with Rose, I felt better about myself and I thought, Of course, Harold and I are equals, in many respects. He's not exactly handsome in the classic sense, although clear-skinned and certainly attractive in that wiry intellectual way. And I may not be a raving beauty, but a lot of women in my aerobics class tell me I'm "exotic" in an unusual way, and they're jealous that my breasts don't sag, now that small breasts are in. Plus, one of my clients said I have incredible vitality and exuberance.

So I think I deserve someone like Harold, and I mean in the good sense and not like bad karma. We're equals. I'm also smart. I have common sense. And I'm intuitive, highly so. I was the one who told Harold he was good enough to start his own firm.

When we were still working at Harned Kelley & Davis, I said, "Harold, this firm knows just what a good deal it has with you. You're the goose who lays the golden egg. If you started your own business today, you'd walk away with more than half of the restaurant clients."

50   And he said, laughing, "Half? Boy, that's love."

And I shouted back, laughing with him, "More than half! You're that good. You're the best there is in restaurant design and development. You know it and I know it, and so do a lot of restaurant developers."

That was the night he decided to "go for it," as he put it, which is a phrase I have personally detested ever since a bank I used to work for adopted the slogan for its employee productivity contest.

But still, I said to Harold, "Harold, I want to help you go for it, too. I mean, you're going to need money to start this business."

He wouldn't hear of taking any money from me, not as a favor, not as a loan, not as an investment, or even as the down payment on a partnership. He said he valued our relationship too much. He didn't want to contaminate it with money. He explained, "I wouldn't want a handout any more than you'd want one. As long as we keep the money thing separate, we'll always be sure of our love for each other."

55 I wanted to protest. I wanted to say, "No! I'm not really this way about money, the way we've been doing it. I'm really into giving freely. I want . . ." But I didn't know where to begin. I wanted to ask him who, what woman, had hurt him this way, that made him so scared about accepting love in all its wonderful forms. But then I heard him saying what I'd been waiting to hear for a long, long time.

"Actually, you could help me out if you moved in with me. I mean, that way I could use the five hundred dollars' rent you paid to me . . ."

"That's a wonderful idea," I said immediately, knowing how embarrassed he was to have to ask me that way. I was so deliriously happy that it didn't matter that the rent on my studio was really only four hundred thirty-five. Besides, Harold's place was much nicer, a two-bedroom flat with a two-hundred-forty-degree view of the bay. It was worth the extra money, no matter whom I shared the place with.

So within the year, Harold and I quit Harned Kelley & Davis and he started Livotny & Associates, and I went to work there as a project coordinator. And no, he didn't get half the restaurant clients of Harned Kelley & Davis. In fact, Harned Kelley & Davis threatened to sue if he walked away with even one client over the next year. So I gave him pep talks in the evening when he was discouraged. I told him how he should do more avant-garde thematic restaurant design, to differentiate himself from the other firms.

"Who needs another brass and oakwood bar and grill?" I said. "Who wants another pasta place in sleek Italian moderno? How many places can you go to with police cars lurching out of the walls? This town is chockablock with restaurants that are just clones of the same old themes. You can find a niche. Do something different every time. Get the Hong Kong investors who are willing to sink some bucks into American ingenuity."

60 He gave me his adoring smile, the one that said, "I love it when you're so naive." And I adored his looking at me like that.

So I stammered out my love. "You . . . you . . . could do new theme eating places . . . a . . . a . . . Home on the Range! All the home-cooked mom stuff, mom at the kitchen range with a gingham apron and mom waitresses leaning over telling you to finish your soup.

"And maybe . . . maybe you could do a novel-menu restaurant . . . foods from fiction . . . sandwiches from Lawrence Sanders murder mysteries, just desserts from Nora Ephron's *Heartburn*. And something else with a magic theme, or jokes and gags, or . . ."

Harold actually listened to me. He took those ideas and he applied them in an educated, methodical way. He made it happen. But still, I remember, it was my idea.

And today Livotny & Associates is a growing firm of twelve full-time people, which specializes in thematic restaurant design, what I still like to call "theme eating." Harold is the concept man, the chief architect, the designer, the person who makes the final sales presentation to a new client. I work under the interior designer, because, as Harold explains, it would not seem fair to the other employees if he promoted me just because we are now married—that was five years ago, two years after he started Livotny & Associates. And even though I am very good at what I do, I have never been formally trained in this area. When I was majoring in Asian-American studies, I took only one relevant course, in theater set design, for a college production of *Madama Butterfly*.

65 At Livotny & Associates, I procure the theme elements. For one restaurant called The Fisherman's Tale, one of my prized findings was a yellow varnished wood boat stenciled with the name "Overbored," and I was the one who thought the menus should dangle from miniature fishing poles, and the napkins be printed with rulers that have inches translating into feet. For a Lawrence of Arabia deli called Tray Sheik, I was the one who thought the place should have a bazaar effect, and I found the replicas of cobras lying on fake Hollywood boulders.

I love my work when I don't think about it too much. And when I do think about it, how much I get paid, how hard I work, how fair Harold is to everybody except me, I get upset.

So really, we're equals, except that Harold makes about seven times more than what I make. He knows this, too, because he signs my monthly check, and then I deposit it into my separate checking account.

Lately, however, this business about being equals started to bother me. It's been on my mind, only I didn't really know it. I just felt a little uneasy about *something*. And then about a week ago, it all became clear. I was putting the breakfast dishes away and Harold was warming up the car so we could go to work. And I saw the newspaper spread open on the kitchen counter, Harold's glasses on top, his favorite coffee mug with the chipped handle off to the side. And for some reason, seeing all these little domestic signs of familiarity, our daily ritual, made me swoon inside. But it was as if I were seeing Harold the first time we made love, this feeling of surrendering everything to him, with abandon, without caring what I got in return.

And when I got into the car, I still had the glow of that feeling and I touched his hand and said, "Harold, I love you." And he looked in the rearview mirror, backing up the car, and said, "I love you, too. Did you lock the door?" And just like that, I started to think, It's just not enough.

70 Harold jingles the car keys and says, "I'm going down the hill to buy stuff for dinner. Steaks okay? Want something special?"

"We're out of rice," I say, discreetly nodding toward my mother, whose back is turned to me. She's looking out the kitchen window, at the trellis of bougainvillea. And then Harold is out the door and I hear the deep rumble of the car and then the sound of crunching gravel as he drives away.

My mother and I are alone in the house. I start to water the plants. She is standing on her tiptoes, peering at a list stuck on our refrigerator door.

The list says "Lena" and "Harold" and under each of our names are things we've bought and how much they cost:

Lena	_Harold_
chicken, veg., bread, broccoli, shampoo, beer $19.63	Garage stuff $25.35
Maria (clean + tip) $65	Bathroom stuff $5.41
groceries (see shop list) $55.15	Car stuff $6.57
petunias, potting soil $14.11	Light Fixtures $87.26
Photo developing $13.83	Road gravel $19.99
	Gas $22.00
	Car Smog Check $35
	Movies & Dinner $65
	Ice Cream $4.50

The way things are going this week, Harold's already spent over a hundred dollars more, so I'll owe him around fifty from my checking account.

75   "What is this writing?" asks my mother in Chinese.

"Oh, nothing really. Just things we share," I say as casually as I can.

And she looks at me and frowns but doesn't say anything. She goes back to reading the list, this time more carefully, moving her finger down each item.

And I feel embarrassed, knowing what she's seeing. I'm relieved that she doesn't see the other half of it, the discussions. Through countless talks, Harold and I reached an understanding about not including personal things like "mascara," and "shaving lotion," "hair spray" or "Bic shavers," "tampons," or "athlete's foot powder."

When we got married at city hall, he insisted on paying the fee. I got my friend Robert to take photos. We held a party at our apartment and everybody brought champagne. And when we bought the house, we agreed that I should pay only a percentage of the mortgage based on what I earn and what he earns, and that I should own an equivalent percentage of community property; this is written in our prenuptial agreement. Since Harold pays more, he had the deciding vote on how the house should look. It is sleek, spare, and what he calls "fluid," nothing to disrupt the line, meaning none of my cluttered look. As for vacations, the one we choose together is fifty-fifty. The others Harold pays for, with the understanding that it's a birthday or Christmas present, or an anniversary gift.

80   And we've had philosophical arguments over things that have gray borders, like my birth control pills, or dinners at home when we entertain people who are really his clients or my old friends from college, or food magazines that I subscribe to but he also reads only because he's bored, not because he would have chosen them for himself.

And we still argue about Mirugai, _the_ cat—not our cat, or my cat, but _the_ cat that was his gift to me for my birthday last year.

"This, you do not share!" exclaims my mother in an astonished voice. And I am startled, thinking she had read my thoughts about Mirugai. But then I see she is pointing to "ice cream" on Harold's list. My mother must remember the incident on the fire escape landing, where she found me, shivering and exhausted, sitting next to that container of regurgitated ice cream. I could never stand the stuff after that. And then I am startled once again to realize that Harold has never noticed that I don't eat any of the ice cream he brings home every Friday evening.

"Why you do this?"

My mother has a wounded sound in her voice, as if I had put the list up to hurt her. I think how to explain this, recalling the words Harold and I have used with each other in the past: "So we can eliminate false dependencies . . . be equals . . . love without obligation . . ." But these are words she could never understand.

85 So instead I tell my mother this: "I don't really know. It's something we started before we got married. And for some reason we never stopped."

When Harold returns from the store, he starts the charcoal. I unload the groceries, marinate the steaks, cook the rice, and set the table. My mother sits on a stool at the granite counter, drinking from a mug of coffee I've poured for her. Every few minutes she wipes the bottom of the mug with a tissue she keeps stuffed in her sweater sleeve.

During dinner, Harold keeps the conversation going. He talks about the plans for the house: the skylights, expanding the deck, planting flower beds of tulips and crocuses, clearing the poison oak, adding another wing, building a Japanese-style tile bathroom. And then he clears the table and starts stacking the plates in the dishwasher.

"Who's ready for dessert?" he asks, reaching into the freezer.

"I'm full," I say.

90 "Lena cannot eat ice cream," says my mother.

"So it seems. She's always on a diet."

"No, she never eat it. She doesn't like."

And now Harold smiles and looks at me puzzled, expecting me to translate what my mother has said.

"It's true," I say evenly. "I've hated ice cream almost all my life."

95 Harold looks at me, as if I, too, were speaking Chinese and he could not understand.

"I guess I assumed you were just trying to lose weight. . . . Oh well."

"She become so thin now you cannot see her," says my mother. "She like a ghost, disappear."

"That's right! Christ, that's great," exclaims Harold, laughing, relieved in thinking my mother is graciously trying to rescue him.

After dinner, I put clean towels on the bed in the guest room. My mother is sitting on the bed. The room has Harold's minimalist look to it: the twin bed with plain white sheets and white blanket, polished wood floors, a bleached oakwood chair, and nothing on the slanted gray walls.

100 The only decoration is an odd-looking piece right next to the bed: an end table made out of a slab of unevenly cut marble and thin crisscrosses of black lacquer wood for the legs. My mother puts her handbag on the table and the cylindrical black vase on top starts to wobble. The freesias in the vase quiver.

"Careful, it's not too sturdy," I say. The table is a poorly designed piece that Harold made in his student days. I've always wondered why he's so proud of it. The lines are clumsy. It doesn't bear any of the traits of "fluidity" that are so important to Harold these days.

"What use for?" asks my mother, jiggling the table with her hand. "You put something else on top, everything fall down. *Chunwang chihan.*"

I leave my mother in her room and go back downstairs. Harold is opening the windows to let the night air in. He does this every evening.

"I'm cold," I say.

105   "What's that?"

"Could you close the windows, please."

He looks at me, sighs and smiles, pulls the windows shut, and then sits down cross-legged on the floor and flips open a magazine. I'm sitting on the sofa, seething, and I don't know why. It's not that Harold has done anything wrong. Harold is just Harold.

And before I even do it, I know I'm starting a fight that is bigger than I know how to handle. But I do it anyway. I go to the refrigerator and I cross out "ice cream" on Harold's side of the list.

"What's going on here?"

110   "I just don't think you should get credit for *your* ice cream anymore."

He shrugs his shoulders, amused. "Suits me."

"Why do you have to be so goddamn fair!" I shout.

Harold puts his magazine down, now wearing his open-mouthed exasperated look. "What is this? Why don't you say what's really the matter?"

"I don't know. . . . I don't know. Everything . . . the way we account for everything. What we share. What we don't share. I'm so tired of it, adding things up, subtracting, making it come out even. I'm sick of it."

115   "You were the one who wanted the cat."

"What are you talking about?"

"All right. If you think I'm being unfair about the exterminators, we'll both pay for it."

"That's not the point!"

"Then tell me, *please,* what is the point?"

120   I start to cry, which I know Harold hates. It always makes him uncomfortable, angry. He thinks it's manipulative. But I can't help it, because I realize now that I don't know what the point of this argument is. Am I asking Harold to support me? Am I asking to pay less than half? Do I really think we should stop accounting for everything? Wouldn't we continue to tally things up in our head? Wouldn't Harold wind up paying more? And then wouldn't I feel worse, less than equal? Or maybe we shouldn't have gotten married in the first place. Maybe Harold is a bad man. Maybe I've made him this way.

None of it seems right. Nothing makes sense. I can admit to nothing and I am in complete despair.

"I just think we have to change things," I say when I think I can control my voice. Only the rest comes out like whining. "We need to think about what our marriage is really based on . . . not this balance sheet, who owes who what."

"Shit," Harold says. And then he sighs and leans back, as if he were thinking about this. Finally he says in what sounds like a hurt voice, "Well, I know our marriage is based on a lot more than a balance sheet. A lot more. And if you don't then I think you should think about what else you want, before you change things."

And now I don't know what to think. What am I saying? What's he saying? We sit in the room, not saying anything. The air feels muggy. I look out the window, and out in the distance is the valley beneath us, a sprinkling of thousands of lights shimmering in the summer fog. And then I hear the sound of glass shattering, upstairs, and a chair scrapes across a wood floor.

125   Harold starts to get up, but I say, "No, I'll go see."

The door is open, but the room is dark, so I call out, "Ma?"

I see it right away: the marble end table collapsed on top of its spindly black legs. Off to the side is the black vase, the smooth cylinder broken in half, the freesias strewn in a puddle of water.

And then I see my mother sitting by the open window, her dark silhouette against the night sky. She turns around in her chair, but I can't see her face.

"Fallen down," she says simply. She doesn't apologize.

130   "It doesn't matter," I say, and I start to pick up the broken glass shards. "I knew it would happen."

"Then why you don't stop it?" asks my mother.

And it's such a simple question.

WRITING ASSIGNMENTS

Analysis

1. Why does Lena's attitude toward the way she and Harold handle finances change?
2. Retell this story from Harold's perspective.
3. Explain the effect that Lena's mother's presence has on Lena, Harold, and their marriage. How do the expression *chunwang chihan* and the broken table relate to the story's theme?
4. How does Cancian's discussion of feminine, masculine, and androgynous conceptions of love help to explain Lena and Harold's differing attitudes toward love and money?
5. Do Tannen's theories help to explain Lena and Harold's problems? That is, how do differing needs for connection (intimacy) and independence (status) contribute to their problems?
6. How do differences in communication styles exacerbate Lena and Harold's marital problems?

7. Explain how Lena's dissatisfaction with her marriage is related to what Cancian calls the powerlessness of feminine love.

Argument

1. Do Lena and Harold love each other? Base your answer on one or more of Cancian's definitions of love (masculine, feminine, or androgynous).
2. Are Lena's resentment and dissatisfaction justified? Explain your answer.
3. If you believe that Lena's resentment is justified, is the way she handles it fair to Harold and effective in resolving their problems?

Personal Writing and Writing from Research

1. How has the handling of money affected your relationship with a friend, lover, or parent? How were emotions connected to finances? Did the way money was handled change over time? Why?
2. Describe and explain your plan for the way a married couple should handle its finances. Does it matter whether both spouses work outside the home, or whether one earns much more than the other?
3. Informally survey other students and write a report comparing the ways they handle financial relationships with members of their family, lovers, friends, or work associates. Analyze how their handling of finances is influenced by their values, relative power in the relationship, the degree of intimacy, and gender.

What We Talk About When We Talk About Love

Raymond Carver

The son of a laborer and a homemaker, Raymond Carver was married and the father of two before he was 20 years old, worked as a manual laborer in his 20s, and died of lung cancer in 1988.

He earned a BA from Humboldt State College in 1963 and an MFA from the University of Iowa in 1966. A prolific writer, he has produced poetry, short fiction, and screenplays. "What We Talk About When We Talk About Love" (1981) comes from the short-story collection of the same name, which focuses on marriage, infidelity, and the collapse of human relationships.

Carver is one of a handful of writers credited with reviving the short story. His stories are generally peopled with the type of working-class and lower-middle-class characters that Carver was familiar with while growing up. Mel, the cardiologist and former seminarian in "What We Talk About . . ." is atypical.

Journal Topics: (1) In a past or current relationship, how did each of you demonstrate love? (2) If you were in a romantic relationship that has ended, compare the way you would have described the other person during the relationship to the way you would describe him or her now.

As You Read: (1) Identify the five couples mentioned in this story and describe the "love" that characterizes each relationship. (2) Do the four speaking characters arrive at any shared understanding about love? (3) What role does alcohol play in this story? (4) What is the significance of Mel's past and present occupations? (5) How do you interpret Mel's thoughts about knights?

My friend Mel McGinnis was talking. Mel McGinnis is a cardiologist, and sometimes that gives him the right.

The four of us were sitting around his kitchen table drinking gin. Sunlight filled the kitchen from the big window behind the sink. There were Mel and me and his second wife, Teresa—Terri, we called her—and my wife, Laura. We lived in Albuquerque then. But we were all from somewhere else.

There was an ice bucket on the table. The gin and the tonic water kept going around, and we somehow got on the subject of love. Mel thought real love was nothing less than spiritual love. He said he'd spent five years in a seminary before quitting to go to medical school. He said he still looked back on those years in the seminary as the most important years in his life.

Terri said the man she lived with before she lived with Mel loved her so much he tried to kill her. Then Terri said, "He beat me up one night. He dragged me around the living room by my ankles. He kept saying, 'I love you, I love you, you bitch.' He went on dragging me around the living room. My head kept knocking on things." Terri looked around the table. "What do you do with love like that?"

5   She was a bone-thin woman with a pretty face, dark eyes, and brown hair that hung down her back. She liked necklaces made of turquoise, and long pendant earrings.

"My God, don't be silly. That's not love, and you know it," Mel said. "I don't know what you'd call it, but I sure know you wouldn't call it love."

"Say what you want to, but I know it was," Terri said. "It may sound crazy to you, but it's true just the same. People are different, Mel. Sure, sometimes he may have acted crazy. Okay. But he loved me. In his own way maybe, but he loved me. There was love there, Mel. Don't say there wasn't."

Mel let out his breath. He held his glass and turned to Laura and me. "The man threatened to kill me," Mel said. He finished his drink and reached for the gin bottle. "Terri's a romantic. Terri's of the kick-me-so-I'll-know-you-love-me school. Terri, hon, don't look that way." Mel reached across the table and touched Terri's cheek with his fingers. He grinned at her.

"Now he wants to make up," Terri said.

10   "Make up what?" Mel said. "What is there to make up? I know what I know. That's all."

"How'd we get started on this subject, anyway?" Terri said. She raised her glass and drank from it. "Mel always has love on his mind," she said. "Don't you, honey?" She smiled, and I thought that was the last of it.

"I just wouldn't call Ed's behavior love. That's all I'm saying, honey," Mel said. "What about you guys?" Mel said to Laura and me. "Does that sound like love to you?"

"I'm the wrong person to ask," I said. "I didn't even know the man. I've only heard his name mentioned in passing. I wouldn't know. You'd have to know the particulars. But I think what you're saying is that love is an absolute."

Mel said, "The kind of love I'm talking about is. The kind of love I'm talking about, you don't try to kill people."

15   Laura said, "I don't know anything about Ed, or anything about the situation. But who can judge anyone else's situation?"

I touched the back of Laura's hand. She gave me a quick smile. I picked up Laura's hand. It was warm, the nails polished, perfectly manicured. I encircled the broad wrist with my fingers, and I held her.

"When I left, he drank rat poison," Terri said. She clasped her arms with her hands. "They took him to the hospital in Sante Fe. That's where we lived then, about ten miles out. They saved his life. But his gums went crazy from it. I mean they pulled away from his teeth. After that, his teeth stood out like fangs. My God," Terri said. She waited a minute, then let go of her arms and picked up her glass.

"What people won't do!" Laura said.

"He's out of the action now," Mel said. "He's dead."

20   Mel handed me the saucer of limes. I took a section, squeezed it over my drink, and stirred the ice cubes with my finger.

"It gets worse," Terri said. "He shot himself in the mouth. But he bungled that too. Poor Ed," she said. Terri shook her head.

"Poor Ed nothing," Mel said. "He was dangerous."

Mel was forty-five years old. He was tall and rangy with curly soft hair. His face and arms were brown from the tennis he played. When he was sober, his gestures, all his movements, were precise, very careful.

"He did love me though, Mel. Grant me that," Terri said. "That's all I'm asking. He didn't love me the way you love me. I'm not saying that. But he loved me. You can grant me that, can't you?"

25   "What do you mean, he bungled it?" I said.

Laura leaned forward with her glass. She put her elbows on the table and held her glass in both hands. She glanced from Mel to Terri and waited with a look of bewilderment on her open face, as if amazed that such things happened to people you were friendly with.

"How'd he bungle it when he killed himself?" I said.

"I'll tell you what happened," Mel said. "He took this twenty-two pistol he'd bought to threaten Terri and me with. Oh, I'm serious, the man was always threatening. You should have seen the way we lived in those days. Like fugitives. I even bought a gun myself. Can you believe it? A guy like me? But I did. I bought one for self-defense and carried it in the glove compartment. Sometimes I'd have to leave the apartment in the middle of the night. To go to the hospital, you know? Terri and I weren't married then, and my first wife had the house and kids, the dog, everything, and Terri and I were living in this apartment here. Sometimes, as I say, I'd get a call in the middle of the night and have to go in to the hospital at two or three in the morning. It'd be dark out there in the parking lot, and I'd break into a sweat before I could even get to my car. I never knew if he was going to come up out of the shrubbery or from behind a car and start shooting. I mean, the man was crazy. He was capable of wiring a bomb, anything. He used to call my service at all hours and say he needed to talk to the doctor, and when I'd return the call, he'd say, 'Son of a bitch, your days are numbered.' Little things like that. It was scary, I'm telling you."

"I still feel sorry for him," Terri said.

30   "It sounds like a nightmare," Laura said. "But what exactly happened after he shot himself?"

Laura is a legal secretary. We'd met in a professional capacity. Before we knew it, it was a courtship. She's thirty-five, three years younger than I am. In addition to being in love, we like each other and enjoy one another's company. She's easy to be with.

"What happened?" Laura said.

Mel said, "He shot himself in the mouth in his room. Someone heard the shot and told the manager. They came in with a passkey, saw what had happened, and called an ambulance. I happened to be there when they brought him in, alive but past recall. The man lived for three days. His head swelled up to twice the size of a normal head. I'd never seen anything like it, and I hope I never do again. Terri wanted to go in and sit with him when she found out about it. We had a fight over it. I didn't think she should see him like that. I didn't think she should see him, and I still don't."

"Who won the fight?" Laura said.

35   "I was in the room with him when he died," Terri said. "He never came up out of it. But I sat with him. He didn't have anyone else."

"He was dangerous," Mel said. "If you call that love, you can have it."

"It was love," Terri said. "Sure, it's abnormal in most people's eyes. But he was willing to die for it. He did die for it."

"I sure as hell wouldn't call it love," Mel said. "I mean, no one knows what he did it for. I've seen a lot of suicides, and I couldn't say anyone ever knew what they did it for."

Mel put his hands behind his neck and tilted his chair back. "I'm not interested in that kind of love," he said. "If that's love, you can have it."

40   Terri said, "We were afraid. Mel even made a will out and wrote to his brother in California who used to be a Green Beret. Mel told him who to look for if something happened to him."

Terri drank from her glass. She said, "But Mel's right—we lived like fugitives. We were afraid. Mel was, weren't you, honey? I even called the police at one point, but they were no help. They said they couldn't do anything until Ed actually did something. Isn't that a laugh?" Terri said.

She poured the last of the gin into her glass and waggled the bottle. Mel got up from the table and went to the cupboard. He took down another bottle.

"Well, Nick and I know what love is," Laura said. "For us, I mean," Laura said. She bumped my knee with her knee. "You're supposed to say something now," Laura said, and turned her smile on me.

For an answer, I took Laura's hand and raised it to my lips. I made a big production out of kissing her hand. Everyone was amused.

45   "We're lucky," I said.

"You guys," Terri said. "Stop that now. You're making me sick. You're still on the honeymoon, for God's sake. You're still gaga, for crying out loud. Just wait. How long have you been together now? How long has it been? A year? Longer than a year?"

"Going on a year and a half," Laura said, flushed and smiling.

"Oh, now," Terri said. "Wait awhile."

She held her drink and gazed at Laura.

50   "I'm only kidding," Terri said.

Mel opened the gin and went around the table with the bottle.

"Here, you guys," he said. "Let's have a toast. I want to propose a toast. A toast to love. To true love," Mel said.

We touched glasses.

"To love," we said.

55   Outside in the backyard, one of the dogs began to bark. The leaves of the aspen that leaned past the window ticked against the glass. The afternoon sun was like a presence in this room, the spacious light of ease and generosity. We could have been anywhere, somewhere enchanted. We raised our glasses again and grinned at each other like children who had agreed on something forbidden.

"I'll tell you what real love is," Mel said. "I mean, I'll give you a good example. And then you can draw your own conclusions." He poured more gin into his glass. He added an ice cube and a sliver of lime. We waited and sipped our drinks. Laura and I touched knees again. I put a hand on her warm thigh and left it there.

"What do any of us really know about love?" Mel said. "It seems to me we're just beginners at love. We say we love each other and we do, I don't doubt it. I love Terri and Terri loves me, and you guys love each other too. You know the kind of love I'm talking about now. Physical love, that impulse that drives you to someone special, as well as love of the other person's being, his or her essence, as it were. Carnal love and, well, call it sentimental love, the day-to-day caring about the other person. But sometimes I have a hard time accounting for the fact that I must have loved my first wife too. But I did, I know I did. So I suppose I am like Terri in that regard. Terri and Ed." He thought about it and then he went on. "There was a time when I thought I loved my first wife more than life itself. But now I hate her guts. I do. How do you explain that? What happened to that love? What happened to it, is what I'd like to know. I wish someone could tell me. Then there's Ed. Okay, we're back to Ed. He loves Terri so much he tries to kill her and he winds up killing himself." Mel stopped talking and swallowed from his glass. "You guys have been together eighteen months and you love each other. It shows all over you. You glow with it. But you both loved other people before you met each other. You've both been married before, just like us. And you probably loved other people before that too, even. Terri and I have been together five years, been married for four. And the terrible thing, the terrible thing is, but the good thing too, the saving grace, you might say, is that if something happened to one of us—excuse me for saying this—but if something happened to one of us tomorrow I think the other one, the other person, would grieve for a while, you know, but then the surviving party would go out and love again, have someone else soon enough. All this, all of this love we're talking about, it would just be a memory. Maybe not even a memory. Am I wrong? Am I way off base? Because I want you to set me straight if you think I'm wrong. I want to know. I mean, I don't know anything, and I'm the first one to admit it."

"Mel, for God's sake," Terri said. She reached out and took hold of his wrist. "Are you getting drunk? Honey? Are you drunk?"

"Honey, I'm just talking," Mel said. "All right? I don't have to be drunk to say what I think. I mean, we're all just talking, right?" Mel said. He fixed his eyes on her.

60   "Sweetie, I'm not criticizing," Terri said.

She picked up her glass.

"I'm not on call today," Mel said. "Let me remind you of that. I am not on call," he said.

"Mel, we love you," Laura said.

Mel looked at Laura. He looked at her as if he could not place her, as if she was not the woman she was.

65   "Love you too, Laura," Mel said. "And you, Nick, love you too. You know something?" Mel said. "You guys are our pals," Mel said.

He picked up his glass.

Mel said, "I was going to tell you about something. I mean, I was going to prove a point. You see, this happened a few months ago, but it's still going on right now, and it ought to make us feel ashamed when we talk like we know what we're talking about when we talk about love."

"Come on now," Terri said. "Don't talk like you're drunk if you're not drunk."

"Just shut up for once in your life," Mel said very quietly. "Will you do me a favor and do that for a minute? So as I was saying, there's this old couple who had this car wreck out on the interstate. A kid hit them and they were all torn to shit and nobody was giving them much chance to pull through."

70   Terri looked at us and then back at Mel. She seemed anxious, or maybe that's too strong a word.

Mel was handing the bottle around the table.

"I was on call that night," Mel said. "It was May or maybe it was June. Terri and I had just sat down to dinner when the hospital called. There'd been this thing out on the interstate. Drunk kid, teenager, plowed his dad's pickup into this camper with this old couple in it. They were up in their mid-seventies, that couple. The kid—eighteen, nineteen, something—he was DOA. Taken the steering wheel through his sternum. The old couple, they were alive, you understand. I mean, just barely. But they had everything. Multiple fractures, internal injuries, hemorrhaging, contusions, lacerations, the works, and they each of them had themselves concussions. They were in a bad way, believe me. And, of course, their age was two strikes against them. I'd say she was worse off than he was. Ruptured spleen along with everything else. Both kneecaps broken. But they'd been wearing their seatbelts and, God knows, that's what saved them for the time being."

"Folks, this is an advertisement for the National Safety Council," Terri said. "This is your spokesman, Dr. Melvin R. McGinnis, talking." Terri laughed. "Mel," she said, "sometimes you're just too much. But I love you, hon," she said.

"Honey, I love you," Mel said.

75   He leaned across the table. Terri met him halfway. They kissed.

"Terri's right," Mel said as he settled himself again. "Get those seatbelts on. But seriously, they were in some shape, those oldsters. By the time I got down there, the kid was dead, as I said. He was off in a corner, laid out on a gurney. I took one look at the old couple and told the ER nurse to get me a neurologist and an orthopedic man and a couple of surgeons down there right away."

He drank from his glass. "I'll try to keep this short," he said. "So we took the two of them up to the OR and worked like fuck on them most of the night. They had these incredible reserves, those two. You see that once in a while. So we did everything that could be done, and toward morning we're giving them a fifty-fifty chance, maybe less than that for her. So here they are, still alive the next morning. So, okay, we move them into the ICU, which is where they both kept plugging away at it for two weeks, hitting it better and better on all the scopes. So we transfer them out to their own room."

Mel stopped talking. "Here," he said, "let's drink this cheapo gin the hell up. Then we're going to dinner, right? Terri and I know a new place. That's where we'll go, to this new place we know about. But we're not going until we finish up this cut-rate, lousy gin."

Terri said, "We haven't actually eaten there yet. But it looks good. From the outside, you know."

80   "I like food," Mel said. "If I had it to do all over again, I'd be a chef, you know? Right, Terri?" Mel said.

He laughed. He fingered the ice in his glass.

"Terri knows," he said. "Terri can tell you. But let me say this. If I could come back again in a different life, a different time and all, you know what? I'd like to come back as a knight. You were pretty safe wearing all that armor. It was all right being a knight until gunpowder and muskets and pistols came along."

"Mel would like to ride a horse and carry a lance," Terri said.

"Carry a woman's scarf with you everywhere," Laura said.

85   "Or just a woman," Mel said.

"Shame on you," Laura said.

Terri said, "Suppose you came back as a serf. The serfs didn't have it so good in those days," Terri said.

"The serfs never had it good," Mel said. "But I guess even the knights were vessels to someone. Isn't that the way it worked? But then everyone is always a vessel to someone. Isn't that right? Terri? But what I liked about knights, besides their ladies, was that they had that suit of armor, you know, and they couldn't get hurt very easy. No cars in those days, you know? No drunk teenagers to tear into your ass."

"Vassals," Terri said.

90   "What?" Mel said.

"Vassals," Terri said. "They were called vassals, not vessels."

"Vassals, vessels," Mel said, "what the fuck's the difference? You knew what I meant anyway. All right," Mel said. "So I'm not educated. I learned my stuff. I'm a heart surgeon, sure, but I'm just a mechanic. I go in and I fuck around and I fix things. Shit," Mel said.

"Modesty doesn't become you," Terri said.

"He's just a humble sawbones," I said. "But sometimes they suffocated in all that armor, Mel. They'd even have heart attacks if it got too hot and they were too tired and worn out. I read somewhere that they'd fall off their horses and not be able to get up because they were too tired to stand with all that armor on them. They got trampled by their own horses sometimes."

95   "That's terrible," Mel said. "That's a terrible thing, Nicky. I guess they'd just lay there and wait until somebody came along and made a shish kebab out of them."

"Some other vessel," Terri said.

"That's right," Mel said. "Some vassal would come along and spear the bastard in the name of love. Or whatever the fuck it was they fought over in those days."

"Same things we fight over these days," Terri said.

Laura said, "Nothing's changed."

100   The color was still high in Laura's cheeks. Her eyes were bright. She brought her glass to her lips.

Mel poured himself another drink. He looked at the label closely as if studying a long row of numbers. Then he slowly put the bottle down on the table and slowly reached for the tonic water.

"What about the old couple?" Laura said. "You didn't finish that story you started."

Laura was having a hard time lighting her cigarette. Her matches kept going out.

The sunshine inside the room was different now, changing, getting thinner. But the leaves outside the window were still shimmering, and I stared at the pattern they made on the panes and on the Formica counter. They weren't the same patterns, of course.

105   "What about the old couple?" I said.

"Older but wiser," Terri said.

Mel stared at her.

Terri said, "Go on with your story, hon. I was only kidding. Then what happened?"

"Terri, sometimes," Mel said.

110   "Please, Mel," Terri said. "Don't always be so serious, sweetie. Can't you take a joke?"

"Where's the joke?" Mel said.

He held his glass and gazed steadily at his wife.

"What happened?" Laura said.

Mel fastened his eyes on Laura. He said, "Laura, if I didn't have Terri and if I didn't love her so much, and if Nick wasn't my best friend, I'd fall in love with you, I'd carry you off, honey," he said.

115   "Tell your story," Terri said. "Then we'll go to that new place, okay?"

"Okay," Mel said. "Where was I?" he said. He stared at the table and then he began again.

"I dropped in to see each of them every day, sometimes twice a day if I was up doing other calls anyway. Casts and bandages, head to foot, the both of them. You know, you've seen it in the movies. That's just the way they looked, just like in the movies. Little eye-holes and nose-holes and mouth-holes. And she had to have her legs slung up on top of it. Well, the husband was very depressed for the longest while. Even after he found out that his wife was going to pull through, he was still very depressed. Not about the accident, though. I mean, the accident was one thing, but it wasn't everything. I'd get up to his mouth-hole, you know, and he'd say no, it wasn't the accident exactly but it was because he couldn't see her through his eye-holes. He said that was what was making him feel so bad. Can you imagine? I'm telling you, the man's heart was breaking because he couldn't turn his goddamn head and see his goddamn wife."

Mel looked around the table and shook his head at what he was going to say.

"I mean, it was killing the old fart just because he couldn't look at the fucking woman."

120   We all looked at Mel.

"Do you see what I'm saying?" he said.

Maybe we were a little drunk by then. I know it was hard keeping things in focus. The light was draining out of the room, going back through the window where it had come from. Yet nobody made a move to get up from the table to turn on the overhead light.

"Listen," Mel said. "Let's finish this fucking gin. There's about enough left here for one shooter all around. Then let's go eat. Let's go to the new place."

"He's depressed," Terri said. "Mel, why don't you take a pill?"

125   Mel shook his head. "I've taken everything there is."

"We all need a pill now and then," I said.

"Some people are born needing them," Terri said.

She was using her finger to rub at something on the table. Then she stopped rubbing.

"I think I want to call my kids," Mel said. "Is that all right with everybody? I'll call my kids," he said.

30   Terri said, "What if Marjorie answers the phone? You guys, you've heard us on the subject of Marjorie? Honey, you know you don't want to talk to Marjorie. It'll make you feel even worse."

"I don't want to talk to Marjorie," Mel said. "But I want to talk to my kids."

"There isn't a day goes by that Mel doesn't say he wishes she'd get married again. Or else die," Terri said. "For one thing," Terri said, "she's bankrupting us. Mel says it's just to spite him that she won't get married again. She has a boyfriend who lives with her and the kids, so Mel is supporting the boyfriend too."

"She's allergic to bees," Mel said. "If I'm not praying she'll get married again, I'm praying she'll get herself stung to death by a swarm of fucking bees."

"Shame on you," Laura said.

35   "Bzzzzzzz," Mel said, turning his fingers into bees and buzzing them at Terri's throat. Then he let his hands drop all the way to his sides.

"She's vicious," Mel said. "Sometimes I think I'll go up there dressed like a bee-keeper. You know, that hat that's like a helmet with the plate that comes down over your face, the big gloves, and the padded coat? I'll knock on the door and let loose a hive of bees in the house. But first I'd make sure the kids were out, of course."

He crossed one leg over the other. It seemed to take him a lot of time to do it. Then he put both feet on the floor and leaned forward, elbows on the table, his chin cupped in his hands.

"Maybe I won't call the kids, after all. Maybe it isn't such a hot idea. Maybe we'll just go eat. How does that sound?"

"Sounds fine to me," I said. "Eat or not eat. Or keep drinking. I could head right on out into the sunset."

40   "What does that mean, honey?" Laura said.

"It just means what I said," I said. "It means I could just keep going. That's all it means."

"I could eat something myself," Laura said. "I don't think I've ever been so hungry in my life. Is there something to nibble on?"

"I'll put out some cheese and crackers," Terri said.

But Terri just sat there. She did not get up to get anything.

45   Mel turned his glass over. He spilled it out on the table.

"Gin's gone," Mel said.

Terri said, "Now what?"

I could hear my heart beating. I could hear everyone's heart. I could hear the human noise we sat there making, not one of us moving, not even when the room went dark.

WRITING ASSIGNMENTS

Analysis

1. Explain the symbolic, or at least suggestive, relevance to the story's themes of Mel's being formerly a seminarian and currently a cardiologist.

2. Explain the thematic significance of Mel's extended digression on armored knights and of the resulting conversation. How is this topic related to Mel's story about the old couple injured in the traffic accident?
3. Compare and contrast the five love relationships mentioned in the story in order to distill insights about the nature of love.
4. How does this story comment on the nature of romantic love?

Argument

1. Does the story suggest that we really don't know what we are talking about when we talk about love?
2. Who has the more "romantic" view of love, Mel or Terri? In answering this question, define what you mean by romantic.
3. Does alcohol impair the thinking of these four people or, by releasing their inhibitions, reveal emotional truths?

Personal Writing and Writing from Research

1. Compare the story's many definitions of love to your own.
2. Research and write an essay about the history and traditions of chivalric love.
3. *Collaborative Project:* Research and report about the history of the institution of marriage, particularly the relationship between love, property, and marriage. This may be a cross-cultural investigation.
4. What is the role of violence in supposedly loving relationships? Research domestic violence.

Roselily

Alice Walker

Born in Georgia, the eighth child in a family of sharecroppers, Alice Walker attended Spellman College and received her BA from Sarah Lawrence College in 1965. She has taught at Wellesley, Yale, and the University of California, Berkeley.

Her collection of poems, *Once* (1968), explores her life as a civil rights worker. *The Third Life of Grange Copeland* (1970), her first novel, focuses on African-American history and traditions, and *Meridian* (1976), her second novel, on the civil rights movement in the 1960s. Her third novel, *The Color Purple* (1982) won a Pulitzer Prize. She has published a fourth novel, *The Temple of My Familiar* (1986), short stories, biographical and critical works, lectures, poems, and essays, including *In Search of Our Mother's Gardens* (1974). Her research on Zora Neale Hurston led to the republication of Hurston's work. *Possessing the Secret of Joy* (1992) focuses on female circumcision. Her work often analyzes the effects of racism and sexism on black women. "Roselily" comes from *Love & Trouble: Stories of Black Women* (1972).

Journal Topics: (1) Describe a relationship that survives even though one or both of the parties is not in love with the other. (2) If not love, what keeps them together? (3) Explain the role of religious belief in shaping your attitude toward marriage.

As You Read: (1) Reconstruct Roselily's past from her thoughts during the wedding. (2) Describe the future that she envisions. Is she wise to marry? (3) Why does *he* marry *her?* (4) What differentiates her husband from the other men she knows?

Dearly Beloved,

1 She dreams; dragging herself across the world. A small girl in her mother's white robe and veil, knee raised waist high through a bowl of quicksand soup. The man who stands beside her is against this standing on the front porch of her house, being married to the sound of cars whizzing by on highway 61.

we are gathered here

2 Like cotton to be weighed. Her fingers at the last minute busily removing dry leaves and twigs. Aware it is a superficial sweep. She knows he blames Mississippi for the respectful way the men turn their heads up in the yard, the women stand waiting and knowledgeable, their children held from mischief by teachings from the wrong God. He glares beyond them to the occupants of the cars, white faces glued to promises beyond a country wedding, noses thrust forward like dogs on a track. For him they usurp the wedding.

in the sight of God

3 Yes, open house. That is what country black folks like. She dreams she does not already have three children. A squeeze around the flowers in her hands chokes off three and four and five years of breath. Instantly she is ashamed and frightened in her superstition. She looks for the first time at the preacher, forces humility into her eyes, as if she believes he is, in fact, a man of God. She can imagine God, a small black boy, timidly pulling the preacher's coattail.

to join this man and this woman

4 She thinks of ropes, chains, handcuffs, his religion. His place of worship. Where she will be required to sit apart with covered head. In Chicago, a word she hears when thinking of smoke, from his description of what a cinder was, which they never had in

Panther Burn. She sees hovering over the heads of the clean neighbors in her front yard black specks falling, clinging, from the sky. But in Chicago. Respect, a chance to build. Her children at last from underneath the detrimental wheel. A chance to be on top. What a relief, she thinks. What a vision, a view, from up so high.

in holy matrimony.

5 Her fourth child she gave away to the child's father who had some money. Certainly a good job. Had gone to Harvard. Was a good man but weak because good language meant so much to him he could not live with Roselily. Could not abide TV in the living room, five beds in three rooms, no Bach except from four to six on Sunday afternoons. No chess at all. She does not forget to worry about her son among his father's people. She wonders if the New England climate will agree with him. If he will ever come down to Mississippi, as his father did, to try to right the country's wrongs. She wonders if he will be stronger than his father. His father cried off and on throughout her pregnancy. Went to skin and bones. Suffered nightmares, retching and falling out of bed. Tried to kill himself. Later told his wife he found the right baby through friends. Vouched for, the sterling qualities that would make up his character.

6 It is not her nature to blame. Still, she is not entirely thankful. She supposes New England, the North, to be quite different from what she knows. It seems right somehow to her that people who move there to live return home completely changed. She thinks of the air, the smoke, the cinders. Imagines cinders big as hailstones; heavy, weighing on the people. Wonders how this pressure finds its way into the veins, roping the springs of laughter.

If there's anybody here that knows a reason why

7 But of course they know no reason why beyond what they daily have come to know. She thinks of the man who will be her husband, feels shut away from him because of the stiff severity of his plain black suit. His religion. A lifetime of black and white. Of veils. Covered head. It is as if her children are already gone from her. Not dead, but exalted on a pedestal, a stalk that has no roots. She wonders how to make new roots. It is beyond her. She wonders what one does with memories in a brand-new life. This had seemed easy, until she thought of it. "The reasons why . . . the people who" . . . she thinks, and does not wonder where the thought is from.

these two should not be joined

8 She thinks of her mother, who is dead. Dead, but still her mother. Joined. This is confusing. Of her father. A gray old man who sold wild mink, rabbit, fox skins to Sears, Roebuck. He stands in the yard, like a man waiting for a train. Her young sisters stand behind her in smooth green dresses, with flowers in their hands and hair. They giggle, she feels, at the absurdity of the wedding. They are ready for something new. She thinks the man beside her should marry one of them. She feels old. Yoked. An

arm seems to reach out from behind her and snatch her backward. She thinks of cemeteries and the long sleep of grandparents mingling in the dirt. She believes that she believes in ghosts. In the soil giving back what it takes.

together,

9   In the city. He sees her in a new way. This she knows, and is grateful. But is it new enough? She cannot always be a bride and virgin, wearing robes and veil. Even now her body itches to be free of satin and voile, organdy and lily of the valley. Memories crash against her. Memories of being bare to the sun. She wonders what it will be like. Not to have to go to a job. Not to work in a sewing plant. Not to worry about learning to sew straight seams in working-men's overalls, jeans, and dress pants. Her place will be in the home, he has said, repeatedly, promising her rest she had prayed for. But now she wonders. When she is rested, what will she do? They will make babies— she thinks practically about her fine brown body, his strong black one. They will be inevitable. Her hands will be full. Full of what? Babies. She is not comforted.

let him speak

10   She wishes she had asked him to explain more of what he meant. But she was impatient. Impatient to be done with sewing. With doing everything for three children, alone. Impatient to leave the girls she had known since childhood, their children growing up, their husbands hanging around her, already old, seedy. Nothing about them that she wanted, or needed. The fathers of her children driving by, waving, not waving; reminders of times she would just as soon forget. Impatient to see the South Side, where they would live and build and be respectable and respected and free. Her husband would free her. A romantic hush. Proposal. Promises. A new life! Respectable, reclaimed, renewed. Free! In robe and veil.

or forever hold

11   She does not even know if she loves him. She loves his sobriety. His refusal to sing just because he knows the tune. She loves his pride. His blackness and his gray car. She loves his understanding of her *condition*. She thinks she loves the effort he will make to redo her into what he truly wants. His love of her makes her completely conscious of how unloved she was before. This is something; though it makes her unbearably sad. Melancholy. She blinks her eyes. Remembers she is finally being married, like other girls. Like other girls, women? Something strains upward behind her eyes. She thinks of the something as a rat trapped, cornered, scurrying to and fro in her head, peering through the windows of her eyes. She wants to live for once. But doesn't know quite what that means. Wonders if she has ever done it. If she ever will. The preacher is odious to her. She wants to strike him out of the way, out of her light, with the back of her hand. It seems to her he has always been standing in front of her, barring her way.

his peace.

12 The rest she does not hear. She feels a kiss, passionate, rousing, within the general pandemonium. Cars drive up blowing their horns. Firecrackers go off. Dogs come from under the house and begin to yelp and bark. Her husband's hand is like the clasp of an iron gate. People congratulate. Her children press against her. They look with awe and distaste mixed with hope at their new father. He stands curiously apart, in spite of the people crowding about to grasp his free hand. He smiles at them all but his eyes are as if turned inward. He knows they cannot understand that he is not a Christian. He will not explain himself. He feels different, he looks it. The old women thought he was like one of their sons except that he had somehow got away from them. Still a son, not a son. Changed.

13 She thinks how it will be later in the night in the silvery gray car. How they will spin through the darkness of Mississippi and in the morning be in Chicago, Illinois. She thinks of Lincoln, the president. That is all she knows about the place. She feels ignorant, *wrong*, backward. She presses her worried fingers into his palm. He is standing in front of her. In the crush of well-wishing people, he does not look back.

WRITING ASSIGNMENTS

Analysis

1. How does the story's structure—its alteration of lines from the wedding service with Roselily's thoughts, and its use of flashback and flashforward—reinforce its themes?
2. Why does Roselily marry a man she may not love?
3. Explain Roselily's attitude toward the role of religion in her life, both the Christianity of her home and her husband's Muslim faith.
4. Explain how images communicate Roselily's feelings and the story's themes.
5. Trace the role of the men in Roselily's life.

Argument

1. Will this marriage improve Roselily's life?
2. Is Roselily taking advantage of the man she is marrying?
3. Does Roselily have any other viable options besides marriage to improve her life?
4. Does Roselily's husband exemplify what Cancian calls "masculine" love?

Personal Writing and Writing from Research

1. In a personal essay, describe and attempt to explain a marriage or long-term relationship with which you are familiar and in which at least one of the participants did not love the other.
2. Trace the development of the Muslim religion in the United States, particularly in the African-American community.

3. *Collaborative Project:* Read *Meridian,* Walker's novel about the experiences of civil rights workers in the 1960s, and other personal, fictional, and nonfictional accounts of that period in order to write a paper about what life was like for those involved in the movement. Focus on the social history and individual experiences rather than on politics. Are any differences in experience or attitude influenced by gender?

4. Compare the traditional roles of Muslim and Christian husbands and wives.

The Marriage Gap

Charisse Jones

In addition to being a personal and emotional commitment, marriage is a social institution affected by economic conditions and society's values. In the 1950s, marriage rates soared and the average age of marrying couples dropped. Since then, marriage rates have steadily declined, in some subcultures more than in others. Reporter Charisse Jones's article, which appeared in the *Los Angeles Times* on March 28, 1993, analyzes the underlying causes, consequences, and personal pain associated with the apparent decline of marriage in the African-American community.

Journal Topics: (1) What attracts you to another person? Are these the same qualities you would look for in a spouse? (2) Are you optimistic about finding a spouse if and when you want to marry? (3) Do you want to marry someone from the same ethnic, racial, or socioeconomic background? Why?

As You Read: (1) Why are marriage rates declining in the African-American community? (2) Which of the causes has to do with individual attitudes? Which, with factors beyond an individual's control? (3) Why are institutions such as churches, the Urban Institute, and the National Council of Negro Women concerned with the decline of marriage?

In many ways, the women are very different. One is a doctor, another a hairdresser, the third is on welfare. But they have at least two things in common.

They are black.

And they are alone.

Barbara, 45, thinks her marital chances may have died in a distant land. "I think my husband may be pushing up daisies in Vietnam," she says of the place where 7,000 black American soldiers lost their lives.

5   Geneva, 31, sometimes blames herself: "You sit back and think 'What's wrong with me that I can't find a good guy?'"

And LaShane, 23, says others too often take what should be hers: "I feel like I'm being cheated," she says of black men who marry non-black women.

Once, she thought she'd marry young, and live happily ever after. But finding a mate, LaShane says, "is turning out to be the most difficult thing for me to achieve."

With a strong desire to marry within their race, and with violence, incarceration, unemployment and other social factors reducing the number of available black men, many black women say they are competing for too few men. And that perceived dearth of marriageable black men has stirred an emotional debate that has reverberated from church workshops to cocktail parties, from popular literature to stage and screen.

Terry McMillan's novel "Waiting to Exhale" struck a nerve with those who claimed they saw themselves in the travails of four black women trying to forge relationships with black men. One of the most provocative scenes in Spike Lee's film, "Jungle Fever," showed black women lamenting the scarcity of potential partners. And in the theater production, "Diary of Black Men," a character boasts that he doesn't need to settle with one woman when black men are in such demand.

10   Many black men, however, say some black women focus on superficial qualities in potential mates, thus ignoring substantial numbers of quality bachelors.

Workshops with such titles as "Surviving the Search for Mr. Right" and "Living in the Spirit of Being Single" are being conducted at black women's conferences nationwide and have heightened a spirited debate.

Yet, despite such discourse, many say not enough serious discussion has been devoted to the decline in black marriage. They emphasize that solutions are critical to avoid a devastating impact on the black community for generations.

"This has nothing short of earthshaking implications for black women, men and children," says Ronald Mincy, senior research associate with the Urban Institute. "No one it seems has the courage to put this on the table and say, 'Listen, we have to deal with this.' . . . We're not effectively coping with this decline in marriage for what it means for the future of our community."

At stake, he and others say, is not just women's personal happiness, but the economic ascent of black America, potentially stymied by shrinking dual-income households. A growing number of women are raising children alone, and children who see no marital relationships in their homes may be less inclined as adults to make such a commitment.

15   The numbers show that black women under 35 are at least twice as likely as their white and Latina counterparts to have never married. And marriage rates have dropped much farther in the past two decades among blacks than any other American ethnic group surveyed. (No figures were available for Asian-Americans.)

For many black women, the fall-out is deeply personal, with emotions ranging from hopelessness to resignation. Some have opted to cross age and racial boundaries; others simply prepare to live their lives alone.

Says Eleanor Hinton Hoyt, national programs director for the National Council of Negro Women: "I think these are very desperate times for black women."

WHAT SHORTAGE?

Not everyone agrees there is a shortage of eligible black men. Some say such a notion has been exploited by those who focus on negatives within the black community. Others claim it is African-American men themselves who sometimes exaggerate the ratio of females to males, using their perceived scarcity to create power over women.

Regardless, the numbers document the shrinking pool of available black men.

20 At first glance, statistics appear to favor black women. For every 1,000 black females born in 1990, there were 29 more black males, according to U.S. Bureau of Health Statistics.

But from that point, the black male's survival odds diminish.

Black males have a slightly higher infant mortality rate than females, and homicide is the leading cause of death for African-American boys ages 15 to 19. One in four black men in their 20s are behind bars, on probation or on parole.

Black men age 20 and older faced a 13.3% national unemployment rate last December [1992]—more than twice that of white males in the same group. Some will be crippled by substance abuse and others will choose a mate of another ethnicity—or their own gender. And some will simply choose not to marry at all.

Such myriad factors severely decrease the number of black men able and willing to marry and support families, many experts say. Thus, fewer black women will marry, and the number of households headed by black females will increase as some women choose to have children without a spouse.

25 No husband or second income means a life of poverty for many single mothers. Nearly 80% of poor black families are headed by black women with no spouse in the home, while 51.2% of all black households headed by women are living below the poverty line, according to the U.S. Census Bureau.

Ultimately, the declining marriage rate spawns economic repercussions that have an impact on the entire black community, researchers say.

"The defining feature of the black middle-class is marriage," says Mincy, explaining that dual-income households are essential for the community's economic status to rise.

"Having to meet the expenses of life, and having little money to put away, inhibits our ability to own businesses, to buy property. . . . One reason the black community has so little wealth is we haven't pooled our incomes despite the fact black women have been working for as long as we can remember."

WHAT MIGHT HAVE BEEN

Lady Cage has struggled alone. And she has little sympathy for divorced women who complain they cannot find new mates when many, like her, have never walked down the aisle.

30 An aspiring businesswoman in her 30s, Cage won't give her age, but acknowledges that in some men's eyes, she's no longer young.

Searching, but not desperate, Cage sometimes ponders what might have been: Kind and loving guys she let go because they didn't fulfill fantasy; marriage proposals in college that she declined.

"Maybe I should have jumped then," she says, laughing. Sometimes "you do regret it." But Cage has not given up hope. She now dates men she once might not have considered. And in the meantime, a job, volunteer work and an exercise routine fill her days.

"I'd rather have a husband and a family," she admits. "But you don't dwell on it. It'll happen. Even with this dwindling pool, it will happen."

Middle- to upper-income black women may be less adversely affected than their lower-income counterparts, but experts say both groups wind up drawing from the same shrunken pool.

35   And that competition, many women say, makes some single black men less willing to settle down with one woman.

"When you talk to guys, a lot feel there's so many black women out here looking for a black man, they don't have to act right," says Lynda Lucas, a 37-year-old divorcee who last December joined a black dating service. "If you don't want them, Mary down the hall [does], and [she'll] do whatever to keep him."

Audrey Chapman tells of moving from Connecticut to Washington: "In Washington the rumor is 7 [females] to 1 [male]. I said, 'People are crazy. There are men all over the place.' But a guy would say that to give himself leverage."

A relationship counselor, Chapman says she understands why some black males trumpet such numbers, regardless of the truth. "I think black men are always seeking some kind of power in this society, and the [people] they seek it with [are] black women," she explains. "They don't have power anywhere else."

FANTASY AND REALITY

To be sure, there are single women who enjoy their independence and have no desire to pursue the stuff of fairy-tales and TV sitcoms.

40   Yet, many women want to marry, no matter their color. "We mirror the larger society," says Barbara Miles, editor of Chocolate Singles, a lifestyle magazine for unmarried blacks. "We raise little girls from the cradle to start picking out their wedding gowns. . . . If they don't live out the fantasy, they get very frustrated."

For a growing number of Americans, the fantasy is simply not reality. From 1970 to 1991, the percentage of married adults nationally dropped from 72 to 61, according to the Census Bureau. The percentages dropped from 73 to 64 for whites and from 62 to 61 for Latinos.

But blacks had the biggest decline—from 64% in 1970 to 44% in 1991.

In some age groups, the number of never-married black women is more than twice that of their white and Latina counterparts. Last year, 41% of black women age 34 and younger had never married, compared to 15% of whites and 20% of Latinas, according to federal statistics.

While noting the effects that violence, incarceration, and unemployment have on limiting the pool of available black men, some experts say the declining marriage rate in the black community simply mirrors the overall decline of matrimony in the U.S. Professionals postponing marriage while pursuing careers, and the growing acceptance of being single also contribute to the decline, they say. Mincy adds that some men may be reluctant to marry women who already have children.

45   Others, however, contend that some black women limit their own chances at marriage by wanting their potential mates to meet unrealistic expectations.

"[They] look for too much in the wrong areas," Chapman says. "By the time we define who this man needs to be, they have eliminated the majority of black men. They want a black Donald Trump, and you can count on one hand the number of men who fit that description."

RAGING DEBATE

The charge that black women want too much is fiercely debated—by men who claim they are hard-working and available, but often ignored; by women who say they simply want a man who will love and respect them; by professionals who defend their desire to marry a man with similar education and income.

"A lot of women should stop relying on TV to tell them what a good black male should be," says 24-year-old Andre Barrington, owner of "Black Obsessions," a L.A.-based video-dating agency. Despite the diminishing pool, he says, "there are [still] quality men out there" eager to marry black women.

A 33-year-old police dispatcher, who did not want his name used, says he's one: "It makes me angry. A lot of guys who do street maintenance are single, a lot of garbage men are single. The guy could be an honest man, but [many women] don't want a man who cleans the streets. It hurts."

50   He is now looking via Barrington's agency. "I very much want a black woman," he says. "But if I can't get a black woman to be with me, what do you think I'm going to do? Turn to another race."

A generation ago, researchers say, expectations for spouses were different. "Our parents were looking for just a good man or good woman, someone who was consistent, dependable, hard working," says counselor Chapman.

Integration helped change that, she says, giving blacks "the illusion that if we acquired what the broader [white] society had then we'd be making it. Everything would be as wonderful for us as it was for them. What we didn't realize was it wasn't wonderful for them either. They were also having problems in their marriages and their families."

But many black women say they just want a "BMW"—a black man working—who will love them and treat them well.

Some professional women have turned from seeking men of similar backgrounds and are considering blue-collar men. But they fear rejection because the men may feel threatened by their income or status.

55   "When you reach a certain level of education and income, you automatically narrow your prospects," says Barbara, the 45-year-old physician who did not want to give her last name. "Regardless of what color a man is, if you're making twice as much money, he's going to be intimidated."

She would like to marry and have a child, Barbara says, but she will not settle for less: "Some women settle for someone who doesn't have the same realm of exposure, or social values. The fact they have an M.R.S. is enough. . . . But that's not fine for me."

While some women have immersed themselves in work and other activities, others have become more proactive—seeking black men from other countries or crossing age, class and racial boundaries to find a mate.

Magazine editor Miles lauds both approaches, adding that less than a decade ago she saw much more desperation among women in unhealthy relationships.

"There was this tenacity to hold on at all costs," she says. "The fear was that if you didn't, you'd end up alone. [Now] I see the panic subsiding . . . because being not married doesn't necessarily mean being without male companionship. . . . There are fewer taboos."

60   Miles notes that many women buying personal ads in her magazine no longer specify only black men.

Though black men are involved in more than 70% of marriages between blacks and whites, the number of black women doing likewise has slowly increased.

Three years ago, Kymberly Jean, 29, opened "Opposites Attract," a dating service that matches different ethnicities. Jean, who dates men of other races, says half her clients are black, including a broad spectrum of women who often consider dating non-blacks as a last resort.

"They're frustrated," she says. "When the women come to me, the main reason they give is 'I'm sick of brothers.' It's not because they're attracted to white men."

HOME ALONE

Lynda Lucas, 37, remembers dateless New Year's Eves, when other women's boyfriends kissed her at midnight. She dreads people constantly asking why an attractive woman such as her is not romantically involved, and she longs for a family.

65   "I've got a career but I don't have anybody to share it with," says Lucas, who has been divorced 10 years. "It's a lot of weekends alone, a lot of holidays alone. You [wonder] what's wrong."

Such loneliness, says NCNW's Hoytt, leads some to date men already involved with other women.

The idea of man-sharing is controversial, with many black women saying they refuse to knowingly participate in such relationships. But Hoytt, a divorcee who has been single for nearly 13 years, did.

"It was a compromise," she says of that now-ended relationship. "I'd rather it not [have been] that way. . . . It was [just] a result of things just being the way they are."

There are efforts to turn things around. Besides dating services, forums in cities such as Los Angeles and Washington have joined black men and women to discuss strengthening relationships.

70   Many also speak of an effort by black professionals to mentor poor children, hoping that positive role models can minimize the hopelessness, violence, and crime that stunt the lives of so many young black men.

Still, some say it will take more.

"The solution is to create meaningful, legitimate employment and ownership opportunities for young black men living in our poorest neighborhoods," says Samuel L. Myers, a human relations and social justice professor at the University of Minnesota. "With that, people will have a vision for a future—violent crime will fall, homicides will be reduced, incarceration will become less of a problem and these guys will be ready to assume their roles" as husbands and fathers.

Meanwhile, some black women have found happiness within themselves.

"We do survive without men," says Claudette Sims, of Houston, a motivational speaker and author who has never married. "We would like to have that family, that nice, special person.

75   "But I think we understand that if we have to go it alone, we will."

WRITING ASSIGNMENTS

Analysis

1. Explain the factors contributing to the decline of marriage in the African-American community.
2. Why is the decline of marriage a matter of concern to anyone other than the individuals who want to marry?
3. How have socioeconomic conditions beyond individual control influenced both men's and women's attitudes toward prospective marriage partners?
4. Compare and contrast Roselily's life, a generation ago and in the rural South, to the lives of today's African-American women as described by Jones.
5. What are the economic consequences, particularly for women and children in the United States, of a decline in marriage?

Argument

1. Does the decline in marriage necessarily indicate a decline in society at large or in a particular community? Explain your answer.
2. Could other social institutions originating in either the community or government successfully compensate for any social problems created by the decline of marriage?
3. Do the standards of traditional masculinity and femininity arouse expectations that make it harder for both men and women in the African-American community to find or to be appropriate marriage partners?

Personal Writing and Writing from Research

1. Watch movies released over the last 10 years that deal with marriage and family in the African-American community, and write a paper on how these movies address the issues raised by Jones.
2. *Collaborative Project:* Survey community-based (e.g., churches, organizations, schools) and commercial (e.g., dating services, personal advertisements, "singles" activities) institutions by which men and women seek company. Compare their respective explicit and implicit criteria for defining attractiveness. If possible, interview participants to evaluate their experiences with these different methods of meeting people. Then write a classification paper on "How to Meet the Right Someone."
3. Write a personal essay in defense of remaining single.

Perspectives on Marriage

Edited by Mary E. Buckley and Gregory F. Augustine Pierce

"Perspectives on Marriage" is used in the premarital counseling program that the Roman Catholic Church offers to couples in the Archdiocese of Los Angeles.

Journal Topics: (1) Draw up a checklist of the marriage-related behaviors and values that you expect in your spouse. Then draw up a complementary checklist for yourself. Compare your lists, and explain why they are similar or different. (2) Do your ideas reflect what Cancian calls an affective (feminine), instrumental (masculine), or androgynous conception of love? (3) Where do your ideas originate: family examples, images drawn from popular culture, religion, experience, or other sources?

As You Read: Complete the following questionnaires based on a past, current, or anticipated relationship with a person whom you had considered or would consider to be a long-term lover or spouse. If possible, have your partner complete the questionnaires, too.

HOW DO YOU SEE ME?

You are invited to compare your views of yourself with your partner's view of you. This exercise emphasizes the fact that the image we have of ourselves is *not* necessarily the image that even those near and dear to us have.

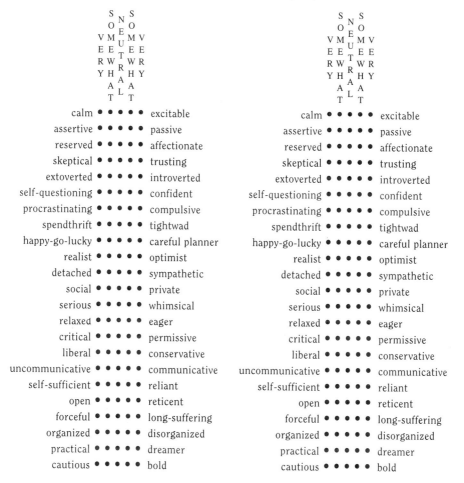

A. You about yourself

B. You about your partner

1. Mark list A about yourself by circling one, *and only one,* of the five dots on each horizontal line (each of the five dots is keyed to the words above: very, somewhat, neutral, etc.). Circle one dot you feel most nearly describes your personality, e.g., in the first line it might be "very excitable" or "somewhat calm." Then proceed to the next line.
2. Next, mark list B about your partner by circling dots which most nearly describe your partner's personality traits.
3. Compare the sheets by holding them side by side. First compare A and D, then compare B and C. Discuss the differences in your perceptions of each other.

HOW DO YOU SEE ME?

You are invited to compare your views of yourself with your partner's view of you. This exercise emphasizes the fact that the image we have of ourselves is *not* necessarily the image that even those near and dear to us have.

C. Your partner about self   *D. Your partner about you*

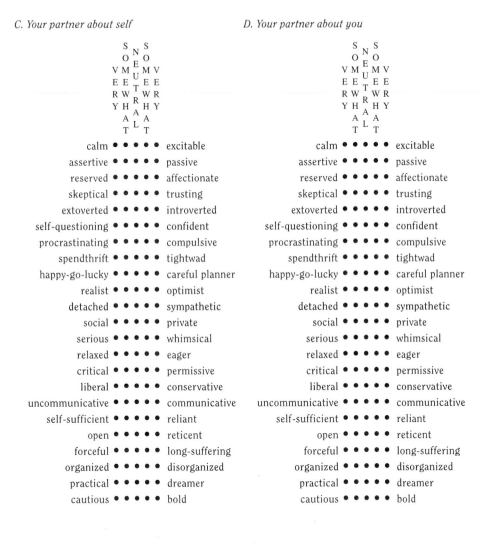

1. Mark list C about yourself by circling one, *and only one,* of the five dots on each horizontal line (each of the five dots is keyed to the words above: very, somewhat, neutral, etc.). Circle one dot you feel most nearly describes your personality, e.g., in the first line it might be "very excitable" or "somewhat calm." Then proceed to the next line.

2. Next, mark list D about your partner by circling dots which most nearly describe your partner's personality traits.
3. Compare the sheets by holding them side by side. First compare A and D, then compare B and C. Discuss the differences in your perceptions of each other.

CLUE EACH OTHER IN

Your partner has traits, qualities, and ways of acting which you especially prize and appreciate, which you wish he or she would develop even more. *But your partner is not a mind reader.* Tell him or her those qualities you find especially attractive. Most certainly love will lead your partner to concentrate on them even more.

Read the qualities presented below, pick out and list the seven you appreciate most in the order of their importance. Feel free to include other qualities not on our list—they might be the most important of all.

Sexually attractive	Dependable	Makes me do new things
Flexible and open	Intelligent	Doesn't blow up
Turns me on physically	Religious	Is interesting and alive
Cares about people	Imaginative	Cares about a home
Understanding	Makes me feel secure	Doesn't push me
Affectionate	Is considerate	Talks to me
Patient with me	Hardworking	Listens to me
Makes me laugh	Is strong	Socially at ease

WHAT I MOST APPRECIATE ABOUT MY PARTNER IS:

1. _____
2. _____
3. _____
4. _____
5. _____
6. _____
7. _____

WHAT I MOST APPRECIATE ABOUT MYSELF IS:

1. _____
2. _____
3. _____
4. _____
5. _____
6. _____
7. _____

TAKE THIS JOB AND SHOVE IT

There are many tasks that need to be done around the house in a marriage. Some of them are paid, most of them are not. Most of us have been raised to expect that certain jobs are done primarily by males and others are done mostly by females. It might be good to be clear before you get married who is going to do what.

Listed below are some common household chores (there is room to add others before you get started). Working separately, mark under the correct column who you think should (S) and who you think will (W)—it's not always the same!—perform each task in your marriage. Then share the results with your partner. Discuss those areas where you have different ideas.

BEAT THE CLOCK

Like money, time is a measure of what we value. There are only 24 hours in a day, 168 hours in a week. Do you and your partner understand and agree on how you will each use this highly prized asset when you are married?

Working alone, look over each of the following activities. Before you begin, add any other major time-consuming activities on the lines provided at the end of the list. Then estimate in the column on the right the number of hours *on the average* you anticipate *you yourself* will spend during the first year of marriage on each activity during a *regular, non-vacation, non-crisis week*. (If you feel you can do two things at once, put the time under one category only.)

Add your hours together and put the total at the bottom. Adjust your estimates until your total is exactly 168! Finally, share your list with your partner and discuss any surprises you find on each other's list.

Activity	*Hours per Week*
Sleeping	_____
Preparing and eating meals at home	_____
Exercising, sports, and personal care	_____
Paid jobs, including commuting	_____
Housework tasks and chores	_____
Shopping and other errands	_____
Childcare	_____
Studying and reading	_____
Watching TV and movies at home	_____
Praying and worshiping	_____
Volunteer activities	_____
Visiting family and friends	_____
Going out for entertainment or meals (together)	_____

Job	Male	Female	Both	Either	Neither	Hire Someone Else
Taking out the garbage						
Doing the dishes						
Making the bed						
Mowing the lawn						
Cooking dinner						
Vacuuming, dusting						
Scrubbing floors						
Washing windows						
Painting the house						
Making breakfast						
Grocery shopping						
Fixing the car						
Taking out the dog (cat)						
Ironing						
Preparing lunch						
Straightening the basement						
Keeping the checkbook						
Decorating the home						
Doing the laundry						
Cleaning the bathroom						
Gardening						
Shoveling snow						
Minor home repairs						

Activity	*Hours per Week*
Going out for entertainment or meals (without your partner)	_____
Hobbies (together)	_____
Hobbies (without your partner)	_____
Talking, cuddling, making love	_____
Doing nothing	
_____	_____
_____	_____
_____	_____
_____	_____
_____	_____
_____	_____
_____	_____
	Total: _____

WRITING ASSIGNMENTS

Analysis

1. Explain how this guide could be applied to the husband and wife in one of the following: "Roselily," "Rice Husband," or "Can a Woman Be Liberated and Married?"
2. Does this guide represent what Cancian calls a feminine, masculine, or androgynous conception of love?
3. How does this guide's approach to marriage tacitly take account of the obstacles to good communication between men and women as described by Tannen?
4. How does this guide reflect changing gender roles in marriage?

Argument

1. Is this guide useful to couples planning to marry?
2. Is there an appropriate balance between attention to behavior and attention to feelings in this guide? If not, explain the changes you would make.

Personal Writing and Writing from Research

1. Explain how you would use Cancian's ideas about love and Tannen's ideas about communication to help you interpret your and your partner's responses to this questionnaire.
2. Describe the additional topics you think this guide should cover, and explain your reasoning.
3. Use your own responses to this questionnaire to describe the marriage you have or hope to have, your specific role in the marriage, and your expectations of your spouse.

4. *Collaborative Project:* Ask a number of married couples in their 30s, 40s, 50s, and 60s to complete the questionnaire and evaluate its relevance to the reality of married life. Do the answers of husbands and wives differ? Do couples of similar ages respond in similar ways? Analyze your findings in terms of changes in gender roles in marriage and changes in marriage itself over the last several decades.

5. Compare other materials used in premarital counseling to "Perspectives on Marriage."

Can a Woman Be Liberated and Married?

Caryl Rivers

Caryl Rivers, born in 1937, is the coauthor with Rosalind Barnett and Grace Baruch of *Beyond Sugar and Spice: How Girls and Women Develop Competence* (1979) and with Alan Lupo of *For Better, For Worse* (1981). She is the author of *Aphrodite at Midcentury: Growing Up Female and Catholic in Postwar America* (1973), *Life Prints: New Patterns of Love and Work for Today's Women* (1983), *Intimate Enemies* (1987), and *Indecent Behavior* (1990). "Can a Woman Be Liberated and Married?" appeared in the *New York Times Magazine* on November 2, 1975.

Journal Topics: (1) Identify a figure from popular culture (films, television, sports, etc.) whose attractiveness you would like to imitate, and explain what it is about this person that makes him or her so attractive. (2) If you ever downplayed, or considered downplaying, some interest or personal trait because you thought it would make you less attractive, describe the situation and how you handled it. (3) How do you anticipate balancing a career and a family, if the situation arises?

As You Read: (1) How does Rivers define a "liberated marriage"? (2) Explain why achieving such a marriage might be easier for Rivers and her husband than for others. (3) How does Rivers explain female hostility toward men? How does she explain male contempt for women? (4) How did having children change the lives of Rivers and her husband?

1   I can remember the exact moment when I was sure I was part of a "liberated" marriage. We were driving along a city street, my husband Alan at the wheel and the two kids, Steven, 8, and Alyssa, 5, in the back seat. Alyssa was clutching a grimy but beloved doll and tugging at the doll's equally grimy and shopworn dress. The overworked threads gave out and the sleeve pulled off. Alyssa looked at the sleeve and

then, ignoring me, handed it to my husband and said, "Will you sew it for me, Daddy?"

2   He didn't sew the dress. He can't sew. I didn't sew the dress. I can't sew either. We gave it to his mother. She's the only one around who isn't all thumbs with a needle. But it was clear that my daughter's question indicated that her mind is—for the time being at least—free of a model of the universe in which the things men do and the things women do are separate spheres, solitary planets that orbit in their own paths, never touching. Since both my husband and I are writers, I suppose she assumes that what grown-ups do is sit in hot stuffy rooms and type a lot, now and then looking up to let out a string of cuss words. It may be the reason she says she would like to stay a kid for a long, long time.

3   I wonder sometimes if, by the time she grows up, society will be on its way to shattering the old sex-role stereotypes that have made so many men and women so miserable. I see young women today who were raised with one set of assumptions about woman's place and then confronted by the women's movement with a whole new lifestyle. Since I teach at the college level, I see a dogged professionalism growing among a great many women students. There is also a growing leeriness about any kind of permanent relationship with men. They prize their new-found freedom and are loath to give it up. The prospect of marriage and children seems terrifying—permanent bondage. I respect their seriousness and their need to achieve on their own. And yet, I wonder if some of them will end up like too many men, who sacrificed their emotional lives and wound up with a pension check, a gold watch and nobody who gives a damn.

4   Can a woman be both liberated and married? And a parent? Can a man? That is a question that is being asked often these days. I think the answer is yes, although one tends to hear more about the failures than the successes—the divorce rate, the runaway wives, the women in consciousness-raising groups who have their consciousnesses lifted right up and out of marriage. I know couples who are splitting up from too much change, too fast. Many of my contemporaries had a decade of very traditional marriages before the women's movement prompted them to try changing their lives. The life they had expected to be heaven when they were 20 turned out to be a source of frustration at 30. Now they are trying to change their way of life and are asking their husbands to adjust to women who are different—often exactly opposite—from the sweet young things they used to be. That sort of wrenching change is what tears marriages apart.

5   I also know couples who are trying to achieve a balance, as my husband and I are doing. It's easier for us because we started out with a set of expectations that weren't so far apart. He knew that I wanted to be a reporter as much as he wanted to be. We both knew we wanted children. I'm convinced that a liberated marriage, like ours, isn't just luck or a gift of Providence. It has a lot to do with what the bride and the bridegroom think they are at the outset and what they want to be.

6   I guess I would define a "liberated" marriage as one in which there is a rough parity of both the dirtwork and the glory—and, life being what it is, there is always more of the former. Everyone's solutions are different; ours is a sort of haphazard taking of

turns. We have no formal contract about who will do what and when; we are not comfortable with rhetoric and don't really use the word "liberated" very much.

7   For a number of years, my husband worked full time and his income was the major one; my part-time income bought the extras. Recently I've been the one to work full time, with his income being supplemental. A rough breakdown of the work would probably go this way. Child care about equal. He handles food shopping, most lunches, the car pool, trash, the dog and miscellaneous tidying. I am in charge of breakfast and dinner, vacuuming, the wash and the ponytail. We both wash dishes. All these chores shift when necessary, the way an outfield shifts over for left-handed hitters. My husband is totally unthreatened by being spotted with a dish towel in his hand. We have no household help, but we do have a baby sitter, a neighbor who comes over when the kids get home from school. She has four kids of her own. Things around the house are rarely dull.

8   We had always planned to have a family and neither of us has ever regretted that decision. The family unit is an emotional center of gravity in our lives. The kids, while they are a lot of work and a lot of worry, are also a constant source of delight—more than I had expected. They break me up constantly. My son, at the family Passover celebration, was asked the ritual question: "Why is this night different from all other nights?" He deadpanned, "Because on all other nights we eat spaghetti." My daughter announced the other day, out of the blue, "I wish my head was flat, like Frankenstein's, so I could carry things on it." In hindsight, my own upbringing was preparation for a liberated marriage.

9   I think, with some puzzlement now and then, of a line that Sylvia Plath wrote: "Every woman adores a fascist/the boot in the face, the brute." That rang false to me when I read it; only a masochist could adore a boot in the face. But then, I have known so many women schooled in masochism. I consider myself a feminist. I've written about women's issues, and I think I understand the twinges, the force, the maddening inconsistencies of the movement. One thing I have never really felt is the rage. I have been angry, resentful, just plain mad—but I have never owned the rage, particularly the sort that is unleashed against men. That kind of fury cannot, I suspect, be fired by proxy. It bears directly on something that has happened *to you*. The well of rage is personal, and why, I wondered, was it lacking in me? I grew up in the fifties, that queen of repressive decades, under the shadow of Anatomy Is Destiny.

10   Many women of my generation wore hobbles on their souls as crippling as the strips of cloth wrapped around the feet of Chinese girl babies to give them a "delicate" walk. Matina Horner, the psychologist who is now president of Radcliffe, discovered the hobbles in her studies of women's fear of success. For many women, particularly bright ones, to succeed in any intellectual task was also to fail as a woman. Those who broke free did not forget the feel of the hobbles. I never knew them. Many women look on men as despots, oppressors, owners of power, brutes. I cannot. I come from a line of liberated men.

11   There was a picture in my parents' house of my grandfather, my mother's father. I never knew him. He died before I was born. In his picture he seemed the very prototype of the Victorian paterfamilias, with his strong jaw and black full mustache. He

raised his children to be hardy, self-reliant and ambitious—and one of them was a girl.

12   My mother was talking about him recently, and she said she had just realized how unusual it was that her father raised her like a boy. She was a tomboy, free to race and run and skin her knees. Chores were equally shared; she was not banished to the kitchen while her brothers did "men's work." Her father emphasized to her the need to be financially independent, and at one point offered to set her up in business. She chose to go to law school instead.

13   My mother met my father in law school. Those were the heady, vigorous years of the thirties, and the momentum of the suffrage movement had not yet waned. Women in the thirties breathed freer air than did my contemporaries. In the fifties, we were rebels without a cause; it was a dull toothache of a decade.

14   I had no strong sense, growing up, that my family was much different from others (although my mother practiced law until I was 5, when she went to join my father at a Navy base in Alabama). My father seemed nicer, funnier, than most fathers, but otherwise I did not perceive him as being that different. I did notice that he was more deeply involved in my life than other girls' fathers were involved in theirs. Those fathers seemed distant—loving, perhaps, but drifting like a cloud, miles above. The father of one of my friends always seemed to be sitting in a chair, smoking a cigar and reading a newspaper, cut off from our lives.

15   For my father, sports was the thread that bound our activities together. I was a baseball fanatic, and every year he and I went to Griffith Stadium to see Harry Truman or Dwight Eisenhower throw out the first ball.

16   When I started to play Catholic Youth Organization basketball in the seventh grade, I inherited a ready-made coach: my father. He had once played semipro basketball, and we had strategy sessions around the dining-room table. When the salt shakers would no longer suffice, the whole family would repair to the living room, where my father would assign positions to my mother, my brother and me, and we would run through a play. He taught me how to use my hips and elbows so the referee wouldn't see, and thanks to him, I was the only girl in the league who could execute a jump shot. (The jump shot was considered, I suppose, too strenuous or too unladylike for girls. This was tommyrot to my father, who knew that ladies didn't win ball games. You had to be aggressive if you wanted to be a good basketball player, he said.)

17   Basketball was serious business at our house. So what if it was only the C.Y.O. girls' team. It did not occur to me that whether or not we beat Blessed Sacrament was not of cosmic concern to everyone. I did notice that there were only a few fathers who went to the girls' games but a lot when the boys played. My father could not live out any fantasies through me. Clearly, I would never be a future Bob Cousy or Sammy Baugh. But our postgame session could not have been more serious if we had been talking about the Knicks or the Celtics instead of the St. Michael's varsity. My father never in any way gave me the impression that what I accomplished was less than it might have been because I was a girl. He was as proud as I of the little cluster of trophies resting on top of the TV set.

18   Later, when I abandoned basketball for tulle ballgowns, with matching pumps and little dabs of perfume behind the ears, the trophies stayed on the TV. At first, I had wanted to pack them away, sure that my boyfriends would think me an Amazon with huge thighs, but my father argued that I had won them, and they ought to stay. He was right, of course. To pack away the trophies would have been betrayal of the rankest order—betrayal of my own past, my accomplishment.

19   Those were the days when women were supposed to be seen but not heard. In an article for The Ladies' Home Journal in 1954, Marlene Dietrich wrote that women should be like moons, floating about the male sun, shining in reflected glory. (The title of the article was "How to Be Loved.") I tried and inevitably flubbed. I was a lousy moon. I tried to lose prettily at tennis. I never lost that instinct for the jugular, developed in those C.Y.O. games. I won arguments with swains about admitting Red China to the U.N. I got good marks. Finally, I faced it. My mother and father had not produced a moon; they taught me to shine on my own.

20   Lacking a proper indoctrination in the national mores, I was a bit slow to sense all the nuances. I was truly puzzled by the male contempt for women that was so openly expressed around me. Men used the word for the female sexual organ as a term of utter scorn, and it was hatred, as much as lust, that dripped through the words of the guy who would mutter on a corner, "I'd like to ——— you, babe!" There was also a female contempt for men that was muted, indirect but had no less a sting.

21   I wonder how many men realize how deep and bitter runs the contempt of women. Barred so often from the arena, where the lights are hot and a man's performance is on display, women have the power of the people in the bleachers. They can criticize, ridicule and demand, safe in the knowledge that the stamina the arena demands will not be asked of them. Their weapon is not the Bronx cheer—that is too direct—but the well-timed laugh, the curl of a lip. If a man could listen in while his sex—or he himself—was being discussed by a group of "traditional, subservient" women, it would chill his blood. I have heard such discussions in which men were reduced to buffoons and incompetents by women who were supposed to love them—and hold them in awe. It is the power of the weak, never openly displayed because there is too much to lose.

22   I was astonished by all this, because contempt was something I had to learn about outside my own home. My mother and my father were equals in their house. If, as the years passed, their marriage was not the paradise that M.-G.-M. said marriage should be, it *was* rooted in the sort of loyalty and trust that can exist only between people of like weight and power. Never, in the entire time I was growing up, did I hear my father put my mother down. Never did I hear her mock him. I grew up believing that is how things were between men and women.

23   It may seem insignificant—or cute—to see ponytailed moppets out there playing shortstop in Little League. But consider. The women those girls will grow up to be will not be inclined to laugh at men when they fail, to mock them when their best turns out to be not good enough. They will have known what it feels like to take a third strike swinging or to bobble a grounder. Contempt will only vanish when women have a chance to play all the games now owned by men.

24   I always wanted to play—ever since I was a kid. I wanted to be where things were happening, not on the sidelines. When Alan and I were married, two years out of grad school, our careers had begun to progress at an even, steady rate. We worked on a small paper in New York State, then went on to jobs reporting politics and urban affairs, he in Baltimore and I in Washington. I must confess that I half-believed his work was more "serious" than mine because he was a man. I was happy, for a time, with the fact that I had been allowed into a man's game.

25   The real changes for us came with the birth of our first child. They had nothing to do with religion. Alan and I had agreed that the children would be raised in the Jewish religion and I would follow my own unorthodox brand of Catholicism. But with Steven's birth, we faced the problem of work roles. Now the responsibility for bringing home the bacon was Alan's. I was determined to continue my career by freelancing, but it was as if a large rock had been placed on the scale of our professional lives—on his side. I accepted the curtailments on my freedom. I did not get upset when he called at 11 and said he was going to have a drink with the other reporters. I know how one likes to talk shop after a hard day. But I had no one to talk shop with. If he called and said he had to miss dinner, I said, "Sure," because I knew about deadlines. But if I was working on a story, there was no one to call and say, "I won't be home," because the baby sitter had deadlines of her own. Sometimes I thought I was living vicariously through my husband's experiences. He was the one in the middle of things and I was on the periphery. I learned a new sensation—the "invisible woman" effect. There were times when we went to parties that people came up eagerly to speak to him and looked through me as if I didn't exist.

26   I became a hoarder of time. My work time was severely rationed. I would rarely ask Alan to give up something he had scheduled to baby-sit while I worked. In my mind I had assigned us places—he was first and I was way behind. I resented this, often. I resented the fact that he simply accepted this, as if it were the way of the world. He never said my work was not important. He was always careful to praise what I had done. But I had the feeling that his work was capital I important and mine was little i important.

27   When he designed a news show for public television and served as its anchorman and news editor, his working day ran from 9 A.M. to 9 P.M. or after. I was home alone night after night with the children. I kept active professionally but it was a great juggling act, calling the baby sitter, making sure Steven had clean underpants and that the meat for dinner was out of the freezer. My husband was exhausted when he came home at night. The 60-hour-plus week left him so frayed it took him half the weekend to get back to normal. I knew how important the idea of the show was to him.

28   At the same time I grew restive about the strain his work put on both of us, how it was beginning to isolate him from the family that was so important to both of us. He would remark, often, that he was missing seeing his daughter grow from an infant into a little girl. This was one of the major factors in his decision to leave television for a magazine job with more reasonable hours. If he had followed the traditional upwardly mobile success pattern, he would have gone on to "bigger" jobs that would have eaten up more and more of his time. Increasingly, I would have had to assume

more and more of the burden of the household and the kids. I suspect that my resentment would have grown like a malevolent weed. He would have been too busy to
see it growing. It could well have choked the life out of our relationship.

29   If the women's movement has had an impact on our personal balance, I guess it is
because I felt more able to articulate my frustrations and he was able to understand
that they were common to a great many women. He has been very considerate about
trying to understand the things that were bugging me, to understand my need to be
serious about my work, and I have tried not to get on a soapbox with movement
speeches. We have the usual yelling matches now and then, but they are usually less
intense than our disagreements over more cosmic issues, such as whether or not
pouring the water from the dog's dish in the kitchen sink is a sanitary practice. I say
the dog germs will gurgle down the sink and disappear and he sees rabies microbes
dancing on the silverware.

30   I have to admit, too, that despite the limits on my freedom in the time I spent at
home, the lack of economic pressure gave me the chance to experiment, to start off
on roads that might lead nowhere. My first book, about growing up as a Catholic in
America, was the result of one of those experiments. I would never have written it if I
had been hiking after some politician on the trail of a headline.

31   I no longer feel that there is an inequality in our professional lives. Sure, I made
sacrifices, but so has he. At different periods of our lives, we have both subsidized
each other's work with time and money, and I have learned a simple truth that I
should have known: You can't have it all, all of the time. Many of the men of my generation thought they could, so they tied themselves to the conveyor belt, thinking
that women would manage their emotions. They wound up with a vacuum where part
of their lives should have been. My husband and I don't want that to happen to us. So
perhaps I will not climb every mountain and ford every stream (a cliché, but my
daughter has played "The Sound of Music" to the point where the sight of whiskers
on kittens makes me want to throw up) but I am damned sure I will get to a lot of
them. My husband will climb back on the merry-go-round but he will know when to
get off. There will be areas in which we can't compete with the people who work 16
hours a day, who eat, live and breathe only for work. So be it. As the children grow
older, some of the old demands they make on us will dwindle, but the parents of teen-
agers assure me that some dandy new ones will arise.

32   I hear some young people talking of the "division of child-care tasks" and it sounds
very clean and scientific, something a computer could manage. It is not like that. As
a reporter in urban America in the sixties and seventies, my husband got acclimated
to the front lines. A black militant once tried to run him over, he patrolled the streets
of New York with the Jewish Defense League, and he got hit with a tomato meant for
Teddy Kennedy when the whites of Boston got upset over busing. He was accustomed
to danger, tension, confusion and chaos—and then came the real test of his mettle:
home.

33   This year, when he got a book contract, we pulled the big switch. He is now working at home, writing. Mornings he also takes care of Alyssa before she goes off
to kindergarten. I work full time, teaching at Boston University. Here, in terms of a

"division of childcare tasks," are a few highlights from an actual day in the life of a liberated man:

34 Somewhere between 6:30 and 7 we struggle out of bed and try to shuffle everybody in and out of one bathroom. Alan makes the bed and I wrestle with the ponytail. I cook bacon and he makes bologna sandwiches. He takes Steven, a third-grader, to school and I get Alyssa in the right coat and shoes for rain or shine. We hop in the car, because Alan will drive me to the university where I have a morning course. The traffic at the entrance to the Sumner Tunnel is its usual incredible snarl. Alyssa announces, brightly, "We are all going to play puppet hands!"

35 Alan moans, audibly. I groan. Puppet hands is a game she invented all by herself. In it, she turns her left hand into Cowey and her right hand into Horsey. The two of them converse in a screechy falsetto that would drive a saint to screaming heresy. But it doesn't stop there. My right hand is Frog and my left hand is Phyllis Frog. Alan's right hand is Fishy and his left hand is Elephant. Elephant is a morose sort, but Fishy has been too engaging for his own good. So Alyssa chants, in a sort of nagging chirp, "Fishy, where are you? Fishy? Fishy? Fiiiissssshhhhyyyyyy!" until her father relents and Fishy speaks.

36 Through the tunnel, up Storrow Drive, Alyssa does puppet hands. My teeth are on edge. Alan drops me off at B.U. Alyssa waves good-by and I hear her saying, "Fishy, Fishy, want to hear me sing?" Alan's knuckles, where he grips the wheel, are turning white.

37 When he and Alyssa arrive home, Alan goes up to the attic-office to work. He has been at the typewriter for half an hour when peculiar sounds, accompanied by a peculiar smell, drift up the stairs. He goes down and discovers that the sounds are being made by Jane, the medium-sized family dog—loyal, dumb and cowardly—who is having an attack of diarrhea on the living-room rug. He drags Jane into the kitchen and starts to swab her off when Alyssa wanders in, wrinkles her nose and says, "I think I have to throw up." He hustles her out of the kitchen. Eventually, he gets back to work.

38 Next comes lunch time and the kindergarten car pool. After the noon car-pool run, there is a precious two and a half hours for work on the book. Then it is time to pick up Steven. Steven's cronies, Joey, Jonathan, Chris and Michael, ride along. Third-grade conversation—and particularly humor—is cheerfully and relentlessly anal. Punch lines involving excrement produce gales of laughter. Alan drives home, attempting to block out the punching, cackling and assorted animal sounds from the back seat.

39 Up in his office, he types vigorously for 12 minutes and eight seconds before he becomes aware of eyes boring into his back. It is Deanna, aged 3, our neighbor's daughter.

40 "Awan," she says. "Can I kiss Jane? Does Jane have jorms?" (Her version of germs.)

41 "You can kiss Jane. She hasn't got germs. Just don't kiss her on the mouth."

42 "Will I get a cold if I kiss Jane, Awan? Does Jane have jorms?"

43 "No jorms. I mean germs."

44 "Do you have jorms, Awan?"

45 "No."

46 "Does Alyssa have jorms?"

47 "No."

48 "Does Alyssa have jorms?"

49 "No. Nobody has jorms!"

50 Steven and Joey come charging in. There is a wounded pigeon on the lawn. Alan hollers at the kids not to touch the pigeon. Pigeons are filthy, plague-carrying birds. He calls the dog officer and waits on the lawn to make sure the pigeon doesn't hobble into the street and get run over, which would upset the children. The dog officer comes and takes the pigeon. Alan goes back to the typewriter. Nothing will come. The muse has vanished. The phone rings. It is I, his loving wife. "Are you having a nice day, dear?"

51 My husband is, I think, one of a growing breed of free men who have not been stamped out of a mold like a chocolate bunny, who can dry a dish or wipe a runny nose without an attack of castration anxiety. I have known too many men struggling honestly with the new ambitions and hopes of women to think the liberated man is a rare species. But there are men—a great many, I suppose—who cannot function in anything but the old way, who must see women as satellites to sustain their own egos. I have known women married to such men: when the women began to grow in their own self-estimation, the marriages broke up.

52 I know other women who are sticking with marriages where there is a great deal of tension about sex roles and division of chores. They stay because they value the relationships and hope things will work out. Sometimes women are afraid to speak out. Other times they bark demands, forgetting that a marriage is not the U.A.W. bargaining table. Some marriages ought to fail, for the sanity of both parties. It is easy to say, in ringing tones, that a woman ought to up and leave any man who isn't liberated. But the formula that works for one person could be deadly for another.

53 I am optimistic, however, for the future of liberated marriage. I think it makes good sense. It is easier than the old model, because it allows both parties more options. I think it must be tough to be a man, looking ahead year after year after year to driving a cab or teaching high-school civics or selling insurance, with no prospects of climbing off the treadmill, even for a while. Is that really much better than the plight of the woman who looks ahead and sees an Everest of dirty dishes and unmade beds?

54 I have a feeling that the men and women of my daughter's generation will be dealing with their expectations earlier and in a more rational way than most of us did. My husband is always saying to Alyssa, "Girls can be doctors" or "Girls can be pilots" or "Girls can be anything they want." He will transmit to her the message my father (and my mother) beamed to me: You are a person of worth, of value, and it is your right to achieve and grow. My husband accorded me that right freely; I did not have to wrest it from him. If I am a free woman, and I believe I am, it is due in no small measure to the fact that I have lived with—and loved and been nurtured by—free men.

WRITING ASSIGNMENTS

Analysis

1. What does Rivers mean by saying, "You can't have it all, all of the time."
2. Trace Rivers's use of imagery and metaphor, and explain how it influences her essay's theme and tone.
3. How does Rivers explain what she describes as pervasive, blatant male contempt for women, and pervasive, but more hidden female contempt for men?
4. Characterize Rivers's attitude toward household responsibilities and family life, and compare it to your own.
5. How will the work world and society generally have to change before marriages like Rivers's become more common?

Argument

1. Do you agree with Rivers that "You can't have it all, all of the time."
2. Do pervasive male contempt for women and a corresponding female contempt for men persist today? If so, how are they expressed?
3. Is Rivers's marriage a realistic model for other couples?
4. Does Rivers's marriage illustrate Tannen's theory that men have a primary need for independence and status, and women, a primary need for connection and intimacy?
5. Is this an androgynous marriage?

Personal Writing and Writing from Research

1. Explain why you would or would not want to be a partner in a marriage like Caryl Rivers's.
2. *Collaborative Project:* Rivers mentions Marlene Dietrich, tacitly acknowledging the influence of movie stars on her own generation. Does this influence persist? Compare and contrast the images of marriage, of husbands' and wives' roles, and of masculinity and femininity in movies from two of the following decades: the 1930s, 1940s, 1950s, 1960s, 1970s, 1980s, and 1990s. Do these images from popular culture correlate with contemporaneous social and political conditions?
3. How did attitudes towards male and female roles and marriage change in the 1970s, the early days of the modern women's movement? Base your research on interviews with men and women who were young adults then, and on material drawn from magazines, films, and books of the period.
4. Rivers says that participation in sports was critical to her development. Extending a sports metaphor, she says that women's "Contempt [for men] will only vanish when women have a chance to play all the games now owned by men." Analyze the role of sports in your development, or trace the changing status of women athletes and athletics since the 1970s and relate these developments to changes in the status of women in society.

Here Comes the Groom
A (Conservative) Case for Gay Marriage

Andrew Sullivan

Andrew Sullivan earned a doctoral degree in government at Harvard University and is the editor of *The New Republic,* where "Here Comes the Groom" appeared in the August 28, 1989, issue. He has written widely on issues concerning gays.

Journal Topics: (1) What is the difference between living together and being married? (2) Are you in favor of legalizing homosexual marriage? Why?

As You Read: (1) Do you agree with the judge's ruling that "'family' merely means an interwoven social life, emotional commitment, and some level of financial interdependence"? (2) What are the public-policy and social problems that the concept of "domestic partnership" raises, according to Sullivan? (3) Why is Sullivan's proposal both radical and conservative?

1 Last month in New York, a court ruled that a gay lover had the right to stay in his deceased partner's rent-control apartment because the lover qualified as a member of the deceased's family. The ruling deftly annoyed almost everybody. Conservatives saw judicial activism in favor of gay rent control: three reasons to be appalled. Chastened liberals (such as the *New York Times* editorial page), while endorsing the recognition of gay relationships, also worried about the abuse of already stretched entitlements that the ruling threatened. What neither side quite contemplated is that they both might be right, and that the way to tackle the issue of unconventional relationships in conventional society is to try something both more radical and more conservative than putting courts in the business of deciding what is and is not a family. That alternative is the legalization of civil gay marriage.

2 The New York rent-control case did not go anywhere near that far, which is the problem. The rent-control regulations merely stipulated that a "family" member had the right to remain in the apartment. The judge ruled that to all intents and purposes a gay lover is part of his lover's family, inasmuch as a "family" merely means an interwoven social life, emotional commitment, and some level of financial interdependence.

3 It's a principle now well established around the country. Several cities have "domestic partnership" laws, which allow relationships that do not fit into the category of heterosexual marriage to be registered with the city and qualify for benefits that up till now have been reserved for straight married couples. San Francisco, Berkeley, Madison, and Los Angeles all have legislation, as does the politically correct

Washington, D.C. suburb, Takoma Park. In these cities, a variety of interpersonal arrangements qualify for health insurance, bereavement leave, insurance, annuity and pension rights, housing rights (such as rent-control apartments), adoption and inheritance rights. Eventually, according to gay lobby groups, the aim is to include federal income tax and veterans' benefits as well. A recent case even involved the right to use a family member's accumulated frequent-flier points. Gays are not the only beneficiaries; heterosexual "live-togethers" also qualify.

4   There's an argument, of course, that the current legal advantages extended to married people unfairly discriminate against people who've shaped their lives in less conventional arrangements. But it doesn't take a genius to see that enshrining in the law a vague principle like "domestic partnership" is an invitation to qualify at little personal cost for a vast array of entitlements otherwise kept crudely under control.

5   To be sure, potential DPs have to prove financial interdependence, shared living arrangements, and a commitment to mutual caring. But they don't need to have a sexual relationship or even closely mirror old-style marriage. In principle, an elderly woman and her live-in nurse could qualify. A couple of uneuphemistically confirmed bachelors could be DPs. So could two close college students, a pair of seminarians, or a couple of frat buddies. Left as it is, the concept of domestic partnership could open a Pandora's box of litigation and subjective judicial decision-making about who qualifies. You either are or are not married; it's not a complex question. Whether you are in a "domestic partnership" is not so clear.

6   More important, the concept of domestic partnership chips away at the prestige of traditional relationships and undermines the priority we give them. This priority is not necessarily a product of heterosexism. Consider heterosexual couples. Society has good reason to extend legal advantages to heterosexuals who choose the formal sanction of marriage over simply living together. They make a deeper commitment to one another and to society; in exchange, society extends certain benefits to them. Marriage provides an anchor, if an arbitrary and weak one, in the chaos of sex and relationships to which we are all prone. It provides a mechanism for emotional stability, economic security, and the healthy rearing of the next generation. We rig the law in its favor not because we disparage all forms of relationships other than the nuclear family, but because we recognize that not to promote marriage would be to ask too much of human virtue. In the context of the weakened family's effect upon the poor, it might also invite social disintegration. One of the worst products of the New Right's "family values" campaign is that its extremism and hatred of diversity has disguised this more measured and more convincing case for the importance of the marital bond.

7   The concept of domestic partnership ignores these concerns, indeed directly attacks them. This is a pity, since one of its most important objectives—providing some civil recognition for gay relationships—is a noble cause and one completely compatible with the defense of the family. But the way to go about it is not to undermine straight marriage; it is to legalize old-style marriage for gays.

8   The gay movement has ducked this issue primarily out of fear of division. Much of the gay leadership clings to notions of gay life as essentially outsider, antibourgeois,

radical. Marriage, for them, is co-optation into straight society. For the Stonewall generation, it is hard to see how this vision of conflict will ever fundamentally change. But for many other gays—my guess, a majority—while they don't deny the importance of rebellion twenty years ago and are grateful for what was done, there's now the sense of a new opportunity. A need to rebel has quietly ceded to a desire to belong. To be gay and to be bourgeois no longer seems such an absurd proposition. Certainly since AIDS, to be gay and to be responsible has become a necessity.

9   Gay marriage squares several circles at the heart of the domestic partnership debate. Unlike domestic partnership, it allows for recognition of gay relationships, while casting no aspersions on traditional marriage. It merely asks that gays be allowed to join in. Unlike domestic partnership, it doesn't open up avenues for heterosexuals to get benefits without the responsibilities of marriage, or a nightmare of definitional litigation. And unlike domestic partnership, it harnesses to an already established social convention the yearnings for stability and acceptance among a fast-maturing gay community.

10   Gay marriage also places more responsibilities upon gays: It says for the first time that gay relationships are not better or worse than straight relationships, and that the same is expected of them. And it's clear and dignified. There's a legal benefit to a clear, common symbol of commitment. There's also a personal benefit. One of the ironies of domestic partnership is that it's not only more complicated than marriage, it's more demanding, requiring an elaborate statement of intent to qualify. It amounts to a substantial invasion of privacy. Why, after all, should gays be required to prove commitment before they get married in a way we would never dream of asking of straights?

11   Legalizing gay marriage would offer homosexuals the same deal society now offers heterosexuals: general social approval and specific legal advantages in exchange for a deeper and harder-to-extract-yourself-from commitment to another human being. Like straight marriage, it would foster social cohesion, emotional security, and economic prudence. Since there's no reason gays should not be allowed to adopt or be foster parents, it could also help nurture children. And its introduction would not be some sort of radical break with social custom. As it has become more acceptable for gay people to acknowledge their loves publicly, more and more have committed themselves to one another for life in full view of their families and their friends. A law institutionalizing gay marriage would merely reinforce a healthy social trend. It would also, in the wake of AIDS, qualify as a genuine public health measure. Those conservatives who deplore promiscuity among some homosexuals should be among the first to support it. Burke could have written a powerful case for it.

12   The argument that gay marriage would subtly undermine the unique legitimacy of straight marriage is based upon a fallacy. For heterosexuals, straight marriage would remain the most significant—and only legal—social bond. Gay marriage could only delegitimize straight marriage if it were a real alternative to it, and this is clearly not true. To put it bluntly, there's precious little evidence that straights could be persuaded by any law to have sex with—let alone marry—someone of their own sex. The only possible effect of this sort would be to persuade gay men and women who force

themselves into heterosexual marriage (often at appalling cost to themselves and their families) to find a focus for their family instincts in a more personally positive environment. But this is clearly a plus, not a minus: Gay marriage could both avoid a lot of tortured families and create the possibility for many happier ones. It is not, in short, a denial of family values. It's an extension of them.

13   Of course, some would claim that any legal recognition of homosexuality is a de facto attack upon heterosexuality. But even the most hardened conservatives recognize that gays are a permanent minority and aren't likely to go away. Since persecution is not an option in a civilized society, why not coax gays into traditional values rather than rail incoherently against them?

14   There's a less elaborate argument for gay marriage: It's good for gays. It provides role models for young gay people who, after the exhilaration of coming out, can easily lapse into short-term relationships and insecurity with no tangible goal in sight. My own guess is that most gays would embrace such a goal with as much (if not more) commitment as straights. Even in our society as it is, many lesbian relationships are virtual textbook cases of monogamous commitment. Legal gay marriage could also help bridge the gulf often found between gays and their parents. It could bring the essence of gay life—a gay couple—into the heart of the traditional straight family in a way the family can most understand and the gay offspring can most easily acknowledge. It could do as much to heal the gay-straight rift as any amount of gay rights legislation.

15   If these arguments sound socially conservative, that's no accident. It's one of the richest ironies of our society's blind spot toward gays that essentially conservative social goals should have the appearance of being so radical. But gay marriage is not a radical step. It avoids the mess of domestic partnership; it is humane; it is conservative in the best sense of the word. It's also practical. Given the fact that we already allow legal gay relationships, what possible social goal is advanced by framing the law to encourage those relationships to be unfaithful, undeveloped, and insecure?

WRITING ASSIGNMENTS

Analysis

1. According to Sullivan, how do individuals and society benefit from marriage?
2. Compare Sullivan's position on the benefits of marriage to attitudes expressed in Jones's article.
3. Identify Sullivan's use of value-laden language, and analyze its effect on the essay's tone.
4. List Sullivan's implicit and explicit assumptions. Are they all generally accepted? Explain how disagreement with any of them might logically undermine Sullivan's argument.

Argument

1. Support or disagree with Sullivan's proposal. In either case, specifically address the points that Sullivan raises.

2. Defend the concept of "domestic partnership" and respond to Sullivan's criticisms of it.
3. Are relationships outside the framework of marriage, whether homosexual or heterosexual, necessarily "unfaithful, undeveloped, and insecure"?

Personal Writing and Writing from Research

1. Describe your own or your family's experience with a homosexual relationship. What would have been the effect of legalizing that relationship through marriage?
2. What is "the Stonewall generation," and is Sullivan's allusive characterization of it accurate?
3. Report on your city's and state's laws governing homosexual rights.

FRIENDS

We cannot pick our family, but we can pick our friends. Furthermore, we can tailor our friendships to suit our personalities and our circumstances, making adjustments as needed. Friends decide when and how often to see each other and how to spend time together. Its voluntary and flexible nature often makes friendship a less complicated, more individualized, more reliably fulfilling, and easier relationship than either family or love relationships. It is no surprise that friendship complements or even compensates for the other important relationships in our lives. We should value it highly.

But ironically, psychotherapist Lillian Rubin says, the accommodating nature of friendship generally guarantees its subordinate status in the hierarchy of affective relationships, below loyalty to family members and lovers. Writing about friendship in "The Neglected Relationship," she notes that we have few words to name—and even fewer rituals or holidays to celebrate—friendship, compared to the wealth of language and ritual we have developed to define and reinforce family and love relationships. While offering both psychological and social explanations, she laments friendship's second-class status.

In "True Friendship Between Men," Stuart Miller defines and celebrates the unique values of close male friendship, while analyzing the cultural obstacles he believes prevent most men from developing such relationships. He directly ties these obstacles to key elements in the American construction of masculinity.

Both Rubin and Miller note that mature men generally speak of youth as the high point of male friendship. Rubin found that the close male friendships of youth generally succumb in a man's maturity to the more insistent demands of work and marriage. She therefore devalues these youthful friendships. But in "The Reunion," Paul Gottlieb testifies to the endurance and importance of such youthful friendships, even when they are interrupted. However, his essay also illustrates Rubin's point that family experiences influence the nature and meaning of friendship in our lives.

In "Focusing on Friends," film director Steve Tesich offers yet another perspective on male friendship. He praises the action orientation, distance, and nonverbal nature of his friendships with men. For some commentators, such as Rubin and Miller, these are precisely the aspects of male behavior that stunt male friendships, but Tesich disagrees. He claims that his male friendships have a greater authenticity and depth than do his highly verbal friendships with women.

Next, Carroll Smith-Rosenberg provides a historical perspective on female friendship in "The Female World of Love and Ritual: Relations Between Women in Nineteenth-Century America." De-emphasizing the psychological underpinnings of friendship that Rubin emphasized, Smith-Rosenberg focuses on the way societally imposed separate spheres for middle-class men and women more than a century ago influenced the quality, content, and expression of female friendship.

In "Friendship, Feminism and Betrayal," Susan Lee analyzes the failure of a once-close friendship. Like Smith-Rosenberg, she views friendship against the backdrop of history, in this case the years before and just after the second women's movement in the 1970s. For her, once women gained greater control over their lives, the responsibilities and terms of friendship changed.

The Neglected Relationship

Lillian B. Rubin

Lillian B. Rubin, a social scientist, psychotherapist, and author, is senior research associate at the Institute for the Study of Social Change at the University of California, Berkeley, where she also received her PhD. Her books include *Busing and Backlash: White Against White in an Urban School District, Worlds of Pain: Life in the Working-Class Family, Women of a Certain Age: The Midlife Search for Self* (1979), *Intimate Strangers: Men and Women Together* (1983), and *Just Friends: The Role of Friendship in Our Lives* (1985), from which this selection is taken.

Journal Topics: (1) How do you define friendship? (2) How has your concept of friendship changed in the last 5, 10, or 15 years? (3) Briefly compare two friendships, one with a male and one with a female, *or* one childhood and one adult friendship.

As You Read: (1) What differences does Rubin see between friendship and kinship, or between friendship and love? (2) How does her definition of ideal friendship compare to the reality of the friendships her interviewees describe? (3) What evidence does Rubin provide to confirm or refute the social significance of friendship? (4) Is Rubin's pool of interviewees representative of American society?

1 . . . Friendship in our society is strictly a private affair. There are no social rituals, no public ceremonies to honor or celebrate friendships of any kind, from the closest to the most distant—not even a linguistic form that distinguishes the formal, impersonal relationship from the informal and personal one.

2 It's not that way everywhere. Some other Western cultures have rituals to mark the progress of a friendship and to give it public legitimacy and form. In Germany, for example, there's a small ceremony called *Duzen,* the name itself signifying the transformation in the relationship. The ritual calls for the two friends, each holding a glass of wine or beer, to entwine arms, thus bringing each other physically close, and to drink up after making a promise of eternal brotherhood with the word *Bruderschaft.* When it's over, the friends will have passed from a relationship that requires the formal *Sie* mode of address to the familiar *Du.*

3 In our own society, no clear lines mark the beginnings of a friendship; often none mark the ending either. Relations of blood generally end in death—clear and unequivocal. But friendships usually just fade away. Beginnings are equally unambiguous in the family: A baby is born and instantly there are mother, father, sister, brother, aunts, uncles, cousins. With marriage also, beginnings and endings are strikingly clear: Marriages start with a wedding and end with death or divorce. But for us, friendship is a *non-event*—a relationship that just *becomes,* that grows, develops, waxes, wanes

THE NEGLECTED RELATIONSHIP • 457

and, too often perhaps, ends, all without ceremony or ritual to give evidence of its existence.

4   Our language offers few possibilities for distinguishing among friendships, the word "friend" being used to refer to a wide range of relationships with varying degrees of closeness and distance. Compare this with kinship and the rich set of descriptive terms the language makes available. The words "mother," "father," "aunt," "uncle," "cousin," all tell us something specific about a person's place in the kin circle. Whether related by blood or by marriage, each relationship has its own designation. There's no ambiguity there; no questions nag us about who is a husband, a wife, a sibling, a child, a parent, a mother-in-law, a brother-in-law. We all know. We know, too, what to expect in those relationships because the rules and boundaries—however imperfectly articulated or realized, however much in flux in this historical moment—are, for most of us, more clearly understood and accepted with kin than they are with friends.

5   But what can we make of this dialogue with a thirty-two-year-old man who spoke with ease and authority about his "fifteen or twenty" intimate friends? No matter how much I probed or prodded, no matter how I phrased and rephrased the questions, he had all the "right" answers. "Yes, I can talk to them about anything, no matter what the problem is," he insisted. "Yes, I can turn to them in any kind of trouble." "Trust," he said, "and joint helpfulness"—these are the central and defining features of friendship for him. "Can you count on all these fifteen or twenty people to be trustworthy and helpful in any situation?" I asked. "Yes," he assured me, "I sure can."

6   "Do you have a best friend?" I asked him, as I had asked everyone else. "Sure do; he's a guy I've known since high school." "How often do you see each other?" Now the answers came with more hesitation. "Well, in fact, we haven't seen each other since he moved east about ten years ago." "How do you stay in touch; by phone?" "Yeah, well, actually, you see, we don't, not really; maybe a couple of times we talked on the phone since he left." "What makes him a best friend then?" I asked as I found myself becoming increasingly nonplussed. "It's just like I said—trust, that's what it is. I know I can absolutely trust him." "Trust him with what?" "With anything I need. I could land on his doorstep in the cold of winter and the dead of night and I know he'd be right there." Flippantly, and without really expecting any surprises in his answer, I wondered, "Just where is this doorstep on which you'd always be welcome to land?" A moment of silence and then, "I'm not sure. You see, he moved a while back and I don't know exactly where he lives now." "How far back?" "I don't remember exactly, a couple of years maybe."

7   Long-distance friendships are, of course, common in our mobile society, many of them representing deep and lasting ties. People speak often of the importance of such friendships, giving evidence of a connection that's undeniable, telling tales of how, after months of separation, they come together and pick up where they left off, as if no time had elapsed. These people, however, know where to find each other, certainly maintain contact more than once in ten years.

8   But I met others who told stories about friendships that, although less extreme than the tale just told, raised similar doubts. Consequently, in forty-four cases (15

percent of those interviewed), where the contradictions seemed very clear, I asked people to refer me on to all those they had named as close friends or best friends. I ended up with the names of 186 people, of whom I contacted 132—some in person, some, who lived in distant places, by telephone. These were relatively brief exchanges since I didn't mean to examine their friendship histories fully, only to discover if the designation of "close" or "best" friend was reciprocal.

9 The results? Eighty-four (64 percent) made no mention of the person I originally interviewed on their list of friends. Sometimes, when I prompted them, they would remember, expressing some mild discomfort at having forgotten this friend while also letting me know this was not an important relationship for them. But often they responded vaguely, acknowledging that they knew him or her but didn't think of the person as a friend. The remaining forty-eight people I contacted listed my respondent as a friend spontaneously, but in only eighteen cases (14 percent) did he or she come anywhere near the top of their list.

10 We have friends, and we have "just" friends; we have good friends, and we have best friends. Yet such is the elusiveness of the idea of "friend" that not even the people involved can always say which is which.

11 "What is a friend?"—a question I asked everyone I talked with. The answers I heard varied somewhat depending on class, gender and generational perspectives. But regardless of the experienced reality of their lives and relationships, most people presented some idealized definition of friendship. *Trust, honesty, respect, commitment, safety, support, generosity, loyalty, mutuality, constancy, understanding, acceptance.* These are the most widely heralded qualities of friendship, the minimum requirements, if you will, to be counted as a friend.

12 Nothing wrong with the list, of course. It just doesn't match up with the friends they described later in our discussion. Yet these are not simply distortions of fact. Rather they are at once the expression of the idealized imagery that talk about friends summons up and the widely shared wish for just such a relationship.

13 Just as with love, the *idea* of friendship stirs yearnings from our infantile past, bringing to life the hope that somewhere, sometime, perfect love, trust, security and safety will be ours once more. Therefore, when the talk turns abstract, as in "What is a friend?," rather than concrete, as in "What is your relationship with Jane like?," we're more likely to respond from the wish than from the reality. It's then that the disparity between the idealized version of *friendship* and the reality of relations with *friends* stands revealed so clearly. It's then, too, that we can see that this paradox is itself a crucial and often overlooked dimension of this whole subject.

14 From the beginning, it was contradictions such as these that made this project alternately exhilarating and aggravating. For without institutional form, without a clearly defined set of norms for behavior or an agreed-upon set of reciprocal rights and obligations, without even a language that makes distinctions between the different kinds of relationships to which we apply the word, there can be no widely shared agreement about what is a friend. Thus it is that one person will claim as a friend someone who doesn't reciprocate; that another who has been called a good friend

says, when I ask him about this relationship, "Oh, yeah, John, we worked together a year or so ago. Haven't seen him since."

15   Yet despite the ambiguity that surrounds friendship in this society, generations of American children have grown up under the influence of an adult world that has brooded more over their social adjustment than their moral development—indeed, often equated the two. By the time a child is two, parents already are concerned about the little one's ability to be sociable, searching anxiously for signs that she or he will be successful in making friends. Soon after, teachers join parents in worrying about the child who spends "too much time alone" or who "has trouble relating to others."

16   Since from our earliest childhood, we have been judged and measured by our ability to make and keep friends, friendship, for us, is not *just* something to be desired. To be without friends is a cause for shame, a stigma, a symptom of personal deficiency that none of us takes lightly. Indeed, in notable ways, our very sense of ourselves is connected to our ability to negotiate the world of friendship. Consequently, the lack of friends can torment even very small children, leaving them with feelings that range from a sense of personal inadequacy to a wish to die. In *The Social World of the Child,* William Damon tells of the eight-year-old girl who said she would "feel like killing [herself]" if she didn't have friends.

17   Who among us has forgotten the agony of standing alone in the schoolyard when others had friends with whom to play? Who cannot recall the youthful dread of being unpopular? Who today can find oneself alone at a cocktail party without discomfort, without being shadowed by the anxieties of the past?

18   Yet until very recently, the subject of adult friendship has been largely absent from the literature of the social and psychological sciences, getting little more than passing reference in studies devoted to other issues. Indeed, so blind have we been to the social and psychological meanings of friendship that anthropologists, trained in the art of studying alien cultures, have paid scant attention to these relationships, even in societies where rituals exist and institutional forms are quite obvious.

19   Our well-developed ideology about marriage and the family, our insistence that these are the relationships that count for the long haul, have, I believe, blinded us to the meaning and importance of friendship in our lives. Until the soaring divorce rate pointed so sharply to a crisis in marriage, we still expected that all our needs for emotional intimacy, social connectedness and intellectual stimulation would be met there. Today we know better. But the knowledge of this reality, no matter how powerfully it has made itself felt, has failed to correct the fantasy.

20   To understand why, we must look to the nuclear family itself—to the many ways it perpetuates itself, not least by creating a set of needs for the kind of intense emotional bonds that are formed there. The isolation of the nuclear family, the privacy of this "sanctum into whose hallowed chambers no outsider has a right of entry," means that it is not just the primary source of survival for the dependent infant, but the wellspring of emotional gratification and identification for the developing child as well.

21   We know, of course, that the emotional needs of infancy and childhood often are not adequately met in the family. Nevertheless, these old emotional connections live inside us with powerful intensity—silken threads that bind us more tightly than any chains. Consequently, we are left forever hungry to feel again the depth of the bond we once knew, to find a new love within which we can experience these old feelings once more. We don't wholly ignore friends, of course. But usually they are a distant second, their place in our lives contingent upon the demands and vicissitudes of love and marriage.

22   The last few years have seen a quickening of interest in friendship among adults, however, an emerging awareness about the importance of friends in our lives. The slim body of existing research tells us that, even where supportive and solid family relationships exist, friends count in any number of ways—from playmates to soul mates. Robert Weiss, who has written extensively on the subject of loneliness, presents convincing evidence that, even when people are comfortably and happily married, the absence of friends exacts a heavy cost in loneliness and isolation. Other studies have found that friends and neighbors provide a more effective support network for schizophrenic women living at home than do members of their family; that friends are more important for maintaining morale in old age than are grandchildren; that divorced women get help with the practical aspects of living from kin, but friends are crucial for the emotional support they offer and the link to the outside world they provide.

23   In another vein, social scientists, worrying about the anomie and alienation of urban life, have brought forth a body of work examining the social networks within which people's lives are embedded. Feminist scholars, attempting to redress the omissions of the past, have produced a small literature showing that women's friendships have always been an important part of their lives and thoughts.

24   Outside the academy as well, several of the major institutions of our society seem to have found their voice on the subject. Look, for example, at the spate of articles about friendship that have recently preoccupied the newspapers and mass-circulation magazines. Notice the major national advertising campaign of the telephone company which exhorts us to "reach out and touch someone," while it shows old and young alike finding new joy in life through a phone call from a friend. In New York City, the telephone company has actually instituted a "Phone-A-Friend" service, in which people who don't have friends of their own can dial a number that will connect them to lonely strangers like themselves. And in northern California, Pacific Bell has just announced a service called Talkline—a program offering teen-agers, adults and seniors their own special numbers that allow them to join a conversation with as many as ten others, all unknown.

25   Even the California State Department of Health has gotten into the act with a series of public service announcements on radio and television extolling the value of friendship for our physical and mental health. "Make a friend," these ads urge. "Friends can be good medicine." Yet the very need for such a campaign is testimony to the ambivalence and ambiguity with which friendship is held in our society. For on the one hand, it tells us that friendship remains our neglected relationship while, at

the same time, acknowledging that from early childhood right on up through old age, friends are crucial to our well-being.

26   To study friendship, then, is to trip over the ambiguity, ambivalence, contradiction and paradox with which this subject is hedged in our society. . . . But this ambiguity is only of interest in the context of some larger understandings about the meaning and purpose friends have in our lives.

27   . . . Friends are central actors in the continuing developmental drama of our adulthood. The burgeoning field of adult development contradicts earlier theories that identity formation is a one-time, all-or-nothing affair that is crystallized in early childhood and determined by the nature of family relations. Rather, most modern theorists now understand the formation of a personal identity as a lifetime process to which our varied experiences in the larger social world, as well as in the family, make their contributions—a process, both conscious and unconscious, in which each of us acts as mediator, in which the experience of the external world is given internal substance and meaning by our own particular integrative and interpretive capacities.

28   From birth onward, we are active and seeking participants in our own development—seeking, in that we continually respond to our internal need for connection with another; active, in that we are in a constant process of internalizing representations of people and objects from the world around us. Our sense of self is formed through this process of internalizing the external world, which, among other things, means making attachments and identifications with others who touch our lives.

29   This is how we come to know who and what we are in the world. Through our connection with others, we develop our sense of our common humanity. Through the images we internalize from the world around us, we eventually take our own measure. A sense of self and personal identity is formed and sharpened in the context of such human interaction—products of the interplay between external and internal, between social experience and its psychological elaboration.

30   In this process, friends count. . . . [O]ur friendships and our developing sense of ourselves are in a complex and continuing interaction, each influencing the other in ways we have not, until now, fully understood. On the one hand, friends have a powerful effect on the development of a full, coherent and satisfactory sense of self; and on the other, the identifications of our earliest childhood years, and the sense of self that grows from them, affect the kinds of friendships we are likely to form in adulthood.

31   Whether child or adult, it is friends who provide a reference outside the family against which to measure and judge ourselves; who help us during passages that require our separation and individuation; who support us as we adapt to new roles and new rules; who heal the hurts and make good the deficits of other relationships in our lives; who offer the place and encouragement for the development of parts of self that, for whatever reasons, are inaccessible in the family context. It's with friends that we test our sense of self-in-the-world, that our often inchoate, intuitive, unarticulated vision of the possibilities of a self-yet-to-become finds expression.

32   In all these ways and more, friendship, as we shall see, finds its long-neglected place in the drama of human development. But since friendships don't exist in isolation

from other important relationships in our lives, in particular those in our nuclear and extended families, we start with a comparison of kinship and friendship.

ABOUT THE STUDY

33 This book is based on in-depth interviews, each lasting several hours, with three hundred men and women, ages twenty-five to fifty-five—people who run the gamut from high-school dropout to college professor, who are single and married, working class and middle class. About two-thirds come from California, where I live and work; the rest are distributed among urban centers across the country. The class composition of the sample is: 22 percent professional upper middle class; 40 percent middle class; 38 percent working class. Class background was determined by a combination of education and occupation.

34   I have, in addition, one hundred interviews with homosexual men and lesbians which focus on their love relationships, their friendships, and the interaction between the two. But since homosexuality raises particular issues around friendship, whether same-sex or cross-sex—issues that deserve a book in their own right—throughout this book I will use these interviews for comparative purposes in specific instances only.

35   Because I was interested in how friendship outside a marriage can affect life inside it, I talked with both partners. Because I wanted to understand friendship from all sides of the interaction, I often interviewed one or more of the people a respondent designated as friends. Wherever possible, I talked to those who were named as best friends. But I did not limit myself to this category alone. Sometimes also I sought out someone who was called a good friend, sometimes someone who was "just a friend," the decision based on what seemed either most problematic or most interesting in the original interview.

36   Right from the beginning, the paradoxical nature of the whole subject of friendship in our society became clear. There was no resistance to participating in the study; indeed, quite the contrary. It made no difference who they were or where they lived; all eagerly granted my request for an interview. But such are the contradictions, both conscious and unconscious, people experience around this issue that it was often harder for them to sort out their friendships, and to speak openly and directly about them, than to discuss the highly personal issues of family life that were the focus of my earlier studies, including even such intimate matters as sexual relations.

WRITING ASSIGNMENTS

Analysis

1. Is Rubin's interview sample broadly representative of American society? If not, whom has she omitted? How might her choice of people to interview have skewed her findings?

2. Develop your own definition of friendship. How do your friendships match up to your general definition? Attempt to explain any discrepancies.
3. Compare and contrast Rubin's and Miller's definitions of the nature and function of friendship. Which, if either, do you find more accurate?

Argument

1. Do you agree with Rubin that friendship takes second place to love and marriage? Why?
2. Rubin says that friendship often has no clear beginning and ending, little language to describe it, and little social or institutional support. Do you agree with Rubin that this amorphousness of friendship is a deficiency? Might it also be an advantage that friendship enjoys over other relationships?

Personal Writing and Writing from Research

1. Rubin cites several feminist studies on female friendship. Use them as the basis for your own assessment of female friendship, either historic or current.
2. *Collaborative Project:* Interview approximately ten members of one of the groups that Rubin identifies—married couples, grandparents, and divorced women—to assess the role of friendship in their lives. Do your findings agree with those of the studies cited by Rubin?
3. Describe how other cultures use ceremonies, rituals, and language to honor and celebrate friendship.
4. Describe a close friendship's origin, development, basis, and expression. How, if at all, does your friend's gender, or your own, influence the nature of this friendship?
5. Rubin says, "To be without friends is a cause for shame, a stigma, a symptom of personal deficiency that none of us takes lightly." Do you agree? Can there be times when the lack of friends is justified, necessary, or just acceptable?

True Friendship Between Men

Stuart Miller

Stuart Miller received his PhD from Yale University and has taught at the University of California, Berkeley; Livingston College; Rutgers University; and the University of New York at Stonybrook. Founder of the Institute of Humanistic Medicine and former director of the Esalen Institute, he is also the author of *Hot Springs* (1971), an account of his experiences in the human potential movement; *The Picaresque Novel* (1967); *Measure, Number and Weight* (1968); *Dimensions of Humanistic Medicine* (1976); *Painted in Blood: Understanding Europeans* (1987); and *Men and Friendship* (1983), from which this selection comes.

Journal Topics: (1) Describe a friendship between two men, both of whom you know well. (2) How, if at all, does friendship between two men, two women, and a man and woman differ?

As You Read: (1) What background factors does Miller see as obstacles to friendship between males? (2) How does Miller define male friendship? (3) According to Miller, how does a man's friendship with another man differ from his friendship with a woman?

The first time I went out interviewing and told someone I was thinking of writing a book on male friendship, it was a sunny spring day in California. I had been divorced for a year and had already started trying to deepen my existing friendships. But it was only recently that the idea to write a book on the subject had occurred to me.

The person I chose was a reliable sort: career man, married, grown children, grandchildren. For a long time he had been head of a humanities department at a university. I respected him. We had first met, years before, because he had defied the university authorities: while not very political himself, he believed in civil liberties and would have resigned, if necessary, to protect those of his students. Indeed, he had been a sort of mentor for me in my youthful days as a professor. So, he was not a friend, because friendship is a more equal relationship, but still someone with whom I felt a personal connection.

Though he had been a teacher for forty-five years before he had retired, gnarled and thin, his western origins still showed through. He was, if you will, the cowboy-scholar. . . . He had the assurance of a man who had risen to the top of his profession even when taking risks.

He squinted at me in the pained way he liked to crease his face when he wanted you to know he was thinking seriously. "Male friendship. You mean you're going to write about homosexuality? That's what everybody will think, at least. Could be dangerous for you."

5   I couldn't believe his reaction. Surely the great tradition of male friendship, celebrated in the West by Homer and Aristotle and Cicero, by Montaigne and Shakespeare and Pope, was what people would think of when I said "male friendship." Surely they would call to mind the expedition of Gilgamesh and Enkidu, the terrible wrath of Achilles at the slaughter of his friend Patrocles, the love of David for Jonathan, which surpassed family and political loyalties, the heroic self-sacrifice of Oliver for his friend Roland. At the very least they would think of the more recent movie images of men loyal to and caring for one another—*The Deerhunter, Butch Cassidy and the Sundance Kid,* and *Breaker Morant.*

"Mebbe," he muttered, "mebbe I'm too affected by the gay scene around here." He didn't sound convinced.

We talked. Yes, he had still a couple of friends. Didn't see them much anymore. Didn't even hear from them much. In fact, the high point, what he really remembered, was in the twenties. . . .

I left the philosopher and walked over to the science building to see another former acquaintance, another retired professor, but this one in his small laboratory. . . . This man, too, had risen to the top of his profession. A renowned scholar, he was short, fat, and cheerful, whereas the first had been tall, thin, and dour.

When I explained what I was up to, he looked uncharacteristically distant as he said, "Mostly it has been death that has deprived me of my friends. You must be careful. You know, of course, that people will think you are writing about homosexuality."

10 "What I'm interested in is the loving relationship between adult men! Is it possible that the situation has gotten so bad that people think male friendship is something queer?"

He smiled sorrowfully.

Everywhere I have gone there has been the same misconception. The bizarre necessity to explain, at the beginning, that my subject is not homosexuality.

The fear of homosexuality and how it affects the possibilities of male friendship in our times are topics that need contemplating, and we will come back to them. The point here, however, is that the estate of male friendship—indeed, of nearly all human relationships—is sufficiently sunk that mere sex remains at the center of people's imaginations. The only moving human relationships that people seem able to conjure up are erotic ones.

It is hard to prove that adult male friendship has died. . . . A recent survey of the readers of *Psychology Today,* purporting to be the most extensive poll of American men and women about friendship, reports that most who responded are satisfied with the quality of their friendships. They confide in their friends, tend to turn to them in times of emotional crises, and tend to find their friends more important as they all get older. The editors see such replies as tending to contradict "clichés" about the impersonality and anomie of life in modern cities. The editors note that the survey results "give cold comfort to social critics."

15 Perhaps. And yet in examining such a survey, one notes that the thousands of people who responded did so voluntarily. One has not yet heard from the nearly three million readers who did not respond. In addition, only a small proportion of those who replied were men, and only fifteen percent were over thirty-five years old. Perhaps the low age of the self-selected sample explains why most respondents reported their friendships had most frequently been formed in childhood. One wonders how events will look to them in a decade or more.

In fact, deep friendship between adult men is quite rare in our society. Most interesting in this regard are the findings of Professor Daniel Levinson's team of social scientists at Yale, the psychologists, sociologists, and anthropologists who patiently studied a cross section of adult American men over many years. In the book *The Seasons of a Man's Life,* they report:

> In our interviews, friendship was largely noticeable by its absence. As a tentative generalization we would say that close friendship with a man or woman is rarely experienced by American men. This is not something that can be adequately determined by a questionnaire or mass survey. The distinction between friend and acquaintance is often blurred. A man may have a wide social network in which he has amicable,

"friendly" relationships with many men and perhaps a few women. In general, however, most men do not have an intimate male friend of the kind that they recall fondly
from boyhood or youth.

Here we get further toward a definition of real male friendship: "the kind" that
men "recall fondly from boyhood or youth."

I have found that friendship, especially adult male friendship, is something impossible to describe in the analytical terms that scientific writers will muster about the subject: "male bonding," "trust," "intimacy," "sharing," "confidant," "helper." The reality
defies all such categories as it eludes, also, "loyalty," "warmth," "affection," "support-
iveness," "common interests," and "common activities." And as it eludes "acceptance"
and "self-disclosure" and even "presence."

. . . As my early interviewing went on, there was reason to think that American men
no longer know what a friend is. If I simply asked them about their friendships, often
they told me everything was fine. Sure, they see people, to a degree confide in people,
to a degree trust people. They have, as the Yale study suggests, a network of relationships. They are not anchorites. But as the psychologist Abraham Maslow put it, that
doesn't mean men have a friend in the world.

20   I talked at length to a man I know who is in his fifties, divorced, and attractive—
not just attractive to women, but to people in general. He is at the center of a vast
professional and social network of contacts. An administrator of a humanitarian institute, he is constantly trying to help others. So he introduces Bill to Joe, in the
hope they will collaborate on a book. And he introduces Arthur to Harry, hoping they
will launch a project in Africa. As time goes on, these people tend to see each other—
first at work, then after work, and they become one another's society. The man who
started it all is pleased, and he is the beneficiary of more and more such successful
pairings. He has lunch or dinner with a "friend" virtually every afternoon and night.
Because he has introduced so many people to one another, these luncheons and dinners are increasingly filled with talk of those mutually related individuals. This man,
more than many people in our society, seems to live supported by a virtual web of
love, one that reaches fifty miles in every direction and is constantly being reinforced
with new knots of meetings and pleasant exchanges.

"I was very sick the other night," he said to me, stirring sugar into his coffee. Indeed, he looked a little paler than usual and his big shoulders seemed to slump. "I
was in my office, a little after five, on Friday, after everyone else had gone home. And
I just fell down. I was hot. Then cold. And my stomach was all knotted up. I could
hardly move."

"Were you conscious?"

"Yes, though mostly of pain."

"Did you call someone?"

25   "No."

"Well, what did you do? You should have called someone."

"I was very afraid, of course. But I waited. And then, crawling, I made it down the
stairs. And somehow, even though it was dark as hell out and raining, I managed to

get into the car and to drive home. I've never been so sick in my life. Really, I thought I might die."

"You should have called someone. Why didn't you call me or one of your other friends?"

"I don't know. I just didn't. And, anyway, it went away the next day."

30 "If anything like this ever happens again you must call me. Please." I tried to get him to look me in the eye and say yes.

"Sure," he said, but I didn't believe him.

How odd that when the crunch comes, he will not call. Does this man have a friend?

. . . Do you love your friend enough to put your life in danger? It is the kind of question that quickly puts facile talk about having friends in perspective.

. . . [But] there's a good chance that the people who might actually save you from Nazis and other assorted monsters might not be friends at all but just plain decent folk. Moreover, the definition posed by the question is simply too behavioral. There is a tendency to define friends merely in terms of action: How often do you *see* them? Would they *help* you? Can you *confide* in them? All important questions. But friendship often does not involve gross behaviors at all. It is, rather, something subtle and inward, a series of inner movements and responses.

35 Let us try another question, then.

You are an adult American male, somewhere past thirty. It is night. You have gotten into bed. With the deliberation that comes at a certain age you close your eyes. You have long since ceased to be sure that they will close by themselves. Now the mind begins its own regular routines: sorting and filing and inventorying your recent experience. What were yesterday's tasks? What will be tomorrow's obligations? Are you up to them? Does your wife still love you? Are the children going to be all right?

As you lie there, waiting for inner quiet, reviewing the day, thinking about tomorrow, wife, child, do you also habitually think about your friend? Do you think with what delight you will see him tomorrow? With what disappointment you won't see him? Do you wonder how he will straighten out *his* family's problems?

When one has a really close friend, his image is part of the carousel of vehicles and beasts that appears at the entrance to one's personal underworld. Like Ulysses, you look forward to seeing the great Achilles that you knew. If at such junctures in life as the space between consciousness and sleep your friend is with you, in your imagination, then you have a friend. If not, if a friend is seldom there, then it doesn't matter how many favors people will do for you, how many rounds of golf you play with them, how much you help one another in your work.

Shakespeare has the phrase for this critical dimension of friendship. As Hamlet is dying, he begs Horatio to live on: "If thou didst ever hold me in thy heart, / Absent thee from felicity a while / And . . . draw thy breath in pain / To tell my story." As much as anything else, friendship is the inner habit of holding someone who is neither spouse nor relative, nor teacher, nor lover, in your heart.

40   Notice here that we are not talking about men in groups; friendship is more selective and personal, almost always two by two. And we are not talking about those exciting, sometimes profound, but necessarily transitory relationships that feed off a
particular social context: comrades in the same political or religious debates and
struggles, co-ideologues, teammates, nor even those bonds formed by living through
dangerous situations together. Many people believe that men in hazardous occupations have friends, but usually, when the danger passes, so does the active being of
friendship; it is replaced by a warm shared nostalgia. True, friendship may sometimes
arise in all such contexts, but it is finally independent of them. Friendship is its own
context.

There are particular experiences when friends are together—perhaps as varied in
their details as the number of men who can make friendships—that also help define
the essence of the relationship. I talked to a man in his fifties who has had his ups and
downs in the world, a writer whose work is marked by its terrifying excursions into
the darker sides of existence: a terrible pain to being human. This man, with a face
roughly torn by lines of care, has his own experience of friendship. Explaining how
with age friendship has become rarer and rarer in his life, he says:

> I think people who develop a real friendship are men who have been very badly hurt
> and unconsciously go to that most exact of human places to heal themselves. In some
> complicated way, friendship at its most perfect is related to deep suffering and deep
> illness; the acute horror of being forced into desolation by a society that clearly has
> little real interest in human values. So when people go toward each other and love
> one another, there's a kind of deep, deep medication. Real friendship, then, is a kind
> of divine act that enables two people to share feelings, to have feelings that life denies
> continually. It's a way of outsmarting life, which is continually getting at you anyway,
> no matter how rich or smart you are . . . It's the one chance you have of getting on
> top of it. It requires all your belief in the possibility that you can walk on water with
> somebody because of the sheer electrical discharge of love. It's a kind of hydrojet
> you're on.

A younger but also middle-aged man, a stout psychotherapist with many children,
describes the moment of friendship:

> A deep and powerful, soft and relaxed quality of simply breathing together. And strong
> moments when one's brain is rapaciously excited around an idea that you're sharing.
> A visceral intimacy, sort of like eating a wonderful meal together. To eat, to be filled,
> no competition; just a kind of gustatory, visceral, endomorphic filling. Very soft. Two
> comrades sitting at the edge of a rock looking at the ocean, or going for a wonderful,
> easy stroll through a city. There is no sense of danger, distrust, threat. The only thing
> that one is on guard about, if at all, is not to say something that will hurt, should it
> come up.

Such descriptions help us recall the experience of friendship and remind us of its
rarity. But there remains the further question: What is the particular note of maleness in experiences of friendship? Many people, in our liberated age especially,

maintain that there is no reality to the idea of male friendship as distinct from a friendship between the sexes or between women. But though the male element in male friendship must ultimately remain a mystery, we can suggest some of its aspects.

There is a particular background to the intimacy one experiences with a close male friend: the usual rivalry and struggle of man against man. In modern competitive society, all men to some extent are seen as potential enemies. In school they are competitors. On the playing field they are competitors. After school hours they are potential aggressors. As we grow to adulthood, they confront us with their criticisms, with their maneuvering for positions in the hierarchies of power, money, celebrity, accomplishment, and the conquest of women. In the bureaucracies within which most of us work, men lie in wait, perhaps to help, perhaps to betray and take our places. In the bureaucracies we deal with—to get our taxes paid, our cars registered, our health care delivered—the strange man can look upon us as an object, as a nuisance, as a potential wrongdoer. On the road, in the heavy steel armor of his automobile, the other man is ever ready to overtake, to pass, to cut off. We live our lives in a world of alien, seemingly tame but, we know, potentially dangerous males.

45   Most of the time we ignore the danger; we smile and stay cheerful, we coyly make gestures of submission or brave our way, we keep our sense of humor, we get by. But one measure of our deep habitual tension is the special relaxation and easiness we feel with a male friend. These are different from the deep comfort a woman lover can give, though all the world's instruments attached to brain and heart would have a hard time measuring the difference. With a male friend, we experience a serene excitement, a softening that thaws the shoulders.

Attending to such sensations, we can think that Wilhelm Reich was not so crazy when he talked about male "body armor." He described how the pliant bodies of male children gradually harden into heavy layers of tissue, adult breastplates, a deep and permanent tightness and tension of neck and gut and thigh, even when the man doesn't exercise. With a real man friend, for some moments, this tight armoring melts. One breathes more slowly and deeply. The back relaxes, and in minute ways even the testicles relax. Safety. The safety that comes from experiencing in an unmediated way that this man among men will not threaten. And that this man will, quite literally, protect your ass, as you will his should other men strike.

Usually, these are unconscious sensations and feelings, but they are nevertheless experienced. A psychologist in his sixties who has an extremely deep relationship with both his wife and one special man friend, has grappled with the notion and come up with this evocative distinction: "With Cynthia, I think, 'She will stand by me in everything, shoulder to shoulder,' but with Michael, I think, 'Back to back—he will help me fight back to back.' "

A tough army colonel tells me, "You know how often, in the most peaceful times and places, you pick a restaurant seat with your back against the wall and facing the door? It's instinctive, unconscious, primitive. And it's not only soldiers who do it—I've noticed it in stockbrokers, lawyers, lots of people. I think one aspect of male friendship is the sense that your back will be covered."

There are other ways to describe the masculine dimensions of friendship. To trust another man fully is to experience the pleasure of moving from expectations of roughness to those of softness and peace. Ordinarily, when we moderns think of other men physically, they are but shaggy creatures to us—rough beards and tough skin—not at all like the women we long to touch. Indeed, the physical attraction women feel for other men baffles us. We shrink from the adult physique of other men the way we often shrink from our own. As the poet Delmore Schwartz put it, we are disgusted with "the heavy bear that goes with me, a manifold honey to smear his face." In deep friendship this cultivated aversion and alienation from masculinity, inevitably including a degree of self-alienation, is from moment to moment forgone.

50   It is not that friends necessarily ever touch. Rather that in friendship we are curiously drawn by the other man's inner beauty past the reflexive aversion to his outer appearance. We are drawn by his wit, the set of his eyes that makes us think we are seen. We are drawn by his apparent gentleness, his directness, his valor. We are drawn by his energy, a male force we share and that reinforces ours just when the world and time seem to have flattened us out altogether. Past the shaggy-beast exterior, the threatening otherness that is also our own physical self, we find a heart that beats with ours, a brain that chimes with ours, an understanding that includes the same masculinity that is, too often, a burden in this life.

A middle-aged police detective hints at the depths of this secret knowledge. "One of the recognitions I share with my present-day friends is that we all have the initiation of maturity. We've had to do certain things to be independent and we know what they are. The shameful ones, the worthy ones, and the breaking of our illusions. You recognize that in the other man, it never has to be spoken, and you build on that."

An aspect of the pleasurable essence of male friendship, then, consists in an imaginative going forth toward and beyond the perpetual threat of combat. It is to enter the shared knowledge of battles lost and won with caring and simple acceptance of mutual maleness.

This experience of generic wariness and repulsion yielding to taking a risk and then to being together is repeated over and over in any real friendship. When it happens, we feel known. Even the beast that is our mutual fate is known. And in some curious way, together we redeem the beast, and we can shout and dance—or we could, if such rejoicings were permitted in our world—with satisfaction at being men.

Then, for no deeper reason than the transient quality of all human satisfaction, the experience is lost and one is again isolated, facing another alien man.

55   This process is nothing exotic; at a certain level of intensity, it can happen in the most ordinary settings and with men who are only casual friends. You have come early to the restaurant where a friend is to meet you for lunch. You sit at the cloth-covered table playing with the silverware. There is a stir in the distance and you raise your eyes. A man approaches. For the instant it seems just another male shape. You keep your armor on. As he comes closer, you see it is your friend, but you are not sure whether he is in a good mood or not. The armor stays on. You smile, you get out of your chair, you hold out the hand to grab the hand, you keep scanning, discreetly, to

see if it's all right. Maybe, now, you'll take your armor off, let it melt away, some or all. Or maybe you'll just keep smiling and busy yourself with "Hello, how are you, how much time will you have, we'd better order, the salmon looks good . . ." Until it fits—if it does, somehow, maybe after a couple of drinks—and by some imperceptible process you are together. But then, during the meal, you may stiffen again, inwardly, at something he said, or you thought he said, and you will reach out imaginary stiff arms to put him off. At the end, when he hurries away as you do, you will with the slightest hidden bitterness forsake him because he forsook you or, in any case, you've got to be a real man, tough and ready, again. Lunch is over. The talk is over. The game is finished.

The experience of meeting another man on that safe inner ground is so special and so important that men will go through rather strange antics to have it. Many commentators have decried the fact that American men, particularly, seem to have to act tough with one another. They have criticized the poking, the proverbial back-slapping, the ironic joking, and the near fighting that men use in approaching one another.

We are all familiar with that rude striking and provoking, even though it is now passing out of fashion. But what is it for? Is it simply a denial of tenderness, a masking of gentler feelings? It is that and also, paradoxically, its opposite. In our culture, where expressing the kinder feelings between adult males is simply not usual, some men evoke those feelings by mock denial. It amounts to a dramatization, almost a parody, of the usual combative relationship between competitive men that can yield itself to real contact.

Joseph Heller reports that he never says sentimental things to his closest friends; for example, that he cares for them. Men don't do that, he insists; it wouldn't seem right. Rather, he makes fun of them. When his friend Mel Brooks interviews him for an article and goes off into a long question in which Brooks is obviously struggling to form his ideas, Heller says, "Oh, but no one cares what *you* think, Mel."

Heller's is a mock assault. It is not intended to hurt. The shock is received as a sting, like the proverbial clap on the back, and a feeling of intimacy and relaxedness is evoked by a kind of magnetic attraction of the opposite. We don't *really* fight, we are really friends. Of course. After much such mutual thumping, softened with enough alcohol, men of this sort will eventually get down to the warmer feelings they cannot easily express. There are even some men who will simply not trust you until they have physically or otherwise fought with you. They must emphasize the armor, use it, before they can allow themselves to put it aside. The famous wrestling scene in D. H. Lawrence's *Women in Love* is of this kind.

60   There are other aspects of the masculine expression of friendship—tendencies toward mutual action or wildness, for example—that are often frustrated by too highly organized a society. One that seems especially important is the admiration close men friends feel for each other. While most of modern life demands that we be ready to compete (thereby ever-honing us to belittle, to criticize, to search for flaws), friendship allows us to esteem the other freely. When men who have close friends or men who in their youth had close friends talk about them, their eyes shine, their faces

light up, and they appreciate, shamelessly, the other's qualities of character, strength, courage, versatility, intelligence, humor, generosity. Such appreciation is in itself a pleasurable release to our otherwise frustrated sense of justice, expressing our best traditional ideas of manliness. More selfishly, those qualities we do admire we magically add, through the bond we feel and in our unconscious imaginations, to our own.

These are some of the special aspects of close male friendship: a willingness to take a dangerous stand for another; a special relaxation and safety; an end to competitiveness, alienation, and self-alienation; a pleasure in doing masculine justice to others, an enhancement of men's own vitality and being. Above all, a holding in the heart.

WRITING ASSIGNMENTS

Analysis

1. Miller cites Joseph Heller's claim that he (Heller) never says sentimental things to his closest [male] friends. Like Steve Tesich, whose essay appears later in this chapter, Heller maintains and values a certain distance from his male friends. Compare Miller's, Heller's, and Tesich's ideas about the role of verbal intimacy in friendships between men.

2. Miller quotes a male psychologist in his 60s who distinguishes between his relationships with his wife and his close friend in this way: in adversity, he is "shoulder to shoulder" with his wife, and "back to back" with his friend. Explore the symbolism of these two images, particularly their relevance to concepts of masculinity and femininity.

3. To what extent might Miller's observations about male friendship reflect his ethnicity (European-American) and class (highly educated and middle class)? If relevant, use your knowledge of another American subculture's attitudes toward friendship to help you develop your response.

Argument

1. Do you agree with Miller that male-male competition, male psychological "armor," male self-alienation, and homophobia all raise obstacles to male friendship?

2. Do you agree with Miller that friendship between men is intrinsically and necessarily different from friendship between a man and woman?

Personal Writing and Writing from Research

1. *Collaborative Project:* Survey historical examples and literary or philosophical depictions of male friendship, beginning with those mentioned by Miller.

2. Compare your definition of male or female friendship with Miller's definition of male friendship.

3. Read Wilhelm Reich on "male armor" and evaluate his assertions by recording your observations of male gestures, posture, and the physical distance maintained in men's interactions with other men. Define and describe the male

population you observe so that your readers know the nature of your study sample.

4. Compare and contrast the images of male friendships in selected television and magazine advertisements. Do these images confirm Miller's analysis of male friendship?

The Reunion

Paul Gottlieb

Paul Gottlieb is publisher and editor-in-chief of the publishing company Harry N. Abrams. "The Reunion" was published in the "About Men" column, which alternates with the "Hers" column, in the *New York Times Magazine.*

Journal Topics: (1) Describe a once-close friendship and attempt to explain why it lapsed. (2) Describe and explain the successful revival of a once-close, then lapsed, friendship. (3) Describe a situation in which loyalty to a friend conflicted with loyalty to a lover or to family.

As You Read: (1) How does Charlie's family background differ from Hugh's and Paul's? (2) How do Charlie's "families" influence his friendships? (3) How does the reunion of these middle-aged friends resemble their youthful friendship? (4) What, if any, are the especially masculine qualities of this friendship?

1 My two best friends from college days are Hugh and Charlie. Hugh and I have remained close for the intervening quarter of a century, but Charlie is another matter altogether. Fifteen years ago, he disappeared completely from our lives. Last December, Hugh and I rediscovered him, and in so doing rediscovered the power of early friendships.

2 We three first met some thirty years ago, in my first week at Swarthmore. I had just turned seventeen, a nervous Brooklyn Tech graduate entering a small Quaker college at the start of everybody else's second semester. In the cavernous commons room of the main building, I spotted two boys who struck me as representing everything college was supposed to be. Hugh was discoursing on the metaphysical poetry of John Donne. Charlie was blowing smoke rings. I could do neither. They were older than I by two years and seemed vastly more knowledgeable. Though Hugh looked like a young Marlon Brando, there was never any question in his or anyone else's mind that he would become a writer. Charlie wore his wavy red hair in a tousled arrangement, as if he had more important matters to think about than his appearance. He would later become a psychologist, but in those days he aspired to the lifestyle and talents of F. Scott Fitzgerald.

3   In the ensuing months, the three of us talked incessantly—about God, about great and not-so-great literature, about our relatively brief past lives, about the nature of man—and we talked an awful lot about girls. That talk at all hours has, I think, something to do with the intensity of friendships formed in early years. Such friendships demand an investment of time that one can rarely afford later, as well as a willingness to be vulnerable, to reveal oneself and to be receptive to new ideas.

4   Hugh and I, both New Yorkers, sprang from relatively similar, stable Jewish backgrounds. Charlie was the only child of a Boston Irish Catholic family: his mother a fragile woman who worked as a nurse and communicated rarely with her son; his father already in the mental hospital that he was never to leave. Over the coming years, Hugh and I were to become variations on the themes of our cultural pasts. Charlie's accomplishment was more awesome: he had to invent himself almost completely. He was the first of us to marry and have a child. In 1955, still in his F. Scott Fitzgerald phase, Charlie wed a Southern debutante. I was best man. Hundreds of elaborately dressed people filled the bride's side of the aisle; on the groom's side, there was Charlie's mother, one aunt and uncle, my family and Hugh.

5   Five years later, Charlie, now recovering from the end of his first marriage, came to New York to do research in psychology. Eventually, he married again, an elegant, reserved woman who seemed uncomfortable with our boisterous behavior. As we each began to raise our own families, Charlie's new wife gradually drew him away from our orbit. We were all too busy to notice what was happening, until one day Charlie and his family simply disappeared from New York. They left no forwarding address. We didn't know where to look for him. Besides, I suppose, Hugh and I were hurt. Charlie, after all, had chosen his new family over our old "family." We went on with our lives. Charlie was now part of our vanished youth.

6   Fifteen years passed. Hugh became a successful novelist; I became a publisher. Then, late in the fall, at a cocktail party, I ran into a woman who knew us all from the old days. "Have you heard about Charlie?" she asked. "He's divorced again and living in Annapolis."

7   Immediately, I knew what I wanted to do. I put my drink down, went into an adjoining room and called Hugh. We agreed that we were going to visit Charlie whether or not he wanted to see us. I managed to get his Annapolis telephone number and nervously called. "Hugh and I are coming to see you," I stammered. "When?" the familiar voice answered, as if we had spoken only the day before.

8   Early one Friday morning last December, Hugh and I took off for Annapolis. The small plane flew not far above the ground, and we fell into silence watching the landscape below. Would our meeting with Charlie be simply a reliving of past associations, or would there be more? Could we get beyond nostalgia for our lost youth and move into a future friendship as well?

9   We arrived at the Baltimore-Washington airport, and as we passed through the landing gate, there was Charlie looking for us. "Oh," I thought, drawing in my breath and my gut, "we are middle-aged for certain." Considerably heavier now, hair thinning, gray mixed with red, Charlie flashed us a familiar grin. We burst into excited shouts like small boys winning a Little League championship. We seized each other joyfully, jumping up and down, whooping, laughing, hugging and kissing. Arm in

arm, we felt invincible, a reunited troika. We raced to the car, hopped in and drove off. Charlie was so excited telling us of his life over the past fifteen years that we completely missed the highway turnoff and had to drive thirty miles out of the way before we came to Annapolis. His parents had both died, he explained. He had gambled everything on his second marriage, hoping it would give him the roots he sought, but, while he had two more children, it had not worked out. He was alone again.

10   We pulled up in front of the hotel where we were to stay. Hugh and I checked in and chose beds as college roommates do, flipping a coin for first choice. Charlie smiled. "Hey, I bought us something." Three identical gift boxes contained three identical knitted ties, maroon with jaunty blue stripes. We laughed and put them on, three aging musketeers in the highest spirits despite the gray and drizzling day.

11   We linked arms to roam the streets of Annapolis. At a restaurant, we began drinking large quantities of wine from pewter tankards. I realized that Hugh and Charlie were sitting side by side as they had been the day I first met them, rattling on about the work of a writer, while I sat quietly, the disciple listening to my elders. We drank more wine, and then reeled from shop to shop, trying on hats, looking at paintings, browsing through antique galleries and bookstores. We flirted with a barmaid who invited us home to bathe in her large zinc tub. (Hugh and I were flattered; to Charlie the invitation was commonplace.) We drank beer and ate dozens of oysters; and, surrounded by the young people from the local college and from the Naval Academy, we briefly found our own youth again, found our young voices and our young minds.

12   That night, Hugh and I lay awake in our hotel beds as we had so often in our college dormitory. We speculated about the nature of our relationships and particularly wondered how we had all influenced each other so many years ago. As we drifted toward sleep, we agreed that the principal quality we had absorbed from Charlie was a sense of wit, that ironic edge that adds zest and spice to thought and language.

13   The next day, we had breakfast with Charlie, admired the view from his small apartment and took turns trying out his water bed. I told him of our conversation the night before, and he laughed.

14   Hugh looked up and said quietly, "Charlie, if we learned wit from you, was there anything you learned from us?"

15   Charlie looked at both of us. "I thought you knew," he said. "Love."

WRITING ASSIGNMENTS

Analysis

1. Describe the circumstances in which this friendship developed and the nature of the friendship. Then compare it to either Miller's or Tesich's view of male friendship.
2. How do Rubin's and Miller's observations help to explain the phases of this friendship and of each man's role in it?
3. What, if anything, characterizes this friendship as a friendship among men?
4. What does Charlie mean when he says he learned "love" from Hugh and Paul?

Argument

1. Does the story of this friendship support or refute Rubin's assertion that commitments to friends take second place to family commitments?
2. Could this friendship just as easily have been a friendship among three women? Explain your answer.

Personal Writing and Writing from Research

1. Compare the friendship described in "Reunion" with one of your own in which once-close friends reunited, or tried to reunite, after falling out of touch.
2. Interview other members of your class, or people a generation older than you, about why their friendships have lapsed or endured. Analyze the contributing factors identified by your interviewees. Explain how your findings have influenced your expectations about the future of your own close friendships.

Focusing on Friends

Steve Tesich

Born in the former Yugoslavia, Steve Tesich immigrated to the United States as a boy. He is author of the novel *Summer Crossing* (1982) and of screenplays that include *Breaking Away* (1978), *Eye Witness* (1980), *Four Friends* (1980), *The World According to Garp* (1982), *American Flyers* (1984), and *Eleni* (1985). The theme of male friendship figures prominently in his screenplays. This essay appeared in the "About Men" column of the *New York Times Magazine*.

Journal Topics: (1) How does putting your feelings into words affect your feelings and the friendship itself? Illustrate your response by describing specific experiences. (2) Do you believe that "actions speak louder than words" when it comes to showing love for another person?

As You Read: (1) What are the shared characteristics of Tesich's male friendships? (2) How do his friendships with males differ from his friendships with women? (3) Why does Tesich believe that he "cheated" or "shortchanged" his women friends by making them the recipients of his uncensored emotions?

1 When I think of people who were my good friends, I see them all, as I do everything else from my life, in cinematic terms. The camera work is entirely different for men and women.

2 I remember all the women in almost extreme close-ups. The settings are different—apartments, restaurants—but they're all interiors, as if I had never spent a single minute with a single woman outside. They're looking right at me, these women in these extreme close-ups; the lighting is exquisite, worthy of a Fellini or Fosse film,

and their lips are moving. They're telling me something important or reacting to something even more important that I've told them. It's the kind of movie where you tell people to keep quiet when they chew their popcorn too loudly.

3   The boys and men who were my friends are in an entirely different movie. No close-ups here. No exquisite lighting. The camera work is rather shaky, but the background is moving. We're going somewhere, on foot, on bicycles, in cars. The ritual of motion, of action, makes up for the inconsequential nature of the dialogue. It's a much sloppier film, this film that is not really a film but a memory of real friends: Slobo, Louie, Sam. Male friends. I've loved all three of them. I assumed they knew this, but I never told them.

4   Quite the contrary is true in my female films. In close-up after close-up, I am telling every woman who I ever loved that I love her, and then lingering on yet another close-up of her face for a reaction. There is a perfectly appropriate musical score playing while I wait. And if I wait long enough, I get an answer. I am loved. I am not loved. Language clears up the suspense. The emotion is nailed down.

5   Therein lies the difference, I think, between my friendships with men and with women. I can tell women I love them. Not only can I tell them, I am compulsive about it. I can hardly wait to tell them. But I can't tell the men. I just can't. And they can't tell me. Emotions are never nailed down. They run wild, and I and my male friends chase after them, on foot, on bicycles, in cars, keeping the quarry in sight but never catching up.

6   My first friend was Slobo. I was still living in Yugoslavia at the time, and not far from my house there was an old German truck left abandoned after the war. It had no wheels. No windshield. No doors. But the steering wheel was intact. Slobo and I flew to America in that truck. It was our airplane. Even now, I remember the background moving as we took off down the street, across Europe, across the Atlantic. We were inseparable. The best of friends. Naturally, not one word concerning the nature of our feelings for one another was ever exchanged. It was all done in actions.

7   The inevitable would happen at least once a day. As we were flying over the Atlantic, there came, out of nowhere, that wonderful moment: engine failure! "We'll have to bail out," I shouted. "*A-a-a-a-a-!*" Slobo made the sound of a failing engine. Then he would turn and look me in the eye: "I can't swim," he'd say. "Fear not," I put my hand on his shoulder, "I'll drag you to shore." And, with that, both of us would tumble out of the truck onto the dusty street. I swam through the dust. Slobo drowned in the dust, coughing, gagging. "Sharks!" he cried. But I always saved him. The next day the ritual would be repeated, only then it would be my turn to say "I can't swim," and Slobo would save me. We saved each other from certain death over a hundred times, until finally a day came when I really left for America with my mother and sister. Slobo and I stood at the train station. We were there to say goodbye, but since we weren't that good at saying things and since he couldn't save me, he just cried until the train started to move.

8   The best friend I had in high school was Louie. It now seems to me that I was totally monogamous when it came to male friends. I would have several girlfriends but only one real male friend. Louie was it at that time. We were both athletes, and one day we decided to "run till we drop." We just wanted to know what it was like. Skinny

Louie set the pace as we ran around our high school track. Lap after lap. Four laps to a mile. Mile after mile we ran. I had the reputation of being a big-time jock. Louie didn't. But this was Louie's day. There was a bounce in his step and, when he turned back to look at me, his eyes were gleaming with the thrill of it all. I finally dropped. Louie still looked fresh; he seemed capable, on that day, of running forever. But we were the best of friends, and so he stopped. "That's it," he lied. "I couldn't go another step farther." It was an act of love. Naturally I said nothing.

9   Louie got killed in Vietnam. Several weeks after his funeral, I went to his mother's house, and, because she was a woman, I tried to tell her how much I had loved her son. It was not a good scene. Although I was telling the truth, my words sounded like lies. It was all very painful and embarrassing. I kept thinking how sorry I was that I had never told Louie himself.

10   Sam is my best friend now, and has been for many years. A few years ago, we were swimming at a beach in East Hampton. The Atlantic! The very Atlantic I had flown over in my German truck with Slobo. We had swum out pretty far from the shore when both of us simultaneously thought we spotted a shark. Water is not only a good conductor of electricity but of panic as well. We began splashing like madmen toward shore. Suddenly, at the height of my panic, I realized how much I loved my friend, what an irreplaceable friend he was, and, although I was the faster swimmer, I fell back to protect him. Naturally, the shark in the end proved to be imaginary. But not my feelings for my friend. For several days after that I wanted to share my discovery with him, to tell him how much I loved him. Fortunately, I didn't.

11   I say fortunately because, on reflection, there seems to be sufficient evidence to indicate that, if anybody was cheated and shortchanged by me, it was the women, the girls, the very recipients of my uncensored emotions. Yes, I could hardly wait to tell them I loved them. I did love them. But once I told them, something stopped. The emotion was nailed down, but with it, the enthusiasm and the energy to prove it was nailed down, too. I can remember my voice saying to almost all of them, at one time or another: "I told you I love you. What else do you want?" I can now recoil at the impatient hostility of that voice, but I can't deny it was mine.

12   The tyranny of self-censorship forced me, in my relations with male friends, to seek alternatives to language. And just because I could never be sure they understood exactly how I felt about them, I was forced to look for ways to prove it. That is, I now think, how it should be. It is time to make adjustments. It is time to pull back the camera, free the women I know, and myself, from those merciless close-ups and have the background move.

WRITING ASSIGNMENTS

Analysis

1. Trace and analyze Tesich's use of cinematic terms to express his experience of friendships with men and women.
2. Use Miller's observations to analyze Tesich's male friendships.

3. Why does Tesich believe that shared activities build a stronger foundation for friendship than verbal communication does?
4. What does this essay reveal about Tesich's assumptions regarding the differences between men's and women's natures and expectations?
5. What does the imagery in Tesich's descriptions of his male friendships reveal about his concept of masculinity?

Argument

1. Agree or disagree with Tesich's preference for shared activity over verbal communication as the strongest foundation of friendship.
2. Do you agree with Tesich about the consequences of talking about feelings: "Language clears up suspense. The emotion is nailed down"? Are these positive consequences for Tesich? Would they be for you?
3. Is Tesich's perspective characteristically masculine?

Personal Writing and Writing from Research

1. In an essay like Tesich's, examine the roles of shared activities and communication about feelings in your friendships with specific men and women.
2. Tesich implies that actions speak louder than words and speak more truthfully. Is it necessary to choose one or the other?

The Female World of Love and Ritual
Relations Between Women in Nineteenth-Century America

Carroll Smith-Rosenberg

A feminist scholar, Carroll Smith-Rosenberg has written numerous essays and articles about women's lives in Victorian America. Many of these articles, including "The Female World of Love and Ritual," which is excerpted here, are collected in *Disorderly Conduct* (1985). With Charles Rosenberg, she wrote "The Female Animal: Medical and Biological Views of Women in 19th Century America," *Journal of American History, 59* (1973): 331–56.

Journal Topics: (1) How do you demonstrate in words and gestures your affection for a close friend? (2) Are there any taboos today on the physical and verbal expressions of love between female friends? Between male friends? If so, describe them.

As You Read: (1) How did social and cultural factors in the lives of nineteenth-century women influence their friendships? (2) How do these friendships resemble and differ from female friendships today? (3) Would a late twentieth-century observer interpret these friendships in the same way that nineteenth-century contemporaries did?

1 . . . [A]n abundance of manuscript evidence suggests that eighteenth- and nineteenth-century women routinely formed emotional ties with other women. Such deeply felt, same-sex friendships were casually accepted in American society. Indeed, from at least the late eighteenth through the mid-nineteenth century, a female world of varied and yet highly structured relationships appears to have been an essential aspect of American society. These relationships ranged from the supportive love of sisters, through the enthusiasms of adolescent girls, to sensual avowals of love by mature women. It was a world in which men made but a shadowy appearance. . . .

2 . . . Intimate friendships between men and men and women and women existed in a larger world of social relations and social values. To interpret such friendships more fully they must be related to the structure of the American family and to the nature of sex-role divisions and of male-female relations both within the family and in society generally. The female friendship must not be seen in isolation; it must be analyzed as one aspect of women's overall relations with one another. . . .

3 This analysis will be based upon the correspondence and diaries of women and men in thirty-five families between the 1760s and the 1880s. These families, though limited in number, represented a broad range of the American middle class, from hard-pressed pioneer families and orphaned girls to daughters of the intellectual and social elite. It includes families from most geographic regions, rural and urban, and a spectrum of Protestant denominations ranging from Mormon to orthodox Quaker. Although scarcely a comprehensive sample of America's increasingly heterogeneous population, it does, I believe, reflect accurately the literate middle class to which the historian working with letters and diaries is necessarily bound. It has involved an analysis of many thousands of letters written to women friends, kin, husbands, brothers, and children at every period of life from adolescence to old age. Some collections encompass virtually entire life spans; one contains over 100,000 letters as well as diaries and account books. It is my contention that an analysis of women's private letters and diaries which were never intended to be published permits the historian to explore a very private world of emotional realities central both to women's lives and to the middle-class family in nineteenth-century America.

4 The question of female friendships is peculiarly elusive; we know so little or perhaps have forgotten so much. An intriguing and almost alien form of human relationship, they flourished in a different social structure and amidst different sexual norms. Before attempting to reconstruct their social setting, therefore, it might be best first to describe two not atypical friendships. These two friendships, intense, loving, and openly avowed, began during the women's adolescence and, despite subsequent marriages and geographic separation, continued throughout their lives. For nearly half a century, these women played a central emotional role in each other's lives, writing time and again of their love and of the pain of separation.

Paradoxically to twentieth-century minds, their love appears to have been both sensual and platonic.

5   Sarah Butler Wister first met Jeannie Field Musgrove while vactioning with her family at Stockbridge, Massachusetts, in the summer of 1849. Jeannie was then sixteen, Sarah fourteen. During two subsequent years spent together in boarding school, they formed a deep and intimate friendship. Sarah began to keep a bouquet of flowers before Jeannie's portrait and wrote complaining of the intensity and anguish of her affection. Both young women assumed nom de plumes, Jeannie a female name, Sarah a male one; they would use these secret names into old age. . . .

6   Sarah's marriage altered neither the frequency of their correspondence nor their desire to be together. In 1864, when twenty-nine, married, and a mother, Sarah wrote to Jeannie: "I shall be entirely alone [this coming week]. I can give you no idea how desperately I shall want you. . . ." After one such visit Jeannie, then a spinster in New York, echoed Sarah's longing: "Dear darling Sarah! How I love you & how happy I have been! You are the joy of my life. . . . I cannot tell you how much happiness you gave me, nor how constantly it is all in my thoughts. . . . My darling how I long for the time when I shall see you. . . ." After another visit Jeannie wrote: "I want you to tell me in your next letter, to assure me, that I am your dearest. . . . I do not doubt you, & I am not jealous but I long to hear you say it once more & it seems already a long time since your voice fell on my ear. So just fill a quarter page with caresses & expressions of endearment. Your silly Angelina." Jeannie ended one letter: "Goodbye my dearest dearest lover—ever your own Angelina." And another, "I will go to bed . . . [though] I could write all night—a thousand kisses—I love you with my whole soul—your Angelina."

7   When Jeannie finally married in 1870 at the age of thirty-seven, Sarah underwent a period of extreme anxiety. Two days before Jeannie's marriage Sarah, then in London, wrote desperately: "Dearest darling—How incessantly have I thought of you these eight days—all today—the entire uncertainty, the distance, the long silence— are all new features in my separation from you grevious to be borne. . . . Oh Jeannie. I have thought & thought & yearned over you these two days. Are you married I wonder? My dearest love to you wherever and *who*ever you are." . . .

8   During the same years that Jeannie and Sarah wrote of their love and need for each other, two slightly younger women began a similar odyssey of love, dependence and—ultimately—physical, though not emotional separation. Molly and Helena met in 1868 while both attended the Cooper Institute School of Design for Women in New York City. For several years these young women studied and explored the city together, visited each other's families, and formed part of a social network of other artistic young women. Gradually, over the years, their initial friendship deepened into a close intimate bond which continued throughout their lives.

9   The letters they wrote to each other during these first five years permit us to reconstruct something of their relationship together. As Molly wrote in one early letter:

> I have not said to you in so many or so few words that I was happy with you during those few so incredibly short weeks but surely you do not need words to tell you what you must know. Those two or three days so dark without, so bright with firelight and

contentment within I shall always remember as proof that, for a time, at least—I fancy for quite a long time—we might be sufficient for each other. We know that we can amuse each other for many idle hours together and now we know that we can also work together. And that means much, don't you think so?

10   She ended: "I shall return in a few days. Imagine yourself kissed many times by one who loved you so dearly."

11   .The intensity and even physical nature of Molly's love was echoed in many of the letters she wrote during the next few years. . . .

12   At the end of the fifth year, however, several crises occurred. The relationship, at least in its intense form, ended, though Molly and Helena continued an intimate and complex relationship for the next half-century. The exact nature of these crises is not completely clear, but it seems to have involved Molly's decision not to live with Helena, as they had originally planned, but to remain at home because of parental insistence. Molly was now in her late twenties. Helena responded with anger and Molly became frantic at the thought that Helena would break off their relationship. Though she wrote distraught letters and made despairing attempts to see Helena, the relationship never regained its former ardor—possibly because Molly had a male suitor. Within six months Helena had decided to marry a man who was, coincidentally, Molly's friend and publisher. Two years later Molly herself finally married. The letters toward the end of this period discuss the transition both women made to having male lovers—Molly spending much time reassuring Helena, who seemed depressed about the end of their relationship and with her forthcoming marriage.

13   It is clearly difficult from a distance of 100 years and from a post-Freudian cultural perspective to decipher the complexities of Molly and Helena's relationship. Certainly Molly and Helena were lovers—emotionally if not physically. The emotional intensity and pathos of their love becomes apparent in several letters Molly wrote Helena during their crisis: "I wanted so to put my arms round my girl of all the girls in the world and tell her . . . I love her as wives do love their husbands, as *friends* who have taken each other for life—and believe in her, as I believe in my God. . . . If I didn't love you do you suppose I'd care about anything or have ridiculous notions and panics and behave like an old fool who ought to know better. I'm going to hang on to your skirts. . . . You can't get away from [my] love." Or as she wrote after Helena's decision to marry: "You know dear Helena, I really was in love with you. It was a passion such as I had never known until I saw you. I don't think it was the noblest way to love you." The theme of intense female love was one Molly again expressed in a letter she wrote to the man Helena was to marry: "Do you know sir, that until you came along I believe that she loved me almost as girls love their lovers. *I know I loved her so.* Don't you wonder that I can stand the sight of you." This was in a letter congratulating them on their forthcoming marriage.

14   The essential question is not whether these women had genital contact and can therefore be defined as heterosexual or homosexual. The twentieth-century tendency to view human love and sexuality within a dichotomized universe of deviance and normality, genitality and platonic love, is alien to the emotions and attitudes of the nineteenth century and fundamentally distorts the nature of these women's

emotional interaction. These letters are significant because they force us to place such female love in a particular historical context. There is every indication that these four women, their husbands and families—all eminently respectable and socially conservative—considered such love both socially acceptable and fully compatible with heterosexual marriage. Emotionally and cognitively, their heterosocial and their homosocial worlds were complementary.

15   . . . What emotional function did such female love serve? What was its place within the hetero and homosocial worlds which women jointly inhabited? Did a spectrum of love-object choices exist in the nineteenth century across which some individuals, at least, were capable of moving? . . .

16   Several factors in American society between the mid-eighteenth and mid-nineteenth centuries may well have permitted women to form a variety of close emotional relationships with other women. American society was characterized in large part by rigid gender-role differentiation within the family and within society as a whole, leading to the emotional segregation of women and men. The roles of daughter and mother shaded imperceptibly and ineluctably into each other, while the biological realities of frequent pregnancies, childbirth, nursing, and menopause bound women together in physical and emotional intimacy. It was within just such a social framework, I would argue, that a specifically female world did indeed develop, a world built around a generic and unself-conscious pattern of single-sex or homosocial networks. These supportive networks were institutionalized in social conventions or rituals which accompanied virtually every important event in a woman's life, from birth to death. Such female relationships were frequently supported and paralleled by severe social restrictions on intimacy between young men and women. Within such a world of emotional richness and complexity devotion to and love of other women became a plausible and socially accepted form of human interaction.

17   An abundance of printed and manuscript sources exists to support such a hypothesis. Etiquette books, advice books on child rearing, religious sermons, guides to young men and young women, medical texts, and school curricula all suggest that late eighteenth- and most nineteenth-century Americans assumed the existence of a world composed of distinctly male and female spheres, spheres determined by the immutable laws of God and nature. The unpublished letters and diaries of Americans during this same period concur, detailing the existence of sexually segregated worlds inhabited by human beings with different values, expectations, and personalities. Contacts between men and women frequently partook of a formality and stiffness quite alien to twentieth-century America and which today we tend to define as "Victorian." Women, however, did not form an isolated and oppressed subcategory in male society. Their letters and diaries indicate that women's sphere had an essential integrity and dignity that grew out of women's shared experiences and mutual affection and that, despite the profound changes which affected American social structure and institutions between the 1760s and the 1870s, retained a constancy and predictability. The ways in which women thought of and interacted with each other remained unchanged. Continuity, not discontinuity, characterized this female world. Molly Hallock's and Jeannie Field's words, emotions, and experiences have direct

parallels in the 1760s and the 1790s. There are indications in contemporary sociological and psychological literature that female closeness and support networks have continued into the twentieth century—not only among ethnic and working-class groups but even among the middle class.

18   Most eighteenth- and nineteenth-century women lived within a world bounded by home, church, and the institution of visiting—that endless trooping of women to each others' homes for social purposes. It was a world inhabited by children and by other women. Women helped each other with domestic chores and in times of sickness, sorrow, or trouble. Entire days, even weeks, might be spent almost exclusively with other women. Urban and town women could devote virtually every day to visits, teas, or shopping trips with other women. Rural women developed a pattern of more extended visits that lasted weeks and sometimes months, at times even dislodging husbands from their beds and bedrooms so that dear friends might spend every hour of every day together. When husbands traveled, wives routinely moved in with other women, invited women friends to teas and suppers, sat together sharing and comparing the letters they had received from other close women friends. Secrets were exchanged and cherished, and the husband's return at times viewed with some ambivalence.

19   Summer vacations were frequently organized to permit old friends to meet at water spas or share a country home. In 1848, for example, a young matron wrote cheerfully to her husband about the delightful time she was having with five close women friends whom she had invited to spend the summer with her; he remained at home alone to face the heat of Philadelphia and a cholera epidemic. Some ninety years earlier, two young Quaker girls commented upon the vacation their aunt had taken alone with another woman; their remarks were openly envious and tell us something of the emotional quality of these friendships: "I hear Aunt is gone with the Friend and wont be back for two weeks, fine times indeed I think the old friends had, taking their pleasure about the country . . . and have the advantage of that fine woman's conversation and instruction, while we poor young girls must spend all spring at home. . . . What a disappointment that we are not together. . . ."

20   Friends did not form isolated dyads but were normally part of highly integrated networks. Knowing each other, perhaps related to each other, they played a central role in holding communities and kin systems together. Especially when families became geographically mobile women's long visits to each other and their frequent letters filled with discussions of marriages and births, illness and deaths, descriptions of growing children, and reminiscences of times and people past provided an important sense of continuity in a rapidly changing society. Central to this female world was an inner core of kin. The ties between sisters, first cousins, aunts, and nieces provided the underlying structure upon which groups of friends and their network of female relatives clustered. Although most of the women within this sample would appear to be living within isolated nuclear families, the emotional ties between nonresidential kin were deep and binding and provided one of the fundamental existential realities of women's lives. . . .

21   Women frequently spent their days within the social confines of such extended families. Sisters-in-law visited each other and, in some families, seemed to spend more time with each other than with their husbands. First cousins cared for each other's babies—for weeks or even months in times of sickness or childbirth. Sisters helped each other with housework, shopped and sewed for each other. Geographic separation was borne with difficulty. A sister's absence for even a week or two could cause loneliness and depression and would be bridged by frequent letters. Sibling rivalry was hardly unknown, but with separation or illness the theme of deep affection and dependency reemerged.

22   . . . Such women, whether friends or relatives, assumed an emotional centrality in each others' lives. In their diaries and letters they wrote of the joy and contentment they felt in each others' company, their sense of isolation and despair when apart. The regularity of their correspondence underlies the sincerity of their words. Women named their daughters after one another and sought to integrate dear friends into their lives after marriage. As one young bride wrote to an old friend shortly after her marriage: "I want to see you and talk with you and feel that we are united by the same bonds of sympathy and congeniality as ever." After years of friendship one aging woman wrote of another: "Time cannot destroy the fascination of her manner . . . her voice is music to the ear. . . ."

23   These female friendships served a number of emotional functions. Within this secure and empathetic world women could share sorrows, anxieties, and joys, confident that other women had experienced similar emotions. One mid-nineteenth-century rural matron in a letter to her daughter discussed this particular aspect of women's friendships: "To have such a friend as thyself to look to and sympathize with her— and enter into all her little needs and in whose bosom she could with freedom pour forth her joys and sorrows—such a friend would very much relieve the tedium of many a wearisome hour. . . ." A generation later Molly more informally underscored the importance of this same function in a letter to Helena: "Suppose I come down . . . [and] spend Sunday with you quietly," she wrote Helena ". . . that means talking all the time until you are relieved of all your latest troubles, and I of mine. . . ." These were frequently troubles that apparently no man could understand. When Anne Jefferis Sheppard was first married, she and her older sister Edith (who then lived with Anne) wrote in detail to their mother of the severe depression and anxiety which they experienced. Moses Sheppard, Anne's husband, added cheerful postscripts to the sisters' letters—which he had clearly not read—remarking on Anne's and Edith's contentment. Theirs was an emotional world to which he had little access.

24   This was, as well, a female world in which hostility and criticism of other women were discouraged, and thus a milieu in which women could develop a sense of inner security and self-esteem. . . . They valued each other. Women, who had little status or power in the larger world of male concerns, possessed status and power in the lives and worlds of other women.

25   An intimate mother-daughter relationship lay at the heart of this female world. The diaries and letters of both mothers and daughters attest to their closeness and

mutual emotional dependency. Expressions of hostility which we would today consider routine on the part of both mothers and daughters seem to have been uncommon indeed. On the contrary, this sample of families indicates that the normal relationship between mother and daughter was one of sympathy and understanding. Only sickness or great geographic distance was allowed to cause extended separation. When marriage did result in such separation, both viewed the distance between them with distress. Something of this sympathy and love between mothers and daughters is evident in a letter Sarah Alden Ripley, at age sixty-nine, wrote her youngest and recently married daughter: "You do not know how much I miss you, not only when I struggle in and out of my mortal envelop and pump my nightly potation and no longer pour into your sympathizing ear my senile gossip, but all the day I muse away, since the sound of your voice no longer rouses me to sympathy with your joys or sorrows. . . ."

26   Central to these mother-daughter relations is what might be described as an apprenticeship system. In those families where the daughter followed the mother into a life of traditional domesticity, mothers and other older women carefully trained daughters in the arts of housewifery and motherhood. Such training undoubtedly occurred throughout a girl's childhood but became more systematized, almost ritualistic, in the years following the end of her formal education and before her marriage. At this time a girl either returned home from boarding school or no longer divided her time between home and school. Rather, she devoted her energies on two tasks: mastering new domestic skills and participating in the visiting and social activities necessary to finding a husband. Under the careful supervision of their mothers and of older female relatives, such late-adolescent girls temporarily took over the household management from their mothers, tended their young nieces and nephews, and helped in childbirth, nursing, and weaning. Such experiences tied the generations together in shared skills and emotional interaction.

27   Daughters were born into a female world. Their mother's life expectations and sympathetic network of friends and relations were among the first realities in the life of the developing child. As long as the mother's domestic role remained relatively stable and few viable alternatives competed with it, daughters tended to accept their mother's world and to turn automatically to other women for support and intimacy. It was within this closed and intimate female world that the young girl grew toward womanhood.

28   One could speculate at length concerning the absence of that mother-daughter hostility today considered almost inevitable to an adolescent's struggle for autonomy and self-identity. It is possible that taboos against female aggression and hostility were sufficiently strong to repress even that between mothers and their adolescent daughters. Yet these letters seem so alive and the interest of daughters in their mothers' affairs so vital and genuine that it is difficult to interpret their closeness exclusively in terms of repression and denial. The functional bond that held mothers and daughters together in a world that permitted few alternatives to domesticity might well have created a source of mutuality and trust absent in societies where greater options were available for daughters than for mothers. Furthermore,

the extended female network—daughter's close ties with her own older sisters, cousins, and aunts—may well have permitted a diffusion and a relaxation of mother-daughter identification and so have aided a daughter in her struggle for identity and autonomy. None of these explanations are mutually exclusive; all may well have inter-acted to produce the degree of empathy evident in those letters and diaries.

29   At some point in adolescence, the young girl began to move outside the matrix of her mother's support group to develop a network of her own. Among the middle class, at least, this transition toward what was at the same time both a limited auton-omy and a repetition of her mother's life seemed to have most frequently coincided with a girl going to school. Indeed education appeared to have played a crucial role in the lives of most of the families in this study. Attending school for a few months, for a year or longer, was common even among daughters of relatively poor families, while middle-class girls routinely spent at least a year at boarding school. These school years ordinarily marked a girl's first separation from home. They served to wean the daughter from her home, to train her in the essential social graces, and, ul-timately, to help introduce her into the marriage market. It was not infrequently a trying emotional experience for both mother and daughter.

30   In this process of leaving one home and adjusting to another, the mother's friends and relatives played a key transitional role. Such older women routinely accepted the role of foster mother; they supervised the young girl's deportment, monitored her health and introduced her to their own network of female friends and kin. Not infre-quently women, friends from their own school years, arranged to send their daugh-ters to the same school so that the girls might form bonds paralleling those their mothers had made. . . .

31   Even more important to this process of maturation than their mother's friends were the female friends young women made at school. Young girls helped each other overcome homesickness and endure the crises of adolescence. They gossiped about beaux, incorporated each other into their own kinship systems, and attended and gave teas and balls together. Older girls in boarding school "adopted" younger ones, who called them "Mother." Dear friends might indeed continue this pattern of adop-tion and mothering throughout their lives; one woman might routinely assume the nurturing role of pseudomother, the other the dependency role of daughter. The pseudomother performed for the other woman all the services which we normally as-sociate with mothers; she went to absurd lengths to purchase items her "daughter" could have obtained from other sources, gave advice and functioned as an idealized figure in her "daughter's" imagination. . . .

32   A comparison of the references to men and women in these young women's let-ters is striking. Boys were obviously indispensable to the elaborate courtship ritual girls engaged in. In these teenage letters and diaries, however, boys appear distant and warded off—an effect produced both by the girl's sense of bonding and by a highly developed and deprecatory whimsy. Girls joked among themselves about the conceit, poor looks or affectations of suitors. Rarely, especially in the eighteenth and early nineteenth centuries, were favorable remarks exchanged. Indeed, while hostil-ity and criticism of other women were so rare as to seem almost tabooed, young

women permitted themselves to express a great deal of hostility toward peer-group men. When unacceptable suitors appeared, girls might even band together to harass them. . . .

33   Even if young men were acceptable suitors, girls referred to them formally and obliquely: "The last week I received the unexpected intelligence of the arrival of a friend in Boston," Sarah Ripley wrote in her diary of the young man to whom she had been engaged for years and whom she would shortly marry. Harriet Manigault assiduously kept a lively and gossipy diary during the three years preceding her marriage, yet did not once comment upon her own engagement nor indeed make any personal references to her fiance—who was never identified as such but always referred to as Mr. Wilcox. The point is not that these young women were hostile to young men. Far from it; they sought marriage and domesticity. Yet in these letters and diaries men appear as an other or out group, segregated into different schools, supported by their own male network of friends and kin, socialized to different behavior, and coached to a proper formality in courtship behavior. As a consequence, relations between young women and men frequently lacked the spontaneity and emotional intimacy that characterized the young girls' ties to each other.

34   Indeed, in sharp contrast to their distant relations with boys, young women's relations with each other were close, often frolicsome, and surprisingly long lasting and devoted. They wrote secret missives to each other, spent long solitary days with each other, curled up together in bed at night to whisper fantasies and secrets. . . .

35   Girls routinely slept together, kissed and hugged each other. Indeed, while waltzing with young men scandalized the otherwise flighty and highly fashionable Harriet Manigault, she considered waltzing with other young women not only acceptable but pleasant.

36   Marriage followed adolescence. With increasing frequency in the nineteenth century, marriage involved a girl's traumatic removal from her mother and her mother's network. It involved, as well, adjustment to a husband, who, because he was male came to marriage with both a different world view and vastly different experiences. Not surprisingly, marriage was an event surrounded with supportive, almost ritualistic, practices. (Weddings are one of the last female rituals remaining in twentieth-century America.) Young women routinely spent the months preceding their marriage almost exclusively with other women—at neighborhood sewing bees and quilting parties or in a round of visits to geographically distant friends and relatives. Ostensibly they went to receive assistance in the practical preparations for their new home—sewing and quilting a trousseau and linen—but of equal importance, they appear to have gained emotional support and reassurance. . . .

37   Sisters, cousins, and friends frequently accompanied newlyweds on their wedding night and wedding trip, which often involved additional family visiting. Such extensive visits presumably served to wean the daughter from her family of origin. . . .

38   Married life, too, was structured about a host of female rituals. Childbirth, especially the birth of the first child, became virtually a *rite de passage,* with a lengthy seclusion of the woman before and after delivery, severe restrictions on her activities, and finally a dramatic reemergence. This seclusion was supervised by mothers,

sisters, and loving friends. Nursing and weaning involved the advice and assistance of female friends and relatives. So did miscarriage. Death, like birth, was structured around elaborate unisexed rituals. When Nelly Parke Custis Lewis rushed to nurse her daughter who was critically ill while away at school, Nelly received support, not from her husband, who remained on their plantation, but from her old school friend, Elizabeth Bordley. Elizabeth aided Nelly in caring for her dying daughter, cared for Nelly's other children, played a major role in the elaborate funeral arrangements (which the father did not attend), and frequently visited the girl's grave at the mother's request. . . .

39   Eighteenth- and nineteenth-century women thus lived in emotional proximity to each other. Friendships and intimacies followed the biological ebb and flow of women's lives. Marriage and pregnancy, childbirth and weaning, sickness and death involved physical and psychic trauma which comfort and sympathy made easier to bear. Intense bonds of love and intimacy bound together those women who, offering each other aid and sympathy, shared such stressful moments.

40   These bonds were often physical as well as emotional. An undeniably romantic and even sensual note frequently marked female relationships. This theme, significant throughout the stages of a woman's life, surfaced first during adolescence. As one teen-ager from a struggling pioneer family in the Ohio Valley wrote in her diary in 1808: "I laid with my dear R[ebecca] and a glorious good talk we had until about 4[A.M.]—O how hard I do *love* her. . . ." Only a few years later Bostonian Euncie Callender carved her initials and Sarah Ripley's into a favorite tree, along with a pledge of eternal love, and then waited breathlessly for Sarah to discover and respond to her declaration of affection. The response appears to have been affirmative. A half-century later urbane and sophisticated Katherine Wharton commented upon meeting an old school chum: "She was a great pet of mine at school & I thought as I watched her light figure how often I had held her in my arms—how dear she had once been to me."

41   . . . How then can we ultimately interpret these long-lived intimate female relationships and integrate them into our understanding of Victorian sexuality? Their ambivalent and romantic rhetoric presents us with an ultimate puzzle: the relationship along the spectrum of human emotions between love, sensuality, and sexuality.

42   . . . It is possible to speculate that in the twentieth century a number of cultural taboos evolved to cut short the homosocial ties of girlhood and to impel the emerging women of thirteen or fourteen toward heterosexual relationships. In contrast, nineteenth-century American society did not taboo close female relationships but rather recognized them as a socially viable form of human contact—and, as such, acceptable throughout a woman's life. Indeed it was not these homosocial ties that were inhibited but rather heterosexual leanings. While closeness, freedom of emotional expression, and uninhibited physical contact characterized women's relationships with each other, the opposite was frequently true of male-female relationships. One could thus argue that within such a world of female support, intimacy, and ritual it was only to be expected that adult women would turn trustingly and lovingly to each

other. It was a behavior they had observed and learned since childhood. A different type of emotional landscape existed in the nineteenth century, one in which Molly and Helena's love became a natural development.

43   Of perhaps equal significance are the implications we can garner from this framework for the understanding of heterosexual marriages in the nineteenth century. If men and women grew up as they did in relatively homogeneous and segregated sexual groups, then marriage represented a major problem in adjustment. From this perspective we could interpret much of the emotional stiffness and distance that we associate with Victorian marriage as a structural consequence of contemporary sex-role differentiation and gender-role socialization. With marriage both women and men had to adjust to life with a person who was, in essence, a member of an alien group.

44   I have thus far substituted a cultural or psychosocial for a psychosexual interpretation of women's emotional bonding. But there are psychosexual implications in this model which I think it only fair to make more explicit. Despite Sigmund Freud's insistence on the bisexuality of us all or the recent American Psychiatric Association decision on homosexuality, many psychiatrists today tend explicitly or implicitly to view homosexuality as a totally alien or pathological behavior—as totally unlike heterosexuality.

WRITING ASSIGNMENTS

Analysis

1. Explain how historical factors influenced the nature and role of female friendships in the nineteenth century.
2. To what extent do social and cultural conditions in the late twentieth century differ from those that Smith-Rosenberg describes? Draw examples of contemporary female friendships from life, literature, the cinema, and television.
3. Despite historical changes, to what extent do female friendships today resemble those of the nineteenth century?
4. How does Smith-Rosenberg explain her assertion about the world of nineteenth-century women: "It was a world in which men made but a shadowy appearance"?
5. How did biology, psychology, and historical-cultural factors all help to shape female friendships in the nineteenth century?

Argument

1. Is the kind of close friendship described by Smith-Rosenberg feasible only for women of a particular social or economic class? Explain your answer.

Personal Writing and Writing from Research

1. Compare and contrast the way nineteenth-century female friends expressed their friendship to the way that you, as a female, do. If you are male, compare

nineteenth-century female friendships to either your own male friendships or to female friendships with which you are familiar.

2. *Collaborative Project:* Compare and contrast your friendships formed in childhood, in the community, at school, and at work. Are the nature and importance of these friendships different for men and women?

3. Interview several generations of men and women in your family about their close friendships. Explain how changing historical conditions helped shape these friendships.

Friendship, Feminism and Betrayal

Susan Lee

Susan Lee has written a novel, *Dear John* (1980) with Sandra Till Robinson, and has another in progress. This article appeared in *The Village Voice* on June 9, 1975.

Journal Topics: (1) Describe a time when a love interest interfered with a friendship. What was your role in this conflict, and how do you explain what happened? In retrospect, would you have handled the situation differently? (2) Do you believe that a real friend is someone who really knows you, faults and all, and accepts you anyway? Or do you believe that a real friend is someone who will expect you to rise above your weaknesses or faults to achieve a mutually shared, but hard to achieve, standard of conduct?

As You Read: (1) What lessons about the relative importance of relationships with females as compared to relationships with males did Lee learn in childhood and adolescence? (2) What does Lee mean when she says, "The given of having friends then was that we understood the same rules. The same given remains except that some of the rules are changing." (3) How does Lee distinguish between friendships and love relationships? (4) Why do both Lee and her friend Linda feel betrayed by each other? (5) What does Lee mean when she says Linda "had become a wife"?

Home for Christmas my first year in college, I spoke to my best friend from high school. Elizabeth and I stayed on the phone for 45 minutes, but we had nothing very much to say to each other. After the conversation, I was upset. I remember wanting to tell my mother, who asked what the matter was, about the weirdness of discovering that this woman and I, who had talked every school day for five years no longer had anything in common. All I could do was cry.

Except for a brief, awkward visit to my house a month later when my father died, a church wedding where Elizabeth married a man I'd gone out with in seventh grade, and two short stopovers in southern New Jersey, I don't remember ever seeing or speaking to her again.

We used to spend hours talking about our relationships with boys. We never discussed our relationship with each other. Except for the few minutes with my mother who told me she thought Elizabeth and I never had anything in common, and my once making a distinction between acquaintances and friends, I'd never spoken about what I considered a real friendship.

Many people have expressed agreement with Cicero that "friendship can only exist between good men." I'm not one of them. As a 30-year-old woman who has had friends since grade school, I have been very concerned with those friendships. Yet only in the last few years have such relationships been acknowledged as being as important as they've always been.

5   It was always commonplace for girls in my high school to spend a great deal of time together. It was also commonplace for a girl to spend Saturdays with another girl listening to Johnny Mathis albums, trying on clothes to find something that fit right, or babysitting and then having the evening that was planned together usurped by some boy calling up for a date. When this happened to me, I felt betrayed. I never said anything. It didn't occur to me that this wasn't the natural order of things. I didn't know anyone who complained, nor do I remember anyone who ever turned down a boy because she'd already made plans with a girl.

One woman I know said that if as a teenager she had told her parents she'd prefer being with a girl than a boy, they would have sent her to a doctor.

Even now, this past summer, when I was home for a few weeks because my mother was sick, my mother only asked questions about the men who called. One night when I was coming into the city, she discovered I was going to see a woman instead of the man who had just called.

All she said was, "Oh?" Within that one word was more archness than I'd ever heard placed in such a small space.

A male friend of mine suggested that, as kids, if a girl could turn down another girl, for a boy, maybe the girls weren't friends. What he didn't understand is how power works, how it matters who gets to set the dates, how important one telephone call can be, and how helpless someone can feel waiting for it.

10   But girls didn't deny each other because we weren't friends. We could only do it because we were and because boys weren't, and because they got to make the call and we didn't.

Still, a friend of mine recently remembered that she once was leaving a girl to go out on a date. Her girlfriend's mother, who was very hurt for her daughter, stopped her and said that when she was young, girls knew the value of friendship.

Now, each of us knows what this woman meant. We might express it in terms of a heightened woman's consciousness. We might talk of it in terms of respect for each of our relationships. My friend didn't. She went out on her date. She knew what was flexible in her life and what wasn't. The given of having friends then was that we understood the same rules. The same given remains except that some of the rules are changing.

The Greeks and Romans featured "friendship" in their society. From what I can tell, such friendship was a code word for male homosexual relationships.

The Old Testament emphasizes loyalty to family. Friendship, as we understand it, was hardly known. The New Testament uses the word "friend" slightly more but is as little interested in the relationships outside the family or group of coreligionists as the Old Testament.

15   While members of African tribes have exchanged names and had friendship ceremonies for generations, friendships have not been considered very important in Western cultures until fairly recently.

It would be difficult to date the advent of magnanimity, trust, and accord first manifesting itself as friendship among westerners. Studying friendship in the Plymouth Bay Colony, one historian decided that friendship, as we know it, did not exist. Far more central was devotion to a religious ideal. If you were in concord with that, you remained in relationship with your neighbors. If not, the relationship would be severed. Very possibly, regardless of your history, you were expelled.

American literature is full of male buddies who are supposedly friends; although they may hardly speak to each other, they would only be too glad to die for each other. I'm not sure if this palship is friendship.

Hardly any fiction deals with friendship between women. Doris Lessing's "The Golden Notebook" uses a relationship between two women as the backdrop for examining one of their lives in depth. Fay Weldon's recent "Female Friends" deals more directly with the subject. The women, unfortunately, are victims who continually slash at each other and whose friendship somehow remains as eternal as the sea.

Many studies have been done about interpersonal relationships. These however, usually deal with dating heterosexual couples. Most, like Erich Fromm in his book about different kinds of love, ignore friendship. The closest Fromm could come was brotherly love. The few that mention friendship concentrate on the architecture of friendship and on the network of who is friendly with whom. The conclusions usually have to do with the proximity of a physical, mental, or emotional sort. One study, for example, reveals that boys of the same height tend to be friends.

20   Friendship has become so institutionalized in our culture that a recent book combined the notion that everyone should have a good friend with the alienated sense that each person should be her or his own best friend.

My guess is that as the family breaks down, friendships will grow in importance. In my own life, as I have relied less and less on the idea of marriage for myself, the more I've come to see the friendships that I've had for years and years as the on-going relationships in my life.

College was a relatively easy place to find people I liked. Condescending as it might have sounded to me then, we each had our futures ahead of us. It seemed possible to get on with a large number of people. Still, most of my college friends and acquaintances disappeared from my life almost as soon as I left the campus. Like Elizabeth and I, we had little more in common than living near each other.

I used to think affection was enough for friendship, but I no longer believe that. Affection can be sufficient for lovers in a way it isn't for friends. But then, people "fall in" love. Someone is a lover after a few days. A friendship, where love develops, often takes years.

A friend is someone I can be myself with; with a lover, I'm all too often someone else, someone I'd rather be. With a friend, I'm a person; with a lover, I'm a person [sic].

25   I can only be myself when there is a shared community of interests between the other person and me. I began to realize how important this was when I got to graduate school in San Francisco and met other people who cared intimately about the same work I did. No longer was someone's impending wedding date the ongoing center of a conversation.

I found people who perceived what went on outside of them and how they acted in the world in many of the same ways I did. I was not as aware of the need for loyalty to friends as I am now. If I fall under the illusion that I was particularly unusual in the way that I treated other women, I remind myself of the green rocking chair in my San Francisco living room. I gave this chair up to any man who came into my house and kept it for myself if another woman was there.

One relationship developed into something more than shared after classroom time. Both Linda and I were dedicated to writing fiction and to working out our lives so that we'd be able to write. And, however different Linda and I were, I was conscious that our friendship had a loyalty and a respect for each other that other friendly relationships did not have.

We spent hours discussing our lives, our work, our dailyness. Where a lover and I take endless time concerning ourselves with ourselves and our specific relationship, Linda and I were spectators at the landscapes of each other's lives. We were more like adjacent lands sharing common borders than the same property itself. It seemed to me that not only did I have my life, but I had hers as well, to see the working out of our goal to become the best writers we possibly could.

A friend like Linda is a reflection of what I value, in a way a lover is not necessarily. I like to be friends with what is best in me and with what I'm interested in. While I, and several of my friends, too often excuse our choice of lovers as irrational or necessary acts, we take the responsibility for whom we've chosen as friends.

30   Still, I'm far more conscious of lovers than I am of friends. Though this is changing, I usually think about friends when something is wrong between us. When I'm in love, I'm almost always aware of my lover.

When I was in California and Linda didn't call or was late for an appointment, I assumed there was a good reason. When a lover messes up, I'm quick to think it's our relationship. Friends don't take things as personally as lovers do. There's less expectation and more politeness with friends, who are taken far more for granted than lovers. Yet the reality in my life is that friends are more constant. Lovers come and go except for those who become my friends and stay near me.

Even understanding this, it didn't occur to me to stay in California because of my friends. Linda, abiding by the same implicit rules I did, never mentioned my remaining to me; I don't know if she thought of it. Another friend confronted me; he asked how I could leave the people I freely acknowledged loving more than anyone else. It was enough for me that I was bored and dissatisfied in San Francisco and wanted to come back to New York.

The following year, I returned to the West Coast for Linda's wedding to another writer. Our relationship had deepened into the assumption that we were each other's friend. Although I had fears about the marriage which Linda was all too aware of, I didn't think of not going to give support. I hoped that if any woman could manage writing and a marriage, Linda would.

I tried seeing her for several weeks yearly in Italy or France where she lived. What I didn't admit to myself after one visit to Praiano was how the three of us were developing. I was writing; Thomas, Linda's husband, was writing; only Linda wasn't.

35   A year and a half later in Paris, I couldn't help seeing what I hadn't wanted to see in Italy. Thomas wrote constantly, and Linda talked about writing. When he worked, we had to whisper. One night when Linda went into her study to work, Thomas interrupted her. I expected her to tell him to leave her alone as she so assiduously left him. Instead, he talked her out of doing anything but spending time with him and me. She acceded to him as she did in much else of what he wanted. She had become a wife.

My visit to Paris was disastrous. Whenever I tried talking about what I found appalling, Linda turned the discussion to my love relationships of the previous year which had not been ones she would have liked to have had. My anger at what I construed as her growing passivity remained unarticulated and high.

I came home and didn't answer a cheery letter ignoring the realities of my stay. A few months later, I wrote a very disturbed explanatory response and did not hear from Linda again.

I knew she'd stopped speaking to her childhood best friend because the woman had once flirted with Thomas. I was aware she'd given me up because of what she thought was an opposite reaction to the man she chose to live with and to the way she led her life.

Six months later, I was speaking to an editor in the publishing house which had signed Thomas's novel and found out Linda and Thomas were in New York for a few weeks.

40   Sorting out my resentment at having lost my closest friendship, I called them. Linda answering, we talked awkwardly and arranged dinner for that night. I thought the two of us might be able to resolve our difficulties. Perhaps I had been wrong. Deep friendship is hard to come by, and I was prepared to do what I could to salvage this one.

When Linda arrived at the restaurant, she said Thomas would be there with some of his friends within half an hour. I was dumbfounded. She and I were to have had dinner alone.

Linda might have missed the American women's movement. Still, she taught a college course on women in Paris. She couldn't be as unaware of turning into a passive, dependent person as she seemed to be. If she and I weren't going to be friends, I at least wanted to make clear what bothered me.

But she didn't want to hear it. As far as she was concerned, I was hostile. Finally, she agreed to meet.

There we were at the Buffalo Road House: I, with a tennis racket, T-shirt, and dungarees; she, with the latest long Parisian swirl skirt. We were surrounded by four booths of male couples who all stopped talking as we began.

45   I gathered they all thought we were the lovers Thomas had believed we were years before. I wanted to turn around and say, "No, no. This is worse. We were friends, and now we're not going to be."

We drank wine and were each very upset. Surprising me, she told me that I had betrayed her. She, who long before defined a friend as someone who knew you and loved you anyway, said I didn't trust her. On my side, I was sure she was the one who betrayed our original friendship. She was the one who'd given up her life for someone else's needs.

I argued, somewhat disingenuously, that I was never hostile to her but to her role as wife. I remember thinking that we were never as close as I had thought.

Linda said, "If Thomas ever was as nasty about you as you've been about him, I would have divorced him a long time ago."

I thought this was not only untrue but gratuitous. Thomas, whose novel includes such lines as, "He stuck his throbbing cock into her Hawaiian cunt," could afford to be magnanimous. There was little reason for him to complain. I could talk all I wanted of the need for women to struggle. While he and his friends discussed how liberated they were, he knew Linda's allegiance and investment were more and more in him and his future and less so in her own.

50   Then she said that since she and I had stopped corresponding, she's started a novel about the friendship between two women and had gotten more than 100 pages into it.

She and I haven't spoken since. I've hoped she would finish that novel. Not only do I want her to write, I want to read about a friendship through her eyes, and I want something to come out of our relationship.

But I'm being disingenuous again. While acting as an external conscience to a friend might sound touching and be theoretically correct, the reshaping of people, luckily for friendship, is traditionally—and usually without success—left to lovers. Linda knew what I was upset about. At one point when I was in Paris talking to Thomas about each of our projects, Linda burst out, "Don't you both see? *I'm* the one in trouble." Thomas denied what I perceived was true. Linda didn't need me to be tiresome or belligerent about it. Even more, she didn't need someone who she sensed didn't trust her enough to overcome it.

While I now know I can no longer be friendly with someone who acts like a "wife," I think Linda was right about my betraying her. I acted like one of the Plymouth Bay colonists. In effect, I said that specific beliefs and actions meant more than our history together.

Still, I'm angry. I know very well that other people's supposedly durable friendships turn out unexpectedly fragile and break fairly easily. Yet, however necessary my betrayal was, this woman and I had made a commitment to each other, the alternative was not to have gone on being friends. We were too on edge with each other to do that. All we could have done was to fade away from each other without having had the courage to talk about our differences at all.

55 When I was young, I thought my friends *had* to act as they did. As a result, I overlooked many decisions that I fundamentally disagreed with. Now, due to the women's movement, I assume each of my friends takes responsibility for her life. Because I no longer consider us powerless, I no longer can forgive acting as if we were.

While a heightened women's consciousness has resulted in our openly valuing friendships more highly than we did before, this same consciousness has caused me, and other women, to demand more of these relationships. The validity of each of our lives has become an issue that might have been passed by before and now can no longer be.

Often, these new pressures are too great for many of these friendships to bear. I know there are no models to go by to put them back together. I know we have to develop new models of not only keeping friendships but having them at all.

Yet to venture that friendships often break apart because of social and political dislocations doesn't alleviate my wanting friendships that last or my being hurt that this relationship with Linda, which I had assumed would be one of these, no longer exists.

Looking back on what happened between us, I can understand the pressures on her to choose as she did. I can wish her well. I can understand my own development which made me make demands that others might find unreasonable. I can do a lot of things, but what I feel—not by Linda so much as by historical circumstance—is cheated.

WRITING ASSIGNMENTS

Analysis

1. Carroll Smith-Rosenberg says that "in the twentieth century a number of cultural taboos evolved to cut short the homosocial ties of girlhood and to impel the emerging women of thirteen or fourteen toward heterosexual relationships." How does Lee's personal essay illustrate this assertion?
2. Compare the close nineteenth-century female friendships described by Smith-Rosenberg to the initial friendship between Susan Lee and Linda. How did the historical backdrops differ, and how did these differences shape the friendships?
3. Compare and contrast Miller's concept of close male friendship with Lee's concept of close female friendship.
4. What does Lee mean when she says of Linda, "She had become a wife."? How does Lee feel about this change? Why?
5. According to Lee, how has the women's movement altered female friendships?
6. Explain the significance of Lee's green rocking chair.

Argument

1. Who betrayed whom, Susan or Linda? Explain your answer in terms of your definition of true friendship.
2. Is Lee too demanding?
3. Is respect essential in true friendship? If you think it is not, what are the essential elements of friendship?
4. Does a friend ever have the right, even the obligation, to try to change his or her friend?

Personal Writing and Writing from Research

1. *Collaborative Project:* Analyze the depiction of friendship in several current television series. Look at male friendships, female friendships, male-female friendships, and at the relationship between friendships and love relationships. Use selections from this chapter to help you interpret what you see.
2. Interview several married couples about how their close friendships changed after they married. Report on your findings, relating them, where applicable, to the ideas introduced in the essays by Rubin, Miller, and Lee.

WORK

In some cultures, people identify themselves by where they come from or who their kin are, because place of origin and family are destiny. In China, where famine has been frequent, the standard greeting is, "Have you eaten yet?" In contrast, Americans are most apt to ask, "What do you do for a living?" because in America, work defines our identity and establishes our status as it does for no other people.

It's easy to understand why. We are a country of immigrants who broke ancient ties to land and kin in order to start anew. We established ourselves by the work we did. Our cultural myths celebrate individualism, hard work, self-reliance, competitiveness, and success. Although we have our aristocrats, we have historically most admired the independent frontiersman, the lonely cowboy, or the little guy who made good. Our heroes have been men who worked, however varied the kind of work they did. But today, many wonder whether men have paid too high a price for this focus on work and on the masculine values associated with it.

And what of women? Although women also worked on farms, on the frontier, in mills, and in factories throughout our history, their socially sanctioned work was to bear children, nurture the family, and uphold morality. A woman's work and status were most often defined by the title of "mother" or "Mrs." Men were supposed "to do," women, "to care." Inevitably, however, women's claim to civil and political rights would include an assertion of economic rights—recognition for the work they have always done, the right to work in occupations once reserved for men, and fair compensation.

When it comes to work, gender and class issues intersect. The Declaration of Independence asserts that all men are created equal; however, some kinds of work command more prestige and higher rewards than others. A gulf exists between the worker and the boss, between those who work with their hands and those who work with their brains, between the strength of muscled endurance and the power of money and prestige.

Furthermore, because the linkage between work and dominance has historically been so integral to masculine identity, men initially responded with ambivalence and resistance to women's attempt to enter the workforce as equals. Many still do. Reflecting their acculturation and historic image as nurturers, women are also often ambivalent. They have struggled, with mixed results, to combine the work ethic and the ethic of care.

These struggles continue for both men and women in the home and on the job. In "The Breadwinner," Mark Gerzon first explores the historical origins of the link between work and masculinity, and then tallies the price both men and women pay for retaining the male breadwinner role. A. M. Homes's fictional portrait of a young lawyer, "Jim Train," also raises questions about the breadwinner's role.

In "Year of the Blue-Collar Guy," Steve Olson energetically celebrates the manliness of blue-collar workers and their under-valued contributions to society. Then Harvey J. Fields shares his ambivalence about his wife's new career in "On-the-Job Training."

Ruth Sidel analyzes "The Real World of Women's Work" against the backdrop of young women's dreams, the messages of popular culture, and economic trends. In

"Only Daughter," Sandra Cisneros shares her struggle to escape a "woman's place" in her Mexican-American community and to win her father's respect for her work.

In "When Feminism Failed," newspaper editor Mary Anne Dolan wonders whether women who have gained access to positions of power and prestige will transform the world of work or simply adopt the "male model." Finally, Faye Fiore surveys the positive changes some women have won in the workplace.

The Breadwinner
Images of Family

Mark Gerzon

Mark Gerzon is the author of *A Childhood for Every Child* (1973), *The Whole World is Watching* (1980), a book about the Sixties generation, and *Coming Into Our Own* (1992), which follows the same generation into midlife. "The Breadwinner: Images of Family," comes from *A Choice of Heroes* (1982), in which Gerzon identifies five archetypes of American masculinity—the Frontiersman, the Soldier, the Breadwinner, the Expert, and the Lord—and examines their usefulness to men today.

Linguists would point out the cultural implications of associating bread, a food staple, with money, an essential medium of exchange in commercial or industrialized societies where few people bake their own bread. "Breadwinner" is thus an even more potent expression than the roughly analogous "bringing home the bacon." Lacking either edible or spendable bread, one starves.

Journal Topics: (1) What do you expect from your work, and how will you integrate your work and personal life? (2) Describe in detail a typical weekday in the life of an adult male or female family member.

As You Read: (1) How effectively do Gerzon's summary of the short story "Lilacs" and his sketch of several "breadwinning" men introduce his essay? (2) How do Gerzon's historical references provide a context for understanding the breadwinner role today? (3) List four criticisms of the breadwinner role.

> Only if we perpetuate the habit of speaking about "the position of women" in a vacuum will we fail to recognize that where one sex suffers, the other sex suffers also.
> —Margaret Mead, *Male and Female,* 1949

In Mary Lavin's short story "Lilacs," an old man, Phelim Malloy, provides for his wife and two daughters by selling manure. The dunghill, located in the corner of their small yard, produces such a foul odor that his wife and his daughters complain constantly.

"But if it could be put somewhere else," suggests his wife, Ros, "and not right under the window of the room where we eat our bit of food."

"What I don't see," interjects his daughter Kate, "is the need for us dealing in dung at all."

His daughter Stacy says nothing; she is in bed with a headache, which afflicts her every Wednesday, when a fresh load of manure is dumped. She wants to have lilacs in the yard and get rid of the smelly muck altogether.

5   But when Malloy suddenly dies, Ros takes over the manure trade. To her daughters' amazement, she argues that they must keep the dunghill where it is. It is their only livelihood.

Soon afterward, unaccustomed to the heavy work, Ros passes away. It is then that Kate, who is concerned about her dowry, leaps to the dung's defense. Then Kate marries, and Stacy becomes the sole mistress of the house. The first thing she plans to do, she tells the family lawyer enthusiastically, is to plant a few lilac trees and get rid of the dunghill.

"But what will you live on, Miss Stacy?" asks the lawyer. And there the story ends.

Poor Phelim Malloy! For decades he made a living that permitted his wife to live comfortably and his daughters to go to boarding school. And he worked knee-deep in manure for most of his adult life.

Neither I nor my friends have such malodorous occupations. Our wives and children live with lilacs, not dung. What we have in common with Phelim Malloy, however, is that our families are becoming aware of how our occupations detract from their lives. They want us to work, of course, but they want us to be husbands and fathers too.

10   Perhaps if I had lived a generation earlier, I could have seen the commuter train that I rode every weekday for more than three years as a symbol of my worldly success. But times have changed. My wife expected to see her husband and expected me to see my children. And I expected it too. Therein was the dilemma. No matter how I stretched myself, I could not be a father *and* a breadwinner.

So the commuter train became, instead, a symbol of my dilemma. In the morning, I would catch the 7:44 or the 8:12. The first would bring me to the office before most of my colleagues; the second, only after everyone else was hard at work. Whenever I could, I took the 8:12. That way I could at least say good-morning to my children.

I would leave the office between five and six, while many of my colleagues were still at work. An hour would pass before I was home. My sons, then both under five, would already have eaten dinner by the time I arrived.

I wanted to be with them, and they wanted to be with me. But it was the end of their day and time for bed. "They're tired," my wife would say to me. "Better let them sleep." Of course, she was right. And yet my day with them, and theirs with me, was just beginning.

I was also tired, quick to lose my temper, and hungry. After several years of this shuttlecock schedule, I was confused too. I was making a living, my wife was taking care of the kids (and teaching part time), and the children were growing up. We were all doing what we were supposed to do, but it was not working—not for me, not for my wife, and not for our children.

15   We are among the lucky ones. My income is higher and my schedule more flexible than most. I miss fewer events in my children's lives than, for example, my friend George, a foreman at a nearby factory. George wants to see his son play football after school "more than anything else in the world," he tells me. His son plays quarterback on his junior high school team, but George has yet to see a game. When the traffic is good, he catches part of the last quarter (by which time the coach has put in the second-string quarterback). When the traffic is bad, his son is already showering in the locker room.

"Paul set a school passing record, but I never saw him complete a single pass," says George. "Again and again I apologized: 'Gee, Paul, sorry I missed the game.' He used to say, 'That's okay, Dad,' but now he just grunts."

George has stopped trying. Paul has stopped caring.

The problem is not limited to clock-punchers. Richard earns twice as much as George but sees his son even less. A sought-after lawyer, Richard reached the top, and stays at the top, by "doing what needs to be done." This means that he may be in Europe or Japan for several weeks or preparing briefs under intense pressure. His job is flexible (at least in theory), so he squeezes out time now and then to watch a baseball game or to reserve a weekend for skiing. But in a competitive world, any time "lost" to family puts his firm at a disadvantage. He may forfeit a client, miss an opportunity, lose the "inside track."

Several years my senior, Richard met me over lunch one day shortly after I had been promoted. I told him how much I regretted missing out on my children's lives. "Welcome to the club!" he replied heartily. Was he sardonically commiserating with me? Or was he genuinely welcoming me to that relatively exclusive professional club whose members' time has such a high market value that they cannot refuse to sell it? I now think he was doing both: congratulating me on my success and forewarning me about its ultimate price. (He is now divorced. His wife has custody of their children.)

20   I used to think that Carl, a professor of history, had this problem solved. When my wife and I both worked, he and his wife once advised us on how to organize a two-career family. Their method was to take turns. When he was under pressure, she would cut back, and when she had to switch into high gear, he would slow down. It all sounded so simple. Most afternoons, Carl could be seen picking up his daughter at school.

What I did not realize was that this freedom from external encumbrances did not resolve his masculine dilemma. When I talked with him a few months later, he was fuming. He resented other faculty members' subtle but unmistakable jokes. "They have no right to question my allocation of time," he argued. "They prefer leisurely lunches or gossiping in the faculty club to spending time with their own children. But why do they try to impose their priorities on me?"

Beneath his irritation, Carl had his own doubts. Although he had tenure, he still felt the spur of academic competition in his flank. "I'm working at a competitive disadvantage," he said. "How can I convince myself, much less them, that my work is to be taken seriously—that I am producing? Maybe I *am* drifting. If I really cared about this book, if I really thought that it was any good, I wouldn't be leading my life like this."

George, Richard, Carl, myself—we were all struggling with a predicament we could not even name. Once we have families, we cannot afford to take our shoulders from the wheel without being inundated with unpaid bills. There is no time left in our lives to think about it. And even if we thought about it, what good would it do? We have to make a living. We have to support our families. Our only way out, it often seems, is to become so successful that at last we can stop. But then it is too late.

Late one night, holding high a blazing torch, Daniel Boone went hunting for deer. After waiting for the gleaming light to reflect in the eyes of his prey, he saw a pair of firelit eyes through the underbrush. He raised his rifle but did not fire. Something about the eyes seemed odd. Moving toward them slowly, he finally realized that they were a woman's. She ran away, but according to legend, Daniel soon came courting and made her his wife.

25   In reality, she was much more than Boone's wife. Nearly as tall as her husband, Rebecca Bryan Boone was a remarkable woman. Single-handedly, and often under harsh frontier conditions, she cared and provided for their children while Daniel was gone for months on various expeditions. When Daniel was kidnapped by the Shawnee, she moved her children hundreds of miles on horseback through hostile Indian territory. When her aging husband was racked by rheumatism, she went hunting and brought back enough game to feed them all. Yet she is depicted in the popular nineteenth-century biographies of the legendary "Col. Daniel Boone" as merely an "amiable Spouse" without any personality of her own. Why, in the legend of Daniel Boone, was the courage and competence of Rebecca Bryan Boone omitted? One suspects that his early biographers, if given the opportunity, would have erased her from the legend altogether.

. . . Whether on the frontier of yesteryear or in the inflationary, urban economy of today, a competent and enterprising woman would be an extraordinary asset. Just as Rebecca's hunting abilities made the Boone family more secure, so today do wives' professional skills enable a family to derive greater rewards from the marketplace and to live more comfortably than would be possible with only a single wage earner.

Yet such a woman has not been highly prized by American men. A woman able to earn enough to support herself and her family did not appeal to us, she threatened us. In a poll conducted in 1946 by *Fortune* magazine, men were asked whether they would prefer to marry a girl who had never worked, one who had been moderately successful in her work, or one who had been very successful. By a wide margin, men preferred the woman of *moderate* success.

Men do not mind a woman who "helps out" or who may "supplement" the family's income. But the notion that one's wife can function just as capably in the marketplace as oneself breeds anxiety. It deprives us of another dimension of heroism—the heroism of The Breadwinner.

The Breadwinner's virtue is equal to his productivity. To his wife and children, he is a hero because he provides for them. To his country, he is a hero because he makes the economy work and grow. The Breadwinner prides himself on his family's material well-being: the more they have, the better a man he is. Even if the Breadwinner's wife works as long and hard as he does, he is nevertheless the provider. If she is employed, he earns more money. If she works as a homemaker, the economy puts money in his pockets and nothing in hers. He can make money; she can only spend it.

30   In an economy that assumes men are the providers and sets wages accordingly, many women need the Breadwinner. Without him, their lives are strained. Consider the plight of women whose husbands are laid off, or who turn to drink, or who are incapacitated by illness or injury, or who abandon their families and evade child support. The wives of such men consider the Breadwinner to be a model of masculinity without equal. They revere the Breadwinner, the man who brings home a paycheck every week and who works year after year without complaint.

    This ideal image of the Breadwinner, however, has been politicized. Instead of inspiring reverence, it triggers debate. Narrow-minded advocates of women's rights declare that the Breadwinner oppresses his wife. According to them, he does not serve his family; he rules over them. He does not take care of his wife; he exploits her. He does not work to provide for his loved ones; he works to achieve success for himself. He is driven by ambition, not love.

    Equally narrow-minded men's rights advocates avow precisely the opposite. The Breadwinner is not the oppressor; he is the victim. "My first wife was completely dependent on me," complained one man. "I was always playing a role of some sort. She wanted me to take on three jobs so she could have the kinds of things she wanted."

    By placing both arguments side by side, it is clear that they are rationales for rage at the other sex. Fortunately for all of us, the truth is both more complex and more human. As Studs Terkel's *Working* poignantly revealed, most men today do not see themselves as powerful, dominating figures. On the contrary, they portray themselves as struggling to find ways to survive and, if possible, to grow, despite the mounting pressures of making enough money to support themselves and their families.

    Our bodies often speak more eloquently than our words. When the twentieth century began, men could expect to live nearly as long as women. A woman's life expectancy was 48 years, a man's 46. But by the mid-1970s, according to the U.S. Department of Health, Education and Welfare, the average woman could expect to live 76.5 years, while the life expectancy of the average man was only 68.7 years. According to some estimates, by the year 2000, men may die a full decade sooner than women.

35   "It is time that men . . . comprehend," advised James Harrison of the Albert Einstein College of Medicine, "that the price paid for belief in the male role is shorter life expectancy. The male sex role will become less hazardous to our health only insofar as it ceases to be defined as opposite to the female role . . ."

    Of the many lethal aspects of masculinity, none is more so than the pressure of work. What is debilitating is not work itself (the chronically unemployed die earlier than other men), but the anxiety and helplessness of bureaucratic employment. Those who are self-employed or who can run their own shop outlive those who are trapped between superior and subordinate. "Longevity depends less upon fitness or genetic inheritance," observed John Stickney in *Self-Made*, a study of entrepreneurship, "than upon work satisfaction, a quality linked to autonomy."

Some men reject the role altogether. Others defend it as the wisdom of tradition. Both responses are oversimplified. All human societies and all human families face the question of how work is to be divided among its members. Every society and every family must find its own answer. In America, our response has varied enormously over our two-hundred-year history.

In colonial America, women had relatively greater occupational freedom than in some later periods. Colonial women were butchers and gunsmiths. They ran mills and shipyards. They worked as midwives and sextons, journalists and printers. They learned a trade, as did men, through apprenticeship. But in the 1800s, a woman's role narrowed. By midcentury, fewer female shopkeepers and business women were at work than before the Revolutionary War. They might be allowed to indulge in such careers before marriage, but once appropriated by a man in marriage, they were, as Alexis de Tocqueville pointed out, "subjected to stricter obligations" than were women in Europe.

Between these two periods came industrialization, a process in which the "home become *divorced* from the workplace," with femininity identified with the former, masculinity with the latter. Before the Industrial Revolution, both sexes usually worked at home. Indeed, home *meant* work. Although women's tasks were different, they were interdependent with men's. They focused on household care: spinning wool and flax, cooking, preserving and curing, animal care, gardening, and countless other productive tasks. But after the Industrial Revolution, concludes historian Amaury de Riencourt, "the wife as the husband's productive partner and fellow worker disappeared."

40   Before industrialization, men frequently took responsibility for training boys as young as six years of age. If a boy did not work with his father, he was apprenticed to another man to learn a trade. Accordingly, most child-rearing manuals in colonial America were written for mothers *and* fathers. Because fathers were nearby, working in a family farm or shop, they played a large role in the rearing of their children, particularly their sons. After industrialization, when men went away to a job, their sons could not follow, and child-rearing advice more often was directed to women only. Boys were still expected to be men, of course, but they spent the first decade of their lives in a world in which they rarely saw grown men at work.

This transition to an industrial society was neither immediate nor simple. Not all men left the farms and family-run shops; not all women lost their productive functions. But the shift was nevertheless profound. The home came to be seen, in Christopher Lasch's phrase, as a "haven in a heartless world."

In marriage, the role of the Breadwinner became paramount. The husband-wife relationship was a union of opposites.

She was:	He was:
family oriented	success oriented
pure	worldly
gentle	aggressive
moral	pragmatic
emotional	rational
delicate	tough
weak	strong

By splitting the national character in half, one feminine and the other masculine, the nineteenth-century family engaged in a holding action against the tumult of history. Women would embody tradition; men would embody change.

Feminist historians have every reason to question this unwritten patriarchal contract that governed the American family. One does not need a lawyer to realize that some of its clauses make it a dangerous document for women to sign. Dare a woman renounce a career so her husband will provide for her? Once a career is foregone, what will assure the quality of his care? Who will guarantee that the contract will be honored? What will happen should the marriage end? Do women want to spend their lives being taken care of by the Breadwinner?

45   These questions were first raised by early feminists, such as Angelina Grimké, Amelia Bloomer, and Charlotte Perkins Gilman. They are now being posed again by today's feminist historians, economists, and sociologists. But one issue rarely raised is: If women were being discriminated against, what was happening to men? Were they ruthlessly forcing the second sex out of the professions and back into the home? Were they reducing women to economic dependence and domestic isolation in order to ensure their own supremacy? Or were they themselves oppressed, struggling workers caught in the grinding gear of industrialization? Were they merely downtrodden and disillusioned men who sought in women a nurturant refuge from a heartless world?

. . . As historian Mary P. Ryan observed, men now labored in "a world gone mad with change, acquisitiveness, and individualism." From countryside to city, from farm to factory, from self-employment to company employee, workers were entering an unfamiliar and often threatening world. The foundations of the marketplace were shifting. While promoting the cult of the true woman, men were becoming enmeshed in its masculine counterpart: the cult of the self-made man. As early as the 1830s, men began to feel the pressure of a new, frustrating, and contradictory definition of success. While fantasizing about the heroic exploits of Daniel Boone or the mythical world of Natty Bumppo, the Breadwinner found himself faced with jobs that were anything but heroic. He was not a solitary figure on the landscape. He was part of an organization that was becoming increasingly complex and bureaucratic. He was not his own boss, but an employee whose livelihood depended on pleasing the man who was.

How, then, was a man to become a success? The hero of Horatio Alger's novels emphasized the importance of dressing neatly and modestly, of being punctual and reliable, of eliminating slang and colloquialism from one's speech. In short, he symbolized "the qualities of character and intellect which make the hero a good employee."

. . . No wonder men felt insecure. They were caught between the too-good-to-be-true heroes of Horatio Alger and an increasingly bureaucratic reality where only aggressive, often ruthless men could become Carnegies and Rockefellers. "The inner conflict in young Americans between the will for righteousness and the will for success," observed historian Bernard Wishy, "must have been extraordinary." The conflict had a direct impact on masculinity, for it was men who were supposed to climb the ladder of success. They placed on women the burden of being righteous because the burden of success was heavy enough.

As Daniel Boone and Davy Crockett etched their virile exploits in the national consciousness, the workingman in Boston, New York, and Philadelphia was caught in the web of industrial civilization. Coping with rent, work, children, and urban life, he had little reason to feel secure, much less heroic. To have a wife at home who took care of him, and who was grateful for his hard-earned wages, was the least he could expect. Regardless of what his work might be, he could feel manly because only men performed his particular function. The most reliable method of ensuring the manliness of the Breadwinner's role was to construct an economy in which only men could be providers, which is precisely what we did. From the Civil War to World War II, women were excluded from the work force to a greater degree than either before or since. "The isolation of women from work was a significant phenomenon," concluded the economist Eli Ginzburg, "for only about eighty years"—roughly from 1860 to 1940.

50   Although Rosie the Riveter led postwar women back into the economy, women are still unable to be the Breadwinner. Even if they are allowed and sometimes even encouraged to bring a second income into the family's bank account, the economy is structured to ensure their continued dependency on the *real* provider. . . .

This sexual division of labor, however, takes its toll on both men and women. The syndromes are so common that they now have names: women suffer from the "Cinderella complex," men from the "Breadwinner complex." "Women are brought up to depend on a man and to feel naked and frightened without one," wrote Cynthia Dowling. "We have been taught to believe that as females we cannot stand alone, that we are too fragile, too delicate, too needful of protection." To avoid being responsible for themselves (and their offspring) and to avoid the hardships and indignities of working for a living, such women cling to men. Even if the relationship is not emotionally fulfilling, at least these wives have a security blanket to protect them from economic woes.

Except for their unhappiness, men who suffer from the Breadwinner complex have precisely the opposite symptoms. They are addicted to their work. Although it causes physical and emotional strain, they climb the ladder of success as quickly as they can.

They feel completely responsible for their families' economic well-being. They are determined to stand alone and to admit to no feelings of weakness or vulnerability. They expect themselves to stand up under the strain. Unable to spend much time or energy on their children, they numb themselves to their fathering role and focus increasingly on their career.

The Cinderella/Breadwinner marriage obviously does not work very well anymore. The husband sees his wife as free from the stress of a job, and envies her; she sees him as having a paying job and social recognition, and envies him. Both of them, observed Margaret Mead in *Male and Female,* are "dissatisfied and inclined to be impatient with the other's discontent."

Even though men are still considered to be the Breadwinner, the two-career family is now common. Old expectations clash with new realities. The Breadwinner still expects to be greeted by the housewife; the working woman expects her husband to share her domestic duties. The Breadwinner expects his wife to be an old-fashioned mother who bakes bread, while she expects him to be a modern father who shares household chores. With work and home no longer divided neatly between the sexes, problems proliferate. When workers in the late sixties were asked about job-related problems, only 1 percent of the conflicts cited related to the family. By the late seventies, the percentage had risen to 25 percent, and it is still rising.

55   A typical conflict is that if the Breadwinner is to compete successfully, his wife and children must move when the company wants to relocate him. His wife's career (if any) and friends must be forfeited. The children's school life must be disrupted. The family, like excess baggage, must be crated and shipped to accompany the Breadwinner on his quest for success.

In addition to practical matters are the interpersonal ones. Unrivaled by any nation on earth, America extols competitiveness. The Breadwinner is willing to compete for success against other men, but not against women. For women, competition has been deemed unfeminine. Nineteenth-century child-rearing manuals enjoined parents to have their daughters avoid the "ruder and more daring gymnastics of boys." Never was she to try to swing higher than her friends, to outdo, to excel. Her virtues rested in solidarity, unity, attachment.

As the sexes split, so do the philosophies of work and family. The capitalist marketplace must be competitive, or waste and corruption ensue. The loving family must be cooperative, or animosity and envy take root.

It is a bizarre division of life. Unwieldy and unworkable, the arrangement is bound to produce tension. Competition cannot be worshiped outside the home and banished within it. A world in which men compete and women cooperate is nothing more than a prescription for inequality.

As long as men cast themselves (or are cast by their wives) as Breadwinners, the pressure on them to achieve will be intense. If a man expects to spend the prime of his life single-handedly supporting his wife, his children, and his home, he has locked himself into a role that cannot help but produce physical and psychological stress. In addition to this stress, he may now bear the resentment of his wife, who is trapped in the home, and the alienation of his children, who complain that he is distant. In such a family, the Breadwinner will neither live long nor live happily. Indeed, the family itself may come apart.

60   Instead of resenting feminists for attempting to rewrite the masculine-feminine contract, we should be grateful. They are challenging a contract that serves us no better than it does them.

WRITING ASSIGNMENTS

Analysis

1. Gerzon describes the traditional husband-wife relationship as a union of opposites. Do the traits he ascribes to the masculine breadwinner still set the standard for the world of work? Draw evidence from the articles in this chapter by Olson, Sidel, and Dolan.
2. Analyze the advantages and disadvantages to men or women of the male breadwinner role.
3. Trace the history of the breadwinner-homemaker role division and try to account for its appeal to men and/or women.
4. Does Gerzon's analysis apply to most working men, or only to some educated, middle-class male workers? Do ethnicity or race affect it?

Argument

1. Does the breadwinner role oppress men, women, both sexes, or neither? Support your answer with evidence from other readings in this chapter and from your personal experience.
2. Is Gerzon's description of the breadwinner accurate? Can it be applied to females as well as to males?
3. Do the traits of a breadwinner have more to do with gender or with having power in a competitive, individualistic, mobile society like ours?
4. Write a defense of the traditional male breadwinner role.
5. Have we changed so much since Gerzon wrote his book (1982) that men and women no longer see the breadwinner role as a measure of masculinity?

Personal Writing and Writing from Research

1. For male students, explore your feelings about being married to a woman who consistently and obviously earns much more money than you. For female students, explore your feelings about being married to a man who consistently and obviously earns much less money than you. In either case, would this earning differential affect your roles within the marriage?
2. *Collaborative Project:* In an update of the 1946 *Fortune* magazine survey mentioned by Gerzon, ask male students on your campus whether they would prefer to marry a woman who had never worked, one who had been moderately successful in her work, or one who had been very successful. Then ask females

the same question about their preference in a husband. In follow-up questions, attempt to discover their reasons. Write a report analyzing the relevance of your findings to contemporary expectations of who will fill the breadwinner role.

3. *Collaborative Project:* Gerzon claims that for many men, "the notion that one's wife can function just as capably in the marketplace as oneself breeds anxiety." To evaluate Gerzon's claim, analyze the content and tone of both traditional and tabloid journalism's and television's coverage of several successful women in different fields to determine whether such women breed anxiety in the general public, their husbands, or in those who write about them. Have attitudes changed? If so, how much?

4. Conduct in-depth interviews with several men and women in traditional marriages to test Gerzon's conclusions: "The Cinderella/Breadwinner marriage obviously does not work very well anymore. The husband sees his wife as free from the stress of a job, and envies her; she sees him as having a paying job and social recognition, and envies him. . . . It is a bizarre division of life. Unwieldy and unworkable, the arrangement is bound to produce tension."

Jim Train

A. M. Homes

In addition to *The Safety of Objects* (1990), the short story collection from which "Jim Train" was taken, A. M. Homes has written two novels, *Jack* (1989) and *In a Country of Mothers* (1993). Reviewers call her work unnerving, funny, and sad. She has been described by her contemporary, the writer David Leavitt, as "what you would get if you crossed David Lynch with John Cheever, and added a bit of Virginia Woolf . . . a portraitist of contemporary life at its most perverse."

Journal Topics: (1) Describe a situation in which you felt you didn't fit in, and then speculate on why you felt like an outsider. (2) Describe how you adjusted to an unfamiliar environment and established in it a comfortable place for yourself.

As You Read: (1) Who are the successful men in this story and what external details signify their success? (2) Compare and contrast Jim Train's role at the office and in his suburban house. (3) Describe Susan Train.

It is Jim's idea to walk every day to and from the station. He thinks of leaving his new home, walking down the sidewalks, past the neighbors' homes, over the small bridge to the train station as a pleasant thing to do, the kind of thing he imagines would keep a man alive.

"It gives me time to think," he tells anyone who asks why he doesn't just have his wife drop him off at the station like all the other men.

"I enjoy large thoughts," he says to his wife one evening. "I need them now. My thoughts are my food," he says. "I have to eat."

Jim pops a section of a Ho-Ho into his mouth; cream filling squirts out onto his lips.

5   "I understand," his wife says, refusing to look at him. The sight of food in a person's mouth makes her ill. "Good night." She turns off the lamp on her side of the bed.

In the morning as he walks, Jim passes unoccupied cars, motors running, warming up, spilling thick exhaust out onto the sidewalks, into the air. He steers around them fully realizing that avoiding the smoke means nothing, toxicity surrounds him.

He weaves down the sidewalk, briefcase in hand, sweating lightly in his overcoat, feeling young, like a boy, looking forward to school and at the same time drawing out his walk so that inevitably he always arrives at the last minute.

On his way into town, he reviews his thoughts, which frequently come to him in the form of a speech. Each day he either adds or subtracts something so that by the time he reaches the station, he has relieved his mind to the extent that when the train pulls in and he squeezes himself into a seat, holding his briefcase on his lap—the weight and trapped heat lowering what is left of his sperm count—he quickly falls asleep.

Jim is a lawyer, as is everyone in New York City, or so it seems. His office is on the thirty-fourth floor of a large midtown office tower. Every morning his first activity after being greeted by his secretary—who bounds towards him, messages in hand, with all the good cheer of a well-bred retriever—is to close his door and call home.

10   "I'm here," he says, as soon as either his wife or the housekeeper picks up the phone.

"Good," the voice on the other end is trained to say.

"Great," Jim says. "Gotta go."

Occasionally when he calls, there is no answer, and Jim gets nervous. His palms sweat, and he finds it difficult to breathe. He sits paralyzed at his desk and pushes the redial button every two minutes until finally someone picks up. It is all he can do to stop himself from hitting redial every minute, or thirty seconds. This did not happen years ago, before they moved out of town. After all, before, if his wife was not home, she was out there somewhere, perhaps walking just below his office window. Now, if she is not home, she is *truly* out there, easily miles from home, possibly in another state.

Each evening, well past eight, when all the offices are empty, Jim goes down the hall, leans back in the senior partner's chair, and looks out over the Manhattan skyline. He relaxes for fifteen or twenty minutes and then on his way out he peeks into the hall, making sure the cleaning lady is at the far end of the floor, unzips his fly, and relieves himself into the large potted plant Patterson keeps by the door.

15 It is Jim's rule that except in cases of extreme emergency, he is not permitted to pee between lunch and the end of the day. By eight o'clock he has collected a sufficient quantity of urine. It is his ritual, his salvation.

Since signing on with Flynch, Peabody, and Patterson, Jim's lost count of how many plants he's killed. Patterson's secretary seems to think their death has to do with the lack of light, the poor quality of air in the building, or possibly a high concentration of lead in the drinking water. The associates make jokes about the horrible smell by Patterson's door. In one the punch line is something about how it's better to drop dead in your tracks than go dripping off like the old man, who in reality is hardly old.

"Not interrupting you, am I?" Patterson says as he walks into Jim's office, laughing, fully aware that there is no such thing as the senior partner interrupting anyone. "You're Flynch-Peabody's Man of the Year."

Jim doesn't know what he's talking about. He feels like a surprise contestant on a game show.

Patterson's secretary comes in with a plaque the size of a coffee table. Patterson himself is grinning from ear to ear. A photographer rushes in and snaps a few pictures of Patterson and Jim standing with the plaque between them. Jim's secretary carries in a large potted plant. Jim blushes deep red and feels his knees turn into rubber bands.

20 This is a joke, a bad joke, Jim thinks. This is Flynch-Peabody's way of saying good-bye.

"You should be proud," Patterson says, shaking Jim's hand. "Not every man is Man of the Year. I never was. Don't think I don't know you're here every night after everyone leaves. I have my spies." He winks at Jim and then leaves.

"Congratulations," Jim's secretary says, still holding the potted plant, which must weigh at least forty pounds. "Where should we put it?"

"Take it home," Jim says. "I have terrible allergies."

His secretary carries the plant out to her desk and Jim calls home again. The line is busy.

25 The shock of the award, the plant in particular, has left him weak. He's still seeing the blue spots from the photographer's flash in front of his eyes. There is no way he can work.

"Early lunch appointment, slipped my mind," Jim says as he passes his secretary's desk on his way out.

I am a self-made man, he tells himself in the elevator. He looks into the silver polish of the control panel and sees his reflection, distorted. I made you and I can break you, any time I want. Something to keep in mind, buddy boy.

Jim takes a long walk, circling the block twice, picking up the power to go farther, then heading in the direction of the river. He thinks about his job, about the view from Patterson's big chair, about how good it feels to finally let go when you've been holding it in all afternoon. Within a half hour, Jim is so fully revived that he marches back to the office.

There are police cars and fire engines everywhere. The street has been sealed off and is filled with people. Jim is panicked and dizzy. No one seems to know what the situation is. He finally spots his secretary, standing tall above the crowd.

30   "I'm so glad you're all right," she says.

"What's going on?" Jim asks.

"Bomb threat," his secretary says.

Jim sees Mr. Patterson leaning on a police car and goes to him.

"Train, Train, I'm so glad they found you," Patterson says. "That's it then, we're all out."

35   "Is there really a bomb?"

Patterson looks grim. "Could be," he says. "Don't really know. We've got a couple of difficult cases coming up, could be related. Remember Wertheimer?" Patterson says, referring to someone who was let go under strange circumstances a few months earlier. "Could be Wertheimer. You never know what a man will do." Patterson nods, tapping his fingers to his head, indicating the possibility of insanity. Train nods vigorously along with Patterson. "Go home," Patterson says. "Call it a day."

Jim shakes his head. "My briefcase is inside. I've got calls to make."

"Go on," Patterson says, flicking his fingers as if shooing Jim away. "Go home."

Jim lingers. He doesn't want to go home. He wants to go to work. He is the Man of the Year. His plaque is up there on the thirty-fourth floor, just next to his desk. He has to decide where to hang it. Jim walks down Lexington Avenue to Forty-second Street, feeling rejected, disconcerted by the absence of his jacket and briefcase.

40   He thinks of a bomb and imagines it buried in Patterson's plant, launching the tall tropical wonder like a missile. The plant crashes through a single window on the thirty-fourth floor as though heaved in anger. A second later all the windows blow out, and a ball of orange fire claims the floor. *Whoosh,* the world is up in smoke.

Jim takes the two-forty train home and walks up the sidewalks, warm and clear with afternoon sun. The streets are full of station wagons, carpools going in all directions. He has the clear impression from the looks drivers give him that the sidewalks are not intended for use by anyone except women with strollers and children under twelve.

He passes the spastic boy that he sees every evening, except in foul weather. The boy is never out in the mornings and Jim imagines that because of his twisted shape it takes a very long time to get him dressed and fed. He stands in matching pants and shirt at the foot of his parents' driveway, frozen in a bent, painful pose, giving Jim a clear idea of what a cast-iron jockey would look like if it were struck by a car or truck.

The boy sees Jim and waves. Jim waves back. He never speaks because he's afraid the boy will talk to him and perhaps he won't understand what the boy is saying and then it will get complicated and even more depressing, so he leaves it at the waving.

On this occasion Jim worries that perhaps he has confused the boy by coming home early and maybe the boy will do something like go inside expecting dinner to be served. Perhaps his mother will think his action is proof of her suspicion that he's regressing and that he really is getting too old and difficult for her to care for and before supper she will call the institution and arrange for them to come and collect him by morning.

45   Jim has the urge to go back down the block and explain his arrival, but the idea of explaining is too exhausting and he resigns himself to feeling guilty.

Jim's key doesn't open the door. Instantly, he's afraid that he has walked to the wrong house, he has forgotten his own address, he will become like the spastic boy and stand frozen at the end of the driveway until someone, his wife he hopes, drives by and recognizes him.

He goes from the kitchen door to the front door and back again. He jumps up and looks in the window and feels comforted when he sees his loafers lying empty in the hall. The familiarity of his belongings and the sensation of being separated from them make him that much more determined to get inside. He breaks the key in half trying to work the lock open.

"Shit," he says.

"Hello?"

50   He hears his neighbor's voice through the bushes at the end of the driveway.

"Is someone there?"

He doesn't answer. He sits on the steps as though he's been sent out as punishment. He is alone in what he thinks of as the middle of nowhere. For five minutes he just sits there, his knees up to his chest, poking the plastic ends of his shoelaces into the eyelets on his shoes, resting.

This would never have happened on 87th Street. He would have gone downstairs and gotten the extra key from the super. He would have run around the corner to the Pearlmans' and waited there in the comfort of their living room. Jim is living in the past, a place where his memory tells him life was easier, almost effortless.

Jim removes his tie and goes into the backyard in his pink oxford-cloth shirt and gray flannel pants. He relieves himself in an azalea bush but it is boring, like being on a camping trip. Little green shoots are poking up all over the yard. His children have left a trowel and a hand rake in the dirt by the driveway and it occurs to Jim that weeding will make him feel better; it will divert his anxious energy. It will make him a farmer, a man he has never been before.

55   He gets down on his hands and knees and begins digging, pulling green things out of the dirt. He makes three stacks of weed balls and is in the process of making a turban out of his shirt when a car pulls into the driveway. He runs around the side of the house, joyous that his family has returned, his shirt wrapped loosely around his head, the sleeves hanging down like floppy ears.

Bill's Repair Man looks at him as though there's some sort of a problem. His expression causes Jim to look down at himself. He's covered with dirt. Clumps of soil are embedded in his chest hair. His gray flannels have grass stains unlike any seen in detergent commercials. One pant leg is ripped open at the knee, the skin under it raw, from when Jim accidently kneeled down hard on a buried rock.

"Doing a little planting?" the repair man asks.

The name sewn on his uniform says Bob even though the truck says Bill. Jim figures that Bob must work for Bill, perhaps they're even related.

"Weeding actually," Jim says, relishing the sensation of explaining himself to a guy with his name sewn on his shirt who clearly doesn't know putting in from taking out, planting from weeding.

60   "I'm here to fix the hot water heater," Bob says.

"There's a little difficulty with the door," Jim says. "My key broke off in the lock."

"Which door?" Bob says.

Jim points up to the kitchen door, and the repair man takes his toolbox out of the truck. Jim follows him up the stairs. Just as they're getting the door open, Jim's wife pulls up in the car. Susan seems surprised by the sight of him and Jim's not sure if it's because he's home hours earlier than usual, or if it's the shirt on his head and the dirt on his chest that have thrown her off guard.

"Daddy!" His daughter Emily hurls herself at him, hugging his knees.

65   "Did you bring me anything?" his older child, Jake, asks.

"Just me," Jim says.

Jake makes a face. He sees the weeds that Jim dug up lying in a heap by the driveway.

"You're in trouble now," Jake says.

"You idiot," Susan screams as she rounds the edge of the car and looks into the backyard. "You dug up my marigolds." She runs through the yard shouting. "What the hell is wrong with you? Are you insane?" Jim charges down the steps and into the yard. He's almost willing to kill Susan to keep the neighbors from hearing her.

70   "Be quiet," he says loudly. "Be quiet."

"You ruined my garden, you fool," Susan screams and then stands silent in the middle of the yard, her arms crossed over her chest.

Bill's Repair Man comes out of the house to get something from his truck. He's grinning and Jim has the urge to punch him, but his children are staring at him, waiting to see what an adult does after being completely humiliated.

Jim walks past all of them, up the steps, and into his house.

There's no reason I should know what a marigold is, he thinks, I'm the Flynch-Peabody Man of the Year.

75   He goes up to the bedroom, empties the contents of the hamper onto the bed, spreads the dirty clothing out evenly, and lies down on top of it. He stares up at the ceiling, sucking his thumb, and occasionally rubbing a soft piece of clothing across his face. This is something he does to relax. He doesn't think it is any stranger than a person taking a Valium, lifting weights, or immersing himself in some kind of tank. Emily comes in with her bottle and lies down next to him.

"You're dirty," Emily says.

Jim nods.

"It's okay." She rests her head on his chest, sucks her bottle, and falls asleep.

The phone rings, Jim gets up carefully, so as not to disturb Emily, and picks up the phone in the hall.

80   "Hi, it's Bill MacArthur."

"Oh, hi Bill, how are you?" Susan says, from the extension in the kitchen.

Jim tries to remember who this Bill is. In the six months they've lived there he's met four Bills, two Bobs, three Roberts, and a Robbie, and he can't tell one from the other.

"Good, good," Bill says. "I'm just getting ready to run the kids down to the park and toss around the ball. I thought maybe you'd like to bring yours."

"What a nice idea."

85 Jim knows that if he'd gone downstairs a minute before and said, Honey, let's take the kids to the park and toss a ball around, she would have looked at him like he was crazy.

"I'll stop by and you can follow me in your car."

Jim tries to imagine who Bill MacArthur is. What's his relation to the real MacArthur? Doesn't he have a job? A family, his own damn wife?

"Kids, kids, where are you?" Susan calls, as she runs up the steps. "Get your shoes on, we're going to the park."

"Can I come with you?" Jim asks, as Susan rubs a damp washcloth over Emily's face, wiping off her sleep and the dirt from Jim's chest.

90 "You have to stay home and re-plant my flowers."

Jim feels as if he's been slam-dunked. How can he do anything when she's running off into the woods chasing wild balls with some guy named Bill?

"Do you wear your ring?" he asks.

"What ring?" Susan says.

"You know, your ring?" Jim spins his wedding band around.

95 "Oh that ring. You scared me for a minute. Of course, except when I'm doing the dishes. What makes you ask?"

MacArthur's horn beeps in front of the house.

Jim stands on the landing, looking out the window. He tries to wave to Bill MacArthur, whoever the hell he is, but MacArthur doesn't see him.

Jim decides to take a shower outside, it will save him the job of cleaning the tub when he's done. He takes a towel and a bar of soap and goes into the yard, hauling the hose after him.

This is what men who don't live in cities do, he thinks, imagining naked men in backyards all over Westchester and up into Connecticut. They shower out-of-doors, like Abe Lincoln. It's the hearty way. The real way.

100 He picks at the dirt embedded in his chest hair, and rubs what he gets between his fingers. He throws the hose over a tree branch and turns on the water—it is cool if not cold. Jim starts to sing. He lathers himself from head to toe, watching the dirt pour off his body in little muddy rivers. He rinses his hair and, when the soap is out of his eyes, looks into the bushes at the far end of the yard. There are two small faces pressed up against the fence. They are giggling. "Look at his pee-pee," a small voice says. Jim turns away. They have ruined his moment. Is a man not free to do as he pleases in his own home, he wonders, to wash his own dirt from his body? Does he need permission? This is not America as Abe Lincoln intended.

He is angry and ashamed. He has the urge to turn the hose on the children but knows it will only start trouble. Instead, he moves cautiously, rinsing himself with his back to them and then wrapping the towel tightly around his waist. Jim carefully collects his clothing, the soap, and the hose, leaving no traces, and walks back towards the house, clean feet squeaking on the grass.

He sits in a straight-back chair in the living room, wet hair slicked back. Susan has bought all new furniture. Nothing is familiar. Nothing is comfortable. Jim goes into the kitchen and tries to make phone calls. His book is in his briefcase at the office. He can't think of where anyone lives and so can't get their numbers from information. He sits in his chair, in the dark, until his wife and children return. They have stopped at McDonald's on their way home; he can smell it on their clothing.

He takes the sleeping Emily, his little french fry, from Susan and carries her up to bed.

"Why were you home this afternoon?" Susan asks when he comes downstairs.

105   He points up towards Emily's bedroom and motions for Susan to whisper. "Bomb threat," he says.

"Nobody else came home early?" Susan says as if she doesn't believe him.

"It wasn't the whole city, just my building, my firm to be exact."

"How odd," she says. "Will you go in tomorrow?"

It has not occurred to Jim that he might not be going to the office in the morning. Susan goes upstairs to remind Jake to put his retainer in. The phone rings and Jim picks it up, hoping it will be someone from work.

110   "Is Susan there?" a male voice asks.

"No, I'm sorry, she's not."

"This is Bob Wellington. I ran into her at the car place the other day and I just wanted to make sure she got her tires rotated all right."

"They seem very well rotated," Jim says.

"How many miles you got on that car?"

115   "I wouldn't know," Jim says.

"Well, remind her to check on the oil change: every thirty-five hundred miles, even though they say you can wait to four or five. Runs the engine down if you wait, kills the car."

"I'll pass the information on."

"Is this her father by chance?" Bob Wellington asks, chuckling.

"No, it's not," Jim says.

120   "Well, good talking to you," Bob says.

"People must think you're divorced," Jim says to Susan, as they undress and get ready for bed. He sees her taking off her slip and underwear and imagines that Susan has secretly gotten a job on her own. She is a suburban callgirl, saving tips to buy a house at the beach. If she works hard enough, she could have a house in the Hamptons by next summer.

"You're at the office a lot," she says.

"What about these other guys, don't they have to work?"

Susan goes downstairs. Jim follows her. She tries to start the dishwasher. It runs for a second, makes a horrible sound, then stops.

125   "Damn," she says.

"Here, let me try." He goes over to the dishwasher, opens the door, closes the door, pushes the start button again, and looks down at the machine. Nothing happens.

"I'll call Robbie Martin," Susan says.

"You don't have to call anybody," Jim says.

"You certainly can't fix it. You have no idea of what to do."

130   It is true Jim doesn't know what to do with anything. Somehow he is content to leave it all alone and assume that it will heal itself.

Jim returns to the bedroom, takes off his pajamas, and dresses again.

"Where are you going?" Susan asks when she sees him dressed and heading for the door.

"Nowhere."

He starts the car and pulls it up close to the house, aiming the lights towards the yard. He flicks on the high beams and gets out. Jim re-plants the marigolds, constantly looking over his shoulder fearful that a band of sixteen-year-olds will mistake the lights for a party. He imagines they will find him, think he is an old man, bind and gag him, then go into his house, turn on the stereo, and eat everything, including his wife and the children.

135   The telephone rings at quarter to six in the morning and Jim immediately thinks of death.

"Hello," he says, waiting for the bad news.

"Mr. Train," his secretary says, "Mr. Patterson's secretary called me and asked me to tell you we won't be opening the office today. The police are still investigating."

"Thanks for letting me know," Train says. "You wouldn't happen to have Howe or Worth's numbers, would you?"

"I'll get them and call back."

140   "No hurry," Train says, hanging up and falling back into a pleasant, productive dream about redesigning the office so that it seems more like a home, with soft couches and televisions; the kind of place where a man could live as well as work.

At seven-thirty Susan gets up. Jim lies in bed and watches her dress.

"Aren't you feeling well?" Susan asks.

"Fine," he says, pulling the blanket up to his chin.

Susan puts on her makeup before her blouse and then makes a big show of getting her blouse over her head without it touching her makeup. Jim is tempted to suggest it would be easier to do it in the reverse, but says nothing. In the mirror Susan's face is pulled down like she's had a stroke, and she's adding more mascara to her eyes, so that her lashes look like licorice sticks.

145   "Why don't you get up," she says. "You can drive Jake to school."

The last time Jim drove him to school, Jake spent the whole ride insulting his father. "You're going the wrong way," he yelled. "Don't you even know where my school is? You missed the short cut." Jim stopped the car at the top of a hill, got out, and walked around to the other side.

"You drive," Jim said.

"Dad," his son whined. "Dad, get back in the car. You're making me late."

Jake sounded exactly like Susan. Jim stood there in the street waiting for the boy to say, You're acting like a child. After ten minutes of absolute silence, Jim got back in and drove the rest of the way to Jake's school.

150   "Are you going to drive him?" Susan asks, putting the finishing touches on her exterior with a sea sponge.

"He can walk," Jim says.

He lies in bed waiting for his secretary to call back. Susan goes downstairs to get the children ready for school and then, without saying good-bye, she leaves with them.

Jim thinks of Patterson's plant and wonders whose plant he'll pee in years from now. He imagines sneaking into the associates' offices after they've left and letting go a little bit in each office, in every corner, revenge against the uncommitted, the false promise of youth and ambition. He sees himself convinced it is his secret, when in reality everyone will know. They'll give new guys cans of air freshener to keep hidden in their desks. New plants will be delivered weekly. No one will dare say anything to Jim because, after all, he is Train, the Train of Flynch, Peabody, Patterson, and Train.

At nine his secretary calls with Howe's number.

155   "Worth is seriously unlisted."

Jim writes the number on the back of a magazine and tells her to have a good day.

"I will," she says. "There's a sale at Macy's."

He lifts himself out of bed tenderly as though just returned from a hernia operation. He takes the steps slowly, as if in pain. How can he be in the house, mid-morning, mid-week, except as a sick person?

Jim calls Howe. The number rings ten times before Howe picks up the phone. Jim stands in the kitchen, the phone tucked under his chin, his free hands randomly plucking bits of food out of the refrigerator and popping them into his mouth.

160   "What took you so long?" Jim asks.

"I thought my wife was going to get it. It's usually for her."

"Any news?" Jim asks.

"My wife is kicking me out of the house. She says I can't come back until six o'clock, preferably seven. I'm driving her crazy."

Jim lets the refrigerator door close, and rinses off his fingers in the sink.

165   "I guess I'll go and buy some shoes, shirts, stuff for the office," Howe says.

"Big sale at Macy's," Jim says.

"Then that's where I'll be. Any details about the bomb?"

"Nothing," Jim says. "You?"

"Last I heard they were still checking. Kind of weird, isn't it?"

170   "It is and it isn't," Jim says.

He thinks of himself as the closest thing the firm has to an in-house philosopher.

"Yeah, guess so," Howe says. "Well, the housekeeper wants to use the phone. I better let her."

Jim's call-waiting beeps.

"See you," Jim says, pressing down the receiver button. "Hello?"

175   "Is this Bill's Repair Man?" a woman's voice asks.

"No, it's not," Jim says. "He was here yesterday."

"This is Jill Robinson. Leave a message for Mrs. Train that I'll meet her at the Chew-Chew, in town, at one?"

A loud noise in the basement/garage startles Jim. He hangs up without saying anything, grabs a butcher knife, and runs downstairs.

"Don't move," he yells at the man stealing his lawnmower.

180 "Who are you?" the man asks.

"The question is who are you?" Jim says, waving the knife around.

"I come to cut the grass, but I don't need this shit," the man says, dropping the mower bag and walking out of the garage to his truck parked in the driveway.

Jim is in the process of reorganizing the cutlery drawer when Susan comes in at noon.

"Why aren't you dressed?" she asks.

185 "I have nothing to do," Jim says, sadly.

Jim is not himself. Without his work, he is a dark and depressed man.

"Get dressed. We'll have lunch in town," Susan says.

"You're meeting Jill Robinson at the Chew-Chew at one."

"Then hurry," Susan says.

190 "Well, hello," Jill says in a voice that's a little too friendly.

It's the first time they've met. Without asking, Jim knows she's a real estate broker—that's what women around here are if they're not social workers, or in rare cases pediatricians. Jill is too hyperactive to be a social worker, too stupid to be a doctor. If Susan weren't there, he'd sit Jill down at the bar and discuss the possibilities of selling his house, or burning it to get the insurance money.

"Is everything all right? You can tell me, I can keep a secret," Jill says.

For how long, Jim wonders, five minutes?

Jill is clearly excited. The only time she's ever seen a husband following his wife around on a weekday is when one of them has just been diagnosed with something horrible, like infertility or breast cancer.

195 "Did you have a doctor's appointment this morning?" Jill asks.

"No," Susan says. "A bomb threat."

Jill's eyes light up. The waitress asks if anyone would like a drink and Jim thinks of having a martini but doesn't because there's something about the way Jill's looking at him that makes him sure she'd tell everyone he was an alcoholic.

"B.L.T. and a Coke," Jim says.

Susan and Jill talk about houses: what's good, bad, broken, and who fixes it. Clearly this is where Bill's Repair Man came from.

200 Jill's been inside every house in the area and keep a running score of who has what in terms of cars, large-screen televisions, walk-in freezers, etc. Jim thinks if she could keep her mouth shut, she'd make a killing as a burglar.

When he can't stand it any longer, he excuses himself from the table by saying he has to make a phone call—"Checking in with the office," he says. Jim goes to the bar and orders a double martini, careful to keep his head low. Through the potted plants he watches Susan and Jill, wondering what Susan sees in Jill—it's not like her to be friends with a woman who frosts her hair. Perhaps she's changing, he thinks—as though this sort of a change is a precursor to something more serious, like Alzheimer's.

He tosses back the martini and returns to the table, face flushed, just as the waitress is putting the lunch plates down. Jim picks at his sandwich carefully, knowing if a leaf of lettuce or a piece of bacon were to lodge in his throat he would be unable or unwilling to free it, and in all likelihood neither would Susan.

He pictures himself choking, looking at Susan and Jill as the world around him gets smaller.

"Should we do something?" Jill will ask—she can never do anything without asking someone's opinion first.

205   "No," Susan will say, "let him go. It's all right."

He imagines himself falling to the floor, Susan and Jill looking at him sweetly for a moment, like he's a child imitating a dog. As his eyes roll back in his head, the women return to their conversation, and the last thing Jim hears has something to do with winterizing.

This is not a solution, he tells himself, ending the choking scenario. This is not the way to go. At the office, at the office, he thinks, sucking on his thoughts like they're lozenges, I'd be talking to my secretary who likes me very much, having a drink in the restaurant next door, buying snacks from the blind man in the lobby, looking out the window, watering Patterson's plant. His eyes water. He almost cries. Everything is okey-dokey, he tells himself. It's going to be all right.

"Aren't you well?" Jill asks Jim.

She is used to men who shovel food into their mouths without looking up until finally, when there is no more, they lift their eyes and burp simultaneously.

210   "Fine, thank you," Jim says.

"Finished?" the waitress asks as she clears the plates.

"Thank you," Jim says, plucking the colored plastic swords from his sandwich before she takes the plate.

"How cute," Jill says.

"Do you want to come with us to the mall?" Susan asks Jim, waving her eyebrows up and down, as though she's making a special offer.

215   "I think I'll just walk home," he says, standing up. "It's a nice day for a walk. Good meeting you." He pumps Jill's hand as though the up-and-down action turns the key to a spring that winds him up so he can toddle home.

It is a beautiful day, the most beautiful day Jim can ever remember seeing. The sky is brilliant blue, the trees are full of leaves, there's a light breeze. It's perfect except the streets are deserted, there are no people, no babysitters, no strollers, nothing. The stillness makes Jim uncomfortable. He feels as though something horrible has happened and everyone except him knew enough to run away. When he turns the next corner, a giant mutant killer will be waiting for him. It will reach down from above the trees and he will never know what hit him. He walks quickly, sure that he will die before he reaches home. He can feel it in his chest. If nothing reaches down to snatch him, it will happen anyway. He will collapse. He will lie crumpled on the sidewalk. The cars driving past him will not see Jim in the suit, they will see only the suit, and think it is a heap of clothing left out for charity to collect. He begins to run. He runs faster and faster until he sees the spastic boy standing in his regular place. The sight of the boy calms him and Jim stops running and begins waving from very far away. The boy waves back.

"I'm home early," he says as soon as he's close enough to talk.

"Did you lose your job?" the boy groans in a voice that is as twisted as his body.

Jim shakes his head. "No."

220 "That's good, I'm happy," the boy says and waves goodbye.

As Jim goes up the steps to the house he thinks about work. If they cancel it again tomorrow he will go in anyway. He will simply arrive at the office. If the guards won't let him upstairs, he will refuse to go home; he will throw himself on their mercy.

WRITING ASSIGNMENTS

Analysis

1. Explain how Jim and Susan Train's marriage illustrates the problems that Gerzon attributes to the typical Breadwinner/Cinderella marriage.
2. As a successful young lawyer, Jim Train is his family's breadwinner. Does he fulfill Gerzon's criteria of the breadwinner ideal?
3. Imagine you were unfamiliar with the American business world and had to figure out who its successful figures were. Trace recurring symbols of status and success in "Jim Train," "The Breadwinner," "On-the-Job Training," and "Year of the Blue-Collar Guy" in order to write a description of the successful executive or professional.
4. What do Jim Train's encounters and exchanges with people in his neighborhood reveal about how others see him and his role?
5. Rewrite selected incidents in this story from Susan Train's point of view.
6. Trace and explain the significance of imagery that associates Jim Train with childishness.
7. How do the women in this story, especially Susan Train, influence Jim Train's self-image?
8. *Collaborative Project:* Write the script for a discussion in which Steve Olson, Jim Train, and Harvey Fields share their experiences and opinions about contemporary American manhood.
9. Explain the irony of the story's last sentence.

Argument

1. Where is Jim Train more at home, in his suburban house or in his office?
2. Who or what is responsible for Jim Train's alienation from his home and family?
3. Is this story just a mean-spirited attack on successful men?
4. Is Jim Train a victim of his circumstances or just a victim of self-pity?
5. Defend or oppose retitling this story, "Invisible Man."

6. What, if any, is the correlation between Jim Train's success at work and his alienation from his family?

Personal Writing and Writing from Research

1. Relate the themes of this story to earlier theoretical studies of alienation, such as David Riesman's *The Lonely Crowd* (1950) and Christopher Lasch's *The Culture of Narcissism* (1979).
2. As a family friend, what advice would you give to either Susan or Jim Train?
3. Compare your handling of an experience during which you felt like an outsider to Jim Train's conduct on his day off at home.
4. Compare the hierarchy and status symbols of an office or business you know well to Jim Train's law firm.

Year of the Blue-Collar Guy

Steve Olson

Steve Olson is a construction worker from Madison, Wisconsin. His essay appeared on November 6, 1989, in *Newsweek's* "My Turn" feature, in which nonprofessional writers have the opportunity to express their opinions about topics that concern all of us.

Journal Topics: (1) What would you say to a visitor from another country who asked you to define and describe a "blue-collar guy." (2) Describe the qualities of the traditional frontier or cowboy hero. Do they have anything in common with your image of a "blue-collar guy"?

As You Read: (1) List the negative stereotypes about blue-collar guys that Olson alludes to or explicitly names. Classify his responses to these stereotypes. (2) Distill Olson's values, particularly his idea of manliness, from this essay. (3) Characterize the essay's tone. Does it change? Describe Olson's intended audience and his purpose.

1 While the learned are attaching appropriate labels to the 1980s and speculating on what the 1990s will bring, I would like to steal 1989 for my own much maligned group and declare it "the year of the blue-collar guy (BCG)." BCGs have been portrayed as beer-drinking, big-bellied, bigoted rednecks who dress badly. Wearing a suit to a cement-finishing job wouldn't be too bright. Watching my tie go around a motor shaft followed by my neck is not the last thing I want to see in this world. But, more to the point, our necks are too big and our arms and shoulders are too awesome to fit suits well without expensive tailoring. Suits are made for white-collar guys.

2 But we need big bellies as ballast to stay on the bar stool while we're drinking beer. And our necks are red from the sun and we are somewhat bigoted. But aren't we all?

At least our bigotry is open and honest and worn out front like a tattoo. White-collar people are bigoted, too. But it's disguised as the pat on the back that holds you back: "You're not good enough so you need affirmative action." BCGs aren't smart enough to be that cynical. I never met a BCG who didn't respect an honest day's work and a job well done—no matter who did it.

3   True enough, BCGs aren't perfect. But, I believe this: we are America's last true romantic heroes. When some 21st-century Louis L'Amour writes about this era he won't eulogize the greedy Wall Street insider. He won't commend the narrow-shouldered, wide-hipped lawyers with six-digit unearned incomes doing the same work women can do. His wide-shouldered heroes will be plucked from the ranks of the blue-collar guy. They are the last vestige of the manly world where strength, skill and hard work are still valued.

4   To some extent our negatives ratings are our own fault. While we were building the world we live in, white-collar types were sitting on their ever-widening butts re-defining the values we live by. One symbol of America's opulent wealth is the number of people who can sit and ponder and comment and write without producing a usable product or skill. Hey, get a real job—make something—then talk. These talkers are the guys we drove from the playgrounds into the libraries when we were young and now for 20 years or more we have endured the revenge of the nerds.

5   BCGs fidgeted our way out of the classroom and into jobs where, it seemed, the only limit to our income was the limit of our physical strength and energy. A co-worker described a BCG as "a guy who is always doing things that end in the letter 'n'—you know—huntin', fishin', workin'. . ." My wise friend is talking energy! I have seen men on the job hand-nail 20 square of shingles (that's 6,480 nails) or more a day, day after day, for weeks. At the same time, they were remodeling their houses, raising children and coaching Little League. I've seen crews frame entire houses in a day—day after day. I've seen guys finish concrete until 11 P.M., go out on a date, then get up at 6 A.M. and do it all over again the next day.

6   These are amazing feats of strength. There should be stadiums full of screaming fans for these guys. I saw a 40-year-old man neatly fold a 350-pound piece of rubber roofing, put it on his shoulder and, alone, carry it up a ladder and deposit it on a roof. Nobody acknowledged it because the event was too common. One day at noon this same fellow wrestled a 22-year-old college summer worker. In the prime of his life, the college kid was a 6-foot-3, 190-pound bodybuilder and he was out of his league. He was on his back to stay in 90 seconds flat.

GREAT SKILLED WORK FORCE

7   Mondays are tough on any job. But in our world this pain is eased by stories of week-end adventure. While white-collar types are debating the value of reading over watching TV, BCGs are doing stuff. I have honest to God heard these things on Monday mornings about BCG weekends: "I tore out a wall and added a room," "I built a garage," "I went walleye fishing Saturday and pheasant hunting Sunday," "I played

touch football both days" (in January), "I went skydiving," "I went to the sports show and wrestled the bear." Pack a good novel into these weekends.

8   My purpose is not so much to put down white-collar people as to stress the importance of blue-collar people to this country. Lawyers, politicians and bureaucrats are necessary parts of the process, but this great skilled work force is so taken for granted it is rarely seen as the luxury it truly is. Our plumbing works, our phones work and repairs are made as quickly as humanly possible. I don't think this is true in all parts of the world. But this blue-collar resource is becoming endangered. Being a tradesman is viewed with such disdain these days that most young people I know treat the trades like a temporary summer job. I've seen young guys take minimum-wage jobs just so they can wear suits. It is as if any job without a dress code is a dead-end job. This is partly our own fault. We even tell our own sons, "Don't be like me, get a job people respect." Blue-collar guys ought to brag more, even swagger a little. We should drive our families past the latest job site and say, "That house was a piece of junk, and now it's the best one on the block. I did that." Nobody will respect us if we don't respect ourselves.

9   Our work is hard, hot, wet, cold and always dirty. It is also often very satisfying. Entailing the use of both brain and body there is a product—a physical result of which to be proud. We have fallen from your roofs, died under heavy equipment and been entombed in your dams. We have done honest, dangerous work. Our skills and energy and strength have transformed lines on paper into physical reality. We are this century's Renaissance men. America could do worse than to honor us. We still do things the old-fashioned way, and we have earned the honor.

WRITING ASSIGNMENTS

Analysis

1. Define blue-collar masculinity according to the criteria Olson establishes. Does his concept of manhood remind you of any mythic American heroes?
2. Write an analysis of Jim Train's problems from Olson's perspective.
3. Synthesize a portrait of white-collar guys based on Olson's essay. Does Olson suggest that they are effeminate?
4. Does Olson's description of manliness omit any necessary or desirable attributes?

Argument

1. Is Gerzon's thesis about the centrality of productive work to American masculinity relevant to Olson's blue-collar guys?
2. Where does Olson's defense of blue-collar guys leave blue-collar gals? Would Olson feel comfortable with women working in the trades?
3. Does society scorn blue-collar guys? Consider the attitudes reflected in popular culture, in schools, in political rhetoric, in your family, and among you and your friends.

Personal Writing and Writing from Research

1. *Collaborative Project:* Trace the history of the working man through his depiction in American folk music.
2. *Collaborative Project:* Research the history of women's entry into once-exclusively male occupations, such as the trades, fire and police work, truck driving, and construction.

On-the-Job Training

Harvey J. Fields

For more information about the *New York Times Magazine* feature "About Men," in which this essay first appeared, see the headnote for David Sherwood in Chapter 3. Harvey J. Fields is rabbi of the Wilshire Boulevard Temple in Los Angeles and is currently at work on his first novel.

Journal Topics: (1) Describe a time when someone close to you made a change in his or her life that you believed to be worthwhile, but found difficult to support. Explain what made the situation difficult, or describe how the difficulty was resolved.

As You Read: (1) Whose job is Fields referring to in his title? (2) How does Fields's daily life change when his wife launches a career outside the home? (3) How does he define the psychological consequences for him of his wife's new career? (4) What are his concerns?

It is 6:30 A.M. and my wife just left for work. Three months ago, she launched a new career as a stockbroker. Together we concluded that it was a good idea. It would boost our income; perhaps more important, it would provide a creative outlet for her talents. "We have a solid marriage. You are young and capable. Look around," I advised. "There are all kinds of opportunities."

We reasoned that her time had arrived. Two of our children are at college; a third is a self-sufficient high school student. For the last twenty-two years, my wife has cared for our needs, run thousands of errands, driven millions of car-pool miles, kept our family finances, been there when the plumber arrived to fix our leaking faucets, and at my side, looking radiant, for a constant stream of professional-social obligations.

Now all of that has changed. And it is not as easy as I thought it would be. Accommodations have to be made. Worries, doubts, little aching jealousies and resentments, and big ones as well, have emerged. Then, while driving to my office and brooding over this transformation erupting in my life, I happened to hear a commentator announce that new research has determined that husbands with working wives have a shorter life expectancy than those with traditional homemaker wives. Icing on the cake, as they say.

During the first few weeks, certain tasks just fell into place. She could no longer deliver and pick up at the cleaner's, or make it to our bank. They were out of her way, but happily right on my route to the office. So were the pharmacy and supermarket.

5   The supermarket. I love the supermarket, but on Sundays. Never during the week, all dressed up in a business suit. Sunday is when a man is supposed to visit the supermarket and fill his cart with all sorts of whims and his favorite beer.

Did I feel queasy pushing a cart around on Tuesday afternoon, holding a long list written on a pink sheet of paper, and with all those women and children staring at me? I did. And I wanted to evaporate when Gwen Sommers cornered me holding a large box of Tide in one hand and a big bottle of Era Plus in the other. With sympathy pouring from her compassionate brown eyes, she asked, "Is everything all right with Sybil?" By that she meant: "You are supposed to be at your office doing a man's job, and Sybil should be here shopping." Of course I wanted to explain, defend, send her home to read *The Feminine Mystique,* but I didn't. Instead, I headed for the checkout line gripping my six-pack of beer, hoping to indicate that all the boxes, cans, fruits and vegetables in my cart were simply the unbridled enthusiasm of a mad male on a shopping spree.

When I reached home, her car was not in the driveway. Another trauma. She was always there to greet me at the door with a warm hug and kiss. Now she was late getting home. The house was dark and empty. No sweet aromas of dinner prepared. Just silence, and all those groceries to bring into the house and put away, and bothersome doubts about how our emerging new arrangement will affect us.

It already has, but you grin and bear the first frustrations. A week after she was hired, we sat down to talk about vacation time. I am tired. It's been a tension-filled year. I need a few weeks to unwind. We have always vacationed together. We would never have considered going off alone. Not us. We are "together" kind of people.

But she is committed to a training program, sixteen weeks of rigorous study. She is flowering with new enthusiasm, and her career demands most of her energy, time and attention. So what about me? A vacation alone? By myself? It hurts, fills me with resentment. What are we married for, anyway?

10   "What about coming up for long weekends?" I suggest. "I will have to check with my boss." It's an innocent remark, but I want to explode. Her boss? I am supposed to be No. 1 in her life. Now, suddenly, she has to get permission from someone else to spend time with me. The gall starts to ooze. I whine inside: "Are we giving up too much? Are we to become roommates sharing the conveniences of a home, the warm memories of rearing our kids, and nothing else?"

One evening, she tells me: "I had lunch today with Tom, George and Steve. We went to this fancy sushi bar. Tom suggested I try it. George says we are going to make a dynamite team. Steve says this. Tom . . . Steve . . . George . . ."

I am not listening to what she is saying. All I hear are male names. All I see are new men in her life: associates, partners, colleagues, customers. All male. All aggressive. All with claims on her.

"Do you know what Jim asked me the other day?" she inquires. I want to stuff my ears, pretend nothing has changed. "What?" I answer, already angry at what I might hear. "I was shocked," she says. "He asked me what I was going to do when the first client came on strong with a proposition and made it clear that, if I wasn't willing, he would take his business elsewhere."

My stomach tightens into an ache. I feel as if I have been hit in the groin. Creeping doubts rumble inside me. I am silent, reflective about it all. The propositions won't be that straightforward. They will come subtly, twisted into all sorts of temptations. The devil always wears angel's garb and his voice is sweet and innocent, even naïve.

15   Later, I laugh at my fears and anxieties. All those years, all my trips, conventions, speaking appearances, alone in hotel rooms in new cities, did she have the same flurry of doubts? Did she wonder about whom I was meeting, and where? How did she make it through all those years, and I can't seem to bear all the questions and confusions for even a month?

And there are other questions. Whose number should be given at the high school in case of emergency? Who is responsible for banking, cleaning, shopping, cooking? How much help can I expect from her when it comes to attending functions related to my career? And is she expecting me to go out and be nice to her clients, rub elbows at office parties with her associates? How shall all of these be sorted out? Who calls the shots?

My stress level is rising. I liked the way we were. We had negotiated a comfortable arrangement. It was smooth, seldom a surprise. Now it's all in flux, and I am scared.

I see myself being stripped of my masculine, dominant, father, success image. There it is. I have said it. We were programmed by parents into believing that the male was the breadwinner. His job was top priority. He was to earn, protect and preside over his family. He was the senior partner; she was the junior partner. But the curtain has fallen on those old assumptions, and it's painful and bewildering.

So I am afraid for us. Human relationships are delicate affairs. Their circuitry is complex and bewildering. They jam, overload and burn out in the most inexplicable ways. The future is no sure bet. That may be tough, but it is the truth.

20   Who knows, if we are lucky, and do our job at communicating, sharing, listening and loving, the fact that my wife just went to work may not shorten my life at all. It may add qualities and dimensions that surprise and enrich us. Let's hope so, because I have just rushed home at lunchtime to meet the plumber, and something has got to make that worthwhile.

WRITING ASSIGNMENTS

Analysis

1. Analyze Fields's feelings about his wife's new career.
2. Classify Fields's complaints into practical inconveniences and psychological concerns. In a letter, advise him on how to handle these issues.
3. Explain how external social pressures aggravate Fields's personal anxieties.
4. To whose "training" does the essay's title refer?

Argument

1. Are you optimistic or pessimistic about the Fieldses' future as individuals and as a couple?
2. Is Fields just spoiled?
3. Is Fields an exceptionally self-aware, fair, and flexible person?

Personal Writing and Writing from Research

1. In a companion essay, speculate on Mrs. Fields's feelings about her new career and the changes in her marriage.
2. *Collaborative Project:* Prepare a demographic study of middle-aged women entering the workforce for the first time. What are their motives and goals? Describe them by educational level, by age, by marital status, whether they have dependent children, and by race and ethnicity.

The Real World of Women's Work

Ruth Sidel

Ruth Sidel based *On Her Own* (1990), from which "The Real World of Women's Work" is taken, on more than 150 open-ended interviews across the country with three groups of people: girls and young women between the ages of 12 and 25; professionals who worked with these girls and young women; and women in their 20s, 30s and 40s. Most of those interviewed were young, from middle-class backgrounds, and from diverse ethnicities and races. Many were college students. Sidel also has written *Women and Children Last: The Plight of Poor Women in Affluent America* (1986).

Journal Topics: (1) Describe your vision of your future work life. What are your criteria for success? (2) Describe your career role models. (3) If you are undecided about your career, what factors are causing your indecision?

As You Read: (1) What are the recurring issues facing women in high-status, high-income professions? (2) Do men face the same issues? What difference does gender make? (3) How is the "male model" of career success defined in this article? (4) What are the implications of recent economic trends for women, especially non-white women, who expect to support themselves and their children? (5) What are the implications of recent economic trends for male breadwinners?

> The male model of work is the working model. It never lets up. If you take time off, you'll get behind—in technical expertise, in publications, in climbing the academic ladder.
>
> Sarah Stark, M.D.
> physician/researcher, New York City

It's horrifying. You have to make a strategy to divide your time between the infant with pneumonia, the screaming baby in a wet diaper, and trying to find a compassionate way to tell another set of parents that their child has just died.

Lynda Levy, R.N.
pediatric nurse, the Bronx

1   Perhaps the most startling aspect of my interviews with young women was their vision of their future work lives. The young women had basically four scenarios for the future: they would enter high-status, high-income professions, such as law, medicine, and business; they would enter more traditional women's occupations, such as art, design, modeling, or the health professions; they would be home with children for the first few years and then find part-time work that was compatible with a primary commitment to child rearing and homemaking; or they could not imagine the future at all. But, with the exception of the last group, the theme that transcends the vast majority of the responses is the desire—indeed, the intention—to be affluent. Perhaps one of the most poignant examples is a seventeen-year-old black high-school senior from California whose mother is on welfare, whose father is "on dope," and whose stepfather "sits around." By the time she is twenty-five, she plans she will be working, have her "own place," and consider having her first child. She doesn't think she will be married—perhaps when she's "older." She would like to have a "BMW convertible" and "a house on a hill" by the time she is thirty. It is not clear whether she plans on acquiring the "house on a hill" on her own or by "marrying someone rich." However they plan to achieve it, the image of "the good life," the affluent life, is the common thread in nearly all the interviews.

2   The other common thread in the beliefs of these young women is that they cannot count on a man—that they are going to have to be able to provide for themselves. If one combines these two dominant expectations, it becomes clear that young women are going to have to earn a very good income indeed in order to provide themselves and their children (if they have any) with the life-styles they desire.

3   If these are the dreams, what is the economic reality for women as we enter the last decade of the twentieth century? Recent headlines tell much of the story: "Making a Living Is NOW a Family Enterprise"; "Top Labor Issue: Jobs for Single Mothers"; "For Women Lawyers, an Uphill Struggle"; "Jobs Go Begging in Human Services"; "Are Women Better Doctors?"; "New York Is Fighting Spread of Sweatshops"; "More Women in Top State Posts"; "Women Gain Little in Academic Jobs"; "Despite Job Gains, Sexual Segregation Remains, U.S. Says."

4   Over the past twenty years, women have entered the labor force in astonishing numbers. During the 1960s the number of women in the labor force grew by 39 percent; during the 1970s, by 41 percent. By March 1986, 64 percent of all women under the age of 65 were in the labor force.

5   Women's entrance into paid employment during this period was not the only dramatic change taking place; women's move into previously male-dominated professions was also dramatic. The number of women entering medicine, for example, has

increased significantly in recent years. In 1970 there were 22,000 active women physicians, comprising 7.1 percent of the profession; by 1986, 79,600 female doctors comprised 15.3 percent of all physicians. According to William Marder, director of the American Medical Association's department of manpower and demographic studies, by 1996 40 percent of new medical-school graduates will be women. If we examine the percentage of female medical students, the numbers are even more startling: in 1949–50 5.7 percent of the applicants and 10.7 percent of the graduates of U.S. medical schools were women; by 1987–88 37 percent of the applicants and 36.5 percent of the first-year students were women.

6   While women are entering medicine in ever-increasing numbers, the professional life of women as a group differs markedly from that of male physicians. They choose different specialities, work fewer hours per week, and see fewer patients. Women are far more likely to choose specialities with regular hours, such as dermatology and pathology, or specialities focusing on doctor-patient relationships, such as family practice, obstetrics and gynecology, pediatrics, and psychiatry. They are far less likely to choose surgery, which is often thought of as the most rigid and hierarchical of the medical specialities and which is known for its years of "infamously arduous training." Perri Klass, a physician who often writes about medicine, particularly as it relates to women, suggests that the reluctance of women to become surgeons may relate to the likelihood of postponing childbearing for the five to seven years of residency.

7   Two of the most pressing questions about women in medicine involve the impact women are having on the profession and the impact the profession is having on women's lives. Klass suggests that the "traditional techniques used by male doctors don't work as well for women"—that women have "more trouble assuming the mantle of all-knowing, paternal medical authority" and therefore rely more on one-to-one relationships, on teaching and empowering their patients and on treating other health workers in a more egalitarian way. If women can influence the practice of medicine in these ways, the profession will indeed benefit from their presence.

8   On the other hand, women are not moving as rapidly as many would like into positions of leadership in the profession or in medical schools. In 1987 only two out of 187 American medical schools had female deans, and out of 2,000 academic departments, only 73 had female chairs.

9   If women are nonetheless having some impact on the medical profession, what of the impact on the lives of women? Many women clearly find great pleasure and fulfillment in their roles as physicians, whether they are treating patients, teaching medical students, doing research, or combining all three. But many find combining medicine with family responsibilities extremely difficult and occasionally impossible. The long hours, the demanding pace, and the often relentlessly competitive nature of medicine, particularly academic medicine, requires serious inroads in time that some female physicians would rather spend in private and familial pursuits.

10   Sarah Stark, a physician in her mid-thirties, talks about the pressures of working in academic medicine. A specialist in a highly technical, extremely competitive

branch of academic medicine, she notes that in her department "the guys" work from seven A.M. until nine P.M. every day. "The male model *is* the working model. It never lets up. If you take time off, you'll get behind—in technical expertise, in publications, in climbing the academic ladder. Competition is encouraged. They think the more scared you are, the more productive you will be. They want you to be scared."

11   She and her husband, also a physician, have decided not to have children at all. She can neither imagine paying someone to raise her children ("And who would be raising the nanny's kids?") nor imagine taking time off from her career for childbearing or child rearing. She describes the options open to female physicians with children: "For women the best scenario is to have no children. Next best is to 'hatch' and go right back to work. If you actually spend some time with your children, you lose respect. When a physician who is a mother is late for a conference, the men *always* comment!"

12   Sarah goes on to talk about the disapproval she receives from the larger society for her decision not to have children: the fellow guests at dinner parties who tell her she will be a "lonely old lady," the taxi drivers who tell her she'll regret the decision "later in life," the "you're unnatural" looks she gets whenever the subject arises. She points out, moreover, that no one reacts the same way when her husband says he isn't planning to have children.

13   She states with considerable feeling that she refuses to be labeled "nonnurturing": "People just do not recognize other ways of nurturing. Anyone who sees me with my patients wouldn't say I'm not nurturing. Anyone who sees me with people whose lives are threatened, with people who are dying, wouldn't say I'm not nurturing. We must begin to have respect for women who choose not to mother and to make their contributions in other ways."

14   Despite the same long periods of training and demanding work, the median income for female physicians in 1986 was just over half that of male physicians, and their net worth only one-third. This discrepancy is in part due to women's relatively recent entrance into medicine and to the fact that they are choosing less lucrative specialties, but it is nonetheless a fact of life. And, of course, females face the same astronomic tuition costs of medical school that males do, the same student loans to repay.

15   While women entering medicine are entering a profession that seems to be, at least temporarily, in decline (there are fewer applicants to medical school each year, and more criticism of the profession from consumers and practitioners alike), women entering law are entering a profession that continues to have great appeal for young people just out of college, for older students, and for some who have already been trained in other professions. In 1988, for example, the nation's 175 accredited law schools were "flooded" with more than 300,000 applications from 75,000 students, an increase of 19 percent over the previous year. In analyzing the reasons for the continued popularity of law as a career, experts point to the visibility of lawyers in the Iran-contra hearings, the popularity and glamour of the television program "L.A. Law," and, of course, the high status and even higher income of many lawyers. In

1987, for example, the median salary of an experienced staff nurse was approximately $24,000, while that of an experienced lawyer was more than $50,000. Moreover, in cities such as New York, lawyers just entering the profession often earn salaries of $70,000 or more. Add in issues of prestige and status and it is not difficult to understand why someone would opt for law rather than for nursing or social work!

16   And indeed, women are becoming lawyers in ever-increasing numbers. In 1979 28 percent of the graduates of law schools were women; by 1988 that figure had risen to 40 percent. But despite high salaries, high status, and high hopes, many women are struggling to find their niche within the profession.

17   A recent article analyzing one of the nation's largest law firms points out that "the partners who actually govern large firms . . . are still overwhelmingly male," that "power comes from time and experience—and the ability to attract major clients on Wall Street . . . still almost exclusively male preserves," and that women are starting to be concerned about personal problems that stem, at least in part, from the "wildly unpredictable hours" and demands of working for a private law firm.

18   In an extraordinarily demanding career such as law, it is "no coincidence that so many women lawyers are unmarried and so few have children." According to one woman, "The basic rule seems to be that either you are married when you start, or you marry the man you were already engaged to or living with, or you stay single." Working most evenings and weekends simply is not conducive to developing new relationships, a process that is time-consuming and often emotionally draining. All too often women working in law firms must choose between a successful professional career and a satisfying personal life. According to Alice Richmond, a recent president of the Massachusetts Bar Association, "We're beginning to see talented, experienced women dropping out of the profession in their thirties. It takes an enormous amount from your soul."

19   Several major firms have recently instituted the option of part-time work, but often such arrangements preclude becoming a partner. In any case, women partners are still a distinct minority. A recent survey by the *National Law Journal* indicates that 90 percent of the partners in the 247 largest firms are white males.

20   According to one woman who is a partner in a major law firm, "I have no doubt that had I had the wonderful husband and two adorable children I thought I wanted years ago, I would not be a partner today." A recent detailed study by the Boston Bar Association of two thousand lawyers in the Boston area found that women were significantly more likely than men to be single, divorced, and without children. Moreover, women lawyers, especially new ones, are more likely to be dissatisfied with their jobs. Yet another lawyer at the same firm sums up the dilemma: "There is no such thing as a superwoman. You live with a constant sense of guilt and divided loyalty. You make accommodations. You can't have it all."

21   There are, of course, other jobs within law—jobs in the public sector, in city, state, or federal government, jobs with voluntary organizations, jobs with a particular perspective, such as civil rights or civil liberties—and while many of them may have more manageable working conditions and lower levels of stress, they usually

pay considerably less, too. For the young lawyer with tuition loans to repay, a high rent to meet each month, and perhaps a yen for a comfortable life-style, earning $33,000 a year at age thirty after three years of law school and a couple of years of clerking does not sound nearly as appealing as earning over twice as much. Even in the public sector, where nine-to-five jobs are more common and part-time jobs are possible, there is often a heavy penalty for choosing to work part-time. According to one lawyer, "There is no question there is a big penalty for working part-time. As it is, the deck [in a New York City agency] is stacked against women, particularly in terms of advancement. Unless somebody acts like a man, she is not perceived as management material."

22   . . . What about women in business, in politics, in academia? The same findings apply to these fields—that women have entered these areas in large numbers but are not moving to the top rungs in any degree comparable to their presence, that there is what has been called a "glass ceiling." In business, for example, it is clear that women own and operate small businesses in much larger numbers than ever before and that they are indeed moving into corporations in significant numbers; but virtually all reports indicate that they are still not reaching the higher levels. According to Rosabeth Moss Kanter, author of the landmark book *Men and Women of the Corporation,* the rules have changed within the corporation. The emphasis today is on risk taking, on the star system among managers. Working steadily and effectively is no longer the way to the top, the road to almost certain promotion. Just as women have gotten a foot on the corporate ladder, the ladder is being snatched away, and instead, "star" performances are being rewarded at all levels. Moreover, according to Kanter, "Flex-time isn't going to help. We're talking about voluntary overtime, about people who think that anyone who just gets through his work isn't doing enough. Day care won't help. These people work at night." Sounds strangely like law and medicine, doesn't it?

23   A study done by the Council on Economic Priorities for *Ms.* magazine in 1987 indicated that there are indeed some corporations that are trying "to meet women halfway." The study stated:

> Although there have been significant improvements for women in the corporate workplace over the last two decades (395 women directors at companies in the two Fortune 500 listings in 1986, compared to only 46 women in 1969), women are seldom found on the top rungs of the corporate ladder. Too much of women's time and energy is still spent not on career development or advancement, but on pursuing equal opportunity, dealing with work-and-family conflicts, and combating sexual harassment.

24   The study further found that nineteen of the twenty companies surveyed had at least one woman on their boards of directors and that fourteen had at least one female corporate vice-president. The percentage of "women officials and managers" ranged from a low of 4 percent at Ford to a high of 81.3 percent at Avon Products; most of the companies are in the 8-to-25 percent range. While several companies

offered flex time and/or job sharing, the majority still treated maternity as a short-term disability, allowing only six to eight weeks of paid leave after delivery plus additional unpaid leave; roughly half of the companies offered unpaid paternal leave. Only four of the twenty companies studied provided either on- or off-site child care. There is no question that conditions are improving for women workers and for families, but these companies seem a long way from "meeting women halfway."

25   But what of the position of women in academia? One would think that academic institutions would be considerably more sensitive to the needs and aspirations of women than, say, corporations, whose bottom line ultimately must reflect a healthy profit. But as in the other fields, in the words of one professor, there has been "progress but no parity."

26   Since 1975 the number of women college presidents has doubled, with women now heading over three hundred of the nation's three thousand colleges. Today women constitute a majority of American college students and receive over one-third of all doctorates, but female professors still have a significantly lower tenure rate than do men and continue to receive significantly lower salaries.

27   In their stimulating and perceptive study *Women of Academe: Outsiders in the Sacred Grove,* Nadya Aisenberg and Mona Harrington explore the reasons "why so many credentialed women . . . [have] ended up—sometimes by choice, usually not—outside the academy." In analyzing the forces that lead to "professional marginality and . . . exclusion from the centers of professional authority," they point out that the quest for professional acceptance and success requires a life of action rather than re-action, an emphasis on one's public role rather than on one's private role, an ability to see oneself and be seen as authoritative rather than submissive, and the opportunity to learn the rules of the game rather than being the quintessential Outsider. In short, female academics, and other professionals as well, must take on those characteristics directly antithetical to the ways in which they were socialized from birth to behave. They must somehow shake off those techniques of "winning a place by ingratiation and self-abnegation" which the authors term the "psychology of the dispossessed" (they might have termed it the "psychology of the oppressed") and instead transform themselves "from a passive to an active persona, from a supportive role player to a central character, a person prepared for autonomy." They must do nothing less than build "a new identity."

28   Aisenberg and Harrington point out how rigid hierarchy, extreme competitiveness among workers for a handful of top positions, and a narrow definition of ability and acceptability foster exclusionary policies that are bound to keep traditional Outsiders—nonwhites, women, people from lower socioeconomic groups—outside the system. This is surely one of the primary functions of such policies. It is important to note, moreover, that while Aisenberg and Harrington are describing academia, they could as well be describing medicine, law, accounting, or any of the elite male-dominated professions.

29   . . . But as great as the gains have been for women in law, medicine, business, and politics at the local level, the vast majority of women still work in service, sales, and clerical jobs; and, for the most part, salaries for these jobs have remained extremely

low. Young women may dream of being a district attorney, a pediatrician, or a highly paid, glamorous model, but the reality is that women workers are far more likely to be salespeople, computer programmers, and lower-level hospital workers.

30   According to the Women's Bureau, more than 53 million women age sixteen and over comprised 45 percent of the total labor force in January 1988. U.S. Department of Labor projections from 1986 to the year 2000 indicate that the labor force will increase by 21 million workers and that women, minorities, and immigrants will account for 90 percent of that increase. The department further estimates that almost all of the increase will be in the service sector, an area in which women are dominant. In 1986 40.5 million women, more than four out of five working women, were employed in the service sector. In health services and social services, women held more than three-fourths of all the jobs.

31   There is both good news and bad news in these data. The good news is that there will be more and more opportunities for women in the labor force during the coming decade. The bad news is that the occupations that will have the greatest increase in job opportunities are those that pay the least: jobs as salespersons; waiters and waitresses; registered nurses; janitors and cleaners; cashiers; general office clerks; food-counter, fountain, and related workers; nurses' aides, orderlies, and attendants; and secretaries. The number of general managers and top executives and truck drivers will also be increasing substantially, but the percentage of women workers in these fields is considerably smaller.

32   Furthermore, if we examine the 1987 median income for full-time, year-round male and female workers in specific occupational groups, we see that substantial income differentials persist even in the highest-paid professions: male executives, administrators, and managerial workers earned $36,155 while females earned $21,874; male professional specialty workers earned $36,098 while females earned $24,565; and male technical and related support workers earned $29,170 while females earned $19,559. Among workers in sales, men earned $27,880 while females earned $14,277, and even among service workers, a female-dominated occupation, men earned $17,320 while women earned only $11,000.

33   It is worth underlining that while the media—TV programs and advertising, news and women's magazines, the "style" sections of the daily newspapers—feature women in upper-middle-class occupations, as the latest achievers of the American Dream, the reality is that most women currently work and will continue to work in the near future in low-status, low-income, often dead-end jobs. This emphasis on the life-styles of the "rich and famous," the upper class and, more recently, the upper middle class, is of course nothing new. The belief that any individual or family can eventually live a life that resembles the lives of those far wealthier or those with high status has fueled the American Dream for over two hundred years and has fueled the consumer society since the Industrial Revolution.

34   . . . Not only are elite high-powered jobs improbable dreams for most young women—and for most young men, for that matter—but while high-income, high-status jobs are touted by the media, by parents, and by peers, jobs in traditional female professions go begging. The United States is today in the midst of a severe

nursing shortage. In 1988, an estimated three hundred thousand nursing jobs were unfilled, and enrollment in schools of nursing was declining. Several factors are responsible for this extraordinarily serious situation: fewer students of high-school age, increased opportunities for young women in other fields, and a general disenchantment with nursing as a career. According to the American Hospital Association, enrollment in nursing schools has declined 10 percent each year since 1974, and in recent years 40 percent of all registered nurses have left the profession to pursue other careers.

35   Salary levels are at least part of that disenchantment. The starting salary for registered nurses averages $20,340 nationally and with experience is likely to rise only to approximately $27,000 a year. As Pam Maraldo, chief executive officer of the National League for Nursing, put it, "Little girls don't want to grow up and be nurses anymore. It's ridiculous that a supervisor at K-Mart makes more than a nurse.". . .

36   But low salaries are not the only reason for nurses' disaffection with the profession. Working conditions often range from difficult to horrendous. Lincoln Hospital, a city hospital in the South Bronx, had ninety nursing vacancies during the winter of 1988. During a recent protest to dramatize conditions at New York City hospitals, Carmen Fascio, head nurse in the emergency room at Lincoln, described a typical day. First she tries to help the twenty to thirty patients who are left over from the previous night, but she is constantly interrupted by ambulance sirens and a steady stream of stabbing and shooting victims and people with heart attacks. "And there I am in the middle of what looks like a war zone in the South Bronx, running around like a chicken without a head, not knowing which way to turn or who to help first. Before you know it, it's lunch time, and there's no way I can be hungry, because how can I eat when there are patients crying near me and families cursing at me?"

37   Lynda Levy is a pediatric nurse at the Bronx Municipal Hospital Center, a teaching hospital located in the northeast Bronx. Each day the pediatric emergency room, staffed with no more than two nurses, sees more than two hundred children. Ms. Levy describes the scene: "It's horrifying. You have to make a strategy to divide your time between the infant with pneumonia, the screaming baby in a wet diaper, and trying to find a compassionate way to tell another set of parents that their child has just died." Is it any wonder we have a nursing shortage?

38   . . . Other health-care professionals are also in increasingly short supply. While the nursing shortage has been developing over the past two decades, the shortage of laboratory technicians, physical therapists, occupational therapists, pharmacists, health aides, and X-ray technicians has emerged only recently. . . .

39   . . . As nursing has lost prestige and professionals over the past twenty years, so has teaching. In 1968, 23.5 percent of all college freshmen were interested in becoming elementary or secondary school teachers; by 1982, only 4.7 percent of students entering college wanted to become teachers. On the other hand, by 1987 the percentage had risen to 8.1. Is this the beginning of a new interest in teaching? What is responsible for this upturn? According to one observer, "The overall climate is good for future teachers: the public is once again interested in education, salaries are up, the jobs are there, and the demographics point to continuing strong demand." Salaries

are indeed up—that is, compared with previous years—but they are hardly *up*. The average beginning salary of teachers across the country in 1987–88 was $18,600 to $19,000; the average salary of teachers in primary and secondary schools is $28,300. Because of the current teacher shortage, many school districts are looking to other countries in order to educate their children. . . .

40   And, of course, preschool teachers, many with bachelor's degrees, a substantial percentage with master's degrees, earn the lowest salaries among all teachers. Many of those valiant professionals who care for our youngest, most vulnerable children for most of their waking days earn no more than poverty wages. *Working Women* magazine certainly provided an apt commentary on American values when it named nursing and teaching as among the "ten worst careers" in 1988!

41   . . . What of part-time jobs, which have grown so much faster than full-time jobs during the 1980s? Nearly 20 million Americans, a large percentage of whom are women, work part-time, and over 5 million would prefer full-time work. Two-thirds of all part-time workers receive no health-insurance benefits; four-fifths are not covered by pension plans at work; and three million part-time workers and their families live in poverty. How does the American Dream look to these workers?

42   What of the millions of temporary jobs that have been created over the last few years? What of these clerical workers, low-level health workers, government workers, and workers in the computer field who earn low wages, have no job security, and often have few benefits? How do they survive when they are laid off?

43   . . . And what about wages and working conditions of nonwhite women? If the work lives of most women in the United States bear little resemblance to young women's fantasies about their future occupational goals, what is the reality for black and Hispanic women? As women as a whole make up over 80 percent of all clerical workers, nearly 25 percent of all working black women are concentrated in just six of forty-eight clerical occupations: file clerks, typists, keypunch operators, teaching assistants, calculating-machine operators, and social-welfare clerks. Among service workers, black women are concentrated in jobs as chambermaids, welfare aides, cleaners, and nurses' aides. While black women are crowded into a few sex-segregated occupations, they are, to a significant extent, working in the least desirable, lowest-paying jobs within these occupations. According to economist Rhonda M. Williams, "Occupational segregation by gender is a longstanding and by now well-known feature of the U.S. economy . . . It is less well-known that the lion's share of the aggregate gender wage gap is attributable to *intra-occupational* [italics in original] wage disparities," that "within occupations men work in high wage firms, women in low wage firms." Even within the same firm, moreover, women tend to work at lower-level jobs, and black women at the lowest-level jobs of all. As Williams states:

> The growing service economy bodes extremely ill for black women, who are consistently the (proportionately) dominant low wage group in each industry: 81.8% of black women are low earners in wholesale, 65.7% in health, 87.9% in retail, and 67.3% in FIRE [finance, insurance, and real estate]. The service economy seems well suited to swell the ranks of low-wage black women.

44   This analysis is corroborated by an examination of the median yearly income of American workers. In 1987, for example, among full-time, year-round workers, white men earned a median yearly wage of $27,468; black men earned $19,385; white women, $17,775; and black women, $16,211. Hispanic workers earned the lowest salaries within each category; Hispanic men earned $17,872 and Hispanic women, $14,893.

45   If we examine the earnings of all persons, including part-time and part-year workers, the pattern remains essentially the same while the income levels are shockingly low: the median yearly income of white males in 1987 was $18,854; of black males, $11,101; of Hispanic males, $12,019; of white females, $8,279; of black females, $6,796; and of Hispanic females, $6,611. During the same year the poverty line for a family of four was $11,611; the only workers whose median incomes were above that level were white and Hispanic males, and the latter were only barely above the line. The median income of all black and Hispanic female workers was less than 60 percent of the poverty line!

46   These numbers take on added significance when we recognize that "since the early 1960s, the part-time workforce has grown nearly three times as fast as the full-time workforce." Approximately one-third of all employed married women, one-fifth of employed divorced, separated, and widowed women, and over one-third of single (never married) women work part-time.

47   The low income of black and Hispanic women is particularly disturbing because of the enormous rise in the number of female-headed families. According to William Julius Wilson:

> Whereas the total number of families grew by 20 percent from 1970 to 1984, the number of female-headed families increased by 51 percent. Moreover, the number of families headed by women with one or more of their children present in the home increased by 77 percent. If the change in family structure was notable for all families in the 1970s, it was close to phenomenal for blacks and Hispanics. Whereas families headed by white women increased by 63 percent, the number of families headed by black and Hispanic women grew by 108 and 164 percent, respectively.

Thus, the vast majority of black and Hispanic women in the work force are not working for the proverbial "pin money"; many of them are working as the sole support of their families; and that is essentially impossible on an income of $6,500 a year for part-time workers and extremely difficult on $15,000 a year, the median income of full-time black and Hispanic female workers.

48   Not only are women's wages problematic, but the stress of being both the primary breadwinner and the primary nurturer is considerable. Most the young women I interviewed recognized that they would be combining work and family roles. Some of them expressed considerable anxiety about how they would mesh the two sets of responsibilities; many seem to take for granted that they would work it all out. Recent studies indicate that managing several complex and often mutually exclusive roles is not as easy as some of them might think and, in fact, can lead to considerable stress. Much of the recent research on stress has focused on males and therefore on the

workplace. Findings about men, however, cannot automatically be assumed to be equally true of women. Many researchers feel that research on women and stress must focus on both family and workplace issues.

49   According to a recent study on women and stress, "the tendency to focus on women's reproductive role has led to the incorrect belief that menopause and the empty nest are central concerns, a belief not supported by empirical research." They go on to suggest that "midlife is not the predominant high-stress period for women," that the "peak 'age of stress'" may be the twenties, when "many young women today face difficult and unfamiliar choices and others struggle to care for young children in isolation and poverty."

50   While women who work outside of the home have often been characterized as having better mental health, being less depressed, and having fewer physical complaints than full-time homemakers, "role overload (having too much to do)" and "role conflict (feeling pulled apart by conflicting demands)" are sources of considerable stress for women. Furthermore, recent research indicates that a work role that combines a low level of control with highly psychologically demanding tasks leads to high levels of stress. . . .

51   Female workers must also return home each night and engage in family roles in which they once again face high demands and little control. It can be argued that women's preoccupation with the well-being of others—husband or partner, children, older family members—frequently makes them vulnerable to frustration and a sense of failure. If low income, inadequate housing, having the sole responsibility for children, and job insecurity are concerns of many women, it becomes clear that stress and all of its physical and mental consequences become additional problems with which millions of women must cope.

52   Many questions remain: why are so many of our young women encouraged to dream the improbable, if not impossible, dream of high-salary, high-status positions while so many urgent, essential jobs remain unfilled? Why do we send the message that success can be found in doing the high-pressure jobs that men have traditionally done when we know that once women take up the challenge and indeed "play the game," they still do not reap the full rewards of their labors? Why do we reward workers in elite male-dominated professions with extraordinarily high salaries and perquisites while others barely scrape by or live in poverty? Why do we make a full commitment to work virtually incompatible with the kind of parenting we feel children need? And why do we make it so very difficult for women and men to both "do" and "care"? . . .

WRITING ASSIGNMENTS

Analysis

1. According to Sidel, how do class background, race, and gender influence the kind of work one does and the pay one receives? Do your observations and personal experiences support Sidel's generalizations?

2. How does Sidel explain the current status of traditionally female occupations, such as nursing, teaching, and secretarial work?
3. What evidence does Sidel provide to show that the "male model" of work and success still prevails in the white-collar world? How does she explain this persistence? Compare her analysis to Mary Anne Dolan's in "When Feminism Failed."
4. Define "overload" and "role conflict" for men and for women.

Argument

1. Have affirmative action programs "leveled the playing field" for working women?
2. Compare Sidel's and Faye Fiore's discussions of how changes in the world of work—such as part-time and flex-time schedules, parental leave, and job sharing—have affected women's careers and general welfare.
3. Can women combine career and personal goals and "have it all"?

Personal Writing and Writing from Research

1. Sidel conducted her interviews during the 1980s, a decade that she and many others call materialistic and greedy. Have values changed in the 1990s?
2. Research one of the professions that Sidel names to explore in greater detail the impact that women are having on the profession, or the impact that the profession is having on women's lives.
3. *Collaborative Project:* Through interviews, explore the experience of professional women in their late 20s, 30s, and early 40s in these areas:

   • career satisfaction
   • trade-offs between work and personal life
   • social pressure to fulfill traditional expectations, such as having children
   • gender-based obstacles, such as sexual harassment or the "glass ceiling"
   • advice they would give to women still in college.

4. Profile one or more very successful women in law, medicine, education, business, or politics. What role did gender play in her/their work life?
5. Profile a woman or women you consider to be your role model(s), and explain why.
6. For female students, in a personal essay reflect on whether Sidel's article has made you reconsider your life goals and career plans.
7. How has the work experience of black women been historically different from the work experience of white women? (See Angela Davis and Betty Friedan in Chapter 2.)

Only Daughter

Sandra Cisneros

Sandra Cisneros, born in Chicago in 1954, is the recipient of two National Education Association fellowships for poetry and fiction. She is the author of *The House on Mango Street* (1984), *Woman Hollering Creek* (1991), and *My Wicked Wicked Ways* (1987), a volume of poetry. She lives in San Antonio, Texas, where, as she says of herself, she is nobody's mother and nobody's wife. "Only Daughter" first appeared in *Glamour,* in the November 1990 issue.

Journal Topics: (1) What do you expect to gain from your college education? (2) Compare your goals to the ones your mother or father have for you. If your goals differ, how have you dealt with the differences? (3) What role has a college education played in your family's history?

As You Read: (1) What was the significance of Cisneros's being "only a daughter" and "the only daughter"? (2) Describe the relationship between Cisneros and her father.

Once, several years ago, when I was just starting out my writing career, I was asked to write my own contributor's note for an anthology I was part of. I wrote: "I am the only daughter in a family of six sons. *That* explains everything."

Well, I've thought about that ever since, and yes, it explains a lot to me, but for the reader's sake I should have written: "I am the only daughter in a *Mexican* family of six sons." Or even: "I am the only daughter of a Mexican father and a Mexican-American mother." Or: "I am the only daughter of a working-class family of nine." All of these had everything to do with who I am today.

I was/am the only daughter and *only* a daughter. Being an only daughter in a family of six sons forced me by circumstance to spend a lot of time by myself because my brothers felt it beneath them to play with a *girl* in public. But that aloneness, that loneliness, was good for a would-be writer—it allowed me time to think and think, to imagine, to read and prepare myself.

Being only a daughter for my father meant my destiny would lead me to become someone's wife. That's what he believed. But when I was in the fifth grade and shared my plans for college with him, I was sure he understood. I remember my father saying, *"Que bueno, ni'ja,* that's good." That meant a lot to me, especially since my brothers thought the idea hilarious. What I didn't realize was that my father thought college was good for girls—good for finding a husband. After four years in college and two more in graduate school, and still no husband, my father shakes his head even now and says I wasted all that education.

5   In retrospect, I'm lucky my father believed daughters were meant for husbands. It meant it didn't matter if I majored in something silly like English. After all, I'd find a

nice professional eventually, right? This allowed me the liberty to putter about embroidering my little poems and stories without my father interrupting with so much as a "What's that you're writing?"

But the truth is, I wanted him to interrupt. I wanted my father to understand what it was I was scribbling, to introduce me as "My only daughter, the writer." Not as "This is only my daughter. She teaches." *Es maestra*—teacher. Not even *profesora*.

In a sense, everything I have ever written has been for him, to win his approval even though I know my father can't read English words, even though my father's only reading includes the brown-ink *Esto* sports magazines from Mexico City and the bloody ¡*Alarma*! magazines that feature yet another sighting of *La Virgen de Guadalupe* on a tortilla or a wife's revenge on her philandering husband by bashing his skull in with a *molcajete* (a kitchen mortar made of volcanic rock). Or the *fotonovelas,* the little picture paperbacks with tragedy and trauma erupting from the characters' mouths in bubbles.

My father represents, then, the public majority. A public who is uninterested in reading, and yet one whom I am writing about and for, and privately trying to woo.

When we were growing up in Chicago, we moved a lot because of my father. He suffered bouts of nostalgia. Then we'd have to let go our flat, store the furniture with mother's relatives, load the station wagon with baggage and bologna sandwiches and head south. To Mexico City.

10   We came back, of course. To yet another Chicago flat, another Chicago neighborhood, another Catholic school. Each time, my father would seek out the parish priest in order to get a tuition break, and complain or boast: "I have seven sons."

He meant *siete hijos,* seven children, but he translated it as "sons." "I have seven sons." To anyone who would listen. The Sears Roebuck employee who sold us the washing machine. The short-order cook where my father ate his ham-and-eggs breakfasts. "I have seven sons." As if he deserved a medal from the state.

My papa. He didn't mean anything by that mistranslation, I'm sure. But somehow I could feel myself being erased. I'd tug my father's sleeve and whisper: "Not seven sons. Six! and *one daughter.*"

When my oldest brother graduated from medical school, he fulfilled my father's dream that we study hard and use this—our heads, instead of this—our hands. Even now my father's hands are thick and yellow, stubbed by a history of hammer and nails and twine and coils and springs. "Use this," my father said, tapping his head, "and not this," showing us those hands. He always looked tired when he said it.

Wasn't college an investment? And hadn't I spent all those years in college? And if I didn't marry, what was it all for? Why would anyone go to college and then choose to be poor? Especially someone who had always been poor.

15   Last year, after ten years of writing professionally, the financial rewards started to trickle in. My second National Endowment for the Arts Fellowship. A guest professorship at the University of California, Berkeley. My book, which sold to a major New York publishing house.

At Christmas, I flew home to Chicago. The house was throbbing, same as always; hot *tamales* and sweet *tamales* hissing in my mother's pressure cooker, and everybody—my mother, six brothers, wives, babies, aunts, cousins—talking too loud and at the same time, like in a Fellini film, because that's just how we are.

I went upstairs to my father's room. One of my stories had just been translated into Spanish and published in an anthology of Chicano writing, and I wanted to show it to him. Ever since he recovered from a stroke two years ago, my father likes to spend his leisure hours horizontally. And that's how I found him, watching a Pedro Infante movie on Galavisión and eating rice pudding.

There was a glass filmed with milk on the bedside table. There were several vials of pills and balled Kleenex. And on the floor, one black sock and a plastic urinal that I didn't want to look at but looked at anyway. Pedro Infante was about to burst into song, and my father was laughing.

I'm not sure if it was because my story was translated into Spanish, or because it was published in Mexico, or perhaps because the story dealt with Tepeyac, the *colonia* my father was raised in and the house he grew up in, but at any rate, my father punched the mute button on his remote control and read my story.

20   I sat on the bed next to my father and waited. He read it very slowly. As if he were reading each line over and over. He laughed at all the right places and read lines he liked out loud. He pointed and asked questions: "Is this So-and-so?" "Yes," I said. He kept reading.

When he was finally finished, after what seemed like hours, my father looked up and asked: "Where can we get more copies of this for the relatives?"

Of all the wonderful things that happened to me last year, that was the most wonderful.

WRITING ASSIGNMENTS

Analysis

1. How do her gender, working-class background, and Mexican-American heritage all help to define Cisneros? Is any one of these factors more important than the others?
2. Explain the significance for Cisneros of being an "only daughter" and "only a daughter."
3. Describe the relationship between Cisneros and her father.

Argument

1. Was her family's attitude more of a hindrance or an additional impetus to Cisneros? What does her story say about the effects of adversity?
2. Are traditional Mexican-American families alone in seeing marriage as a girl's destiny and college merely as a way to achieve it?

Personal Writing and Writing from Research

1. Describe your own experience of pursuing an identity or goals that your family did not understand or support.

2. Cisneros suggests that her father's indifference to her writing was both a sorrow and a liberation. Describe an interest that you either abandoned for lack of encouragement or developed because you were free to pursue it without interference.

When Feminism Failed

Mary Anne Dolan

Mary Anne Dolan worked briefly in politics in the mid-1960s, then joined the *Washington Star*. During her nine years there, she eventually became assistant managing editor. She was the editor of the *Los Angeles Herald Examiner* for seven years, winning the Women's Golden Flame Award in 1980. She is now a syndicated columnist and television commentator based in Los Angeles. "When Feminism Failed" first appeared June 26, 1988, in the *New York Times Magazine*.

Journal Topics: (1) Calling on your own work experiences, do women behave differently from men? Describe the setting and the similar or different behaviors. (2) If you have not held a job, ask the same questions about male and female behavior in the classroom.

As You Read: (1) List the specific evidence supporting Dolan's conclusion that feminism failed during her editorship at the *Los Angeles Herald Examiner*. (2) Deduce from that evidence a definition of what would have constituted success. (3) According to Dolan, who is responsible for this failure? Do you agree that it was a failure?

The first tremor struck me at a meeting one early morning in 1983. I was sitting in my office at the large table where, as editor of the *Los Angeles Herald Examiner*, I planned daily editions with the news staff.

Gwen Jones, the fashion editor, had strolled in while I was reading that day's papers and asked if we could chat. She had been worrying about coming to me for a long time, she said. But we went back a ways together and trusted each other and, she'd determined, "I thought you should know."

Gwen, a young feminist-leaning journalist, was concerned about the women I'd put in charge of large departments of the paper, specifically hers. It was great to have female executives, she said, but not if they didn't listen and didn't support you and seemed only concerned about building their own bureaucracies. Things were changing at the newspaper, she said. Issues were being politicized, meetings were stultifying. In general, her department's morale was down and the writers were dispirited. It wasn't—I remember her words—"fun anymore."

Others—male and female—had tried to make the same point; this time, something caught in my heart.

5   But I forged ahead with what I thought of as an experiment in "management by family." It was my privilege and ultimately my duty.

I had come to the editorship of the *Herald* after nearly 10 years in executive newspaper jobs and after many more years working with colleagues to promote a greater role for women in journalism. In Washington, we had organized in Nora Ephron's apartment house, we had changed the concept of "society pages," we had marched on the Gridiron. We had succeeded in getting women like me into newspaper training programs and onto national and foreign news desks.

I had begun as a clerk, answering telephones and carrying lunches for the women's department of the now-defunct *Washington Star*. In 1981, when I was touted as the first woman in America to rise through the ranks to the editorship of a major metropolitan newspaper, there was no way I was not going to bring other women with me.

This was a moment when the promise of the women's movement could be fulfilled. We had permission at last. The joint belonged to us! We would bring all those "female" qualities we had been boasting about on placards for years in through the front door, into the open of the newsroom. We would be a family. Between male and female would be respect and generosity and adaptability and warmth and comity and nurturing. Such an environment would make the most of our talents and, centrally, of our work. We would have honest conflict and competition, but also compromise and consensus and, therefore, success. We would make mincemeat of the male business model.

In no time, the *Herald* had what we believed was the first 50/50 male/female masthead in the country. We had the first female circulation director. We had a woman as sports columnist and a woman as editor of the editorial pages. There were many women in middle echelons, including the business editor. We were determined to show that women could do as well as men at running a big paper. By the time I left the paper five years later to return to writing, I still believed this to be true, but I also knew it would take a long time to get beyond the male models so many women had adopted.

10   Looking back, I can say that of the women I appointed to top-level positions, only one truly resisted the cliched power traps and rose to the kind of heights Betty Friedan predicted what she wrote *The Feminine Mystique* 25 years ago. Only one learned to "compete not as a woman or a man but as a human being."

It wasn't that all the men at the *Herald* were wise and wonderful as leaders (though many of them were). Nor did all the women in positions of responsibility abuse their power. What happened was that, by and large, they took on the worst—sometimes hilarious—aspects of the stereotypical corporate ladder-climbing male. As soon as masthead status was achieved, the power grab began.

The number of formal meetings, with "boss" at the head of the table, quadrupled; there were premeetings and postmeetings. Words like "facilitate" and "strategize" came into vogue. Everyone was suddenly afraid that somebody else knew something she didn't. Or had a more impressive title.

Office geography became as important in what had once been our cranky *Citizen Kane* newsroom as it is in the West Wing of the White House. Secretaries began acting like palace guards.

There were memos everywhere, multicopied and held with brightly colored plastic paper clips representing various fiefdoms. If you didn't have a "record" of a conversation, the conversation hadn't taken place.

15   Where there was opportunity to deal with people openly and with ease, many female managers were wary. They acted out a script that was part Osgood Conklin, part J.R. Ewing, part M.B.A./One-Minute-Manager and a tiny bit Mom. Many spent a good deal of time seeking out the nearest male authority figures. A succession of male general managers was courted. Male executives from Hearst, the parent company in New York, who flew in on business were afforded a coquettish new brand of ancient pagan king worship.

It took me a while to catch on to all this. For one thing, I hadn't expected it. For another, I didn't want to see it. To me, the women I had imported as managers and editors appeared wise, funny, mature. But to the staff they were brittle, conniving, power-hungry and unyielding. One after another, close friends of mine tried to convey to me what was happening; some even feared I would lose my job to one of the women they saw as plotting against me. (I guffawed at this notion, and in this, at least, I was right. After I left, none of these women were given a shot at the editorship and all but one have since left the paper.) At some point in all this, a male columnist and friend of many years' standing suggested I procure a new kind of bulletproof vest—for my back.

I can see now how my own background and my cheery belief in the accomplishments of the American women's movement may have impaired my vision. I can hear Germaine Greer snickering, but it seemed to me then, and it seems to me still, that we have much to applaud in our society's progress toward equality between the sexes. Thanks to brothers who always treated me as a peer, parents who admirably delivered roots and wings, and mentors—men and women both—I developed personal confidence and greater confidence in women as leaders.

At the *Herald,* I was criticized for being too strident on some matters (boycotting redundant meetings—with the general manager and business administration of the paper, for example) and too soft on others (spending too much time, emotion and money coaxing a series of stories out of a slow-producing correspondent in Nicaragua). But my working model was well-known: trying to build enthusiasm and excitement through the sheer creative spin of work. The challenge was daunting: the *Herald* was facing off day-to-day against the monolithic *Los Angeles Times.* We had fewer people and severely limited resources. I fought for staff and money but also for paint and library research equipment and, sometimes, flowers. I often wandered into the newsroom offering some treat or other, prompting some staffers to buzz: "Here comes Rosalynn Carter with cookies for the earth-quake victims."

Bringing women to the center of this challenge was a simple, natural joy. They were experienced professionals who rightly demanded good titles and good salaries, and got them, just as I had. Not one had reason to feel financially insecure or psychologically threatened. Yet the fact was, many of these women were content to go along with a humanizing philosophy in the workplace as a diversion only. Their essential creed was an ancient one, the male one: power first.

20   In the newsroom, the effects of these conflicting creeds became obvious. It was, as Gwen had said, not good. Curiously, the sense of family that suffered was, I think, what had initially attracted the women I had hired.

In the end, the realization of how truly stymied we women still were by our lack of female models and our lack of confidence to do things differently left me as dispirited as many of us felt after the Vice Presidential campaign of Geraldine Ferraro.

The clearest thing I could say at the time was that women—or men—who have never felt empowered, whether by parents or teachers or mentors, cannot be expected to know how to handle this commodity, as hot and alien as some radioactive substance. No one wakes up in the morning and naturally knows what to do, or what not to do, with power—how to avoid addiction to it, how to protect it, how to give it away. By the time I wore "Editor" on my metaphoric green eyeshade, I had not learned it all, but I knew I had been excellently taught. And it troubled me that, somehow, I had not done enough.

A friend sent me back to Steven Spielberg's movie *Gremlins*. In it, she reminded me, the adventurer who brings the adorable little magwai out of an exotic China-town lair is advised by an Ancient One: never lead it to water and don't let it eat after midnight.

"When you brought women into a strange land," she said, "the same rules applied. You gave women water—power—and, optimistically, you left them alone. Like gremlins, they turned into monsters."

25   Surely that wasn't inevitable, was it?

Still, mine was only one case history, an experiment. It had been an exhausting and profoundly disappointing chapter in my career, but instructive. When I left the *Herald* in 1985, I tucked it under my arm until I could know how, or why, to pass it along.

My experiment came back to me with the full force of an earthquake almost three years later. I was having a conversation with Alexander Astin, a professor of higher education at the University of California at Los Angeles. As director of an annual national survey of college freshmen, Astin has for 22 years collected data on the hopes and dreams of the young. "Students are a pretty good barometer on society," he was saying, "and what they're teaching us is that society's values have shifted." Of 1987's roughly 290,000 freshmen, a record 75.6 percent said that "being very well off financially" was a top goal, considerably more than in 1986 and nearly twice the 1970 percentage.

That, in itself, was not what intrigued me. Rather, it was that during that same period—as female enrollment swelled to equal and, in some parts of the country, exceed male enrollment—the interest in "developing a meaningful philosophy of life" reached an all-time low. From a peak of 82.9 percent in the freshmen class of 1967, this interest has nose-dived to a 39.4 rating. The mind and matter values had virtually flip-flopped.

I asked Astin what he thought accounted for that extreme swing. He touched his fingertips together, paused, and answered: "The women's movement."

30   I knew what he meant. I thought about the fact that while I was seeing startlingly diminished evidence of a social conscience and beneficence in my own age group, studies showed young people were turning to materialism like flies to butter. There had to be a deeper cause than the Reagan era and Wall Street. The most significant social movement of my lifetime—the women's movement—had to have played a key role.

"A large part of the thinking behind the women's movement said that the goodies in this society were disproportionately reserved for the men," Astin said, "and that there were obstacles to women having access to these goodies. . . . It was one thing to resent not being free to become a doctor or lawyer or business person because of an expectation that a woman should take care of a man and raise kids. But I think it was something else to emphasize women having an opportunity to go out and make a killing just like the guys. . . ."

Had the tangible goals of the movement survived, but without the philosophical underpinnings that had made them so supremely important? Had status, money, power become, in themselves, the rewards? "In every trend," Astin told me, "the men are now taking their leads from the women. . . . But, in one of the great ironies, the women have come to resemble the old male models."

I dragged myself back to my office in Westwood that afternoon, realizing as I walked along the sidewalk, somewhere between the U.C.L.A. Student Union and my Videotheque store, that if we were passing on to our children merely the values of power, money, and status, it was because those were what we were clinging to. What was missing in the "new" women I saw at the *Herald* and elsewhere was the joyful "I am." What remained was the fearful "I want."

The more time I've spent with female professionals in Los Angeles and other cities, the more I have noticed a shift away from the attitudes of the 60's and 70's—that talk of strength and sisterhood—to the hard-edged, glitzy patois of the 80's. Women's anger toward men is, I believe, even greater now than before. Devotion to success at the expense of personal well-being is rampant. Something is seriously askew.

35   What of the legacy of the women's movement? Some argue that we have, as a society, moved forward under its continuing influence. Others subscribe to the "critical mass" theory—that is, that only when enough women (or blacks or Hispanics or homosexuals) gain power does an evolutionary movement toward equality occur. I find that the latter theory is quickly embraced by those who prefer to ignore the negative

female leadership styles they see around them. But many of those I interviewed for this article argued that both men and women are furthering the problem by refusing to deal with it honestly.

"Let's face it," said one man, "those of us who would like to learn management techniques from our female boss don't even know what to say when we see her hire and promote women and then set up rivalries with them. If we confront her, we're 'just being men'; if we don't, we're 'wimps.'"

Or this, from a woman, an entertainment executive in Hollywood: "I think women dress like men and act like men in the office because corporate males love it; it doesn't threaten their sexuality."

At a conclave held in February at the University of Southern California to examine the effects of the women's movement on the media, Anne Taylor Fleming, a writer and television commentator, addressed fellow panel members at the summary session of the meeting: "We talk a lot about women getting 'access' to male worlds—the power and the money—but a part of me is saying, 'Do I want that? Is that what we want? Didn't we want to redefine that terrain? Didn't we want to figure out a way to help men be more genteel, more gentle?' I don't see it happening."

"What I worry about is that along with making the breakthroughs, we are acceding to the styles of male behavior. I think it bodes ill certainly for women, probably for men and for all our children."

40   Fleming's point, applauded by the audience, was not picked up by the moderator, Betty Friedan. It was significant, I thought, that the subject was being dodged. Others agreed. Said one frustrated conferee: "This is no time to be semi-honest."

"I will tell you exactly what I see and it's not good," said Judy Miller, vice president of marketing at Braun & Company, a Los Angeles public relations firm. She is also president of the powerful Los Angeles Trusteeship for the Betterment of Women, a mother and a community leader.

"I see two types of women in the U.S. corporate culture—the young M.B.A. women and the 'super bitches.' The younger women come out of graduate schools with all the degrees, full of training and enthusiasm and no people skills. They figure they just do the job required, get paid big money fast and that's that. They have no ability to interact, no ability to work with teams, no talent at delegating and no willingness to give credit rather than hog it.

"The new generation of M.B.A.'s has been trained like men and they come in and act like little automatons, as if they've rejected their instinctive skills. Very, very few women are good all-round contributors. Most couldn't care less, refuse to play and then hit a ceiling and are not promoted. They blame the system or the men who, right now, are acting like better contributors than the women."

And the older workers?

45   "They used to be queen bees. Now, they're super bitches. They feel 'entitled'—to power, to huge salaries, to treating others, especially women, with disdain and an arrogance that says, 'I don't need anybody.' They all go off and tell dirty jokes with the guys, completely rejecting their own femininity and becoming sexist counterparts.

"I tell myself that we may be sensitive to this because any women out there who makes it still represents every woman," Miller said. "Or I think, 'Maybe there are enough women doing things that we're just seeing universally held bad human traits coming out.' I don't know."

At the U.S.C. conference, entitled "Women, Men and Media: Breakthroughs and Backlash," Betty Friedan asked a distinguished group of national media figures the following question: "Are women going to move to money rather than social consciousness?"

Howard Rosenberg, the *Los Angeles Times* television critic, said: "If we labor under the assumption that women are somehow going to be of a higher consciousness than men, we are wrong."

Esther Shapiro, a television producer ("Dynasty"), said: "Well, women have an equal opportunity to be as ruthless as they want."

50   The question, to me, is not whether women can be as ruthless as men; we all know the answer to that. But is it so unreasonable to expect, as we did during the height of the woman's movement, that women can be humanizers?

In the unique laboratory that was the *Herald*, women given large doses of power were transmogrified by it. Faced with the freedom to behave differently from the iconic male executive, the new women chose the course of least change.

Can we avoid imitating the very worst, rather than the best, of the male model? Can we spare our children our mistakes? The U.C.L.A. data would suggest that the next generation is patterning itself after women who, perhaps involuntarily, are helping to reinforce rather than reinvent the models of the past.

I am haunted by the ancient words of Euripides:

> The Gods
> Visit the sins of the fathers
> upon the children

Of the many aftershocks I've felt since leaving the *Herald*, the strongest came on the day Gwen Jones died. She was 37, beautiful, wise and withered to death by cancer. On a February day, we gathered in a large church in Altadena, Calif., to mourn her.

55   A friend warned me that this occasion would be tough on many levels, not the least being that it was the first real "family reunion" of the old Heraldites. "Don't worry if it isn't there anymore. Offices really can't be families, you know."

But it was there all right.

We wept and sang and hugged and cheered Gwen for bringing us back together. Despite those who had tried to politicize us, fragment us, defeat us, it had happened. We were family. The younger female executives came excitedly to talk about their new babies and their husbands as well as their work.

Only one of the former "power women" showed up. Unsurprisingly, she created the only power pew in this most non-hierarchical of environments. She sat with the current and former publishers of the newspaper, both men, one at each elbow.

The women I have watched most carefully are those who richly deserved and won the opportunity to effect change. These are not downtrodden females. I cannot think of one out of the 40 or 50 who immediately march before my eyes who is not attractive, possessed of wit and capable of warmth.

60 No, this monster is within. Out of some ancient fear that the power is not truly ours, we set about destroying it. Like slaves who can't give up their masters, we cling either to male bosses or to male models. We are responsible for keeping alive the "He-Tarzan, Me-Jane" ethic, rendering ourselves powerless all over again. But somehow comfortable.

We ought to ask again: What do we want? If it is not to reach within ourselves and out to men, to humanize institutions and to pass on a different set of standards to our children, then what?

The "new female model" Betty Friedan called for in "The Second Stage"—the synthesis of "female experiences and female values"—has not yet formed. It is, perhaps, in the bulbs, as Eleanor Holmes Norton says, and will flower when the earth is warm enough. But it is time to be sure we are teaching the young well.

One can only hope that when Gwen's 6-year-old daughter, Jasmine, is ready, the garden will be in full bloom.

WRITING ASSIGNMENTS

Analysis

1. Distill Dolan's definition of feminism from her essay and compare it to competing definitions exemplified by the women executives at the *Herald*. Which do you support?
2. *Collaborative Project:* Identify the following women mentioned by Dolan and explain her allusions to them: Germaine Greer, Nora Ephron, Betty Friedan, Rosalynn Carter, Geraldine Ferraro, and Eleanor Holmes Norton. To what extent do they represent different faces of feminism?
3. Explain the relationship that Dolan sees between masculinity and power. Is she right?
4. Why do Dolan and Professor Astin attribute the diminished social conscience and increased materialism of the 1980s to the women's movement?

Argument

1. Infer from her essay what Dolan means by the "male business model." Do you agree with Dolan's explanation of why her women executives adopted it?
2. Compare and contrast Sidel's and Dolan's explanations for why women in powerful positions or prestigious professions are "acceding to the styles of male behavior." Then, in an essay, answer Dolan's question: "Can we avoid imitating the very worst, rather than the best, of the male model?"
3. Based on this essay, do you think that Dolan is hostile to men?

4. Do you agree with Dolan that most of her female executives "sold out" feminism's goals and principles by making "status, money, power . . . the rewards"?

Personal Writing and Writing from Research

1. Research and report on the role of women in journalism today.
2. *Collaborative Project:* Have each member of the group informally define feminism. After discussing these definitions, have each person write a position paper on feminism today, incorporating additional research if needed.

Women's Career-Family Juggling Act
Corporations Are Taking Notice

Faye Fiore

This article, by reporter Faye Fiore, appeared in the *Los Angeles Times* on December 13, 1992, several months after then-President Bush vetoed the Family Leave Bill, and several months before Congress passed it again and President Clinton signed it into law. The issues that this article raises persist. Other recent articles have documented the efforts of fathers to combine career with significant parenting. Most such studies focus on middle-class professionals.

Journal Topics: (1) Describe a situation in which there were competing, legitimate demands on your time. How did you handle this conflict? Would you handle it differently today? Could the context of the conflict have been changed to reduce the pressure on you?

As You Read: (1) How do the changes that Fiore describes benefit working mothers and their employers? (2) What are the disadvantages to the employee and to the employer? (3) Are the working mothers described in this article representative of working women in general?

Impressions mattered the morning Demetra Lambros raced to meet one of her law firm's newest clients. She put on mascara and rehearsed her presentation in the cab on the way to a stately Washington, D.C., office. She gave a firm handshake to all the gentlemen present, set her briefcase squarely on the table, opened the client's file and watched blankly as a pacifier came flying out.

"Oops," said Lambros, fast-track lawyer three days a week and full-time mommy the other four.

For professional women, the conflict between work and family dates at least from the emergence of feminism. But economic circumstances are finally beginning to imbue some women with the power to manage the conflict to their advantage. Perhaps for the first time since women broke into the corporate club, they are using their leverage to demand jobs that accommodate *them.*

They are negotiating flexible work schedules, scaling back to 20-hour weeks and working from computers at home. Companies downsizing amid the economy's relentless squeeze are increasingly receptive to women's offers to job share, sacrifice health benefits and forgo raises in exchange for a little more time with their children.

5   "I have a real job and I still see my baby," said Lambros, a 33-year-old law firm associate. "He is the most important thing in the world to me. If this place had not helped me work out a part-time schedule, I would not have come back."

With 45% of the American work force made up of women, experts say Corporate America is waking up to the idea that the rigid 9-to-5 day and 40-hour week are luxuries that it can no longer afford—not if it hopes to retain women workers who have become pillars in its ranks.

"Listen up guys: . . . You cannot cut out half the labor force and expect to be a successful corporation," said Charles Boesel, spokesman for the Women's Bureau at the U.S. Department of Labor. "If you want to retain the best and the brightest, you have to hire women . . . and have programs in place that keep them happy."

The American labor force is growing older. More men are retiring at one end and more women are entering at the other. Women will make up two-thirds of the net gain in workers by 2005; three-fourths will become pregnant during their working lives, according to Labor Department forecasts.

More men are taking greater roles in parenting and housekeeping. Still, the strides made by generations of women who broke sex barriers on the job have left today's employed mothers with one foot in the '90s and the other in the '50s.

10   "The woman is the one who gets the call when the kid swallows the Ping-Pong ball. She is the one who goes to the Mommy and Me classes," said Sheila Kuehl, managing director of California Women's Law Center, a nonprofit women's civil rights firm. "Most professional women start out thinking they can do both, and they do it by making appointments with their kids."

The career-family juggling act appears to be taking its toll.

In a survey of 1,400 women conducted this year by the Ms. Foundation for Women and the Center for Policy Alternatives in New York, one-quarter said their greatest personal struggle was inflexible work hours.

Germany, France and Sweden have been helping parents balance career and family since the 1960s with flexible work hours. In America, though, only a sliver of the work force can opt for anything less than a rigid, full-time schedule.

Those who are cutting such deals tend to be college-educated professionals with career experience too valuable to lose; employers accommodate them because they like them.

15   Dr. Jamie Baker Knauss, a 39-year-old Pasadena pediatrician and mother of two boys, delayed starting her practice for two years until she found a group of doctors flexible enough to share her patient load so she could work three days a week.

Ellen McDonnell, a 37-year-old mother of two girls and senior producer of National Public Radio's Morning Edition, works one day a week out of her Maryland home, a diaper pail beside her desk.

Assistant U.S. Atty. Leslie Swain, the 39-year-old mother of two girls, was one of the first federal prosecutors in Los Angeles to work a three-day week—a schedule once considered impossible for a trial attorney.

"Being a lawyer is what I wanted to do as far back as I can remember," she said. "But being a mother is what puts a bounce in my step."

Despite studies showing that workplace flexibility leads to reduced turnover, absenteeism and tardiness and improved loyalty and morale, most corporations have resisted making it a policy.

20   Experts say the resistance stems in part from an age-old work ethic: Good employees are at their desks eight hours a day; those who are not must not be working.

"A major project is coming, something has to be done by Friday and all of a sudden it's: 'Whoops, this person has Friday off.' That happens one or two times in the private sector and people go through the roof," said Glenn Meister, a consultant in the Los Angeles office of A. Foster Higgins & Co., a benefits firm.

But several employers who offer flexible schedules said most conflicts can be resolved—if both the employer and worker are willing to bend. Prosecutor Swain plans to abandon her part-time schedule whenever she has a case in trial. Pediatrician Knauss often uses her evenings to return patient phone calls.

In fact, several employers said they usually get more than three days' work for three days' pay because the part-time employee is focused on the job rather than tugged by a neglected family. The largest criminal fine ever levied in a defense contracting fraud case was won by Assistant U.S. Atty. Julie Fox Blackshaw, a part-time Los Angeles prosecutor and the mother of 22-month-old Jessica.

"We have no complaints," said U.S. Atty. Terree Bowers, Blackshaw's boss.

25   If regard for the changing American family does not move corporations to accommodate working mothers, the bottom line might, experts say.

Employees who work shorter hours with reduced benefits fit into the needs of many companies forced to cut costs and downsize in these recessionary times, Meister said. Employers say flexible scheduling allows them to keep experienced workers and reduce costly turnover.

Alan Murray, deputy chief of the Wall Street Journal's bureau in Washington, D.C.—where several reporters have shared beats and have worked part-time—said flexible scheduling has allowed the newspaper to hold onto experienced women journalists.

"It has been a big payoff for us," Murray said. "This company has always believed the Wall Street Journal is as good as its people . . . and we have to do what's necessary to keep them. If that means letting them work three days a week, we try to do it."

A 1987 task force at Aetna Life & Casualty in Hartford, Conn., found that one-fourth of mothers who took a maternity leave never came back. By its own estimates, Aetna was losing more than $1 million annually in employee turnover; every worker saved was money in the company's pocket.

30   Aetna instituted a family-leave policy and flextime, which required workers to be in the office between 9 and 3 and left to them when they put in the other 90 minutes of the workday. Within four years, only 9% of mothers were failing to return from maternity leave, said Michelle Carpenter, manager of Aetna's work/family strategies unit.

     But even women who have the option of scaling back say there is a stigma attached to working less. They believe that they are no longer considered serious players, that they fall out of the loop for promotions. Many describe a nagging ambivalence: Once they felt guilty about spending too much time at work; now they feel guilty about not spending enough.

     "There was a time I would have killed to be on a big, important, fast-moving criminal case," said one mother working part-time as an attorney. "Now I feel like I'm living in a world of young whippersnappers and I can't compete."

     Maura Thorpe would tell her it is worth it.

     It is almost noon, and Thorpe is positioned at her computer in an upstairs study of a white fixer-upper in the San Gabriel Valley. She is professionally dressed in a straight black skirt and low heels. Three little girls, all under age 5, are playing at her feet. At 30, she is eight months pregnant with her fourth child.

35   Thorpe works at home three days a week as an appellate attorney for the state of California while a baby-sitter watches the children. "I think about how I could jump in and be the best appellate lawyer, the best criminal lawyer, and then I think, what am I saying?" she muses, straightening 3-year-old Denny's ponytail. "I love picking them up from school. They are always beaming about the project they did or the kid they played with. When they're hurt, they want their mom and no one else. And that's special to me."

WRITING ASSIGNMENTS

Analysis

1. Compare the advantages and disadvantages to workers and employers of the workplace changes described by Fiore.

Argument

1. Should the employment options described in this article be available to men?
2. If the employment options described in this article were available to men, would men use them? Explain and defend your answer.
3. Why might some employees object to these employment options?

Personal Writing and Writing from Research

1. *Collaborative Project:* Using the library or primary research at an accessible employer, evaluate the success of alternative employment policies such as those described by Fiore.
2. Interview older members of your own family about how alternative work schedules would have affected their lives. Report on your findings.

POPULAR CULTURE

SYLVIA   by Nicole Hollander

On "A Prairie Home Companion," radio humorist Garrison Keillor says of the inhabitants of his mythical town, Lake Wobegon:

"All the women are strong, all the men are good-looking, and all the children are above average."

Of course, they aren't. Keillor's description makes us smile because, as children, we all want to be "above average," but averages being what they are, we can't be. The humor of his description of the town's men and women is just as gently far-fetched. It comes from reversing gender stereotypes: *women* are supposed to be beautiful, and *men* are supposed to be strong. Lake Wobegon thus promises release from both the law of averages and cultural dictates. No wonder it is both a popular and a mythical place.

The beauty queen and the star athlete, those familiar icons of popular culture, symbolize what Americans believe to be quintessential femininity and masculinity. The two parts of this chapter examine some of the enduring and changing ways that popular culture defines gender roles through images of beauty and sports.

BEAUTY

American women spend billions of dollars annually on products promising youth, slenderness, and beauty. Are women foolish? Perhaps not, because even women who crash the glass ceiling seldom escape the pinch of the glass slipper. When Bill Clinton ran for president, the media reported that his wife, Hillary Rodham Clinton, a brilliant and successful lawyer, wore a size 6, and favored bright colors. Her mid-campaign switch from long hair and headband to a stylish short cut generated more coverage than her previous 20 years of work as a lawyer and advocate for children. And it is possible that more Americans know that the first lady appeared in high-fashion photographs in *Vogue* magazine than that she has long been an advocate for children and educational reform.

In the chapter's opening section, "A Woman's Beauty: Put-Down or Power Source?" Susan Sontag meditates on the privileges and burdens of beauty for women today.

One enduring American icon of female beauty is the Barbie doll. Marge Piercy's poem "Barbie Doll" links Barbie to the destructive power of the beauty ideal. But Helen Cordes's journalistic essay "What a Doll!" presents both Barbie's detractors and defenders.

The average American woman is expected, like Barbie, to be slender. Over the last 100 years, mainstream American culture has admired thinner and thinner women. In the 1960s, the most celebrated model was nicknamed Twiggy in recognition of her shape. Since then, more curvaceous models have come into and gone out of vogue, but the ideal female form remains substantially thinner than is healthy or even possible for most women. In "Fasting Girls: The Emerging Ideal of Slenderness in American Culture," Joan Jacobs Brumberg analyzes the historical origins and economic underpinnings of the American preference for thinness.

In "Beauty and the Backlash," Susan Faludi updates Brumberg's analysis of the economics of the beauty business and the costs that women pay for competing in a lifelong and very serious beauty pageant. Like Brumberg, Faludi asserts that beauty is a political issue.

Combining the language of advertising, the promises of the beauty industry, and the archetypes of the fairy tale, Helena Maria Viramontes in "Miss Clairol" looks at a Latina's preparations for a big date through the eyes of her pre-adolescent daughter.

In the last selection in the first part of this chapter, John Updike revisits, from one man's perspective, the topic that Susan Sontag introduced, the relationship between beauty, women, and power.

SPORTS

Although Bonnie Blair has won five Olympic gold medals for speed skating, the women most likely to appear in *Sports Illustrated* are still the svelte beauties in the annual swimsuit issue. Or they are athletes reduced to caricatures: Nancy Kerrigan, ice princess as victim, or Tonya Harding, the brash upstart from the wrong side of town. It is not surprising that the world of sports remains largely a male preserve because it enshrines traditionally masculine values: mastery, strength, competitiveness, determination, aggressiveness, and stoicism.

In "Why Sports Is a Drag," journalist Dave Barry exaggerates contrasting male and female attitudes toward sports in order to poke fun at the American male obsession with sports—an obsession he shares.

In American popular culture, athletics includes both individual and team competitive sports, but the biggest money and attention go to team sports. Here the stars are winners who achieve fame and fortune by dominating their sport and their peers.

What does football, the quintessentially American sport, reveal about us? Cultural anthropologist and football fan W. Arens decodes the masculine meanings of football in "Professional Football: An American Symbol and Ritual." Next, Mark Kram's profile of football safety Joey Browner, "No Pain, No Game," raises disturbing questions about the linkage between football and American popular culture's glorification of violence. Gary Gildner's poem, "First Practice," further underscores the connections between competitive contact sports, violence, and masculinity.

In contrast, Leonard Kriegel's "Taking It" offers a more positive, but still ambivalent, reflection on the connection between American masculinity and the values of sports.

Jennifer Briggs's love of sports inspired her to become a sportswriter. In "My Life in the Locker Room," she chronicles the resistance she encountered in fulfilling her dream. Finally, in "The Unbound Foot: Women and Athletics," biologist Anne Fausto-Sterling traces improvements in women's athletic performance while examining the interplay between biology and culture in athletics.

BEAUTY

A Woman's Beauty
Put-Down or Power Source?

Susan Sontag

Besides her many articles and reviews, which have established her as a formidable polemicist and rigorous intellectual, Susan Sontag has published three collections of essays, *Against Interpretation* (1966), *Styles of Radical Will* (1969), and *Under the Sign of Saturn* (1980). Her book-length essays are *Trip to Hanoi* (1969), *On Photography* (1976), *Illness as Metaphor* (1978), and *AIDS and Its Metaphors* (1989). She has also written two novels, *The Benefactor* (1963) and *Death Kit* (1967), and a volume of short stories, *I etcetera* (1978).

One commentator notes that Sontag's essays reflect "thought unfinished, thought still being formulated. . . . Although Sontag's writing includes quotable aphoristic statements, it is designed more to provoke thought than to conclude it, to explore ideas rather than explain them. The forms of her essays, moreover, often reflect her restlessly inquiring mind." "A Woman's Beauty," which exemplifies these qualities, first appeared in *Vogue* magazine in 1975.

Journal Topics: (1) Under what circumstances is beauty an asset? Is it ever a liability? (2) Is human beauty more often associated with men or women? Why?

As You Read: (1) How do historical references provide a context for Sontag's analysis of the role of beauty today? (2) How does Sontag define women's association with beauty? (3) What are the advantages and disadvantages of this association to women?

1   For the Greeks, beauty was a virtue: a kind of excellence. Persons then were assumed to be what we now have to call—lamely, enviously—*whole* persons. If it did occur to the Greeks to distinguish between a person's "inside" and "outside," they still expected that inner beauty would be matched by beauty of the other kind. The

well-born young Athenians who gathered around Socrates found it quite paradoxical that their hero was so intelligent, so brave, so honorable, so seductive—and so ugly. One of Socrates' main pedagogical acts was to be ugly—and teach those innocent, no doubt splendid-looking disciples of his how full of paradoxes life really was.

2   They may have resisted Socrates' lesson. We do not. Several thousand years later, we are more wary of the enchantments of beauty. We not only split off—with the greatest facility—the "inside" (character, intellect) from the "outside" (looks); but we are actually surprised when someone who is beautiful is also intelligent, talented, good.

3   It was principally the influence of Christianity that deprived beauty of the central place it had in classical ideals of human excellence. By limiting excellence (*virtus* in Latin) to *moral* virtue only, Christianity set beauty adrift—as an alienated, arbitrary, superficial enchantment. And beauty has continued to lose prestige. For close to two centuries it has become a convention to attribute beauty to only one of the two sexes: the sex which, however Fair, is always Second. Associating beauty with women has put beauty even further on the defensive, morally.

4   A beautiful woman, we say in English. But a handsome man. "Handsome" is the masculine equivalent of—and refusal of—a compliment which has accumulated certain demeaning overtones, by being reserved for women only. That one can call a man "beautiful" in French and in Italian suggests that Catholic countries—unlike those countries shaped by the Protestant version of Christianity—still retain some vestiges of the pagan admiration for beauty. But the difference, if one exists, is of degree only. In every modern country that is Christian or post-Christian, women *are* the beautiful sex—to the detriment of the notion of beauty as well as of women.

5   To be called beautiful is thought to name something essential to women's character and concerns. (In contrast to men—whose essence is to be strong, or effective, or competent.) It does not take someone in the throes of advanced feminist awareness to perceive that the way women are taught to be involved with beauty encourages narcissism, reinforces dependence and immaturity. Everybody (women and men) knows that. For it is "everybody," a whole society, that has identified being feminine with caring about how one *looks*. (In contrast to being masculine—which is identified with caring about what one *is* and *does* and only secondarily, if at all, about how one looks.) Given these stereotypes, it is no wonder that beauty enjoys, at best, a rather mixed reputation.

6   It is not, of course, the desire to be beautiful that is wrong but the obligation to be—or to try. What is accepted by most women as a flattering idealization of their sex is a way of making women feel inferior to what they actually are—or normally grow to be. For the ideal of beauty is administered as a form of self-oppression. Women are taught to see their bodies in *parts,* and to evaluate each part separately. Breasts, feet, hips, waistline, neck, eyes, nose, complexion, hair, and so on—each in turn is submitted to an anxious, fretful, often despairing scrutiny. Even if some pass muster, some will always be found wanting. Nothing less than perfection will do.

7   In men, good looks is a whole, something taken in at a glance. It does not need to be confirmed by giving measurements of different regions of the body, nobody encourages a man to dissect his appearance, feature by feature. As for perfection, that is

considered trivial—almost unmanly. Indeed, in the ideally good-looking man a small imperfection or blemish is considered positively desirable. According to one movie critic (a woman) who is a declared Robert Redford fan, it is having that cluster of skin-colored moles on one cheek that saves Redford from being merely a "pretty face." Think of the depreciation of women—as well as of beauty—that is implied in that judgment.

8   "The privileges of beauty are immense," said Cocteau. To be sure, beauty is a form of power. And deservedly so. What is lamentable is that it is the only form of power that most women are encouraged to seek. This power is always conceived in relation to men; it is not the power to do but the power to attract. It is a power that negates itself. For this power is not one that can be chosen freely—at least, not by women—or renounced without social censure.

9   To preen, for a woman, can never be just a pleasure. It is also a duty. It is her work. If a woman does real work—and even if she has clambered up to a leading position in politics, law, medicine, business, or whatever—she is always under pressure to confess that she still works at being attractive. But in so far as she is keeping up as one of the Fair Sex, she brings under suspicion her very capacity to be objective, professional, authoritative, thoughtful. Damned if they do—women are. And damned if they don't.

10   One could hardly ask for more important evidence of the dangers of considering persons as split between what is "inside" and what is "outside" than that interminable half-comic half-tragic tale, the oppression of women. How easy it is to start off by defining women as caretakers of their surfaces, and then to disparage them (or find them adorable) for being "superficial." It is a crude trap, and it has worked for too long. But to get out of the trap requires that women get some critical distance from that excellence and privilege which is beauty, enough distance to see how much beauty itself has been abridged in order to prop up the mythology of the "feminine." There should be a way of saving beauty *from* women—and *for* them.

WRITING ASSIGNMENTS

Analysis

1. In what sense is beauty a form of power?
2. In what sense is beauty a liability?
3. According to Sontag, how has the association of beauty with women contributed to the devaluation of both women and beauty?
4. Why does Sontag say that women are "damned if they do. . . . And damned if they don't" take their looks seriously?
5. Is beauty necessarily gendered? Survey examples of "the beautiful" that carry neither masculine nor feminine connotations. You may want to compare Sontag's ideas with John Updike's in "The Female Body," later in this chapter.
6. Compare and contrast specific contemporary American exemplars of masculine and feminine beauty. In what ways, if any, do these role models of attractiveness also define contemporary gender roles?

Argument

1. Sontag claims, ". . . we are actually surprised when someone who is beautiful is also intelligent, talented, good." Do you agree?
2. Is Sontag correct when she says the standards of beauty applied to women are more exacting, detailed, and oppressive than those applied to men?
3. Are men less concerned than women with their looks?
4. Is a person who believes that beauty is extremely important therefore shallow, lacking in intelligence, or even morally suspect?

Personal Writing and Writing from Research

1. In a personal essay, explain your criteria for human beauty and describe someone who fulfills your definition.
2. Compare the tables of contents and the advertising in two popular magazines, one directed at women and the other at men, to determine how much they reinforce traditional femininity's concern with beauty and masculinity's concern with power and performance.
3. *Collaborative Project:* Compare and contrast standards of human beauty by examining the ideals of beauty within different historical periods, countries, or American subcultures. Also consult Joan Jacobs Brumberg's "Fasting Girls," later in this chapter.
4. Write a research paper in which you explain and illustrate the classical Greek attitude toward beauty.

Barbie Doll

Marge Piercy
Please see the headnote on Marge Piercy in Chapter 5, page 369.

What a Doll!

Helen Cordes
In the notoriously fickle toy business, where one year's best seller is likely to bomb the next, the Barbie doll seems practically eternal. Introduced in 1959, Barbie is the world's best-selling doll. Annual sales, including her accessories, continue to rise, topping $1 billion in 1993. The average American girl owns eight Barbie dolls and buys two or three new ones a year. Barbie is sold around the world, including in poorer countries, such as China and Portugal.

Journal Topics: (1) What role, if any, did the Barbie doll play in your childhood? Was she popular among your friends, with members of your family, or with you?

(2) Does she communicate a positive or negative image to girls? (3) What was your favorite childhood toy or game? (4) How did your parents influence your taste in toys? (5) Do toys exert a lasting influence on children?

As You Read: (1) How is the self-image of the girl in Piercy's "Barbie Doll" formed? (2) Describe the poem's tone and identify the phrases and words that establish the tone. (3) In "What a Doll!" Cordes points out that "Barbie was an astronaut years before Sally Ride. . . ." Why is this worth noting?

BARBIE DOLL

1969

This girlchild was born as usual
and presented dolls that did pee-pee
and miniature GE stoves and irons
and wee lipsticks the color of cherry candy.
5　Then in the magic of puberty, a classmate said:
You have a great big nose and fat legs.

She was healthy, tested intelligent,
possessed strong arms and back,
abundant sexual drive and manual dexterity.
10　She went to and fro apologizing.
Everyone saw a fat nose on thick legs.

She was advised to play coy,
exhorted to come on hearty,
exercise, diet, smile and wheedle.
15　Her good nature wore out
like a fan belt.

So she cut off her nose and her legs
and offered them up.
In the casket displayed on satin she lay
20　with the undertaker's cosmetics painted on,
a turned-up putty nose,
dressed in a pink and white nightie.
Doesn't she look pretty? everyone said.
Consummation at last.
25　To every woman a happy ending.

WHAT A DOLL!

1　Can anyone with a social conscience find anything good to say about Barbie? Please. If Barbie were real, she'd measure 36-18-33. Can there be any doubt that with crisis-level anorexia rates, Barbie's hands are bloody? Would Barbie ever wear a T-shirt saying "Live simply so that others may simply live"? Barbie's very existence preaches consumerism—she's nothing without profligate products ranging from toenail polish to a pink RV camper to haul around her never-quite-big-enough wardrobe.

2   Or are there other ways to look at Barbie? Among the unlikely voices rising in defense of Barbie are those of feminist moms who see daughters absorbing—what?!—messages of power from Barbie (who, incidentally, comes in many versions of dolls of color). And at the same time cutting-edge artists are using Barbie to pose provocative questions about sex, power, and gender.

3   Barbie's detractors and supporters can't argue with one fact: Barbie is here to stay. After three decades, sales only continue to climb, with Barbies living in nearly every U.S. and Canadian household that has children and residing in 67 other countries as well. Massive merchandising efforts include *Barbie* magazine and a new Barbie compact disc.

4   Monolithic marketing of this 11-inch über doll may make some parents even more resolved to ignore their child's begging for Barbies. But journalist and mother Marnie Jackson explains in the leftist Canadian *This Magazine* (Dec./Jan. 1991) why parents should avoid the hard line on Barbie, as well as on other not politically correct toys such as toy guns and Nintendos. While denying "bad" toys may help parents feel more in control over "bad" influences, how much lasting weight will a Barbie or a plastic Uzi carry in the long run? The lasting values kids will have, Jackson writes, are those that are "intrinsic in the sort of relationships we have with our children, arising out of the ordinary, humdrum way a family works and plays."

5   Besides, she notes, when today's savvy kids see parents assigning moral judgments to toys, they see bargaining possibilities. If the new "Happy To Be Me" doll—she's a Barbie-like doll touted as more realistic, with real-life measurements of 36-27-38—is OK, why not Barbie? If a water pistol is OK, why not a toy M-16? Despite a fondness for the M-16, Jackson's son, she reports, continues to be a generally non-violent, consistently kind kid.

6   As for Barbie dolls, how kids play with them is telling, Jackson says. Her observations are borne out by testimonials I've heard from many former Barbie fans (now grownup feminists) whose Barbie persona was a woman of power who—even at her most generous—never deferred to Ken.

Barbie fan Diane Bracuk would not be surprised. In *Parenting* (Aug. 1991), Bracuk claims Barbie was a "truly revolutionary doll, one that inspired, rather than oppressed, young girls' imaginations." Proof? Particularly in Barbie's pioneer years, she represented a liberating counter to the omnipresent image of woman as housewife drudge. Barbie was an astronaut years before Sally Ride, and her mid-'60s appearance as "Career Girl" Barbie predated many of her real-life counterparts' entry into the work world. Barbie was not a kept woman. Bracuk notes: While she dates Ken, she never marries him, ostensibly paying the Barbie Dream Home mortgage herself.

But does Barbie have it all? This chipper "icon of American womanhood" has an irresistible dark side that's surfacing in artists' imaginations. As humorist Alice Kahn reports in the *New York Times* (Sept. 29, 1991), Barbie's showing up in places like the cult documentary *Superstar: The Karen Carpenter Story,* where her miniature plastic starring role makes Carpenter's death from anorexia nervosa "seem even more poignant and senseless," Kahn notes. California artist Ken Botto, who Kahn labels "a leading practitioner of Barbie noire," creates Barbie tableaux. In one of them, Barbie towers over a comatose Ken. Botto sees Barbie as "a reflection on what we think of femininity. It's not flattering."

WRITING ASSIGNMENTS

Analysis

1. Why does Piercy title her poem "Barbie Doll" when Barbie isn't even mentioned in the poem?
2. How does Piercy's "Barbie Doll" develop ideas presented in Lieberman's essay in Chapter 4, " 'Some Day My Prince Will Come': Female Acculturation Through the Fairy Tale," and Susan Faludi's "Beauty and the Backlash," which appears in this chapter.
3. Trace the ways that Piercy's poem suggests that gender roles are culturally constructed rather than innate.
4. Analyze the tone and meaning of the poem's last line.
5. Analyze the ways that popular toys affect boys' self-esteem and concept of masculinity.
6. How do toys influence the development of a child's gender role?

Argument

1. "Barbie Doll" was written in 1969. Are young girls today more or less likely to be subjected to the social pressures experienced by the girl in this poem?
2. Is Barbie a "materialistic bimbo or feminist trailblazer"? For a research paper, survey Barbie dolls currently on the market, survey your contemporaries, and analyze articles about the Barbie doll, including those cited by Cordes.

Personal Writing and Writing from Research

1. Write a poem comparable to Piercy's, but from a young boy's perspective.
2. Write a poem or short story in which a girl or boy successfully resists the social conditioning illustrated in "Barbie Doll."
3. *Collaborative Project:* After defining a sample population, analyze the relationship between gender role conditioning and contemporary tastes in children's toys. Visit local toy stores, child care centers, and elementary schools, and interview their personnel.

Fasting Girls
The Emerging Ideal of Slenderness in American Culture

Joan Jacobs Brumberg

This historical analysis is an excerpt from Brumberg's book, *Fasting Girls: The Emergence of Anorexia Nervosa as a Modern Disease* (1988).

Journal Topics: (1) Describe and compare your concept of the ideal female and male figures. (2) How is your self-image affected by advertisements for clothing, health, and beauty products, or by shopping for clothing? (3) Explore the connotations of these adjectives: svelte, slender, slim, thin, skinny, scrawny. (4) Why might individuals feel guilty about their weight? (5) Is slenderness as important to men as it is to women? (6) How do attitudes toward slenderness vary among different ethnic groups?

As You Read: (1) How did the democratization of fashion through ready-to-wear clothing influence attitudes toward female body size and shape? (2) What role did advertising play in shaping ideals? (3) How have specific historical events and underlying cultural values influenced attitudes toward female body size and shape?

1   Within the first two decades of the twentieth century, even before the advent of the flapper, the voice of American women revealed that the female struggle with weight was under way and was becoming intensely personal. As early as 1907 an *Atlantic Monthly* article described the reaction of a woman trying on a dress she had not worn for over a year: "The gown was neither more [n]or less than anticipated. But I . . . *the fault was on me* . . . I was more! Gasping I hooked it together. The gown was hopeless, and I . . . I am fat." . . . By the twentieth century . . . overweight in women was not only a physical liability, it was a character flaw and a social impediment.

2   Early in the century elite American women began to take body weight seriously as fat became an aesthetic liability for those who followed the world of haute couture. Since the mid-nineteenth century wealthy Americans—the wives of J. P. Morgan, Cornelius Vanderbilt, and Harry Harkness Flagler, for instance—had traveled to Paris to purchase the latest creations from couturier collections such as those on view at Maison Worth on the famed rue de la Paix. The couturier was not just a dressmaker who made clothes for an individual woman; rather, the couturier fashioned "a look" or a collection of dresses for an abstraction—the stylish woman. In order to be stylish and wear couturier clothes, a woman's body had to conform to the dress rather than the dress to the body, as had been the case when the traditional dressmaker fitted each garment. . . .

3   In 1908 the world of women's fashion was revolutionized by Paul Poiret, whose new silhouette was slim and straight. . . . Almost immediately women of style began to purchase new kinds of undergarments that would make Poiret's look possible; for example, the traditional hourglass corset was cast aside for a rubber girdle to retract the hips.

4   After World War I the French continued to set the fashion standard for style-conscious American women. In 1922 Jeanne Lanvin's chemise, a straight frock with a simple bateau neckline, was transformed by Gabrielle Chanel into the uniform of the flapper. Chanel dropped the waistline to the hips and began to expose more of the leg: in 1922 she moved her hemlines to midcalf, and in 1926–27 the ideal hem was raised to just below the knee. In order to look good in Chanel's fashionable little dress, its wearer had to think not only about the appearance of her legs but about the smoothness of her form. Women who wore the flapper uniform turned to flattening brassieres constructed of shoulder straps and a single band of material that encased the body from chest to waist. In 1914 a French physician commented on the revised dimensions of women's bodies: "Nowadays it is not the fashion to be corpulent; the proper thing is to have a slight, graceful figure far removed from embonpoint, and *a fortiori* from obesity. For once, the physician is called upon to interest himself in the question of feminine aesthetics."

5   The slenderized fashion image of the French was picked up and promoted by America's burgeoning ready-to-wear garment industry. Stimulated by the popularity of the Gibson girl and the shirtwaist craze of the 1890s, ready-to-wear production in the United States accelerated in the first two decades of the twentieth century. Chanel's chemise dress was a further boon to the garment industry. Because of its simple cut, the chemise was easy to copy and produce, realities that explain its quick adoption as the uniform of the 1920s. According to a 1923 *Vogue,* the American ready-to-wear industry successfully democratized French fashion: "Today, the mode which originates in Paris is a factor in the lives of women of every rank, from the highest to the lowest."

6   In order to market ready-to-wear clothing, the industry turned in the 1920s to standard sizing, an innovation that put increased emphasis on personal body size and gave legitimacy to the idea of a normative size range. For women, shopping for ready-to-wear clothes in the bustling department stores of the early twentieth century

fostered heightened concern about body size. With a dressmaker, every style was theoretically available to every body; with standard sizing, items of clothing could be identified as desirable, only to be rejected on the grounds of fit. (For women the cost of altering a ready-made garment was an "add-on"; for men it was not.) Female figure flaws became a source of frustration and embarrassment, not easily hidden from those who accompanied the shopper or from salesclerks. Experiences in department-store dressing rooms created a host of new anxieties for women and girls who could not fit into stylish clothing. In a 1924 testimonial for an obesity cure, a formerly overweight woman articulated the power of dress size in her thinking about dieting and about herself: "My heart seemed to beat with joy at the prospect of getting into one of the chic ready-made dresses at a store."

7   Ironically, standard sizing created an unexpected experience of frustration in a marketplace that otherwise was offering a continually expansive opportunity for gratification via purchasable goods. Because many manufacturers of stylish women's garments did not make clothing in large sizes, heavy women were at the greatest disadvantage. In addition to the moral cachet of overweight, the standardization of garment production precluded fat women's participation in the mainstream of fashion. This situation became worse as the century progressed. Fashion photography was professionalized, a development that paralleled the growth of modern advertising, and models became slimmer both to compensate for the distortions of the camera and to accommodate the new merchandising canon—modern fashion was best displayed on a lean body.

8   The appearance in 1918 of America's first best-selling weight-control book confirmed that weight was a source of anxiety among women and that fat was out of fashion. *Diet and Health with a Key to the Calories* by Lulu Hunt Peters was directed at a female audience and based on the assumption that most readers wanted to lose rather than gain weight. . . . "You should know and also use the word calorie as frequently, or more frequently, than you use the words foot, yard, quart, gallon and so forth. . . . Hereafter you are going to eat calories of food. Instead of saying one slice of bread, or a piece of pie, you will say 100 calories of bread, 350 calories of pie."

9   Peters' book was popular because it was personal and timely. Her 1918 appeal was related to food shortages caused by the exigencies of the war in Europe. Peters told her readers that it was "more important than ever to reduce" and recommended the formation of local Watch Your Weight Anti-Kaiser Classes. "There are hundreds of thousands of individuals all over America who are hoarding food," she wrote. "They have vast amounts of this valuable commodity stored away in their own anatomy." In good-humored fashion Peters portrayed her own calorie counting as both an act of patriotism and humanitarianism:

> I am reducing and the money that I can save will help keep a child from starving . . .
> [I am explaining to my friends] that for every pang of hunger we feel we can have a
> double joy, that of knowing we are saving worse pangs in some little children, and
> that of knowing that for every pang we feel we lose a pound. A pang's a pound the
> world around we'll say.

10   But Peters showed herself to be more than simply an informative and patriotic physician. Confessing that she once weighed as much as 200 pounds, the author also understood that heavy women were ashamed of their bulk and unlikely to reveal their actual weight. Peters observed that it was not a happy situation for fat women. "You are viewed with distrust, suspicion, and even aversion," she told her overweight readers.

11   Although she tried to make light of the hunger pains suffered by dieters and adorned her book with playful illustrations, Peters' point was clear: dieting was a lonely struggle that involved renunciation and psychological pain. For some women, such as herself, the struggle was for a lifetime. Although she was able to control her weight at 150 pounds, the author confessed it was not easy. "No matter how hard I work—no matter how much I exercise, no matter what I suffer," lamented Peters, "I will always have to watch my weight, I will always have to count my calories."

12   Peters' book was among the first to articulate the new secular credo of physical denial: modern women suffered to be beautiful (thin) rather than pious. Peters' language and thinking reverberated with references to religious ideas of temptation and sin. For the modern female dieter, sweets, particularly chocolate, were the ultimate temptation. Eating chocolate violated the morality of the dieter and her dedication to her ideal, a slim body. Peters joked about her cravings ("My idea of heaven is a place with me and mine on a cloud of whipped cream") but she was adamant about the fact that indulgence must ultimately be paid for. "If you think you will die unless you have some chocolate creams [go on a] *debauch*," she advised. "'Eat 10 or so' but then *repent* with a 50-calorie dinner of bouillon and crackers." (Italics added.)

13   Although the damage done by chocolate creams could be mediated by either fasting or more rigid dieting, Peters explained that there was a psychological cost in yielding to the temptation of candy or rich desserts. Like so many modern dieters, Peters wrote about the issue of guilt followed by redemption through parsimonious eating: "Every supposed pleasure in sin [eating] will furnish more than its equivalent of pain [dieting]." But appetite control was not only a question of learning to delay gratification, it was also an issue of self-esteem. "You will be tempted quite frequently, and you will have to choose whether you will enjoy yourself hugely in the twenty minutes or so that you will be consuming the excess calories, or whether you will dislike yourself cordially for the two or three days you lose by your lack of will power." For Peters dieting had as much to do with the mind as with the body. "There is a great deal of psychology to reducing," she wrote astutely. In fact, with the popularization of the concept of calorie counting, physical features once regarded as natural—such as appetite and body weight—were designated as objects of conscious control. The notion of weight control through restriction of calories implied that overweight resulted solely from lack of control; to be a fat woman constituted a failure of personal morality.

14   The tendency to talk about female dieting as a moral issue was particularly strong among the popular beauty experts, that is, those in the fashion and cosmetics industry who sold scientific advice on how to become and stay beautiful. Many early-twentieth-

century beauty culturists, including Grace Peckham Murray, Helena Rubinstein, and Hazel Bishop, studied chemistry and medical specialties such as dermatology. The creams and lotions they created, as well as the electrical gadgets they promoted, were intended to bring the findings of modern chemistry and physiology to the problem of female beauty. Nevertheless, women could not rely entirely on scientifically achieved results. The beauty experts also preached the credo of self-denial: to be beautiful, most women must suffer.

15   Because they regarded fat women as an affront to their faith, some were willing to criminalize as well as medicalize obesity. In 1902 *Vogue* speculated, "To judge by the efforts of the majority of women to attain slender and sylph-like proportions, one would fancy it a crime to be fat." By 1918 the message was more distinct: "There is one crime against the modern ethics of beauty which is unpardonable; far better it is to commit any number of petty crimes than to be guilty of the sin of growing fat." By 1930 there was no turning back. Helena Rubinstein, a high priestess of the faith, articulated in *The Art of Feminine Beauty* the moral and aesthetic dictum that would govern the lives of subsequent generations of women: "An abundance of fat is something repulsive and not in accord with the principles that rule our conception of the beautiful. . . ."

WRITING ASSIGNMENTS

Analysis

1. What are the connotations of female "slenderness" in contemporary American culture? How is a woman's weight linked to images of her health, fitness, social class, ethnicity, age, and life-style?
2. Explain the connection, first made by Dr. Lulu Hunt Peters, between moral virtue, or character, and slenderness. Does this linkage persist today?
3. How did the mass-marketing of clothing (the ready-to-wear garment industry) and advertising influence popular attitudes toward women's body size and shape?
4. Explore the ways that contemporary American society punishes "overweight" people through criticism, ridicule, and ostracism.
5. Compare and contrast the popular images of "thin" men and "thin" women. How are these images related to gender roles?

Argument

1. To what extent is concern about one's weight appropriate?
2. Is being overweight ugly, dangerous, or morally wrong? Why or why not?
3. Who are more severely criticized when they are overweight—women or men? Why?
4. Are men as preoccupied as women with their own size and weight? Explain your answer.

Personal Writing and Writing from Research

1. Trace the depictions over time or across cultures, in sculpture or in painting, of woman's ideal size. Explore how these images reflect a woman's social role.
2. *Collaborative Project:* In a research paper, survey the popular culture of food—as expressed in advertisements, cookbooks, food packaging, songs, movies, and verbal expressions—and analyze the link between moral values and social status, on the one hand, and particular foods or body size on the other. For example, consider the symbolism of chocolate, "natural" foods, sweet foods, and milk, or the link between particular foods and athletes, successful persons, families, men, women, the old or young, or the sexually appealing.
3. Thinness, like a tanned skin, was once a sign of lower social and economic status. Trace and explain changes in attitudes toward tanned skin or thinness, either across cultures or historically.
4. Compare attitudinal differences toward slenderness among individuals of different ethnicities or races; among adolescents, young adults, the middle-aged, the elderly; between men and women; among persons of working class, middle-class and upper-class social status.
5. How have issues of body size and shape personally affected you?

Beauty and the Backlash

Susan Faludi

Susan Faludi is no stranger to controversy. As editor of her high-school paper, she wrote about school meetings of born-again Christians that violated the separation of church and state. The meetings were halted. On an Elks scholarship, and with money earned from cleaning toilets, Faludi attended Harvard, where she graduated summa cum laude. As managing editor of the *Harvard Crimson,* she wrote about sexual harassment on campus. Her story about a male professor, published over the objections of a dean, caused the university to ask the professor to take a leave of absence. Faludi won a Pulitzer Prize for explanatory journalism for her *Wall Street Journal* article on the human cost of the multibillion-dollar leveraged buyout of Safeway. Hers is thoroughly researched, activist journalism.

Faludi began *Backlash* after reading a *Newsweek* article about a 1986 Harvard-Yale marriage study, which reported that women of a certain age were more likely to be shot by a terrorist than to marry. The study, given wide coverage, panicked many women. Faludi, then in her late 20s, researched the study and found it full of errors; she also discovered that the *Newsweek* article had compounded the errors through exaggeration. She saw this one incident as evidence of a pervasive, often insidious, campaign by political leaders, the courts, Hollywood, and the mass media to convince women that feminism was their enemy and that independence would make them unstable and unmarriageable. Their goal, she believed, was to drive women back into traditionally feminine roles. After four years of exhaustive research that confirmed her hunch, Faludi published *Backlash* in October 1991, in the wake of the Anita Hill-Clarence Thomas hearings. The book became a controversial best seller and earned Faludi the National Book Critics Circle prize for nonfiction.

Journal Topics: (1) Are men or are women more fearful of aging? Why? (2) Describe your own experiences, or those of someone you know, with cosmetic surgery. (3) Under what circumstances would you have cosmetic surgery? (4) Name and describe the contemporary advertising model, or television or film star, who is most like your ideal of masculine or feminine good looks.

As You Read: (1) Explain the purpose and effect of Faludi's extended anecdotes, such as the stories of mannequin sculptor Robert Filoso and plastic surgeon Dr. Robert Harvey. (2) When, if ever, does attention to beauty become dangerous?

1 With the aid of a metal rod, the first woman of "the New Generation" stands in Robert Filoso's Los Angeles workshop, her feet dangling a few inches off the floor. Her clay arms are bandaged in gauze strips and her face hooded in a plastic bag, knotted at the neck to keep out dust motes. A single speck could cause a blemish.

2 "There are no imperfections in my models," the thirty-eight-year-old mannequin sculptor explains. "They all have to be taken out." The dank environment inside the bag, however, has bred its own facial flaws. Between the woman's parted lips, a green mold is growing.

3 On this April morning in 1988, Filoso is at work on the model that will set the standard for the following year. Ever since he brought "the new realism" to female mannequins—chiseling detailed vertebrae, toes, and nipples—Filoso has led the $1.2 billion dummy industry, serving all the better retailers. This year, he is making some major changes. His New Generation woman has shrunk in height, gained almost three inches on her breasts, shed an inch from her waist, and developed three sets of eyelashes. The new vital statistics, 34-23-36, are voluptuous by mannequin standards, but the Lacroix era of strapless gowns and bone-tight bodices requires bigger busts and wasp waists. "Fashion," Filoso says, "determines the shape of my girls."

4 The sculptor gingerly unwinds the cloth strips and hands them to his assistant and model, Laurie Rothey. "It seems like so many of the girls are getting breast implants," Rothey is saying as they work, and she isn't referring to the mannequins. "It's the only way you can get jobs because big breasts are all the [modeling] agencies are hiring now. . . ."

5   . . . Later that day . . . Filoso describes his vision for the New Generation. He pictures an in-shape upscale Marilyn Monroe, a "curvy but thin" society lady who can "afford to go to Bergdorf Goodman's and buy anything." Their poses, too, he says, will be "more feminine, more contained. . . . In the 1970s, mannequins were always out there, reaching for something. Now they are pulling into themselves." That's the way it is for real women in the '80s, too, he says: "Now you can be yourself, you can be a lady. You don't have to be a powerhouse."

6   In Filoso's opinion, these developments are a big improvement over the '70s, when women "didn't care" about their appearance. "The stores didn't want beautiful mannequins, because they were afraid women customers would look at them and say, 'God, I could never look like that in a million years.'" That era, Filoso is happy to report, has passed. "Now, mannequins are really coming to life. They are going to start getting prettier again—more like the fashion photography you'd see in old magazines from the 1950s." And what of female customers who might say, as he put it, "God, I could never look like that in a million years"? But that's the good news, Filoso says. "Today, women can look at a beautiful mannequin in a store and say, 'I want to look like her,' and they actually can! They can go to their doctor and say, 'Doc, I want these cheekbones.' 'Doc, I want these breasts.'"

7   He sighs. "If I were smart, I would have become a plastic surgeon."

8   During the '80s, mannequins set the beauty trends—and real women were expected to follow. The dummies were "coming to life," while the ladies were breathing anesthesia and going under the knife. The beautiful industry promoted a "return to femininity" as if it were a revival of natural womanhood—a flowering of all those innate female qualities supposedly suppressed in the feminist '70s. Yet the "feminine" traits the industry celebrated most were grossly unnatural—and achieved with increasingly harsh, unhealthy, and punitive measures.

9   The beauty industry, of course, has never been an advocate of feminist aspirations. This is not to say that its promoters have a conscious political program against women's rights, just a commercial mandate to improve on the bottom line. And the formula the industry has counted on for many years—aggravating women's low self-esteem and high anxiety about a "feminine" appearance—has always served them well. (American women, according to surveys by the Kinsey Institute, have more negative feelings about their bodies than women in any other culture studied.) The beauty makers' motives aren't particularly thought out or deep. Their overwrought and incessant instructions to women are more mindless than programmatic; their frenetic noise generators create more static than substance. But even so, in the '80s the beauty industry belonged to the cultural loop that produced backlash feedback. Inevitably, publicists for the beauty companies would pick up on the warning signals circulating about the toll of women's equality, too—and amplify them for their own purposes.

10   "Is your face paying the price of success?" worried a 1988 Nivea skin cream ad, in which a business-suited woman with a briefcase rushes a child to day care—and catches a glimpse of her career-pitted skin in a store window. If only she were less

successful, her visage would be more radiant. "The impact of work stress . . . can play havoc with your complexion," *Mademoiselle* warned; it can cause "a bad case of dandruff," "an eventual loss of hair" and, worst of all, weight gain. Most at risk, the magazine claimed, are "high-achieving women," whose comely appearance can be ravaged by "executive stress." In ad after ad, the beauty industry hammered home its version of the backlash thesis: women's professional progress had downgraded their looks; equality had created worry lines and cellulite. This message was barely updated from a century earlier, when the late Victorian beauty press had warned women that their quest for higher education and employment was causing "a general lapse of attractiveness" and "spoiling complexions."

11   The beauty merchants incited fear about the cost of women's occupational success largely because they feared, rightly, that that success had cost *them*—in profits. Since the rise of the women's movement in the '70s, cosmetics and fragrance companies had suffered a decade of flat-to-declining sales, hair-product merchandisers had fallen into a prolonged slump, and hairdressers had watched helplessly as masses of female customers who were opting for simple low-cost cuts defected to discount unisex salons. In 1981, Revlon's earnings fell for the first time since 1968; by the following year, the company's profits had plunged a record 40 percent. The industry aimed to restore its own economic health by persuading women that *they* were the ailing patients—and professionalism their ailment. Beauty became medicalized as its lab-coated army of promoters, and real doctors, prescribed physician-endorsed potions, injections for the skin, chemical "treatments" for the hair, plastic surgery for virtually every inch of the torso. (One doctor even promised to reduce women's height by sawing their leg bones.) Physicians and hospital administrators, struggling with their own financial difficulties, joined the industry in this campaign. Dermatologists faced with a shrinking teen market switched from treating adolescent pimples to "curing" adult female wrinkles. Gynecologists and obstetricians frustrated with a sluggish birthrate and skyrocketing malpractice premiums traded their forceps for liposuction scrapers. Hospitals facing revenue shortfalls opened cosmetic-surgery divisions and sponsored extreme and costly liquid-protein diet programs.

12   The beauty industry may seem the most superficial of the cultural institutions participating in the backlash, but its impact on women was, in many respects, the most intimately destructive—to both female bodies and minds. Following the orders of the '80s beauty doctors made many women literally ill. Antiwrinkle treatments exposed them to carcinogens. Acid face peels burned their skin. Silicone injections left painful deformities. "Cosmetic" liposuction caused severe complications, infections, and even death. Internalized, the decade's beauty dictates played a role in exacerbating an epidemic of eating disorders. And the beauty industry helped to deepen the psychic isolation that so many women felt in the '80s, by reinforcing the representation of women's problems as purely personal ills, unrelated to social pressures and curable only to the degree that the individual woman succeeded in fitting the universal standard—by physically changing herself.

13   The emblems of pulchritude marketed in the '80s—frailty, pallor, puerility—were all beauty marks handed down by previous backlash eras. Historically, the backlash

Venus has been an enervated invalid recovering on the chaise longue, an ornamental and genteel lady sipping tea in the drawing room, a child bride shielded from the sun. During the late Victorian era, the beauty industry glorified a cult of invalidism—and profited from it by promoting near-toxic potions that induced a chalky visage. The wasting-away look helped in part to unleash the nation's first dieting mania and the emergence of anorexia in young women. In times of backlash, the beauty standard converges with the social campaign against wayward women, allying itself with "traditional" morality; a porcelain and unblemished exterior becomes proof of a woman's internal purity, obedience, and restraint. The beautiful backlash woman is controlled in both senses of the word. Her physique has been domesticated, her appearance tamed and manicured as the grounds of a gentleman's estate.

14   By contrast, athleticism, health, and vivid color are the defining properties of female beauty during periods when the culture is more receptive to women's quest for independence. In the late 1910s and early 1920s, female athletes began to eclipse movie stars as the nation's beauty archetypes; Coco Chanel's tan launched a nationwide vogue in ruddy outdoor looks; and Helena Rubinstein's brightly tinted cosmetics made loud and flamboyant colors acceptable. By the late 1920s and '30s, however, the beauty press denounced women who tanned their faces and companies fired women who showed up at work sporting flashy makeup colors. Again, during World War II, invigorated and sun-tanned beauties received all the praise. *Harper's Bazaar* described "the New American Look of 1943" this way: "Her face is out in the open and so is she. Her figure is lithe and strong. Its lines are lines of action. The glamour girl is no more." With the war over, however, the beauty industry restored that girl—encouraged by a new breed of motivational research consultants who advised cosmetics companies to paint more passive images of femininity. Beauty publicists instructed women to inflate their breasts with padding or silicone, to frost their hair with carcinogenic dyes, to make themselves look paler by whitening their face and lips with titanium—to emulate, in short, that most bleached and medicalized glamour girl of them all, Marilyn Monroe.

15   Under the '80s backlash, the pattern would repeat, as "Action Beauty," as it was so labeled and exalted in '70s women's magazines, gave way to a sickbed aesthetic. It was a comprehensive transformation carried out at every level of the beauty culture—from the most superficially applied scent to the most invasive and dangerous operations.

FROM CHARLIE TO OPHELIA

16   In the winter of 1973, Charles Revson called a high-level meeting of Revlon executives. He had a revolutionary concept, he told them: a fragrance that celebrated women's liberation. (It actually wasn't that revolutionary: in the 1910s, perfume companies like Shalimar replaced weak lavenders with strong musks and marketed them to liberated New Women.) The Revlon team code-named the plan "Cosmo," and they spent the next several months taking groups of women out to lunch and asking them what they wanted in a perfume.

17   The women told the Revlon interviewers that they were sick of hearing that fragrances were supposed to be defining them; they wanted a perfume that reflected the new self-image they had defined for themselves. The company's market researchers considered this and eventually came up with a fragrance called Charlie, which they represented in ads with a confident and single working woman who signs her own checks, pops into nightclubs on her own, and even asks men to dance. Revlon introduced Charlie in 1973—and sold out its stock within weeks. Less than a year into its launch, Charlie had become the nation's best-selling fragrance.

18   "Charlie symbolized that new lifestyle," Revlon executive vice president Lawrence Wechsler recalls, "that said, you can be anything you want to be, you can do anything you want to do, without any criticism being directed at you. If you want to wear pantsuits at the office instead of a skirt, fine." The success of the Charlie ad campaign inspired nearly a dozen knockoffs, from Max Factor's Maxi ("When I'm in the Mood, There's No Stopping Me") to Chanel's Cristalle ("Celebrate Yourself"), each featuring heroines who were brash, independent, and sexually assertive. Superathletes abounded, from Coty's ice-skating champion, Smitty, to Fabergé's roller-skating dynamo, Babe ("the fragrance for the fabulous new woman you're becoming")—in homage to Olympian Babe Didrikson Zaharias.

19   Suddenly in 1982, Revlon retired the old Charlie ad campaign and replaced her with a woman who was seeking marriage and a family. The change wasn't inspired by a decline in sales; Revlon's managers just "sensed" that Charlie's time had passed. "We had gone a little too far with the whole women's liberation thing," Wechsler says. "And it wasn't an issue anymore, anyway. There were more important issues now, like drugs. And then there's the biological clock. There's a need now for a woman to be less striving." But the cancellation of the Charlie ad campaign, he insists, is actually a sign of women's "progress." The American woman has come so far, he says, "she doesn't have to be so assertive anymore. She can be more womanly."

20   The new campaign, however, didn't appeal to female customers and Revlon had to replace it again in 1986. This time the company did away with the character of Charlie altogether and offered an assortment of anonymous women who were identified as "very Charlie" types (in an ad campaign created by Malcolm MacDougall, the same ad executive who produced *Good Housekeeping's* New Traditional woman). In a sense, the company had come full circle: once again, the fragrance was defining the standard that women had to meet.

21   At least the "very Charlie" women were still walking and showing signs of life. By the mid-'80s, many of the fragrance ladies had turned into immobilized, chalky figurines. The perfume industry had decided to sell weaker fragrances to weaker women, and both the scent and the scented were toned down. . . .

22   . . . As the fragrance industry geared up its second strategy, the marriage pitch, demure and alabaster brides soon proliferated in perfume ads, displacing the self-confident single women. In 1985, Estee Lauder unveiled Beautiful, the fragrance "for all your beautiful moments." But the only "moment" the ads ever depicted was a wedding day. (The "Beautiful Moments" campaign for women happened to coincide with Omega watches' "Significant Moments" campaign for men, making for an

unintentionally instructive back-to-back contrast in many magazines: on one page, she lowered her veil; on the next, he raised his fist to celebrate "the pure joy of victory.") . . .

23   Women in the fragrance ads who weren't having babies were being turned into them—as one company after another selected a prepubescent girl as the new icon of femininity. "Perfume is one of the great pleasures of being a woman," the caption read in *Vogue,* accompanying a photo of a baby-girl Lolita, her face heavily made up and blond curls falling suggestively across cherubic cheeks. "In praise of woman," was the 1989 ad slogan for Lord & Taylor's perfume Krizia, but the only woman praised in this ad was a preschooler dressed in Victorian clothes, her eyes cast demurely downward. "You're a wholesome woman from the very beginning," murmured still another perfume ad—of a ladylike five year old. Even one of Revlon's new "very Charlie" types was under ten.

24   But none of these marketing strategies paid off. . . .

25   With the lures of wealth, marriage, and infancy proving insufficient inducement, the perfume ad campaigns pushed idealization of weak and yielding women to its logical extreme—and wheeled out the female corpse. In Yves Saint Laurent's Opium ads, a woman was stretched out as if on a bier, her eyes sealed shut, a funereal floral arrangement by her ashen face. In Jovan's Florals ads, a modern-day Ophelia slipped into supreme repose, her naked body strewn with black and white orchids. The morbid scene sported this caption: "Every woman's right to a little indulgence."

KEEPING A DAILY DE-AGING DIARY

26   The cosmetics industry adopted a familiar Victorian maxim about children as its latest makeup "trend" in the late '80s. As a feature headline put it, "The Makeup Message for the Summer: Be Seen But Not Heard." The beautiful woman was the quiet one. *Mademoiselle's* cosmetics articles praised the "muted" look, warned against "a mouth that roars," and reminded women that "being a lady is better . . . better than power, better than money." *Vogue* placed a finger to women's lips and appealed for silence: "There's a new sense of attractiveness in makeup. . . . [N]othing ever 'shouts.'" Ten years earlier, makeup, like fragrance, came in relentlessly "spirited" and "exuberant" colors with "muscle." The "Outspoken Chanel" woman wore nail and face color as loud as her new "confidence" and "witty voice." Now cosmetics tiptoed, ghostly, across the skin. Partly, of course, this new beauty rule was just the by-product of that time-honored all-American sales strategy: Create demand simply by reversing the dictates of style. But the selection of the muffled maiden as the new ideal was also a revealing one, a more reassuring image for beauty merchants who were unnerved by women's desertion of the cosmetics counter.

27   The makeup marketers rolled out the refined upper-class lady, too; like the fragrance sellers, they hoped to make more money off fewer women by exhorting affluent baby-boom women to purchase aristocratic-sounding beauty products—with matching high-class prices. But again this marketing maneuver backfired. The

heaviest users of makeup are teens and working-class women—and the formidable price tags on these new "elite" makeups just scared them off. The makeup companies' tactics only caused their earnings to fall more sharply—soon, leading securities analysts were warning investors to avoid all cosmetics stocks.

28   Finally, though, these companies came up with a more lucrative way to harness backlash attitudes to their sales needs. Many major cosmetics companies began peddling costly medicinal-sounding potions that claimed to revert older female skin to baby-pale youth and to shield women's "sensitive" complexions from the ravages of environmental, and especially professional, exposure. By exploiting universal fears of mortality in the huge and aging baby-boom population—exploiting it in women only, of course—the industry finally managed to elevate its financial state.

29   By the late '80s, entering a cosmetics department was like stumbling into a stylish sanitarium. The salesclerks were wearing white nurse uniforms, and the treatments were costly and time-consuming regimens with medicinal names and packages, accompanied by physicians' endorsements. Clarins's $92 "Biological Tightener" came in a twenty-day treatment rack lined with test-tube-shaped "ampoules." Glycel, an "antiaging" cream, boasted the support of heart surgeon Dr. Christiaan Barnard. La Prairie offered "cellular therapy" from their "world-renowned medical facility" in Switzerland—and its $225 bottles were filled with "capsules" and came with little spoons for proper dosage. Clinique's "medically trained" staff urged women to exfoliate daily, chart their epidermal progress in a "Daily Dè-Aging Workbook," and monitor skin health on the company's "computer"—a plastic board with sliding buttons that was closer to a Fisher-Price Busybox than a MacIntosh.

30   References to female fertility were replete at the cosmetics counter, too, as the beauty industry moved to exploit the "biological-clock" anxieties that popular culture had done so much to inflame. The labels of dozens of beauty treatments claimed remedial gynecological ingredients: "sheep placentas," "bovine embryos," and even, bizarrely, "human placental protein." Also on display, in keeping with the demands of '80s backlash fashion, were $50 "breast creams" and "bust milks" to boost a woman's bra size—products not seen in department stores since the 1950s.

31   To promote their skin "treatments," cosmetics companies employed traditional scare tactics about skin damage ("Premature Aging: Don't Let It Happen to You," Ultima II ads warned—it's "every skin-conscious woman's worse nightmare come true"), but they delivered these fear-inducing messages now with pseudofeminist language about taking control. The ad agency that created Oil of Olay's successful '80s campaign—which shifted the company's focus from older women with real wrinkles to baby-boom women with imaginary ones—employed what its executives labeled "the control concept." Its age-terrorized but take-charge female model vowed, "I don't intend to grow old gracefully. . . . I intend to fight it every step of the way." Chanel ads even advised professional women to use antiwrinkle creams to improve their work status; fighting wrinkles, they informed, was "a smart career move."

32   While cosmetics companies used the vocabulary of women's liberation for marketing purposes, they also claimed that the fruits of that liberation were eroding women's appearance. Career "stress" was the real destroyer of feminine beauty, the cosmetics

industry insisted. The fluorescent office lights and even the daily commute posed a greater threat to female skin than intensive tanning, Ultima II ads insisted. "Dermatologists have agreed that you accumulate far more damage during the year going to and from work than in two weeks of concentrated sunbathing."

33   The beauty companies fared better hawking antiwrinkle potions than traditional scents and cosmetics because backlash appeals in this venue were able to couple female awareness of ancient cultural fears of the older woman with modern realities of the baby-boom woman's aging demographic. This was a most effective combination. By 1985, a cosmetics trade association survey of skin-care professionals found that 97 percent had noticed that their clients were markedly more worried and upset about the threat of wrinkles than just a few years earlier. By 1986, skin-cream annual sales had doubled in five years to $1.9 billion. And for the first time, many department-store cosmetics counters were selling more skin-treatment products than color makeup. At I. Magnin, these treatments made up 70 percent of all cosmetics sales.

34   The popularity of high-priced antiwrinkle creams could hardly be attributed to improvements in the lotions' efficacy. The claims made on behalf of high-priced anti-aging products were virtually all fraudulent, the promises of "cell renewal," "DNA repair," and age "reversal" so ludicrous that even the Reagan-era U.S. Food and Drug Administration issued cease and desist orders against twenty-three of the cosmetic firms. Promises to protect women's health by shielding their skin from the sun were similarly phony. Skin-care companies cashed in with sunblocks claiming protection factors as high as 34; researchers and the FDA could find no effectiveness over 15. And while it would be nice to believe that beauty companies simply wanted to guard women's skin from carcinogenic rays, they showed no such vigilance against cancer when publicizing one of their most highly touted skin-treatment innovations of the decade: Retin-A.

35   A century earlier, women were encouraged to consume "Fowler's Solution," an arsenic-laced acne cream, to revitalize aging skin; it made them sick, some fatally. In the '80s, beauty doctors dispensed a prescription acne ointment reputed to possess antiaging properties. Retin-A, however, also had caused cancer in mice and an oral version of the drug, Accutane, was linked to birth defects. Moreover, Retin-A seemed more effective at burning women's faces than burnishing them. In the one study testing the cream's effect on wrinkles—sponsored by Retin-A's own maker, Ortho Pharmaceutical Corp.—73 percent of the participants who took Retin-A needed topical steroids to reduce the painful swelling and 20 percent developed such severe dermatitis that they had to drop out of the study. (On the other hand, the study found that Retin-A gave *one* of the participants a "much improved" facial appearance.)

36   The dermatologist who had conducted this lone study, John Voorhees, agreed to serve as Ortho's chief promoter of Retin-A. Needless to say, the dermatology chairman from the University of Michigan didn't dwell on the medical dangers when he endorsed Retin-A at a news conference in the Rainbow Room in Manhattan—a publicity stunt that caused Johnson & Johnson's stock price to leap eight points in two days. The media dubbed Voorhees the '80s Ponce de Leon; *USA Today* declared his discovery "a miracle." In one year, Retin-A sales rose 350 percent to $67 million,

pharmacies sold out of the $25 tubes, dermatologists' office visits skyrocketed and doctors set up Retin-A shopping-mall "clinics" that drew hundreds of women. The FDA had not approved Retin-A's use for wrinkles, but dermatologists dispensed it for that purpose anyway, simply claiming on the prescription forms that their middle-aged female patients were suffering from adolescent acne breakouts. On paper anyway, the doctors had succeeded in turning grown women back into pimply teenage girls. . . .

THE BREAST MAN OF SAN FRANCISCO

37   Over lunch at San Francisco's all-male Bohemian Club, the businessmen are discussing their wives. "My wife is forty but she looks thirty," plastic surgeon Dr. Robert Harvey tells them. So far, all he's had to do is a few facial collagen injections to smooth her crow's feet. "Eventually, she'll probably want a tummy tuck." The men nod genially and spear bits of lobster salad. The few women present—at lunch, the club admits women as "escorted" guests—say nothing.

38   At this noon repast, Dr. Robert Harvey, the national spokesman of the Breast Council, is the featured speaker. This is, in fact, his second appearance. "The Breast Man of San Francisco," as some of his staff and colleagues refer to him, Harvey is said to be the city's leading breast enlargement surgeon—no small feat in a city boasting one of the nation's highest plastic surgeon-to-patient ratios.

39   With lunch over, the Breast Man pulls down a movie screen and dims the lights. The first set of slides are almost all photos of Asian women whose features he has Occidentalized—making them, in Harvey's opinion, "more feminine." As the before-and-after pictures flash by, Harvey tells the men how one woman came in complaining about the shape of her nose. She was "partly correct," he says; her nose "needed" changing, but not in the way she had imagined.

40   Back at the office later that day, one of Harvey's "patient counselors" rattles off a long list of Harvey's press and public appearances: *"Good Housekeeping, Harper's Bazaar,* the 'Dean Edell Show'—we've got a video of that if you want to see it. . . ." Then there are the speaking engagements: "The Decathalon Club, the San Francisco Rotary Club, the Daly City Rotary Club, the Press Club. . . ." The list is surprisingly long on men's associations. "They tell their wives about it," she explains. "The men's clubs are very revenue-producing."

41   Harvey's patient counselor (who has since relocated) was herself a prime revenue-producer for the doctor. When prospective clients called, she told them to come on in and look at her breasts. She had hers expanded from 34B to 34C a few years ago. She told the women, "I can say that personally I feel more confident. I feel more like a woman." (She doesn't, however, feel confident enough to have her name used; some of the men closest to her, she explains, don't know she had the operation.) She served as an effective marketing tool, she says. "They feel safe if they can talk to a non-threatening [woman] first. That way they don't feel like a guy is trying to sell them something." Her assistance was a real boon, helping Harvey's breast business to double in three years. Harvey liked to call her "my right arm."

42   For patients nervous about surgery, Harvey's counselor suggested they start out with a facial injection of collagen. At $270 per cc, one collagen injection lasts about six months. "It's a good way for them to get their feet wet. It helps them cross the bridge to surgery." She administered several injections a day—"seven is my max." In one year, she says, this procedure alone quadrupled Harvey's revenues. He didn't pay her a commission on the surgical patients she brought into his practice this way, but she says she doesn't mind; she's just "grateful" that he let her perform the operation. Anyway, Harvey rewards his employees in other ways: for their birthdays, he has given nearly half the women on his staff free cosmetic surgery.

43   Harvey originally became a plastic surgeon "for altruistic reasons"; he wanted to work with burn patients. But he soon switched to cosmetic procedures, which are "more artistic"—and far more lucrative. Sitting in an office stocked with antiques and coffee-table books on Leonardo da Vinci, Harvey explains, "It's very individual. We are sculptors." He has never had plastic surgery himself. "I guess my nose isn't great, but it just doesn't bother me." From his desk drawer, Harvey pulls out samples of the various "choices" now available to women seeking breast implants. They can choose between silicon-based, water-based and "the adjustable." The last comes with a sort of plastic straw that sticks out of a woman's armpit after the operation. If she doesn't like the size, he can add or subtract silicone through the straw: "That way the lady can feel she has some control. She can make adjustments."

44   Most women who want breast implants are "self-motivated," he says. By that, he means they aren't expanding their breasts to please a man. "They are part of that Me Generation. They are doing it for themselves. Most times, their husbands or boyfriends like them just the way they are." That doesn't stop him, however, from maintaining his full schedule of men's-club speaking engagements.

45   "I've never met anyone post-op who wasn't just thrilled," Harvey's counselor says, as she provides a list of five satisfied customers. "The results are excellent," Harvey says. "Only five percent have to get their implants removed."

46   But the very first woman on the list belongs to that five percent. A year earlier, Harvey had injected silicone gel implants through this woman's armpit into her breasts. A few weeks later, her breasts started hurting. Then they hardened into "rocks." Then the left implant started rising.

47   "It just got worse until it felt like the implant was stuck under my armpit," says the woman, an engineer in nearby Silicon Valley. "I couldn't move it. I'd use my bicep and two arms and my boyfriend would help me and it still wouldn't move. I tried tying an Ace bandage around my chest to keep them in line. I was getting afraid." She called Harvey and he told her, she recalls, "not to worry, it would go down."

48   Instead, it rose higher. She went to the medical school library and started reading about breast surgery. The studies she read in the professional literature informed her that breast implants injected through the armpit fail 40 percent of the time, not 5 percent. (Harvey says he got the 5 percent figure from an unwritten, unpublished study he conducted of two hundred of his own patients.) After a year of anguish, she finally had Harvey remove the implants. He installed a new set through the nipples, a procedure that leaves a scar but has a lower failure rate. So far, she says, it seems to be working out. She says she bears Dr. Harvey no ill-will. "At first," she says, "I was

kind of angry, but he was very good about helping me with my problem. I was really grateful for his patience. He didn't even charge me for the second operation."

49   Asked about this woman's experience later, Harvey blames it on the patient. "She probably wasn't massaging enough," he says.

COSMETIC SURGERY: CANCER AND OTHER "VARIATIONS FROM THE IDEAL"

50   Starting in 1983, the American Society of Plastic and Reconstructive Surgeons launched a "practice enhancement" campaign, issuing a flood of press releases, "pre- and post-op photos," and patient "education" brochures and videotapes. They billed "body sculpturing" as safe, effective, affordable—and even essential to women's mental health. "There is a body of medical information that these deformities [small breasts] are really a disease," a statement issued by the society asserted; left uncorrected, flat-chestedness causes "a total lack of well-being." To fight this grave mental health hazard, the society was soon offering a financing plan for consumers—"no down payment" and credit approval within twenty-four hours.

51   The inspiration for the society's PR blitzkrieg was the usual one—a little problem with supply and demand. While the ranks of plastic surgeons had quintupled since the 1960s, patient enthusiasm hadn't kept pace. By 1981, the flood of doctors into cosmetic surgery had made it the fastest-growing specialty in American medicine, and they simply needed more bodies. Plastic surgeons started seeking publicity in a systematic way. By the mid-'80s, their appeals overran magazines and newspapers, offering "low monthly payment plans," acceptance of all credit cards, convenient evening and Saturday surgery sessions. A single issue of *Los Angeles* magazine contained more than two dozen such ads.

52   The surgeons marketed their services as self-image enhancers for women—and as strategies for expanding women's opportunities. Cosmetic surgery can even help women "pursue career goals," an ad in the *New York Times* promised. With liposuction, "you can feel more confident about yourself," the Center for Aesthetic & Reconstructive Surgery said. "Most important," you can exercise a "choice"—although by that, the ad copy referred only to "your choice of physician."

53   From *Vogue* to *Time,* the media assisted the doctors, producing dozens of stories urging women to "invest," as a *Wall Street Journal* article put it, in breast expansion and liposuction. "Go curvy," *Mademoiselle* exhorted. "Add a bit above the waist"; it's easy and you can "go back to work in five days, and to aerobics in six weeks." "Attention, front and center!" the magazine demanded again, three issues later. "The lush bust is back"—and breast implants are the ideal way of "getting a boost." A feature in *Ladies' Home Journal* lauded three generations of women in one family who have "taken control" of their appearances by taking to the operating table: grandmother had a $5,000 face-lift, mother a $3,000 breast implant (after her husband admitted that the idea of big breasts "would indeed be exciting"), and daughter a $4,000 nose job. "I decided that feeling good about my body was worth the risk," the mother

explained. TV talk shows conducted contests for free cosmetic surgery; radio stations gave away breast implants as promotions. Even *Ms.* deemed plastic surgery a way of "reinventing" yourself—a strategy for women who "dare to take control of their lives."

54 Soon, the propaganda circle was complete: cosmetic surgeons clipped these articles and added them to their résumés and advertisements, as if media publicity were proof of their own professional excellence. "Dr. Gaynor is often called 'the King of Liposuction,'" an ad for dermatologist Dr. Alan Gaynor boasted. "He has appeared as a liposuction expert on TV dozens of times, as well as in *Time* magazine and the *Wall Street Journal,* and most local newspapers."

55 The campaign worked. By 1988, the cosmetic surgeons' caseload had more than doubled, to 750,000 annually. And that was counting only the doctors certified in plastic surgery; the total annual figure was estimated in excess of 1.5 million. More than two million women, or one in sixty, were sporting the $2,000 to $4,000 breast implants—making breast enlargement the most common cosmetic operation. More than a hundred thousand had undergone the $4,000-plus liposuction surgery, a procedure that was unknown a decade ago. (By 1987, the average plastic surgeon cleared a *profit* of $180,000 a year.) About 85 percent of the patients were women—and they weren't spoiled dowagers. A 1987 survey by a plastic surgery association found that about half their patients made less than $25,000 a year; these women took out loans and even mortgaged homes to pay the surgery bill.

56 Publicity, not breakthroughs in medical technology, had made all the difference. Plastic surgery was as dangerous as ever; in fact, the operations would become even riskier as the big profits lured droves of untrained practitioners from other specialties. In 1988, a congressional investigation turned up widespread charlatanry, ill-equipped facilities, major injuries, and even deaths from botched operations. Other studies found that at least 15 percent of cosmetic surgery caused hemorrhages, facial nerve damage, bad scars, or complications from anesthesia. Follow-up operations to correct mistakes filled a two-volume, 1,134-page reference manual, *The Unfortunate Result in Plastic Surgery.* Plastic surgeons were devoting as much as a quarter of their practices to correcting their colleagues' errors.

57 For breast implants, in at least 20 percent of the cases, repeat surgery was required to remedy the ensuing pain, infection, blood clots, or implant ruptures. A 1987 study in the *Annals of Plastic Surgery* reported that the implants failed as much as 50 percent of the time and had to be removed. In 1988, investigators at the FDA's Product Surveillance division found that the failure rate of breast implants was among the highest of any surgery-related procedure under their purview. But rather than take action, the FDA stopped monitoring failure rates altogether—because consulting doctors couldn't decide what constituted "failure."

58 Contracture of scar tissue around the implant, separation from the breast tissue, and painful hardening of the breasts occurred in one-third of women who had the operation. The medical literature reported that 75 percent of women had some degree of contracture, 20 percent of it severe. Implants also caused scarring, infection, skin necrosis, and blood clots. And if the implants ruptured, the leaking could cause

toxicity, lupus, rheumatoid arthritis, and autoimmune diseases such as scleroderma. The implants also could interfere with nursing, prevent cancer detection, and numb sensitivity. In 1989, a Florida woman died during breast enlargement surgery. While the cause, an overdose of anesthesia, was only indirectly related to the procedure, it's still fair to describe her as a backlash victim: a model with two children, she had the operation because the modeling agencies were demanding women with big breasts.

59   In 1982, the FDA declared breast implants "a potentially unreasonable risk of injury." Yet the federal agency did not pursue further research. And when a 1988 study by Dow Corning Corporation found that silicone gel implants caused cancer in more than 23 percent of rats tested, the FDA dismissed the findings. "The risk to humans, if it exists at all, would be low," FDA commissioner Dr. Frank Young said. Not until April 1991, after still more federal research linking foam-coated implants to cancer surfaced and after a congressional subcommittee intervened, did the FDA finally break down and give the implant manufacturers ninety days to demonstrate that their devices were safe or take them off the market. A nervous Bristol-Myers Squibb Co. wasted no time yanking its two brands from the shelves.

60   To these problems, the American Society of Plastic and Reconstructive Surgeons responded with a "position statement," written as a press release, which offered "reassurance to the nearly 94,000 women who undergo breast enlargement every year." Women with breast implants "are at no increased risk of delayed cancer diagnosis," the statement soothed, without offering any medical evidence to back its claim. It did, however, propose that "the real causes of late diagnosis are ignorance, complacency, neglect, and denial." In other words, the woman's fault.

61   The track record of liposuction, the scraping and vacuuming of fat deposits, was no better. Between 1984 and 1986, the number of liposuction operations rose 78 percent—but the procedure barely worked. Liposuction removed only one to two pounds of fat, had no mitigating effect on the unseemly "dimpling" effect of cellulite, and, in fact, often made it worse. The procedure also could produce permanent bagginess in the skin and edema, just two of the "variations from the ideal" that the plastic surgery society cataloged in its own report. Another "variation" on the list: "pain."

62   . . . By 1987, only five years after the fat-scraping technique was introduced in the United States, the plastic surgery society had counted eleven deaths from liposuction. A 1988 congressional subcommittee placed the death toll at twenty. And the figure is probably higher, because patients' families are often reluctant to report that the cause of death is this "vanity" procedure. . . .

63   . . . Surgeons also marketed the injection of liquid silicone straight into the face. *Vogue* described it this way: "Plastic surgery used to be a dramatic process, but new techniques now allow doctors to make smaller, sculptural facial changes." This "new" technique was actually an old practice that had been used by doctors in the last backlash era to expand breasts—and abandoned as too dangerous. It was no better the second time around; thousands of women who tried it developed severe facial pain, numbing, ulcerations, and hideous deformities. One Los Angeles plastic surgeon, Dr. Jack Startz, devastated the faces of hundreds of the two thousand women he injected with liquid silicone. He later committed suicide.

64   For the most part, these doctors were not operating on women who might actually benefit from plastic surgery. In fact, the number of reconstructive operations to aid burn victims and breast cancer patients declined in the late '80s. For many plastic surgeons, helping to boost women's self-esteem wasn't the main appeal of their profession. Despite the ads, the doctors were less interested in improving their patients' sense of "control" than they were in improving their own control over their patients. "To me," said plastic surgeon Kurt Wagner, who operated on his wife's physique nine times, "surgery is like being in the arena where decisions are made and no one can tell me what to do." Women under anesthesia don't talk back.

WRITING ASSIGNMENTS

Analysis

1. Explain how Faludi uses logic, organization, evidence, and tone to develop her thesis.
2. Trace the way that concern over profits, independent of a backlash motive or ideology, influences trends in the beauty industry.
3. How does Faludi explain the history of "Charlie" perfume?
4. According to Faludi, why are women's fears of aging easier to exploit than men's? Is she right?
5. Explain how race or class affect ideals of masculine or feminine looks. Provide examples.

Argument

1. Should the availability of cosmetic products and procedures be more strictly regulated? Explain and illustrate your answer.
2. Should the marketing and advertising of cosmetic products and procedures be more strictly regulated? Explain and illustrate your answer.
3. Recommend an appropriate health care policy toward elective or cosmetic plastic surgery. Consider such issues as insurance coverage, truth in advertising, consumer education, the cost of research, and the allocation of resources by medical schools (to train doctors) and by hospitals (of space).

Personal Writing and Writing from Research

1. Explain the effect that using or not using cosmetic products has had on your self-image. If relevant, trace changes in your attitude over time.
2. Analyze the effect that your using or not using cosmetic products has had on people close to you (e.g., family, friends, colleagues).
3. Describe your personal tastes in one or more beauty products designed for men or women, and analyze how advertising has shaped these tastes.
4. Trace the advertising strategy during the 1990s of a particular cosmetic product (e.g., perfume) or brand (e.g., Clinique) mentioned by Faludi. How does

the 1990s marketing of this product or specific line compare to its 1980s image?

5. Analyze and compare the gender-role messages contained in a sampling of advertisements for cosmetic products, electronic equipment, automobiles, or food and drink products.

6. *Collaborative Project:* Analyze the editorial and advertising content of a magazine with a primarily male or female readership in order to discover other elements of its readers' demographic profile (i.e., age, class, region, and race). In a research paper, assess the messages about gender roles that are part of the magazine's advertisements.

7. Analyze the gender-role messages of a television program, including its advertisements.

8. Analyze the gender images that underlie the advertising for a male cosmetic or clothing line.

9. Basing your position on library research and on interviews with people who have had cosmetic surgery, explain when and why you would—or would not—recommend cosmetic surgery to others or choose it for yourself.

Miss Clairol

Helena Maria Viramontes

Born in 1954 and raised in East Los Angeles in an extended working-class Chicana family that included nine children, Helena Maria Viramontes began writing fiction in 1975. Like other women writers of color, such as Alice Walker, Paule Marshall, and Maxine Hong Kingston, she credits her mother for her creative imagination. She often writes about the courage of women who live under oppressive conditions, because she wants "to do justice to their voices. To tell these women, in my own gentle way, that I will fight for them, that they provide me with my own source of humanity." "Miss Clairol" first appeared in 1980 and was published in *Chicana Creativity and Criticism: Charting New Frontiers in American Literature.*

Journal Topics: (1) Describe in detail your memories of the way an older female or male member of your family worked on her or his appearance prior to an important occasion. (2) How do your ideas about what is attractive differ from those of your same-sex parent? (3) Describe a specific time when you felt really pleased with your personal appearance; what contributed to this feeling?

As You Read: (1) In what ways is Champ like and unlike her mother, Arlene? (2) Do you think Champ will eventually imitate her mother? (3) Why is this date so important to Arlene?

Arlene and Champ walk to K-Mart. The store is full of bins mounted with bargain buys from T-shirts to rubber sandals. They go to aisle 23, Cosmetics. Arlene, wearing bell bottom jeans two sizes too small, can't bend down to the Miss Clairol boxes, asks Champ.

–Which one mamá–asks Champ, chewing her thumb nail.

–Shit, mija, I dunno.–Arlene smacks her gum, contemplating the decision.–Maybe I need a change, tú sabes. What do you think?–She holds up a few blond strands with black roots. Arlene has burned the softness of her hair with peroxide; her hair is stiff, breaks at the ends and she needs plenty of Aqua Net hairspray to tease and tame her ratted hair, then folds it back into a high lump behind her head. For the last few months she has been a platinum "Light Ash" blond, before that a Miss Clairol "Flame" redhead, before that Champ couldn't even identify the color—somewhere between orange and brown, a "Sun Bronze." The only way Champ knows her mother's true hair color is by her roots which, like death, inevitably rise to the truth.

–I hate it, tú sabes, when I can't decide.–Arlene is wearing a pink, strapless tube top. Her stomach spills over the hip hugger jeans. Spits the gum onto the floor.–Fuck it.–And Champ follows her to the rows of nailpolish, next to the Maybelline rack of make-up, across the false eyelashes that look like insects on display in clear, plastic boxes. Arlene pulls out a particular color of nailpolish, looks at the bottom of the bottle for the price, puts it back, gets another. She has a tattoo of purple XXX's on her left finger like a ring. She finally settles for a purple-blackish color, Ripe Plum, that Champ thinks looks like the color of Frankenstein's nails. She looks at her own stubby nails, chewed and gnawed.

5   Walking over to the eyeshadows, Arlene slowly slinks out another stick of gum from her back pocket, unwraps and crumbles the wrapper into a little ball, lets it drop on the floor. Smacks the gum.

–Grandpa Ham used to make chains with these gum wrappers–she says, toeing the wrapper on the floor with her rubber sandals, her toes dotted with old nailpolish.–He started one, tú sabes, that went from room to room. That was before he went nuts–she says, looking at the price of magenta eyeshadow.–Sabes que? What do you think?–lifting the eyeshadow to Champ.

–I dunno know–responds Champ, shrugging her shoulders the way she always does when she is listening to something else, her own heartbeat, what Gregorio said on the phone yesterday, shrugs her shoulders when Miss Smith says OFELIA, answer my question. She is too busy thinking of things people otherwise dismiss like parentheses, but sticks to her like gum, like a hole on a shirt, like a tattoo, and sometimes she wishes she weren't born with such adhesiveness. The chain went from room to room, round and round like a web, she remembers. That was before he went nuts.

–Champ. You listening? Or in lala land again?–Arlene has her arms akimbo on a fold of flesh, pissed.

–I said, I dunno know.–Champ whines back, still looking at the wrapper on the floor.

10   –Well you better learn, tú sabes, and fast too. Now think, will this color go good with Pancha's blue dress?–Pancha is Arlene's comadre. Since Arlene has a special

date tonight, she lent Arlene her royal blue dress that she keeps in a plastic bag at the end of her closet. The dress is made of chiffon, with satin-like material underlining, so that when Arlene first tried it on and strutted about, it crinkled sounds of elegance. The dress fits too tight. Her plump arms squeeze through, her hips breathe in and hold their breath, the seams do all they can to keep the body contained. But Arlene doesn't care as long as it sounds right.

–I think it will–Champ says, and Arlene is very pleased.

–Think so? So do I mija.–

They walk out the double doors and Champ never remembers her mother paying.

It is four in the afternoon, but already Arlene is preparing for the date. She scrubs the tub, Art Labo on the radio, drops crystals of Jean Nate into the running water, lemon scent rises with the steam. The bathroom door ajar, she removes her top and her breasts flop and sag, pushes her jeans down with some difficulty, kicks them off, and steps in the tub.

15   –Mija. MIJA–she yells.–Mija, give me a few bobby pins.–She is worried about her hair frizzing and so wants to pin it up.

Her mother's voice is faint because Champ is in the closet. There are piles of clothes on the floor, hangers thrown askew and tangled, shoes all piled up or thrown on the top shelf. Champ is looking for her mother's special dress. Pancha says every girl has one at the end of her closet.

–Goddamn it Champ.–

Amidst the dirty laundry, the black hole of the closet, she finds nothing.

–NOW–

20   –Alright, ALRIGHT. Cheeze amá, stop yelling–says Champ, and goes in the steamy bathroom, checks the drawers, hairbrushes jump out, rollers, strands of hair, rummages through bars of soap, combs, eyeshadows, finds nothing; pulls open another drawer, powder, empty bottles of oil, manicure scissors, kotex, dye instructions crinkled and botched, finally, a few bobby pins.

After Arlene pins up her hair, she asks Champ,–Sabes que? Should I wear my hair up? Do I look good with it up?–Champ is sitting on the toilet.

–Yea, amá, you look real pretty.–

–Thanks mija–says Arlene.–Sabes que? When you get older I'll show you how you can look just as pretty–and she puts her head back, relaxes, like the Calgon commercials.

Champ lays on her stomach, T.V. on to some variety show with pogo stick dancers dressed in outfits of stretchy material and glitter. She is wearing one of Gregorio's white T-shirts, the ones he washes and bleaches himself so that the whiteness is impeccable. It drapes over her deflated ten year old body like a dress. She is busy cutting out Miss Breck models from the stacks of old magazines Pancha found in the back of her mother's garage. Champ collects the array of honey colored haired women, puts them in a shoe box with all her other special things.

25   Arlene is in the bathroom, wrapped in a towel. She has painted her eyebrows so that the two are arched and even, penciled thin and high. The magenta shades her eyelids. The towel slips, reveals one nipple blind from a cigarette burn, a date to forget. She rewraps the towel, likes her reflection, turns to her profile for additional inspection. She feels good, turns up the radio to . . . your love. For your loveeeee, I will do anything, I will do anything, forrr your love. For your kiss . . .

     Champ looks on. From the open bathroom door, she can see Arlene, anticipation burning like a cigarette from her lips, sliding her shoulders to the ahhhh ahhhhh, and pouting her lips until the song ends. And Champ likes her mother that way.

     Arlene carefully stretches black eyeliner, like a fallen question mark, outlines each eye. The work is delicate, her hand trembles cautiously, stops the process to review the face with each line. Arlene the mirror is not Arlene the face who has worn too many relationships, gotten too little sleep. The last touch is the chalky, beige lipstick.

     By the time she is finished, her ashtray is full of cigarette butts, Champ's variety show is over, and Jackie Gleason's dancing girls come on to make kaleidoscope patterns with their long legs and arms. Gregorio is still not home, and Champ goes over to the window, checks the houses, the streets, corners, roams the sky with her eyes.

     Arlene sits on the toilet, stretches up her nylons, clips them to her girdle. She feels good thinking about the way he will unsnap her nylons, and she will unroll them slowly, point her toes when she does.

30   Champ opens a can of Campbell soup, finds a perfect pot in the middle of a stack of dishes, pulls it out to the threatening rumble of the tower. She washes it out, pours the contents of the red can, turns the knob. After it boils, she puts the pot on the sink for it to cool down. She searches for a spoon.

     Arlene is romantic. When Champ begins her period, she will tell her things that only women can know. She will tell her about the first time she made love with a boy, her awkwardness and shyness forcing them to go under the house, where the cool, refined soil made a soft mattress. How she closed her eyes and wondered what to expect, of how the penis was the softest skin she had ever felt against her, how it tickled her, searched for a place to connect. She was eleven and his name was Harry.

     She will not not tell Champ that her first fuck was a guy named Puppet who ejaculated prematurely, at the sight of her apricot vagina, so plump and fuzzy.–Pendejo–she said–you got it all over me.–She rubbed the gooey substance off her legs, her belly in disgust. Ran home to tell Rat and Pancha, her mouth open with laughter.

     Arlene powder puffs under her arms, between her breasts, tilts a bottle of *Love Cries* perfume and dabs behind her ears, neck and breasts for those tight caressing songs which permit them to grind their bodies together until she can feel a bulge in his pants and she knows she's in for the night.

     Jackie Gleason is a bartender in a saloon. He wears a black bow tie, a white apron, and is polishing a glass. Champ is watching him, sitting in the radius of the gray light, eating her soup from the pot.

35   Arlene is a romantic. She will dance until Pancha's dress turns a different color, dance until her hair becomes undone, her hips jiggering and quaking beneath a new

pair of hosiery, her mascara shadowing under her eyes from the perspiration of the ritual, dance spinning herself into Miss Clairol, and stopping only when it is time to return to the sewing factory, time to wait out the next date, time to change hair color. Time to remember or to forget.

Champ sees Arlene from the window. She can almost hear Arlene's nylons rubbing against one another, hear the crinkling sound of satin when she gets in the blue and white shark-finned Dodge. Champ yells goodbye. It all sounds so right to Arlene who is too busy cranking up the window to hear her daughter.

WRITING ASSIGNMENTS

Analysis

1. Explain how "Miss Clairol" ironically echoes the conventions of traditional fairy tales, "Cinderella" in particular. You may want to consult Lieberman's article in Chapter 4, " 'Some Day My Prince Will Come': Female Acculturation Through the Fairy Tale."
2. Why does Viramontes mention so many beauty products and identify many of them by brand name?
3. We are twice told that "Arlene is romantic" and "a romantic." What does this mean?
4. Using Sontag's categories, is beauty a "put-down or power source" in this story?
5. Explain the significance of the title.
6. How do Arlene's economic status and ethnicity help shape her attitudes and actions?
7. How does Champ's presence in the story influence the reader's response to Arlene?
8. Why are men mentioned but never seen or heard?
9. Explain the significance of Arlene's two versions of her first experience with sexual intercourse.
10. How has popular culture shaped Arlene's understanding of beauty and of the connection between beauty and romance?

Argument

1. Does the story criticize or sympathize with Arlene?
2. Is "Miss Clairol" a modern fairy tale? Does it have a happy ending?

Personal Writing and Writing from Research

1. Whether you are male or female, compare your memories of getting ready for a "big date" with Arlene's.
2. Rewrite "Miss Clairol" from the perspective of someone from a different socioeconomic, racial, or ethnic background.

The Female Body

John Updike

John Updike, born in 1932, is an amazingly prolific author who has written 16 novels—the most widely known being the *Rabbit* books—15 books of poetry, 21 short-story collections, 11 books of essays, and numerous occasional pieces. As one commentator notes, he has earned "virtually every American literary award, repeated bestseller-dom, and the near royal status of the American author-celebrity." Still, he has critics. As another commentator says, ". . . those who admire the work consider him one of the keepers of the language; those who don't say he writes beautifully about nothing very much."

In response, Updike says, "Everything can be as interesting as every other thing. An old milk carton is worth a rose. . . I like middles. It is in the middles that extremes clash, where ambiguity restlessly rules. . . . There's a 'yes-but' quality about my writing that evades entirely pleasing anybody."

His short essay "The Female Body" originally appeared in the *Michigan Quarterly Review* (1990) with the title "Venus and Others." It illustrates what some praise as his "lush and elegantly wrought style," a style which others find "overly lyrical, bloated." In it he probes a favorite theme, the pervasive, subversive power of sexuality.

Journal Topics: (1) Compare the way men regard the female body with the way women regard the male body. Do the two sexes view each other differently? (2) Write a description of either an idealized male or female body. (3) Is it possible for men and women to interact without awareness of each other's bodies? Is a sexual undercurrent necessarily, inevitably present?

As You Read: (1) What evidence does Updike present to show that "on this planet, the female body is the prime aesthetic object"? (2) According to Updike, does the beauty of the female body give women power? If so, what kind of power? (3) How does Updike explain the "paradoxical contradictoriness of male attitudes toward the female and her body"?

1   "Thy navel is like a round goblet, which wanteth not liquor," says the male voice in the Song of Solomon, "thy belly is like a heap of wheat set about with lilies. Thy two breasts are like two young roes that are twins." Robert Graves, in *Watch the Northwind Rise,* quotes a vernacular rendering of these verses which goes, "Your belly's like a heap of wheat,/ Your breasts like two young roes./ O come to bed with me, my

sweet,/ And take off all your clo'es!" A naked woman is, for most men, the most beautiful thing they will ever see. On this planet, the female body is the prime aesthetic object, re-created not only in statuary and painting but in the form of door knockers, nutcrackers, lamp stands, and caryatids. For the Victorians, it was everywhere, naked in brass, while their real women were swaddled and padded and reinforced like furniture; in this century, the female body haunts merchandising from top to bottom, from the silky epidermal feel of a soft cigarette pack to the rumpy curves of a Porsche. The female body is a masterpiece of market design, persuading the race to procreate generation after generation, extracting semen from mesmerized men with the ease of a pickpocket at a girlie show.

2   This captivating mechanism pays a price for its own complexity: cancer attacks breasts and ovaries, menstrual cramps and hysteria impair performance. Its season of bloom, of potential fertility, is shorter than that of the male body, though more piquant and powerful. Kafka, in a letter to Max Brod, unchivalrously remarked of women, "Not until summer does one really see their curious kind of flesh in quantities. It is soft flesh, retentive of a great deal of water, slightly puffy, and keeps its freshness only a few days." He goes on, with his scrupulous fairness: "Actually, of course, it stands up pretty well, but that is only proof of the brevity of human life." Just so, the actuarial longer-lastingness of the female body demonstrates the relative biological disposability of the male and the salubrious effects of lifelong exercise in the form of housework.

3   If the main social fact about the female body is its attractiveness, the main political fact is its weakness, compared with the male body. There may be some feminists ardent enough to dispute this, but the truth is elemental. As Elizabeth Hardwick, reviewing Simone de Beauvoir's *The Second Sex,* put it with admirable firmness, "Women are certainly physically inferior to men and if this were not the case the whole history of the world would be different. . . . Any woman who ever had her wrist twisted by a man recognizes a fact of nature as humbling as a cyclone to a frail tree branch." This fact lies behind many facts of feminine circumstances, such as the use of women as domestic drudges and beasts of burden in the world's fundamental economy, and the superior attentiveness and subtlety of women in the private maneuvers of advanced societies. "The fastidiousness of women," Stendhal wrote in *On Love,* "is the result of that perilous situation in which they find themselves placed so early, and of the necessity they are under of spending their lives among cruel and charming enemies."

4   This physical weakness and the cruelties that result are the truth but not all the truth, and from the standpoint of the species not even the main truth. An interesting thought-experiment, for an adult male, is to try to look at a prepubescent girl, one of ten or eleven, say, with the eyes again of a boy the same age. The relative weakness, the arresting curves, the female fastidiousness, are not yet in place, but the magic is—the siren song, the strange simultaneous call to be kind and to conquer, the swooning wish to place one's life *beside* this other. To be sure, cultural inducements to heterosexuality bombard us from infancy; but they fall, generally, upon terrifically receptive ground.

5   The female body is, in its ability to conceive and carry a fetus and to nurse an infant, our life's vehicle—it is the engine and the tracks. Male sexuality, then, returning to this primal source, drinks at the spring of being and enters the murky region, where up is down and death is life, of mythology. The paradoxical contradictoriness of male attitudes toward the female and her body—the impulses to exalt and debase, to serve and enslave, to injure and comfort, to reverence and mock—goes back to some point of origin where emotions are not yet differentiated and energy has no distinct direction. The sex act itself, from the male point of view, is a paradox, a transformation of his thrusts into pleasure, a poke in the gut that is gratefully received. Sadism and masochism naturally flirt on the edges of our, as Katherine Mansfield said, "profound and terrible . . . desire to establish contact."

6   And naturally modern women feel a personal impatience with being mythologized, with being envisioned (talk about hysteria!) as madonnas and whores, earth-mothers and vampires, helpless little girls and implacable dominatrices, and with male inability to see sex simply for what it is. What is it? A biological function and procedure, presumably, on a plane with eating and defecation, just as women are, properly regarded, equally entitled human beings and political entities with minds of their own. Well, men *have* been known, inadvertently, in lapses of distraction or satiety, to see the female body as just a body, very like their own, built for locomotion as well as procreation, an upright watery stalk temporarily withstanding, with its miraculous molecular chain reactions, the forces of gravity and entropy. It is a lucid but dispirited moment, seeing a nude woman as a kind of man, only smaller, lighter-framed, without a beard, but matching men tuft for tuft otherwise, and with bumps, soft swellings, unmale emphases stiffened with fat, softly swayed by gravity . . . a heap of wheat set about with lilies . . . those catenary curves, that curious, considerate absence . . . the moment of lucid vision passes.

7   In asking forgiveness of women for our mythologizing of their bodies, for being *unreal* about them, we can only appeal to their own sexuality, which is different but not basically different, perhaps, from our own. For women, too, there seems to be that tangle of supplication and possessiveness, that descent toward infantile undifferentiation, that omnipotent helplessness, that merger with the cosmic mother-warmth, that flushed pulse-quickened leap into overestimation, projection, general mix-up.

8   The Song of Solomon has two voices: there is a female extoller as well. She claims, "My beloved is white and ruddy, the chiefest among ten thousand. His head is as the most fine gold, his locks are bushy, and black as a raven. . . . His belly is as bright ivory overlaid with sapphires," etc. Can it be that the male body—its bulky shoulders, its narrow hips, its thick-veined feet and hands, its defenseless boneless belly above the one-eyed priapic oddity—may also loom as a glorious message from the deep? In Margaret Atwood's last novel, *Cat's Eye,* the heroine, in one of the many striking passages about growing up female and human, reflects upon the teenage boys she talks to on the telephone: "The serious part is their bodies. I sit in the hall with the cradled telephone, and what I hear is their bodies. I don't listen much to the words but to the silences, and in the silences these bodies recreate themselves, are created by me, take

form." Some of this is sexual, she reflects, and some is not. Some is purely visual: "The faces of the boys change so much, they soften, open up, they ache. The body is pure energy, solidified light." For male and female alike, the bodies of the other sex are messages signaling what we must do—they are glowing signifiers of our own necessities.

WRITING ASSIGNMENTS

Analysis

1. How does Updike explain and support his claim that, "On this planet, the female body is the prime aesthetic object"? Is his evidence convincing?
2. Are there cultures where the female body is not the prime aesthetic object? How can these cultural differences be explained?
3. If Updike is correct that men and women cannot avoid being aware of and obsessed by each other's bodies, what political, economic, and social consequences follow?
4. Compare Updike's comments on the female body to Susan Sontag's in "A Woman's Beauty: Put-Down or Power Source?" earlier in this chapter.
5. How does Updike's perspective explain the male and female behavior and attitudes described earlier in this chapter by Susan Faludi, Joan Jacobs Brumberg, or Helena Maria Viramontes?
6. How does advertising use the subliminal appeal of the female body to sell products?
7. What are the consequences of Updike's position for women's access to traditionally male fields?

Argument

1. Updike attempts to explain the "paradoxical contradictoriness of male attitudes toward the female and her body." Do you agree with him? If not, what are alternative explanations?
2. Do you agree with Updike that human sexuality makes it impossible for both men and women to avoid being obsessed with each other's bodies?
3. Are women's attitudes toward men's bodies the same as men's attitudes toward women's?

Personal Writing and Writing from Research

1. *Collaborative Project:* Do a cross-cultural comparison of the artistic depiction of the female body. You may want to draw your evidence from Western, Indian, Chinese, Native-American, or African art.
2. Drawing examples from different historical periods, compare several literary tributes to female beauty. How does the definition of female beauty change? What effects does female beauty have on the male viewer and on the women themselves?

SPORTS

Why Sports Is a Drag

Dave Barry

A Pulitzer Prize-winning journalist for the *Miami Herald,* humorist Dave Barry satirizes many aspects of contemporary American culture. His books include *Babies and Other Hazards of Sex* (1984), *Claw Your Way to the Top* (1986), *Homes and Other Black Holes* (1988), *Dave Barry Talks Back* (1992), *Dave Barry Does Japan* (1993), and *Dave Barry Is Not Making This Up* (1994). "Why Sports Is a Drag" was published in *Dave Barry's Greatest Hits* (1988).

Journal Topics: (1) Do men and women behave differently when they watch or play sports? If so, describe the differences. (2) Do men take sports more seriously than women? Why? (3) Who is your favorite male or female sports figure? Why?

As You Read: (1) Find five examples of exaggeration in Barry's essay and explain their effect on you as a reader and on the essay's tone. (2) Summarize the differences, according to Barry, between male and female attitudes toward sports. (3) How does Barry's account of his own attitude toward sports affect what he says about other men? (4) Does Barry really believe that "sports is a drag"?

1   Mankind's yearning to engage in sports is older than recorded history, dating back to the time, millions of years ago, when the first primitive man picked up a crude club and a round rock, tossed the rock into the air, and whomped the club into the sloping forehead of the first primitive umpire. What inner force drove this first athlete? Your guess is as good as mine. Better, probably, because you haven't had four beers. All I know is, whatever the reason, Mankind is still nuts about sports. As Howard Cosell, who may not be the most likable person in the world but is certainly one of the most obnoxious, put it: "In terms of Mankind and sports, blah blah blah blah the 1954 Brooklyn Dodgers."

2   Notice that Howard and I both use the term "Mankind." Womankind really isn't into sports in the same way. I realize things have changed since my high-school days, when sports were considered unfeminine and your average girls' gym class consisted of six girls in those gym outfits colored Digestive Enzyme Green running around waving field-hockey sticks and squealing, and 127 girls on the sidelines in civilian clothing, claiming it was That Time of the Month. I realize that today you have a number of top female athletes such as Martina Navratilova who can run like deer and bench-press Chevrolet pickup trucks. But to be brutally frank, women as a group have a long way to go before they reach the level of intensity and dedication to sports that enables men to be such incredible jerks about it.

3   If you don't believe me, go to your local racquetball club and observe the difference between the way men and women play. Where I play, the women tend to gather
on the court in groups of random sizes—sometimes three, sometimes five, as if it
were a Jane Fonda workout—and the way they play is, one of them will hit the ball at
the wall and the rest of them will admire the shot and compliment her quite sincerely, and then they all sort of relax, as if they're thinking, well, thank goodness
that's over with, and they always seem very surprised when the ball comes *back*. If
one of them has the presence of mind to take another swing, and if she actually hits
the ball, everybody is *very* complimentary. If she misses it, the others all tell her what
a *good* try she made, really, then they all laugh and act very relieved because they
know they have some time to talk before the ball comes bouncing off that darned *wall*
again.

4   Meanwhile, over in the next court, you will have two males wearing various knee
braces and wrist bands and special leatheroid racquetball gloves, hurling themselves
into the walls like musk oxen on Dexedrine, and after every single point one or both
them will yell "S—!" in the self-reproving tone of voice you might use if you had just
accidentally shot your grandmother. American men tend to take their sports seriously, much more seriously than they take family matters or Asia.

5   This is why it's usually a mistake for men and women to play on teams together. I
sometimes play in a coed slow-pitch softball league, where the rules say you have to
have two women on the field. The teams always have one of the women play catcher,
because in slow-pitch softball the batters hit just about every pitch, so it wouldn't really hurt you much if you had a deceased person at catcher. Our team usually puts the
other woman at second base, where the maximum possible number of males can get
there on short notice to help out in case of emergency. As far as I can tell, our second
basewoman is a pretty good baseball player, better than I am anyway, but there's no
way to know for sure because if the ball gets anywhere near her, a male comes barg-
ing over from, say, right field, to deal with it. She's been on the team for three seasons now, but the males still don't trust her. They know that if she had to choose
between catching a fly ball and saving an infant's life, deep in her soul, she would
probably elect to save the infant's life, without even considering whether there were
men on base.

6   This difference in attitude between men and women carries over to the area of
talking about sports, especially sporting events that took place long ago. Take the
1960 World Series. If we were to look at it objectively, we would have to agree that the
outcome of the 1960 World Series no longer matters. You could make a fairly strong
case that it didn't really matter in 1960. Women know this, which is why you almost
never hear them mention the 1960 World Series, whereas you take virtually any male
over age 35 and even if he can't remember which of his children has diabetes, he can
remember exactly how Pirates shortstop Bill Mazeroski hit the ninth-inning home
run that beat the Yankees, and he will take every available opportunity to discuss it at
length with other males.

7   See that? Out there in Readerland, you females just read right through that last
sentence, nodding in agreement, but you males leaped from your chairs and shouted:

"Mazeroski wasn't a SHORTSTOP! Mazeroski played SECOND BASE!" Every male in America has millions of perfectly good brain cells devoted to information like this. We can't help it. We have no perspective. I have a friend named Buzz, a successful businessman and the most rational person you ever want to meet, and the high point of his entire life is the time he got Stan Albeck, the coach of the New Jersey Nets, to look directly at him during a professional basketball game and make a very personal remark rhyming with "duck shoe." I should explain that Buzz and I have season tickets to the Philadelphia 76ers, so naturally we hate the Nets a great deal. It was a great honor when Albeck singled Buzz out of the crowd for recognition. The rest of us males congratulated Buzz as if he'd won the Nobel Prize for Physics.

8   It's silly, really, this male lack of perspective, and it can lead to unnecessary tragedy, such as soccer-riot deaths and the University of Texas. What is even more tragic is that women are losing perspective, too. Even as you read these words, women are writing vicious letters to the editor, expressing great fury at me for suggesting they don't take their racquetball seriously. Soon they will be droning on about the importance of relief pitching.

WRITING ASSIGNMENTS

Analysis

1. Explain how the humor of Barry's piece plays with masculine and feminine stereotypes.
2. Analyze the tone of "Why Sports Is a Drag." How does Barry's persona or role in the essay influence its tone?
3. What, if anything, is Barry really criticizing?

Argument

1. Does Barry's piece accept the validity of the masculine and feminine stereotypes that it invokes?
2. Barry claims, "Womankind really isn't into sports in the same way [as mankind]." Do you agree?

Personal Writing and Writing from Research

1. Compare your memories of the attitudes that male and female high-school students had toward sports with Barry's. Have times changed?
2. Compare Barry's work with that of other writers who also use humor to write about sports.
3. Write your own humorous essay about some aspect of sports.

Professional Football
An American Symbol and Ritual

W. Arens

A cultural anthropologist, "W." Arens has done fieldwork in Africa and has published articles in scholarly journals on ethnicity and change. As "Bill" Arens, he is an avid football fan. In this essay, he uses the tools of his discipline to probe football's cultural meanings. When a shorter version of this essay appeared in the sports pages of the *New York Times,* he received a number of letters raising serious allegations about his patriotism, intelligence, and masculinity.

Journal Topics: (1) Describe the rituals associated with a sport that you play or have played. (2) Do you think that a culture's games say something important about that culture? (3) What is your favorite spectator sport? Why? (4) Which sport do you think is most characteristically American? Why?

As You Read: (1) According to Arens, why is football the quintessential American sport? (2) Why does Arens say that a football game, admittedly violent, better "symbolizes the way in which our society carries out violence than does a sport [like boxing] that relies on naked individual force"? (3) Why is football an especially masculine sport? (4) What are the elements of ritual associated with a football game?

> O, you sir, you! Come you hither, sir. Who am I, sir?
>
> **OSWALD:** My lady's father.
>
> **LEAR:** 'My lady's father'! my lord's knave! you whoreson dog! you slave! you cur!
>
> **OSWALD:** I am none of these, my lord; I beseech your pardon.
>
> **LEAR:** Do you bandy looks with me, you rascal? [striking him.]
>
> **OSWALD:** I'll not be strucken, my lord.
>
> **KENT:** Nor trip'd neither, you base football player.
>
> *King Lear,* Act I, Scene 4

> A school without football is in danger of deteriorating into a medieval study hall.
>
> —Vince Lombardi

1   Attitudes toward football players have obviously changed since Shakespeare's time. Today the once "base football player" occupies the throne and rules the land. In fact, to have played too many games without a helmet seems to be a prerequisite for high office in our country. The prominent role football assumes in our society deserves comment. I would contend that although only a game, it has much to say about who and what we are as a people.

2   Although I am a professional anthropologist by training and have carried out fieldwork in another culture, this essay owes its impetus to the years I have sat in front of a television watching hundreds of football contests. Out of a feeling of guilt, I began to muse in a more academic fashion about this game and turned to the numerous books written by players and also to the rare anthropological accounts of sport in other societies. This has led me to believe that if an anthropologist from another planet visited here he would be struck by the American fixation on this game and would report on it with the glee and romantic intoxication anthropologists normally reserve for the exotic rituals of a newly discovered tribe. This assertion is based on the theory that certain significant symbols are the key to understanding a culture. It might be a dreadful thought, but nonetheless true, that if we understood the meaning of football we might better understand ourselves.

3   I emphasize a symbolic analysis because this game that intrigues us so much is engaged in by relatively few, but highly skilled individuals. Most of us at one time or another have played golf, tennis, basketball, softball, or even baseball, but only the "pros" play football. Touch football must be discounted because it lacks the essential ingredients of violent physical contact and complexity of game plan. The pleasure derived from football therefore is almost totally vicarious. This sport's images and messages satisfy our collective mind, not our individual bodies.

4   An appreciation of this argument requires an initial short detour in time to examine the evolution of this American sport from its European origins. The enshrined mythology states that the game was first played by a group of English soldiers who celebrated their victory over a Viking settlement by entering the losers' burial ground and using the skulls of the enemies' dead in a kicking match. Sometime later, an animal's inflated bladder was substituted for the skull, and the sport of "Dane's Head" became known as football. During the early Middle Ages, the game was a disorganized all-day competition between neighboring towns. The ball was placed midway between two villages and the object was to kick it along the countryside into the village and finally onto the green of the opposing community for a score. The game became so popular with the English peasantry that Henry II banned the pastime in the twelfth century because it interfered with the practice of archery. The sport was not reinstated until the seventeenth century, by which time the longbow had become an obsolete weapon.

5   According to Reisman and Denny (1969), who have charted the game's evolution, the kicking aspect remained dominant until 1823 when, as popular legend has it, a scoundrel named William Ellis, of Rugby School, "with a fine disregard for the rules of football, as played in his time, first took the ball in his arms and ran with it." This innovation on soccer was institutionalized at the school, and shortly thereafter was adopted by others; hence the name "rugby"—and the association of this sport in England with the educated elite.

6   Although both games were exported to America, only rugby was modified in the new setting. The claim has been made by the participants, and officially adopted by the National Collegiate Athletic Association, that the first intercollegiate game took place between Rutgers and Princeton in 1869. However, since that contest followed

soccer rules, the honor of having played the first game of what was to emerge as American football rightly should go to Harvard and McGill in 1874, when rugby regulations were the order of the day. In the remaining decades of the nineteenth century, the sport began to take on a more American form as a definite line of scrimmage and the center snap replaced the swaying "scrum" and "heal out" of English rugby. This meant that possession of the ball was now given to one team at a time. However, the introduction of the forward pass in the early years of this century signaled the most radical break with the past. These revisions on rugby resulted in greater structure and order, but at the same time more variety and flexibility, because running, kicking, and forward passing were incorporated as offensive maneuvers. Football had become an American game.

7   As a result of this process, football has emerged as an item of our cultural inventory that we share with no other country but Canada, where it is not nearly so popular. Does football's uniqueness and popularity say something essential about our culture? Rather than dismiss this question as trivial, we should be aware that we share our language, kinship system, religions, political and economic institutions, and a variety of other traits with many nations, but not our premier spectator sport. This is important when we consider that other societies have taken up baseball, a variation of cricket, and basketball, a homegrown product. Like English beer, the American brand of football is unexportable, even to the colonies. No one else can imagine what the natives see in it. On the other hand, soccer, the world's number one sport, has not been a popular success in America. In a peculiar social inversion, though, the educated and well-traveled American middle class has taken some interest in this sport of the European working classes. Nonetheless, football is uniquely American and little else can be included in this category.

8   Also, football, as compared to our language and many values, is not forced upon us. It is an optional aspect of our culture's inventions, which individuals choose to accept. Our society, like any other complex one, is divided by race, ethnicity, income, political affiliation, and regionalism. However, 79 percent of all the households in the country tuned in the first Super Bowl on TV, implying that the event cut through many of the divisive factors just mentioned. Personally, I can think of precious little else that I have in common with our former or current president, with a rural Texan, or an urban black other than a mutual passion for this game. Football represents not only "Middle America," as is so often claimed, but the whole of America. When we consider football, we are focusing on one of the few things we share with no one outside our borders, but do share with almost everyone within it.

9   The salient features of the game and of the society that created and nourishes it reflect some striking similarities. The sport combines the qualities of group coordination through a complex division of labor and minute specialization more than any other that comes to mind. Every sport exhibits these characteristics to an extent, but in football the process has surely reached the zenith. Every professional and major college team finds it necessary today to include a player whose only function is place kicking, and another for punting. Some have individuals whose sole responsibility is to center or hold the ball for the point after touchdown. Football is also a game in

which success now demands an extensive reliance on sophisticated electronic technology from telephones to computers while the match is in progress. In short, football, as opposed to its ancestor, rugby, epitomizes the spirit and form of contemporary American society.

10 Violence is another of our society's most apparent features. This quality of American life and its expression in football clearly accounts for some of the game's appeal. That football involves legitimate bodily contact and territorial incursion defines it as an aggressive sport par excellence. It is hardly surprising therefore that books by participants are replete with symbolic references to war. For example, Jerry Kramer, a Green Bay Packer during their glory years of the 1960s, divides his book, *Instant Replay,* into the following sections: Preliminary Skirmishes; Basic Training; Mock Warfare; Armed Combat; War's End. Frank Leahy, a former coach of Notre Dame and in his time a living symbol of America, wrote in his memoirs:

> . . . the Stars and Stripes have never taken second place on any battlefield. With this in mind, we ask you to think back and ask yourself where our young men developed the qualities that go to make up a good fighting man. . . . These traits are something that cannot be found in textbooks nor can they be learned in the lecture room. It is on the athletic fields that our boys acquire these winning ways that are as much a part of the American life as are freedom of speech and of the press (1949: 230).

11 Mike Holovak (1967), a former coach of the New England Patriots, waxed even more lyrical in reminiscing about his World War II military service. He refers to those years as the time he was on "the first team" in the "South Pacific playground" where the tracers arched out "like a long touchdown pass" and the artillery fired "orange blobs—just like a football."

12 To single out violence as the sole or even primary reason for the game's popularity is a tempting oversimplification. There are more violent sports available to us, such as boxing, which allows for an even greater display of legitimate blood spilling. Yet, boxing's popularity has waned over the last few decades. Its decline corresponds with the increased interest in professional football, in which aggression is acted out in a more tactical and sophisticated context. Football's violence is expressed within the framework of teamwork, specialization, mechanization, and variation, and this combination accounts for its appeal. A football contest more adequately symbolizes the way in which our society carries out violence than does a sport that relies on naked individual force. An explanation of football's popularity on the basis of violence alone also overlooks the fact that we are not unique in this respect. There have been many other violent nations, but they did not enshrine football as a national symbol.

13 Although the "national pastime" may not have suffered the same fate as boxing, interest in baseball has also ebbed. If my analysis of football is correct, then baseball is not in step with the times either. The action in baseball does not entail the degree of complexity, coordination, and specialization that now captures our fancy. I think this is what people mean when they say that baseball is boring. The recent introduction of the designated hitter and the occasional base-running specialist who never bats or fields are moves to inject specialization and heighten the game's appeal to

modern America. In essence, baseball belongs to another era, when life was a bit less complicated.

14   To return to our original interest, one final point must be made on the symbolism of football. Earlier I wrote that football represented the whole of America and overcame traditional differences in our society. However, the importance of the division between the sexes, which has more recently become part of our consciousness, was not mentioned. Football plays a part in representing this dichotomy in our society because it is a male preserve that manifests and symbolizes both the physical and cultural values of masculinity. Entrance into the arena of football competition depends on muscle power and speed possessed by very few males and beyond that of most females. Women can and have excelled in a variety of other sports, but football generally excludes them from participation. It was reported in a local newspaper that during a game between female teams the players' husbands appeared on the sidelines in women's clothes and wigs. The message was clear: if the women were going to act as men, then the men were going to transform themselves into women. These "rituals of rebellion" involving an inversion of sex roles have often been recorded by anthropologists. It is not surprising that this symbolic rebellion in our culture was aimed at a bastion of male supremacy.

15   If this argument seems farfetched, consider the extent to which the equipment accents the male physique. The donning of the required items results in an enlarged head and shoulders and a narrowed waist, with the lower torso poured into skin-tight trousers accented only by a metal cod-piece. The result is not an expression, but an exaggeration of maleness. Dressed in this manner, the players engage in handholding, hugging, and bottom patting, which would be ludicrous and disapproved in any other context. Yet, this is accepted on the gridiron without a second thought. Admittedly, there are good reasons for wearing the gear, but does that mean we must dismiss the symbolic significance of the visual impression? The game could just as easily be played without the major items, such as the helmet, shoulder pads, and cleats. They are as much offensive as defensive in function. Indeed, in comparison rugby players seem to manage quite well in the flimsiest of uniforms.

16   The preceding discussion puts us in a better position to ask the question hinted at earlier—are we in effect dealing with an American ritual of some meaning? The answer depends upon how ritual is defined. A broad anthropological view suggests that it is a standardized, repetitive activity carried out for the purpose of expressing and communicating basic cultural ideals and symbols. A ritual therefore does not necessarily imply communication with the supernatural. The inauguration of a president or the playing of the national anthem are common examples of nonreligious rituals in America. An objective evaluation of the problem also demands recognizing that an act can have a sacred and a secular character at the same time. Consequently, at one level, football can be viewed simply as a sport and at another level as a public ritual. Considering some of the players' activities from this perspective furnishes some interesting and supportive observations.

17   If we view the game as a ritual and therefore in some respects as a sacred activity, we would expect the participants to disengage themselves from the profane world of

everyday affairs. This is a common aspect of ritual behavior in any part of the world. Especially relevant for the participants is the avoidance of what anthropologists refer to as "pollution"—an impure ritual state—as the result of contact with contaminating acts or situations. Association with this profane realm renders a participant symbolically unfit to engage in a sacred performance.

18   In many rituals performed entirely for and by males, sexual contact with females must be avoided. Abstinence under these conditions is almost a cultural universal because the sexual act is an expression of man's animal or profane nature. In many a rite of passage for boys about to enter adulthood, the participants are taken out of the community, isolated from the opposite sex, and may not be seen by them. In other societies, prior to a significant activity such as the hunt or warfare, the community members are admonished to refrain from sexual behavior for fear of disastrous consequences. Is it really surprising then that in the world of sport, and with football in particular, sex before the event is viewed with suspicion? In this context I am reminded of Hoebel's (1960) statement that: "The Cheyenne feeling about male sexuality is that it is something to be husbanded and kept in reserve as a source of strength for the great crises of war." This compares well with the attitude at the virtually monastic world of football training camps. At these facilities all of the players, including those married, are sequestered together during practice days. They are allowed to visit their wives, who must be living off the grounds, on Saturday night only, since there is no practice on Sunday. As is to be expected they must return to the all-male atmosphere on Sunday evening in consideration of Monday's activities. The result is that sex and football, the profane and the sacred, are segregated in time and space. During the season a variation of the procedure prevails. The players and staff spend Saturday night together since the contest takes place on Sunday. In each instance there is a clear-cut attempt to avoid the symbolic danger of contact with females prior to the event.

19   This was impressed on me when I traveled with my university's team by chartered bus to a game to be played at the opponent's field. Since there were a few unoccupied seats, two of the players asked the coach if their girlfriends could ride along. He said in all seriousness that they could not ride to the game with us, but that they could join us on the bus on the way home. A writer who spent the season with the Rice University football squad mentioned a similar instance (Tippette, 1973). When the team bus pulled up in front of the dormitory where they would spend the night on the opponent's campus, a number of the girls from the college entered the vehicle and began to flirt with the players. The Rice coach, who was in an accompanying car, stormed onto the bus and ordered the girls off immediately. He then told the players that they should have known better, since the incident was a dirty trick instigated by their foe. Dirty trick or not, somebody planned the exercise, well aware of the unsettling effect that it would have on the team.

20   One further example is from the professional arena. Describing the night before the first Super Bowl, when the Green Bay Packers were allowed to bring along their wives as a reward for championship play, Jerry Kramer wrote: "My wife's been here for the past few days, and so has Chandler's. Tonight we're putting the girls in one

room, and Danny and I are sharing one. It's better for the girls to be away from us tonight. We're always grumpy and grouchy before a game" (1968).

21   There are, of course, some perfectly reasonable arguments for segregating the players prior to a game. For one, the coaches argue that they are assured that the team members get an undistracted night's sleep. Thus it is assumed that the players will be better able to concentrate on the upcoming event. At the same time, when these vignettes are considered, the theme of possible pollution through contact with females is not altogether absent. In any event, the inhibition of sexual activity prior to an athletic event has no apparent scientific rationale. The latest position based on research argues that sex is actually beneficial, since it induces a more restful night's sleep.

22   The *New York Times* recently reported that a British physician who has advised and interviewed his country's Olympic competitors mentioned that one informant admitted setting the world record in a middle distance track event an hour after sexual intercourse. Another confessed that he ran the mile in less than four minutes an hour and a half after the same activity. One must look beyond rationality for an explanation of the negative attitude toward sex on the part of the elders who control professional football. However, if we grant that the sport involves a significant ritual element, then the idea does make some sense. From this standpoint scientific reasoning is not relevant.

23   Accounts of rituals in other cultures also indicate the prevalent belief in symbolic contamination through contact with illness or physical imperfection. Examples of this sort of avoidance also crop up in football. Players report that those who become sick to their stomachs in the summer heat of training camp are avoided and become the objects of ridicule. In a similar vein, participants are rightfully admonished to stay away from an injured player so that the trainer can attend to him. However, they do not appear to need the advice since after a momentary glance they studiously avoid a downed colleague. Injured, inactive players on the team I was associated with as faculty sponsor were not allowed to mingle with the active participants during the game. The loquacious professional Jerry Kramer also writes that when he was hurt and disabled, he felt like an "outsider," "isolated" and "separated" from the rest of the group. Others have written that they were ignored during these times by their teammates and coaches. I do not want to push this argument too far because there are many sound reasons to explain this patterned reaction. At the same time, I can think of similar arguments for the behavior of people in other cultures after having come into contact with illness or death.

24   Eating is another profane act, since it is a further indication of our animal nature. As in every society, contact with certain foods renders an individual unfit to participate in rituals. However, in contrast to sexuality and physical imperfection, nourishment cannot be avoided for any length of time. Instead, under controlled conditions, the act of eating is incorporated into the ritual, and the food becomes charged with a sacred character. Consequently, not just any type of food is acceptable, but only specified types with symbolic significance may be ingested by ritual participants. What would be more appropriate in our society than males eating beef prior to the great

event? Imagine the scorn that would be heaped upon a team if it were known that they prepared themselves for the competition by eating chicken.

25   The problem with a purely functional interpretation is that this meat, which, it is believed, must be eaten on the day of the competition, is not converted into potential energy until hours after the game has ended. Although the players must appear for this meal because it is part of the ritual, actually very few eat what is presented to them. Instead, in contradiction to the ritual experts, the participants prefer a high-energy snack, such as a pill, which they realize has more immediate value. Nevertheless, those who control the players' behavior, as in the other instances, adhere to a less functional course by forcing their charges to confront a meaningful symbolic substance. If this situation were presented to an anthropologist in the heart of the Amazon, I wonder how long it would take to suggest ritual cannibalism on the part of the natives.

26   I have tried to make it clear that I am well aware that there are a number of secular, functional explanations for the behavior that has been described. However, it bears repeating that a ritual has a variety of levels, components and consequences. The slaughter of a white bull during a rite of passage for males among cattle-keeping people in Africa has an obvious nutritional benefit for those who consume it. At the same time, though, this does not obviate the ritual significance of the act. If I am making too much of the symbolic element of American football, then perhaps we ought to reconsider the ease with which we accept this type of analysis for other supposedly simpler cultures. Accounts of team log racing among the Shavante Indians of Brazil as an attempt to restore harmony to a social order beset by political divisions (Maybury-Lewis, 1967) and the analysis of cock fighting in Bali (Geertz, 1972) as an expression of national character, have caused little stir. Unless we consider ourselves something special, our own society is equally suited to such anthropological studies. It is reasonable that if other people express their basic cultural themes in symbolic rituals, then we are likely to do the same.

References

Geertz, Clifford, 1972, "Deep Play: Notes on a Balinese Cockfight." *Daedalus.* Winter.

Hoebel, E. Adamson, 1960, *The Cheyenne.* New York: Holt, Rinehart and Winston.

Holovak, Mike, 1967, *Violence Every Sunday.* New York: Coward-McCann.

Kramer, Jerry, 1968, *Instant Replay.* New York and Cleveland: World Publishing Company.

Leahy, Frank, 1949, *Notre Dame Football.* New York: Prentice-Hall.

Maybury-Lewis, David, 1967, *Akwe-shavante Society.* Oxford: Clarendon Press.

Reisman, David and Denny, Reuel, 1969, "Football in America: A Study in Cultural Diffusion." In J. W. Lory, Jr. and G. S. Kenyon, eds., *Sport, Culture and Society.* New York: Macmillan.

Tippette, Giles, 1973, *Saturday's Children.* New York: Macmillan.

WRITING ASSIGNMENTS

Analysis

1. How has modern technology influenced the experience of playing and watching football?
2. As Arens notes, the worlds of sports, business, and war borrow each other's language and concepts. Find additional examples of this borrowing, and analyze its significance.
3. Arens claims that football represents "the whole of America." To what extent does this "whole" include women?

Argument

1. Explain why you agree or disagree with Arens's characterization of football as the quintessential American sport.
2. Arens claims that, "Football plays a part in representing this dichotomy [between the sexes] in our society because it is a male preserve that manifests and symbolizes both the physical and cultural values of masculinity." Do you agree?

Personal Writing and Writing from Research

1. Following Arens's model, analyze another sport. Include its history, its essential characteristics, its role in contemporary culture, and its rituals.
2. Analyze the cultural meanings of the beauty pageant. How might the beauty pageant's symbolic value for American femininity be compared to football's symbolic value for American masculinity?
3. Define the elements and analyze the significance of another secular American ritual such as the prom, a graduation exercise, a political convention, a presidential inauguration, a parade, the World Series, or the Academy Awards.

No Pain, No Game

Mark Kram

Mark Kram was a minor league ballplayer before becoming a sportswriter. He wrote for the *Baltimore Sun* before becoming a senior sportswriter for *Sports Illustrated*. Currently he is a screenwriter and a contributing editor to *Esquire*, where this profile was published in 1992. Sports commentator Frank Deford says of "No Pain, No Game" that Kram's "fascination with the brutality that men do to their fellows in the name of sport has never seemed more eloquently put than in this piece on football violence." He has also written memorably about boxing.

Journal Topics: (1) Do you believe that professional sports, particularly football, are too violent? (2) Does the public want football, or other sports, to be violent? (3) If you were ever injured playing a contact sport or another sport, describe how you dealt with the injury and how your coach, peers, and others expected you to deal with it.

As You Read: (1) How does the opening paragraph set up the rest of the article? (2) Identify the uses of drugs, according to Kram and Joey Browner, in contemporary football. (3) List both Kram's and Browner's uses of animal imagery, and explain their effect. (4) Why does Browner continue to play?

Observe, please, the human skeleton, 208 bones perfectly wrought and arranged; the feet built on blocks, the shinbones like a Doric column. Imagine an engineer being told to come up with the vertebral column from scratch. After years, he might produce a primitive facsimile, only to hear the utterly mad suggestion: Okay, now lay a nerve cord of a million wires through the column, immune to injury from *any* movement. Everywhere the eye goes over the skeleton, there is a new composition: the voluting Ionic thigh, Corinthian capitals, Gothic buttresses, baroque portals. While high above, the skull roof arches like the cupola of a Renaissance cathedral, the repository of a brain that has taken all this frozen music to the bottom of the ocean, to the moon, and to a pro football field—the most antithetical place on earth for the aesthetic appreciation of 208 bones.

After nine years in the NFL, Joey Browner of the Vikings is a scholar of the terrain and a rapt listener to the skeleton, the latter being rather noisy right now and animated in his mind. It is Monday morning, and all over the land the bill is being presented to some large, tough men for playing so fearlessly with the equation of mass times velocity; only the backup quarterback bullets out of bed on recovery day. The rest will gimp, hobble, or crawl to the bathroom, where contusions are counted like scattered coins, and broken noses, ballooned with mucus and blood, feel like massive ice floes. Browner unpacks each leg from the bed as if they were rare glassware, then stands up. The feet and calves throb from the turf. The precious knees have no complaint. The thigh is still properly Ionic. The vertebral column whimpers for a moment. Not a bad Monday, he figures, until he tries to raise his right arm.

The bathroom mirror tells him it's still of a piece. It's partially numb, the hand is hard to close, and the upper arm feels as if it's been set upon by the tiny teeth of small fish. Pain is a personal insult—and not good for business; he knows the politics of injury in the NFL. Annoyed, his mind caroms through the fog of plays from the day before, finally stops on a helmet, sunlit and scratched, a blur with a wicked angle that ripped into his upper arm like a piece of space junk in orbit. He rubs *dipjajong*—an Oriental balm—on the point of impact, dresses slowly, then slides into an expensive massage chair as he begins to decompress to a background tape of Chopin nocturnes, quieting and ruminative, perfect for firing off Zen bolts of self-healing concentration to his arm.

By the next morning, after re-creating his Monday damage probe, he appears more worried about his garden of collard greens and flower bed of perennials; given the shape of his arm, most of hypochondriacal America would now be envisioning amputation. That is what Browner would like to do, so eager is he to conceal the injury, so confident is he that he could play with one and a half arms. At six-three, 230 pounds, he is a diligent smasher of cupolas, who has made more than one thousand tackles in his career. He is the first $1 million safety in NFL history; a six-time All-Pro; and a two-time conscriptee to the all-Madden team, an honor given out to those who have no aversion to dirt, blood, and freeway collision.

5   His only peer is Ronnie Lott, with whom he played at USC. Lott put the safety position on the map, invested it with identity, separated it from the slugging linebackers and the butterfly cornerbacks. It is the new glamour position in the NFL, due in part to CBS's John Madden, a joyful and precise bone counter who always knows where the wreckage will lie. With schedule parity, the outlawing of the spear, the clothesline, and the chop block, with excessive holding, and so many tinkerings to increase scoring, pro football veered toward the static on TV. Madden, it's clear, wanted to bring some good old whomp back to the game, and he found his men in players like Lott and Browner. Now the cameras are sensitive to the work of safeties, the blackjacks of the defensive secondary.

Of all hitters, they have the best of it: time and space for fierce acceleration, usually brutal angles, and wide receivers who come to them like scraps of meat being tossed into a kennel. Lott delineates their predatory zest in his book, *Total Impact,* saying that during a hit, "my eyes close, roll back into my head . . . snot sprays out of my nostrils, covering my mouth and cheeks." His ears ring, his brain goes blank, and he gasps for air. He goes on to broaden the picture: "If you want to find out if you can handle being hit by Ronnie Lott, here's what you do. Grab a football, throw it in the air, and have your best friend belt you with a baseball bat. No shoulder pads. No helmet. Just you, your best friend, and the biggest Louisville Slugger you can find."

Like medical students, pro players do not often dwell on the reality of the vivisection room, so Lott is an exception, a brilliant emoter with a legitimate portfolio, but still a man who has a lot of pages to fill with body parts and brute-man evocations. Browner has no marquee to live up to—except on the field. He is a star, though not easily accessible in media-tranquil Minnesota, distant from the hype apparatus on both coasts, part of a team that always seems to avoid the glory portioned to it annually in preseason forecasts.

Tuesdays are black days at a losing team's quarters, soft on the body and miserable for the mind. It is the day when coaches slap cassettes of failure into machines, vanish, then emerge with performances graded, carefully selecting their scapegoats. Good humor is bankrupt. On this Tuesday, Viking coach Jerry Burns looks much like Livia in *I, Claudius,* who in so many words scorches her gladiators, saying: "There will be plenty of money for the living and a decent burial for the dead. But if you let me down again, I'll break you, I'll send the lot of you to the mines of New Media." Browner smiles at the notion. "That's it—pro football," he says. "You don't need me."

"No tears like Lott?" he is asked.

10   "No tears," he says. "I guess I don't have much of a waterworks."

"No snot?"

He laughs: "He must have some nose."

"What's total impact?"

"Like a train speeding up your spinal cord and coming out your ear. When it's bad."

15   "When it's good?"

"When you're the train. Going through 'em and then coming out and feeling like all their organs are hanging off the engine."

"You need rage for that?"

"Oh, yeah," he says. "The real kind. No chemicals."

"Chemicals? Like amphetamines?"

20   "Well, I don't know that," he says, shifting in his chair. "Just let's say that you can run into some abnormal folks out there. I keep an eye on the droolers."

"Your rage, then?"

"From pure hitting," he says. "Controlled by years of Zen study. I'm like the sun and storm, which moves through bamboo. Hollow on the inside, hard and bright on the outside. Dumb rage chains you up. But I got a lot of bad sky if I gotta go with a moment."

"Ever make the perfect hit?"

"I've been looking for it for years."

25   "What would it feel like?"

"It would *feel* like you've launched a wide receiver so far he's splashed and blinkin' like a number on the scoreboard. That's what you're after mostly."

"Sounds terrible."

"It's the game," he says, coolly. "If you can't go to stud anymore, you're gone."

"I get the picture."

30   "How can you?" he asks, with a tight grin. "You'd have to put on the gear for the real picture."

There is no dramaturgy with Browner, just a monotone voice, a somnolent gaze that seems uninterested in cheerful coexistence. Or, perhaps, he is a model of stately calm. His natural bent is to listen. He does come close to the psychological sketch work of Dr. Arnold Mandell, a psychiatrist with the San Diego Chargers some years back who visited the dark corners of a football player's mind. Now in Florida, Mandell says: "Take quarterbacks: two dominant types who succeed—the arrogant limit-testers and the hyperreligious with the calm of a believer. Wide receivers: quite interested in their own welfare; they strive for elegance, being pretty, the stuff of actors. Defensive backs: very smart, given to loneliness, alienation; they hate structure, destroy without conscience, especially safeties."

Is that right? "I don't know," says Joey. "But it's not good for business if you care for a second whether blood is bubbling out of a guy's mouth." Highlighted by cornices of high bone, his eyes are cold and pale, like those of a leopard, an animal whose biomechanics he has studied and will often watch in wildlife films before a game. An all-purpose predator with a quick pounce, no wasted motion, the leopard can go up a tree for a monkey ("just like going up for a wide receiver") or move out from behind a bush with a brutal rush of energy ("just what you need for those warthog running backs"). The mind tries for the image of him moving like a projectile, so massive and quick, hurling into muscle and bone. . . .

Browner offers to bring you closer to the moment of impact. He puts some tape into the machine and turns off the lights. The figures up on the screen are black and white, flying about like bats in a silent, horrific dream. Suddenly, there is Christian Okoye, of the Chiefs, six-one, 260 pounds, a frightful excrescence from the gene pool, rocketing into the secondary, with Joey meeting him point blank—and then wobbling off of him like a blown tire. "*Boooom!*" he says. "A head full of flies. For me. I learned. You don't hit Okoye. He hits you. You have to put a meltdown on him. First the upper body, then slide to the waist, then down to the legs—and pray for the cavalry." Another snapshot, a wide receiver climbing for the ball, with Browner firing toward him. "*Whaaack!*" he says. "There goes his helmet. There goes the ball. And his heart. Sometimes. You hope." The receiver sprawls on the ground, his legs kicking. Browner looks down at him. Without taunting or joy, more like a man admiring a fresco. "I'm looking at his eye dilating," he says. "Just looking at the artwork. The trouble is, on the next play I could be the painting." . . .

". . . The film seems eerie without sound."

35   "That's how it is out there. You don't hear. You're in another zone."

"So why not pad helmets? That's been suggested by some critics."

"Are you kidding?" he says. "Sound sells in the living rooms. Puts backsides in BarcaLoungers for hours. The sound of violence, man. Without it, the NFL would be a Japanese tea ceremony."

The sound, though, is just the aural rumor of conflict, much like the echo of considerable ram horn after a territorial sorting-out high up in the mountain rocks. NFL Films, the official conveyer of sensory tease, tries mightily to bottle the ingredient, catching the thwack of ricocheting helmets, the seismic crash of plastic pads, and every reaction to pain from gasp to groan. Network coverage has to settle for what enters the living room as a strangulated muffle. But in the end, the sound becomes commonplace, with the hardcore voyeur, rapidly inured in these times, wondering: *What is it really like down there?* It has the same dulling result as special effects in movies; more is never enough, and he knows there is *more*. Like Browner says: "Whatever a fan thinks he's seeing or hearing has to be multiplied a hundred times—and they should imagine themselves in the middle of all this with an injury that would keep them home from work in real life for a couple of weeks."

What they are not seeing, hearing—and feeling—is the hitting and acceleration of 250-pound packages: kinetic energy, result of the mass times speed equation. "Kinetic energy," says Mandell, "is the force that dents cars on collision." He recalls the first hit he ever saw on the sidelines with the Chargers. "My nervous system," he says, "never really recovered until close to the end of the game. The running back was down on his back. His mouth was twitching. His eyes were closed. Our linebacker was down, too, holding his shoulder and whimpering quietly. I asked him at halftime what the hit felt like. He said: 'It felt warm all over.'"...

40   ... It is Pete Gent's suspicion (the ex-Cowboy and author of *North Dallas Forty*) that the NFL intruded heavily on descriptions of violence, as it has with the more killer-ape philosophies of certain coaches. If so, it is a censorship of nicety, an NFL public relations device to obscure its primary gravity—choreographed violence.

But claw and tooth are fast gaining in the language in the booth, as if the networks are saying, Well, for all these millions, why should we struggle with euphemism during a head sapping? Incapable of delicate evasion, John Madden was the pioneer. Ever since, the veld has grown louder in decibel and candid depiction. Thus, we now have Dan Dierdorf on *Monday Night Football,* part troll, part Enrico Fermi of line play and Mother Teresa during the interlude of injury (caring isn't out—not yet). There's Joe Theismann of ESPN—few better with physicality, especially with the root-canal work done on quarterbacks. Even the benignity of Frank Gifford seems on the verge of collapse. He blurted recently: "People have to understand today it's a violent, vicious game." All that remains to complete the push toward veracity is the addition of Mike Ditka to the corps. He said in a recent interview: "I love to see people hit people. Fair, square, within the rules of the game. If people don't like it, they shouldn't watch."

Big Mike seems to be playing fast and loose with TV ratings—the grenade on the head of the pin. Or is he? He's not all *Homo erectus,* he knows the show biz fastened heavily to the dreadful physics of the game. "Violence is what the NFL sells," Jon Morris of the Bears, a fifteen-year veteran, once said. "They say they don't, but they do." The NFL hates the V-word; socially, it's a hot button more than ever. Like drugs, violence carries with it the threat of reform from explainers who dog the content of movies and TV for sources as to why we are nearly the most violent society on earth. Pete Rozelle was quick to respond when John Underwood wrote a superb series in *Sports Illustrated* on NFL brutality a decade back. He condemned the series, calling it irresponsible, though some wits thought he did so only because Underwood explored the possibility of padding helmets.

Admittedly, it is not easy to control a game that is inherently destructive to the body. Tip the rules to the defense, and you have nothing more than gang war; move them too far toward the offense, and you have mostly conflict without resistance. Part of the NFL dilemma is in its struggle between illusion and reality; it wants to stir the blood without you really absorbing that it is blood. It also luxuriates in its image of the American war game, strives to be the perfect metaphor for Clausewitz's ponderings about real war tactics (circa 1819, i.e., stint on blood and you lose). The warrior ethic is central to the game, and no coach or player can succeed without astute attention to the precise fashioning of a warrior mentality (loss of self), defined by Ernie Barnes, formerly of the Colts and Chargers, as "the aggressive nature that knows no safety zones."

Whatever normal is, sustaining that degree of pure aggression for sixteen, seventeen Sundays each season (military officers will tell you it's not attainable regularly in real combat) can't be part of it. "It's a war in every sense of the word," wrote Jack

Tatum of the Raiders in *They Call Me Assassin*. Tatum, maybe the preeminent hitter of all time, broke the neck of receiver Darryl Stingley, putting him in a wheelchair for life; by most opinions, it was a legal hit. He elaborated: "Those hours before a game are lonely and tough. I think about, even fear, what can happen." If a merciless intimidator like Tatum could have fear about himself and others, it becomes plain that before each game players must find a room down a dark and distant hall not reachable by ordinary minds.

45   So how do they get there, free from fear for body and performance? "When I went to the Colts," says Barnes, "and saw giant stars like Gino Marchetti and Big Daddy Lipscomb throwing up before a game, I knew this was serious shit, and I had to get where they were living in their heads." Job security, more money, and artificial vendettas flamed by coaches and the press can help to a limited point. So can acute memory selection, the combing of the mind for enraging moments. With the Lions, Alex Karras took the memory of his father dying and leaving the family poor; the anger of his having to choose football over drama school because of money kept him sufficiently lethal. If there is no moment, one has to be imagined. "I had to think of stuff," said Jean Fugett of the Cowboys. The guy opposite him had to become the man who "raped my mother."

But for years, the most effective path to the room was the use of amphetamines. Hardly a book by an ex-player can be opened without finding talk about speed. Fran Tarkenton cites the use of "all sorts" of uppers, especially by defensive linemen seeking "the final plateau of endurance and competitive zeal." Johnny Sample of the Jets said they ate them "like candy." Tom Bass even wrote a poem about "the man" (speed), a crutch he depended on more than his playbook. Dave Meggysey observed that the "violent and brutal" player on television is merely "a synthetic product." Bernie Parrish of the Browns outlined how he was up to fifteen five-milligram tablets before each game, "in the never-ending search for the magic elixir." The NFL evaded reality, just as it would do with the proliferation of cocaine and steroids in the eighties.

The authority on speed and pro football is Dr. Mandell, an internationally respected psychiatrist when he broke the silence. He joined the Chargers at the behest of owner Gene Klein and found a netherland of drugs, mainly speed. One player told him "the difference between a star and a superstar was a superdose." Mandell tried to wean the players off speed and to circumvent the use of dangerous street product. He began by counseling and prescribing slowly diminishing doses, the way you handle most habits. When the NFL found out, it banned him from the Chargers. Mandell went public with his findings, telling of widespread drug use, of how he had proposed urine tests and was rebuffed. The NFL went after his license, he says, and the upshot was that after a fifteen-day hearing—with Dr. Jonas Salk as one of his character witnesses—he was put on five-year probation; he resigned his post at the University of California–San Diego, where he had helped set up the medical school.

"Large doses of amphetamines," he says now, "induce prepsychotic paranoid rage."

"What's that mean?" he is asked.

50   "The killer of presidents," he says.

"How would this show up on the field?"

"One long temper tantrum," he says. "Late hits, kicks to the body and head, overkill mauling of the quarterback."

"How about before a game?"

"Aberrant behavior. When I first got up close in a dressing room, it was like being in another world. Lockers being torn apart. Players staring catatonically into mirrors. I was afraid to go to the center of the room for fear of bumping one of them."

55 "Is speed still in use?"

"I don't know," he says. "I'd be surprised if it wasn't, especially among older players who have seen and heard it all and find it hard to get it up. Speed opened the door for cocaine. After speed, cocaine mellows you down." He pauses, says thoughtfully: "The game exacts a terrible toll on players."

Joey Browner is asked: "At what age would you take your pension?"

"At forty-five," he says.

"The earliest age, right?

60 "Yeah."

"Should the NFL fund a longevity study for players?"

"Certainly."

"Are they interested in the well-being of players? Long term or short term?"

"Short term."

65 "Any physical disabilities?"

"Can't write a long time with my right hand. This finger here [forefinger] can't go back. It goes numb."

"How hard will the transition be from football?"

"I'll miss the hitting," he says.

"If someone told you that you might be losing ten to twenty years on your life, would you do it again?"

70 "Wouldn't think twice. It's a powerful thing in me."

"They say an NFL player of seven years takes 130,000 full-speed hits. Sound right?"

"Easy. And I remember every one."

Browner was answering modified questions put to 440 ex-players during a 1988 *Los Angeles Times* survey. Seventy-eight percent of the players said they had disabilities, 60 percent said the NFL was not interested in their well-being, and 78 percent wanted a longevity study. Browner was with the majority on each question. What jolted the most was that pro football players (66 percent of them) seem to be certain they are dying before their time, and that 55 percent would play again, regardless. The early death rate has long been a whisper, without scientific foundation. "We're now trying to get to the bottom of this idea," says Dr. Sherry Baron, who recently began a study for the National Institute for Occupational Safety and Health. "From the replies we get, a lot of players are nervous out there."

The Jobs Rated Almanac seemed to put the NFL player near the coal miner when it ranked 250 occupations for work environment. Judged on stress, outlook, physical demands, security, and income, the NFL player rose out of the bottom ten only in income. With good reason. . . . Pete Gent says: "I went to an orthopedic surgeon, and he told me I had the skeleton of a seventy-year-old man."

75   Pro football players will do anything to keep taking the next step. As it is noted in Ecclesiastes, *There is a season*—one time, baby. To that end, they will balloon up or sharpen bodies to murderous specification (steroids), and few are the ones who will resist the Novocain and the long needles of muscle-freeing, tissue-rotting cortisone. Whatever it takes to keep the life. A recent report from Ball State University reveals the brevity and psychic pain: One out of three players leaves because of injury; 40 percent have financial difficulties, and one of three is divorced within six months; many remember the anxiety of career separation setting in within hours of knowing it was over.

. . . On Saturday, Joey Browner begins to feel the gathering sound of Sunday, bloody Sunday. He goes to his dojo for his work on *iaido,* an art of Japanese swordsmanship—not like karate, just exact, ceremonial patterns of cutting designed to put the mind out there on the dangerous edge of things. He can't work the long katana now because, after thirty needles in his arm a couple of days before, it was found that he had nerve damage. So, wearing a robe, he merely extends the katana, his gaze fixed on the dancing beams of the blade, making you think of twinkling spinal lights. What does he see? The heads of clever, arrogant running backs? Who knows? He's looking and he sees what he sees. And after a half hour you can almost catch in his eyes the rush of the leopard toward cover behind the bush where he can already view the whole terrible beauty of the game, just a pure expression of gunshot hits, all of it for the crowd that wants to feel its own alphaness, for the crowd that hears no screams other than its own, and isn't it all so natural, he thinks, a connective to prehistoric hunting bands and as instinctually human as the impulse to go down and look at the bright, pounding sea.

WRITING ASSIGNMENTS

Analysis

1. Should Kram's title be read as an assertion, a protest, or a question? Explain your answer.
2. Explain the role of the media, the fans, management, and the players themselves in making football an exceptionally violent sport.
3. How could football be made less violent and safer?
4. Analyze Kram's attitude toward Browner. Is it mostly admiring or critical?
5. Analyze how the use of animal imagery influences the article's tone and themes.
6. After a lengthy discussion of drugs and injuries, Kram concludes the article with an evocation of Browner, on Saturday, preparing for another "bloody" Sunday. Analyze the effectiveness of this conclusion.

Argument

1. Contemporary American football has been compared to Roman gladiatorial contests. Is this a valid comparison?
2. Do you agree that "the warrior ethic is central to the game"?
3. As if he had entered Browner's mind, Kram writes, ". . . isn't it all so natural, he [Browner] thinks, a connective to prehistoric hunting bands and as instinctually human as the impulse to go down and look at the bright, pounding sea." Does Kram share the view he attributes to Browner? Do you?
4. In the previous article, cultural anthropologist Arens calls football the quintessential American game and claims that it symbolizes the cultural and physical values of masculinity. If Arens is correct, is Joey Browner the epitome of American manhood?

Personal Writing and Writing from Research

1. Compare your feelings about and experiences in a particular sport to Joey Browner's.
2. Profile an athlete at your school.
3. Survey your contemporaries about their experiences with sports-related injuries. How do the kind and number of injuries vary from sport to sport? Have injuries influenced the players' desire to continue playing?
4. *Collaborative Project:* Analyze the media's handling of violence, conflict, and injury in their coverage of a contact-sport event. Consider radio, television, and print coverage.
5. *Collaborative Project:* Interview male and female athletes at your school who play the same sport to discover whether their attitudes toward and experiences in their sport reflect gender differences. Write a research paper analyzing your findings.

First Practice

Gary Gildner

Gildner, born in 1938, teaches English at Drake University in Iowa. His books of poetry include *Digging for Indians* (1971), *Nails* (1975), *Letters from Vicksburg* (1976), *Out of This World* (1975), *The Runner and Other Poems* (1978), and *Blue Like the Heavens* (1984). "First Practice" appeared in his first volume of poetry, *First Practice* (1969).

Journal Topics: (1) If you have ever played a team sport, describe your "first practice." (2) What role has team sports played in your life? (3) What role has sports and athletics played in the life of the schools you've attended? (4) What are the values you associate with sports?

As You Read: (1) Why does Clifford Hill ask if "there were any girls present"? (2) Why does he call these schoolboys "men" rather than boys? (3) What vision of sports and sportsmanship does Hill convey in his short speech?

<blockquote>

After the doctor checked to see
we weren't ruptured,
the man with the short cigar took us
under the grade school,
5 where we went in case of attack
or storm, and said
he was Clifford Hill, he was
a man who believed dogs
ate dogs, he had once killed
10 for his country, and if
there were any girls present
for them to leave now.
                   No one
left. OK, he said, I take
that to mean you are hungry
15 men who hate to lose as much
as I do. OK. Then
he made two lines of us
facing each other,
and across the way, he said,
20 is the man you hate most
in the world,
and if we are to win
that title I want to see how.

But I don't want to see
25 any marks when you're dressed,
he said. He said, *Now.*

</blockquote>

Taking It

Leonard Kriegel

Kriegel, the author of the novel *Quitting Time* and a collection of essays, *Falling,* is a professor of English and director of the Center for Worker Education at the City University of New York. Please see the headnote for David Sherwood's essay in Chapter 3 for more information on "About Men," the *New York Times Magazine* column in which "Taking It" appeared.

Journal Topics: (1) What is meant by the expression, "Be a man!"? (2) Describe how you have dealt with a particular adversity. What character traits did you develop from this experience?

As You Read: (1) Who were Kriegel's heroes, and how were the qualities that he attributed to them related to his sense of manhood? (2) What role does Kriegel's mother play in his battle against polio, and why is he less ready to acknowledge her role?

1   In 1944, at the age of eleven, I had polio. I spent the next two years of my life in an orthopedic hospital, appropriately called a reconstruction home. By 1946, when I returned to my native Bronx, polio had reconstructed me to the point that I walked very haltingly on steel braces and crutches.

2   But polio also taught me that, if I were to survive, I would have to become a man—and become a man quickly. "Be a man!" my immigrant father urged, by which he meant "become an American." For, in 1946, this country had very specific expectations about how a man faced adversity. Endurance, courage, determination, stoicism—these might right the balance with fate.

3   "I couldn't take it, and I took it," says the wheelchair-doomed poolroom entrepreneur William Einhorn in Saul Bellow's *The Adventures of Augie March*. "And I *can't* take it, yet I do take it." In 1953, when I first read these words, I knew that Einhorn spoke for me—as he spoke for scores of other men who had confronted the legacy of a maiming disease by risking whatever they possessed of substance in a country that believed that such risks were a man's wagers against his fate.

4   How one faced adversity was, like most of American life, in part a question of gender. Simply put, a woman endured, but a man fought back. You were better off struggling against the effects of polio as a man than as a woman, for polio was a disease that one confronted by being tough, aggressive, decisive, by assuming that all limitations could be overcome, beaten, conquered. In short, by being "a man." Even the vocabulary of rehabilitation was masculine. One "beat" polio by outmuscling the disease. At the age of eighteen, I felt that I was "a better man" than my friends because I had "overcome a handicap." And I had, in the process, showed that I could "take it." In the world of American men, to take it was a sign that you were among the elect. An assumption my "normal" friends shared. "You're lucky," my closest friend said to me during an intensely painful crisis in his own life. "You had polio." He meant it. We both believed it.

5   Obviously, I wasn't lucky. By nineteen, I was already beginning to understand—slowly, painfully, but inexorably—that disease is never "conquered" or "overcome."

Still, I looked upon resistance to polio as the essence of my manhood. As an American, I was self-reliant. I could create my own possibilities from life. And so I walked mile after mile on braces and crutches. I did hundreds of push-ups every day to build my arms, chest, and shoulders. I lifted weights to the point that I would collapse, exhausted but strengthened, on the floor. And through it all, my desire to create a "normal" life for myself was transformed into a desire to become the man my disease had decreed I should be.

6   I took my heroes where I found them—a strange, disparate company of men: Hemingway, whom I would write of years later as "my nurse"; Peter Reiser, whom I dreamed of replacing in Ebbets Field's pastures and whose penchant for crashing into outfield walls fused in my mind with my own war against the virus; Franklin Delano Roosevelt, who had scornfully faced polio with aristocratic disdain and patrician distance (a historian acquaintance recently disabused me of that myth, a myth perpetrated, let me add, by almost all of Roosevelt's biographers); Henry Fonda and Gary Cooper, in whose resolute Anglo-Saxon faces Hollywood blended the simplicity, strength and courage a man needed if he was going to survive as a man; any number of boxers in whom heart, discipline and training combined to stave off defeats the boy's limitations made inevitable. These were the "manly" images I conjured up as I walked those miles of Bronx streets, as I did those relentless push-ups, as I moved up and down one subway staircase after another by turning each concrete step into a personal insult. And they were still the images when, fifteen years later, married, the father of two sons of my own, a Fulbright professor in the Netherlands, I would grab hold of vertical poles in a train in The Hague and swing my brace-bound body across the dead space between platform and carriage, filled with self-congratulatory vanity as amazement spread over the features of the Dutch conductor.

7   It is easy to dismiss such images as adolescent. Undoubtedly they were. But they helped remind me, time and time again, of how men handled their diseases and their pain. Of course, I realized even then that it was not the idea of manhood alone that had helped me fashion a life out of polio. I might write of Hemingway as "my nurse," but it was an immigrant Jewish mother—already transformed into a cliché by scores of male Jewish writers—who serviced my crippled body's needs and who fed me love, patience and care even as I fed her the rhetoric of my rage.

8   But it was the need to prove myself an American man—tough, resilient, independent, able to take it—that pulled me through the war with the virus. I have, of course, been reminded again and again of the price extracted for such ideas about manhood. And I am willing to admit that my sons may be better off in a country in which "manhood" will mean little more than, say, the name for an after-shave lotion. It is forty years since my war with the virus began. At fifty-one, even an American man knows that mortality is the only legacy and defeat the only guarantee. At fifty-one, my legs still encased in braces and crutches still beneath my shoulders, my elbows are increasingly arthritic from all those streets walked and weights lifted and stairs climbed. At fifty-one, my shoulders burn with pain from all those push-ups done so relentlessly. And at fifty-one, pain merely bores—and hurts.

9   Still, I remain an American man. If I know where I'm going, I know, too, where I have been. Best of all, I know the price I have paid. A man endures his diseases until he recognizes in them his vanity. He can't take it, but he takes it. Once, I relished my ability to take it. Now I find myself wishing that taking it were easier. In such quiet surrenders do we American men call it quits with our diseases.

WRITING ASSIGNMENTS

Analysis

1. How did Kriegel extend the ethic of masculine toughness beyond polio to other areas of his life?
2. Claiming that his struggle against polio made him a man, Kriegel defines American manhood as "endurance, courage, determination, [and] stoicism. . . ." Compare him to football safety Joey Browner, profiled in the previous article.
3. Kriegel says, "How one faced adversity was, like most of American life, in part a question of gender. Simply put, a woman endured, but a man fought back." Identify and describe other situations in which American responses could be described as gender-conditioned.
4. From the perspective of middle age, does Kriegel still believe that his masculinity enabled him to "beat" polio?
5. Kriegel concludes, "In such quiet surrenders do we American men call it quits with our diseases." To what diseases besides polio is he referring?

Argument

1. Has Kriegel's model of manhood served him well?
2. Is Kriegel right to say that how one faces adversity is a "question of gender"?

Personal Writing and Writing from Research

1. Compare your heroes to Kriegel's.
2. Describe how you faced a specific adversity. Was your response conditioned by your concepts of masculinity and femininity?
3. Have recent changes in the law and in social attitudes made life less difficult for persons with disabilities?

My Life in the Locker Room

Jennifer Briggs

Jennifer Briggs was one of the first ball girls for the Texas Rangers. From 1980 to 1994, she worked for the *Fort Worth Star-Telegram*, part of that time as a major-league baseball columnist. She is the coauthor of *Nolan Ryan: The Authorized Pictorial Biography* and currently is a freelance writer based in the Dallas-Fort Worth area.

Journal Topics: (1) Can a woman sportswriter do the job as effectively as a man? (2) What advantages and disadvantages does a woman sportswriter face? (3) Describe your idea of the atmosphere, people, and behavior in "the locker room."

As You Read: (1) How do Briggs's experiences as a sportswriter show that, for many people, the world of sports remains a male preserve? (2) How is sexuality or sexual innuendo used both on and off the job to exclude, intimidate, or trivialize Briggs? (3) Are men the only ones who give Briggs a hard time?

I was twenty-two years old and the first woman ever to cover sports for the *Fort Worth Star-Telegram.* Up until then, my assignments had been small-time: high school games and features on father-daughter doubles teams and Hacky Sack demonstrations. But now it was late September, and my editor wanted me to interview Mr. October about what it was like not to make the playoffs.

I'd heard the stories: the tales of women who felt forced to make a stand at the clubhouse door; of the way you're supposed to never look down at your notepad, or a player might think you're snagging a glimpse at his crotch; about how you've always got to be prepared with a one-liner, even if it means worrying more about snappy comebacks than snappy stories.

Dressed in a pair of virgin white flats, I trudged through the Arlington Stadium tunnel—a conglomeration of dirt and spit and sunflower seeds, caked to the walkway like 10,000-year-old bat guano at Carlsbad Caverns—dreading the task before me. It would be the last day ever for those white shoes—and my first of many covering professional sports.

. . . It was mostly worn, ectoplasm-green indoor-outdoor carpeting—and stares. But on top of it being my first foray behind the red door, I was scared because of *who* I was interviewing: a superstar with a surly streak. I fully expected trouble. This was baptism by back draft, not fire.

5   But I couldn't back out. In many ways, I had made a career choice when I walked through that locker room door.

"May I talk to you?" I asked Reggie, as everyone watched and listened.

He did not answer.

"Can I talk to you for a minute," I said. . . .

. . . A simple no would have sufficed. But instead, the man who is an idol to thousands of children launched into a verbal tirade, loudly insulting my intelligence and shouting for someone to remove me from the clubhouse.

10   Here I was in my white flats, some fresh-out-of-college madras plaid skirt, one of those ridiculous spiked hairdos with tails we all wore back then, and probably enough add-a-beads to shame any Alpha Chi.

And there was Reggie, in nothing but sanitary socks.

His voice was growing louder. Mine, firmer.

Now almost everyone had stopped watching football and was watching me and Reggie. "Is she *supposed* to be here?" he demanded. "You can't be in here now."

"Are you going to talk to me or not?" I asked one more time, interrupting.

15   He wouldn't answer.

"All right, *heck* with it then," I said. I spun around and walked out—past the staring faces, through the red door, down the 10,000-year-old bat-guano tunnel—and emerged into the dugout and the light of the real world, where I was nothing but a kid reporter who didn't get the story. It was the last time I would ever try to interview Reggie. And it was my first failure covering sports. But it wouldn't be my last.

Long before I was allowed to eat fish with bones, could go all night without peeing in my bed, or understood *Gilligan's Island* wasn't real, I loved baseball. It's the reason I'm a sportswriter, and I learned it from my dad. Back then, almost thirty years ago, passion for the national pastime was an heirloom fathers passed to their sons. But a little girl with blond pin curls somehow slipped into the line of succession. I don't have a radio talk show yet, but I now make my living writing about sports—at the moment, mostly the Texas Rangers. Covering major league baseball full time is my goal.

. . . I've wanted to write stories about baseball since I was ten years old—to write words so good that people would read them twice. I used to write Dallas Cowboys columns in blue Crayola on a Big Chief tablet in the part of my sister's walk-in closet I had designated as the press box. Bell bottoms hung over my head as I berated Tom Landry for not getting rid of Mike Clark or praised Roger Staubach the way little kids now get all slobbery over Nolan Ryan.

I never told my friends. I always won the big awards in elementary school, went to football games, and performed in talent shows. What kind of a goob would they take me for if they knew? But after getting home from school, I'd quickly skip back to the sports section of the evening *Star-Telegram* to compare my work to that of the pros. Sometimes I'd turn the sound down on the TV and try to do baseball play-by-play, too. I can look back now and see I was sunk early, my heart hopelessly immersed in a severely codependent relationship with a kids' game played by grown-ups.

20   It began when I was three and my daddy took me to Turnpike Stadium—now Arlington Stadium—to see the old minor league Spurs. We lived in Arlington, about five miles from the ball park. He carried me to the back of the outfield wall and climbed the slatted boards with his right arm and clutched me in his left. Then he held my head over the top of the wall in center. And there, not 1,000 days after I had emerged from the darkness of the womb, hundreds of bright light bulbs made me squint as I watched the first half-inning of my life, the last three outs of a Spurs game.

All I remember is green and light and the security of my daddy's arms.

. . . One night in the stands, I had my Helen-Keller-at-the-well experience. Suddenly it all made sense: the way the numbers went across in a line on a scoreboard, what the three numbers at the end of the nine meant, even why the shortstop didn't have a bag. "He just doesn't" was suddenly sufficient and I knew a grown-up secret, like writing checks, making babies, or reading words.

My daddy and I saw our first major league game together on Opening Night here in 1972. Some summers we went to twenty games; others we went to about fifty-six.

... He'd pull me out of school at lunch once a year to go to the spring baseball luncheon and take me to games early so I could collect autographs. The balls with the signatures still sit on my mantel, most reading like the tombstones of major league also-rans.

25   When I was fourteen, I heard from a friend that the Rangers would soon be hiring ball girls. The rumor was bogus, but it planted an idea. I began a one-kid campaign to institute ball girls at Arlington Stadium—as well as to become the first.

I wrote management—repeatedly. The executive types weren't too hot on the idea. So when I was about sixteen, I wrote every major league club with ball girls and asked about the pros and cons. I sent copies of their responses to the Rangers' front office. I corresponded with them for another two years before the call finally came.

They were trying ball girls.

They picked three—Cindy, because she was a perky cheerleader at the University of Texas at Arlington; Jamie, because she had modeling experience; and me, because I was a pest.

We shagged foul balls, but in retrospect, I guess we were more decorative than functional. They used to have us dance to the "Cotton-Eyed Joe" in the seventh inning, and for a while we shook pom-poms during rallies—acts I now, as a baseball purist, consider heresy. But hey, I was the center of attention on a baseball field; I could sell out for that.

30   The next year, I was booted because I couldn't do backflips.

But by then I had gotten to know the sportswriters and broadcasters, and the *Star-Telegram* offered me a job—in sports—typing in scores and answering the phone.

I dropped my plans to go to the University of Texas and study broadcasting. I had enough natural talent, I felt certain, that with one high heel in the door, I could work my way into a writer's job—maybe even someday cover baseball.

The realities of the corporate world and the attitudes of Texas high school and college coaches quickly clouded my idealistic vision of a quick ascent from eighteen-year-old ball girl phenom to big-league ace baseball writer.

You see, folks in the world of sports weren't use to working with a "fee-male." And you know, they all say that word so well.

35   I started out in the office, taking scores on the phone and taking heat from the guys. Writing this the other night, tears filled my eyes, and I got that precry phlegm in my throat. I was surprised to realize that some of the wounds still hurt.

It wasn't Reggie or pro-locker-room banter.

It was an area high school coach who routinely tried to get me to drop by his house when his wife was out of town; when I refused for the third time, he refused to provide any more than perfunctory answers to my story questions.

It was when all the guys were inside doing interviews, and I was standing in the rain, makeup peeling, outside the high school locker room at Fort Worth's Farrington Field, waiting beneath the six-foot-long "No Women" sign for the players to come to the doorway. It was walking into the football locker room at the University of Texas in Austin and having a large man with burnt-orange pants and dark white face pick me up by my underarms and deposit me outside the door.

God, I hate making a scene.

40 I have complained little through the years because the last thing I ever wanted to do was to single myself out from the guys. I didn't want to be branded as some woman on a crusade. I've never been on any campaign to debunk the myth that testicles are somehow inherent to a full understanding of balls.

I just wanted to cover sports.

But much of the early abuse came from the place I least expected it—my own paper.

Like a lot of kids starting out, I'd do office work all week and help cover games on the weekends—anything for a chance to prove my worth as a sportswriter. During my first four years at the *Star-Telegram* I took one day off to model at an auto show and five days off to get married. Those years were perhaps the most trying. There was a sports editor who would stop by every time he saw me eating, stare at me, and say in all seriousness, "Jenn, if you get fat, we won't love you no more." I could see my worth resided within the confines of a B cup and size six jeans. I wanted to cry each time he said that.

The guys screamed at me and demanded to know if I was "on the rag" when I was surly; yet they could scream and be surly at me all they wanted.

45 One editor in the chain of sports command kept trying to get me to check into the Worthington Hotel with him after work. Another superior had his assistant let me off early so he could be waiting for me in the parking lot.

He said he wanted to talk. I got in the car.

"Jenn," he asked, "do you want to be treated like an eighteen-year-old kid or a woman?"

At first, I thought he meant on the job. He meant on the bed.

I never went near a bedroom with any of them, but I told him "a woman" because I didn't know how answering "eighteen" to this loaded question would affect my precarious career.

50 I was quite confused. My most innocent comments were greeted with sexual innuendo. I'm no wimp; I can take a lot. I know people make sexual comments to one another, and they are not always inappropriate. But this was something else.

All the culprits are either long gone or have actually apologized, saying they just didn't know better at the time.

But how was I supposed to do my job with all that crap going on? I had to think as much about how to handle the next unwanted advance or suggestive quip as I did trying to figure the Mavericks' averages.

Some readers had similar problems accepting a woman. I can't remember the number of times I've picked up the phone in the sports department, answered some trivia question, and, when the answer didn't win the guy a bar bet, had the caller demand, "Put a man on this phone." Some simply called me a "stupid bitch" and hung up.

I know they don't know what they're talking about. But the remarks still hurt.

55 For years I was hopelessly mired in phone answering and score taking, watching as others in similar positions moved up and on. . . .

I was close to giving up. I seriously considered taking a job as a researcher for a law firm.

But one thing kept me in sports: I got a Rangers media pass every year. It was the lonely thread that tied me to my game.

In the arbitrary world of newspaper politics, the arrival of a new sports editor breathed life into my career. I began investigating the pay-for-play scandals of the Southwest Conference. I broke several stories, one of which won a national award for investigative sports reporting.

I remember hiding in a tree outside a North Dallas bank waiting for an SMU running back because we had heard this was where he picked up his money. Then there was the time we had a story about an SWC coach paying players, and I appeared one morning at the school where he was an assistant. Tipped off to my presence, the coach broke into a near run when I headed towards him in the hall. He ran into a dark office where I found him hiding under the desk.

60   Hey, this is pretty cool, I thought. When you've got dirt on them, all the condescending good-ol'-boy stuff goes out the window.

I was actually in charge.

An SMU booster threatened to have my legs broken—and I was delighted. That's something he'd say to anyone, I realized.

While all this was going on, I began helping out with Dallas Cowboys sidebar articles and weekend coverage of the Rangers. I helped cover the team for the Associated Press.

. . . Oh sure, little stuff happened, like the time one of the Oakland A's made a big point of standing next to me naked in the middle of the clubhouse or one of the Los Angeles Raiders chucked a set of shoulder pads at my butt.

65   Then there was the occasion Rangers manager Doug Rader spat corn on me after I asked a dumb question. Of course, Rader would have spat corn at anybody.

By then, I had become accustomed to the nudity and byplay of the locker room. I've always considered the real hurdle of all this to be players' perception of me, not suppressing my thoughts. . . .

The players didn't know I'd grown up with games or that my best friends had usually been crude guys or that I could open a beer bottle with my incisors or that I liked to fish as much as they did. They didn't know, and it made me feel awkward that they didn't know that this stuff really didn't bother me outside of the fact that I felt obligated to respond with a remark, which took away from my ability to do my job.

I was nervous the first time I entered the Rangers locker room, about seven years ago. Not about naked bodies or about crude remarks but about how they would *think* I felt—and how I intended to respond with confidence, no matter what happened.

. . . The first thing I saw was four guys in a big shower.

70   Because of my vantage point, it appeared I would have to walk through the shower, through the four wet, naked men, to get to the actual locker-room area. I retreated back behind the door before anyone could see me.

Maybe I didn't belong here. Maybe I'd never fit in.

. . . But I had a deadline. I had to go in.

I wasn't afraid of naked men. I was afraid of the unknown.

A few feet in, I realized a hall ran in front of the showers. You take a right turn before you have to walk straight into the naked men and the soap.

75   The first Ranger I interviewed was drying his stomach with a towel. Before I could utter a word, he said, "Wait, let me rub it, it will get hard."

That seemed like such a dumb thing to say. I mean, I know how penises work. And I know how smartass remarks work, too. The latter are supposed to be more humorous than the former, though adulthood has taught me different.

I'll always remember that no one else laughed, for whatever reason, and that made me feel good.

So I went about my business. I asked my question; he answered.

. . . I was in the visiting clubhouse waiting to interview one of the Oakland A's this year when one of the players called, "Here, pussy"—as though he were calling a cat. But of course, he hadn't lost Fluffy; he'd found a woman in his locker room.

80   It doesn't make me angry anymore; it just seems silly and absurd. But some paranoia lingers. Sometimes I'm kind of quiet in a group interview, and I have this feeling other reporters will think it's because I'm a dumb ol' girl.

I'm a general-assignment sports reporter now, which means I do whatever they ask of me. My aim as a writer is to make the people I cover seem human to the readers. You can't do this without asking about their dogs and their mom and what bugs them even worse than dropping the soap in the shower. It seems logical to me. I mean, we know a guy is probably happy to be a number-one draft choice, but what makes him real is how he is like or unlike us. It's the way we measure all people, the *Homo sapiens* equivalent of sniffing butts by the fire hydrant.

But I don't think it seems very logical to some of the other reporters. Sometimes I will request an interview at someone's house, and my peers act as though it's weird. But how can you really profile a guy if you haven't seen his coffee table or the junk stuck to his fridge?

Sometimes before the game when everyone is milling about, I go sit around the corner in equipment manager Joe Macko's office and visit for a while just so I don't wear out my welcome in the room o' nakedness. Some nights I walk out the back door where all the wives are waiting, and they stare at me strangely, as though they think I'm the woman *Cosmo* warned them about or something.

. . . I really want to be as unobtrusive as possible, so I will turn away from someone who is dressing or, if I have the time, wait until he has put his shorts on before I approach. I've been around long enough now that if they see me turn away, they probably know it isn't because I'm scared or intimidated. I like to think I've earned a little respect.

85   . . . The most puzzled responses to my job come from the friends and acquaintances in my personal life. Kids at the tanning salon want to know if I date the players. Friends at Bible study ask if the players are mean to me. And then there's the guy—almost any guy in any bar in town—who subjects me to a sports-trivia quiz during the usual getting-acquainted foreplay.

. . . And of course, women everywhere want to know about that great walled fortress of wet boy flesh, the locker room.

We're sitting around the salon one day making bets on when the rest of the country will catch on that Ross Perot is a weasel when someone says he finished ahead of Bush and Clinton in another poll. . . .

Donna doesn't like politics, so she asks what it is I do for the paper again. Donna doesn't like newspapers either. Donna is a good argument for euthanasia.

The immediate response is curiosity: Do I get to go in the locker room?

90   Well, yeah.

So you've been in the Mavericks locker room? Yeah.

And you won't believe this, and I swear it's true: the immediate response of three women who don't even like sports outside of bungee jumping at Baja is, "You've seen Ro Blackman *naked?*"

Well, I guess I had; I wasn't sure.

I'm sure he's been naked in the room where I was at some time. But the point is that you don't even think much about people being naked after a while, and unless you have some peculiar reason for remembering, you don't know who you have seen naked because they all kind of waltz in and out of the shower naked, just one wet butt covered with soap film after another.

95   I tried to explain that it is probably a lot like being a male gynecologist: the daily procession of personal parts becomes so routine that it ceases to be of anything but professional interest.

Yet I wonder. When men gather at bars and golf courses and any of the other traditional salt licks for male bonding, do they ask the gynecologist what Mrs. Holcombe's hooters look like? Do they want to know if it's hard for him to keep his professionalism with his hand inserted in some babe's bodily cavity—and whether it's scary?

I doubt it.

Donna persists.

"I can't believe you are not in love with these men," she says, biting her cuticle. I try to explain, which is difficult because Donna and I are on different sexual wavelengths. . . .

100   . . . Actually, I tell them, one of the most peculiar side effects of my job is that it seems to run off men in personal relationships. Oh sure, at first they think it's pretty cool that you're the only person at a party who can remember Neil Lomax's name or that you can name all the Rangers managers in eighteen seconds—with a shot in your mouth.

But that's while they are still trying to maneuver you quickly into bed. During this phase of courtship, most men would be reassuring Lassie that her role as a dog star doesn't matter, that they just like her nice, shiny coat.

For most of the guys that hang around for more than three dates, my job suddenly becomes a problem. Apparently a guy has to be awfully secure not to be intimidated by my frequent trips into locker rooms (as though I'm doing comparative shopping) or by my knowing a good bit about sports.

. . . The dirty little secret I've discovered is how little men know about sports, since this is what men are supposed to know more about than women. Most of the men I've dated certainly don't know about the social fraying of America or why it might be at all amusing that a guy named Fujimori is in charge of Peru, so you'd certainly hope they knew some inane facts about NFL rushers. All most know how to do is bitch about the Cowboys and Mavericks and Rangers—about their (a) record, (b) salaries, (c) coach or manager—and praise the "kick-butt" barbecue they make before watching eighteen hours of football on Sundays. That's before they tell me I don't have any business in the locker room.

I have assimilated to a large degree but probably never will completely.
105   . . . I can understand the athletes being naturally uncertain what to make of women, of me.

Many of the women they're around—other than the reasonably stable ones like their wives and mothers—are groupies. I understand that uniforms—unless they say, "Eb, your man who wears the star" on the lapel—are a great aphrodisiac in contemporary culture. . . .

Yet anyone who gets self-worth through random sex with a professional athlete is not exactly MENSA material. So you've got all these big-haired babes who think the electoral college is a beauty school, ready to hoist their miniskirts for the first athlete who comes along. And then you've got this woman who comes in to interview them, maybe with big hair and a short skirt too, depending on the humidity and what's off at the cleaners that day.

So why are they going to think the reporter is any different at first? Logic says they might not. So I remain cautious, probably overly cautious, about appearances.

. . . No less than two or three times a home stand, the feeling hits again—almost always as I walk down that tunnel from the upper deck that spits you out in back of home plate. It's just before batting practice, about 4:30 P.M. The TCBY people are pouring half gallons of yogurt stuff into the soft-serve machines; a guy is sweeping up peanuts in three-quarter time. I think how cool it is to watch a stadium yawn to life. Last night's trash still blows, even though people are sweeping all over the place. It reminds me of a debutante waking up in last night's party dress, reeking of beer.
110   About two yards down, I see legs behind the batting cage. Someone has come out early for batting practice. In a few more feet, the torsos appear and the warm breeze melts around my face. Near the field, I can see it is Al Newman and somebody. Always Al Newman, and he's always smiling because he's kind of happy to be here too.

The grass spreads out in the shape of a precious gem, and there are fans here and there who have come to see batting practice just because it's relaxing. Then it hits me: My job means I get to be around this game and write about it. And it's O.K. to spit your sunflower seed hulls on the floor. I head down the steps, past the seats where I couldn't even afford to sit when I was a kid, open heaven's gate, and walk onto the field.

Sometimes I take a seat in the dugout, where a few of the guys are filtering in, grabbing bats and bubble gum. For a minute, before I start to work, I smell the bubble gum in the breeze and look at the kids leaning over the dugout and the boys of summer in it.

And every once in a while I think about slatted billboards and a daddy's arms.

The other night, there were two girls in the clubhouse after the game. They were reporters and looked young enough to remind me of my old days—except they weren't wearing white flats.

115   No one did or said anything off-color. But there were a few giggles. And a few guys maybe flounced around a little more just for brief amusement. Quite normal, nothing harmful.

I mentioned this to someone later.

I noted being in the middle of the room when a player came out of the shower, spotted me, and turned around and went back in. A few minutes later he came back out wearing a towel.

By now I wouldn't really notice if he'd worn a towel or hadn't. But it struck me that something had changed: that my presence was no longer cause for flouncing; that I'd somehow earned this strange sign of courtesy and respect.

"Jenn," my friend told me, "I guess you rate a towel now."

WRITING ASSIGNMENTS

Analysis

1. Classify and explain the obstacles Briggs faced in becoming a sportswriter.
2. Analyze the role of sexual harassment in Briggs's career.
3. Briggs, a pioneer, denies being a crusader: ". . . the last thing I ever wanted to do was to single myself out from the guys. I didn't want to be branded as some woman on a crusade. I've never been on any campaign to debunk the myth that testicles are somehow inherent to a full understanding of balls." Given the experiences that she describes, explain whether her attitude helped or hindered her.
4. In what ways is Briggs traditionally feminine? In what ways is she not?
5. Describe Jennifer Briggs. In particular, explain how Briggs's choice of words and use of humor characterize her.
6. Analyze the ways that Briggs modified her behavior and appearance to cope with and reduce resistance to her as a sportswriter. Were these measures effective?

Argument

1. In "Taking It," Kriegel says that women endure adversity, but men fight back. Do Briggs's struggle to become a sportswriter and Kriegel's struggle with polio illustrate gender-based differences in dealing with adversity?
2. Is Briggs, despite her success, still something of an outsider in the world of sports?
3. Does Briggs enjoy any advantages as a sportswriter because she is a woman?
4. Does Briggs's experience confirm Updike's position in "The Female Body" that sexuality inevitably affects male-female interactions?

Personal Writing and Writing from Research

1. Trace and analyze your own experiences as a pioneer, whether it be as the first person in your family to attend college, to leave home to attend college, to have a romantic relationship with a person from another religion or ethnicity, etc.
2. Trace the career of another pioneer who, like Briggs, crossed the gender line in a formerly all-female or all-male field, or who integrated a formerly racially segregated field.
3. Briggs is not the only woman sportswriter to describe her experiences. In a research paper, compare women sportswriters' experiences.
4. Research and report on what role, if any, gender plays in how sports are covered at your school or by your local media.

The Unbound Foot
Women and Athletics

Anne Fausto-Sterling

Anne Fausto-Sterling was trained to do laboratory research in developmental genetics, an area that represents a cross between embryology (the study of the development from single egg cells into complex, many-celled organisms) and genetics (the study of the mechanisms of inheritance). A feminist and associate professor of biology and medicine at Brown University, she says, "Where I differ from some of those I take to task is in *not* [italics added] denying my politics. Scientists who do deny their politics—who claim to be objective and unemotional about gender while living in a world where even boats and automobiles are identified by sex—are fooling themselves and the public at large." "The Unbound Foot" is excerpted from her 1985 book, *Myths of Gender.*

Journal Topics: (1) Describe your understanding of the differences between male and female athletic performance. How do you explain these differences?

As You Read: (1) What specific cultural evidence does Fausto-Sterling introduce to help explain differences in male and female athletic performance? (2) What role does she assign to biology, specifically to the role of hormones?

1 ... Let me begin with the obvious. Except for the incongruous cases of sexual development, men and women have different reproductive systems and organs. They also have hormones that may differ in amount although not in kind. These

differences may be small or large, depending on biological rhythms, life cycle rhythms, stress, and both lifelong and immediate individual experience. On average men are a bit taller and a bit stronger than women. Obviously a physiological, inherent, natural difference, you say? Here I begin to hedge my bets, a hedging that I can perhaps illustrate most usefully by examining male/female differences in athletic performance.

2   It is easy to forget that only in very recent times have girls been allowed, even as young children, to roam free and to train their bodies. Athenian women had permission neither to watch nor to participate in the original Olympic games; not until 1984 did females officially run in the Olympic marathon. One nineteenth-century American writer considered woman to be a true physical oddity: "The width of her pelvis and the consequent separation . . . of the heads of her thighbones *render even walking difficult*"[1] (emphasis added), while a well-known twentieth-century "sports philosopher" suggested that "one way of dealing with these disparities between the athletic promise and achievements of men and women is to view women as truncated males."[2] Only within the last decade have educators even considered the idea that boys and girls should or could receive the same athletic training. The argument has always been that the biological differences between boys and girls and men and women prevent their competition on the athletic field. Yet one need only read the following poignant account of Chinese foot binding to remember that we still do not know how far a female athlete might have gone had she, from infancy, used her body as fully and as freely as do many little boys:

> They did not begin to bind my feet until I was seven because I loved so much to run and play. . . . [Then] they had to draw the bindings tighter than usual. My feet hurt so much that for two years I had to crawl on my hands and knees. Sometimes at night . . . I could not sleep. I stuck my feet under my mother and she lay on them so they hurt less . . . by the time I was eleven my feet did not hurt and by the time I was thirteen they were finished.[3]

3   The knowledge that women's feet have only recently been unbound, however, cannot hide the fact that grown men and women look different, that they are sexually dimorphic. Although humans are among the least dimorphic of primates, the fact that the average adult female weighs 10 percent less than the average male (among gorillas the average female weighs 50 percent less than the average male) remains obvious. So too do the variety of other physical characteristics, particularly adult muscle shape and size and the amount and distribution of body fat. Hormones most likely are an important factor in the development of height, muscle size, and fat distribution, although their specific mode of action is a matter of some dispute.[4]

4   During their early years, girls and boys are quite similar in height. By the early teens girls, who mature earlier but stop growing sooner, spurt ahead, but boys continue to grow for three to five years longer and thus on average reach a taller height. One college athletic recruiter commented that it is easier to recruit female athletes as first-year students because they are a known quantity, whereas the changes in height and strength for boys continue throughout the college years. The key hormone in this

growth process is called, appropriately enough, *growth* hormone. The pituitary gland that produces it probably uses a somewhat different biological clock in males than in females, but even this is not certain. Some reports suggest that exercise can affect the short-term synthesis of growth hormone; thus the different activity levels of boys and girls could alter growth hormone metabolism.[5] There are some suggestions that physical training in children leads to more vigorous growth.[6] Even today the amount of physical activity that boys and girls engage in varies greatly, although the differences must certainly be less than they were a hundred years ago. As social restrictions on little girls continue to fall by the wayside, it will be of interest to see whether one result is a decrease in the 10 percent height difference between men and women. My suspicion is that, given widespread changes leading to equal physical activity for boys and girls in an environment with adequate nutrition, the male/female height dimorphism will decrease by a few percentage points but will not disappear altogether.

5   About 25 percent of the body weight of nonathletic women is fat, in contrast to the 15 percent of the average untrained man's body weight.[7] (The fact that women usually have more of that fat in their breasts and legs is no secret.) This physical difference appears at puberty and, although poorly understood, is thought to result from the greater amount of estrogen active in the female. As anyone who has ever dieted knows, however, body fat is not constant. The amount present in the bodies of highly trained female long-distance runners approaches that of similarly trained men,[8] although what is there is still differently distributed. Some physicians think that the difference in fat content between average college-aged men and women is primarily due to differences in life-style.[9] This, too, only changing social customs will allow us to know for sure.

6   Height and shape differences are not absolute, but it may be that strength differences are. During development the cells that become muscle fuse with one another to form large fibers. The number of fibers in each individual becomes fixed during the first few years of life, and subsequent muscle growth consists only of increases in the length and width of such fibers. Much of the muscle size differences between males and females result from disparities in fiber growth rather than fiber number. Both hormones and physical activity play a role. Growth hormone differences may account for the fact that girls' muscles grow to their maximum size at an earlier age, while the combination of a more prolonged period of growth hormone synthesis in boys and increases in testosterone level may, together, account for the greater muscle bulk evident as young men mature.

7   The belief that testosterone builds muscle strength has contributed to a controversy in the sports world. Should athletes take androgen-like drugs—paying the price in future health problems—in order to build up their bodies? Although these chemicals do promote weight gain and increased thigh circumference, controlled studies show no significant differences in strength between men who do and do not take these drugs. Ironically, the total amount of blood testosterone has been shown to decrease in men taking the externally supplied androgen, a change mediated by the lowered blood concentrations of a hormone-binding protein.[10] Despite such studies, belief in

the effectiveness of androgenic drugs remains, continuing to provide serious difficulties for athletes, their physicians, and the organizers of athletic events.

8   Even for height, body shape, muscle fiber number, and physical differences in muscle shape, hormones alone tell only a partial story. This is made clear from an observation of Balinese men recorded by the anthropologist Margaret Mead.

> The arms of the men are almost as free of heavy muscle as those of the women, yet the potentiality for the development of heavy muscle is there; when Balinese work as dock-coolies . . . their muscles develop and harden. But in their own villages they prefer to carry rather than lift, and to summon many hands to every task. . . . *If we knew no other people than the Balinese we would never guess that men were so made that they could develop heavy muscles.*[11] [Emphasis added]

9   The question of muscle strength seems to be somewhat separate from that of shape. Some estimates suggest that even highly trained athletes use only 20 percent of their muscle potential, and changes in strength may well involve not only increases in muscle bulk but, perhaps as important, changes in the use of muscle that is already present. Strength is the ability of an individual to exert force against some external resistance, and different parts of the body have different strengths. The average strength differences between men and women result at least in part from men's larger size. The upper body strength of the average female (that is, strength derived from arms and shoulders) is about half that of the average male although, when matched for size, a woman has 80 percent of a man's upper body strength. The lower body strength of the average woman reaches 70 percent of the average man's, and when the comparison is made between individuals of the same weight a woman's lower body strength approaches 93 percent of a man's. Leg strength measured relative to lean body weight (leaving out the fat differences) actually shows women's legs to be 5.8 percent stronger than men's.[12] One implication of these data is that sports emphasizing upper body strength will probably always offer males an advantage—as long as they are played in a culture such as ours, rather than in a place like Bali. Advantages accruing to men in other sports such as running, however, may be due only to differences in leg length, rather than strength.

10   In this discussion of differences between untrained men and women, the relative influences of height, fat content, strength of hormones, and environment cannot be easily untangled. At the moment it appears that differences in the timing of growth hormone synthesis during childhood and adolescence may account for male/female height differences and may also be a component of differences in muscle development. On the other hand, it remains possible (and only time will tell) that at least some of the height and strength dimorphism between males and females would diminish in a culture in which girls from infancy on engaged in the same amount and kind of physical activity as boys. It is my own guess, though, that even then small average differences would remain. Finally, it behooves us to remember that the amount of variation among men and among women is greater than that between the sexes. Thus no two differently sexed individuals can be assumed, sight unseen, to have different heights, shapes, or strengths.

11   Looking at highly trained athletes offers another view of physical differences between men and women. Although one assumes that both groups will compare more closely because they have had a greater chance through training to develop their potential, few female athletes begin to train as early or have the same opportunities and training as do male athletes. One sport in which differences in body composition redound to women's advantage is marathon swimming, women's greater body fat providing increased buoyancy and protection against the cold. Here women hold the world record, a title that came easily once it became acceptable for females to try the feat. The first woman ever to swim the English Channel (Gertrude Ederle in 1926) not only astounded the world by succeeding at all, but she broke the men's record by two hours! In fact she so took the public by surprise that a London newspaper did not have time to withdraw an editorial claiming that her failure (expected when the paper went to press) demonstrated that women were physically inferior to men and their entry into competitive athletics a hopeless enterprise.[13]

12   Between 1964 and 1984 women marathon runners have knocked more than an hour-and-a-half off their running times, while men's times during that same period have decreased by only a few minutes. The relative differences between men's and women's times in shorter running events have also fallen considerably since the 1930s. In 1934, for example, the women's time for the 100-meter run was 13.5 percent lower than the men's, but by 1974 the difference had decreased to 9.1 percent. There are similar trends in swimming (with the possible exception of the 100-meter event). In all swimming and track events in the 1976 Olympics, females were 89 to 93 percent as fast as men—that is, females were 10 percent slower.[14] If the gap between highly trained male and female athletes were to continue to close at the current rate, in thirty to forty years men and women would compete in these sports on an equal basis.[15] It is, of course, also possible that the rate of female improvement will level off. In that case we will have a better idea of just how different the physical capacities of the male and female body are. One way to guess about the outcome is to look at male and female differences in a country where training and coaching methods seem comparable for both sexes. East German female swimmers, for example, swim a mere 3 percent more slowly than the men (for the 100- and 400-meter freestyle). The difference is there, but it isn't much!

13   In some sports, for example tennis, where the essential overhand serve relies heavily on upper body strength, and basketball, where upper body strength and absolute height are vital, men and women will probably always perform differently. Others, such as gymnastics, may well turn out to favor women. Whatever the outcome, however, it has become clear that girls and women can be excellent athletes, and it has become increasingly acceptable for the average girl to learn to enjoy using her body in physical activity. There are hormonal bases for some of the physical differences between adult men and women. Yet even these interact with culture and socialization to produce the final product. No matter how our ideas about male and female physique evolve in the coming years, one thing remains certain: our cultural conceptions will change the way our bodies grow, and how our bodies grow will change the way our culture views them.

Notes

1. A. Walker, *Woman Physiologically Considered* (New York: J. and H. G. Langley, 1843), 8.

2. P. Weiss, *Sport: A Philosophical Inquiry* (Carbondale, Ill.: Southern Illinois University Press, 1969), 215.

3. Ida Pruitt, *A Daughter of Han* (New Haven: Yale University Press, 1945), 22.

4. S. B. Stromme, D. Meen, and A. Arkvaag, "Effects of an Androgenic-Anabolic Steroid on Strength Development and Plasma Testosterone Levels in Normal Males," *Medicine and Science in Sports* 6(1974):203–8.

5. J. R. Sutton et al., "Hormonal Changes During Exercise," *Lancet* 2(1968):1304; and J. Roth et al., "Secretion of Human Growth Hormone: Physiologic and Experimental Modification," *Metabolism* 12(1963):577–79.

6. G. M. Andrew et al., "Heart and Lung Functions in Swimmers and Non-Athletes During Growth," *Journal of Applied Physiology* 32(1972):245–61.

7. J. H. Wilmore, "They Told Me You Couldn't Compete with Men and You, Like a Fool, Believed Them. Here's Hope," *Women Sports* 1(1974):40–43, 83.

8. J. H. Wilmore, C. H. Brown, and J. A. Davis, "Body Physique and Composition of the Female Distance Runner," *Annals of the New York Academy of Sciences* 301(1977):764–76.

9. J. H. Wilmore and C. H. Brown, "Physiological Profiles of Women Distance Runners," *Medicine and Science in Sports* 6(1974):173–81.

10. S. B. Stromme, D. Meen, and A. Arkvaag, "Effects of an Androgenic-Anabolic Steroid."

11. Margaret Mead, *Male and Female* (New York: Morrow, 1949), 175.

12. J. Hudson, "Physical Parameters Used for Female Exclusion from Law Enforcement and Athletics," in *Women and Sport: From Myth to Reality,* ed. Carole A. Oglesby (Philadelphia: Lea and Febiger, 1978).

13. S. L. Twin, *Out of the Bleachers* (Westbury, N.Y.: Feminist Press, 1979); and Nina Kusick, "The History of Women's Participation in the Marathon," *Annals of the New York Academy of Science* 301(1977):862–76.

14. J. Hudson, "Physical Parameters Used for Female Exclusion."

15. Ken Dyer, "Female Athletes are Catching Up," *New Scientist,* 22 Sept. 1977, 722–23.

WRITING ASSIGNMENTS

Analysis

1. How do culture and biology interact to produce differences in male and female athletic performance?

2. Analyze the cultural changes that have contributed to improved female athletic performance in recent years.

3. Why has female athletic performance improved more rapidly in recent years than male athletic performance?

4. Characterize the tone of this selection. How do Fausto-Sterling's choice of words and use of evidence influence the effectiveness of her presentation?

Argument

1. Should female athletes and women's athletic programs receive resources equal to those given to male athletes and to men's athletic programs on college and university campuses? In high schools?
2. Should American women—both as players and spectators—make athletics as central to their lives as American men have?

Personal Writing and Writing from Research

1. How did the "culture" of your family or community influence your attitude toward athletics?
2. Compare the cultural messages about athletics delivered to males and to females by your family or community.
3. Research the history of women's participation and achievement in a particular sport.
4. Trace the history and current status of women's athletics at your school. Compare your findings to comparable data about the men's athletic program.
5. Trace the history of a specific ethnic or racial group's exclusion from or participation in a sport.
6. Analyze the coverage of female athletes in your local newspaper or in a sports magazine. Does it reflect any gender bias?

LITERARY CREDITS

Maya Angelou "Family Affairs" from *Shaker, Why Don't You Sing?* by Maya Angelou. Copyright © 1983 by Maya Angelou. Reprinted by permission of Random House, Inc.

Maya Angelou "A Job on the Streetcars" from *I Know Why the Caged Bird Sings* by Maya Angelou. Copyright © 1969 by Maya Angelou. Reprinted by permission of Random House, Inc.

W. Arens "Professional Football: An American Symbol and Ritual" by W. Arens reprinted by permission from Susan Montague.

David P. Barash "Sexism: Strategies of Reproduction, or When is Beeswax Like a Ferrari?" excerpt from *The Whispering Within* by David P. Barash. Copyright © 1979 by David P. Barash. Reprinted by permission of HarperCollins Publisher, Inc.

Dave Barry "Why Sports Is a Drag" from *Dave Barry's Greatest Hits* by Dave Barry. Copyright © 1988 by Dave Barry. Reprinted by permission of Crown Publishers, Inc.

Sandra L. Bem "Transforming the Debate on Sexual Inequality: From Biological Difference to Institutionalized Androcentrism," a lecture, from *The Lenses of Gender* by Sandra Bem by permission of the publisher, Yale University Press. Copyright © 1993 by Yale University Press.

Jennifer Briggs "My Life in the Locker Room" by Jennifer Briggs is reprinted by permission of *The Dallas Observer,* copyright © 1992.

Harry Brod "Scholarly Studies of Men: The New Field Is an Essential Complement to Women's Studies" from *Against the Tide* by Michael S. Kimmel and Thomas E. Mosmiller. Copyright © 1992 by Michael S. Kimmel and Thomas E. Mosmiller. Reprinted by permission of Beacon Press.

Joan Jacobs Brumberg Excerpt from Chapter 9, "Fasting Girls: The Emerging Ideal of Slenderness in American Culture," reprinted by permission of the publishers from *Fasting Girls: The Emergence of Anorexia Nervosa as a Modern Disease* by Joan Jacobs Brumberg, Cambridge, Mass.: Harvard University Press, Copyright © 1988 by the President and Fellows of Harvard College.

Mary E. Buckley Excerpt from *Perspectives on Marriage* edited by Mary E. Buckley and Gregory F. Augustine Pierce. Copyright © 1992 ACTA Publications, 4848 N. Clark Street, Chicago, IL 60640 (312) 271-1030. Used with permission. All rights reserved.

Francesca M. Cancian "Feminine and Masculine Love" from *Love in America* by Francesca Cancian, copyright © 1987. Reprinted with the permission of Cambridge University Press.

Raymond Carver "What We Talk About When We Talk About Love" from *What We Talk About When We Talk About Love* by Raymond Carver. Copyright © 1981 by Raymond Carver. Reprinted by permission of Alfred A. Knopf, Inc.

Sandra Cisneros "Only Daughter" reprinted courtesy of *Glamour* Magazine. Copyright © 1990 by The Conde Nast Publications, Inc.

Jan Clausen "Daddy" is reprinted from *Mother, Sister, Daughter, Lover* (Freedom, CA: The Crossing Press). Copyright © Jan Clausen, 1980.

Helen Cordes "What a Doll!" by Helen Cordes, reprinted with permission of

December 25, 1983. Copyright © 1983 by The New York Times Company. Reprinted by permission.

Stephen Jay Gould "Biological Potentiality vs. Biological Determinism," reprinted from *Ever Since Darwin: Reflections in Natural History* by Stephen Jay Gould with the permission of W. W. Norton & Company, Inc. Copyright © 1977 by Stephen Jay Gould.

Patricia Albjerg Graham Excerpt from "Expansion and Exclusion: A History of Women in American Higher Education" from *Signs: Journal of Women in Culture and Society,* V3, #4, published by the University of Chicago Press. Copyright © 1978 by the University of Chicago Press.

A. M. Homes "Jim Train" reprinted from *The Safety of Objects* by A. M. Homes with permission of W. W. Norton & Company, Inc. Copyright © 1990 by A. M. Homes.

bell hooks "Black Women and Feminism" from *Talking Back, Thinking Feminist, Thinking Black* by bell hooks, copyright © 1989. By permission of South End Press.

Charisse Jones "The Marriage Gap" by Charisse Jones from *The L. A. Times,* March 28, 1993. Copyright © 1993, *Los Angeles Times.* Reprinted by permission.

David Michael Kaplan "Doe Season" by David Michael Kaplan first appeared in *The Atlantic Monthly.* It also appeared in *Comfort* by David Michael Kaplan and *Best American Short Stories,* 1986. Copyright © 1985 by David Michael Kaplan. Reprinted by permission of Brandt & Brandt Literary Agents, Inc.

Bel Kaufman "Sunday in the Park" from *To Be a Man.* Bel Kaufman is the author of the best seller *Up the Down Staircase.*

Mirra Komarovsky "College Men: Gender Roles in Transition," an essay given at Oberlin College Conference, March,

1983. Copyright © 1987 by the Board of Trustees of the University of Illinois. Used with the permission of the author and of the University of Illinois Press.

Mark Kram "No Pain, No Game" from *Esquire Magazine,* January, 1992. Copyright © 1992 by Mark Kram.

Leonard Kriegel "Taking It" from About Men, *The New York Times Magazine,* June 9, 1985. Copyright © 1985 by The New York Times Company. Reprinted by permission.

Susan Lee "Friendship, Feminism and Betrayal" from *The Village Voice,* June 9, 1975. Copyright © 1975 by *The Village Voice.*

Marcia R. Lieberman "Someday My Prince Will Come: Female Acculturation Through the Fairy Tale" from *College English,* December, 1972. Copyright © 1972 by the National Council of Teachers of English. Reprinted with permission.

Audre Lorde "Hanging Fire" reprinted from *The Black Unicorn* by Audre Lorde, with permission of W. W. Norton & Company, Inc. Copyright © 1978 by Audre Lorde.

John McCluskey, Jr. "Forty in the Shade" from *Mr. America's Last Season Blues* by John McCluskey, Jr. Copyright © 1983 by the author, published by Louisiana State University Press. Used with permission.

Stuart Miller Excerpt from "True Friendship Between Men" from *Men and Friendship.* Copyright © 1983 by Stuart Miller. Reprinted by permission of Houghton Mifflin Co. All rights reserved.

Sue Miller Excerpt from *Family Pictures* by Sue Miller. Copyright © 1990 by Sue Miller. Reprinted by permission of HarperCollins Publisher, Inc.

Sharon Olds "Rite of Passage" from *The Dead and the Living* by Sharon Olds. Copyright © 1983 by Sharon Olds.

August 31, 1970. Copyright © 1970 by Gloria Steinem.

Andrew Sullivan "Here Comes the Groom" from *The New Republic,* August 28, 1989. Reprinted by permission of *The New Republic,* copyright © 1989, The New Republic, Inc.

Amy Tan "Rice Husband" reprinted by permission of G. P. Putnam's Sons from *The Joy Luck Club* by Amy Tan. Copyright © 1989 by Amy Tan.

Deborah Tannen Text excerpt from "Intimacy and Independence" from *You Just Don't Understand* by Deborah Tannen, Ph.D. Copyright © 1990 by Deborah Tannen, Ph.D. By permission of William Morrow & Company, Inc.

Steve Tesich "Focusing on Friends" from About Men, *The New York Times Magazine,* December 4, 1983. Copyright © 1983 by The New York Times Company. Reprinted by permission.

Cooper Thompson "A New Vision of Masculinity" from *Changing Men,* Spring, 1985. Copyright © 1985 by Cooper Thompson.

John Updike "The Female Body" from *Odd Jobs* by John Updike. Copyright © 1991 by John Updike. Reprinted by permission of Alfred A. Knopf, Inc.

Helena Maria Viramontes "Growing" by Helena Maria Viramontes is reprinted with permission from the publisher of *The Moths and Other Stories* (Houston: Arte Publico Press-University of Houston, 1985.)

Helena Maria Viramontes "Miss Clairol" from *Chicana Creativity and Criticism.* Reprinted by permission of Marie Brown Associates. Copyright © 1988, Helena Viramontes.

Alice Walker "Roselily" from *In Love & Trouble: Stories of Black Women,* copyright © 1972 by Alice Walker, reprinted by permission of Harcourt Brace & Company.

Mitsuye Yamada "Invisibility Is an Unnatural Disaster: Reflections of an Asian American Woman" by Mitsuye Yamada from *This Bridge Called My Back* © 1983, edited by Cherrie Moraga and Gloria Angaldua. Used by permission of the author and of Kitchen Table Press, P.O. Box 908, Latham, NY 12110.

Hisaye Yamamoto "Seventeen Syllables" by Hisaye Yamamoto from *Seventeen Syllables and Other Stories,* copyright © 1988 by Hisaye Yamamoto and Kitchen Table: Women of Color Press, P.O. Box 908, Latham, NY 12110.

Jose Zuniga "My Life in the Military Closet" from *The New York Times Magazine,* July 11, 1993. Copyright © 1993 by The New York Times Company. Reprinted by permission.

ART/PHOTO CREDITS

INDEX